Crime and Punishment in Indonesia

Indonesia's criminal law system faces major challenges. Despite the country's transition to democracy, both the Criminal Code and the Criminal Procedure Code are badly out of date, the former only superficially changed since colonial times and the latter remaining as it was under Soeharto's authoritarian New Order regime.

Law enforcement officers and judges are widely seen as corrupt or incompetent, and new laws, including new Islamic laws passed at the regional level, often contradict the Criminal Code and national statutes, including human rights laws.

This book, based on extensive original research by leading scholars in the field, provides an overall assessment of the state of criminal law, law enforcement and penal policy in Indonesia, considers in depth a wide range of specific areas of criminal law, and discusses recent efforts at reform and their prospects for success.

Tim Lindsey is Malcolm Smith Professor of Asian Law, and Director of the Centre for Indonesian Law, Islam and Society at the University of Melbourne.

Helen Pausacker is Deputy Director of the Centre for Indonesian Law, Islam and Society and a Principal Research Assistant in the Asian Law Centre, the University of Melbourne.

Routledge Law in Asia

Series editors
Randall Peerenboom
Pip Nicholson
Michael Ng

13 **Juries in the Japanese Legal System**
The Continuing Struggle for Citizen Participation and Democracy
Dimitri Vanoverbeke

14 **Confucian Constitutionalism in East Asia**
Bui Ngoc Son

15 **Religion, Law and Intolerance in Indonesia**
Tim Lindsey and Helen Pausacker

16 **Constitutional Interpretation in Singapore**
Theory and Practice
Jaclyn L. Neo

17 **Politics and Constitutions in Southeast Asia**
Marco Bünte and Björn Dressel

18 **Law and Society in Malaysia**
Pluralism, Religion and Ethnicity
Edited by Andrew Harding and Dian Shah

19 **Judicial Reform in Taiwan**
Democratization and the Diffusion of War
Edited by Neil Chisholm

20 **Constitutional Change in Singapore**
Reforming the Elected Presidency
Edited by Jaclyn L. Neo and Swati S. Jhaveri

21 **Crime and Punishment in Indonesia**
Edited by Tim Lindsey and Helen Pausacker

Crime and Punishment in Indonesia

Edited by Tim Lindsey
and Helen Pausacker

Routledge
Taylor & Francis Group
LONDON AND NEW YORK

First published 2021
by Routledge
2 Park Square, Milton Park, Abingdon, Oxon OX14 4RN

and by Routledge
52 Vanderbilt Avenue, New York, NY 10017

Routledge is an imprint of the Taylor & Francis Group, an informa business

British Library Cataloguing-in-Publication Data
A catalogue record for this book is available from the British Library

Library of Congress Cataloging-in-Publication Data
A catalog record has been requested for this book

ISBN: 978-1-138-31738-3 (hbk)
ISBN: 978-0-429-45524-7 (ebk)

Typeset in Times New Roman
by Newgen Publishing UK

This book is dedicated to the late Munir Said Thalib and all those lawyers, scholars and activists who work tirelessly for law reform in Indonesia.

Geoff Todd, 'Crime and Punishment in Indonesia', 2020. Acrylic and charcoal on paper 110cm x 75cm. Published with kind permission of the artist.

Contents

Contributors

Dina Afrianty is a research fellow at the La Trobe University Law School. She is the author of *Women and Sharia Law in Indonesia: Local Women's NGOs and the reform of Islamic Law in Aceh* (Routledge 2015). Her current research focuses on the intersectionality of gender, law and religion in the context of Indonesia's democratic transition. Dina is the founder and current President of Australia-Indonesia Disability Research and Advocacy Network (AIDRAN). She is also a research fellow at the Center of Social Difference at Columbia University, an Associate of the Centre for Indonesian Law, Islam and Society (CILIS) at the University of Melbourne, and an Associate of the State Islamic University in Jakarta.

Rifqi Sjarief Assegaf is currently completing his PhD at Melbourne Law School. He previously worked in the President's Delivery Unit (UKP4, Unit Kerja Presiden untuk Pengawasan dan Pengendaliuan Pembangunan) and the Satuan Tugas Pemberantasan Mafia Hukum (Presidential Task Force to Eradicate Judicial Corruption). Prior to that, he served as Executive Director of LeIP (2003–2007), a non-governmental organisation concentrating on judicial reform that he co-established. Rifqi's main interests are legal and judicial reform, anti-corruption, and access to information; he is actively involved in research, legal drafting and policy advocacy in those areas. In 2005, he received The Asia Foundation 50th Anniversary Award in Recognition of Outstanding Contribution to Law Reform in Indonesia.

Simon Butt is Professor of Indonesian Law and Associate Director (Indonesia) of the Centre for Asian and Pacific Law at the University of Sydney, where he teaches and researches Indonesian law. He has previously held an Australian Research Council Australian Postdoctoral Research Fellowship and now holds an Australian Research Council Future Fellowship. He completed a doctoral thesis on Indonesia's Constitutional Court, and researches and teaches in Bahasa Indonesia. He has written widely on aspects of Indonesian law, including *The Constitutional Court and Democracy* (Brill 2015), *Corruption and Law in Indonesia* (Routledge 2012), *The Constitution of Indonesia: A Contextual Analysis* (Hart 2012, co-authored with Tim Lindsey), and *Indonesian Law* (Oxford 2018, co-authored with Tim Lindsey).

Apsari Dewi has a PhD from the University of Melbourne. Her doctoral thesis examined the strengths and limitations of international extradition between Indonesia and Australia. She also holds a Bachelor of Laws from Udayana University of Bali and a Master of Laws from the University of Melbourne. Dewi's specialisation is Indonesian criminal law and international crime cooperation. Before commencing her PhD research, she was the Head of the International Cooperation Section of the Attorney General's Office of the Republic of Indonesia and has many years' experience working as a public prosecutor in Denpasar, Bali, and North Jakarta.

Ricky Gunawan is an Indonesian human rights lawyer and former Director of the Community Legal Aid Institute (LBHM), a leading legal aid organisation based in Jakarta, which he co-founded in 2007. He specialises in access to justice, torture, death penalty, mental health, human rights and drugs policy. Ricky lectures at Atmajaya Catholic University and Jentera Law School, where he teaches Drugs Law and Policy. He earned his law degree from the University of Indonesia and holds an MA in Theory and Practice of Human Rights, from the University of Essex, UK with a full scholarship from the Open Society Foundation. In 2017, he won the British Council Award for Social Impact in Indonesia, recognising his contribution and commitment to positive social change and improving lives. In 2019, he was a Global Justice Fellow at the Centre for Criminology, University of Oxford

Nadirsyah Hosen has been working as a Senior Lecturer in the Faculty of Law, Monash University since July 2015. Prior to this, he was an Associate Professor in the School of Law, University of Wollongong. He has a Bachelor's degree from UIN Syarif Hidayatullah Jakarta; a Graduate Diploma in Islamic Studies and Master of Arts with Honours from the University of New England; and a Master of Laws in Comparative Law from Charles Darwin University. He completed his first PhD (Law) at the University of Wollongong and a second PhD (Islamic Law) at the National University of Singapore.

Stephanie Juwana earned her Bachelor of Laws from the University of Indonesia, in 2016, where her studies focused on international maritime law. She was a special advisor to the Minister of Marine Affairs and Fisheries and the Presidential Task Force to Combat Illegal Fishing from 2017 to 2019. Her work mostly relates to capacity-building for law enforcement officers, fisheries resources management, compliance analysis, and international law and relations, but she has also been involved in policy-making and law drafting. She was a contributor to the High-Level Panel for a Sustainable Ocean Economy's Blue Paper 15 on Illegal, Unreported and Unregulated Fishing and Associated Drivers. Prior to working with the dential Task Force to Combat Illegal Fishing, she was legal counsel at the Lubis Ganie Surowidjaja law firm.

Josi Khatarina holds a PhD from the University of Melbourne. Her areas of interest are environmental law and governance and she works as a senior researcher for the Indonesian Centre for Environmental Law (ICEL). Previously, Josi worked as a senior legal specialist at the REDD+ Agency, where she was involved in various law reform initiatives including a licence review, a multi-door approach to enforcement, indigenous community lands, and development of a roadmap for legal reform on natural resources and environmental management. Before that, Josi was an assistant to the Satuan Tugas Pemberantasan Mafia Hukum (Presidential Task Force to Eradicate Judicial Corruption). Early in her career, Josi initiated and headed a national coalition to advocate for the Freedom of Information Law, which was enacted in 2008.

Tim Lindsey is Redmond Barry Distinguished Professor, Malcolm Smith Professor of Asian Law, and Director of the Centre for Indonesian Law, Islam and Society (CILIS) at the University of Melbourne. He was an Australian Research Council Federation Fellow from 2006 to 2011 and a long-serving member, and then chair, of the Board of the Australia-Indonesia Institute. Tim is also a founder and an Executive Editor of the *Australian Journal of Asian Law*. His more than 100 publications include: *Indonesia: Law & Society* (in its second edition); *The Constitution of Indonesia: A Contextual Analysis* (with Simon Butt); and a monograph series, *Islam and Law in Southeast Asia* (three volumes: Indonesia, Singapore, and Malaysia and Brunei, the last two with Kerstin Steiner), as well as *Drugs Law and Legal Practice in Southeast Asia* (2016, with Pip Nicholson); *Religion, Law and Intolerance in Indonesia* (2016, edited with Helen Pausacker); and *Indonesian Law* (with Simon Butt).

Tim Mann is the editor of the *Indonesia at Melbourne* blog, Associate Director of the Centre for Indonesian Law, Islam and Society (CILIS), and a PhD student at Melbourne Law School since 2018, researching legal aid in Indonesia. Before joining CILIS in 2015, Tim spent several years working as a programme officer at The Asia Foundation in Jakarta, partnering with a broad range of Indonesian civil society organisations implementing programmes on religious freedom, human rights, public policy research and civic participation. In addition to his work with the University of Melbourne, Tim continues to work as a consultant on development projects in Indonesia. Tim holds a Master of Development Studies from the University of Melbourne.

Lilis Mulyani works at the Indonesian Institute of Sciences (LIPI) in Jakarta, where she researches land law and agrarian studies, human rights, and legal methodology. Lilis is currently a PhD candidate at the Melbourne

Law School and holds an LLM in Public and International Law, also from Melbourne Law School. Her PhD thesis examines the legal personality of groups and land rights. Her research focuses on Indonesia's Agrarian Law, which has created inequality between groups of people, with powerful institutions such as the state and corporations dominating land use and land control. Lilis has a particular interest in customary and peasant communities.

Raynov Tumorang Pamintori joined Reprieve in March 2015 and is now the South-East Asia Research Fellow on the Death Penalty Team. Prior to joining Reprieve, Raynov worked as a project assistant at Indonesia's National Development Planning Agency, where he supported research on an integrated criminal justice system. During his final year in law school, he also served as a research assistant to the Indonesia Judicial Monitoring Society of the Faculty of Law of the University of Indonesia. There he was involved in research projects related to judicial reform and court monitoring activities. Raynov holds a Bachelor's degree in Law from the Faculty of Law of the University of Indonesia.

Helen Pausacker is Deputy Director of the Centre for Indonesian Law, Islam and Society (CILIS) and a Principal Research Assistant in the Asian Law Centre, both at the University of Melbourne. She is also an Executive Editor of the *Australian Journal of Asian Law*. Helen is an Arts graduate of the University of Melbourne (BA Hons, BLitt and Graduate Certificate in Gender and Development) and Monash University (MA) and holds a PhD from Melbourne Law School. Her publications include *Behind the Shadows: Understanding a Wayang Performance* (1996) and, as editor (with Tim Lindsey), *Chinese Indonesians: Remembering, Distorting, Forgetting* (2005), and *Religion, Law and Intolerance in Indonesia* (2016).

Daniel Peterson is the author of *Islam, Blasphemy, and Human Rights in Indonesia: The Trial of Ahok* (Routledge). Daniel holds a PhD from Australian Catholic University. He is also a qualified lawyer and teacher, fluent in Indonesian, and an Associate of the Centre for Indonesian Law, Islam and Society (CILIS) at the University of Melbourne.

Mas Achmad Santosa is a well-known legal and judicial reform activist in Indonesia. He was appointed by President Susilo Bambang Yudhoyono in 2009 as an acting Commissioner of the Corruption Eradication Commission (KPK) and a member of the Presidential Task Force to Combat Judicial Mafia led by Prof. Kuntoro Mangkusubroto. From 2012 to 2014 he was Deputy Minister/Deputy Head of the Presidential Delivery Unit for Monitoring, Evaluation and Oversight for Development. In 2014, the Minister of Marine Affairs and Fisheries, Susi Pujiastuti, made him head of the Task Force to Combat Illegal, Unreported and Unregulated Fishing. From 2015 to 2019, he was the coordinator of a special advisors group in the Presidential Task Force to Combat Illegal Fishing (Task Force

115). He obtained his Bachelor of Laws from the University of Indonesia (1983) prior to an LLM from the Osgoode Hall Law School of York University, Toronto, Canada (1990) and then a PhD from the University of Indonesia.

Ken M. P. Setiawan is a Lecturer in Asian and Indonesian Studies at the Asia Institute, the University of Melbourne, and an Associate of the Centre for Indonesian Law, Islam and Society (CILIS) at the Melbourne Law School. Her research interests include globalisation and human rights as well as historical violence and transitional justice. She has widely published on the politics of human rights in Indonesia. Ken is the author of *Promoting Human Rights: National Human Rights Commissions in Indonesia and Malaysia* (Leiden University Press 2013).

Leopold (Leo) Sudaryono, is completing a doctorate in criminology at the Australian National University, investigating ways to improve the management of criminal justice systems, including prisons, in Indonesia. Leo has worked for The Asia Foundation since 2006. Prior to that he was a senior programme officer for Oxfam GB in Indonesia and a lawyer at the Legal Aid Institute (LBH) Jakarta in early 1998. He was also a member of the legal staff at KontraS, where he worked closely with the late human rights activist Munir and others in advocating the return of kidnapped pro-democracy activists. Leo has a Bachelor in Law from Diponegoro University, Semarang (1998); a Master's Degree in Human Rights and Civil Liberties (LLM) from the University of Leicester (2002, funded by FCO Chevening); and a Transitional Justice Diploma from the University of Cape Town, South Africa (2005).

Acknowledgements

It is impossible to fully understand Indonesia's troubled legal system without insights into its complex and largely dysfunctional criminal justice system, so often the source of major debate in that country. This volume grew from a small attempt to do this, in the form of a roundtable conference on crime and punishment in Indonesia, convened by the Centre for Indonesian Law, Islam and Society (CILIS) on 29 November 2017 at the University of Melbourne.

The aim of this event was to investigate in detail some of the more controversial problems in contemporary criminal law in Indonesia. The chapters by Dina Afrianty and Tim Mann, Rifqi Sjarief Assegaf, Simon Butt, Apsari Dewi, Ricky Gunawan, Nadirsyah Hosen, Josi Khatarina, Tim Lindsey, Lilis Mulyani, Helen Pausacker, Daniel Peterson, and Ken M. P. Setiawan all originate from this conference. Other chapters were commissioned to fill some obvious gaps in subject matter, although, as we explain in Chapter 1, we have not attempted to cover all aspects of Indonesian criminal law.

The administration of the conference was expertly handled by Kathryn Taylor and Mary Kozlovski, Our thanks also go to the members of CILIS, particularly Tim Mann, for assistance during the editing and proofing process, and to our Dean, Professor Pip Nicholson, and former Dean, Professor Carolyn Evans, for their strong commitment to the study of Indonesian law in the Melbourne Law School. We are also grateful to Professors Michael Ng, Randy Peerenboom and (again) Pip Nicholson, the series editors of Routledge's 'Law in Asia' series, for their support for this project. Tim also expresses his deep gratitude to Allison Stekelenburg for her enthusiasm and relentless support for his work on Indonesia.

Finally, special thanks must go to Peter Sowden, our Routledge editor. This is our second book with Peter and it has again been a pleasure to work with him.

Tim Lindsey and Helen Pausacker
Melbourne, May 2020

Terminology

Non-English terms

Because individual chapters in this book will be read separately from others, a translation of non-English terms used is provided in parentheses or a note the first time each term appears in a chapter. The term is also italicised on first use in that chapter. Most non-English terms also appear in the glossary.

Indonesian usage

For simplicity, 'Law' has been preferred to 'Act' or 'Basic Law', in translating the terms *undang-undang* and *undang-undang pokok*. 'Elucidation' or 'explanatory memorandum' is used for *penjelasan*. For convenience, the term 'Article' (*pasal*) is taken to cover sub-articles (*ayat*), paragraphs, etc.

Different authors in this book have sometimes used slightly different but accurate translations of some Indonesian terms, including passages in legislation and names of institutions. Because these usages reflect their stylistic preferences and their interpretation of the original Indonesian we have not sought to achieve complete standardisation.

The modern Indonesian standard orthography – determined by the Indonesian Ministry of Education since 17 August 1972 – is used for all Indonesian words unless *ejaan lama* (old spelling) is used in quotation, name or title. In the case of names, the spelling used by the person named has been preferred where it is known, thus 'Soeharto' rather than 'Suharto'.

Arabic terms

There is no standard spelling of Arabic terms in Indonesian. Different spellings are often used interchangeably and variations can commonly be found even within individual documents. Different authors in this book therefore sometimes use a range of spelling styles for words derived from Arabic. Again, we have not sought to achieve complete standardisation.

Abbreviations

Acronym/abbreviation (Indonesian full title)	English
ACC	Anti-corruption Court
AGO	Attorney General's Office
Agra (Aliansi Gerakan Reforma Agraria)	Alliance of Agrarian Reform Movement
AILA (Aliansi Cinta Keluarga Indonesia)	Family Love Alliance (*aila* also means 'big family' in Arabic)
AKKBB (Aliansi Kebangsaan untuk Kebebasan Beragama dan Berkeyakinan)	National Alliance for the Freedom of Religions and Beliefs
AMAN (Aliansi Masyarakat Adat Nusantara)	Adat Communities Alliance in Nusantara
API (Aliansi Petani Indonesia)	Indonesian Peasant Alliance
Babinsa (Bintara Pembina Desa)	army non-commissioned officers, charged with keeping the peace locally
BAP (*Berita Acara Pemeriksaan*)	police report
binmas (*bina masyarakat*)	community policing
BKSDA *Balai Konservasi Sumber Daya Alam*	Natural Resource Conservation Council
BNN (Badan Narkotika Nasional Republik Indonesia)	Indonesian National Narcotics Agency
BPHN (Badan Pembinaan Hukum Nasional)	National Law Development Agency
BUMN (Badan Usaha Milik Negara)	State owned company
CV (*Commanditaire Vennootschap*)	limited partnership
DPD (Dewan Perwakilan Daerah)	Regional Representative Assembly
DPR (Dewan Perwakilan Rakyat)	Peoples' Representative Assembly, the national legislature

DPRD (Dewan Perwakilan Rakyat Daerah)	Regional People's Representative Assembly
EGP	Era Giat Prima, a finance company
e-KTP (*Kartu Tanda Penduduk Elektronik*)	national electronic identity card
FIELD	Farmers Initiative for Ecological Livelihood and Democracy
FKWI (Forum Komunikasi Waria Indonesia)	Indonesian Transgender Communication Forum
Formabes (Forum Madura Bersatu)	United Madura Front
FPI (Front Pembela Islam)	Islamic Defenders Front
Fraksi ABRI (Fraksi Angkatan Bersenjata Republik Indonesia)	Armed Forces Fraction
FUI (Front Umat Islam)	Muslim Community Front
gakkum (*penegakan hukum*)	law enforcement
GAM (Gerakan Aceh Merdeka)	Free Aceh Movement
GBHN (Garis-garis Besar Haluan Negara)	Broad Outlines of State Policy
gerpol (*gerilya politik*)	'political guerillas', a derogatory term used for left-leaning, particularly underground, movements or activists
Golkar (Golongan Karya)	'Functional Group', the political party of former Presidents Soeharto and Habibie
GPK (Gerakan Pemuda Ka'bah)	Ka'bah Youth Movement
hansip (*pertahanan sipil*)	civil defence force, a village security officer
HIR (Herziene Indonesisch Regelment)	Civil Procedure Code (colonial code for Java and Madura)
HRCL	Human Rights Court Law, 2000
HRW	Human Rights Watch
ICCPR	International Covenant on Civil and Political Rights
ICJR	Institute for Criminal Justice Reform
IHCS	Indonesian Human Rights Committee for Social Justice
intelkam (*intelijensi dan keamanan*)	[police] intelligence
IPPHTI (Ikatan Petani Pengendalian Hama Terpadu Indonesia)	Indonesian Farmers Association for Pest Control
ITK (*Indikator Tata Kelola*)	indicator
JKPP (Jaringan Kerja untuk Pemetaan Partisipatif)	Working Network for Participatory Mapping

JMSPS (Jaringan Masyarakat Sipil Peduli Syariah)	Civil Society Network for Shari'a (Aceh)
KAMMI (Kesatuan Aksi Mahasiswa Indonesia)	Indonesian Muslim Students' Action Front
Kiara (Koalisi Rakyat untuk Keadilan Perikanan)	The People's Coalition for Fisheries Justice
KIBAR (Kediri Bersama Rakyat)	Kediri Stands with the People
KKN (Korupsi, Kolusi, Nepotisme)	corruption, collusion and nepotism
KNPA (Komite Nasional Pembaruan Agraria)	National Committee for Agrarian Reform
Komnas HAM (Komisi Nasional Hak Asasi Manusia)	National Commission for Human Rights
KontraS (Komisi Untuk Orang Hilang dan Korban Tindak Kekerasan)	Commission for the Disappeared and Victims of Violence
Kopkamtib (Komando Operasi Pemulihan Keamanan dan Ketertiban)	Operational Command for the Restoration of Security and Order
Kostrad (Komando Strategis Angkatan Darat)	Army Strategic Reserve
Kowani (Kongres Wanita Indonesia)	Indonesian Women's Congress,
KPA (Konsorsium Pembaruan Agraria)	Consortium for Agrarian Reform
KPK (Komisi Pemberantasan Korupsi)	Corruption Eradication Commission
kristal (*krisis total*)	total crisis
KUHAP (*Kitab Undang-undang Hukum Pidana*)	Criminal Procedure Code
KUHP (*Kitab Undang-undang Hukum Pidana*)	Criminal Code
KUHPerdata (*Kitab Undang-Undang Hukum Perdata*)	Civil Code
lantas (*lalu lintas*)	traffic unit
LBH (Lembaga Bantuan Hukum)	Legal Aid Institute
LBH APIK (Lembaga Bantuan Hukum – Asosiasi Perempuan Indonesia untuk Keadilan)	Indonesian Women's Association for Justice – Legal Aid Institute
LBH Masyarakat	Community Legal Aid Institute
LeIP (Lembaga Kajian dan Advokasi untuk Independensi Peradilan)	Indonesian Institute for Independent Judiciary
LGBTIQ, LGBT	Lesbian, Gay, Bisexual, Transgender, Intersex, Queer – Indonesians more commonly use LGBT

LPSK (Lembaga Perlindungan Saksi dan Korban)	witness protection agency
MAKI (Perkumpulan Masyarakat Anti Korupsi)	Indonesian Anti-Corruption Community
MenPUPERA (Menteri Pekerjaan Umum dan Perumahan Rakyat)	Ministry of Public Work and Public Housing
Monas (Monumen Nasional)	National Monument
MPR (Majelis Permusyawaratan Rakyat)	People's Consultative Assembly
MPU (Majelis Permusyawaratan Ulama)	Ulama Deliberative Assembly (Acehnese ulama council)
MUI (Majelis Ulama Indonesia)	Indonesian Council of Ulama
NGO	Non-Government Organisation
NPWP (Nomor Pokok Wajib Pajak)	tax file number
NU (Nahdlatul Ulama)	literally, 'Awakening of Ulama', the largest Indonesian Islamic non-government organisation
P2TP2A (Pusat Pelayanan Terpadu Pemberdayaan Perempuan dan Anak)	Integrated Care Centre for the Empowerment of Women and Children
Parman (*Partisipasi teman*)	friends' contributions [to police non-budgetary sources of income]
Parmas (*Partisipasi masyarakat*)	victims' contribution [to police non-budgetary sources of income]
Parmin (*Partisipasi kriminil*)	criminals' contribution [to police non-budgetary sources of income], or bribes
PDI-P (Partai Demokrasi Indonesia – Perjuangan)	Indonesian Democracy Party – Struggle
PDSKJI (Perhimpunan Dokter Spesialis Kedokteran Jiwa Indonesia)	Indonesian Psychiatric Association
Peperti (Penguasa Perang Tinggi)	Supreme War Authority
perda (*peraturan daerah*)	Local (or regional) regulation
Perpu (Peraturan Pemerintah Pengganti Undang-undang)	Government Regulation in Lieu of Law
Petrus (*penembak misterius*)	mysterious shooters (1983–5)
Pid.B (Pidana Biasa)	Regular criminal case
Pid.C (Pidana Cepat)	Fast-tracked criminal case (expedited hearing)
PILNET	Public Interest Lawyers Network
PK (*peninjauan kembali*)	judicial reconsideration
PKBI (Perkumpulan Keluarga Berencana Indonesia)	Indonesia Planned Parenthood Association

PKI (Partai Komunis Indonesia)	Indonesian Communist Party
PKS (Partai Keadilan Sejahtera)	Justice and Prosperity Party
Polda (*Polisi daerah*)	police – regional level
Polres (*Polisi resort*)	police – district level
Polri (*Polisi Republik Indonesia)*	Indonesian police
Polsek (*Kepolisian sektor*)	police – sub-district police office
PON (Peran Olahraga Nasional)	National Games
PPNS (Penyidik Pegawai Negeri Sipil)	civil servant investigators
PPP (Partai Persatuan Pembangunan)	United Development Party
Prolegnas (*Program Legislasi Nasional*)	National Legislation Programme
PT (*Perseroan Terbatas*)	limited liability company
PT BISI	Benih Inti Subur Intani Company
PTPN (PT Perkebunan Nusantara)	Indonesia Plantation Company
PTSP (Perizinan Terpadu Satu Pintu)	One-Stop Integrated Service
Rbg. (*Rechtsreglement Buitengewesten*) (Dut.)	Legal Procedure Regulation for Areas Outside of Java and Madura (colonial legislation)
RUU KUHAP (*Rancangan Undang-Undang Kitab Undang-undang Hukum Pidana*)	draft Criminal Procedure Code
RUU KUHP (*Rancangan Undang-Undang Kitab Undang-undang Hukum Pidana*)	Draft Criminal Code
sabhara (*samapta bhayangkara*)	general security unit of police (riot police and first dispatch for crimes)
SBSI (Serikat Buruh Sejahtera Indonesia)	Prosperous Workers Union of Indonesia
sembako (sembilan bahan pokok)	the nine basic household needs, defined as: rice, sugar, cooking oil or (or margarine), beef/chicken, eggs, milk, kerosene, and salt
SIPERIBUN (Sistem Informasi Perizinan Perkebunan)	Information system for the licensing of plantations
SIT (Surat Izin Terbit)	Licence to Publish
SIUP (Surat Izin Usaha Perdagangan)	Trading permit
SIUPP (Surat Izin Usaha Penerbitan Pers)	Licence for a Publishing Firm

SKPP (*Surat Keputusan Penghentian Penuntutan)*	Prosecution Termination Orders
SKSHH (*Surat Keterangan Sahnya Hasil Hutan*)	Certificate of Validity of Forest Product
SOMO (Stichting Onderzoek Multinationale Ondernemingen) (Dut.)	Centre for Research on Multinational Corporations
SP3 (*Surat Perintah Penghentian Penyidikan*)	Investigation Termination Orders
SPDP (*Surat Pemberitahuan Dimulainya Penyidikan*)	letter informing a suspect that investigation has commenced
SPI (Serikat Petani Indonesia)	Indonesian Peasant Union
Sprindik (*Surat Perintah Penyidikan)*	investigation order
SPSI (Serikat Petani Kelapa Sawit)	Palm-oil Farmers Association
SQBM (Standardisasi, Mutu dan Pembinaan Usaha)	Standardisation, Quality and Business Monitoring
UAE	United Arab Emirates
UDHR	Universal Declaration of Human Rights
UIN (Universitas Islam Negara)	State Islamic University
UN	United Nations
UNDP	United Nations Development Programme
UPR	Universal Periodic Review
VOC (Vereenigde Oost-Indische Compagnie) (Dut.)	Dutch East India Company
Walhi (Wahana Lingkungan Hidup Indonesia)	Indonesian Forum for the Environment
WH (Wilayatul Hisbah)	Shari'a police (Aceh)
WHO	World Health Organization
WvS (Wetboek van Strafrecht Nederlandsch Indie)	Criminal Code for the Dutch East Indies (for Europeans)

Glossary

'uqubat	punishments
acara pemeriksaan biasa	ordinary examination
acara pemeriksaan cepat	expedited examination
acara pemeriksaan singkat	summary examination
acara pidana cepat	expedited case
actus reus (Lat.)	action or conduct which is a constituent element of a crime, as opposed to the mental state of the accused
ada siksa kubur (Ar.)	torture in the grave
adat	traditional or customary 'law'
adzan (Ar.)	call to prayer
ahli telematika	telematics expert (who deals with telecommunications and computer science)
akhlak (Ar.)	morality
Aksi Bela Islam	Action to Defend Islam
alasan pembenar	defences
alat bukti yang sah	piece of valid evidence
Aliansi Kebangsaan untuk Kebebasan Beragama dan Berkeyakinan	National Alliance for Religious Freedom
Aliansi Nasional Reformasi KUHP	National Alliance for the Reform of the Criminal Code
Allahu Akbar (Ar.)	God is Great
al-man'u (Ar.)	prevention
al-qat'u, qat'a (Ar.)	amputation
amar ma'ruf nahi mungkar (Ar.)	commanding good and preventing evil
amicus curiae (Lat.)	someone who is not a party to a case and may or may not have been solicited by a party and who assists a court by offering information, expertise, or insight that has a bearing on the issues in the case

aqidah (Ar. *'aqīda*)	belief, faith, creed
Arus Pelangi	'Rainbow Flow', an LGBT advocacy group
auliya (Ar.)	leader, loyal friend
aurat (Ar. *awra*)	parts of a person's body (different for men and women), which according to Islamic law should be covered when outside the family environment
aznan	Muslim call to prayer
Badan Anggaran	Budgetary Agency
bakpao	Chinese steamed bun
banci	transvestite, transsexual
banding	appeal
basah	wet
batal demi hukum	legally void
Bataviasche Statuten	Colonial legal code for Batavia (now Jakarta)
bea perolehan hak atas tanah dan bangunan	transfer duty for the acquisition of rights over land and buildings
bebas murni	full acquittal
bebas tidak murni	qualified acquittal
bedaya	Javanese dance
berita acara	dossier
berita acara pemeriksaan	summary of records of interviews of witnesses
Berita Acara Persidangan	minutes of court session
berkas	dossier of evidence
berkas terpisah	separate prosecution
berlebihan	disproportionate, exaggerated
Bina Desa	Village Development
bissu	half-man/half-woman – although not necessarily biologically intersex – priests (one of five gender classifications of Buginese in South Sulawesi)
Buku Pedoman Penyelenggaran Organisasi	book of administrative guidelines
Burgerlijk Rechtsvordering	Colonial civil code for European residents of Dutch East Indies
cabul, perbuatan cabul	indecent acts
calabai	'female-acting' biological men (one of five gender classifications of Buginese in South Sulawesi)

calalai	'male-acting' biological women (one of five gender classifications of Buginese in South Sulawesi)
ceroboh	careless
chador	long, shapeless, drably-coloured garment, worn by some Muslim women
delik aduan	complaint offence, that police cannot investigate without a victim submitting a complaint
delik biasa	normal offence, initiated by the police
demi hukum	according to law
Dewan Pertimbangan	Advisory Council
dibodohi	fooled
dibohongi	misled, lied to
ditutup demi hukum	[case] closed by the operation of law
divisualisasikan	viewed
efek jera	deterrent effect
ekonomi syari'ah	shari'ah economy
ekstradisi	extradition
fatwa (pl fatawa)	Islamic legal opinion
Forum Anti Penistaan Agama	Anti-Religious Defamation Forum
Fraksi Karya Pembangunan	The Development Faction
gallon	bottled water (large size)
gangguan usaha perkebunan	disruption of plantation business
gayr ma'qul al-ma'na (Ar.)	unreasonable
gemblak	'kept boy' of *warok*, who dresses as a woman (Ponorogo, East Java, also known as *janthil*)
Gerakan Nasional Pengawal Fatwa MUI	National Movement to Guard MUI Fatwa
Gerakan Reformis Islam	Islamic Reform Movement
golongan rakyat Indonesia	group of Indonesian people
habeas corpus (Lat.)	ruling allowing a person to be brought before a court to determine whether there is legal authority to detain the person
hadd or had (pl. hudud) (Ar.)	specific punishment fixed in the Qur'an for a crime
hadith (Ar., alternative local spelling: *hadis*)	records of the words, deeds and circumstances of the Prophet Muhammad

hajj, haji (Ar. *hajjun*)	annual Islamic pilgrimage to Mecca between the eighth and thirteenth days of the month of *dhul hiijati* to perform specific rites
hakim	judge
hakim ketua	chair of a panel of judges (hearing a case)
hakim pemeriksa pendahuluan	investigating judge
halal (Ar. *ḥalāl*)	permissible, lawful
Herziening van Arresten en Vonnissen, also simply known as 'herziening' (Dut.)	final case review
hibah (Ar. *hiba*)	Charitable bequest/gift of one's wealth given during one's lifetime, or stipulated in a will to be distributed posthumously
Hizbut Tahrir; *Hizb ut-Tahrir* (Ar.)	Party of Liberation, founded 1953 in Jerusalem, an international Islamic political organisation, which also had an Indonesian branch
homoseksual	homosexual
Hoogerechtshof (Dut.)	Supreme Court (colonial)
Hudud (Ar.)	specific punishment fixed in the Qur'an for a crime
hujjah (Ar.)	evidence, proof
hukum acara cepat	fast or expedited legal process
hukum jinayat	Islamic criminal law
hukum positif	positive law
Hukum Revolusi	Revolutionary Law
hukum yang hidup dalam masyarakat	living law (lit. law that lives in society)
ihtimal (Ar.)	possibility
ijtihad (Ar. *ijtihād*)	legal reasoning and interpretation of *Sharī'ah* (Islamic legal theory)
ikhtilath (Ar.)	intermingling (flirting, touching, hugging and kissing)
infaq (also spelled infak) (Ar. *infaq*)	*sadaqa* (giving) for the family; providing the family with its basic needs, see nafkah
Insiden Monas	'Monas Incident', 1 June 2009, peaceful march in support of the *Pancasila*, attacked by FPI
Iqta'u 'anni lisanah/lisanaha' (Ar.)	literally 'cut me off from his/her tongue'

Islam kaffah	Islam in its totality
Jaksa	Public prosecutor
Jaksa Agung	Indonesia's combined Prosecutor General and Attorney General
Jamaah	congregation, group
janthil	'kept boy' of *warok*, who dresses as a woman (Ponorogo, East Java, also known as *gemblak*)
jarimah	Islamic law offences
Jaringan Lesbian dan Gay Indonesia	Indonesian Network of Lesbians and Gays
jilbab	headscarf worn by Muslim women
jinayah, jinayat	Islamic criminal law
kafir (Ar. *kāfir*)	a person who does not believe in Islam
kamar	room
Kamisan	'Thursdays', protest by survivors of human rights violations outside Presidential Palace in Jakarta
Kartu Jakarta Pintar	Smart Jakarta Card
kasasi	cassation
kasasi demi kepentingan hukum	cassation in the interests of law
kasus cadangan	reserve cases
keamanan dan ketertiban	security and order
kedaluwarsa	limitations period
Kehakiman	Ministry of Judicial Affairs
kejahatan	felony, criminal
kejahatan-kejahatan terhadap kesusilaan	moral crimes
keji	despicable
kekuatan hukum tetap	binding or permanent legal force
kenakalan	wayward behaviour, naughtiness
keong/buka keong	snail shell/open the shell: unlock the cell door (colloq.)
kepribadian	identity
keputusan/putusan	judicial decision
keresahan di masyarakat	social unrest
kering	dry
kesusilaan	morality
keterangan ahli	expert testimony
keterangan saksi	witness testimony
ketertiban hukum	legal order
ketua	chair
khalwat (also: khalwa) (Ar.)	prohibited proximity between unrelated persons of the opposite sex, without a third party present

khamar (Ar.)	alcohol, the consumption, producing, storing, selling or gifting of alcoholic beverages
kitab tafsir	exegesis manuscripts
Koalisi Rakyat untuk Kedaulatan Pangan	People's Coalition for Food Sovereignty
Koalisi untuk Kedaulatan Benih Petani	Farmers Seed Sovereignty Coalition
Komisi Kerukunan Umat Beragama	Religious Communities Harmony Commission
Kompilasi (also known as 'Kompilasi Hukum Islam')	Compilation of Islamic Law, the 1991 Indonesian codification of Islamic law on marriage, inheritance and waqf
Koninklijk Besluit (Dut.)	Royal Decree
kurungan	'confinement', light imprisonment (one year, or one year and four months for concurrent crimes); detention
landraden	land councils
Laskar Pembela Islam	FPI's militia
lesbi	lesbian
lese majeste	'injured majesty', offence of insulting the ruler
lex certa (Lat.)	legal certainty
limitatif	limited, restricted
liwath (Ar.)	sodomy
ludruk	drama in which women characters are portrayed by men (Surabaya, East Java)
ma'qul al-ma'na	has a rational intent and understanding
macem-macem itu	suchlike
mafia peradilan	Judicial mafia
Mahkamah Agung	Supreme Court, Indonesia's highest appeal court
Mahkamah Konstitusi	Constitutional Court
Mahkamah Syariah	shari'a courts (Aceh)
Mahram (Ar.)	a close male relative, who one is not allowed to marry, and who therefore can act as a chaperone for a Muslim woman
mairil	younger, prettier boy in a homoerotic relationship in a *pesantren* (Islamic boarding school)
maisir (Ar.)	gambling

majelis taklim	non-formal Islamic education
makunrai	'female-acting' biological women (one of five gender classifications of Buginese in South Sulawesi)
Mama minta pulsa	'Mummy asks for phone credit' – a common fraudulent text message in Indonesia
maqasid	objective
masih banyak lagi	many others
melakukan perbuatan cabul dengan jenis kelamin yang sama	antara sesama orang dewasa conducting an indecent act with an adult of the same sex
melanggar kesopanan	violating decency
melanggar kesusilaan (*aanstotelijk voor de eerbarheid, openbare schennis der eerbarheid* – Dut.)	violating morality
melecehkan	abuse
memanfaatkan	to use
membangkit nafsu birahi	arouse sexual desire
membebaskan dari seluruh dakwaan	acquitted of all charges
memiliki	owning
memperdengarkan	allow to be heard
memperkaya	enrich
memperoleh keyakinan	strong belief
mempertontonkan	to show
mengganggu usaha/bisnis	disrupt business
menghancurkan atau memusnahkan	destroy or exterminate
menghina	to insult
menguntungkan	to profit
menguasai	possessing
menimbang	consider
mens rea (Lat.)	mental element of a crime: a person's intention to commit a crime or knowledge that one's action or lack of action would cause a crime to be committed
menyebarkan	distribute
menyelit	male–male relationship between adult man and youth (Bali)
menyimpan	to save or store
merendahkan	degrade

meresahkan masyarakat	disturb the public peace
merugikan/merusak akhlak	damaging morality
meyelenggarakan	hold [an event]
moral agama	religious morals
muatan pornografi	'pornographic flavour'
multitafsir	multiple interpretations
musahaqah (Ar.)	lesbian sex
mushollah (also spelled mushalla, Ar. *musalla*)	prayer room
mushtarak (Ar.)	ambiguous
mustahil	inconceivable
mutlak	absolute
nabi	apostle, prophet, messenger
Nabi Besar	the 'Big Prophet', the Prophet Muhammad
nafsu birahi	sexual desire
nasi cadong	poor quality steamed rice with tofu/tempe and stewed vegetables, served in prison
nasi goreng	fried rice
nasi padang	rice with spicy chicken or meat, originating from Padang, West Sumatra (often served with separate dishes)
naskah akademik	formal academic study that precedes the drafting of a Bill
natuurlijke person (Dut.)	individual
Nawa Cita	nine-point plan (for Jokowi's first term as President)
negara hukum	law state, rule of law, state based on law. French equivalent: *État de droit*
nilai kesusilaan	moral values
niqab	women's Islamic clothing, which covers the face
Nota Keberatan	Notice of Objection
Nota Kesepahaman Bersama	Joint Agreement
Nota Pembelaan	Notice of Defence
Nota Pendapat	Prosecutor's Note
novum	new determinative evidence or circumstances (a ground for judicial reconsideration)
oroane	'male-acting' biological men (one of five gender classifications of Buginese in South Sulawesi)

padu-serasi	coherency-compatibility
pajak bumi dan bangunan	land and building tax
pakai	use, wear
Pancasila	'five principles', the Indonesian national ideology: 1. belief in an Almighty God, 2. just humanitarianism, 3. unity of Indonesia, 4. democracy guided by consultation and 5. social justice.
Pangéran	Javanese royalty
Panitera Muda Pidana	Head of Clerks for Criminal Cases
Papa Minta Saham	'Papa Wants Shares' (nickname for scandal involving Setya Novanto's attempt to extort shares from Freeport McMoRan)
pelanggaran	violations, misdemeanours, less serious crimes
pelanggaran hak asasi manusia yang berat	gross human rights violations
pelayanan masyarakat	public service (by police, such as traffic or vehicle and driver registration)
pelecehan seksual	sexual abuse
pemeriksaan	trial
pemeriksaan tambahan	investigation
pemerkosaan	rape
pemimpin	leader
pencurian	theft
pencurian dengan kekerasan	theft with violence
pencurian dengan pemberatan	aggravated theft
pendapat dan sikap	opinion and stance
penetapan	judicial order
penetapan fungsi hutan	determination of forest function: stage one of forest establishment
pengadilan negeri	district court
pengadilan tinggi	high court
penghinaan	insult
penghinaan ringan	minor insult or slander
pengulu	religious official
Peninjauan kembali	judicial reconsideration, the final form of 'appeal' to the Supreme Court
penjelasan	elucidation, explanatory memorandum
penodaan	staining, disgracing, desecrating, dishonouring, blaspheme
penodaan agama	blasphemy

penyelidikan	preliminary investigation
penyelundupan hukum	'trafficking in law'
penyidikan	investigation
peradilan agama	religious court (Indonesia's Islamic courts)
peraturan perundang-undangan	statutes and regulations
perbuatan cabul	see: *cabul*
perda	regional or local regulation
perkawinan	marriage
perlakuan yang tak menyenangkan	'offensive treatment' offence
perlindungan hak asasi manusia	protection of human rights
permufakatan jahat	malicious intent
pertimbangan	considerations
petunjuk	indication, circumstantial evidence
Piagam Jakarta	Jakarta Charter, first draft of the 1945 Constitution containing a controversial provision in the preamble that would require Muslims to practise Islamic law. This provision was deleted in 1945.
pidana pengawasan	supervised detention
pidana tutupan	confinement (a form of punishment)
pihak ketiga yang berkepentingan	interested third parties
piket	shift
pistole	the right for a prison inmate to improve his or her prison conditions at his or her own expense
poel van verwording (Dut.)	cesspool of vice
Pola Bangunan Pemasyarakatan	Building Standards for Correction Facilities
porno, pornografi	pornography
pornoaksi	porno-action
prapenuntutan	pre-charge
praperadilan	pretrial procedure in the Code of Criminal Procedure / pretrial hearings
preman	gangster, thug
premim remedium (Lat.)	first resort
Pusaka	heirloom, bequest (forest people's programme in Indonesia)
Puteri Indonesia	Indonesian Princess (beauty contest)
qadzaf (Ar.)	accusing someone of rape, without being able to present four witnesses

qanun (local variant *kanun*)	regional Islamic legislation, positive law, law promulgated by Muslim rulers
Qanun Acara Jinayat	Aceh's Islamic Criminal Procedure Code
Qanun Jinayat	Aceh's Islamic Criminal Code
qat'ul yad (Ar.)	amputation of the hand
qishash, qishas/diat (Ar.)	offences for which compensation or 'retaliation'/'settlement of accounts' may be part of the punishment. The right for a victim to demand the same deed as they suffered – for example, in the case of murder, a murder victim's heirs might demand the murderer's execution
Qur'an (Ar., also spelled *Quran* and *Koran*)	Islamic holy book, believed by Muslims to be the Word of God
Raden van Justitie	courts of justice (colonial)
rasa kesusilaan	moral feelings
rechtspersoonlijkeid (Dut.)	legal person
Reformasi	Reformation, term used for period after the fall of Soeharto in 1998
Reglement op de Strafvordering	Civil Code for Europeans (colonial)
reiningsproces (Dut.)	cleansing process
reserse	criminal detective unit of police
Residentiegerechten	residency courts (colonial)
respondeat superior (Lat.)	doctrine that a party is responsible for acts of their agents
Rois Syuriah (Ar.)	Advisory Leader
saksi fakta	factual witnesses
saksi pelapor	reporting witnesses
sawit	palm oil
schoonmaak (Dut.)	cleaning
secara melawan hukum	illegally
shadaqah, also spelled *sadaqah*, *shodaqah* and *sedekah* (Ar. *sadaqa*)	voluntary charity or giving (zakat is differentiated from *shadaqa* in the Qur'an and Hadith)
societas delinquere non potest (Lat.)	corporations cannot commit a crime
sodomi	sodomy
Solidaritas Perempuan	Women's Solidarity
Staatsblad (Dut.)	bulletin of acts and orders
standar biaya konsumsi tahanan	standard cost for the daily rations (in prison)

Strafvordering (Dut.)	colonial Criminal Code for Europeans
Strafwet voor Inlanders (Dut.)	colonial Criminal Code for 'natives'
surat	document
surat dakwaan	initial indictment letter
surat edaran	Circular Letter, a form of practice note issued by the Supreme Court
Surat Gubernur DKI Jakarta	Governor of Jakarta Letter
surat penghentian penuntutan	written statement explaining why prosecution is terminated
surat pengukuran tanah	land survey document
surat perintah penahanan	detention order
surat teguran	reprimand
surat tuntutan	formal charge
ta'abbudi	ritual only, rituals that cannot be changed
ta'aqquli (Ar.)	reasonable
ta'zir (Ar. *Ta'dhir*)	discretionary punishment, that is, one in which there is scope for both judicial and legislative discretion
tabayyun (Ar.)	seeking clarification
tausiyah or tawṣiya (Ar. awṣā, yūṣī, tawṣiya)	advice from Muslim leaders/scholars that is not a formal *fatwa*
tazir hadd	punishment for a crime that does not have strict requirements of *hadd* punishments
teman setia	loyal friend
tertangkap tangan	caught in the act
testimonium de auditu (Lat.)	prohibition of hearsay
tiang listrik	electricity pole
tidak berdasar	baseless
tidak lengkap	incomplete
tidak pasti	unverified, uncertain
tidak patut	unfit
tidak tepat	inappropriate
tindak pidana	criminal acts
tindak pidana dalam masa perang atau konflik bersenjata	crimes committed in times of war or armed conflict
tindakan penyimpangan yang dilakukan didepan umum	deviant behaviour in public
uang kebersamaan	collective money, paid by prison inmates
ucapan	utterance
Uitlevering van Vreemdelingen (Dut.)	Extradition of Foreigners

ulama (Ar. *alim* – the Arabic plural is *ulama*, but the term ulama is often used in the singular in Indonesia, also spelled *ulema*)	Muslim religious scholars
ulayat	communal title, customary lands
ulayat kaum	clan's communal lands
ultimum remedium	last resort
umma (also ummat, umat and ummah) Islam (Ar. *ummat al-Islam*)	Muslim community
umrah	lesser pilgrimage to Mecca
undang-undang	Law, statute (produced by the national legislature, the DPR)
undang-undang khusus	special laws
Undang-undang Melaka	Laws of Malacca
Undang-undang Tindak Pidana Khusus	Special Crime Statute
undang-undang umum	general laws
upaya hukum luar biasa	extraordinary legal measure (refers to judicial reconsideration)
vies gedoe (Dut.)	dirty stuff
wadam	transvestite, transsexual, combination of 'Hawa Adam' (Eve and Adam)
wakaf (Ar. *waqf*, also spelled *waqaf* or *waqf*)	Islamic charitable foundation, trust or endowment, pious donations
warga negara	citizens
waria	transvestite, transsexual, combination of 'wanita pria' (woman and man)
waris	inheritance
warok	man of prowess, who will often have a young male companion (Ponorogo, East Java)
wayang kulit	shadow puppet performance
wayang wong (Javanese), wayang orang (Indonesian)	dance adaptation of wayang kulit
wethistoirsche interpretative (Dut.)	purposive interpretation of legislation
Wilayatul Hisbah	religious or shari'a 'police' (in Aceh)
Yayasan Putri Waria Indonesia	Foundation for Indonesian Women Transsexuals/Transvestites
Yurisprudensi	Jurisprudence (leading Supreme Court decisions)

yurisprudensi tetap	fixed jurisprudence (Supreme Court decisions usually seen as binding)
zakat (Ar. *zaka* or *zakat*)	charitable contribution required to be made by a Muslim in accordance with Muslim law, Islamic alms-giving
zawajir (Ar.)	deterrence
zedenschoonmaak (Dut.)	moral cleaning
zina (sometimes also spelled 'zinah')	extra-marital relations, adultery, sexual intercourse out of marriage

1 Crime and punishment in Indonesia

Tim Lindsey and Helen Pausacker

The drafting and enforcement of criminal law is the result of a complex interaction between the state, society and individuals. Criminal law is a way of articulating and applying normative ideas about what a community should be like (Case et al. 2017: 55–80). This means it often has profound political significance. It is therefore no surprise that as Indonesia has transitioned from a colonial regime to a dictatorship, then to a democracy (albeit an imperfect one), criminal justice, or, more often, criminal injustice, has played a prominent part in key political events.

That is true of the defence oration of Soekarno at his trial by the Dutch in 1930, a text that could never have prevented his conviction for subversion but which, as *Indonesia Menggugat* [Indonesia Accuses], became a foundational document for Indonesian nationalist resistance (Abdullah 2009: 43–5). It was true of the notorious Kopkamtib[1] military tribunals that sent hundreds of thousands of suspected communists to death or lengthy imprisonment in the mid-sixties, as the armed forces purged the political left and toppled Soekarno from the Presidency he had held since 1945. It is true of the absence – even now – of trials of those who organised those tribunals, as well as the extra-judicial murders of thousands more leftists around the same time. It is true of the political theatre staged by the Legal Aid Institute (Lembaga Bantuan Hukum, LBH) under Soeharto's New Order in the 1980s and 1990s, which turned the subversion trials of doomed dissidents into powerful critiques of the regime (Lev 1996). It is true of the nominal trials that eventually convicted only a handful of soldiers for the murders of students and dissidents in the months leading up to the collapse of the New Order in 1998, amid the chaos of the Asian Financial Crisis (Setiawan, Chapter 4, this volume; US Department of State 1999). It is true of the equally disappointing trials that eventually acquitted those prosecuted for human rights abuses in the violence that preceded East Timor's secession from Indonesia.[2] It is true of the trials of bankers implicated in the brazen theft of bail-out funds pumped into Indonesia after 1999 to salvage the country's shattered financial sector – some of which were still on appeal ten years later. It is true of the 2017 blasphemy trial of Basuki Tjahaja Purnama ('Ahok'), Jakarta's ethnic Chinese Christian governor, as he campaigned to retain office, an event that polarised the nation and brought more than 700,000 anti-Ahok protesters on the streets of the capital (Butt 2017; Peterson, Chapter 15). These are just a few examples; there are many more.

Despite the key role crime and punishment have always played in politics in Indonesia – or perhaps because of it – few Indonesians have confidence in their nation's criminal justice system. They have many reasons for this, but a key one is that too many defendants seem to be convicted in the face of inadequate evidence and blatant disregard for criminal procedural law and defendants' rights. In fact, most Indonesians are familiar with a parade of notorious high-profile trials that have produced results that many observers (including overseas governments and investors, as well as Indonesians) consider blatantly unjust, or at best highly questionable. Well-known examples include the Manulife case, where a foreign insurance company executive was held in prison on dubious fraud charges as leverage in a wider shareholder battle for control of a lucrative business (Linnan 2008). Another was the notorious Jakarta International School scandal, where school staff, including a Canadian teacher, Neil Bantleman, were convicted of child abuse on the flimsiest of evidence, much of which seemed to be manufactured (Paddock 2019). Or the Jessica Wongso case, where a woman was convicted of murdering a friend in a Jakarta café by poisoning her coffee, when not only was there no real evidence ever presented to show she administered poison to her friend, but there was not even reliable evidence that her friend's death was the result of poison in the first place (Budiari 2016; Heriyanto 2016). Yet another example was the Antasari Azhar case, where the former chair of the Corruption Eradication Commission (KPK, Komisi Pemberantasan Korupsi) was imprisoned for the murder of man in an alleged love triangle. He was convicted despite the weak evidence adduced, which seemed to give weight to Azhar's claims that he was framed because of the KPK's success in investigating corruption among law enforcement officials (Coren 2010).

There are also plenty of other, equally controversial cases where the opposite happens: defendants – usually wealthy and politically powerful – are acquitted despite seemingly convincing evidence of their guilt, with courts performing interpretative gymnastics or relying on technical sleight of hand to justify their ruling. One of the best known involved Setya Novanto, the Speaker of the national legislature, the DPR (Dewan Perwakilan Rakyat, People's Representative Assembly) and former Golkar Party Chairman, who was able to persuade the courts to dramatically reinterpret criminal procedure law to halt a police investigation of him for corruption (Mann, Chapter 5, this volume).

However, the criminal cases that concern Indonesians are not just about the elite in the capital city either. The country has repeatedly been scandalised by the prosecution of villagers and the poorest of the poor for thefts of the most petty kind – Cacao seeds, a pair of plastic sandals, old plates, fallen branches in a forest – with convictions and hefty prison terms imposed in some cases (Assegaf, Chapter 9, this volume). Some of these cases involved villagers foraging on what were once their traditional lands (Mulyani, Chapter 14, this volume). Few doubt that many of the judges in these cases were simply following the wishes of powerful local business interests, such as plantation owners, logging and mining companies, and the like. These powerful groups, which routinely exploit poorly drafted and implemented state regulation of the resources and forests sectors, have been able to use criminal law as an effective tool in their efforts to divest local communities – often traditional groups – of land rights and access to resources they have enjoyed for generations. Cases like this reinforce popular perceptions that, as Indonesians often say, the 'law is like a knife, *tumpul ke atas, tajam ke bawah*': blunt upwards but sharp downwards.

One does not need to look far for explanations for disturbing acquittals and convictions of the kinds just described. Indeed, it is widely accepted in Indonesia that the criminal justice system in Indonesia is permeated by corruption, from top to bottom, and therefore routinely abused by the wealthy and influential. Responsibility for this is usually said to rest with the infamous 'judicial mafia' (*mafia peradilan*), a term popularly used In Indonesia to refer to all corrupt law enforcers. Successive presidents and chief justices have repeatedly publicly bewailed the judicial mafia and vowed to eradicate it (Butt and Lindsey 2011; Goodpaster 2002). They have little to show for their efforts beyond the occasional scalp of a token police officer, prosecutor or judge, usually taken by the now-beleaguered and politically constrained KPK (Satuan Tugas 2010), although the 2013 imprisoning for life of Akil Mochtar, the Chief Justice of the Constitutional Court, for taking bribes in electoral disputes was undoubtedly a significant achievement in itself.

One of the consequences of the persistent corruption of criminal law enforcement (and sometimes a cause of it) in Indonesia is continuing low levels of competence among many police, prosecutors and judges. This contributes to the common pattern of closing ranks when the conduct of a particular case comes under fire, no matter how egregious. Often this is also done to protect the corrupt system but there are times when even honest law enforcers do the same thing. It is a brave – and rare – Indonesian judge who is prepared to incur the enmity of local police and prosecutors or his or her peers on the bench, let alone the Supreme Court, which has control over judicial career paths. The Supreme Court will reverse lower courts in the most controversial cases, and sometimes even overturn itself, but this is often when the criticism is too intense, and it cannot resist the institutional urge to realign itself with public opinion. Or it might simply be because the bench has been bribed.

The road to dysfunction

The dysfunction of Indonesia's criminal justice is no recent aberration. In fact, it is the result of long trajectory that Lev (1996, 1999) traces to the collapse of parliamentary democracy in that late 1950s, but which has antecedents in the ideological debates of nationalist leaders in the years leading to the declaration of independence in 1945. The debates then about the form the new republic would take included contests between advocates of a liberal democratic republic, supporters of a socialist system, those who called for an Islamic state, and proponents of authoritarianism or, in Indonesian political thought, 'Integralism' (Bourchier 1998; Lubis 1993). Eventually, a democratic model was agreed upon but the task of drafting the constitution was given to the foremost proponent of Integralism, Professor Soepomo. Integralism takes what history has proven to be the naïve view that state and society are identical and unified and therefore there is no need for rights or checks and balances, as the state, embodied in a charismatic ruler, will always have the interests of the people at heart. Predictably, the document Soepomo produced established a very powerful presidency and gave limited authority to the other organs of state. It also conferred no rights on citizens, leaving them instead to be dealt with by the legislature, at its discretion. This set a model for criminal justice that empowered the state, saw the courts essentially as an arm of the executive, and paid little attention to rights.

This model has proved persistent and influential in Indonesian legal culture ever since. That is so even though Indonesia soon adopted liberal democratic constitutions, first on a federal model in 1949 and then as a unitary state in 1950. In fact, the next seven years was a unique period of relative integrity for the criminal justice system, with a high sense of professionalism among lawyers and judges, reflecting the lengthy charter of rights, separation of powers and judicial independence guaranteed in these two constitutions (Lev 1996). This system began to unravel in 1957, when President Soekarno declared a form of emergency rule, suspending most state institutions. It finally came to an end two years later, when he unilaterally (and unconstitutionally) abolished the liberal democratic constitution and reintroduced the Integralist constitution of 1945, allowing him to rule directly (Butt and Lindsey 2018: 7–8). The promulgation of what he called 'Revolutionary Law' (*Hukum Revolusi*) and the power he asserted to intervene in the legal process and overrule court decisions as he saw fit soon led to a rapid deterioration of professionalism across the legal sector, and the politicising of the criminal process. The result was, as Lev (1999) says, harsh laws, unfair trials, incompetent prosecutions, judicial errors, and disproportionate sentences.

When Soeharto toppled Soekarno, taking power in 1966, his promises to restore legality and the rule of law (*negara hukum*) were welcomed but quickly proved illusory. Instead, Soeharto continued the arbitrary rule of his predecessor, and in some respects even extended it, facilitated by a military bureaucracy that quickly took control of government (Lubis 1993). Despite swinging Indonesia from the political left to the right, Soeharto's New Order retained the Integralist model developed under Soekarno, with all the problems for criminal justice just described but now complicated by a new problem, as corruption became commonplace (Pompe 2005). This certainly took the form of political influence – so-called 'telephone justice', where law enforcers waited for a call from the presidential palace relaying instructions before making decisions (Zifcak 1999) – but an elaborate system of institutionalised state-sanctioned bribery also emerged. It famously stretched from police stations, to prosecutors' offices, to the steps of the courts (where 'casebrokers' waited, clipboards in hands, to collect and distribute bribes), to judges' chambers, to the palace, which was believed to receive a cut of most illegal payments made to state officials. In time, this vast and highly organised system of corruption became the only effective way for defendants to deal with criminal charges, and it was effective against almost anything but direct intervention by the First Family (Lindsey 1999; Pemberton 1999; Southwood and Flanagan 1983).

Soeharto fell in 1998 amid riots triggered by *kristal* (*krisis total*, total crisis), the political and economic chaos delivered by Indonesia's catastrophic financial collapse after the rupiah was floated in 1997. The 1945 Constitution was soon comprehensively revised to deliver another swing of the political pendulum, this time back towards liberal democracy. The amended 1945 Constitution that was finalised in 2002 after four years of heated legislative debate would have been almost unrecognisable to Professor Soepomo. It had been expanded from 71 to 199 articles,[3] so that 89 per cent were new or amended (Horowitz 2013). It was now was far more similar to the liberal democratic constitution of 1950 than the sparse 'lightning constitution' he had written. It contained, among other things, a lengthy charter of rights, separation of powers, a Constitutional Court (for the first time), guarantees of free and fair elections, and provisions that forced the military out of politics and back into the barracks. Judicial independence was also guaranteed. As a result, the Supreme Court was taken out from under the long-standing control of the Ministry of Judicial Affairs (*Kehakiman*) and given independent authority over Indonesia's courts. Judges across the country were given salary increases, bigger court budgets, and improved judicial education (Pompe 2005).

These changes were dramatic and far-reaching, and led to the creation of new, much more open society and a far more democratic political system. However, they have not proved sufficient to resolve the deep problems the criminal justice system inherited from the first two presidencies, in particular the lack of judicial professionalism and the traditions of institutionalised collusion between police, prosecutors and judges. The courts have gone 'from non-independence to independence without accountability' and are highly resistant to efforts to introduce oversight (Hosen 2017: 187). It follows that while political interference does seem to have decreased significantly (Butt and Lindsey 2011), there is no evidence that the entrenched system of corruption developed under the New Order has decreased as well. In fact, judicial corruption convictions confirm that it is alive and well (Butt and Lindsey 2011; Jakarta Globe 2012; Jakarta Post 2011; Satuan Tugas 2010). As the United Nations Special Rapporteur on the Independence of Judges and Lawyers who visited Indonesia in 2002 concluded:

> allegations of widespread corruption are real. Though there is no doubt that there are some honest judges, the integrity of these judges is tainted by unabated and widespread judicial corruption.
>
> (Cumaraswamy 2003: 18)

A failing system

Today, more than two decades since Soeharto resigned, Indonesia's criminal justice system seems strained close to breaking point. Few who are involved in it can honestly speak well of it. To be sure, there are certainly courageous lawyers – private, NGO and state – who are committed to justice and the rule of law, but the task they face is overwhelming. Because very little of the complex machinery of criminal law enforcement works as it should, it is hugely difficult for an honest lawyer to find a foothold. For starters, the legislative foundations of the criminal justice system are two hangovers of previous eras: the re-enacted colonial Criminal Code of 1918, and the Soeharto-era Criminal Procedure Code of 1981 (Fitzpatrick 1999), and even the few relatively progressive aspects of the latter are ignored. Both statutes are flawed and outdated documents that need reform, but the bills to replace them currently before the national legislature, the DPR, are, in many respects, little better, and in some respects much worse, as explained below. Efforts over many years to patch up their shortcomings by passing other regulation has led to a forest of 'special purpose' statutes and regulations, many overlapping and some contradicting one another (Butt and Lindsey Chapters 2 and 3, this volume; Butt and Lindsey 2018: 186–7). They include aspirational human rights laws that have never been properly applied.

Likewise, the institutions entrusted with the enforcement of these laws, police, prosecutors and judges, rarely function as they should, as suggested above. Too many police are corrupt, routinely use violence, and ignore the rights of defendants enshrined in legislation, including basic rights to legal advice. Too many prosecutors remain among the less reformed and most corrupt public servants in Indonesia, and routinely monetise *basah* (wet) criminal cases, where funds can be extracted, and neglect or mishandle *kering* (dry) cases that cannot be monetised. And the courts – which usually ignore or cover-up the behaviour of police and prosecutors – are too often showpieces for 'institutional resistance' to reform (Aspandi 2002; Lev 1996; Yunto 2008), rather than the forum that ensures reforms are implemented. Three of the most serious problems are the lack of weight given to the presumption of innocence, the general paucity and weakness of judicial reasoning in criminal judgments, and gross inconsistencies in sentencing, something that is usually hard to explain other than by assuming corruption, incompetence, or, charitably, very poor training.

It is true that, as argued above, most of these problems are long-standing but a good deal have worsened over the last fifteen years. There are many reasons for this, including President Susilo Bambang Yudhoyono's reluctance to take firm action to support reform, a failing that became more obvious in the course of his second term (2009–14), and the limited interest President Joko Widodo ('Jokowi') has in legal issues and his even more limited enthusiasm for law reform, both of which were apparent even in his first term (2014–19). However, part of the explanation must also include growing social conservativism and, in particular, the rise of religious intolerance among Indonesia's Muslim majority. This is often manipulated by members of the elite for political gain, usually at the expense of vulnerable people such as LGBT[4] individuals, minority religions, and Indonesia's many unorthodox religious groups, which are often reported by Islamist groups to police for prosecution for a range of moral offences (Lindsey and Pausacker 2016). The use of Islamic norms in legislation to achieve these ends by creating new moral offences, typically produced by politicians with an eye on the ballot box rather than the scriptures, has been increasingly problematic since around 2005 (Buehler 2016). This is especially true of Aceh, the only province in Indonesia with the legal right to apply shari'a, where rights – especially of women and minority groups – are increasingly curtailed.

All these factors, combined with politicians' now-entrenched penchant for criminalisation as the preferred policy response to the many issues that come before the nation's national and regional legislatures, have led to extreme levels of prison overcrowding. This has created horrific conditions for the quarter of a million Indonesians now incarcerated. Sadly, this abusive neglect also extends to the death penalty, which (as is so often the case elsewhere in the world) became a tool for political popularity in President Jokowi's first term, from 2014 to 2019. The complex criminal law in this area has at times been openly flouted by the government, with tragic consequences (Gunawan and Pamintori, Chapter 11).

The result is that Indonesia has a criminal justice system that is failing. For the state, it is not a reliable instrument of policy, an effective way to impose its will on society and individuals, because it is subject to corruption, resistance and incompetence. For the same reasons, it offers society little protection from corrupt individuals, who, if they have political financial and political means, can easily subvert the system. On the other hand, individuals who lack political or financial means find the system offers them little or no defence against state and society, should either decide to mobilise the criminal justice system against them.

Crime and punishment in this book

This book is not an attempt to provide a comprehensive overview of Indonesia's criminal justice system; that has been done elsewhere.[5] It does not pretend to cover all aspects of criminal law enforcement, or to capture every one of the many challenges this troubled system faces; that would be beyond the reach of even multiple volumes. Rather this book presents a series of in-depth studies of some of the major problems just described, snapshots that together offer insights into a complex criminal justice system in crisis by locating it in Indonesia's complex wider social and political contexts.

The book begins with an overview of Indonesia's two flawed criminal law codes. The first two chapters in this part are introductory in nature. They are intended to provide the reader who lacks prior knowledge of the codes with descriptive background information, and act as reference that we hope will be useful as they read the other chapters. In Chapter 2, Tim Lindsey and Simon Butt discuss the Criminal Code. In the following chapter, they discuss the Criminal Procedure Code.

In Chapter 4, Ken M. P. Setiawan considers the possible inclusion of the crime of genocide and other crimes against humanity in the draft Criminal Code currently before the DPR. She examines these concepts in international and national law, then discusses the reasons for the inclusion of these extraordinary crimes in the draft Criminal Code. Finally, she considers what such inclusions may mean for Law No. 26 of 2000 on the Human Rights Courts, which currently regulates the crime of genocide and crimes against humanity. She argues that the codification of these crimes in the Criminal Code is problematic, as it diminishes the extraordinary character of the offences. Their inclusion in the Criminal Code, she says, may contribute to continuing current patterns of impunity for such offences, rather than combating it.

The second part of the book deals with crime, reform and the Courts. In Chapter 5, Tim Mann examines *praperadilan,* the contentious pretrial procedure in the Code of Criminal Procedure, first introduced in 1981. In recent years, the pretrial mechanism has been subject to multiple challenges in the Constitutional Court. He examines the evolving practice of pretrial hearings, including recent Constitutional Court decisions and Supreme Court guidelines that have altered the nature of these proceedings. As a case study, he examines the legal troubles of prominent politician Setya Novanto and explains how Novanto was able to exploit the pretrial motion mechanism to dodge prosecution.

In the following chapter, Tim Lindsey examines the Supreme Court's final stage of appeal, the PK (*peninjauan kembali*) or judicial reconsideration. The provisions of the Code of Criminal Procedure that establish judicial reconsideration have been the source of much controversy and continual re-interpretation, particularly as they apply to criminal cases. He examines two issues that have been particularly problematic: whether more than one application for judicial reconsideration is permitted, and whether prosecutors are entitled to apply for judicial reconsideration of acquittals. Despite repeated interventions by the DPR, the executive and the Constitutional Court, these two much-debated issues still lack full resolution, largely because the Supreme Court has consistently resisted interpretations that favour the rights of defendants. The Supreme Court's interpretations could well be confirmed if the draft Criminal Code now before the DPR is passed. The result is that this 'extraordinary legal mechanism' seems to have become detached from its original purpose – providing a last chance to defendants who have suffered manifest injustice.

In Chapter 7, Apsari Dewi rethinks Indonesia's Extradition Law, another legacy of the Dutch colonial era. Extradition law has developed slowly in Indonesia, with the Dutch legislation only replaced by an Indonesian statute in 1979, which remains in force. She discusses whether this Law meets modern standards of extradition and, in particular, whether it achieves an appropriate balance between good international relations, effective prosecution of transnational crime, and protection of human rights. Dewi concludes that it does not, and recommends urgent reforms to bring extradition practice in Indonesia into line with international practice.

The third part of the book examines penalties and sentencing. In Chapter 8, Leopold Sudaryono looks at prison overcrowding, which, as mentioned, has reached crisis point in Indonesia, with the number of inmates doubling in just five years from 71,000 to 139,000 from 2004 to 2009, and then almost doubling again to 226,000 in 2016, a growth rate four times the global average. In many major cities in Indonesia, prisons hold up to 520 per cent of their official capacity. Sudaryono finds that overcrowding means the prisons are unable to function properly and that inmates' daily lives are adversely affected. He examines changes in penal policy in Indonesia after the 1998 reforms, including the political enthusiasm for creating more and more new criminal offences, and explains how these factors drive prison overcrowding.

In Chapter 9, Rifqi S. Assegaf examines sentencing for minor property offences and how this has been affected by the Supreme Court's Regulation No. 2 of 2012, which increased the threshold loss required for offences to be considered a minor offence under the Criminal Code. Specifically, the regulation changed the threshold for minor theft and embezzlement from smaller than or equal to Rp. 250 to Rp. 2,500,000 and increased the fine for offences from Rp. 250 to Rp. 250,000. This should make it much harder for police to detain petty offenders before trial, while at the same time creating realistic fines that are better deterrents and offer judges alternatives to incarceration when sentencing. However, Assegaf argues that this regulation, while much-needed, is still not effective for a number of reasons, including: the resistant attitude of judges; lack of awareness or understanding of the regulation; practical issues (such the police's strong preference for pretrial detention); and, of course, corruption.

The following chapter is also by Rifqi S. Assegaf. In it, he finds that there is an increasing trend for the national legislature to create so-called 'special criminal statutes' with mandatory minimum penalties. From 1997 to 2014, for example, 219 new offences were introduced that had mandatory minimum sentences. Indonesian law enforcement officials have resisted some of these, with many judges simply refusing to impose the minimum penalties required. Assegaf argues that while the public generally expects the courts to impose severe sentences in these cases, the gravity of the offences and the culpabilities of the offenders are, in reality, extremely, diverse. They range from low-level officials who received only small profits for assisting an offence, to high-ranking officials and businesspersons who obtain huge profits and cause significant loss to state finances.

In Chapter 11, Ricky Gunawan and Raynov T. Pamintori discuss the increasing use of the death penalty between 2015 and 2016, when Indonesia carried out three rounds of executions, executing a total of eighteen people, all drug offenders. Human rights organisations, both domestic and abroad, criticised President Jokowi's use of the death penalty and executions to address what he claimed was a national 'drugs emergency'. Gunawan and Pamintori argue that the death penalty does not deter drug crimes and, in Indonesia's flawed justice system, the risk of miscarriage of justice means there is a real possibility of executing innocent people. Despite this, the general public in Indonesia still firmly supports the death penalty, believing it has a deterrent effect. Gunawan and Pamintori also consider the prospects for abolition of the death penalty, finding that while it is unlikely at present, there is some prospect of reducing how often the death sentence is imposed and actually carried out.

The fourth part of the book examines crime and the environment. Mas Achmad Santosa and Stephanie Juwana argue in Chapter 12 that although Indonesian law has made some effort to conceptualise corporate criminal liability in relation to environmental damage, it has not yet developed as it should. Their chapter provides an overview of the historical development of corporate criminal liability in Indonesia and the laws regulating it, examining four environmental cases in which corporations were tried and punished. Santosa and Juwana show that law enforcers lack a shared common understanding of a corporate crime. They explore how these different conceptualisations drive discrepancies in the application of corporate criminal liability that have allowed companies to escape punishment for causing serious environmental damage.

Josi Khatarina examines non-compliance with the natural resources licensing regime for palm oil in the following chapter. She finds that, following trends in other natural resources management laws, the 2014 Plantation Law introduced heavy criminal sanctions for officials who issue licences not in accordance with existing laws and regulations. These penalties were introduced after research had shown that there was widespread non-compliance by local governments with national guidelines for the issue of plantation licences. However, Khatarina finds that there is still no sign of these new punitive provisions being used, and non-compliant licences continue to be issued. She argues this is largely because of lack of commitment and capacity on the part of the government agencies responsible for implementing them, and their entrenched reluctance to cooperate on enforcement.

In Chapter 14, Lilis Mulyani examines criminal injustice and land conflicts in Indonesia, arguing that these typically occur because of contestation between holders of registered land rights and traditional communities who rely on informal, traditional rights. Regional and local governments favour businesses seeking land for economic extraction, with many licences and formal land titles acquired by bypassing proper procedures. Title holders then use the state law enforcement apparatus to enforce their 'rights', and local people are criminalised for accessing land that they could formerly freely access, or which was owned by their community, or even their own families. This has excluded many local people from their ancient customary lands, particularly those living in traditional communities. Mulyani argues that these land conflicts should be resolved not by criminal law but by policies that create more just and equal access to land, and in particular, recognition of traditional rights to customary lands or communal title (*ulayat*).

The fifth part of the book examines crime and religion. In Chapter 15, Daniel Peterson examines the legal arguments mounted by Ahok's legal team against the blasphemy charges their client faced, charges made stronger by the 2010 landmark decision of the Constitutional Court to uphold Indonesia's blasphemy law. Peterson examines Ahok's lawyers' legal defences, including those based on constitutional and statutory human rights guarantees (freedom of expression and procedural fairness), as well as an evidence-based response to the charge of blasphemy and the lesser charge of inciting hatred against a group. He also considers use by the prosecutor of a *fatwa* (religious legal opinion) of MUI (Majelis Ulama Indonesia, Indonesia's influential Council of Ulama), concluding that it deeply prejudiced Ahok's right to a fair trial.

In Chapter 16, Helen Pausacker examines the increasing number of laws that criminalise Indonesian lesbian, gay, bisexual and transgender (LGBT) people. Although homosexuality is not illegal per se at the national level in Indonesia, more and more discriminatory laws are being passed in a number of regions, particularly Aceh. Indonesian LGBT people now also face the possibility of imprisonment under national laws, such as the 2008 Pornography Law, which criminalises public sexual conduct. Finally, Pausacker details debate underway about whether homosexuality should be included as a crime in any new criminal code.

In the following chapter, Helen Pausacker compares the cases of Habib Rizieq Shihab, leader of the FPI (Front Pembela Islam, Islamic Defenders Front) and Nazril Irham, a member of boy-band Peterpan (now Noah), known as Ariel. Both were charged under the 2008 Pornography Law. Rizieq's case related to screenshots of salacious WhatsApp conversations that went viral on the internet. Ultimately, these charges were dropped. On the other hand, Ariel was imprisoned after videos of sexual activity with two ex-girlfriends went public. The provisions of the Pornography Law allow the production of pornography for personal purposes but do not allow distribution of pornography. Both cases seem to have been misconceived, because neither Rizieq nor Nazril were accused of personally uploading the material to the internet, and the people who did upload it were never charged. In fact, it seems there was no real investigation to find who perpetrated the uploading. Pausacker asks whether the Pornography Law is being (mis)used for political purposes to punish people for perceived immoral behaviour.

In Chapter 18, Nadirsyah Hosen examines Islamic *hudud* (Islamic criminal law, specific punishment fixed in the Qur'an for a crime), punishment, focusing on the common claim of Islamist hardliners that applying *hudud* punishments, particularly amputation of the hands of thieves, would free Indonesia from corruption. Hosen tests this assumption by, first, looking at the interpretation of the relevant Qur'anic verses in a modern context; second, by evaluating the current situation of Indonesian corruption; and, finally, by comparing Indonesia with other countries. He argues that Islamic *hudud* is decidedly not the solution to Indonesia's entrenched corruption problems.

The sixth, and final, part of the book discusses criminal law in Aceh which is, as mentioned, the only province in Indonesia that has the legal power to apply shari'a. In Chapter 19, Tim Mann and Dina Afrianty examine the *Qanun Jinayat*, Aceh's Islamic Criminal Code, passed by the DPRA (Dewan Perwakilan Rakyat Aceh, Aceh's People's Representative Council under regional autonomy laws in 2014. They discuss the fact that the Qanun Jinayat introduces several Islamic criminal law offences that are not covered by the national Criminal Code and extends punishment for them to non-Muslims, including the internationally-condemned public caning of two men for consensual homosexual sex in May 2017. They detail the points of conflict between the Criminal Code, other national laws and the *Qanun Jinayat*. In conclusion, Mann and Afrianty reflect on the prospects for reform of criminal law in Aceh in the future.

In Chapter 20, Simon Butt critiques decisions of Indonesia's Supreme Court dealing with the validity of Qanun, laws passed by Aceh's provincial legislature, and, in particular, the court's 2015 decision to throw out an application for judicial review of Aceh's Qanun Jinayat on a technicality.[6] Butt argues that the Court should have proceeded to hear the case, which raised very important questions about the operation of Indonesian criminal law. He comments that the decision reflects the court's strong tendency to rely on formalistic justifications as way to avoid deciding politically difficult cases, particularly those dealing with the status of Islamic law.

Conclusion

In late 2019, Indonesia's criminal justice system once again became the subject of major national political controversy. With a newly-elected DPR due to be sworn in on 1 October, the outgoing members had flagged their determination to pass a new criminal code before their term ended. The draft code included many highly controversial provisions, including, among others, some that would make it an offence to criticise either the president (as had been the case until a similar provision was struck down by the Constitutional Court in 2006)[7] or the courts. Other provisions would criminalise most forms of extramarital sex and would facilitate persecution of LGBT Indonesians. There was no public consensus in support of the draft code, and these and many other provisions were hotly contested by a range of interest groups, including conservative Muslim groups and progressive civil society activist groups.[8]

In fact, fear the draft code would soon become law helped sparked some of the largest student demonstrations in Indonesia since the fall of Soeharto in 1998. Thousands of students and members of civil society marched in cities across Indonesia under the banner 'Reform Corrupted' (*Reformasi Dikorupsi*) (LBH 2019). Their objections to the code were accompanied by protests against another statute passed by the DPR shortly before it turned its attention to the Criminal Code: Law No. 2 of 2019 on the Second Amendment of Law No. 30 of 2002 on the KPK. This now prevents the KPK from conducting wiretaps, searches and seizures without permission from a new supervisory board appointed by the president. Protesters saw this Law as a defensive measure by the government intended to gut the highly-regarded KPK, preventing it from conducting the fearless investigations of corruption among the political, bureaucratic and business elites for which it became famous, and which no other Indonesian agency has ever been able to achieve. The protests soon became violent, with three dead and 273 hospitalised on one night in Jakarta alone (Wijaya 2019; Prabowo 2019). Police arrested more than a thousand students, detained many of them without charge, and, according to legal aid lawyers, denied many access to legal counsel (Briantika 2020; LBH 2019; Lokataru 2019), Under pressure from President Jokowi, the DPR relented, and agreed to leave a decision on the Criminal Code to the incoming DPR. Jokowi, however, resisted demonstrators' calls to use his power to issue an emergency regulation to repeal the new KPK Law.

As mentioned, the draft Criminal Code remains before the new DPR, and there can be little doubt that if politicians move to pass it, it will again generate enormous public opposition, as there is still no social consensus in support of it. The multifaceted dysfunction of the national criminal justice system, and its deeply politicised nature, means that any changes to any part of it – for better or worse – will have direct impact on most Indonesians, whether rich or poor, and deep ramifications for how Indonesian state and society operates. A new Criminal Code would affect every social group in Indonesia, although in very different ways. The interests of politicians are diverse; for example, some are concerned to cater to religiously intolerant identity politics, while others seek legitimacy by opposing that. Most, however, are unified by a fear of increased transparency, given corruption is as engrained in Indonesian politics as much as it in the courts, and it ties politicians to corrupt businesses and the judicial mafia. This sets them at all odds with most of the public. While the public may be divided over many issues, including morally conservative regulation, most generally want greater accountability from the elites that rule them, and would particularly like to see law makers and law enforcers reined in.

These divergent interests mean that national agreement about the kind of criminal justice reform that, as this book aims to demonstrate, Indonesia urgently needs, is likely to remain elusive. It also means that even if reforms of the kind proposed by the contributors to this volume are passed into law, it will be extraordinarily difficult for them to be fully and fairly implemented.

Notes

1 Kopkamtib (Komando Operasi Pemulihan Keamanan dan Ketertiban, Operational Command for the Restoration of Security and Order) was established in late 1965 after the attempted coup, to 'cleanse' or 'annihilate' members of the PKI (Partai Komunis Indonesia, Indonesian Communist Party). See Robinson 2019: 63.
2 Setiawan, Chapter 4, this volume; Human Rights Watch (2002); and see Butt and Lindsey (2018: 276) for a table summarising the outcomes in these trials and the related appeals.
3 This calculation counts each sub-article separately to reach 199 articles. See Asshiddiqie (2017).
4 In many Western countries, it is now common to use the acronym LGBTIQ or LGBTQI, or even LGBTIQ++, which adds 'intersex' and 'queer' to the list of terms. It is currently rare for Indonesians to add these terms, so we have adopted the four-letter acronym, as used in Indonesia.
5 There are many detailed Indonesian language commentaries on criminal law. See for example, Sugandhi (1981) and Soesilo (1974). For an English language summary, see Butt and Lindsey (2018).
6 Supreme Court Decision No. 60 P/HUM/2015
7 Constitutional Court Decision No. 013-022/PUU-IV/2006.
8 For a summary of the more problematic provisions of the draft code, see Butt and Lindsey, Chapter 2, this volume.

References

Abdullah, Taufik 2009. *Indonesia: Towards Democracy*. Singapore: ISEAS

Aspandi, Ali 2002. *Menggugat Sistem Hukum Peradilan Indonesia Yang Penuh Ketidakpastian* Jakarta: Lembaga Kajia Strategis Hukum Indonesia dan Lutfansah Mediatama

Asshiddiqie, Jimly 2017. *Indonesian Post-Crisis Constitutional Reform: an Incremental Big-Bang Constitutional Change between 1999–2002* https://law.unimelb.edu.au/__data/assets/pdf_file/0010/2607391/Indonesia-Asshidique.pdf

Bourchier, David 1998. 'Positivism and Romanticism in Indonesian Legal Thought', in Tim Lindsey (ed.), *Indonesia: Law and Society.* Sydney: Federation Press, pp. 186–96

Briantika, Adi 2020. 'Koalisi Kritik KomnasHAM Soal Pendataan Aksi 'Reformasi Dikorupsi, *Tirto.id*, 31 January https://tirto.id/koalisi-kritik-komnas-ham-soal-pendataan-aksi-reformasi-dikorupsi-ev6e

Budiari, Indra 2016. 'Court Drama Ends as Jessica Gets 20 Years', *The Jakarta Post*, 28 October www.thejakartapost.com/news/2016/10/28/court-drama-ends-as-jessica-gets-20-years.html

Buehler, Michael 2016. *The Politics of Shari'a Law: Islamist Activists and the State in Democratic Indonesia*. Cambridge: Cambridge University Press

Butt, Simon 2017. 'Why is Ahok in Prison? A Legal Analysis of the Decision', *Indonesia at Melbourne*, 6 June https://indonesiaatmelbourne.unimelb.edu.au/why-is-ahok-in-prison-a-legal-analysis-of-the-decision/

Butt, Simon and Lindsey, Tim 2011. 'Judicial Mafia: Corruption and the Courts in Indonesia', in E. Aspinall and G. Van Klinken (eds.), *The State and Illegality in Indonesia.* Leiden: KITLV Press, pp. 189–216

Butt, Simon and Lindsey, Tim 2012. *The Constitution of Indonesia: A Contextual Analysis.* Oxford: Hart Publishing

Butt, Simon and Lindsey, Tim 2018. *Indonesian Law.* Oxford University Press

Case, Steve; Johnson, Phil; Manlow, David; Smith, Roger; and Williams, Kate (2017) *Criminology*. Oxford University Press

Coren, Anna 2010. 'Former Amto-Graft Chief Murder Case Raises Corruption Woes', *CNN*, 12 February http://edition.cnn.com/2010/WORLD/asiapcf/02/12/indonesia.corruption.antasari.trial/index.html

Cumaraswamy Param 2003. *Report of the Special Rapporteur on the Independence of Judges and Lawyers, Mr. Param Cumaraswamy (E/CN.4/2003/65/Add.2)*. New York: United Nations

Fitzpatrick, Daniel 1999. 'Culture, Ideology and Human Rights: The Case of Indonesia's Code of Criminal Procedure', in Tim Lindsey (ed.), *Indonesia: Law and Society*, 1st edn. Sydney: Federation Press, pp. 339–55

Goodpaster, Gary 2002. 'Reflections on Corruption in Indonesia', in Timothy Lindsey and H. W. Dick (eds.), *Corruption in Asia: Rethinking the Governance Paradigm.* Sydney: Federation Press, pp. 87–108

Heriyanto, Devina 2016. 'Q&A: Looking into Jessica's Harrowing Hours – Is She Guilty?', *The Jakarta Post*, 24 August www.thejakartapost.com/academia/2016/08/24/qa-looking-into-jessicas-harrowing-hours-is-she-guilty.html

Horowitz, Donald L 2013. *Constitutional Change and Democracy in Indonesia.* Cambridge: Cambridge University Press

Hosen, Nadirsyah 2017. 'The Indonesian Courts', in H.P. Lee and Marilyn Pittard, *Asia Pacific Judiciaries: Independence, Impartiality and Integrity*. Cambridge: Cambridge University Press, pp. 186–208

Human Rights Watch 2002. 'Indonesia's Court for East Timor a "Whitewash"', 20 December www.hrw.org/news/2002/12/20/indonesias-court-east-timor-whitewash

ICW 2001. *Menyingkap Tabir Mafia Peradilan (Hasil Monitoring Peradilan ICW)* Jakarta: Indonesian Corruption Watch

Jakarta Globe 2012. 'Criticism as Indonesia Judge Gets Just Four Years Jail for Corruption', *Jakarta Globe*, 29 February

Jakarta Post 2011. 'Police, Court Officials Top List of Judicial Mafia Reports', *The Jakarta Post*, 31 December

LBH 2019. *Reformasi Dikorupsi, Demokrasi Direpresi.* Jakarta: Lembaga Bantuan Hukum www.bantuanhukum.or.id/web/wp-content/uploads/2019/12/Catahu-2019-reformasi-dikorupsi.pdf

Lev, Daniel S. 1996. 'Between State and Society: Professional Lawyers and Reform in Indonesia', in Daniel S. Lev and Ruth McVey (eds.), *Making Indonesia.* Ithaca: Cornell University Press, pp. 144–63

Lev, Daniel S. 1999. 'The Criminal Regime: Criminal Process in Indonesia', in Vincente L. Rafael (eds.), *Figures of Criminality in Indonesia, The Philippines, and Colonial Vietnam*. Ithaca: Cornell University Press, pp. 175–92

Lindsey, Tim 1999. '"Corruption" as Rational Response in the ASPAL State: The Failure of Reformasi Hukum', in Drew Duncan and Tim Lindsey (eds.), *Indonesia after Soeharto: Reformasi & Reaction*. Victoria BC: CAPI, pp. 176–88

Lindsey, Tim and Pausacker, Helen 2016. *Religion, Law and Intolerance in Indonesia.* London: Routledge

Linnan, David 2008. 'Commercial Law Enforcement in Indonesia: The Manulife Case', in Tim Lindsey (ed.), *Indonesia: Law and Society*, 2nd edn. Sydney: Federation Press, pp. 596–619

Lokataru 2019. *Hadiah Kayu Untuk Para Demonstran.* Jakarta: Lokataru https://lokataru.id/wp-content/uploads/2019/12/hadiah-kayu-2.pdf

Lubis, Todung Mulya 1993. *In Search of Human Rights: Legal-Political Dilemmas of Indonesia's New Order, 1966–1990.* Jakarta: Gramedia Pustaka Utama

Paddock, Richard C. 2019. 'Indonesia Frees Canadian Accused of Using Magical Powers to Abuse Children', *The New York Times*, 12 July www.nytimes.com/2019/07/12/world/asia/bantleman-canada-teacher-indonesia-abuse-clemency.html

Pemberton, John 1999. 'Open Secrets: Excerpts from Conversations with a Javanese Lawyer, and a Comment', in Vicente Rafel and Rudolf Mrazek (eds.), *Figures of Criminality in Indonesia, the Philippines, and Colonial Vietnam.* Ithaca: Southeast Asia Program Publications Southeast Asia Program Cornell University, pp. 193–209

Pompe, Sebastiaan 2005. *The Indonesian Supreme Court: A Study of Institutional Collapse.* Ithaca: Cornell University Press

Prabowo, Haris 2019. 'Korban Demo Mahasiswa, Anies: Semalam 273, Sekarang 19 Orang', *Tirto id.*, 25 September <https://tirto.id/korban-demo-mahasiswa-anies-semalam-273-sekarang-19-orang-eiHQ>

Robinson, Geoffrey B. 2019. *The Killing Season: A History of Indonesian Massacres.* Princeton and Oxford: Princeton University Press

Satuan Tugas Pemberantasan Mafia Hukum 2010. *Mafia Hukum: Modus Operandi, Akar Permasalahan dan Strategi Penanggulangan.* Jakarta: Satuan Tugas Pemberantasan Mafia Hukum

Soesilo, Raden 1974. *Kitab Undang-Undang Hukum Pidana (K.U.H.P.) Serta Komentar-Komentarnya Lengkap Pasal Demi Pasal, Untuk Para Pajabat Kepolisian Kejaksaan Pamong-Praja Dsb.* Jakarta: Politeia

Southwood, Julie and Flanagan, Patrick 1983. *Indonesia: Law, Propaganda and Terror.* London: Zed

Sugandhi, R. 1981. *Kitab Undang-Undang Hukum Pidana (K.U.H.P.) dengan Penjelasannya.* Jakarta: Usaha Nasional 1981

US Department of State 1999. 'Indonesia Country Report on Human Rights Practices for 1998', 26 February https://fas.org/irp/world/indonesia/indonesia-1998.htm

Wijaya, Callistasia 2019. 'Lebih 50 Demonstran Meninggal Saat Unjuk Rasa sepanjang 2019: "Sangat Mengerikan terjadi di Negara Demokrasi"', *BBC*, 30 October www.bbc.com/indonesia/indonesia-50217875

Yunto, E. 2008. 'Mencermati Pemberian SP3 Kasus Korupsi', *Hukumonline*, 25 November

Zifcak, Spencer 1999. '"But a Shadow of Justice": Political Trials in Indonesia', in Tim Lindsey (ed.), *Indonesia: Law and Society*, 1st edn. Sydney: Federation Press, pp. 355–66

Laws and regulations

Criminal Code of 1918 (Wetboek van Strafrecht Nederlandsch Indie)

Criminal Code (*Kitab Undang-Undang Hukum Pidana*, KUHP: Law No. 1 of 1946 as amended by Law No. 27 of 1999 on the Indonesian Criminal Code)
Criminal Procedure Code of 1981 (Kitab Undang-undang Hukum Acara Pidana, KUHAP)
Law No. 1 of 1979 on Extradition
Law No. 26 of 2000 on the Human Rights Courts
Law No. 44 of 2008 on Pornography
Law No. 39 of 2014 on Plantation
Law No. 2 of 2019 on the Second Amendment of Law No. 30 of 2002 on the KPK (Komisi Pemberantasan Korupsi, The Corruption Eradication Commission)
Qanun Aceh No. 6 of 2014 on Islamic Criminal Law (*Hukum Jinayat*)
Supreme Court Regulation No. 2 of 2012 on the Adjustment of Fine Limits for Minor Crimes and Fine Amounts in the Criminal Code

Court cases

Constitutional Court Decision No. 013-022/PUU-IV/2006 (*Lèse Majesté* case)
Supreme Court Decision No. 60 P/HUM/2015

Part I

The criminal law codes

2 The Criminal Code

Simon Butt and Tim Lindsey[1]

Indonesia's *Kitab Undang-Undang Hukum Pidana* (KUHP) or Criminal Code contains the definitions of various criminal acts and the penalties applicable to those who perform them. It is the main source of 'substantive' criminal law.[2] This chapter offers an introductory account of its content and application, as background to other, more narrowly focused, chapters of this book. The procedural aspects of criminal law, including rules about police investigations, prosecutions and trials, are covered in the KUHAP (*Kitab Undang-Undang Hukum Acara Pidana* or Criminal Procedure Code), which is discussed in the next chapter.

KUHP is a creation of Dutch colonialism. After issuing a series of criminal laws that applied to different ethnic groups,[3] the Dutch finally enacted a universal Criminal Code for the Dutch East Indies – the *Wetboek van Strafwet Nederlandsch Indie* (WvS) – in 1918. This Code was applied until Independence in 1945 and was soon adopted by the new Indonesian government, with very few changes, through passage of Law No. 1 of 1946 on Criminal Law.[4] The main effects of this law were to rename the WvS the 'KUHP' (*Kitab Undang-Undang Hukum Pidana* or Criminal Code) (art. 6) and to replace each reference to the 'Dutch East Indies' with 'Indonesia' (art. 1). KUHP was initially applied in Java and Madura,[5] and was extended to the remainder of Indonesia in 1958.[6]

'Special' criminal laws

KUHP has been amended several times, but never comprehensively. Reform to Indonesian criminal law has instead been primarily achieved through the passage of 'special' (*khusus*) criminal law statutes that deal with specific crimes. Most of these statutes have been enacted to provide more effective regulatory regimes for existing offences than KUHP offered; others seek to respond to new problems or issues, usually by creating new offences. Importantly, these special statutes generally replace any KUHP provisions dealing with the same subject matter. They also alter the criminal procedures applied in the investigation, prosecution, and trial of the offences they describe, at least to the extent that they contradict the KUHAP.[7]

The subject matter of these specific-purpose criminal statutes is varied and includes, among others:

- economic crimes (Emergency Law No. 7 of 1955 on Investigation, Prosecution and Trial of Economic Crimes);
- subversion (Law No. 11/PNPS/1963 on Eradication of Subversive Activity, revoked by Law No. 26 of 1999);
- road traffic (Law No. 14 of 1992 on Traffic and Road Transport);
- psychotropic substances (Law No. 5 of 1997 on Psychotropics);
- corruption (Law No. 31 of 1999 on Eradication of Criminal Acts of Corruption, amended by Law No. 20 of 2001);
- terrorism (Law No. 15 of 2003 on Adoption of Interim Emergency Law No. 1 of 2002 on the Eradication of Terrorist Acts);
- pornography (Law No. 44 of 2008 on Pornography);
- narcotics (Law No. 35 of 2009 on Narcotics);
- money laundering (Law No. 8 of 2010 on Criminal Acts of Money Laundering); and
- funding of terrorism (Law No. 9 of 2013 on the Prevention and Eradication of Criminal Acts of Money Laundering).

Criminal offences are also created by other laws that might not be seen as obviously criminal in nature, such as those regulating the environment, land rights and intellectual property rights, among many others. There are too many of these 'non-KUHP' offences to cover exhaustively in this chapter, but many are discussed elsewhere in this book.[8] In the rest of this chapter, we offer an overview of the contents of KUHP, in order of its content, as background for many of the other chapters in the book, and then outline proposals for its reform.

Content of KUHP

KUHP is divided into three 'books':

- Book I: General Provisions (arts. 1–103). This book relates to the application of the Code and includes general principles of criminal law.
- Book II: Crimes (arts. 104–488).
- Book III: Violations or Misdemeanours (arts. 489–569).

Book I: General provisions

Article 1(1) of KUHP establishes a fundamental principle of Indonesian criminal law found in all developed legal systems: criminal liability can be established only for conduct prohibited by law. Criminal laws cannot, therefore, operate retrospectively, so that if no applicable law exists when the act is committed, there can be no criminal culpability. However, if the applicable law is changed after that act occurred, then the most favourable of the pre- and post-conduct laws must be applied to the defendant (art. 1(2)).

Indonesian criminal law applies to 'every person who commits a crime in Indonesia' (art. 2). In other words, it applies in the entire territory of Indonesia, to citizens and non-citizens alike. This territory includes Indonesian airspace, territorial waters, and Indonesia-flagged ships and airplanes (art. 3).

Extra-territoriality

KUHP also purports to have some extra-territorial operation, subject to restrictions imposed by international law (art. 9). It applies outside Indonesia to citizens and non-citizens who commit crimes against the national security of Indonesia listed in art. 4. These include treason (arts. 104, 106, 107, 110, 111 bis (1)), rebellion (art. 108), and attacking the president or vice-president (art.131). Also with purported extra-territorial operation are crimes related to currency, stamps and marks issued by the Indonesian government (art. 4(2)); forgery of some types of documents (art. 4(3)); piracy and hijacking (arts. 438, 444–7, and 479(j)); and crimes that could jeopardise civil aviation safety (art. 479(1)(m), (n), and (o)).

The Code also purports to apply extra-territorially to its own nationals who violate provisions of Chapters 1 and 2 of Book II and arts. 160, 161, 240, 279, 450, and 451 (art. 5(1)), which contain offences related to national security and crimes against the dignity of the president and vice-president.[9] Failing to uphold one's duty to defend the nation (art. 240), bigamy (art. 279), and piracy (arts. 450 and 451) are also extra-territorial crimes. More expansively, KUHP applies to overseas Indonesian nationals who commit an act that violates both KUHP and the criminal law of the country where the act was committed (art. 5(2)). However, the death penalty cannot be applied against an Indonesian citizen for a crime committed overseas if the other country does not impose the death penalty for that crime (art. 6).

Inchoate offences

KUHP contains provisions on inchoate offences, such as intent, attempt, and facilitation. Those who incite, compel, or participate in the commission of a crime are punished as perpetrators and face the same penalties (art. 55(1)). The same goes for those who persuade a person to commit a crime by providing an opportunity, the means, or information for a crime to be committed (art. 55(2)).

Attempt to commit a serious offence (*kejahatan*, or felony) is punishable under KUHP if intent is apparent from the commencement of performance of the offence, but performance is not completed for reasons independent of the offender's own will (art. 53(1)). A person is an accessory if they intentionally help when a crime is committed, or provide the opportunity, means, or information to commit a crime (art. 56). Accessories and attempters generally face a sentence 'discount' of one-third less than the primary punishment for the crime (arts. 53(2) and 57). But if the maximum punishment for the primary offence is capital punishment or life imprisonment, they face a maximum punishment of fifteen years' imprisonment (arts. 53(3), 57(1)–(2)).

Being an accessory after the fact is also prohibited. Article 221(1) imposes up to nine months imprisonment or a fine for assisting or concealing a person who has committed an offence in order to evade an investigation or prosecution, or destroying, removing or concealing goods related to the offence for the same purpose. However, art. 221(2) specifies that art. 221(1) does not apply to spouses, former spouses or other close family members of perpetrators. They, therefore, cannot be held culpable as accessories.

Complaint offences

Indonesian criminal law categorises offences as *delik biasa* (normal offences) or *delik aduan* (complaint offences). *Delik biasa* are processed by the police regardless of whether a victim or third party makes a complaint. If a victim alerts police to a *delik biasa* by reporting it, but subsequently withdraws that report, police can still pursue the case.

By contrast, *delik aduan* are only considered to be crimes if they are reported to police. If a victim reports a *delik biasa* to the police but subsequently withdraws that report, the police must drop the case. Examples of such offences include: adultery (art. 284); sex with a female between the ages of twelve and fifteen years (art. 287); criminal defamation (art. 310); breach of confidentiality (art. 322); and abduction (art. 332).

Articles 72–5 describe the procedure for making complaints. Notably, the Criminal Code allows for the parents, spouse, or children of a deceased victim to make a report on his or her behalf (unless the deceased wished no complaint to be made) (art. 73). Minors under the age of sixteen years against whom a criminal act has been perpetrated need a parent or guardian to complain on their behalf (art. 72). Indonesian residents must file their complaint within six months of learning that the act was committed; those residing outside Indonesia have nine months (art. 74(1)).

Once a complaint is lodged, a complainant has three months to retract it if they wish the police to drop the case (art. 75). If the complaint alleges rape, arts. 72, 73, and 75 do not apply (art. 284(3)), and the complaint can be withdrawn before the trial commences (art. 284(4)).

Defences and aggravating factors

Chapter III of Book I outlines defences (*alasan pembenar*), and mitigating and aggravating factors. Offenders can neither be found guilty nor punished if they have a mental illness (art. 44(1)), or if they were affected by duress (art. 48). For the duress defence to apply, the pressure must have been such that the defendant could not reasonably avoided it in the circumstances (Soesilo 1974: 54). For example, if a defendant is forced to commit a crime under threat of being immediately shot (Sugandhi 1981), the physical and mental coercion may have left the defendant little choice, or none, but to commit the crime. Soesilo (1981: 54) suggests that whether duress existed must be assessed by balancing various factors, including the degree of power the compeller had over the defendant; whether the defendant could have escaped or avoided the situation; and whether committing the act was a reasonable response considering the level of force or threat exerted.

Offenders are not to be punished if they act to defend their own, or another person's, body, morality, or property against direct unlawful assault or immediate threat (art. 49(1)), even if that response is excessive (art. 49(2)). Other defences are that the act was required by statute (art. 50) or under an official order issued by a competent authority (art. 51).

KUHP's criminal penalties can be increased by one-third in two circumstances. The first is where an official commits a punishable act and, in doing so, violates his or her official duties or uses the power, opportunity, or means granted by his or her office (art. 52). The second is where the offender uses the Indonesian flag when committing a crime (art. 52a).

Sentencing and punishment

KUHP distinguishes between 'primary' and 'secondary' (or 'additional') punishments. Primary punishments include capital punishment, imprisonment, confinement, fines, and 'closed detention',[10] which resembles house arrest (art. 10a). Additional punishments include the withdrawal of certain rights, forfeiture of specific property, and publication of the relevant judgment (art. 10b).

Imprisonment can either be for life or for a fixed period (art. 12(1)). This period may vary between one day and fifteen years, which can be extended to a maximum of twenty years if the offence attracts a potential death sentence or life imprisonment. A sentence exceeding fifteen years may be imposed for concurrent crimes or recidivism, or where the aggravating factors under art. 52, described above, apply (art. 12(3)). However, a 'fixed period' can never exceed twenty years (art. 12(4)).

A unique type of punishment imposed in Indonesia is *kurungan* – 'confinement' or light imprisonment. *Kurungan* can be for a maximum period of one year, or one year and four months in the case of concurrent crimes, recidivism, or aggravating circumstances (arts. 18(1) and (2)). As discussed below, KUHP allows a convicted person to choose *kurungan* instead of paying a fine (art. 31(1)) and those unable to pay a fine will enter *kurungan* (art. 30(2)). *Kurungan* inmates are allowed certain privileges, including the '*pistole*' right, under which an inmate can improve his or her conditions, for example, by bringing in household goods, a television, mattress, or food at his or her own expense (arts. 20–23).

KUHP stipulates that male inmates can be required to work during the term of their imprisonment, unless serving life imprisonment or unfit to do so (arts. 24–25).

Fines

Article 30 of KUHP sets a minimum fine of Rp. 3.75 (equivalent to US$0.0002). As mentioned, a judge can impose *kurungan* instead of a fine, though for no longer than six months, except in cases of concurrent crimes, recidivism, or aggravating circumstances, for which the maximum term is eight months (art. 30(2)–(5)). Payment of the fine immediately releases the offender from *kurungan* (art. 31(2)). Judges can consider time served when deciding the duration of *kurungan* or the amount of a fine (art. 33(1)).

Recent adjustments to fine amounts

As mentioned, KUHP remains largely unchanged from the WvS enacted by the Dutch in 1918. The fines mentioned in the Code are therefore now miniscule because of inflation and various economic crises. The government increased the value of all fines in the early 1960s[11] but did not increase them again until recently, as discussed below. One result of this is that fines have long been almost meaningless as punishments, leaving many judges feeling compelled to imprison. This has contributed to Indonesia's high levels of incarceration and prison overcrowding, discussed by Sudaryono in Chapter 8 of this book.

A related problem – primarily with theft-related crimes – is that the seriousness of offences and the punishment associated with them is determined by the monetary value of goods stolen. So, for example, arts. 362 and 364 of KUHP state that theft of goods worth over Rp. 250 (equivalent to about US$0.02) attracts a maximum sentence of five years of imprisonment. According to art. 364, theft of goods valued at less than Rp. 250 should be considered minor theft and attract a maximum of three months.[12] As discussed in more detail in Chapters 10 (Assegaf) and 14 (Mulyani), police have been criticised for overusing this provision to detain anyone accused of theft of items of very little value, including a few cacao pods, or a pair of plastic sandals (Nusrat 2009; Tedjakusuma 2012). Because art. 21 of the KUHAP allows police to detain anyone suspected of a crime carrying a sentence of five years or more, this has also contributed to the high rates of pre-trial detention throughout Indonesia, as Sudaryono explains in Chapter 8.

In response to public dissatisfaction,[13] Supreme Court Regulation No. 2 of 2012 on the Adjustment of Fine Limits for Minor Crimes and Fine Amounts in the Criminal Code, was issued. The Regulation notes that, between 1960 and 2012, the value of gold per gram increased by 10,000-fold, such that the previously stipulated limitation of Rp. 250 should be increased to Rp. 2.5 million. Accordingly, the regulation increased the threshold value mentioned under arts. 364 (minor theft), 373 (minor fraud), 379 (minor deception), 384 (minor deception by a seller), 407(1) (minor destruction), and 482 (minor buying and selling of stolen goods), from Rp. 250 to Rp. 2.5 million. The Regulation establishes that crimes involving theft of goods worth less than Rp. 2.5 million should be heard as an expedited case (*acara pidana cepat*), under arts. 205–10 of KUHAP, discussed in Chapter 3 of this book.[14] The 2012 Supreme Court Regulation increases the maximum fine for all other crimes described in KUHP by 1,000-fold.[15] Article 4 of the 2012 Regulation instructs judges to consider these changes when sentencing but many do not do so, as Assegaf also shows in Chapter 9.

While the Regulation may have provided a short-term fix for inappropriately low fines, it does not provide an enduring solution such as by producing a formula that allows for currency fluctuation. We believe the Regulation was intended as a stop-gap measure, in anticipation of a new Criminal Code, which, as discussed below, seeks to address this issue. Unfortunately, as at the time of writing, this bill was still being debated in the national legislature, as it has been for some years.

The death penalty

The death penalty is prescribed for several offences in the Criminal Code, and for narcotics, terrorism, corruption, and human rights offences under 'special' laws, discussed above. Despite being available for many offences, the death penalty has, since the collapse of the New Order, been used primarily in drug cases, and in some terrorism and premeditated murder cases. The following crimes are punishable by death under KUHP:

- Premeditated murder (art. 340).
- Aggravated robbery by two or more persons that results in severe injury or death (art. 365(4)).
- Extortion resulting in severe injury or death (art. 368).
- Piracy resulting in death (art. 444).
- Hijacking offences that result in death or destruction of an aircraft (art. 479k(2)).
- Sabotaging or tampering with an aircraft resulting in death or destruction of the aircraft (art. 479o(2)).
- Treason with intent to kill the president or vice-president or deprive them of their ability to govern (art. 104).
- Premeditated murder of the head of a friendly state (art. 140).
- Collusion with foreign powers intended to cause and resulting in hostilities; and assisting the enemy or prejudicing the state in time of war, such as through betrayal, destruction, or demoralisation (arts. 111 and 124(3)).[16]

None of these provisions require judges to hand down the death penalty; in Indonesia its imposition is always discretionary (Butt 2014). Indeed, some laws seek to prevent or delay its imposition where it would be otherwise available. For example, art. 44 of the Criminal Code states that offenders with a mental illness cannot be held responsible for a crime committed although Indonesian judges appear to have sometimes ignored this restriction. Pregnancy provides only a temporary reprieve from execution, which can be performed forty days after the woman gives birth.[17]

Executions have increased since President Joko Widodo (Jokowi) took office in late 2014. Jokowi has publicly committed his government to a hard-line approach to drugs, as Gunawan and Pamintori explain in Chapter 11. He appears to believe that his country is in the grips of a drug 'emergency' (Marwati 2016) and sees the death penalty as a crucial element in the eradication of narcotics (McRae 2015). For example, between January and April 2015, fourteen people were executed. Almost immediately, the government then announced plans to execute a similar number (Okezone 2015). Although fourteen executions were planned for the morning of 29 July 2016, ten inmates were given last-minute reprieves (Chapter 11 offers an account of these events). Nevertheless, in the current climate, it seems unlikely that those convicted of drug-related offences will receive clemency, which is also discussed in Chapter 11. At time of writing approximately 150 people were on death row in Indonesia (Media Indonesia 2016).

Books II and III: Offences

As mentioned, KUHP is divided into three 'books', with Book II dealing with Crimes (Articles 104–488), and Book III Violations or Misdemeanours (Articles 489–569). In this section, we consider only offences from these books that tend to attract controversy.

Defamation

Article 310 of KUHP imposes up to nine months' imprisonment for 'anyone who intentionally attacks the reputation or honour of another person by alleging a certain fact, with the clear intention of making that fact publicly known'. If the attack is written, published, shown, or broadcast publicly, the sentence can increase to one year and four months. If a public official is defamed during performance of his or her duties, the penalty can be increased by one-third (art. 316).

An allegedly offensive act will not be considered defamatory if done in the public interest or in self-defence (art. 310). Truth is not a defence, although proving it can assist a defendant to make out public interest or self-defence. If the defendant attempts to prove the truth of the allegation but fails, an increased term of up to four years' imprisonment can apply (art. 311).

Criminal defamation is often used by powerful political or business figures to silence their critics.[18] Of course, this is highly problematic from a democratic perspective.

Hate speech

Article 156 states that 'any person who publicly expresses animosity, hatred or insults against a group of Indonesian citizens, faces up to four years' imprisonment'. Here, 'group' refers to all groups in Indonesian society, based on differences of race, country of origin, religion, place of birth, descent, citizenship, or position, according to the laws of the state.

Despite this wide definition, Indonesian police have rarely acted against perpetrators of hate speech (Gumilang 2015).

Prostitution

Prostitution is not explicitly forbidden under Indonesian law. KUHP indirectly addresses it by prohibiting intermediaries from initiating or facilitating 'indecent activities' (*cabul*) and imposing a maximum sentence of one year and six months (art. 296). Similarly, art. 506 imposes *kurungan* of up to one year for those who profit from the prostitution of women. Law No. 21 of 2007 on the Eradication of Human Trafficking also creates offences of sexual exploitation (arts. 1–6 and 12).

Homosexuality

As Pausacker explains in Chapter 16, at the time of writing, homosexuality is not forbidden by national laws in Indonesia, despite being condemned in some Indonesian communities. According to art. 292 of KUHP, adults who engage in 'indecent activities' with a minor of the same gender face up to five years' imprisonment. This provision, along with arts. 284 on adultery and 285 on rape, was challenged before the Constitutional Court, which handed down its decision in late 2017.[19] The applicants – who included a conservative Muslim group called the 'Family Love Alliance' (AILA, Aliansi Cinta Keluarga Indonesia) – had asked the Court to change art. 292 so that it applied to all indecent acts between people of the same gender, regardless of their age. A five-to-four majority rejected the request, deciding that it did not have jurisdiction to criminalise particular acts, because this was a matter for the legislature. The minority held that it would have allowed the application, primarily because Indonesia is a religious state and all religions practised in Indonesia prohibit intercourse between people of the same gender.

'Sodomy' (*liwath*) and lesbian sex (*musahaqah*) are prohibited under Aceh's shari'a criminal code, the Qanun Jinayat, discussed in Chapters 19 (Mann and Afrianty) and 20 (Butt). Punishments for violations include up to 100 lashes with a cane, a fine of 1,000 grams of gold, or 100 months in prison (arts. 63 and 64). Also discussed below is the draft revision KUHP now before the DPR (Dewan Perwakilan Rakyat, Peoples' Representative Assembly, the national legislature), which, if passed in its current form, would criminalise public affection between people of the same gender.

Blasphemy

Article 156a of KUHP was inserted by the passage of Presidential Instruction 1 PNPS/ 1965, which was confirmed as a statute by Law No. 5 of 1969 (commonly called 'the Blasphemy Law'). Article 156a imposes up to five years' imprisonment for persons who publicly and intentionally express feelings or behaviour of hostility, abuse, or disparage one of the six recognised religions in Indonesia. Although this provision has existed for over half a century, it was used sparingly under the New Order regime. Since the fall of Soeharto in 1998, however, at least 120 people have been convicted for blasphemy (Crouch 2012). In Chapter 15 of this book, Peterson discusses one of the most controversial of these convictions, that of the former governor of Jakarta, Basuki Tjahaya Purnama (better known as 'Ahok').

In 2009, a coalition of human rights and religious freedom activists challenged the constitutionality of art. 156a in the Constitutional Court.[20] The applicants argued, among other things, that this provision violated art. 28E of the Constitution, which states that 'every person has the right to adhere to a religion and worship according to his or her religion'. They also objected to the state playing a role in determining orthodoxy for a religion. The challenge prompted a heated national debate. Opponents of the challenge referred to art. 28J(2) of the Constitution, which provides that:

> in exercising his or her rights and freedom, every person must be subject to the restrictions stipulated in laws and regulations with the intention of guaranteeing the recognition of and respect for the rights and freedoms of other people and to fulfil fair demands in accordance with the considerations of moral and religious values, security, and public order in a democratic society.

On 19 April 2010, the Constitutional Court rejected the application, holding that art. 28J(2) justified art. 156a. In doing so, however, it mentioned that although the government only recognised six official religions (Islam, Protestantism, Catholicism, Buddhism, Hinduism, and Confucianism), it should 'leave alone' followers of other faiths (Hapsari 2010). This has, unfortunately, done little to prevent attacks on those whose beliefs are seen as unorthodox.

Reform of the Criminal Code

The Constitutional Court has effected some reform of KUHP in cases where it has struck down provisions as contrary to the Constitution. Among these were arts. 134, 136, and 137 – the so-called '*lese majeste*' ('injured majesty', offence of insulting the ruler) provisions. The first few years after Soeharto's resignation witnessed a period of relative political openness, with citizens and activists able to criticise the president without fear of legal reprisal. However, government opponents soon began to be targeted by arts. 134, 136, and 137, particularly during the presidency of Megawati Soekarnoputri (Human Rights Watch 2003, 2010). In 2006, the Constitutional Court ruled that these provisions were unconstitutional.[21] The Court held that the articles 'decreased the freedom to express thoughts and opinions, freedom of information, and legal certainty' and found that the penalties under art. 134 could be used to 'obstruct the process of democracy'. The Court also noted that the provisions had been introduced by the Dutch for use against the indigenous Indonesian population during the colonial period and that it was, therefore, not appropriate that they be applied against citizens in independent Indonesia.

One year later, the Constitutional Court also revoked arts. 154 and 155 of KUHP, which the New Order had also used to restrict freedom of expression.[22] Article 154 had provided:

> Any person who publicly expresses feelings of hostility, hatred or contempt towards the Government of Indonesia faces a prison sentence of up to seven years or a fine of Rp. 4,500.

Article 155(1), meanwhile, stated:

> Any person who publicly broadcasts, shows or displays writings or drawings that contain hostility, hatred or contempt towards the Government of Indonesia, with the intention that such content becomes known by the public, faces a prison sentence of up to four years and six months, or a fine of Rp. 4,500.

The Court held that both provisions:

> give rise to the tendency for abuse of power, because they can easily be interpreted according to the inclinations of authorities. A citizen who intends to deliver a criticism or opinion to the government – as is their right under the 1945 Constitution – could easily be accused of making a statement of 'hostility hatred or contempt' against the Government of Indonesia.[23]

The Constitutional Court also made a significant amendment to KUHP when it removed the 'offensive treatment' offence (*perlakuan yang tak menyenangkan*). Originally, art. 335(1) stated that anyone who, 'with violence or threat of violence, forces another person to do or not do something, or allows something to happen, that is offensive to that other person or another person' faces one year's imprisonment or a fine of Rp. 4,500. This provision was challenged in 2013 by a defendant accused of 'offensive treatment'. The Court decided that the concept was vague and subjective, and thus violated the constitutional right to legal certainty and broader concepts of justice.[24]

Various other provisions in KUHP have been revoked through passage of specific laws intended to replace them. For example, the Corruption Law[25] repealed arts. 209–10 (on giving gifts to officials); arts. 387–8 (fraudulent behaviour by a contractor, buildings expert or supplier who thereby endangers people, goods, or the state during a time of war); and arts. 415–20, 423, 425, and 435 (offences perpetrated by officials).[26] Law No. 21 of 2007 on the Eradication of People Smuggling likewise revoked art. 297 of KUHP (trafficking of women and underage boys); and art. 324 (slavery).[27]

Draft bill for reform of KUHP

Despite these various piecemeal changes, it has long been clear that KUHP, a colonial inheritance now more than a century old, is no longer suitable as the basic source of criminal law in Indonesia and needs replacement. For decades, successive governments have considered doing this and produced various drafts for discussion. In fact, the DPR has included a draft KUHP and draft KUHAP in the annual list of priority bills for deliberation since 2015, but whether they will be passed and, if so, when is still uncertain.

One reason for the slow pace of criminal law reform is the sheer size of the codes, which makes holding detailed or focused discussions difficult for the legislature. Previous iterations of the draft codes have sparked nationwide controversies over specific articles, which have also stalled negotiations. Their deliberation has also often been overtaken by more pressing legislation, and by political events. For example, an attempt to deliberate a new code foundered in 2014, after the country and the legislature became preoccupied by legislative and presidential elections held that year. In 2019, the legislature attempted again to pass the 2015 KUHP draft but this triggered fatal riots by students and civil society groups objecting to many of its more controversial provisions,[28] and debate was abandoned at the request of the president. At the time of writing, in early 2020, this draft was again before the legislature.

The 2015 RUU KUHP (*Rancangan Undang-Undang Kitab Undang-undang Hukum Pidana,* Draft Criminal Code) contains 786 articles, which is considerably more than KUHP's 569 articles, but is divided into two books instead of three. The first book contains general provisions (*aturan umum*); and the second covers criminal acts (*tindak pidana*), including both 'crimes' (*kejahatan*) and 'violations' (*pelanggaran*), to which KUHP dedicated separate books.

In the following paragraphs, we discuss some of the more notable provisions of these two books, with the caveat that these provisions might be changed before enactment, if they are enacted at all.

Book I

Adat

One criticism of the RUU KUHP is that it increases legal uncertainty rather than reduces it. Article 1(1) resembles the current Code, stating that

'A person can only be convicted or charged if their behaviour is a criminal act as described in laws and regulations existing when the act was committed'. Article 1(2) appears to strengthen art. 1(1) by prohibiting the use of analogies to determine whether a criminal act has occurred. This seems designed to preclude law enforcement officials from broadly interpreting code provisions to capture criminal acts that are not explicitly prohibited, thereby increasing 'legal certainty'. Article 2(1), however, seems to reverse this, by stating that art. 1(1) must not 'reduce the effectiveness of "living law" (*hukum yang hidup*) in the community, which can determine that a person should be punished, even though their acts are not prohibited by written law'. The academic draft (*naskah akademis*) accompanying the RUU KUHP states that 'the inclusion of crimes based on living law, or what was previously known as customary (*adat*) law, is intended to satisfy the community's sense of justice' (Ministry of Justice and Human Rights 2013). Adat or 'living law' is dynamic and varies significantly across Indonesia, thereby considerably increasing legal uncertainty. We expect that identifying the 'living law' will be highly fraught, not least because 'living law' is rarely, if ever, written'. We fear that unpopular community members might face criminal allegations for violating adat principles that they did not know existed, or that were concocted by other community members or even law enforcement officials after the commission of the act for which punishment is sought. The scope for abuse of art. 2(1) to criminalise otherwise legal behaviour seems very high.

The RUU KUHP mentions adat or 'living law' in other provisions, which add significant weight to the concerns just described. Article 68 states that adat obligations can be imposed as standalone punishments and in addition to more conventional criminal punishments, such as incarceration or fines. Article 68(3) largely affirms art. 2(1), stating that adat punishments can be issued even for acts that are not proscribed as criminal acts. Similarly, art. 102 permits judges to enforce adat obligations or impose adat penalties – particularly if the act constitutes no crime elsewhere defined in the RUU KUHP – or instead to simply issue a fine or award compensation. The RUU KUHP also contemplates living law being a mitigating (art. 139(h)) or aggravating (art. 141(i)) factor in sentencing.

Penalties

The RUU KUHP introduces a new categorisation of sanctions. The primary penalties, in order of severity are: imprisonment; confinement (*pidana tutupan*); supervised detention (*pidana pengawasan*); fines; and community service (art. 66). Community service can be substituted for offences carrying less than six months' imprisonment or a relatively minor fine (art. 88(1)). The maximum community service sentence is 240 hours for offenders over 18 years and 120 hours for offenders under that age (art. 88(4)).

Notably, the RUU KUHP no longer categorises death as a primary penalty. It can be handed down 'as an alternative ... as a last resort to "nurture" or "placate" (*mengayomi*) the community' (art. 89). Importantly, the RUU KUHP also establishes a ten-year probationary period for death sentences (art. 91(1)).[29] If an offender on 'death row' demonstrates good behaviour during this period, exhibits remorse, and the public reaction to the crime is not too great, the sentence can be changed from death to imprisonment (art. 91(2)). In any event, execution can take place only after the president has rejected a clemency request (art. 90(1)). Even if the clemency request is rejected, if execution does not occur within ten years, the death penalty can be converted to a life sentence by presidential decision (art. 92).

Fines

The RUU KUHP overcomes the problem of having to regularly adjust the fine amounts in the Code. Article 82 prescribes six categories of fines. Each crime that attracts a fine refers to one of these categories, rather than a specific sum, as in the original KUHP. Fine amounts in each category can be altered through government regulation (art. 82(7)). The fine amounts in the draft are realistic penalties:

- Category I: Rp. 10 million.
- Category II: Rp. 50 million.
- Category III: Rp. 150 million.
- Category IV: Rp. 500 million.
- Category V: Rp. 2 billion.
- Category VI: Rp. 15 billion

Corporations

As discussed in Chapter 12 (Santosa and Juwana), the RUU KUHP introduces criminal sanctions for corporations (art. 48). A corporation can be held criminally culpable for the acts of persons holding functional positions in the corporation while working for the corporation or pursuing its interests in the field of business of that corporation (art. 49). If a corporation performs a criminal act, the corporation, its boards, and its directors can be held responsible (art. 50).

The RUU KUHP imposes heavy fines upon functional position-holders found guilty of the criminal acts of a corporation (art. 82). Any convicted person or entity unable to pay a fine within a court-specified period will have the fine taken from their income and assets (art. 84(2)). If this cannot be achieved, the RUU KUHP provides for revocation of a company's licence or even its dissolution (art. 87).

Book II

The RUU KUHP has been widely criticised for its preoccupation with 'moral' issues – for example adultery, cohabitation, and birth control. It is also problematic because it reinstates provisions that restrict freedom of the press and freedom of expression that were previously invalidated by the Constitutional Court.

Homosexuality

Article 495 of the RUU KUHP, the so-called 'LGBT Article', has been one of its most controversial new provisions. As a result, it has undergone many changes during drafting but the most recent version seen by the authors would make it a criminal offence to perform 'indecent acts' (*perbuatan cabul*) with a person of the same sex in public, punishable by eighteen months' imprisonment or a Category II fine (art. 495(1)(a)). 'Indecent acts' with a person of the same sex that involve force, violence, or the threat of violence, or that are published in the form of pornography, would be punishable by nine years' imprisonment or a Category III fine (art. 495(1)(b)–(c)). If done with a person who was known, or should have been known, to be under the age of eighteen, they would be punishable by twelve years' imprisonment or a Category IV fine (art. 495(2)), or, if accompanied by violence or the threat of violence, fifteen years' imprisonment or a Category V fine (art. 495(3)) (Erdianto 2017). If passed in this form, the criminalisation of indecent acts would, as Pausacker points out in Chapter 16, probably extend to most public affection between people of the same gender.

Adultery

Article 284 of the existing KUHP, which regulates *zina* or adultery, only applies to married persons having intercourse with a person other than their husband or wife. The constitutionality of art. 284 was challenged before the Constitutional Court as part of the case involving art. 292 on same-sex intercourse. The applicants had asked the Court to expand the definition of art. 284 to include any form of sexual intercourse other than between a married man and woman. A slim majority refused on the ground that expanding art. 284 involved norm reformulation, which was a task for the legislature.

The RUU KUHP expands the types of behaviour considered *zina* in the current Code. According to art. 484(1)(e), an unmarried man and an unmarried woman who have sexual intercourse face up to five years' imprisonment. This new offence is a complaint offence (*delik aduan*), meaning that an aggrieved third party must report it to police or prosecutors before charges can be laid (art. 484(2)). A complaint can be withdrawn, but only before court proceedings commence (art. 484(4)). Unmarried heterosexual couples who live together also face imprisonment of up to one year or a Category II fine (art. 488). This provision proved very controversial in Indonesia, and its potentially extremely wide application helped spark the 2019 riots.

Birth control and abortion

The current KUHP restricts offering or promoting to minors devices intended to prevent or abort pregnancy (art. 283(1)). The RUU KUHP tightens these restrictions. Under art. 481, any person who displays a tool to prevent pregnancy, or broadcasts or displays information on how to obtain such a tool, faces a Category I fine. Article 482 provides for the same penalty for a tool or device to abort pregnancy. Article 483 states that officials engaged in family planning and sexual health programmes are not subject to arts. 481 and 482.

Restrictions on abortion are more severe. A person who offers, or advises about, medication to terminate a pregnancy faces seven years' imprisonment or a Category IV fine (art. 501(1)). Offenders performing this act in the course of their duties can have their professional licences revoked (art. 501(2)). Doctors who perform abortions for medical reasons are exempted (art. 501(3)).

Freedom of expression

Democracy activists have expressed concern about the proposed reinstatement of provisions restricting freedom of expression. Any person who publicly insults the recognised government, resulting in disorder in the community, faces up to three years in prison or a Category IV fine (art. 284). The same punishment applies to any person who publicly broadcasts, shows, or displays writings, images, or recordings that insult the recognised government and result in disorder in the community (art. 285). These two articles essentially reintroduce arts. 154 and 155 of KUHP, which, as mentioned, the Constitutional Court invalidated in 2007.

Likewise, the RUU KUHP reinstates the '*lese majeste*' articles on publicly insulting the president or vice-president, which impose up to five years' imprisonment or a Category IV fine (arts. 263–4). As also mentioned earlier, the Constitutional Court invalidated the equivalent KUHP provisions in 2006.

Freedom of the press

Human rights activists are concerned that the RUU KUHP will threaten press freedom. The draft introduces two particularly problematic articles. The first is art. 309(1), which prohibits the broadcasting and distribution of fabricated news resulting in disturbance or unrest in the community and imposes a sentence of up to two years in prison or a Category III fine for doing so. The second, art. 310, is more dangerous for journalists. It states that any person who broadcasts or distributes news that is unverified (*tidak pasti*), disproportionate or exaggerated (*berlebihan*), or incomplete (*tidak lengkap*), resulting in disturbance in the community, will be liable to up to one year in prison or a Category II fine.

Crimes against national ideology

More than fifty years have passed since the bloody aftermath of the 1965 coup attempt, when hundreds of thousands of communists were killed and imprisoned and the Indonesian Communist Party was destroyed. However, anti-communist discourse remains deeply entrenched in Indonesia. One of the key tools used by the New Order regime in its campaign against communism was Provisional People's Consultative Assembly Decision No. XXV/1966, which prohibited the promotion of Marxism/Leninism. Despite periodic attempts to repeal the Decision, it remains in force in democratic Indonesia. The RUU KUHP contains several provisions that draw directly from this New Order relic.

Any person who publicly spreads or promotes – verbally, in writing, or through any other media – Marxism/Leninism or communist teachings, intending to alter or replace Pancasila as the state ideology, faces imprisonment for up to seven years (art. 219(1)). Heavier penalties apply if community unrest ensues (art. 219(2)). Establishing an organisation based on communist teachings attracts a maximum prison sentence of ten years (art. 220(a)).

Similarly, any person who publicly states an intention – verbally, in writing, or through any other media – to eliminate or replace Pancasila as the state ideology will be liable to up to five years in prison (art. 221(1)).

Religion

Finally, the RUU KUHP introduces increased restrictions on religion and religious life. Unfortunately, these largely follow the spirit of art. 156a of KUHP, which, as mentioned, has been widely used in the post-Soeharto period to attack religious minorities and unorthodox groups.

Publicly insulting a religion in Indonesia can result in a two-year prison sentence or Category III fine (art. 348). If the insult is contained in a recording, document, or image for public dissemination, up to five years' imprisonment or a Category IV fine can be imposed (art. 349(1)). Activists have expressed concern that 'a religion in Indonesia' will likely be interpreted as only protecting the six official religions, and then only the orthodox versions of them.

Lastly, any person who publicly incites violence, intending to eliminate an official religion in Indonesia, faces up to four years in prison or a Category IV fine (art. 350).

Conclusion

As a country with a very traditional civil law legal system inherited from its Dutch colonisers, Indonesia relies heavily on statutes as the principal source of its criminal law. Unfortunately, its principal source of substantive criminal law, KUHP, is over a century old and was designed for very different circumstances to those that prevail in modern Indonesia. It is clearly outdated and needs wholesale reform.

These problems have been aggravated by the piecemeal attempts that have been made to repair KUHP over the last six decades. These have taken four forms: limited direct amendment of some provisions of KUHP by statute; more extensive replacement of provisions by 'special' statutes dealing with particular areas of law that overlap with KUHP; various government agencies (such as the Supreme Court) passing low-level regulations in an attempt to remedy specific problems in KUHP; and, since 2003, interventions by Constitutional Court striking out or reinterpreting particular provisions of KUHP that it considers are contrary to the Constitution.

The result is an increasingly problematic and complex criminal law system that is sometimes internally conflicted, as many of the chapters of this book demonstrate. There is a clear consensus that KUHP needs to be replaced, but, equally clearly, there is no consensus as to the content of that replacement. This is because creating a new Criminal Code requires consideration of almost every aspect of substantive criminal law. Indonesia is a country that has always been famous for its social and cultural diversity, and it has been increasingly polarised over religious and political differences in the last decade, often manifesting as deep division over moral and social values. This means finding agreement over criminal laws that will directly define sexual freedoms, human rights, or citizen's rights to oppose or criticise the government, among many other things, is extremely difficult.

While politicians may be able to negotiate deals among themselves over the content of the RUU KUHP, those settlements rarely achieve uniform popular support. An example is political defamation, which many civil society groups see as a direct threat to their own activities as well as the basic freedoms of all citizens. This, combined with wider anxieties over 'moral panic' provisions that would criminalise much sexual behaviour, has been enough to spark public resistance to the RUU KUHP, at times including major demonstrations, rioting and even violence.

For all these reasons, although the RUU KUHP is, as mentioned, before the national legislature as we write and marked as a priority bill, its fate – and that of Indonesian criminal law more widely – remains entirely unpredictable. The only thing that is almost certain is that any new Criminal Code will be highly controversial, whatever its content, and likely to be subject to continued efforts to amend it and interventions by the Constitutional Court. These efforts and interventions will probably be driven and contested by civil society groups, both progressive and conservative.

Notes

1 We are grateful to Tim Mann for his important contribution to the research on which this chapter is based. It draws on material in Butt and Lindsey (2018).

2 Because Indonesia adopted a form of the civil law system from the Dutch, judicial decisions (*putusan*) are generally not considered a source of law, as they are in common law countries. Instead, reliance is placed largely on statutes and other

regulations (*peraturan perundang-undangan*), usually referred to as 'positive law' (*hukum positif*), in determining applicable law. The term 'law' in Indonesia can in certain circumstances be understood as embracing many forms of bureaucratic decisions. Article 7(1) of Law No. 12 of 2011 on Lawmaking establishes a so-called 'hierarchy of laws', that is, a formal order of priority or ranking of some of these instruments.

3 Dutch presence in the archipelago was first established through the Dutch East India Company (Vereenigde Oost-Indische Compagnie, VOC), founded in 1602. In 1800, after the VOC went bankrupt, the Netherlands government took control of the VOC-administered colonies and the region became known as the Netherlands East Indies. The earliest colonial legal code, the *Bataviasche Statuten*, was developed for the city of Batavia (now Jakarta) by the Dutch East India Company, and was first promulgated in 1642 by the Governor General, Anthony van Diemen. However, customary, or *adat*, law applied to Indonesians living elsewhere. Dutch administrators long resisted calls to enact a single Criminal Code applicable to all. In 1867, a Criminal Code that applied only to Europeans (the *Wetboek van Strafrecht*) was issued, and in 1872, a Criminal Code for 'natives' (*Strafwet voor Inlanders*) followed. This was predominantly based on the Code for Europeans, although it included some additional offences that applied specifically to 'natives' (Cribb 2010). A pluralistic judicial system thus evolved, where criminal cases involving indigenous people were tried in 'regional courts' (*landraden*, or 'land councils'), and cases involving Europeans were heard in the first instance residency courts (*Residentiegerechten*), six regional appellate courts, the courts of justice (*Raden van Justitie*), and the Supreme Court (*Hoogerechtshof*). See Lev (1985: 59; and 1972) and Vandenbosch (1944: 193–4).

4 Article 1 states that Indonesia's criminal law is the law that existed on 8 March 1942. This date was chosen to 'reset' the criminal law to what it was under Dutch rule immediately before the Japanese occupation.

5 Article 17, 1946 Criminal Law.

6 Law No. 73 of 1958.

7 As we show in the next chapter, many special statutes seek to make investigation, prosecution, and trial of particular offences easier or more effective, including by giving police greater investigative powers, permitting civil servant investigators to assist police, allowing prosecutors to adduce a wider range of evidence, and allowing cases to be heard by ad hoc judges

8 For environmental crimes, see Chapters 14 (Mulyani) and 12 (Santosa and Juwana). For land-related crimes, see Chapter 14 (Mulyani) and 13 (Khatarina).

9 Articles 134, 136, and 137, which deal with defaming or insulting the president and vice-president, were invalidated by Constitutional Court Decision No. 013-022/PUU-IV/2006.

10 Closed detention was added by Law No. 20 of 1946 and is expanded upon in Government Regulation No. 8 of 1948.

11 Interim Emergency Law No. 16 of 1960 on Changes to the Criminal Code; Interim Emergency Law No. 18 of 1960 on Amendments to the Fine Amounts in the KUHP and in other Criminal Provisions in Force Before 17 August 1945, endorsed by the DPR as statutes through Law No. 1 of 1961 on Legalisation of all Emergency Laws Passed Before 1 January 1961 to Become Law.

12 Article 364 states that goods stolen must be valued at less than Rp. 25 to be considered a minor crime. This value was increased to Rp. 250 by Government

Regulation in Lieu of Law No. 16 of 1960 on Changes to the Criminal Code, increasing the amounts listed under arts. 364, 373, 379, 384, and 407.

13 The elucidation (explanatory memorandum) to Supreme Court Regulation No. 2 of 2012 explicitly addresses growing public frustration with the state's heavy-handed approach to petty crime. It states that 'the community finds it grossly unfair that such cases attract a sentence of five years in prison as described under art. 362, which they consider out of step with the value of the goods stolen'. See also Assegaf, Chapter 9.

14 Article 2(2), Supreme Court Regulation No. 2 of 2012 on Fine Limits for Minor Crimes and Fine Amounts in the Criminal Code.

15 With the exception of the crimes in arts. 303(1)–(2),because those offences had already been amended by Law No. 7 of 1947 on Gambling.

16 For a full account of offences in other statutes and regulations that attract the death penalty, see Butt and Lindsey (2018: 193–5).

17 See also Law No. 11 of 2012 on the Juvenile Justice System, which grants children the right not to receive the death penalty or a life sentence (art. 6(f)). Instead, the maximum penalty is ten years for children found guilty of a crime for which the death penalty or life imprisonment could otherwise be imposed: art. 43. Despite this provision, Indonesian judges have, in fact, imposed the death sentence on minors. See Soares (2015).

18 Complaints now often use KUHP in conjunction with art. 27(3) of Law No. 11 of 2008 on Information and Electronic Transactions (as amended by Law No. 19 of 2016), if the alleged defamation was conveyed electronically.

19 Constitutional Court Decision No. 46/PUU-XIV/2016.

20 Constitutional Court Decision No. 140/PUU-VII/2009.

21 Constitutional Court Decision No. 013-022/PUU-IV/2006.

22 Constitutional Court Decision No. 6/PUU-V/2007.

23 Constitutional Court Decision No. 6/PUU-V/2007, para [3.18.6], p 77.

24 Constitutional Court Decision No. 1/PUU-XI/2013, para [3.16].

25 Law No. 20 of 2001 Amending Law No. 31 of 1999 on Eradication of Corruption.

26 Article 43B, Law No. 20 of 2001 on the Revision of Law No. 31 of 1999 on the Eradication of Corruption.

27 Article 65, Law No. 21 of 2007 on the Eradication of People Smuggling.

28 Protesters were also objecting to Law No. 2 of 2019 on the Second Amendment of Law No. 30 of 2002 on the the Corruption Eradication Commission (KPK, Komisi Pemberantas Tindak Pidana Korupsi. This prevents the KPK from conducting wiretaps, searches and seizures without permission from a new supervisory board appointed by the president. See Chapter 1 (Lindsey and Pausacker).

29 This probationary period may apply if: there is no strong community reaction; the convicted person shows regret and a desire to improve; the role of the convicted person in the crime was not especially important; or there are other mitigating factors (art. 91(1)).

References

Butt, Simon 2014. 'Judicial Responses to the Death Penalty in Indonesia', *Alternative Law Journal* 39(2): 134

Butt, Simon and Lindsey, Tim 2018. *Indonesian Law*. Oxford University Press

Cribb, Robert 2010. 'Legal Pluralism and Criminal Law in the Dutch Colonial Order', *Indonesia* 90: 63

Crouch, Melissa 2012. 'Indonesia's Blasphemy Law: Bleak Outlook for Minority Religions', *Asia Pacific Bulletin* 146, 26 January www.eastwestcenter.org/publications/indonesias-blasphemy-law-bleak-outlook-minority-religions

Erdianto, Kristian 2017. 'DPR-Pemerintah Belum Sepakat, Pasal LGBT dalam RKUHP Ditunda' *Kompas.com*, 5 February https://nasional.kompas.com/read/2018/02/05/20140041/dpr-pemerintah-belum-sepakat-pasal-lgbt-dalam-rkuhp-ditunda

Gumilang, Prima 2015. 'Kapolri: Banyak Polisi Tidak Paham Ujaran Kebencian', *CNN Indonesia,* 5 November

Hapsari, Arghea Desafti 2010. 'Court Upholds Blasphemy Law', *The Jakarta Post*, 20 April

Human Rights Watch 2003. 'A Return to the New Order? Political Prisoners in Megawati's Indonesia', *Human Rights Watch* 15(4), July www.hrw.org/sites/default/files/reports/indon0703.pdf

Human Rights Watch 2010. 'Turning Critics into Criminals: The Human Rights Consequences of Criminal Defamation Law in Indonesia', May www.hrw.org/en/reports/2010/05/04/turning-critics-criminals-0

Lev, D. 1972. *Islamic Courts in Indonesia: A Study in the Political Bases of Legal Institutions.* Berkeley: University of California Press

Lev, Daniel S. 1985. 'Colonial Law and the Genesis of the Indonesian State', *Indonesia* 40: 57

Marwati 2016. 'President Jokowi: Four State Problem Have [sic] to Be Resolved Immediately', *Universitas Gadjah Mada News*, 10 December http://ugm.ac.id/en/news/9558-president. jokowi:.four.state.problem.have.to.be.resolved.immediately

McNusrat, Madina 2009. 'Duh ... Tiga Buah Kakao Menyeret Minah ke Meja Hijau ...', *Kompas* 19 November

McRae, Dave 2015. '"Jokowi" and His Firing Squads', *Strategic Review* 5: 29–32

Media Indonesia 2016. 'Pelaksanaan Hukuman Mati Tidak Akan Surut', *Media Indonesia*, 23 May http://mediaindonesia.com/news/read/46705/pelaksanaan-hukuman-mati-tidak-akan-surut/2016-05-23

Ministry of Justice and Human Rights 2013. *Draft Naskah Akademik Rancangan Undang-Undang tentang Kitab Undang-Undang Hukum Pidana*. Jakarta: National Law Development Agency, Ministry of Justice and Human Rights

Okezone 2015. 'Jaksa Agung: Eksekusi Mati Tahap Tiga Setelah Lebaran', *Okezone News*, 30 May

Soares, Singgih 2015. 'Indonesian Justice Tainted by Death Sentence against Minor', *Tempo*, 22 March

Soesilo, Raden 1974. *Kitab Undang-Undang Hukum Pidana (K.U.H.P.) serta Komentar-Komentarnya Lengkap Pasal demi Pasal, untuk Para Pajabat Kepolisian Kejaksaan Pamong-Praja Dsb*. Bogor: Politeia

Sugandhi, R 1981. *Kitab Undang-Undang Hukum Pidana (K.U.H.P.) dengan Penjelasannya*. Jakarta: Usaha Nasional

Tedjasukmana, Jason 2012. 'Sandals and Solidarity: Why Indonesians Are Using Flip-Flops as Symbols of Protest', *Time*, 6 January

Vandenbosch, Amry 1944. *The Dutch East Indies: Its Government, Problems, and Politics*. University of California Press, pp. 193–4

Laws and regulations

Bataviasche Statuten of 1642 (earliest colonial legal code for Batavia by the Dutch East India Company (Vereenigde Oost-Indische Compagnie, VOC)
Wetboek van Strafrecht of 1867 (colonial Criminal Code that applied only to Europeans)
Strafwet voor Inlanders of 1872 (Criminal Code for 'natives')
Wetboek van Strafrecht Nederlandsch Indie 1918
1945 Constitution (*Undang-undang Dasar*)
MPRS (Provisional People's Consultative Assembly) Decision No. XXV/1966 (which prohibited the promotion of Marxism/Leninism)
Criminal Code (*Kitab Undang-Undang Hukum Pidana*, KUHP: Law No. 1 of 1946 as amended by Law No. 27 of 1999 on the Indonesian Criminal Code)
KUHAP (*Kitab Undang-Undang Hukum Acara Pidana* or Criminal Procedure Code)
Law No. 1 of 1946 on Criminal Law
Law No. 20 of 1946 on Confinement Punishment
Law No. 7 of 1947 on Gambling
Emergency Law No. 7 of 1955 on Investigation, Prosecution and Trial of Economic Crimes
Law No. 73 of 1958, KUHP, the Criminal Code
Law No. 11/PNPS/1963 on Eradication of Subversive Activity (revoked by Law No. 26 of 1999)
Interim Emergency Law No. 16 of 1960 on Changes to the Criminal Code
Interim Emergency Law No. 18 of 1960 on Amendments to the Fine Amounts in the KUHP
Law No. 1 of 1961 on Legalisation of all Emergency Laws Passed before 1 January 1961 to Become Law
Law No. 12 of 1992 on Road Traffic
Law No. 5 of 1997 on Psychotropic Substances
Law No. 26 of 1999, revoking Law No. 11/PNPS/1963 on Eradication of Subversive Activity
Law No. 31 of 1999 on the Eradication of Corruption (amended by Law No. 20 of 2001)
Law No. 20 of 2001 Amending Law No. 31 of 1999 on Eradication of Corruption
Law No. 20 of 2001 on the Revision of Law No. 31 of 1999 on the Eradication of Corruption
Law No. 15 of 2003 on Adoption of Interim Emergency Law No. 1 of 2002 on the Eradication of Terrorist Acts
Law No. 21 of 2007 on the Eradication of People Smuggling
Law No. 11 of 2008 on Information and Electronic Transactions, as amended by Law No. 19 of 2016
Law No. 44 of 2008 on Pornography
Law No. 35 of 2009 on Narcotics
Law No. 8 of 2010 on the Prevention and Combating of Money Laundering
Law No. 12 of 2011 on Lawmaking
Law No. 11 of 2012 on the Juvenile Justice System
Law No. 9 of 2013 on the Prevention and Eradication of Terrorism Financing
Law No. 19 of 2016, amending Law No. 11 of 2008 on Information and Electronic Transactions

Presidential Instruction 1 PNPS/ 1965 and endorsed as a statute by Law No. 5 of 1969 (commonly called 'the Blasphemy Law')
Government Regulation No. 8 of 1948 on Confinement Punishment
Government Regulation in Lieu of Law No. 16 of 1960 on Supreme Court Regulation No. 2 of 2012 on Fine Limits for Minor Crimes and Fine Amounts in the Criminal Code
Supreme Court Regulation No. 2 of 2012 on the Adjustment of Fine Limits for Minor Crimes and Fine Amounts in the Criminal Code

Court decisions

Constitutional Court Decision No. 013-022/PUU-IV/2006 (*Lèse Majesté* case)
Constitutional Court Decision No. 6/ PUU-V/2007 (*Hate Sowing* case)
Constitutional Court Decision No. 140/PUU-VII/2009 (*Blasphemy Law* case)
Constitutional Court Decision No. 1/PUU-XI/2013 (*Offensive Treatment case*)
Constitutional Court Decision No. 46/PUU-XIV/2016 (*Indecent Activities/ Family Love Alliance case*)

3 The Criminal Procedure Code

Simon Butt and Tim Lindsey[1]

The *Kitab Undang-undang Hukum Acara Pidana* or KUHAP (Law No. 8 of 1981) is Indonesia's Code of Criminal Procedure. It governs the roles of the police and prosecutors, the law on arrests, warrants, detention, searches, legal aid, evidence, trials and appeals in most types of cases. Unlike the Criminal Code, which was first passed in 1918, KUHAP is not a colonial legacy. Rather it was developed by the Indonesian government as a major reform to meet the contemporary needs of the administration of criminal justice, replacing the Dutch procedural code that had been in place since 1926.[2] At the time, the Soeharto government claimed KUHAP reflected international norms, particularly human rights (Lev 1996: 156; Lubis 1993). However, it is a flawed statute, like the Criminal Code, and is routinely flouted (Lev 1996: 157). From the start, it has failed to achieve its objectives and needs fundamental reform or replacement.

KUHAP divides criminal procedure into four distinct stages. The first is the preliminary investigation (*penyelidikan*), to determine whether a crime has been committed.[3] The second is the main investigation (*penyidikan*), which is intended to obtain more information and evidence of the crime, and name a suspect or suspects.[4] At this stage, pre-trial hearings (*praperadilan*) may also take place. The third stage is prosecution, where prosecutors prepare their case against the defendant for presentation before a court.[5] This is followed by the trial, at which a panel of (usually three) judges examine the case, decides whether the defendant is guilty or innocent and, if guilty, imposes a punishment. Appeals may then follow. In this chapter, we consider provisions of KUHAP and other laws that regulate each of these five stages, with a particular focus on the rights of suspects and defendants. In doing so, our aim is to provide a brief, descriptive overview of criminal procedure law in Indonesia to assist readers and as background to other chapters in this book.

Several themes emerge from the discussion in this chapter. First, the procedural stages just described are generally treated as strict divisions. This is particularly true of primary investigation and prosecution. In practice, this division has undermined cooperation between police and prosecutors, thereby impeding their work and perpetuating the institutional rivalry that has long existed between them (Wagner and Jacobs 2008: 201–2).

Second, KUHAP is far from comprehensive. Many other statutes and regulations have been enacted to fill in gaps, or to provide more detail. There are, for example, specific statutes concerning the police (Law No. 2 of 2002), the public prosecution (Law No. 16 of 2004), and every branch of the courts, all of which bear on criminal procedure. Many 'special' (*khusus*) criminal laws have also been enacted to deal with particular offences – such as terrorism, narcotics offences and money-laundering – and most of these contain their own criminal procedures that prevail over KUHAP to the extent of any inconsistency. A good example of this is Law No. 20 of 2001 amending Law No. 31 of 1999 on the Eradication of Corruption, which Assegaf discusses in Chapter 10 of this book.

Various statutes and subordinate regulations cover other issues related to criminal procedure, such as clemency applications, remissions, and parole. Further, the Constitutional Court has issued many important decisions in this area that have had a significant impact on the content of criminal procedure law. This judicial development of the law has occurred even though Indonesia follows the European Civil Law tradition, which relies principally on law made by the legislature and executive and usually accords no formal legal status to judicial decisions as a source of law. Accordingly, while it is true to say that KUHAP is the starting point for Indonesian criminal procedural law, this body of law is now found in a complex and diffuse range of sources.

Third, KUHAP may look adequate 'on paper' but is often ignored in practice, particularly by police (Fitzpatrick 2008; Lev 1996). When first enacted, KUHAP was, as mentioned (and as Lindsey discusses further in Chapter 6), heralded as a victory for human rights, at least compared with its colonial predecessor. This was because it purported to grant suspects and defendants procedural rights that they did not have under the previous law. However, KUHAP has, unfortunately, not lived up to these expectations. There are numerous reasons for this, including that its provisions are vaguely worded, do not cover some key areas, and impose no sanctions for non-compliance by law enforcement officials. The same shortcomings apply to most of the other laws that bear on criminal process in Indonesia.

Finally, Indonesian criminal procedure law is now out-of-date and, as mentioned, is in urgent need of a complete overhaul. Lawyers and activists have repeatedly called for amendments to, or even replacement of, the diverse body of laws that make up Indonesia's criminal procedure law, including KUHAP itself. We consider some of the more recent proposals for reform – which have their own shortcomings – at the end of this chapter.

Investigation

As mentioned, investigations begin with *penyelidikan* – an initial stage during which police[6] collect evidence and determine whether a crime has been committed. KUHAP states that these investigations are to be conducted by preliminary investigators (*penyelidik*) (art. 4). However, some special criminal laws authorise certain other state officials to conduct these investigations and then to proceed to primary investigations. Officials and employees of the National Narcotics Agency (BNN, Badan Narkotika Nasional Republik Indonesia) and the Corruption Eradication Commission (KPK, Komisi Pemberantasan Korupsi) are among those who have these investigatory powers.[7]

When undertaking their investigations, preliminary investigators can generally receive reports and complaints about crimes, search for information and evidence, and stop people they deem suspicious to inspect their identification (art. 5(1)(a)). On the order of a primary investigator (*penyidik*), preliminary investigators can also arrest and detain a person; conduct body and property searches; seize documents; take fingerprints and photos; and bring a person before a prosecutor (art. 5(1)(b)).

If, when these preliminary investigations are complete, police believe that a crime was committed, the case will advance to the primary investigation (*penyidikan*) stage. Here, police continue to gather evidence, question witnesses, continue crime scene investigations, and, if necessary, conduct crime scene reconstructions. They also identify suspects. Primary investigators have powers very similar to those possessed by preliminary investigators, but do not need approval by a more senior investigator. The primary investigator can call on experts to assist in the case; stop an investigation; or take other necessary action according to the law (art. 7). KUHAP also allows assistant investigators to be appointed, if required (art. 10–12).

Investigators compile a dossier (*berita acara*) about the investigation, which contains: records of interview of suspect and witnesses; documentation relating to arrests, detentions, property searches and seizures; documentary evidence; crime scene assessments; relevant court rulings or determinations; and material relevant to the investigation (art. 75). This dossier is then handed over to prosecutors. If prosecutors believe that the dossier contains insufficient evidence to proceed to prosecute, they can return the dossier to investigators, along with instructions about what further information is required (art. 110(2)). The police investigation is considered complete if prosecutors do not return the dossier within fourteen days (art. 110(4)).

Any person who experiences or witnesses a crime, including a victim of that crime, can report it to investigators (art. 108(1)). If a preliminary investigator receives such a report, or catches a person in the process of committing a crime, then he or she must commence a preliminary investigation. He or she must prepare a report for a primary investigator (art. 102), who then coordinates, supervises, and guides the preliminary investigator (art. 105). Likewise, any primary investigator who learns of, or receives a report or complaint about, an activity that could reasonably be suspected to constitute a crime must immediately investigate (art. 106). Before the investigation process begins, investigators must inform suspects about their right to legal counsel (art. 114). The police must report any investigations they commence to prosecutors. Similarly, if police stop an investigation, they must inform prosecutors, and the suspect or the suspect's family (art. 109).

KUHAP empowers investigators to call suspects or witnesses for questioning. The request must clearly state the reason for questioning and give reasonable notice. If the suspect or witness does not attend, the investigator can call the person to appear at another time, and order an official to bring the suspect or witness to him or her (art. 112). Investigators can also call on experts to assist their investigations (art. 120(1)).

While Indonesia has no formal plea-bargaining system, the police often exercise discretion when laying charges through an informal system called 'reserve cases' (*kasus cadangan*). Under this practice, police charge a suspect with only one of multiple potential crimes for which they might be responsible, reserving the right to press further charges in order to secure the suspect's cooperation. This usually takes place without court or prosecutor involvement, and is a process widely seen as open to corruption, often exploited by police to extort suspects.

As mentioned, once the investigation is complete, the investigator must hand over the case file to prosecutors, who then decide whether sufficient evidence exists to prosecute. If the evidence is insufficient, prosecutors return the case file with a request for further information (art. 110(2)).

Arrest

KUHAP allows police and other appointed state officials to arrest a person who is 'strongly suspected' of a crime, based on 'sufficient preliminary evidence' (arts. 16–17).[8] In 1984, the Supreme Court Chief Justice, the prosecutor general, the Justice Minister, and the police chief decided that 'sufficient preliminary evidence' was a police report and one other piece of evidence. Nevertheless, considerable debate remains about what evidence is sufficient and what is not (Hamzah 2014).[9]

Arrest ordinarily requires a warrant, which must identify the person to be arrested, outline the suspected crime, and state the place of interrogation (art. 18(1)). The warrant need not be issued by a court – an order from a superior officer will usually suffice. Those suspected of less serious crimes (*pelanggaran*) can be arrested only if they have been called several times for questioning but failed to attend, without lawful excuse (art. 19(2)). The police must provide a copy of the warrant to the family of the person arrested 'immediately' following the arrest (art. 18(3)). Where an offender is caught in the act (*tertangkap tangan*), however, no warrant is required (art. 18(2)).

Article 18(3) was challenged in the Constitutional Court by Hendry Batoarung Ma'dika, who was detained by police for twenty-four days before a copy of his arrest warrant was provided to his family.[10] The Court held that 'immediately' should be understood as 'immediately, and no more than seven days'. For the Court, seventy-two hours was sufficient time to deliver a copy to the family but it decided that seven days was an appropriate period that could be applied uniformly across Indonesia, given its size and variable geographic conditions.[11]

Searches

KUHAP permits primary investigators to search a suspect's body or house for the purposes of the investigation (art. 32). For house searches, investigators must first obtain a search warrant from the local district court chief judge (art. 33(1)). In urgent circumstances, however, investigators can, without a warrant, search the place where the suspect resides, the crime scene, and other relevant accommodation and public places (art. 34(1)). Unfortunately, however, KUHAP does not stipulate what constitutes an 'urgent circumstance', which allows police to simply unilaterally determine that this precondition has been met, and search without a warrant.

KUHAP allows preliminary investigators to search the clothing and possessions of persons who they strongly suspect are carrying items that should be confiscated (art. 37).

Confiscation

An investigator can only confiscate goods with written approval from the relevant district court. In pressing circumstances, investigators can confiscate movable objects but must immediately report this to that court (art. 38). The following items can be confiscated:

- property suspected to have been partly or wholly obtained through criminal means;
- property used to commit or prepare for a crime;
- items used to impede a criminal investigation; and
- other items directly connected to a crime (art. 39).

If a person is caught 'red-handed', investigators can confiscate items used, or suspected to have been used, to commit the crime, and other items with evidentiary value (art. 40).

Custody (temporary detention)

Primary investigators, preliminary investigators (if ordered by a primary investigator), prosecutors, and judges can detain suspected offenders or defendants, but detention is not mandatory. Under KUHAP detention is legal only if the alleged crime is an offence specified in art. 21(4)(b) or carries a penalty of at least five years' imprisonment (art. 21(4)(a)). The detention should also be supported by 'sufficient evidence' to 'strongly suspect' that the prospective detainee committed the offence and is likely to: not attend trial;

Table 3.1 Detention limits under the KUHAP

Phase of criminal procedure	*Limits of detention*	*Relevant legislation*
Arrest and preliminary investigation (*penyelidikan*)	24 hours	KUHAP, art. 19(1)
Primary investigation (*penyidikan*)	60 days (20 days, extendable by 40 days)	KUHAP, arts. 20(1), 24
Trial (*pemeriksaan*)	90 days (30 days, extendable by 60 days, with approval of a high court judge)	KUHAP, arts. 20(3), 26
Appeal	90 days (30 days, extendable with approval of a high court judge)	KUHAP, arts. 20(3), 27
Cassation	110 days (50 days, extendable by 60 days, with approval of the Chief Justice of the Supreme Court)	KUHAP, arts. 20(3), 28

damage or dispose of evidence; or repeat the offence (art. 21(1)). Detention can be: in a state facility; at home, under observation from authorities; or 'city detention', where the suspect must report to authorities at specified intervals (art. 22(1)–(3)).

KUHAP specifies clear time limits for permissible detention during each stage of the criminal procedure, as Table 3.1 shows.[12]

Detention can be extended by a further sixty days if the alleged crime carries a penalty of nine years' imprisonment or more.[13] This extension can be sought during the investigation, prosecution, or trial stages, and must be ordered by a district court judge, a high court judge, or the Supreme Court, according to the stage the process has reached (art. 29).

Unfortunately, these time limits are honoured more in the breach than the observance. The processes described above present many opportunities for corruption, and widespread evidence exists of the routine abuse of the pre-trial detention process, often involving serious violations of human rights. Until recently, police were able to detain suspects in cases of suspected theft involving goods valued at more than Rp. 250 (equivalent to about US$ 0.02). In 2012, the Supreme Court issued a regulation raising the minimum threshold to Rp. 2.5 million (about US$ 200)[14] but this is not always applied in practice, as Assegaf shows in Chapter 9.

During a visit to Indonesia in 2007, the UN special rapporteur on torture, Manfred Nowak, found that, as standard procedure, Indonesian police detained suspects for the full sixty days during primary investigations. This is much longer than permitted under international law (Nowak 2008). He noted that prolonged detention not only increases opportunities for abuse but also gives time for signs of physical abuse to disappear before detainees are released or transferred. Nowak expressed concern that pre-trial detainees and convicted prisoners are often housed together in Indonesian prisons, which is another clear violation of international standards.

Unfortunately, deaths in police custody are not uncommon, including deaths of minors (Budiari 2015; Haryanto 2012). Nowak heard many allegations of police torture and ill-treatment, and concluded that torture was 'routine practice' in police stations in many parts of Indonesia. Jakarta and other metropolitan areas of Java (Nowak 2008: 12). He also received reports, corroborated by forensic medical analysis, of: beatings, including with wooden sticks, chains, iron bars, and hammers; kicking with heavy boots; electrocution; and shots fired into detainees' legs. Other reports have described sexual violence (Perkumpulan Lembaga Bantuan Hukum Masyarakat 2012). Detainees interviewed by Nowak (2008: 12) reported that torture is used primarily to elicit confessions or information on drug suppliers, but also simply to extract bribes.

Bail

KUHP permits bail under certain conditions. An investigator, prosecutor, or judge may, at the request of the suspect or defendant, suspend or postpone detention. A personal or financial guarantee and other conditions can be imposed on the release from detention (art. 31(1)). The general elucidation (*penjelasan*, explanatory memorandum) to KUHAP provides examples of such conditions: regularly reporting to authorities (for example daily, or once every three days); and remaining at home or in a particular city. If these conditions are not met, then the suspension of detention can be revoked (art. 31(2)).

Government Regulation No. 27 of 1983 on the Implementation of the Criminal Procedure Code explains bail procedures, including payment of financial guarantees. The relevant authority – police, during the investigation stage; prosecutors, while the case is being prepared for court; and the court, once the trial has started – determines the amount payable. The suspect or their legal representative must deliver the bail money directly to the district court clerk, who must confirm receipt of the funds. If the suspect or defendant flees, and cannot be found after three months, the money is transferred to the state (art. 35).

As for personal guarantees, anyone with a relationship to the suspect – including a legal representative or family member – can give one. They can do this by signing a statement promising to pay a specified amount to the relevant authorities if the accused absconds. Again, if the suspect or defendant cannot be found within three months, the money is forfeited to the state (art. 36).

In practice, district court clerks are notorious for refusing to sign confirmation receipts and not returning the funds once the case has concluded. According to some reports, bail money is often handed to investigating police officers or prosecutors, with the expectation that they will then deliver it to the court, although this rarely happens. Accordingly, criminal lawyers tend to recommend personal guarantees over directly-paid financial guarantees (Hukumonline 2005).

Rights of the accused

KUHAP contains procedural safeguards intended to protect the rights of suspects and defendants. These include the rights to: the presumption of innocence; legal counsel; and be free of the burden of proof. Commentators have identified a major gap between procedural rules and actual practice, stemming from vague or inadequate regulations (Fitzpatrick 2008; Strang 2008: 188–7) insufficient knowledge of procedures, and a willingness to flagrantly violate them. Of course, this is detrimental to the rights of defendants and significantly reduces the rigour and quality of police investigations.[15]

Right to silence

KUHAP does not grant a clear right against self-incrimination. Article 66 states that defendants do not bear the burden of proof but debate has arisen about whether this equates to the right to silence (Fitzpatrick 2008: 507), and in practice, judges tend to draw inferences of guilt from a defendant's failure to speak at trial.

Interrogation and other rights

Suspects have the rights to be interrogated promptly after arrest and be clearly informed of the allegations against them in language they understand at the beginning of interrogation (arts. 50–1). During investigation and trial, suspects and defendants also have the rights to freely provide investigators, prosecutors, and the court with information and use an interpreter at all times (arts. 52 and 53(1)).

KUHAP also grants suspects and defendants the right to:

- contact and receive visits from:
  - a private doctor for health purposes, whether connected with the case or not (art. 58);
  - family, household members, or anyone else whose assistance is required. These people must be informed of detention by a relevant officer, so that the suspect or defendant can receive legal assistance or security for bail or for any other family or business purpose (arts. 59–61);
  - a member of the clergy of any religion (art. 63);
- correspond with their family or legal counsel at any time and receive writing materials for this purpose. Officials must not examine this

correspondence, unless they suspect that correspondence is being abused. If this happens, documents must be stamped and returned to suspects to indicate that they have been intercepted and scrutinised (art. 62);
- be tried in open court (art. 64); and
- present witnesses beneficial to their case (art. 65).

Right to counsel

Once detained, suspects and defendants may contact their legal counsel, and foreign citizens can contact diplomatic representatives (art. 57). Suspects and defendants have the right to assistance from legal counsel of their choosing during investigations, and at every other stage of the criminal process (arts. 54–5). That legal representative must have access to the suspect or defendant at all stages. Investigators, prosecutors, and corrections staff must not listen in on any conversations or meetings held between a suspect or defendant and their lawyer, unless the alleged offence threatens national security (art. 71). This is a very broad exemption that is sometimes used by police to justify intrusion. The legal representative also has the right to access the police investigation report or dossier about the accused or defendant upon request and to send and receive written correspondence on behalf of the accused (arts. 72–3).

The state must provide free legal assistance to persons accused of crimes that carry fifteen years' imprisonment or more, or the death penalty, and to those facing a sentence of five years' or more who cannot afford legal representation (art. 56). In practice, most detainees have no lawyer present during police questioning. This is partly because the police do not have to inform them of this right, so many detainees are not aware of it and hence do not demand it (Fitzpatrick 2008: 507). Worse, some detainees report that police threaten violence or tougher penalties if they ask for or get a lawyer. Many detainees succumb to this pressure, declining legal counsel, even if offered (Perkumpulan Lembaga Bantuan Hukum 2012).

Challenges to arrest or detention

One of KUHAP's most-heralded reforms was the introduction of pre-trial hearings (*praperadilan*) (arts. 77–83), discussed in detail by Mann in Chapter 5. This mechanism allows a suspect, his or her family, or legal counsel to challenge the legality of an arrest or detention, such as where an arrest was made without a valid warrant (arts. 77 and 79). It has been loosely compared to the principle of *habeas corpus* in common law countries but is far narrower and much more restricted.

A single judge hears the challenge and must reach a decision within ten days of the application being made (arts. 78 and 82(1)). Importantly, there is no right of appeal from a pre-trial determination to a high court or the

Supreme Court, and if an issue relating to arrest or detention is not raised in a pre-trial hearing, courts usually refuse to allow it to be raised at trial (Fitzpatrick 2008: 506). If the *praperadilan* judge finds the arrest or detention to be unlawful, then the accused is released (art. 82(3)(a)). A suspect or accused person is entitled to compensation for unlawful detention (art. 95),[16] but this is very rarely received.

Scholars have documented serious shortcomings with the pre-trial hearing process in practice. Chief among these is that any complaints about arrest or detention are first lodged with the police – the very subject of the complaint (Fitzpatrick 2008: 506). Further concerns include an undersupply of lawyers, especially in rural areas, and detainees being intimidated by police into not seeking legal counsel (Perkumpulan Lembaga Bantuan Hukum 2012), even though they are entitled to it, as discussed above. Also, police officers are not explicitly required by law to attend pre-trial hearings. Some therefore fail to appear, causing delays to proceedings; others appear only after trials have started, by which stage judges will not usually allow the legality of arrests and detentions to be contested. Finally, because pre-trial hearings are decided by a single judge and determinations cannot be appealed, standards of decision-making are generally low, with outcomes notorious for lack of uniformity and predictability (Fitzpatrick 2008: 506).

Under art. 80 of KUHAP, investigators, prosecutors, or interested third parties can also challenge the termination of investigations or prosecutions through *praperadilan* proceedings. This avenue is intended as a check on the power of police and prosecutors to drop cases, which they have often done in controversial circumstances, raising concerns about bribery. In May 2013, the Constitutional Court expanded the class of applicants who can challenge a termination.[17] In this case, an NGO, the Indonesian Anti-Corruption Community (Perkumpulan Masyarakat Anti Korupsi, MAKI), challenged the constitutionality of art. 80. The South Jakarta District Court had regularly refused to allow it to challenge terminations of corruption investigations using *praperadilan* proceedings, on grounds that MAKI was not an 'interested third party' (Hukumonline 2013a, 2013b). The Court held that the phrase 'interested third parties' (*pihak ketiga yang berkepentingan*) must be interpreted broadly, beyond just victims or informants to also include non-governmental and community organisations.[18]

In 2015, the Constitutional Court also expanded what can be challenged in pre-trial motions, to allow applicants to challenge the legality of being formally named a suspect.[19] Formally upgrading the status of a person of interest or witness to a 'suspect' has important implications, discussed below. In our view, this decision is understandable, in theory at least, but it has been criticised by anti-corruption activists for allowing alleged corruptors to challenge their being named a suspect, successfully in some cases (The Jakarta Post 2015; Saragih 2015; Assegaf 2015), as Mann explains in Chapter 5 of this book.

Being named a suspect

In Indonesia, being 'named a suspect' is loosely equivalent to being charged in common law countries. Article 1(14) of KUHAP states that a 'suspect' is a person who, based on preliminary evidence, is suspected of committing an offence. Police Chief Regulation No. 14 of 2012 on the Management of Criminal Investigations repeats the definition (art. 1(10)) and defines 'preliminary evidence' as a police report and one other piece of legal evidence (art. 1(21)).

Once named a suspect, the person will be further investigated and, depending on the weight of the evidence police obtain, may be prosecuted. Investigations are not time-limited, so once a person is named a suspect, he or she will usually be under investigation until police issue a formal directive (an SP3 or *Surat Perintah Penghentian Penyidikan*)[20] to stop it. An investigation can be stopped if: there is insufficient evidence; the act committed was not a crime; or 'according to law' (*demi hukum*) if the suspect dies, the limitation period for the offence (*kedaluwarsa*) has passed or the complaint is revoked (for *delik aduan* cases, where a complaint is a necessary for an investigation to proceed); or a judge has already made a legally binding decision in relation to the same act (art. 76 of the Regulation; art. 109 of KUHAP). It is widely believed that police sometimes intentionally keep unmeritorious investigations on foot for many years in order to place pressure on their critics or political enemies, or just to extort bribes.

Prosecution

As mentioned, once the police or civil servant investigators have completed their investigations, they hand over the case, including the dossier of evidence (*berkas*), to prosecutors. Prosecutors then have seven days to determine whether to return it for further investigation, along with instructions (arts. 110(2), 137(1), and 138 of KUHAP). If returned, investigators then have fourteen days to complete the investigation, following these instructions, and return the dossier to prosecutors. Dossiers are commonly sent back and forth repeatedly and, in some cases, police choose to drop cases rather than investigate further (Strang 2008: 198).

A prosecutor can decide not to prosecute if insufficient evidence exists, the alleged offence does not constitute a criminal act, or the case is closed by law (*ditutup demi hukum*) (art. 140(2a)) – that is, it cannot proceed, for example, because the accused has died. If the prosecution chooses this course, it must issue a written statement explaining why prosecution was terminated (*surat penghentian penuntutan*). This decision is not final: 'the public prosecutor can prosecute the accused if later it is clear that a new reason exists' to do so (art. 140(d)).

Prosecutors can terminate a case or refuse to prosecute, even if sufficient prima facie evidence exists that would otherwise enable prosecution. Law No. 16 of 2004 on Public Prosecution allows the Jaksa Agung (Indonesia's combined Prosecutor and Attorney General) to 'put aside' a case if the 'public interest' so requires (art. 35(c)). 'Public interest' is vaguely defined as 'the interest of the nation and state and/or the wider community' (elucidation to art. 35(c)). Before exercising this power, the prosecutor general must first consider the opinions of state institutions with authority over the issues involved in the case.

Once satisfied with the dossier, the prosecutor prepares a formal indictment and delivers it to the relevant district court, which will set trial date (arts. 140(1) and 152). At this stage, the case file usually contains:

(a) the arrest warrant;
(b) the detention order;
(c) the provision under which the suspect is charged;
(d) a crime scene report;
(e) a list of exhibits for trial;
(f) the names of witnesses interviewed and a summary of their records of interview (*berita acara pemeriksaan*);
(g) a legal analysis; and
(h) a conclusion.

Prosecutors can terminate the prosecution or revise the indictment once, but not within seven days before the trial commences. The defendant, his or her legal counsel, and the investigator must be informed of any amendments (art. 144).

Limitations on prosecution

Limitation periods

Articles 78 to 80 of the Criminal Code (KUHP) set time periods, after the expiry of which defendants cannot be prosecuted. For crimes carrying a prison sentence of three years or less, the limitations period (*kedaluwarsa*) is six years. For crimes carrying a prison sentence of more than three years, the period is twelve years. For crimes carrying the death penalty or life imprisonment, it is eighteen years. For people under the age of eighteen years when the offence was committed, the period is reduced by one-third (art. 78). Limitation periods run from the day after the offence was committed (except in several specified circumstances) and cease upon prosecution (arts. 79–80).

Double jeopardy

The KUHP protects against double jeopardy (*nebis in idem*). Article 76 states:

> Except where it is still possible for a judge's decision to be reconsidered, a person may not be prosecuted twice for an act about which an Indonesian judge has already adjudicated, in a decision that has become binding.

This 'double jeopardy' prohibition is repeated in art. 18(5) of Law No. 39 of 1999 on Human Rights:

> No person can be prosecuted for a second time for the same case for an act that has been the subject of a court decision that has legally binding force.

Thus, once an Indonesian judge has handed down a decision against the defendant that has acquired 'binding legal force' – that is, one against which no further appeal is possible – the defendant cannot be prosecuted again for an act covered by that decision.

Trial procedure

Chapter XVI of KUHAP covers trial procedure. As the Indonesian legal system is a civil law system, nearly all district court (*pengadilan negeri*) cases are heard by a panel of three judges and juries are not used. One of the judges is the chair (*hakim ketua*) and is usually more senior than the other two. Typically, the judges produce a single, joint judicial decision (*putusan*), although dissenting opinions are permitted. Civil law systems are 'inquisitorial', meaning the judges inquire into the truth of what has occurred. The judges control the proceedings and can directly question witnesses if they choose.

KUHAP recognises three types of trials: ordinary examinations (*acara pemeriksaan biasa*); summary examinations (*acara pemeriksaan singkat*); and expedited examinations (*acara pemeriksaan cepat*). Expedited cases involve crimes that attract up to three months' detention (*kurungan*) or a Rp. 7,500 fine; and minor insult or slander (*penghinaan ringan*) (art. 205(1)).

Expedited cases are heard by a single judge, must commence within three days of filing, are decided in a single day and cannot be appealed (arts. 205(3) and 207(1)(b)). Witnesses can be called but do not need to testify under oath (art. 208). Summary examination, meanwhile, is used for simple crimes not mentioned in art. 205 to which the application of the law is straightforward, and which the public prosecutor considers will be easily proved (art. 203(1)). The public prosecutor presents the accused, plus any witnesses, experts, interpreters, and evidence (art. 203(2)). If the judge believes further investigation is required, the judge can give prosecutors up to fourteen additional days. If prosecutors fail to complete their investigation within this period, the judge can order that the case be heard as an 'ordinary examination' (art. 203(3)).

Ordinary examinations, or *acara pemeriksaan biasa*, proceed as follows. When a district court head receives a case file from prosecutors, he or she first determines whether the case appears to fall within the court's jurisdiction. If it does, then he or she selects the judges to hear the case, who then determine the date for the trial (art. 152(1)). Judges, prosecutors, or clerks must recuse themselves if they have a blood or marital relation up to the third degree, or are, or were, married to the defendant or his or her legal representative (art. 157).

Presiding judges are expected to have read the case file before the case commences. Much anecdotal evidence suggests, however, that judges routinely fail to do this and are, therefore, ill-prepared to handle and decide their cases.

The language of the trial is Indonesian and the chair (*ketua*) of the panel of judges must ensure that the defendant and witnesses can answer questions freely. Trials must be open and public, unless issues of morality or juvenile offenders are involved. Failure to meet these conditions renders any decision reached invalid (*batal demi hukum*) (art. 153(1)–(4)), although, again, these rules are rarely paid anything more than lip service.

When the trial commences, the chair must confirm the defendant's personal details and ask whether he or she completely understands the charges (art. 155). The prosecution then reads out the indictment, which contains the alleged facts and criminal offence, including relevant provisions of the KUHP or other criminal laws. The defendant or his or her legal representative can object to the court's jurisdiction or the indictment. After hearing from the public prosecutor, the judges decide this matter. If the court agrees with the defendant, the case proceeds no further (art. 156(1)–(2)).

Judges must hear testimony from all witnesses named in the case file, beginning with any victim statements. Each witness must recite an oath or swear according to his or her religion that he or she will provide a truthful recollection of events (art. 160). If testimony by a witness differs from his or her statement recorded in the case file, the chair must remind the witness of the obligation to be truthful and ask for an explanation for the discrepancy (art. 163). Penalties apply for providing a false statement (art. 174).

Judges, prosecutors, and the defendant or his or her legal counsel can question witnesses (art. 165) but must not 'ensnare' the witness or defendant with those questions (art. 166). Witnesses with obligations to safeguard secrets because of their occupation, position, or the esteem in which they are held, may ask to be excused from testifying. This includes officials with obligations to maintain the confidentiality of state secrets. Judges decide on the soundness of the reasons offered, when deciding whether to excuse them (art. 170(1)–(2)). All relevant evidence must be shown to the defendant (and witnesses, if necessary). The judge chairing the panel of judges is also required to show all pieces of evidence to the accused (and any witnesses, if necessary) for comment (art. 181(1)–(2)).

Following witness examination, the prosecutor proposes a sentencing demand, and the accused presents his or her defence. The prosecutor can respond, but the defendant always has the opportunity to speak last. The sentencing demand, defence, and response to the defence are provided in writing, read out in court, and submitted to the chair (art. 182(1)). The chair then declares that the examination has concluded, although it can be reopened if requested by the prosecutor or defendant (art. 182(2)).

The judges then deliberate in private, with the chair asking the opinions of the other judges on the panel, from youngest to oldest, to reach a decision. While a unanimous decision is ideal, a majority of the panel carries the day. If no majority is achieved, then the decision most favourable to the defendant is adopted (art. 182(5)–(6)). Given that panels comprise an odd number, this rule appears applicable only if one judge suffers misfortune during the trial that prevents them participating in deliberations. In any case, dissenting judgments are relatively uncommon.

Presumption of innocence

As noted in the previous chapter, KUHAP contains no clear, comprehensive articulation of a defendant's fundamental rights or the principles that underpin many criminal justice systems, such as the right to remain silent or the presumption of innocence. However, defendants have the right to be presumed innocent until proved guilty. Article 8(1) of Law No. 48 of 2009 on Judicial Power states that every person suspected, arrested, detained, prosecuted, or summoned before the courts must be considered not guilty until a judicial decision of binding legal authority establishes guilt.

KUHAP, meanwhile, places the burden of proof to establish guilt on prosecutors (art. 66). That onus is, however, reversed in rare instances. This is true, for example, for defendants charged under art. 98 of the Law No. 35 of 2009 on Narcotics, who bear the burden to demonstrate that certain assets are not proceeds of drug-related crime.

Law No. 39 of 1999 on Human Rights also provides for defendants' rights. For example, art. 18, which implements art. 14(2) of the International Covenant on Civil and Political Rights, provides the presumption of innocence to all persons arrested, detained, or prosecuted on suspicion of committing a crime, until otherwise proven guilty in court. Likewise, the Constitutional Court has held that the presumption of innocence is implicit in the declaration, contained in art. 1(3) of the Constitution, that Indonesia is a rule of law state (*negara hukum*).[21]

Evidence and witnesses

Judges cannot convict a defendant unless they have the strong belief (*memperoleh keyakinan*) that a crime has taken place and that the accused committed it. This strong belief must be supported by at least two 'pieces of valid evidence' (*alat bukti yang sah*) (art. 183 of KUHAP).

Article 184 of KUHAP identifies five types of legally admissible evidence:

- witness testimony;
- expert evidence;
- documents/letters;

- indications (*petunjuk*); and
- testimony of the defendant.

A witness is someone who provides a statement for an investigation, prosecution, or trial about what he or she heard, saw, or experienced first-hand (art. 1(26)). However, the testimony of only one witness will not suffice; at least two are required (art. 185(2)), or one witness' testimony must be supported by another piece of valid evidence (art. 185(3)). A defendant's statement is admissible if made before the court but must also be supported by at least one other form of evidence (art. 189(2)).

Use of documentary evidence is restricted under art. 184(1)(c). This provision requires that to be 'valid evidence' documents must be 'official documents' produced by 'public officials' about events or circumstances they heard, saw, or experienced, including: records of interview (art. 187(a)); and documents containing expert opinions (art. 187(b)), including affidavits; and 'other documents', provided they 'have a connection with the substance of another piece of evidence' (art. 187(c)).

Petunjuk, loosely translatable as 'circumstantial evidence', is notoriously difficult to describe and apply (Harahap 2000). The formal definition of *petunjuk* evidence encompasses:

> acts, events or circumstances which, because they are consistent with each other, or with the crime itself, indicate that a crime has been committed and the identity of the perpetrator.
>
> (art. 188(1))

This will usually be indirect evidence, relied upon when direct evidence – such as eyewitness testimony – is lacking. Like other forms of evidence, use of petunjuk evidence is limited by KUHAP. For example, like witness testimony, a sole piece of petunjuk evidence will be insufficient. It must be corroborated by at least one other form of petunjuk evidence or another type of valid evidence before it can formally be considered valid evidence.

Conspicuous in their absence from art. 184 are types of evidence relied upon in many trials around the world, such as photographs, telephone recordings, videos, electronic transmissions, and the like. This means that incontrovertible evidence, such as a reliable video footage showing the accused committing a crime, even if corroborated by one type of evidence acknowledged in art. 184, was, for many decades, insufficient to ensure conviction. In practice, their admissibility – primarily as petunjuk evidence – has depended on the inclinations of the presiding judges. However, in 2008, more modern types of evidence, such as video and sound recordings, and electronic information, were added to types of valid evidence that prosecutors can used to prove guilt. Article 5(1) of Indonesia's Law No. 11 of 2008 on Information and Electronic Transactions (as amended by Law No. 19 of 2016) states that 'electronic information' and 'electronic documents' are valid evidence, and art. 5(2) states that art. 5(1) is intended to expand the type of evidence that can be used in criminal procedural law.[22]

Article 185 of KUHAP specifies how judges should weigh up evidence. They must assess: consistency between witness statements and other types of evidence; the motive a witness may have to provide a particular explanation; the lifestyle and morality of a witness; and all other matters that could influence the plausibility of the testimony.

In 2011, the Constitutional Court expanded the definition of 'witness' to include people beyond those who 'heard, saw or experienced' the crime, as defined in art. 1(26).[23] The applicant, former Law and Human Rights Minister Yusril Ihza Mahendra, who was facing corruption charges, objected to the narrow definition of 'witness'. He had wanted to call Vice-President Jusuf Kalla, and former Presidents Megawati Soekarnoputri and Susilo Bambang Yudhoyono as witnesses for the defence under art. 65 of KUHAP, which allows a defendant to put forward a favourable witness or expert. But prosecutors objected because these people did not directly experience the alleged crime. The Court held that the definition of 'witnesses' did not need to be confined to the art. 1(26) categories. The precise implications of this decision are not clear, but it seems possible that defendants can now call witnesses to provide an alibi or attest to their good character. Nevertheless, well-founded concerns have been raised about the willingness of investigators and prosecutors to give effect to this decision (Hukumonline 2011).

Appeals

Both defendant and prosecution can appeal a decision, unless it arose from an expedited procedure, in which case an appeal is not available. Appeals (*banding*) from first instance district courts are heard in the high court (*pengadilan tinggi*) located in the capital of each province (art. 87). Appeals must be lodged at the district court where the case was first heard within seven days of the first instance decision (art. 233).[24] If the defendant does not do this, then he or she is deemed to have accepted the decision (art. 234(1)) and it becomes enforceable. This time limit is usually very strictly applied, and the courts routinely reject late applications, regardless of the reason for delay.

A panel of at least three high court judges review each appeal. There are usually no hearings and no opportunity for verbal submissions, with the panel relying exclusively on the appeal documents (art. 238(1)). If the high court believes that the district court negligently applied the law, made a mistake, or was not complete in its examination, the high court can remit the case to the same district court with an order to correct, or can make the correction itself (art. 240(1)). If necessary, the high court can vacate a district court decision before issuing its own (art. 240(2)).

If dissatisfied with the high court decision, parties can apply for cassation (*kasasi*) by the Supreme Court (Mahkamah Agung, Indonesia's highest appeal court). They have fourteen days from the date of the high court decision, or from being informed of that decision (arts. 244 and 245(1)), after which the application will usually be rejected, regardless of the merits, and the high court decision becomes enforceable. In addition, prosecutors can apply for 'cassation in the interests of law' (*kasasi demi kepentingan hukum*). Any penalty imposed by the Supreme Court in such a cassation cannot exceed that imposed at the initial trial.[25]

In a cassation, the Supreme Court can overturn decisions of lower courts if, for example, they lacked, or exceeded their, jurisdiction, or wrongly applied the law or broke it (art. 253(1)). Formally, the purpose of cassation is to ensure correct application of the law, but in practice, the Supreme Court generally treats it as if were an 'appeal' and reconsiders matters of fact if it wishes to, usually by characterising factual matters as involving problems of law (Butt and Lindsey 2018: 87).However, the Supreme Court's approach to cassation is inconsistent, sometimes being open to reviewing facts and sometimes insisting strictly on only considering legal issues

A cassation decision has permanent binding force, and is immediately executable, although problems with enforcement are very common (Butt and Lindsey 2018: 87).

Appeals against acquittals

KUHAP appears to prohibit the Supreme Court from hearing cassations against acquittals. Article 244 states:

> the accused or prosecutor may file a cassation appeal at the Supreme Court for all judgments on criminal cases handed down by a court other than the Supreme Court, *except for acquittals*.[26]

In 2013, the Constitutional Court changed this. It heard a challenge to art. 244 submitted by a former civil servant from West Sumatra, who had been acquitted by the Padang corruption court. The applicant argued that art. 244 did not provide a sufficiently clear prohibition against prosecutors filing a cassation appeal against his acquittal, and as a result, his constitutional right to legal certainty was violated (Hukumonline 2013c). The Constitutional Court granted the application but, instead of clarifying that acquittals could not be appealed, it deleted the term 'except for acquittals' from art. 244 – a result far from what the applicant sought. Since this decision, all acquittals can be appealed (Hukumonline 2013b).

Reconsideration

Although not strictly an appeal, KUHAP also provides another avenue that strongly resembles an appeal – judicial reconsideration (*peninjauan kembali* or PK).

Reconsideration enables the Supreme Court to reopen a decision of any court (other than the Constitutional Court) that is of 'binding legal force',[27] including the Supreme Court's own cassation decisions (art. 263). Applications are lodged with the court that first handled the case, which sends the application to the Supreme Court. There is no time limit on when they may be lodged (art. 264(3)).

To seek judicial reconsideration, the applicant must point to: new determinative evidence or circumstances (commonly known as a *novum*); inconsistent lower court decisions; or judicial error (art. 263(2)). Applicants can often meet at least one of these, and one rarely hears of applications being rejected for failing to meet at least one ground. If the application is based on a *novum*, the case will usually be remitted temporarily to the district court that originally heard the matter. It will examine the new evidence, including hearing any witnesses, and then return the case to the Supreme Court, along with a summary of evidence taken. Formally, any penalty issued in a reconsideration decision must not exceed that of the decision being appealed (art. 266(3)), although this rule is sometimes ignored.

In 2013, the Constitutional Court removed the restrictions in art. 268(3) of KUHAP that prevented a person lodging more than one application for judicial reconsideration application,[28] but the Supreme Court circumvented this by relying on provisions in other laws that limit reconsiderations to just one,[29] which the Constitutional Court did not deal with in its decision. In 2016 and 2017,[30] however, the Constitutional Court held that because the substance of these laws were the same as art. 268(3), they were no longer binding as far as they related to criminal cases. The Supreme Court seems to have accepted this and has now heard a significant number of second reconsideration applications (Kepaniteraan Mahkamah Agung RI 2017). Lawyers have indicated, however, that the Supreme Court more strictly applies the grounds in second reconsideration applications, such that a truly new *novum* is required. This and other controversies relating to judicial reconsideration are considered in more detail by Lindsey in Chapter 6 of this book.

Compensation and rehabilitation

KUHAP gives individuals the right to compensation if arrested, detained, prosecuted, or sentenced without a valid legal reason, or if mistakes were made about the person's identity or the law applied (art. 1(22)). Individuals also have the right to 'restoration' of their previous position, dignity, and status (Chapter XII of KUHAP). Compensation and rehabilitation can be awarded in a pre-trial hearing, if the judge finds that an arrest or detention was illegal (art. 77(b)).

Government Regulation No. 92 of 2015 significantly changed the way compensation is calculated. Under its predecessor, individuals could only demand between Rp. 5,000 and Rp. 1 million (US$ 0.35–74). The 2015 Regulation increases the range from Rp. 500,000 to Rp. 100 million (US$ 37–7,400). The

2015 Regulation also permits the award of Rp. 25 million to Rp. 300 million, if law enforcement officials cause serious injuries or disabilities that interfere with an individual's ability to work. Compensation increases to between Rp. 50 million and Rp. 600 million if illegal arrest, detention, prosecution, trial, mistaken identity or misapplication of the law, results in death (art. 9). The 2015 Regulation requires the Ministry of Finance to pay compensation within fourteen working days of receiving the request (art. 11(2)).

KUHAP reform

The national legislature, the DPR (Dewan Perwakilan Rakyat, Peoples' Representative Assembly) has included a draft Criminal Code (RUU KUHP, *Rancangan Undang-Undang Kitab Undang-undang Hukum Pidana*) and a draft Criminal Procedure Code (RUU KUHAP, *Rancangan Undang-Undang Kitab Undang-undang Hukum Pidana*) on its list of priority bills for discussion every year since 2015. Neither have yet been passed, largely due to the challenges of building broad political and social consensus on their contents, largely because of the far-reaching implications of many of the provisions they contain.

The RUU KUHAP contains 286 articles, as does the existing Code. Here we consider four contentious issues regulated in the most recent publicly circulated version of the draft, noting that its contents may well change significantly before it is enacted, if that ever happens.

First, the draft contains provisions on investigating judges (*hakim pemeriksa pendahuluan*). While apparently intended to replace *praperadilan*, investigating judges have far greater powers, including to assess the legality of arrest, detention, search, seizure of goods, and the tapping of communications. They can also: cancel or suspend detentions; rule that statements made by suspects violate their right against self-incrimination; declare that an investigation or prosecution was conducted for an improper purpose; exclude improperly obtained evidence; ensure that suspects and defendants have legal representation; and, perhaps most controversially, decide whether a case should progress to prosecution (art. 111(1) of the RUU KUHAP).

The draft also gives investigating judges exclusive power to order the detention of people suspected of committing an offence carrying a sentence of five years' imprisonment or more, or a specified offence (art. 59(1)). Police need to present the suspects they want detained before the investigating judge. Only in emergency circumstances can investigators detain a suspect on their own without authorisation from an investigating judge (Hukumonline 2013d).

While investigating judges appear to be a boon for the rights of suspects and defendants, concern has been expressed about how such powers could be misused to limit the powers of investigators or prosecutors, particularly in corruption cases (Hukumonline 2013e; f). Reformists also anticipate that the powers of investigating judges and ordinary law enforcers might overlap, causing jurisdictional conflicts.

A second issue is wiretapping, which KUHAP does not cover. Under the draft, wiretapping is permitted in relation to twenty 'serious' crimes, including state security offences, abduction, kidnapping, violent theft, extortion, threats, people trafficking, smuggling, corruption, money laundering, counterfeiting, immigration crime, weapons, terrorism, gross human rights violations, narcotics, rape, murder, illegal mining, illegal fishing, and illegal logging (art. 83(2)). An investigating judge must authorise these wiretaps. Authorisation expires after thirty days but can be extended for another thirty days (art. 83(6)) (Hukumonline 2013g).

These provisions are highly contentious, particularly if they apply to the Corruption Eradication Commission (KPK), which can already wiretap and record conversations when investigating or prosecuting.[31] However, under amendments to the KPK Law,[32] the KPK now requires wiretapping preapproval from its new Oversight Board. It is unclear whether, if the RUU KUHAP is enacted, the KPK will need authorisation from its Oversight Board, an investigating judge, or both. Either way, anti-corruption activists see any oversight of the KPK's wiretapping powers as likely to reduce the Commission's effectiveness, and the enactment of the amendments to the KPK Law triggered widespread protests in 2019.

Third, the draft gives power to prosecutors to nominate 'crown' or state witnesses. These are suspects or defendants who played a minor role in a particular criminal act. They can be released from prosecution for helping to reveal the involvement of others in the act. Even those playing a larger role in the criminal act can win a reduced sentence by admitting guilt and 'informing' on others, at the discretion of the judge (art. 200). Presumably, this will potentially enable figures more culpable than others in a criminal enterprise or plot to win reduced sentences by incriminating smaller players.

Finally, Indonesian judges have long bewailed the absence of power to punish contempt of court, as can judges in common law countries. Controversial and high-profile trials are often accompanied by aggressive demonstrations, both within and outside the courtroom, that disrupt proceedings, and are thought to unduly influence judges to side with perceived public sentiment. Article 212 of the draft would, for the first time, give judges a clear power to prevent this. Specifically, it requires that judges be shown respect by all those present in the courtroom, and empowers judges to throw out those who misbehave, after a warning, and have them charged with an offence. While the need for such powers is understandable, the poor reputation of judges in Indonesia has led many to fear that these powers will be used improperly to silence criticism, intimidate litigants, prevent monitoring for corrupt behaviour, and reduce transparency in hearings.

Conclusion

KUHAP sets the broad structural and procedural framework for Indonesian criminal law, from preliminary investigation through to final Supreme Court reconsideration case review. It also defines the roles and powers of law enforcers and establishes the rights of citizens accused of criminal offences.

KUHAP is fundamentally important to the criminal justice system of Indonesia. It is, therefore, highly problematic that, although, as Lindsey shows in Chapter 6, the objectives of its drafters were expressed in aspirational terms that reflect international norms of fairness and justice, KUHAP is, in reality, an inadequate and problematic document. Certainly, many of its provisions establish norms or institutions intended to protect the rights of citizens embroiled in the criminal justice system – suspects, detained and accused persons, and convicts. But these provisions are compromised by others that dilute their effectiveness or, in some cases, by law enforcers who simply ignore them, with the result that 'institutional resistance' (Lev 1996: 157) renders the protections futile.

This is not an accident. KUHAP was the creation of an authoritarian government notorious for its distaste for rule of law (*negara hukum*) and, in particular, the rights of citizens. It was produced as a response to international criticism of Indonesia's lack of respect for human rights and, in particular, the rights of accused persons. It was intended as a sop, a way to counter that criticism at a time when the government felt vulnerable to foreign condemnation. This is why many of the rights conferred were counterbalanced by limitations and conditions that favour the state. It is therefore not surprising that many of its protections for accused persons – even those few that are clear – have too often been ignored by police and other law enforcers.

In these circumstances, the need for reform of KUHAP has long been obvious but the draft bill currently proposed, while an improvement in some respects, will not resolve all its problems.

Notes

1 This chapter draws on material in Butt and Lindsey (2018). We thank Tim Mann for his excellent research.

2 HIR: *Herziene Inlandsch Reglement* or Civil Procedure Code. The Dutch introduced the *HIR* in 1926. It regulated procedural law, both civil and criminal, but applied only to the islands of Java and Madura. A further statute was enacted in 1927 to cover the areas outside Java and Madura, known as the 'Legal Procedure Regulation for Areas Outside Java and Madura' (*Rechtsreglement Buitengewesten* or Rbg).

3 Articles 1(4), (5), 4, 5, and Chapter XIV, Part 1, KUHAP.

4 Articles 1(1), (2), (3), 6–8, and Chapter XIV, Part 2, KUHAP.

5 Articles 1(6), (7), 13–15, and Chapter XV, KUHAP.

6 Police responsibility is divided by administrative region. The national police (*kepolisian nasional*) has jurisdiction over all Indonesia; regional police (*kepolisian daerah*) in their provinces; 'resort police' (*kepolisian resort*) in counties and cities (*kabupaten/kota*); and sectoral police (*kepolisian sektor*) at the sub-district level: art. 4, Government Regulation No. 23 of 2007.

7 Article 70(i), Law No. 35 of 2009 on Narcotics; art. 6(c), Law No. 30 of 2002 on the Corruption Eradication Commission (as amended by Law No. 19 of 2019).

8 In the accompanying elucidation, 'sufficient preliminary evidence' is defined as 'preliminary evidence to suspect a crime' in accordance with art. 1(14).
9 The Constitutional Court has declared that 'sufficient preliminary evidence' in art. 1(14) means two pieces of formally valid legal evidence, but this decision was issued in the context of a challenge to the sufficiency of evidence required to name a person a suspect in the context of a pre-trial challenge, discussed below: Decision No. 21/PUU-XII/2014. It is, therefore, unclear whether the decision extends to arrests.
10 Constitutional Court Decision No. 3/PUU-XI/2013, p. 4.
11 Constitutional Court Decision No. 3/PUU-XI/2013, pp. 32–4.
12 Other statutes provide for different limits of detention. Under art. 76 of the 2009 Narcotics Law, for example, State Narcotics Agency (BNN) investigators may detain a person for seventy-two hours, with the possibility of extension for a further seventy-two hours.
13 The same extension is applicable if the suspect suffers from serious physical or mental illness, as evidenced by a doctor's certificate.
14 Article 1, Supreme Court Regulation No. 2 of 2012 on Adjustment of Limits for Minor Crimes and Fines in the Criminal Code.
15 For example, there is no legislation or set of overarching rules authorising police use of wiretapping, and they are known to use it without legal authority. This means that when police tap phones in investigations, they cannot use the evidence obtained in court but, at the same time, citizens whose privacy is violated have no recourse: Strang (2008: 198).
16 See also arts. 77(b) and 81.
17 Constitutional Court Decision No. 98/PUU-X/2012.
18 See para [5.1] of 98/PUU-X/2012. The inclusion of NGOs in the understanding of 'interested third parties' was also considered in Constitutional Court Decision No. 76/PUU-X/2012 but that application involved an attempt to limit the meaning of that phrase, which was rejected because the court viewed it as wide enough to encompass NGOs.
19 Constitutional Court Decision No. 21/PUU-XII/2014.
20 Investigation Termination Order.
21 Constitutional Court Decision No. 133/PUU-VII/2009, at para [4.3].
22 Article 44(b) restates that electronic information and documents can be used for investigations, prosecutions and trials.
23 Constitutional Court Decision No. 49/PUU-VIII/2010.
24 Article 236 states that the district court clerk must send a copy of the decision, the case file, and evidence to the high court within fourteen days of the appeal being lodged.
25 Article 259(2), KUHAP. See also Kristianto et al. 2009: 340.
26 Emphasis added. See Hukumonline 2012.
27 That is, a decision in respect of which rights of appeal have been exhausted.
28 Constitutional Court Decision No. 34/PUU-XI/2013.
29 Namely, art. 24 (2), Law No. 48 of 2009 on Judicial Power; and art. 66(1), Law No. 14 of 1985 on the Supreme Court, as amended by Law No. 5 of 2004.
30 Constitutional Court Decisions Nos. 108/PUU-XIV/2016, 1/PUU-XV/2017, and 23/PUU-XV/2017.
31 Article 12(1), Law No. 30 of 2002 on the Corruption Eradication Commission.
32 Article 12B, Law No. 19 of 2019 amending Law No. 30 of 2002 on the Corruption Eradication Commission.

References

Assegaf, Rifqi 2015. 'Pretrial Hearings: Who Will Fix the Mess?', *Indonesia at Melbourne*, 7 July http://indonesiaatmelbourne.unimelb.edu.au/pretrial-hearings-who-will-fix-the-mess/

Budiari, Indra 2015. 'Cleaners' Families Reveal Police Torture to Kompolnas', *The Jakarta Post*, 18 February www.thejakartapost.com/news/2015/02/18/cleaners-families-reveal-police-torture-kompolnas.html

Butt, Simon and Lindsey, Tim 2018. Indonesian Law. Oxford University Press.

Fitzpatrick, Daniel 2008. 'Culture, Ideology and Human Rights: The Case of Indonesia's Code of Criminal Procedure', in Tim Lindsey (ed.), *Indonesia: Law and Society*, 2nd edn. Annandale: Federation Press, pp. 499–514.

Hamzah, Chandra 2014. *Penjelasan Hukum (Restatement) Tentang Bukti Permulaan Yang Cukup*. Jakarta: Pusat Studi Hukum dan Kebijakan http://pshk.or.id/site/sites/default/files/Dokumen%20penelitian/Penjelasan%20Hukum%20Tentang%20Bukti%20Permulaan%20Yang%20Cukup.pdf

Harahap, Yahya 2000. *Pembahasan Permasalahan dan Penerapan KUHAP: Pemeriksaan Sidang Pengadilan, Banding, Kasasi dan Peninjauan Kembali,* 2nd edn. Jakarta: Sinar Grafika

Haryanto, Ulma 2012. 'Police in West Sumatra Tortured Brothers to Death: Komnas Ham', *Jakarta Globe*, 25 January http://jakartaglobe.id/archive/police-in-west-sumatra-tortured-brothers-to-death-komnas-ham/

Hukumonline 2005. 'Penangguhan Penahanan dengan Uang Jaminan Perlu Diperjelas', *Hukumonline*, 28 July

Hukumonline 2011. 'Advokat Ragu Penyidik Patuhi Putusan MK', *Hukumonline*, 24 August www.hukumonline.com/berita/baca/lt4e54f084b1ed5/advokat-ragu-penyidik-patuhi-putusan-mk

Hukumonline 2012. 'MA Protes Larangan Kasasi Vonis Bebas', *Hukumonline*, 12 July www.hukumonline.com/berita/baca/lt4ffe97b185446/ma-protes-larangan-kasasi-vonis-bebas

Hukumonline 2013a. 'Kejaksaan Akui Legal Standing LSM', *Hukumonline*, 23 January www.hukumonline.com/berita/baca/lt50ff8b8824e42/kejaksaan-akui-ilegal-standing-i-lsm

Hukumonline 2013b. 'MK Tegaskan LSM Bisa Ajukan Praperadilan', *Hukumonline*, 21 May www.hukumonline.com/berita/baca/lt519b604ebe2e3/mk-tegaskan-lsm-bisa-ajukan-praperadilan

Hukumonline 2013c. 'Pelarangan Kasasi Atas Vonis Bebas Dibatalkan', *Hukumonline*, 28 March www.hukumonline.com/berita/baca/lt51544359991le/pelarangan-kasasi-atas-vonis-bebas-dibatalkan

Hukumonline 2013d. 'Bebas Murni Atau Tidak Murni Sudah Tak Relevan', *Hukumonline*, 28 October www.hukumonline.com/berita/baca/lt526dcda563378/bebas-murni-atau-tidak-murni-sudah-tak-relevan

Hukumonline 2013e. 'Menahan Tersangka, Kewenangan Hakim Pemeriksa Pendahuluan', *Hukumonline*, 11 April www.hukumonline.com/berita/baca/lt51665dd4d9028/menahan-tersangka--kewenangan-hakim-pemeriksa-pendahuluan

Hukumonline 2013f. 'Ahli Kritik Hakim Komisaris di RKUHAP', *Hukumonline*, 15 March www.hukumonline.com/berita/baca/lt51431dd699b58/ahli-kritik-hakim-komisaris-di-rkuhap

Hukumonline 2013g. 'Aturan Penyadapan, Memangkas KPK', *Hukumonline*, 21 March www.hukumonline.com/berita/baca/lt514abdf2afade/aturan-penyadapan--memangkas-kpk

The Jakarta Post 2015. 'Former Makassar Mayor Wins Pre-Trial Court Decision', *The Jakarta Post*, 12 May www.thejakartapost.com/news/2015/05/12/former-makassar-mayor-wins-pretrial-court-decision.html

Kepaniteraan Mahkama Agung RI 2017. *Kegiatan 2016* https://kepaniteraan.mahkamahagung.go.id/index.php/kegiatan/1410-inilah-putusan-yang-diajukan-peninjauan-kembali-di-tahun-2016

Kristianto, Agustinus Edy; Zen, A. Patra M.; and Martha, Carolina S. 2009. *Panduan Bantuan Hukum di Indonesia: Pedoman Anda Memahami dan Menyelesaikan Masalah Hukum*. Jakarta: YLBH PSHK

Lev, Daniel S. 1996. 'Between State and Society: Professional Lawyers and Reform in Indonesia', in Daniel S. Lev and Ruth McVey (eds.), *Making Indonesia*. Ithaca: Cornell University Press, pp. 145–63

Lubis, Todung Mulya 1993. *In Search of Human Rights: Legal-Political Dilemmas of Indonesia's New Order, 1966–1990*. Jakarta: Gramedia Pustaka Utama

Nowak, Manfred 2008. *Report of the Special Rapporteur on Torture and Other Cruel, Inhuman or Degrading Treatment or Punishment, Manfred Nowak: Addendum: Mission to Indonesia*. New York: United Nations

Perkumpulan Lembaga Bantuan Hukum Masyarakat 2012. 'Revealing the Practice of Violations of the Rights of the Accused during the Investigation Stage: Case Study of the Accused of Drug Offense in Jakarta'. Jakarta: LBH Masyarakat http://lbhmasyarakat.org/admin/dataupload/Documentation%20on%20the%20Violation%20of%20the%20Rights%20of%20the%20Suspect,%20July%202012.pdf

Saragih, Bagus B. T. 2015. 'Hadi's Pre-Trial Victory a 'Disaster' for KPK', *The Jakarta Post*, 26 May www.thejakartapost.com/news/2015/05/26/hadi-s-pretrial-victory-a-disaster-kpk.html

Strang, Robert R. 2008. '"More Adversarial, But Not Completely Adversarial": Reformasi of the Indonesian Criminal Procedure Code', *Fordham International Law Journal* 32(1): 188

Wagner, Benjamin B. and Jacobs, Leslie Gielow 2008. 'Retooling Law Enforcement to Investigate and Prosecute Entrenched Corruption: Key Criminal Procedure Reforms for Indonesia and Other Nations', *University of Pennsylvania Journal of International Economic Law* 30: 183

Laws and regulations

Rechtsreglement Buitengewesten (Rbg.) of 1927 (Legal Procedure Regulation for Areas Outside of Java and Madura)

Criminal Code (*Kitab Undang-Undang Hukum Pidana*, KUHP: Law No. 1 of 1946 as amended by Law No. 27 of 1999 on the Indonesian Criminal Code)

Civil Procedure Code (Herziene *Inlandsch Reglement*, HIR) of 1926

Criminal Procedure Code Law (*Kitab Undang-undang Hukum Acara Pidana*, KUHAP), Law No. 8 of 1981

Law No. 31 of 1999 on the Eradication of Corruption

Law No. 39 of 1999 on Human Rights

Law No. 14 of 1985 on the Supreme Court, as amended by Law No. 5 of 2004

Law No. 19 of 2019 amending Law No. 30 of 2002 on the KPK
Law No. 2 of 2002 on Police
Law No. 20 of 2001 amending Law No. 31 of 1999 on the Eradication of Corruption
Law No. 30 of 2002 on the Corruption Eradication Commission
Law No. 16 of 2004 on the Prosecution Service
Law No. 11 of 2008 on Information and Electronic Transactions, as amended by Law No. 19 of 2016
Law No. 35 of 2009 on Narcotics
Law No. 48 of 2009 on Judicial Power
Law No. 19 of 2019 amending Law No. 30 of 2002 on the Corruption Eradication Commission
Government Regulation No. 27 of 1983 on the Implementation of the Criminal Procedure Code
Government Regulation No. 23 of 2007 on the Jurisdiction of the Indonesian National Police
Government Regulation No. 92 of 2015
Supreme Court Regulation No. 2 of 2012 on Adjustment of Limits for Minor Crimes and Fines in the Criminal Code
Police Chief Regulation No. 14 of 2012 on the Management of Criminal Investigations

Court cases

Constitutional Court Decision No. 133/PUU-VII/2009 (*Bibit and Chandra case*)
Constitutional Court Decision No. 45/PUU-VIII/2010 (*Mahendra case*)
Constitutional Court Decision No. 76/PUU-X/2012 (*Praperadilan NGO case*)
Constitutional Court Decision No. 98/PUU-X/2012 (*Termination of Prosecution case*)
Constitutional Court Decision No. 3/PUU-XI/2013 (*Ma'dika arrest case*)
Constitutional Court Decision No. 34/PUU-XI/2013 (*Multiple Reconsideration case*)
Constitutional Court Decision No. 21/PUU-XII/2014 (*Setya Novanto Praperadilan case*)
Constitutional Court Decisions No. 108/PUU-XIV/2016 (*Multiple Reconsideration case*)
Constitutional Court Decision No. 1/PUU-XV/2017 (*Multiple Reconsideration case*)
Constitutional Court Decision No. 23/PUU-XV/2017 (*Multiple Reconsideration case*)

4 Ordinary laws and extraordinary crimes

Criminalising genocide and crimes against humanity in the draft Criminal Code?

Ken M. P. Setiawan

Every Thursday since 2007, survivors of human rights violations, their family members and representatives of human rights organisations gather in front of the Presidential Palace in Jakarta. This is Indonesia's longest-running human rights protest, and it is known as Kamisan ('Thursdays'). While initially staged as a protest by those affected by human rights violations under the authoritarian New Order (1965–98), over time the gathering has also offered a platform for protests against more recent violations. The ongoing presence of those directly affected by human rights violations, and their consistent calls to hold perpetrators of serious crimes to account, makes it clear that the Indonesian legal system has largely failed to establish an effective human rights framework.

After the end of authoritarianism in 1998, Indonesia witnessed many political and legal reforms. In the realm of human rights this included the ratification of international treaties, the enactment of domestic laws, and the introduction of new mechanisms and the strengthening of existing institutions charged with the promotion and protection of human rights. However, in practice it has proven to be extremely difficult to hold violators of human rights to account in a court of law. Less than a handful of cases have been heard by the Human Rights Court,[1] while the investigations of other cases have come to a standstill in the Attorney General's Office (*Kejaksaan*). It is thus evident that Indonesia's criminal justice system has limited ability to adequately respond to serious human rights violations (Clarke 2008; Herbert 2008). It is in this light that proposed revisions to the KUHP (*Kitab Undang-Undang Hukum Pidana*, Criminal Code), which seek to insert new offences of gross human rights violations into the Code, are particularly relevant.

The chapter will start by briefly looking back at serious human rights violations committed under the rule of President Soeharto. It then discusses human rights law reforms after 1998, paying particular attention to Law No. 26 of 2000 on the Human Rights Courts. That Law's definitions of the crime of genocide and crimes against humanity will be analysed vis-à-vis their conceptualisations in international law, as well as the processes of bringing human rights crimes to trial. The chapter will then turn to an analysis of the provisions relating to gross human rights proposed in the Draft Criminal Code. While acknowledging that it may be some time before these proposed revisions become law – if at all – the suggested amendments offer a lens through which it is possible to discuss the broader issue of human rights reform in Indonesia, and the prosecution of gross human rights crimes in particular. By placing the proposed amendments in the wider context of human rights reform in Indonesia, and drawing on Otto's (2002) concept of 'Real Legal Certainty', this chapter seeks to explore to what extent legal reform may improve accountability for gross human rights crimes.

Gross human rights violations under Indonesia's New Order

The failures of the Indonesian human rights system are perhaps best demonstrated by the fact that twenty years after the fall of authoritarianism, justice is yet to be delivered for crimes committed under the repressive regime of President Soeharto (1966–98). Both international and domestic human rights organisations have consistently raised the need for Indonesia to provide redress for these victims (Human Rights Watch 2017). Addressing past crimes is widely regarded as a crucial step in a country's transition process to more democratic forms of governance. From this perspective, legal processes are used to forge both a symbolic and actual break with the past. Recently, particular attention has been given to the 1965–6 violence that formed the basis of Soeharto's New Order (Kuddus 2017: 45), largely as a result of domestic and international advocacy.

On 30 September 1965, a group calling itself the '30 September Movement' kidnapped and killed six high-ranking military officers and a lieutenant. The Army Strategic Reserve (Kostrad, Komando Strategis Angkatan Darat), under the command of then Major General Soeharto, swiftly suppressed the Movement and attributed the murders to the PKI (Partai Komunis Indonesia, Indonesian Communist Party). Consequently, a violent campaign against members of the PKI and its sympathisers was instigated across Indonesia. It is estimated that the army and army-affiliated militias killed approximately 500,000 people, while an additional 600,000–750,000 were detained, often for lengthy periods of time without trial (McGregor 2013: 138). They suffered from inadequate rations, were denied adequate medical treatment, and were subjected to torture and other forms of inhumane treatment, as well as sexual violence. Those who survived persecution in connection with the 1965 violence were denied an array of civil rights upon their release, and suffered systematic discrimination and exclusion in their communities. The persecution of the PKI and its affiliated organisations led to the destruction of the Indonesian political left.[2]

The patterns of the violence used by the military in 1965 and 1966 were replicated in other settings. During the Indonesian occupation of East Timor (1975–99), for example, the military used killings, mass detention, torture, sexual abuse and long-term imprisonment to crush opposition. Similar methods were used against political opposition in territories with separatist claims, such as Papua[3] and Aceh, as well as dissidents (Drexler 2008: 2). Other, 'smaller-scale military attacks on civilians' (Lindsey 2001: 286) included the 1983–5 Petrus (*penembak misterius*, mysterious shooters) killings, in which disguised members of the military abducted and murdered gangsters on the orders of Soeharto (Lindsey 2001: 288); the 1984 Tanjung Priok killings, in which the military opened fire on demonstrators (Sulistiyanto 2007: 77); the 1989 Talangsari case in which the military attacked an Islamic minority group, killing over 100 (Utami 2017: 52); and the 1997–98 disappearances of twenty-five pro-democracy activists, of whom the fate of thirteen remains unknown (Setiawan 2016: 18). Other well-known examples of military violence during the New Order towards regime critics are the murders of labour activist Marsinah (1996) and journalist Udin (Lindsey 2001: 286).

Indonesians were well-aware of the violence perpetrated by the security forces. Fear and violence were constant elements of New Order state and society. Human rights violations were not isolated incidents, but a systematic part of state policy and behaviour towards those considered enemies of the regime (Heryanto and Mandal 2003: 4–6). The final weeks of the New Order regime made this once again clear. Severe violence perpetrated by the security forces erupted across the country and, in particular, in Jakarta. In May 1998, military agents were the key instigators of looting and violence directed particularly at the ethnic Chinese community (Purdey 2006: 127–8). The military also opened fire on student protestors, killing four and wounding nearly 700, in what is known as the Trisakti killings (Setiawan 2016: 24).[4] The violence perpetrated by the military towards the end of the Soeharto regime brought the armed forces into further disrepute and strongly influenced calls within Indonesia and abroad to hold those responsible to account (McGregor and Setiawan 2019).

'Real Legal Certainty' and gross human rights violations

Until legislative reform in the area of human rights took place after 1998, Indonesian law included very few provisions for the protection of human rights in general. Legal provisions criminalising serious human rights crimes were absent altogether. The original 1945 Constitution,[5] for instance, included minimal human rights guarantees. Most of these were in Chapter X, which deals with citizens (*warga negara*).[6] The inclusion of only very limited human rights in the 1945 Constitution was the result of the 'integralist' theory of the state, which largely excluded ideas of individual rights.[7] The notion of an integralistic state also gave the President extensive powers over the executive (Bourchier 2015; Lubis 1993). While the colonial era Criminal Code that applied under the New Order – and which still applies today – includes several relevant 'conventional' offences, including murder, arson, assault, torture, rape, the destruction of property, kidnapping and criminal conspiracy (see Butt and Lindsey, Chapter 3, this volume), there were no specific provisions with regards to gross human rights crimes. Moreover, the available provisions meant little in cases where the security forces were involved. There was thus virtually no legal redress for the abuse of state power against its citizens.

This brings me to a discussion of Otto's concept of 'Real Legal Certainty'. This refers to the existence of predictable rules as well as their legal interpretation and application by the judiciary and other law enforcement organisations (Otto 2002: 24). Using this conceptualisation, it is evident that while there were some legal norms during the New Order, they were far from sufficient for the prosecution of gross human rights crimes. In addition, the relevant authorities often did not apply those legal norms that did exist. While this was, in itself, a major problem, a more pressing concern was that under the New Order judicial independence was eroded and law became a tool of the state. In such circumstances, Indonesians were unlikely to benefit from formal legal certainty.

People need 'Real Legal Certainty'. This is defined by Otto as the extent to which in a given situation: there are clear, consistent and accessible legal rules issued or acknowledged by the state; these rules are applied by government institutions; citizens (generally) conform to such rules; the rules are consistently applied by independent and impartial judges in the case of dispute settlement; and these judicial decisions are put into practice. In summary, the existence of Real Legal Certainty can be determined by legal rules, legal institutions and the wider social context in which they operate (Otto 2002: 25).

Real Legal Certainty is often difficult to achieve because of various factors. Otto has distinguished four categories of so-called 'countervailing forces', namely: social and cultural values; political power structures; the economic interests of powerful groups; and the capacities of the institutions of the state (Otto 2002: 29). While Otto has mainly considered these factors separately from each other, when applied to New Order Indonesia it is evident that they may also overlap. At first glance, political power structures can be identified as undermining Real Legal Certainty, and the military's control over politics effectively prevented the application of human rights norms (McGregor and Setiawan 2019). At the same time, military dominance was strongly tied to the economic interests of the ruling elites and the limited power of state institutions. Similarly, the New Order's criticism of the international human rights regime in the 1990s under the banner of 'Asian values' illustrated how notions of cultural particularism were being used as political tools to avoid responsibility for the protection of human rights (Setiawan 2013: 34). As such, it is clear that the factors that negated the chances of Real Legal Certainty under the New Order were intertwined with one another, rather than isolated in individual categories.

Human rights reforms after 1998

The resignation of Soeharto in 1998 saw a wave of optimism in both Indonesia and globally regarding the democratic trajectory of the nation, including justice for gross human rights crimes. The question of the criminalisation and prosecution of human rights crimes in Indonesia entered the political and legal arena influenced by domestic and international pressure to address the involvement of the military in violence against civilians (Lindsey 2008: 28). This led to the military's withdrawal from its political role, as well as a number of human rights reforms.

The post-1998 period saw Indonesia's swift acceptance of key international human rights treaties, including the International Covenant on Civil and Political Rights (ICCPR), and the International Covenant of Economic, Social and Cultural Rights (ICESCR). However, Indonesia has not ratified any of the Optional Protocols that allow for individual complaints to be brought to the United Nations. It has also not ratified the Rome Statute, which allows for the prosecution of individuals for gross human rights crimes. Despite these lacunae, human rights norms are now – at least formally – firmly entrenched in the Indonesian legal system.

As a result of these reforms, the relevant framework for the prosecution of human rights violations, in addition to provisions in the Criminal Code that pre-date 1998, now consists of the amended 1945 Constitution, Law No. 39 of 1999 on Human Rights, and Law No. 26 of 2000 on the Human Rights Court (HRCL).[8] The process of prosecuting gross violations of human rights includes decisions made by, and interactions between, the various institutions and agencies that have been given those responsibilities through the legislation in place. As will be discussed in more detail below, they include the national legislature, the DPR (Dewan Perwakilan Rakyat), the courts, Komnas HAM (Komisi Nasional Hak Asasi Manusia, the National Human Rights Commission), and the office of the Jaksa Agung, the combined Prosecutor General and Attorney General (AGO).[9] The establishment of this extensive framework, in combination with the end of authoritarianism and the retreat of the military in politics, suggested that there was a more conducive environment for Real Legal Certainty.

The first of the new human rights Laws passed in the *Reformasi* era was the Human Rights Law of 1999. This includes a provision for the establishment of Human Rights Courts to prosecute gross human rights violations.[10] The Law's Elucidation states that 'Indonesia's history [...] has witnessed human rights violations [...] of which many fall within the category of gross human rights violations'. It defines these as 'mass killings (genocide), arbitrary or extra judicial killings, torture, enforced disappearance, slavery and systematic discrimination'. The Human Rights Law also determined that specialised courts would be established within four years,[11] and that human rights abuses would be tried by existing courts in the interim.[12]

The large-scale abuses that took place in Indonesian-occupied East Timor[13] in the lead-up to, and following, the 1999 independence referendum, triggered increased pressure on Indonesia for a more comprehensive human rights framework in line with international standards (Herbert 2008: 460). This led the Habibie government to issue an interim emergency law, Government Regulation in Lieu of Law (Peraturan Pemerintah Pengganti Undang-undang, Perpu) No. 1 of 1999, which was passed in an effort to prevent Indonesia being subjected to an international human rights tribunal (Cammack 2016: 191; Dewi, Niemann and Triatmodjo 2017: 31). This Regulation formed the basis of the 2000 Human Rights Courts Law (HRCL), which provides for the establishment of permanent human rights courts, as well as ad hoc courts for cases that occurred before the Law's enactment.

Before moving to a discussion of the provisions in the HRCL related to gross human rights violations, it is necessary to briefly discuss the second round of amendments to the 1945 Constitution. These occurred after the enactment of the Human Rights Law and the Perpu, and a few months before the HRCL was passed. This amendment cycle saw the addition of a specific chapter (Chapter XA) on human rights, which was largely modelled on the Universal Declaration of Human Rights (UDHR), once again underlining Indonesia's acceptance of the international human rights regime (Lindsey 2008: 29).

A particular important article in this chapter relevant to the prosecution of human rights crimes is art. 28I(1) or the principle against retroactivity. According to this provision 'the right not to be prosecuted under retrospective laws is a human right that may not be diminished under any circumstances'. The dominant interpretation of this article is that crimes that occurred prior to 2000, and are not included in the pre-existing Criminal Code, cannot be prosecuted. However, customary international law holds that gross violations can be prosecuted retrospectively (Clarke 2008: 438), and Indonesian civil society organisations have warned that the Constitutional principle against retroactivity could shield perpetrators of human rights abuses from being held to account. I will revisit this constitutional provision vis-à-vis the proposed amendments to the Criminal Code later in this chapter, but will first turn to an examination of these crimes in the HRCL, which to date is the most relevant piece of Indonesian legislation dealing with gross human rights violations and the prosecution of these crimes in a court of law.

Extraordinary crimes in the Human Rights Courts Law

Law No. 26 of 2000 on the Human Rights Courts defines 'gross human rights violations' (*pelanggaran hak asasi manusia yang berat*) as the crime of genocide and crimes against humanity.[14] The 'crime of genocide' is defined in the HRCL as

> any act committed with the intent to destroy or exterminate (*menghancurkan atau memusnahkan*), in whole or in part, a national, racial, ethnic or religious group, by killing members of the group, causing serious bodily or mental harm to members of the group; deliberately

> inflicting on the group living conditions to bring about its physical destruction in whole or in part; imposing measures intended to prevent births within the group; or forcibly transferring children of the group to another.[15]

The Law defines 'crimes against humanity' as

> any of the following acts when committed as part of a widespread or systematic attack where it is known that the attack is directly aimed at the civilian population, in the form of: murder; extermination; enslavement; deportation or forcible transfer of the population; deprivation of liberty or other arbitrary deprivations of physical liberty in violation of fundamental rules of international law; torture; rape, sexual slavery, enforced prostitution, forced pregnancy, enforced sterilisation or other forms of sexual violence of comparable gravity; persecution of any group or collectivity based on political, racial, national, ethnic, cultural, religious, gender or other grounds that are universally recognised as prohibited under international law; enforced disappearance of persons; or the crime of apartheid.[16]

The Elucidation of the HRCL states that these definitions are based on the 1998 Rome Statute. This is the treaty that established the International Criminal Court (ICC), which has the jurisdiction to prosecute individuals for international crimes of genocide, crimes against humanity, war crimes, and the crime of aggression. The latter two crimes have not been included in the HRCL.

The HRCL's provisions on command responsibility also appear to have been based on those in the Rome Statute. This article holds military commanders responsible for crimes committed 'by troops under his or her effective command and control, or effective authority and control as the case may be, as a result of his or her failure to exercise control properly over such forces'.[17] This requires evidence that the commander knew, or had reason to know, that a subordinate committed a crime[18] and failed to take measures to prevent or repress them or report the subordinate to the competent authorities for further inquiry, investigation and prosecution.[19] The HRCL also stipulates that police and civilian commanders can be held liable for the actions of their subordinates.[20]

The use of the definitions from international law, and, in particular, the Rome Statute in the HRCL is interesting, considering that Indonesia is yet to sign the Statute. Indonesia's reluctance to become a state party to this treaty has been attributed to government fears that ratification may lead to it being held to account for human rights violations in an international court (Hukumonline 2013).[21] Nevertheless, the fact that the drafters of the HRCL have based its core definitions on the Rome Statute illustrates that international human rights concepts command authority in the Indonesian context. Also, it reflects the demands of legal reform in the immediate post-authoritarian context – in which the Law was drafted – that saw increased pressure on Indonesia to develop a legal framework largely consistent with international norms.

A particular interesting point is that the Elucidation (explanatory memorandum) to the HRCL underlines that gross human rights violations constitute 'extraordinary crimes'. As such, these crimes 'have a broad impact both at the national and international level and *are not criminal acts that are regulated in the Criminal Code*' (emphasis added). This appears to confirm the view of the drafters of the HRCL that these crimes cannot, or should not, be provided for in the Criminal Code.

The penal provisions in the HRCL include prison sentences of at least ten and no more than twenty-five years for those found guilty of the crime of genocide. Life imprisonment and the death penalty may also be imposed.[22] These punishments also apply to those found guilty of a number of crimes against humanity, namely killing, extermination, deportation or forcible relocation, deprivation of liberty, and apartheid.[23] Those found guilty of enslavement and torture are subject to a minimum of five or maximum of fifteen years' imprisonment.[24] Sexual violence, persecution and enforced disappearance are punishable by a minimum imprisonment of ten, and maximum of twenty, years.[25] These penalties are, with the exception of the death penalty, largely consistent with the provisions of the Rome Statute, which state that imprisonment may not exceed a maximum of thirty years and that life imprisonment must be justified by the extreme gravity of the crime.[26]

The Human Rights Courts Law provides for the establishment of two types of courts: the permanent human rights courts for violations that occurred after the HRCL was passed,[27] and the ad hoc courts for cases that occurred before 2000.[28] In the process of bringing cases of gross human rights violations to court, a key role is played by Komnas HAM, which has the sole authority to conduct preliminary investigations (*penyelidikan*).[29] If Komnas HAM is of the opinion that there is sufficient evidence of gross human rights violations, it can forward its findings to the Attorney General's Office, which then conducts the main investigation (*penyidikan*) in such cases.[30] If the AGO's investigation also finds evidence of severe human rights violations, prosecution can take place through a permanent or ad hoc court, depending on when the crimes took place. Because of their special nature, ad hoc courts require approval by the DPR and are formally established by Presidential Decision.[31] While on paper this process appears to be straightforward, in practice it has been convoluted, with limited outcomes.

Human Rights Courts in Indonesia

Since 1998, Komnas HAM has completed many investigations of cases where it suspected the gross violation of human rights. Only three of these cases – East Timor, Tanjung Priok and Abepura – have been heard in a Human

Rights Court. One of the main stumbling blocks in this process has been the AGO's reluctance to follow up on Komnas HAM's investigations, using various, and sometimes creative, reasons to justify its inaction.

For example, in 2002, responding to Komnas HAM's investigation into the Trisakti, Semanggi I and Semanggi II cases, the AGO claimed that the documents submitted by the Commission were incomplete. After the required documents were delivered, it was argued that Komnas HAM's inquiry was not valid, as the members of the investigation team had not been sworn in. Three years later, the AGO stated it would not open an investigation into the case, as it believed there were no indications of gross violations of human rights, thereby dismissing Komnas HAM's findings altogether. Komnas HAM's investigations into the May 1998 violence and human rights violations in Papua[32] were rejected on similar grounds. In 2006, the AGO stated it would not follow up on Komnas HAM's findings regarding the 1997–8 disappearances of activists until the DPR approved the establishment of an ad hoc court. In 2012, the AGO returned Komnas HAM's reports on the 1965–6 violence and the Petrus killings, arguing that these would be difficult to investigate as they occurred too long ago (Setiawan 2016: 24–5).

The three cases that have proceeded to the Human Rights Courts have not led to the punishment of violators of gross human rights crimes. The first ad hoc human rights tribunal was held in 2002 and 2003 to try Indonesian officials for crimes committed in the lead-up to, and following, the 1999 independence referendum in East Timor. The Court tried eighteen defendants from the military, the police and the civil administration. They were all indicted for crimes against humanity, specifically murder or assault as part of a widespread, and systematic, attack directed at civilians. They were also charged in relation to acts committed by subordinates. However, only six defendants were convicted at trial and all were eventually acquitted on appeal. Analyses of these trials have shown that the court failed to identify and punish perpetrators (Cammack 2016: 191).

The ad hoc Human Rights Court for East Timor increased calls to address human rights crimes that occurred in Indonesia. Influenced by the rise of political Islam in the early *Reformasi* period, victims and survivors of the 1984 Tanjung Priok case called for trials of military commanders who served at the time. An ad hoc Human Rights Court for Tanjung Priok was held between 2003 and 2004. Fourteen defendants were indicted for crimes against humanity. Only two were convicted (to three and ten years' imprisonment respectively), but even these were overturned on appeal (Sulistiyanto 2007: 88).

A similar pattern was discernible in the Abepura tribunal,[33] which was the first and only case to be heard at a permanent Human Rights Court. Proceedings were held between 2004 and 2005 in the court in Makassar, where only two defendants stood trial, far less the twenty-four persons identified by Komnas HAM in its investigation as being responsible for the crimes committed. Both defendants were indicted for crimes against humanity, including murder, assault and torture. They were not held responsible for crimes committed by their subordinates, although testimonies of survivors clearly identified the chain of command (Elsam 2004: 10–11). The court acquitted both men and victims' claims for compensation were dismissed (Feith 2006).

In short, the cases heard by the Human Rights Courts have been unsuccessful, as in all proceedings only a few convictions were secured, and all were eventually overturned on appeal. This has been largely attributed to weaknesses in the prosecution. In all three cases, discrepancies existed between the findings of Komnas HAM's investigations and the charges that defendants faced. The proceedings were also influenced by the presence of security forces during hearings, intimidating victims who gave testimony, and possibly also judges (Cammack 2016; Elsam 2004; Sulistiyanto 2007). By holding the lower- and middle-ranked officials to account, the courts have largely ignored the element of command responsibility. As such, it is evident that the Indonesian military has been able to operate largely without reference to law (Fitzpatrick 2008).

While the HRCL codified gross human rights crimes in Indonesian law and established a new mechanism for the prosecution of such serious offences, in practice this Law has been largely ineffective. The repeated refusal of the AGO to follow up on investigations by Komnas HAM, the minimal amount of cases heard by the courts, and the disappointing outcomes of trial proceedings have preserved impunity, rather than broken it. This is the result of a number of intertwined factors, such as weaknesses in the prosecution, as well as significant external pressure on the court and witnesses, including from the military. The legal process in this regard is also weakened by endemic corruption and a lack of independence of judges (Clarke 2008: 433; Herbert 2008: 459).

In addition, the HRCL itself has also contributed to these outcomes because of a lack of clarity in some provisions of the Law. The HRCL, for instance, does not specify exactly what evidence Komnas HAM needs to present to the AGO or whether the Commission's investigators need to be sworn in (as is the case for AGO investigators). In the case of the ad hoc courts, the Law does not explicitly state whether an investigation by the AGO should be preceded by the establishment of an ad hoc court or followed by it. These loopholes in the Law have provided the AGO with reasons to postpone further investigations or abandon them altogether.

The ambiguities in the HRCL illustrate that there are insufficient clear and consistent legal rules for the prosecution of gross human rights violations. In addition, the implementation of the HRCL, as well as broader goals of human rights reform, are undermined by various factors, including a weak judicial system and the ongoing influence of powerful interest groups, particularly the security forces (Setiawan 2016: 23–8). These 'illiberal' forces are unlikely to withdraw from the socio-political context; in fact they appear to have been gaining traction (McGregor and Setiawan 2019). This poses significant challenges for achieving Real Legal Certainty, which is dependent on a state and society 'oriented towards a legal system, and a legal system that has succeeded in being the major normative frame of reference' (Otto 2002: 25).

Extraordinary crimes in the Draft Criminal Code

The failure of the existing human rights framework to deliver justice for gross human rights violations underlines the necessity for legal reform in this area. Both Komnas HAM and human rights organisations in Indonesia have long advocated for amendment of the 1999 Human Rights Law and the 2000 HRCL. While both laws have been included in the 2015–19 Prolegnas (*Program Legislasi Nasional,* National Legislation Programme), it does not appear that amendment of these laws is imminent. Instead, it is proposed that gross human rights violations will be introduced in the new Criminal Code. As discussed earlier in this chapter, the KUHP is limited in its capacity to enable the prosecution of gross human rights violations. It does not include provisions on crimes against humanity or the crime of genocide, nor does it criminalise command responsibility, a crucial element for holding the architects of gross violations to account. As such, the Criminal Code as it stands is of little relevance for the prosecution of serious human rights crimes.

A key driver for the revision of the Criminal Code is the desire of lawmakers to include all criminal acts in an effort to comprehensively codify Indonesian criminal law. It is from this perspective that gross human rights violations were also included in the Draft. In this section I will discuss the Draft Code's provisions on gross crimes against human rights in Chapter IX of the second 'book', or part, of that Code. This chapter identifies gross human rights crimes as the crime of genocide (art. 400), crimes against humanity (art. 401), as well as crimes committed in times of war or armed conflict (art. 402). Furthermore, art. 403 states that when these crimes occur, those in command (military, police or otherwise) are responsible for crimes committed by their subordinates.

The Draft Criminal Code defines genocide as acts 'exclusively aimed at denying the existence of a societal group based on skin colour, religion, gender, age or physical or mental disabilities'.[34] The Draft Criminal Code determines that this crime is punishable

> by death or life imprisonment, or imprisonment of at least five years and at most twenty years, [for] every person who committed with the intent of destroying or eliminating whole or in part a national, racial, ethnic or religious group; killing members of the group; causing serious bodily or mental harm to members of the group; inflicting on the group conditions of life calculated to bring about its physical destruction whole or in part; imposing measures to prevent births within the group; forcibly transferring children of the group to another group.[35]

The next article (art. 401) stipulates that crimes against humanity attract the same penalties. It defines crimes against humanity in line with the provisions in the HRCL, adding to the list of offences 'other inhuman acts that are similar to those that lead to either severe mental or physical suffering'.[36] For both crime of genocide and crimes against humanity, the Draft Code determines that any person aiding and abetting such crimes will be subject to the same punishments.[37]

In addition to crimes against humanity and the crime of genocide, the Draft Criminal Code also identifies crimes committed in times of war or armed conflict (*tindak pidana dalam masa perang atau konflik bersenjata*) as a gross human rights violation. These crimes include

> killing; torture or inhuman treatment, including biological experiments; causing great suffering or serious injury to body or health; extensive destruction and appropriation of property, not justified by military necessity and carried out unlawfully and wantonly; compelling a prisoner of war or other protected persons to serve in the forces of a hostile power; to deprive prisoners or other protected persons of the rights to a fair and regular trial; unlawful eviction or deportation, transfer, or unlawful confinement; or the taking of hostages.[38]

These offences, too, are punishable by death, life imprisonment or a prison sentence of at least five, and at most twenty, years.[39] The inclusion of crimes committed in war or armed conflict broadens the scope of gross human rights violations compared to that in the HRCL. This is negated by art. 405, however, which states that the provision does not apply to situations 'related to internal tensions, such as riots, violence that is separate and sporadic in nature or other acts that have similar characteristics'. The provision will therefore not be able to be applied to one of Indonesia's most pressing human rights concerns: crimes in internal armed conflict.

The Draft Criminal Code also includes provisions regarding command responsibility. Article 403 stipulates 'a military commander or person effectively acting as a military commander shall be held criminally responsible for gross human rights crimes'.[40] This includes cases where the military commander knew, or should have known, that the forces were committing or about to commit such crimes,[41] and where he or she failed to take all necessary measures to prevent these acts, or to bring the matter to other authorities for investigation and prosecution.[42] Similar provisions apply to 'superiors, whether from the police force or other civil groups'.[43] Commanders found guilty of these crimes may be subjected to the death penalty, life imprisonment, or a prison sentence of at least five years and not more than twenty years.[44]

There are a number of differences between the provisions in the Draft Criminal Code and the HRCL. This is particularly evident in the addition of

Table 4.1 Penalties for gross human rights crimes in Law No. 26 of 2000 on the Human Rights Courts and the Draft Criminal Code

	Law No. 26 of 2000 on the Human Rights Courts	*Draft Criminal Code*
Crime of genocide	Capital punishment, life imprisonment or a prison sentence between ten and twenty-five years	Capital punishment, life imprisonment or a prison sentence between five and twenty years
Crimes against humanity	Capital punishment, life imprisonment or a prison sentence between ten and twenty-five years for murder, extermination, deportation or forcible relocation, deprivation of liberty and apartheid. A prison sentence between ten and twenty years for sexual violence, persecution and enforced disappearance. A prison sentence between five and fifteen years for enslavement and torture.	Capital punishment, life imprisonment or a prison sentence between five and twenty years
Crimes committed in times of war and armed conflict	-	Capital punishment, life imprisonment or a prison sentence between five and twenty years
Command responsibility	Penalty in accordance with the crimes committed.	Capital punishment, life imprisonment or a prison sentence between five and twenty years

crimes committed in times of war and armed conflict, which are currently not offences under the HRCL. The HRCL, however, requires 'malicious intent' (*permufakatan jahat*), a term absent from the Draft Criminal Code. This is a significant omission, as the element of intent is a key element of international law on the crime of genocide (Schabas 2009: 241). The main difference is, however, that the penalties for gross human rights crimes have been lowered in the Draft Criminal Code as regards imprisonment (see Table 4.1). The Draft Criminal Code also applies the same penalties to all gross violations of human rights, while the HRCL applies different penalties for crimes against humanity.

The Elucidation to the Draft Criminal Code states that the crimes included in this chapter have been modelled on international law. Specifically, it states that the definition of the crime of genocide was based on the 1948 International Convention on the Prevention and Punishment of the Crime of Genocide, whereas the definition of war crimes is based on the 1949 Geneva

Convention for the Protection of Victims of War. The Elucidation states that these conventions are relevant to Indonesian law, as Indonesia is a member of the United Nations and therefore bound by its statutes. This perhaps explains why the Elucidation does not mention the Rome Statute, to which Indonesia is not a party. Yet, the fact that there is no reference to the Rome Statute is puzzling, as it can be regarded as a more recent international standard on gross human rights violations. It was also crucial in informing the draft of the HRCL, regardless of Indonesia's ratification status, and the wording of the provisions of the Draft Criminal Code are very similar to those in the Rome Statute.

The Elucidation also states that the provisions on gross human rights violations do not apply to 'acts that are aimed at the assimilation of those groups into Indonesian society, for instance through education, guidance, and others, to raise their living conditions so they can play an appropriate role in societal life'.[45] Should the Draft Criminal Code be passed in its current form, this provision may serve to preclude the prosecution of human rights crimes that occur in some parts of Indonesia, specifically Papua. Here, the government has long claimed that its actions are in the interest of the development of Papua within the context of the Indonesian state.

While acknowledging that these provisions have not been enacted yet, and taking into account the lengthy process of criminal law reform in Indonesia, the proposed inclusion in the Criminal Code of gross human rights violations, or the so-called extraordinary crimes of international law, should prompt serious reflection on what these additions may mean for the prosecution of human rights crimes. Komnas HAM has been critical of these proposals, and Commissioner Roichatul Aswidah (who between 2012 and 2017 was also chair of the Commission's team dealing with past human rights violations) has stated that 'extraordinary crimes have a special character and are different from ordinary crimes' (Kompas 2017). As such, Komnas HAM is of the opinion that 'the inclusion of these crimes in the Draft Criminal Code reduces their character from extraordinary to ordinary crimes' and has the potential to entrench impunity. The Commission instead argued for the enactment of a new Law on Gross Human Rights Violations to replace the HRCL (Suara 2017). This Law would also detail the process of investigating and prosecuting gross human rights violations, addressing some of the problems that have arisen between Komnas HAM and the AGO. The positioning of Komnas HAM with regard to the provisions of the Draft Criminal Code has been shared by many NGOs, such as those in the National Alliance for the Reform of the Criminal Code (Aliansi Nasional Reformasi KUHP), who also argue that amendments to the HRCL would be more appropriate.

In addition, the proposed provisions have the potential to create a two-track method for prosecuting gross human rights violations: under both the 2000 Human Rights Courts Law and the Criminal Code. While prosecutions under the Criminal Code may offer a 'fall-back position' (Herbert 2008: 460) where such endeavours fail in the HRCL, the inconsistencies between the provisions in the Criminal Code and the HRCL pertaining to punishments are highly problematic. Furthermore, additional problems may arise considering the hierarchy of laws and the relationship between the Criminal Code, the HRCL and the Constitution. Of particular concern would be how the new provisions in the Criminal Code relate to the Constitutional principle against retroactivity and, in particular, whether Indonesia would follow international interpretations that gross human rights crimes can, in fact, be prosecuted retrospectively. The proposed additions to the Criminal Code regarding serious human rights crimes thus appear to muddy the waters even further.

Conclusion

The proposed inclusion of gross human rights violations in the Draft Criminal Code has been mainly driven by a desire to fully codify Indonesian criminal law, rather than to improve the prosecution of serious human rights crimes. The proposed amendments to the Draft Criminal Code are largely consistent with international and national law where it concerns the definitions of gross human rights violations. They also include crimes of war and aggression, which are not offences under Indonesian law as it currently stands. However, this chapter has also outlined some inconsistencies between the proposed additions to the Criminal Code and Law No. 26 of 2000 on the Human Rights Courts, most importantly in terms of penal provisions. Moreover, concerns have been raised about the potential incorporation of these extraordinary crimes in Criminal Code. This includes what has been labelled as the 'degradation' of the special characteristic of gross human rights violations, as well as uncertainties that may emerge as a result of a two-track system for the prosecution of human rights crimes. As such, the inclusion of gross human rights crimes in the Criminal Code will most likely not contribute to holding those accountable for human rights violations to account.

This chapter has placed the proposed inclusions of gross human rights violations in the Draft Criminal Code in the broader context of human rights reform in Indonesia. It has used the concept of Real Legal Certainty as an analytical tool to discuss to what extent laws and legal reform contribute to bring perpetrators of past human rights crimes to justice. The presence or absence of Real Legal Certainty can be attributed to legal rules, institutions, and the wider contexts in which they operate. This reflects the fact that the effective implementation of laws is dependent on multiple factors. While the existence of clear legal norms is important for attaining Real Legal Certainty, it is also dependent on the consistent application of these rules by government institutions and the judiciary. Citizens, too, need to conform to these rules as much as possible. At the same time, that process is both supported and negated by various factors, including the interests of powerful groups and the capacities of state institutions. While on paper the powers of state institutions involved in the promotion and protection of human rights have been significantly strengthened in the post-authoritarian period, in practice this has barely translated into meaningful change. This can, in part, be attributed to weaknesses in legal drafting, as illustrated by the complicated process of prosecuting gross human rights violations. However, what has been more concerning in the Indonesian context is that powerful interest groups and, in particular, the military continue to yield significant power over the legal process, resulting in impunity persisting.

In a context where it is evident that the law and legal institutions cannot be used instrumentally to effect change, the addition of gross human rights crimes to the Draft Criminal Code has little meaning. Should these changes be passed they will only further weaken the human rights framework. For any reforms to have the desired effect – to come to a situation where human rights norms are recognised in law, where the state and its agencies refrain from infringing on these rights, and where there is redress should these infringements occur – substantial political, social and ideological change is required.

Notes

1 Tribunals were held for: violations in the lead-up to, and following, East Timor's independence referendum in 1999; the 1984 Tanjung Priok massacres; and crimes committed in Abepura in 2003 (Setiawan 2019).

2 Recent scholarship has argued that the annihilation of the leftist movement in Indonesia constitutes a genocide (see, for instance, Melvin and Pohlman 2018). However, the drafters of the Convention on the Prevention and Punishment of the Crime of Genocide (1948) explicitly excluded political groups from its scope (Schabas 2009: 117).

3 In this chapter, the term 'Papua' is used to refer to the entire western half of the island of New Guinea, which is Indonesian territory. It comprises the provinces of Papua and West Papua.

4 The Trisakti killings are usually referred to together with the Semanggi I and Semanggi II cases, although these took place after Soeharto's resignation (Setiawan 2016: 24).

5 From 1949 to 1959, Indonesia mostly adhered to the 1950 Provisional Constitution, which recognised individual rights in relation to the state, including freedom from torture or other forms of cruel, inhuman or degrading treatment or punishment (art. 11). For an extensive discussion, see Lubis 1993: 60–85.

6 These provisions concern citizenship (art. 26), equality before the law (art. 27), freedom of association and speech (art. 28), freedom of religion (art. 29), participation in national defence (art. 30), and the right to education and (art. 31). In addition, art. 34 stipulates that the poor and abandoned children will be looked after by the state.

7 The notion of human rights was, however, not entirely alien to Indonesia. Some drafters of the 1945 Constitution, such as Muhammad Yamin and Muhammad Hatta, believed that it was very important to have provisions on 'citizens' rights' in the Constitution, taking inspiration from the 1776 American Declaration of Independence and the 1787 Bill of Rights (Lubis 1993).

8 The framework nominally also includes Law No. 27 of 2004 on the Truth and Reconciliation Commission, which provides for cases of human rights violations to be settled outside court. However, in 2006 the Constitutional Court struck down this Law, finding it to be unconstitutional. Under the presidency of Joko Widodo, new non-judicial mechanisms have been introduced to deal with past human rights violations. As these mechanisms do not include prosecution, they are not included in this chapter. For a detailed overview of the initiatives introduced under Joko Widodo, see McGregor and Setiawan 2019.
9 For a detailed flowchart, see Herbert 2008: 472.
10 Article 104(1).
11 Article 104(2).
12 Article 104(3).
13 While the country is now increasingly referred to as Timor-Leste, I use East Timor in this chapter, as this is how the Indonesia human rights tribunal dealing with that country referred to it.
14 Article 7.
15 Article 8.
16 Article 9.
17 Article 42(1).
18 Article 42(1)(a).
19 Article 42(1)(b).
20 Article 42(2).
21 The ICC does not replace the authority of national courts, and only investigates and prosecutes these crimes where states have proved unable or unwilling to do so. The court only has jurisdiction over crimes when they are committed in in the territory of a state party or are committed by a national of a state party.
22 Article 36.
23 Article 37.
24 Articles 38 and 39.
25 Article 40 (1).
26 Article 77.
27 Article 2.
28 Article 43(1).
29 Article 18(1).
30 Article 20(1), art. 21(1).
31 Article 43(2).
32 These are the cases of Wasior (2001) and Wamena (2003).
33 On 7 December 2000, an unidentified group of people attacked the police headquarters in Abepura, Papua. In this attack, two police officers and a security guard died. Brimob (Korps Brigade Mobil, Mobile Brigade Corps) paramilitary police troops retaliated by attacking civilians. The investigation by Komnas HAM stated that these attacks led to the deaths of two persons and 105 were tortured (Elsam 2004: 4–5).
34 Elucidation to the Draft Criminal Code.
35 Article 400.
36 Article 401(1)(k).
37 For the crime of genocide: art. 400 (2); for crimes against humanity: art. 401(2).
38 Article 402.
39 Article 402.

40 Article 403(a).
41 Article 403(a)(1).
42 Article 403(a)(2).
43 Article 403(b).
44 Article 403.
45 Elucidation on art. 400.

References

Bourchier, David 2015. *Illiberal Democracy in Indonesia. The Ideology of the Family State*. Abingdon and New York: Routledge

Cammack, Mark 2016. 'Crimes against Humanity in East Timor. The Indonesian Ad Hoc Human Rights Court Hearings', in Kirsten Sellars (ed.), *Trials for International Crimes in Asia*. Cambridge University Press, pp. 191–225

Clarke, Ross 2008. 'The Bali Bombing, East Timor Trials and the Aceh Human Rights Court – Retrospectivity, Impunity and Constitutionalism', in Timothy Lindsey (ed.), *Indonesia: Law and Society,* 2nd edn. Sydney: The Federation Press, pp. 430–55

Dewi, Yustina Trihoni Nalesti, Niemann, Grant R. and Triatmodjo, Marsudi 2017. 'Indonesia's Human Rights Court: Need for Reform', *Asia-Pacific Journal on Human Rights and the Law* 18(1): 28–47

Drexler, Elizabeth 2008. *Aceh, Indonesia: Securing the Insecure State*. Philadelphia: University of Pennsylvania Press

Elsam (Lembaga Studi dan Advokasi Masyarakat) 2004. *Laporan Pemantauan Pengadilan Hak Asasi Manusia Kasus Abepura. Perkara Johny Wainal Usman dan Daud Sihombing*. Jakarta: Elsam

Feith, Annie 2006. 'Justice for Papuans?', *Inside Indonesia* no. 87, July–September

Fitzpatrick, Daniel 2008. 'Culture, Ideology and Human Rights: The Case of Indonesia's Code of Criminal Procedure', in Timothy Lindsey (ed.), *Indonesia: Law and Society,* 2nd edn. Sydney: The Federation Press, pp. 499–514

Herbert, Jeff 2008. 'The Legal Framework of Human Rights in Indonesia', in Timothy Lindsey (ed.), *Indonesia: Law and Society,* 2nd edn. Sydney: The Federation Press, pp. 456–82

Heryanto, Ariel and Mandal, Sumit K. 2003. 'Challenges to Authoritarianism in Indonesia and Malaysia', in Ariel Heryanto and Sumit K. Mandal (eds.), *Challenging Authoritarianism in Southeasi Asia: Comparing Indonesia and Malaysia*. London: RoutledgeCurzon, pp. 1–23

Hukumonline 2013. 'Pemerintah Masih Takut Meratifikasi Statuta Roma', 17 July www.hukumonline.com/berita/baca/lt51e6c2ca4777c/pemerintah-masih-takut-meratifikasi-statuta-roma

Human Rights Watch 2017. 'World Report 2017: Indonesia', *Human Rights Watch*, 28 December www.hrw.org/world-report/2017/countrychapters/indonesia

Kompas 2017. 'Komnas HAM Berharap KUHP Tak Atur Kejahatan Genosida', 14 June nasional.kompas.com/read/2017/06/14/22015271/komnas.ham.berharap.kuhp.tak.atur.kejahatan.genosida

Kuddus, Rohana 2017. 'The Ghosts of 1965. Politics and Memory in Indonesia', *New Left Review* 104: 45–92

Lindsey, Tim 2001. 'The Criminal State: Premanisme and the New Indonesia', in Grayson Lloyd and Shannon Smith (eds.), *Indonesia Today: Challenges of History*. Lanham etc.: Rowman & Littlefield Publishers Inc., pp. 283–97

Lindsey, Timothy 2008. 'Constitutional Reform in Indonesia: Muddling Towards Democracy', in Timothy Lindsey (ed.), *Indonesia: Law and Society,* 2nd edn. Sydney: The Federation Press, pp. 23–47

Lubis, Todung Mulya 1993. *In Search of Human Rights. Legal-Political Dilemmas of Indonesia's New Order, 1966–1990*. Jakarta: PT Gramedia Pustaka Utama

McGregor, Katharine E. 2013. 'Mass Violence in the Indonesian Transition from Sukarno to Suharto', Global Dialogue 15(1): 133–44

McGregor, Katharine and Setiawan, Ken 2019. 'Shifting from International to "Indonesian" Justice Measures: Two Decades of Addressing Past Human Rights Violations', *Journal of Contemporary Asia*. 49(5): 837–61

Melvin, Jess and Pohlman, Annie 2018. 'A Case for Genocide: Indonesia 1965–1966', in Katharine McGregor, Jess Melvin and Annie Pohlman (eds.), *The Indonesian Genocide of 1965: Causes, Dynamics and Legacies*. London: Palgrave Macmillan, pp. 27–47

Otto, Jan Michiel 2002. 'Toward an Analytical Framework: Real Legal Certainty and Its Explanatory Factors', in Jianfu Chen, Yuwen Li and Jan Michiel Otto (eds.), *Implementation of Law in the People's Republic of China*. The Hague etc.: Kluwer Law International, pp. 23–34

Purdey, Jemma 2006. *Anti-Chinese Violence in Indonesia 1996–1999*. National University of Singapore Press

Schabas, William 2009. *Genocide in International Law: The Crime of Crimes*. Cambridge University Press

Setiawan, Ken 2013. *Promoting Human Rights. National Human Rights Commissions in Indonesia and Malaysia*. Leiden University Press

Setiawan, Ken 2016. 'From Hope to Disillusion: The Paradox of Komnas HAM, the Indonesian National Human Rights Commission', *Bijdragen tot de Taal-, Land- en Volkenkunde* 172(1): 1–32

Setiawan, Ken 2019. 'The Human Rights Courts: Embedding Impunity', in Melissa Crouch (ed.), *The Politics of Court Reform: Judicial Change and Legal Culture in Indonesia*. Cambridge: Cambridge University Press. pp. 287–310

Suara 2017. 'Komnas HAM dan LSM Hukum Tolak Tipsus Masuk KUHP', 14 June www.suara.com/news/2017/06/14/155605/komnas-ham-dan-lsm-hukum-tolak-tipsus-masuk-kuhp

Sulistiyanto, Priyambudi. 2007. 'Politics of Justice and Reconciliation in Post-Suharto Indonesia', *Journal of Contemporary Asia* 37(1): 73–94

Utami, Penny Naluria 2017. 'Pemulihan Hak Ekonomi dan Sosial Korban Pelanggaran Berat Hak Asasi Manusia Dalam Peristiwa Talangsari 1989', *Jurnal HAM* 8(1): 51–65

Legislation

1945 Constitution (UUD 1945, *Undang-Undang Dasar 1945*)

Criminal Code (*Kitab Undang-Undang Hukum Pidana*, KUHP: Law No. 1 of 1946 as amended by Law No. 27 of 1999 on the Indonesian Criminal Code)Draft Criminal Code (RUU KUHP, *Rancangan Undang-Undang Kitab Undang-Undang Hukum Pidana*)

Geneva Convention on the Protection of Victims of War

Government Regulation in Lieu of Law No. 1 of 1999 on the Human Rights Courts

International Convention on the Prevention and Punishment of the Crime of Genocide
International Covenant on Civil and Political Rights
International Covenant on Economic, Social and Cultural Rights
Law No. 39 of 1999 on Human Rights
Law No. 26 of 2000 on the Human Rights Courts
Law No. 27 of 2004 on the Truth and Reconciliation Commission
Rome Statute on the International Criminal Court
Universal Declaration of Human Rights

Part II

Crime, reform and the Courts

5 Pretrial hearings

Safeguarding human rights or a gift to corruptors?

Tim Mann

The former Speaker of Indonesia's DPR (Dewan Perwakilan Rakyat, People's Representative Assembly, the national legislature) and former Golkar Party Chairman, Setya Novanto, escaped corruption charges so many times that foreign journalists started calling him 'Mr Teflon' (McBeth 2017a, 2017b). The controversial politician had been implicated in numerous high-profile corruption cases over the past two decades (including a scandal involving the bailout of Bank Bali in 1999, and an apparent attempt to extort shares from mining giant Freeport in 2015), but he always managed to avoid legal consequences.

In July 2017, however, the KPK (Komisi Pemberantasan Korupsi, Corruption Eradication Commission) named him a suspect in one of the largest corruption scandals in Indonesian history – the embezzlement of Rp. 2.3 trillion (US$ 172 million) from a national electronic identity card (e-KTP, *Kartu Tanda Penduduk Elektronik*) project. Novanto was accused of being a central figure in the scheme, and reportedly received US$ 7.3 million himself. It wasn't long before his non-stick coating finally wore out. On 24 April 2018, the Jakarta Corruption Court (which is housed in the Central Jakarta District Court) sentenced him to fifteen years in prison for his role in the case. He will be prevented from holding public office for five years after he is released (ABC 2018).

At one point, however, it looked like Novanto would escape charges yet again. In September 2017, he successfully challenged his 'suspect' status in a pretrial hearing, or *praperadilan* (Kahfi 2017). His brief escape was just the latest in an increasingly long line of corruption suspects evading charges using pretrial hearings. What began as a mechanism to strengthen protection of suspects from arbitrary arrest and detention has now emerged as one of the most common strategies used by corrupt officials to evade charges.

This chapter examines the contentious pretrial procedure in detail. It begins with a brief discussion of Indonesia's KUHAP (*Kitab Undang-Undang Acara Pidana,* Criminal Procedure Code), which first introduced the pretrial mechanism in 1981. In recent years, the mechanism has become highly controversial and has been subject to multiple challenges at the Constitutional Court. The chapter examines the evolving regulation and practice of pretrial hearings, including recent Constitutional Court decisions and Supreme Court guidelines that have altered the nature of these proceedings. Finally, the chapter looks at the convoluted legal troubles Novanto experienced, and how he was able to exploit the pretrial motion mechanism to dodge prosecution, before being finally forced to face the consequences.

A new procedural code

When it was introduced in 1981, the Indonesian Criminal Procedure Code was considered one of the landmark reforms of the post-Independence period (Lev 2008: 59). It replaced the Dutch colonial procedural code, the *Herziene Inlandsch Reglement* or HIR, which regulated procedural law, both criminal and civil, for Indonesians (or 'natives'). Introduced as the *Indisch Reglement* in 1848 and initially only applying to residents of Java and Madura, it was revised in 1926 and amended as the HIR in 1941.

During the colonial period, European residents were subject to separate codes for civil (*Burgerlijk Rechtsvordering*) and criminal (*Strafvordering*) matters, which contained protections of personal rights similar to those in the Netherlands (Lev 1985: 61). However, unlike the codes that applied to Dutch residents, the IR/HIR provided little protection for the rights of defendants. The HIR allowed suspects to be detained indefinitely, as police or prosecutors needed only apply to the chair of the local court to have detention extended for thirty-day periods. This meant that defendants were sometimes detained for years at a time, with no legal recourse to challenge their detention (ICJR 2014: 27). The HIR also only provided for legal counsel at the time of trial, not during preliminary interrogation, leaving the door open to the use of torture and abuse to extract confessions (Hart 1987: 175).

The introduction of the KUHAP was therefore intended to provide a better balance between the needs of law enforcement officials to arrest and detain people suspected of committing an offence and the rights of the accused. It cemented a number of safeguards to protect the rights of defendants, such as the principle of the presumption of innocence,[1] the right to prompt interrogation (and trial) after arrest (art. 50), and the right to legal counsel (art. 54)[2] (Fitzpatrick 2008: 504).

One of the most important reforms introduced by the KUHAP was providing district courts with the authority to hear pretrial motions. District courts are authorised to hear pretrial proceedings to rule on:

a) the legality of arrest or detention, at the request of the suspect, his family, or other party on behalf of the subject;
b) the legality of the termination of an investigation or prosecution, on request, to uphold law and justice; and
c) a request for compensation and rehabilitation by a suspect, his or her family, or other party, if a case does not progress to trial (art. 1(10), see also art. 77)

Pretrial hearings were reportedly introduced in an attempt to incorporate the concept of *habeas corpus* into the Indonesian legal system, although the form that resulted is much more limited, as will be shown later in this chapter.[3]

The KUHAP was instituted following major criticism of the treatment of defendants under the HIR, and there can be no doubt that the reforms introduced through the KUHAP were an advance. However, in many ways, they were not much more than a nod to human rights norms – the design of the mechanism provided many loopholes for police and prosecutors to continue to behave unethically. According to the late legal scholar and reformer Adnan Buyung Nasution, when the pretrial hearing concept was originally proposed, it was in a much stronger form than the final form adopted (Hukumonline 2003). In any case, the human rights reforms introduced through the KUHAP have not been effective in defending or protecting human rights. Continuing high levels of torture and forced confessions in the decades since the KUHAP was implemented are stark evidence of how little difference the new protections have made (US Department of State 2016).

A major disappointment in the implementation of the revised KUHAP relates to the function of pretrial hearings. Before examining how they have been exploited by corruption suspects in recent years, it is important to first look in detail at the pretrial procedure as described in the KUHAP, particularly as it relates to suspects.

Key elements of the pretrial mechanism

The pretrial mechanism allows a suspect to challenge the legality of arrest or detention (art. 77). A request can be submitted by the suspect, his family or legal representative to the head of the district court. The application must include the reasons for the challenge (art. 79).[4]

Pretrial hearings are intended to be an expedited procedure. They are chaired by a single judge, who is appointed by the chair of the relevant district court and is assisted by a clerk (art. 78(2)). The appointment of the judge is at the discretion of the head of the court, and there are no formal procedures regulating the appointment of judges in pretrial motions (ICJR 2014: 46). The appointed judge is responsible for setting the date of the hearing within three days of receiving a pretrial hearing application (art. 82(1)(a)).

At the hearing, the judge hears testimony from the suspect or accused, as well as the relevant authority, such as the police investigator or prosecutor (art. 82(1)(b)). This is to be completed promptly and a decision handed down within seven days (art. 82(1)(c)).

These time limits have important consequences. If the district court trial itself begins and the pretrial process has yet to reach a decision, the pretrial motion is thrown out (art. 82(1)(d)). Further, there are no regulations compelling officials to appear in court. This means that police investigators and prosecutors often avoid, or fail to attend, pretrial hearings to delay proceedings, in the hope that the trial will begin and the pretrial motion will be dismissed (Fitzpatrick 2008: 506).

Meanwhile, as mentioned, art. 77 states that district courts have the authority to hear and rule on the legality of arrest, detention, the termination of investigation or prosecution, and compensation or rehabilitation. However, art. 78(1) states that the institution or mechanism responsible for executing this authority is the pretrial hearing, effectively restricting challenges to arrest or detention to pretrial hearings, and not the trial itself. There are therefore significant incentives for police and prosecutors to avoid having arrest and detention procedures raised in a pretrial process. Comments made by government figures during the deliberation process before the passage of the KUHAP suggest that incorporating these types of loopholes into the procedure was intentional. The Soeharto government never intended the pretrial process to introduce strong oversight of the behaviour of police investigators and prosecutors (ICJR 2014: 27–36).

If the pretrial hearing finds an arrest or detention to be unlawful, then the accused must be immediately released and an amount of compensation or rehabilitation determined (art. 82(3)(a) and (c)). Although it is not mentioned explicitly in the definition of pretrial hearings under arts. 1(10) or 77 of the KUHAP, a pretrial hearing may also decide that a confiscated item is not required as evidence, in which case it must be immediately returned to the accused or whomever it was obtained from (art. 82(1)(b) and 82(3)(d)).

The KUHAP states that decisions on the legality of arrest or detention, or compensation in pretrial hearings cannot be appealed (art. 83(1)). However, a decision in a pretrial hearing at the stage of investigation by police (*penyelidikan*) does not preclude a suspect submitting a pretrial application at the next stage of investigation (*penyidikan*), which is conducted by prosecutors (art. 82(1)(e)). A suspect could, for example, file a pretrial motion challenging the legality of arrest, and a second challenging the legality of detention.

The KUHAP does not describe the procedural law for pretrial applications and hearings in detail. In practice, the suspect or accused is responsible for proving that his or her detention was illegal. The suspect or accused is generally termed an 'applicant' and the relevant official (police officer, prosecutor or other investigator, for example from the KPK) is generally referred to as a 'defendant' (ICJR 2014: 44). Although the KUHAP does not specify how to submit an application, in general they are submitted directly to the head of the relevant district court, rather than being sent by post.

The application should include the complete identity of the applicant and respondent and a detailed explanation of the reasons for the submission, as well as the losses suffered because of the actions of the respondent (ICJR 2014: 45). As noted above, the head of the court should appoint the judge and clerk and set the trial date within three days of receiving the application. Judges call on applicants, 'defendants' or witnesses by means of written summons. According to the KUHAP, a summons to an investigation or interrogation must be delivered at least three days before the person is scheduled to attend (art. 227(1)). This can make it difficult for a judge to reach a decision in the required seven days.

The hearing itself usually begins with a recitation of the pretrial request. The respondent or defendant is then provided with a chance to respond with a counter argument. The applicant may reply again, and the defendant is then provided with a chance for a rebuttal. Witnesses, evidence and documents are examined, and then the judge will issue his or her decision (ICJR 2014: 46). The KUHAP does not specify if judges must reach their decision within seven days of the application being registered or the date of the first hearing. In practice, it is common for pretrial hearings to extend for about nineteen business days from the time the application is submitted (ICJR 2014: 6).

Having established the general procedures for pretrial motions, it is important to consider the elements that can be challenged in a pretrial motion.

Challenging the legality of arrest and detention

Under the KUHAP, police may arrest a person who they 'strongly suspect' of committing a crime, based on 'sufficient preliminary evidence' (art. 17). Arrest may be for a maximum of twenty-four hours (art. 19(1)), after which detention must be ordered. The KUHAP does not define what constitutes 'sufficient preliminary evidence' and it has been the subject of some debate in Indonesia. However, the KUHAP also states that a judge may only convict a defendant if he or she is convinced, on the basis of at least two pieces of legal evidence, that a criminal act occurred, and the accused committed it (art. 183). Legal evidence is further defined as witness testimony, expert testimony, documents, circumstantial evidence (or 'indications', *petunjuk*), or the testimony of the accused (art. 184).

In 1984, a meeting of the Chief Justice of the Supreme Court, the Prosecutor General, the Minister of Justice and the Chief of Police decided that 'sufficient preliminary evidence' constituted a police report and one other piece of evidence. Police Chief Regulation 14 of 2014 defines sufficient preliminary evidence in the same manner.[5] Police chief regulations tend to be highly influential on how lower ranking police conduct operations in the field, and has generally determined how police have interpreted the phrase. In 2015, the Constitutional Court made its own ruling on the matter, stating that the phrases 'preliminary evidence', 'sufficient preliminary evidence' and 'sufficient evidence' in arts. 1(14), 17, and 21(1) of the KUHAP were unconstitutional unless they were understood to mean at least two pieces of evidence as described under art. 184.[6]

In addition to 'sufficient preliminary evidence', police must also have an arrest warrant, except in cases where the accused is caught in the act (*tertangkap tangan*). The warrant should include the identity of the accused, the reason for arrest, brief details of the alleged offence and the place of interrogation (art. 18(1), (2)). A copy of the warrant must also be sent to the family of the suspect or accused immediately after arrest (art. 18(3)).

The KUHAP also allows suspects to challenge the legality of their detention at a pretrial hearing. 'Detention' is defined under the KUHAP as the placement of a suspect or the accused in a certain place by an investigator, prosecutor or judge with a ruling, in accordance with the procedures regulated by the KUHAP (art. 1(21)). So, what qualifies as 'legal detention'? First, it must be ordered by a competent authority – an investigator, prosecutor or judge, depending on the stage of the legal process (art. 20). According to the KUHAP, an investigator can order detention of a suspect or accused person who is 'strongly suspected' of committing a criminal offence 'based on sufficient evidence'. Detention should only be ordered 'in circumstances that raise concern that the suspect or accused will escape, damage or destroy evidence and/or repeat the offence' (art. 21(1)). To detain a suspect, police investigators or prosecutors must also obtain a detention order (*surat perintah penahanan*) that includes the identity of the suspect or accused, the reason for detention, brief details of the alleged offence, and the place where he or she will be held (art. 21(2)).

Detention can also only be ordered for offences that carry a sentence of five years or more in prison, or for a number of specified offences (art. 21(4)). Controversially, arts. 362 and 364 of the Criminal Code (KUHP) state that people who steal items worth more than Rp. 250 (about US 2¢) face a maximum sentence of five years in prison.[7] Police had routinely exploited this provision to detain people accused of stealing low-value goods. Public anger over police detention of poor citizens over accusations of minor theft – such as the notorious case of a child accused of stealing a policeman's flip-flop sandal – prompted the Supreme Court to pass Regulation No. 2 of 2012 on Adjustment of Limits for Minor Crimes and Fines in the Criminal Code, which increased the threshold from Rp. 250 to Rp. 2.5 million (about US$ 200). But police and prosecutors have largely ignored this regulation, and have continued to detain people based on the old amount (Domingo and Sudaryono 2016: 19).[8]

In summary, there are several aspects that must be fulfilled for detention to be considered legal (in addition to it being ordered by a competent authority – an investigator, prosecutor or judge):

1) it must be in relation to an offence carrying a sentence of five years or more or a specified offence;
2) there must be sufficient evidence;
3) the subjective aspects of art. 21(1) must be satisfied (strong suspicion and concern that the suspect or accused will escape, destroy evidence or repeat the offence); and
4) the letter of detention must be complete and be copied to the suspect's family.

A 2014 study of eighty pretrial hearings by the Institute for Criminal Justice Reform (ICJR) found that judges mostly considered these elements to be alternative in nature rather than cumulative (ICJR 2014: 64).

A particular problem is how judges deal with the subjective element of ‘concern’ that the suspect or accused may escape, damage or destroy evidence or repeat the crime. Police have full discretion to determine whether these conditions exist, and police generally claim that they do, regardless of the specifics of a case. In a 2007 visit to Indonesia, the UN Special Rapporteur on Torture found that it was ‘standard procedure’ for police investigators to detain suspects for the full sixty-one days allowed under the KUHAP (UN Human Rights Council 2008: 12).

Pretrial hearings are the only avenue available for a suspect or the accused to challenge this aspect of their detention. However, there are no standards or indicators against which this ‘concern’ can be measured. And it is very difficult for applicants in pretrial hearings to prove to a judge that there was no reason for concern. In any case, available evidence suggests that when judges deal with the issue at all, they treat it in a cursory manner. The ICJR report found that when the issue was raised in pretrial hearings, many investigators and prosecutors simply restated art. 21(1) as giving them a discretionary right, without elaborating the specifics of their ‘concern’, and this was usually accepted by judges (ICJR 2014: 63).

There do not appear to be any examples of suspects using pretrial motions to challenge detention by police or prosecutors for the theft of items worth less than Rp. 2.5 million (but more than Rp. 250), although there would appear to be grounds under art. 21(4). A concern is that the adjustment to the Rp. 250 value has only been made by Supreme Court regulation and is yet to be reflected in the KUHAP (see Assegaf, Chapter 9). A strict reading of the KUHAP could therefore rule that detention was legal. A further complicating factor is that the people arrested for minor theft are usually poor and often lack the resources to mount a pretrial application. The ICJR study referred to above found that of eighty pretrial decisions studied, only three were filed by the suspect or accused – the remaining seventy-seven were filed by legal representatives (ICJR 2014: 52). This suggests that pretrial hearings continue to be an option used primarily by middle-class or elite applicants.

Pretrial hearings would also appear to be the appropriate forum for deciding whether ‘sufficient preliminary evidence’ or ‘sufficient evidence’ has been obtained to justify arrest or detention. In practice, however, judges have interpreted this element of the pretrial hearing in a very narrow and formal sense, focusing on the fulfilment of administrative requirements, such as the presence of an arrest warrant (Aries 2017).[9] Judges almost never rule on whether sufficient evidence has been obtained, as they consider this aspect to be entering the material aspects of the case, which they say is the authority of the judges at the trial itself (ICJR 2014: 71).

Suspect status as a matter that can be challenged

This began to change, however, in early 2015, when South Jakarta District Court Judge Sarpin Rizaldi issued a controversial decision in favour of police chief candidate Budi Gunawan. Newly-elected President Joko Widodo had selected Gunawan as the sole candidate to replace Sutarman as police chief in early 2015. The nomination was immediately unpopular and was widely assumed to have the fingerprints of Megawati Soekarnoputri, Widodo's party leader and former President, all over it, as Gunawan had served as her aide when she was president, from 2001–4. The nomination was also condemned by anti-corruption activists, because Gunawan was among several police profiled in an explosive 2010 *Tempo* magazine issue on senior police with suspiciously large bank accounts (Tempo 2010). Soon after Gunawan's name was announced, the KPK revealed that it had been investigating him for more than six months over suspicious transactions that took place when he served as head of the Career Development Agency at National Police Headquarters from 2003 to 2006 (Sinaga 2015).

One day before he was scheduled to undergo a 'fit and proper' test at the House of Representatives (Dewan Perwakilan Rakyat, DPR), on 13 January, the KPK named Gunawan as suspected of corruption. Being declared a suspect (*terdakwa*) is loosely equivalent to being charged in common law countries. The DPR was seemingly unfussed by this development, however, and Gunawan passed his 'fit and proper' test and was confirmed in a DPR plenary hearing on 15 January.

On 19 January, Gunawan submitted a pretrial application at the South Jakarta District Court, which has long had a reputation for being corrupt.[10] Judge Sarpin closely reviewed the KPK's 'Investigation Order' (*Surat Perintah Penyidikan, Sprindik*), and made the surprising decision that Gunawan's suspect status was illegal.[11] This went beyond the remit of pretrial hearings as described under art. 77 of the KUHAP, and was one of the first times the scope of pretrial hearings had been interpreted as extending to the naming of suspects.[12]

Sarpin's ruling rested on a dubious interpretation of the Law No. 30 of 2002 on the Corruption Eradication Commission to find that Gunawan was not a 'legal subject' who could be investigated by the KPK. Article 11 of the Law on the KPK states that it has the authority to investigate and prosecute corruption crime:

a) involving law enforcement officials and state officials;
b) causing disturbance in the community; and
c) resulting in state losses of more than Rp. 1 billion.

Sarpin ruled that at the time of the offence Gunawan was not a 'law enforcement' official, because his position as head of the Career Development Agency comprised assistance to the leadership and staff operations.

Sarpin further relied on the definition of 'state official' in arts. 1(1) and 2 of Law No. 28 of 1999 on State Officials Who Are Clean and Free from Corruption, Collusion and Nepotism. The judge ruled that as a senior 'Echelon II A1' position, the role of the head of the Staff Development

Agency did not fit the definition of state official.[13] According to Sarpin, 11(b) did not apply either, because he was relatively unknown to the community before he was nominated as police chief. Finally, Sarpin held, the KPK's investigation order, a *Surat Perintah Penyidikan* or *Sprindik*, accused Gunawan of receiving 'gifts', not of causing state losses, so 11(c) could not apply either. Sarpin found that as the investigation could not be considered legal, then the *Sprindik* and Gunawan's status as a suspect should not be considered legal either.[14] In his decision, Sarpin made specific reference to Gunawan's suspect status, finding it to be illegal.[15]

The Sarpin decision sent shockwaves through the Indonesian political establishment and in doing so exposed one of the core weaknesses of the pretrial process. Because pretrial motions are decided by a single judge and cannot be appealed, they are highly vulnerable to the whims of the deciding judge and are 'notorious for lack of uniformity and predictability' (Fitzpatrick 2008: 506).

As a civil law system, Indonesia does not have a formal system of precedent, but there were immediate concerns that Sarpin's decision would encourage other alleged corruptors to follow in Gunawan's footsteps and challenge their suspect status. On 28 April, the Constitutional Court made sure that this would be the case. The court ruled that art. 77(a) of the KUHAP, which describes the scope of pretrial hearings, was unconstitutional unless it was interpreted to extend to the naming of suspects (as well as body/property searches and seizure of goods or property). The Constitutional Court argued that naming someone a suspect involved a restriction of civil rights or freedoms and so it was necessary to provide the accused with a mechanism to challenge abuses of power.

In its ruling, the Court noted that while they were intended to strengthen protection of human rights, pretrial hearings had become simply formal processes that were limited to examining administrative requirements and, as such, were far from the true intention of pretrial hearings.[16] Its decision also recognised the weight that being named a suspect carries in the Indonesian legal system. The Court said that when the KUHAP was first implemented in 1981, being named a suspect was not a major cause for concern in the Indonesian community. But, over time, being named a suspect has come to have significant implications. The Court stated that the KUHAP did not contain a system of checks and balances to assess the validity of the acquisition of evidence, or a way to exclude evidence obtained illegally, as in the United States.[17] The decision also noted that being named a suspect did not have a clear time limit, meaning that individuals were forced by the state to accept their suspect status without any legal means to question the legality or purpose of being labelled as such. Extending the scope of pretrial hearings to include suspect status, the Court argued, was important to protect individuals from ill treatment by investigators.[18]

It therefore seems that the primary motivation of the Constitutional Court in ruling that the scope of pretrial hearings should be extended to cover naming someone a suspect was to strengthen human rights protections for suspects. However, as it came on the back of the Gunawan decision at the South Jakarta District Court, observers were concerned that it would be interpreted as giving the green light to corruption suspects to challenge their suspect status. Sure enough, on 12 May 2015, just three months after the Gunawan decision, the former Makassar mayor, Ilham Arief Sirajuddin, also successfully challenged his status as a suspect at the South Jakarta District Court (Jakarta Post 2015). Judge Yuningtyas Upiek Kartikawati ruled that the KPK did not have two valid pieces of evidence, and as such, Sirajuddin's suspect status was illegal.[19] Two weeks later, on 26 May, former Supreme Audit Agency (BPK) Chairman Hadi Poernomo had his status as a suspect revoked as well. South Jakarta District Court Judge Haswandi made the somewhat puzzling decision that his investigation was invalid because it had been conducted by KPK investigators, not police or prosecutors (Saragih 2015). Over the past few years, several high-profile corruption suspects have now had their suspect statuses quashed in pretrial hearings, including former Minister Dahlan Iskan, former Sabu Raijua District Head Marthen Dira Tome, and Nganjuk District Head Taufiqurrahman.

Although this is a deeply worrying trend, it is important to recognise that, on balance, corruption suspects do not do so well in pretrial hearings, as Table 5.1 shows. Before the Budi Gunawan decision, the KPK had never lost a pretrial challenge. According to KPK Chair Agus Rahardjo, between 2004 and 2014, there were thirty-two pretrial challenges to KPK investigations – none of which were successful (Republika 2016). In 2015, however, the KPK faced twenty-six pretrial challenges, and ultimately lost three, including the Gunawan case (KPK 2016: 17). In 2016, fifteen of the cases the KPK was investigating were challenged by corruption suspects in pretrial hearings. Only one of these suspects – Marthen Dira Tome – was successful (KPK 2017: 249; Aziz 2017). Likewise, in 2017, the KPK's Annual Report lists twenty-seven pretrial cases, with corruption suspects winning just two – Setya Novanto and Taufiqurrahman (KPK 2018: 344–5).[20]

Table 5.1 Pretrial challenges faced and lost by KPK 2004–17

Year	*Pretrial challenges*	*Challenges lost by KPK*
2004–2014	32	0
2015	26	3
2016	15	1
2017	27	2

Source: KPK reports, Aziz 2017.[1]

[1] Note that this table refers only to corruption cases investigated by the KPK, and not cases investigated by police or the prosecutor's office.

Challenging the seizure of goods and body or property searches

A strict reading of art. 77 of the KUHAP would suggest that the seizure of items and searches do not fall within the scope of pretrial hearings. As noted above, arts. 82(1)(b) and 82(3)(d) of the KUHAP provide, however, that pretrial hearings may rule that seized items are not valid evidence. An aspect of the 2015 Constitutional Court decision that is often overlooked is that it also concluded that body and property searches and seizure of property were within the remit of pretrial hearings.[21] In doing so, the Court referred to one of its own earlier decisions, No 65/PUU-IX/2011 of 1 May 2012, in which it stated that one of the objectives of pretrial hearings were to prevent arbitrary actions by investigators or prosecutors when conducting arrest, searches, seizure of property, investigation, prosecution, and the termination of investigation or prosecution.[22] Again, this decision, while seemingly sound, has the potential to allow corruption suspects to have evidence obtained excluded from their trials. Although he was ultimately unsuccessful, this was an avenue that disgraced, corrupt former DPR member and Democratic Party politician Muhammad Nazaruddin attempted in 2011 (Waskita 2011).

Challenging the dropping of investigations

The KUHAP allows police investigators, prosecutors and 'concerned third parties' to submit pretrial motions to challenge the termination of investigation or prosecution by law enforcement officials (arts. 77(a), 80, 82, 83). As mentioned above, investigation or prosecution can only be dropped when police or prosecutors issue formal directives, known as Investigation Termination Orders (*Surat Perintah Penghentian Penyidikan*, SP3) when issued by police, and Prosecution Termination Orders (*Surat Keputusan Penghentian Penuntutan*, SKPP) when issued by prosecutors.[23] The rationale for provisions to allow police, prosecutors and third parties to dispute the dropping of investigations in pretrial proceedings is clear – it can provide a safeguard against the possibility of suspects bribing police or prosecutors to have their cases dropped.

The KUHAP lists the reasons for terminating an investigation or prosecution as: failure to obtain sufficient evidence; that the act was not a criminal offence, or for legal reasons (*demi hukum*), for example, the suspect has died, has already been tried for the same offence; or the expiry of a limitations period (*kedaluwarsa*) (arts. 109(2) and 140(2)).

The general procedure for pretrial hearings to challenge the termination of an investigation or prosecution is largely unchanged from the procedure for hearings on arrest or detention. Until recently, however, decisions on the dropping of investigations could be appealed to the relevant provincial High Court (art. 83(2)). But in May 2012, the Constitutional Court ruled that art. 83(2) violated the Constitution and did not have binding legal force, because it treated investigators and prosecutors differently from suspects, who cannot appeal pretrial decisions.[24] The Court believed that this inequality did not provide for legal certainty.

In addition to appeals to the relevant provincial High Court being disallowed, Law No. 5 of 2004 on the Supreme Court dictates that the Supreme Court may not hear cassation appeals on pretrial decisions (art. 45A(2)(a)). In 2016, the Supreme Court passed a regulation forbidding reconsideration requests (*peninjauan kembali*, PK) on pretrial decisions (art. 3).[25] This regulation was published in part to correct a Supreme Court circular from 2014, which stated that PK hearings were permitted for pretrial decisions in cases where there were indications of 'trafficking in law' (*penyelundupan hukum*), essentially corruption.[26] The regulation noted that the phrase *penyelundupan hukum* was prone to multiple interpretations and could contribute to conflicting decisions or legal uncertainty.

The Supreme Court handed down another important decision on this aspect of pretrial hearings one year earlier. A civil society organisation called the Indonesian Anti-Corruption Community (Perkumpulan Masyarakat Anti Korupsi, MAKI) challenged the constitutionality of art. 80, referring specifically to the phrase 'concerned third parties', which is not defined in the KUHAP.[27] MAKI was motivated to challenge the article because it had submitted pretrial applications to dispute the dropping of corruption cases but had several of them rejected on the grounds that civil society organisations did not have the legal standing to submit a pretrial application. In May 2013, however, the Constitutional Court ruled that art. 80 was unconstitutional unless it was understood to extend to victims, informants and nongovernmental and community organisations.[28]

Challenging the delayed processing of investigations

Just as police and prosecutors often terminate cases under suspicious circumstances, they may sometimes intentionally neglect to terminate a case when it serves their interests. As a SP3 or SKPP is required to terminate an investigation or prosecution, police and prosecutors will sometimes avoid terminating weak cases, using the 'suspect' status as a threat against the accused, insinuating that the investigation could be revived at any moment. For example, on 25 March 2015, the Indonesian National Police named former Deputy Justice and Human Rights Minister Denny Indrayana a suspect over what many consider to be trumped-up corruption charges relating to an online passport payment gateway that he introduced when in government (Sundaryani 2015). Denny has stated that he believes the case was retaliation for his impassioned public defence of the KPK in its dispute with the police in early 2015. five years later, he remains a suspect, with no sign of progress in his case but facing the continued possibility of detention at the whim of the police.

Although the matter is not addressed explicitly in the KUHAP, in at least one case, a district court has granted a pretrial application that contested a delay in bringing a case to trial. Muspani, a former member of the national

Regional Representatives Assembly (Dewan Perwakilan Daerah, DPD), filed a pretrial motion with the Central Jakarta District Court in relation to the case of former Bengkulu Governor Agusrin Maryono Najamuddin, who was accused of corruption in the management of land and building tax (*pajak bumi dan bangunan*) and transfer duty for the acquisition of rights over land and buildings (*bea perolehan hak atas tanah dan bangunan*). State prosecutors and KPK investigators began investigating the case in 2007 and in 2009 the chief justice of the Supreme Court issued a decision directing the Central Jakarta District Court to hear and rule on the case.[29] In his pretrial application, Muspani said that he believed prosecutors had already issued an SKPP terminating the prosecution process but had not made it public. In the pretrial hearing in November 2010, Judge Supraja ruled in favour of Muspani, deciding that prosecutors must immediately refer the case to the Central Jakarta District Court for trial (Hukumonline 2010). The Central Jakarta District Court initially cleared former Governor Agusrin of the corruption charges, under suspicious circumstances (Sari 2011), however a cassation appeal to the Supreme Court eventually saw him sentenced to four years in prison (Hukumonline 2012).[30]

Compensation and rehabilitation

Another aspect of pretrial hearings, which will not be discussed in detail here, is the authority to request compensation or rehabilitation for arrest or detention. The KUHAP provides that suspects, accused or convicted people have the right to demand compensation for unlawful arrest, detention, prosecution, conviction, or 'other acts', because of mistaken identity or errors in application of the law (art. 95(1)).[31] Applications by suspects or their beneficiaries for compensation for unlawful arrest, detention, or other acts, and for cases that do not progress to trial are heard in, and follow, the procedures of pretrial hearings (art. 95(2),(5)). Decisions are made in the form of a judicial order (*penetapan*) (art. 96(1)). Similarly, a suspect can also request rehabilitation for unlawful arrest or detention for cases that do not progress to trial (art. 97(3)). Requests can be filed by a suspect, his or her family, or legal counsel at the relevant district court within fourteen days of a decision on the legality of arrest or detention.[32]

Supreme Court Regulation No. 4 of 2016

Perhaps sensing the confusion resulting from the multiple Constitutional Court rulings on pretrial hearings, in 2016, the Supreme Court sought to clarify the scope of pretrial hearings. In Supreme Court Regulation No. 4 of 2016, it confirmed that pretrial hearings are to rule on:

a) the legality of arrest, detention, the termination of investigation or prosecution, declaring a person a suspect, seizure [of goods] and searches; and

b) compensation and rehabilitation for individuals whose case was terminated at the investigation or prosecution stages (art. 2(1)).

Although pretrial hearings have long been criticised for having an inordinate focus on surface level administrative requirements, the Supreme Court reinforced this approach in the expanded scope to cover the naming of suspects. The regulation states that 'pretrial examinations on the legality of naming someone a suspect [should] examine only the formal legal aspects' – that is, whether there are at least two pieces of legal evidence – and should not rule on the substance of the case (art. 2(2)). Importantly, the decision also stated that a pretrial hearing that finds a suspect was named a suspect in violation of the law does not remove the authority of an investigator to name the person a suspect at a later stage, provided that two new valid pieces of evidence are found in relation to the substance of the case (art. 2(3)).

Given that it has been such a contentious procedure, it is not surprising that the regulation of pretrial hearings is dynamic and continues to evolve. This chapter now turns to examination of the case of disgraced politician Setya Novanto, which serves to illustrate many of the recent challenges associated with pretrial hearings in Indonesia.

Setya Novanto: Untouchable no more

The case of controversial politician Setya Novanto is one of the most well-known cases of what has become a depressingly familiar pattern – corruption suspects using pretrial hearings to challenge their suspect status. It demonstrates the evolution of pretrial hearings from a mechanism ostensibly designed to protect the rights of defendants into a tool often used by corruptors to try to avoid being penalised for their crimes. Novanto had been a member of the DPR for the Golkar Party since 1999. He was implicated in scandal since then, and, as mentioned, was, for a long time, able to dodge charges.

His questionable dealings are numerous and complicated (and even include a bizarre appearance at a Donald Trump campaign rally in 2015). They are worth recapping briefly here, if only to illustrate his remarkable knack for avoiding the courts. They extend back to around the time he was first elected as a member of the DPR for Golkar in 1999. In mid-1999, Bank Bali paid an inflated commission to finance company Era Giat Prima (EGP), of which Novanto was president-director, to help it recover debts from a failed bank that had been taken over by the Indonesian Bank Restructuring Agency (IBRA). Within days of EGP receiving funds, multiple transfers were made to politicians, lawmakers and public officials (Crouch 2010: 219). While Bank Indonesia Director Syahril Sabirin, EGP Principal Director Djoko Tjandra, and IBRA Deputy Pande Lubis were all convicted in the scandal, Novanto emerged unscathed.

Several other controversies followed. In 2006, for example, he was questioned by prosecutors after he and fellow Golkar politician Nurdin Halid were implicated in the removal of 60,000 tonnes of imported Vietnamese rice from customs storage in 2003. Only a fraction of the required customs duty had been paid (Budiarti and Barus 2006). In 2004, Asia Pasific Eco Lestari (APEL), a company owned by Novanto, illegally imported more than 1,000 tonnes of toxic waste disguised as organic fertiliser into Indonesia from Singapore. Novanto claimed he had resigned from the company in 2003, but documents emerged showing that he had signed an agreement between APEL and the Singaporean firm on 29 June 2004 (Liputan6 2005).

In 2013, KPK investigators raided his office in the DPR complex over suspicions of a connection to the 2012 National Games (PON, Peran Olahraga Nasional) corruption scandal involving former Riau Governor Rusli Zainal. Rusli was eventually found guilty of ordering the delivery of Rp. 9 billion in bribes to Novanto and another Golkar legislator, Kahar Muzakkir. Novanto denied that he had received a bribe, however, and was only ever questioned as a witness (Liputan6 2013; Syukur 2014).

One of Novanto's closest shaves came in 2015, when a recording emerged of him allegedly attempting to extort a 20 per cent stake in the Indonesian arm of mining behemoth Freeport McMoRan in exchange for guaranteeing the extension of its contract (Jensen and Da Costa 2015). The scandal became known as *Papa Minta Saham* ('Papa Wants Shares'), mimicking fraudulent text messages that are common in Indonesia, supposedly from one's mother asking for phone credit – *Mama minta pulsa*. Novanto was then serving as Speaker of the DPR, a position he had secured in the wake of the deeply polarised 2014 presidential election, at which Golkar backed Prabowo Subianto, who lost.[33] Following a brutal and public House Ethics Council investigation, Novanto resigned as Speaker in December 2015. However, in April 2016, the Attorney General's Office put the case on hold, claiming that they could not investigate the case further because a key figure present in the recorded meeting, oil tycoon Muhammad Reza Chalid, had fled overseas (Rahadian 2016).

Novanto's rehabilitation was miraculous. Novanto was elected chair of Golkar a month later and immediately announced that Golkar would join Joko Widodo's ruling coalition (Tempo 2016). Novanto also challenged elements of the 2008 Information and Electronic Transactions Law on the admissibility of recorded evidence in the Constitutional Court. In September 2016, the Court ruled that digital recordings could only be considered valid evidence if ordered by police, prosecutors or other law enforcement officials.[34] This meant that the recording of Novanto – which was made by Freeport Indonesia President Director Maroef Sjamsoeddin – could not be used to prosecute him. In late September, the House Ethics Council 'restored his name', and by November, he was back in the Speaker's chair (Reuters 2016; Tashandra 2016).

But the worst was still to come. Indications of corruption in the tender process for the e-KTP scheme first became public in 2011 (Pakpahan 2011). The project was marked up to Rp. 5.8 trillion, reportedly resulting in state losses of Rp. 2.3 trillion (US$ 172 million). As early as 2013, corruption convict and former Democratic Party Treasurer Muhammad Nazaruddin named Novanto as a key architect of the scheme (Tribun News 2013). It was not until 2017, however, that the case was blown wide open. A mammoth investigation by the KPK over a number of years questioned 294 witnesses, including former and current members of the DPR, state officials, and e-KTP project winners (Arkhelaus W 2017). Eventually more than seventy lawmakers and every political party in DPR Commission II, which was responsible for approving the budget for the project, became implicated in the case. Many observers have referred to the e-KTP scandal as the largest corruption case ever pursued by the KPK. It has also been a goldmine for Indonesia's lively online community and its enthusiastic meme generators, who dealt with their frustration by mocking Novanto mercilessly on social media. In April 2017, the KPK issued a travel ban to prevent Novanto from travelling overseas, and on 17 July, the KPK announced that it had finally named him a corruption suspect. On 11 April, one of the KPK's most senior investigators, Novel Baswedan, was attacked with acid returning home from morning prayers. Many observers speculated on whether this attack was linked to his investigation of the e-KTP scheme (Indrayana 2017).

Pretrial hearing

Novanto repeatedly refused to attend questioning by KPK investigators – both before and after he was named a suspect.[35] Soon after he was named a suspect, Novanto sought to challenge his suspect status in a pretrial hearing, and his application was registered with the South Jakarta District Court on 4 September 2017. Judge Cepi Iskandar was selected to hear the case and set a date for the first hearing of 12 September. The KPK submitted a request to delay the hearing by three weeks so it could prepare administrative requirements, and a new date of 20 September was set for the first hearing (Taher 2017).

Novanto's argument rested on several claims. First, he argued that the KPK had named him a suspect before conducting a legal investigation process, primarily because the KPK published its Investigation Order (*Surat Perintah Penyidikan,* or *Sprindik*)[36] and named him a suspect on 17 July, but he only received a letter informing him that investigation had commenced (*Surat Pemberitahuan Dimulainya Penyidikan*, or SPDP) on 18 July.[37] He claimed that he had not been interviewed as a potential suspect or asked to provide testimony in the case against him.[38] Further, the KPK accused Novanto of engaging in corruption with Ministry of Home Affairs officials Irman and Sugiharto, who were sentenced to seven and five years in prison, respectively, for their roles in the e-KTP case by the Central Jakarta District

Court.[39] Novanto argued that he should not have been named a suspect on this basis because he was not mentioned in the judges' decision.[40] Novanto also argued that the statements of witnesses in the Irman and Sugiharto case could not be used as evidence to name Novanto a suspect, because this evidence was only valid for their cases. Further, he said that at the time the crime allegedly occurred, he was head of the Golkar faction in the House of Representatives, and did not have the authority to direct other lawmakers to commit the crime of which he was accused.[41] Novanto also argued that the KPK investigators appointed to conduct the investigation had been incorrectly appointed.[42] Finally, Novanto's pretrial application argued that the KPK had abused its power in issuing a travel ban against him on 10 April, given that he was only a witness at the time, and was not named a suspect until 17 July.[43]

Judge Iskandar reached a decision on 29 September. Anti-corruption activists were highly critical of the hearing, during which Iskandar refused to allow the KPK to play a recording that apparently provided strong evidence of Novanto's involvement and questioned the 'ad hoc' nature of the KPK as an institution (Kumparan 2017). The final decision is 237 pages long and, like most Indonesian legal decisions, highly repetitive and poorly written, with many long, run-on, sentences.

The judge acknowledged both that Novanto believed he should not have been named a suspect because his name was not mentioned in the Irman and Sugiharto decision, and conversely, that the KPK believed the same case showed clear evidence of Novanto's involvement. But Iskandar said his role was simply to determine whether Novanto had been named a suspect in line with legal procedure, not to determine whether corruption had occurred. By connecting the Irman and Sugiharto decision to Novanto's case, the judge said, both Novanto and the KPK were asking him to consider the substance of the case, which was beyond the scope of pretrial hearings. As such, he said, the matter needed no further consideration.[44]

To consider the matter of the timing of Novanto's suspect status, Iskandar reviewed provisions on preliminary investigation (*penyelidikan*) and investigation (*penyidikan*) in the 2002 Law on the KPK, the KUHAP and the KPK's standard operating procedures. Iskandar stated there was evidence that KPK had named Novanto a suspect at the commencement of the investigation (*penyidikan*) process.[45] Although there is no regulation explicitly dictating the stage of the investigation process at which a person can be named a suspect, Iskandar based his decision on art. 1(2) of the KUHAP, which states that 'investigation is a series of acts by an investigator in matters and by means regulated in this Law to look for and gather evidence with which to clarify whether an offence has occurred and to locate the suspect'. It was his belief, Iskandar continued, that naming a suspect should come at the end of the investigation process, to protect the rights of the accused. This would provide enough time to examine evidence to determine if it was valid or not, and consider whether it was obtained in a legal manner, before taking the step of naming someone a suspect.[46] Particularly interesting in this component of the decision is Iskandar's deployment of the language of human rights to justify his interpretation. He said that one of the reasons that investigations were divided into preliminary investigation and investigation stages was to ensure that preliminary investigators and investigators were cautious, and avoided methods that could be considered an abuse of power in obtaining legal evidence.[47]

In fact, the KUHAP indicates that investigators can name a person a suspect at any stage of the investigation. Article 1(14) describes a suspect as 'a person who, by virtue of his behaviour or condition, based on preliminary evidence, can be reasonably suspected of having committed an offence'. The minimum requirement therefore is possessing preliminary evidence. It is true that in most cases, the investigator will obtain this evidence from an investigation, as described in art. 1(2) of the KUHAP. As Iskandar suggests, this is an important means of ensuring accountability of investigators – one would not want police to name a person a suspect without first investigating the case correctly. But when investigating a suspect, investigators may also obtain information or evidence of the involvement of another person. In these circumstances, investigators are able to issue a new SPDP (informing prosecutors or the suspect that a new investigation has commenced) and name the new suspect straight away. This is what occurred in Novanto's case.

Controversially, Iskandar stated that all the evidence that the KPK had submitted, including three examinations of Novanto as a witness (on 13 December, 10 January and 14 July), was obtained through the development of cases against Irman, Sugiharto and businessman Andi Agustinus [alias Andi Narogong]. Iskandar stated that the KPK had violated its procedures by using the investigation orders from other cases in the investigation of Novanto's case.[48] Any evidence against Novanto should have been collected after 17 July, he said, when the investigation order for Novanto was issued by the KPK.[49] This raised questions, the judge continued, as to when the KPK was able to obtain two sufficient pieces of evidence and examine the accused before naming him a suspect.[50] This was a highly unusual interpretation of criminal procedural law. Irman and Sugiharto had been convicted following witness statements made before a court in relation to the same case in which Novanto was allegedly involved. Further, regarding confiscated evidence, the KUHAP clearly indicates that evidence in one case can be used for further cases. Article 46(2) states that

> after a case has been decided, confiscated items should be returned to the person(s) named in the decision, except if the decision states the item should be seized by the state, to be destroyed or damaged so that it may no longer be used, *or if it is needed as evidence in another case*.

Finally, Iskandar addressed the matter of improper temporary appointment of police investigators to the KPK but noted that because Novanto failed to mention which investigators he was impugning, he was not able to consider the issue.[51]

Iskandar concluded that in naming Novanto a suspect, the KPK had not followed the procedures and provisions of Law No. 30 of 2002 on the Corruption Eradication Commission, the KUHAP and the standard operating procedures of the KPK, and so his suspect status was illegal.[52] The judge ordered the KPK to terminate its investigation into Novanto and Mr Teflon walked free again.

Second time lucky

Despite their disappointment at the setback, KPK officials privately expressed confidence that they had so much evidence against Novanto that it would not be long before they named him a suspect again. They publicly recalled the Supreme Court's recent clarification that even if a pretrial decision has ruled that an accused person's suspect status was illegal, this did not eliminate the possibility that he or she could be named a suspect in the future, provided two new pieces of evidence could be found. The KPK then attempted to call in Novanto for questioning as a witness in relation to the e-KTP case on several further occasions but Novanto always had an excuse. Once he said he could not attend because he was visiting his constituents while the DPR was in recess. On other occasions, he said the KPK had not obtained the required written permission from the president, in accordance with Law No. 17 of 2014 on Legislative Bodies, 'the MD3 Law' (Tempo 2017).

Although its attempts to question Novanto were unsuccessful, on 10 November, the KPK formally announced it had named him a suspect again. The KPK made it clear that it had issued an Investigation Order on 31 October and sent an SPDP letter to inform Novanto that the investigation had commenced on 3 November (Fatmawati 2017). Novanto began scrambling. On 13 November, he filed a Constitutional Court challenge to arts. 46(1)-(2) and 12 of the 2002 Law on the Corruption Eradication Commission, which relate to the KPK's investigating authority and its authority to request that the Directorate General of Immigration place a travel ban on a person.[53] On 15 November, Novanto declined to be questioned again, stating that he would wait for the outcome of the Constitutional Court challenge (Belarminus 2017b). The same day, he filed another pretrial hearing with the South Jakarta District Court (Medistiara 2017).

The KPK's patience with Novanto's continual sidestepping was wearing thin, and on 15 November it issued a warrant for his arrest (Belarminus 2017c). Later that evening, KPK investigators arrived at his house to arrest him but Novanto was nowhere to be found (Hakim 2017b). In perhaps the most ludicrous aspect of the whole saga, Novanto disappeared for nearly twenty-four hours, only to emerge on the evening of 16 November at Medika Permata Hijau Hospital, after reportedly being involved in a car accident with an electricity pole. Novanto's lawyer, Fredrich Yunadi, claimed that Novanto had been on the way to the KPK to turn himself in for questioning when the crash occurred. He said the politician had suffered serious injuries, including a swelling the size of a *bakpao* (Chinese steamed bun) on his head (Tashandra 2017).

Indonesian social media users, who had developed a degree of gallows humour about Novanto's attempts to evade the law, would have none of it. They were more worried about the 'real victim' of the crash, the electricity pole, and quickly pushed the hashtag #savetianglistrik ('save the electricity pole') into the list of trending topics on Twitter. Internet users mocked the seemingly minor nature of the crash, posting images of the pole being rushed to hospital and recording melodramatic video tributes to the pole (BBC 2017). On 17 November, Novanto was transferred to Cipto Mangkusomo Hospital, and on 19 November its medical director confirmed what everyone already knew – Novanto did not need to be hospitalised. KPK investigators had finally got their man, and he was detained for further interrogation (Ihsanuddin 2017).

Several months later, the truth of the farcical incident became clear. Novanto's former lawyer, Yunadi, and a Medika Permata Hijau Hospital doctor, Bimanesh Sutarjo, have now been sentenced to seven years and three years in prison, respectively, for obstructing an investigation into a corruption suspect (Rachman 2018; Sheany 2018). During their trials, multiple witnesses testified that the crash was staged. Two Medika Permata Hijau Hospital nurses said that Novanto never had a *bakpao* sized lump on his head (BBC 2018). It also emerged that Yunadi had booked a VIP room on level 3 of Medika Permata Hijau Hospital *before* the accident was supposed to have occurred (Gabrillin 2018; Rachman 2018).

The South Jakarta District Court appointed Judge Kusno to rule on Novanto's pretrial application and set a date of 30 November for the first hearing. The KPK asked for the hearing to be delayed for three weeks, but Kusno granted only a week, and rescheduled the date of the first hearing to 7 December (Belarminus 2017d). The KPK was not going to let Novanto get away again, and worked hard to finalise their investigation into him, so that the trial proper could begin and Novanto's pretrial case thrown out – despite the suspect's unhelpful tendency to 'fall asleep' during his interrogation by KPK officials (Aji 2017).

The KPK submitted Novanto's case file to the Jakarta Corruption Court on 6 December, and 13 December was set for the first hearing of the trial itself (Putra 2017). In accordance with art. 82(1)(d) of the KUHAP, this left only four working days for Judge Kusno to decide on the pretrial motion before it would be thrown out. For once, time was not on Novanto's side and on 14 December, Judge Kusno ruled that the pretrial hearing had, indeed, been thrown out, meaning that Mr Teflon would finally be forced to have his day in court (Belarminus 2017e). Novanto's long run of good luck finally ran out, and he was sentenced to fifteen years behind bars.

Conclusion

When pretrial hearings were introduced through the 1981 KUHAP, there were hopes that the process would be able to make amends for the widespread violations of defendants' rights that had occurred under the HIR. However, the reality has failed to meet the hopes of reformers, with principles of due process routinely violated, and torture and forced confessions common.

One of the fundamental concerns for defendants' rights is that applications for pretrial hearings can only be made after the arrest and detention has occurred. Investigators are not obliged to prove to a court that their actions in arresting or detaining a person are justified unless the suspect or accused files a pretrial motion. This leaves considerable room for abuse of power by investigators and creates incentives for officials to deny access to or discourage accused individuals from accessing legal counsel.

Further, although the pretrial hearing would appear to be the most appropriate forum for reviewing whether sufficient preliminary evidence has been obtained to warrant arrest or detention, judges have typically only wanted to review administrative aspects of arrest or detention, such as whether an arrest warrant has been obtained and a copy of the detention order delivered to family members. Judges in pretrial hearings will often not consider whether sufficient evidence has been obtained to suggest that a crime has been committed by the accused. A focus on the administrative aspects of detention means that pretrial hearings almost never question the authority of police or prosecutors to detain suspects over 'concern' that they will escape, damage or destroy evidence, or repeat the act. Judges in pretrial hearings regularly dismiss this aspect as the discretionary right of investigators and prosecutors and refuse to question it.

Another weakness of pretrial motions is that they are decided by single judges and outcomes cannot be appealed. This has led to some rather strange legal reasoning used by judges in pretrial hearings, especially in cases involving corruption suspects, as judges are safe from the scrutiny of their peers or an appeals court, which creates obvious opportunities for corrupt behaviour.

Despite the recent popularity of pretrial hearings among corruption suspects, given the large number of criminal cases handled by Indonesian courts every year, use of pretrial hearings by suspects remains limited. It is also an avenue more likely to be pursued by middle class or wealthy defendants. As noted, pretrial applications are overwhelmingly submitted by legal representatives. Poorer defendants – who may have been refused access to legal assistance, or discouraged from accessing it – are often unaware of the pretrial option.

The evolution of pretrial hearings from a mechanism supposedly designed to protect the rights of defendants from repressive actions by the state into a tool used by state officials to escape corruption charges is consistent with a broader trend in Indonesia. The past few years have seen officials and organisations exploit the tools of democracy to undermine democracy and the rule of law. In 2014, for example, democratically elected members of the House of Representatives passed a new Law to end direct elections for district and provincial leaders, and hand the power to select local leaders to regional legislatures (DPRD, Dewan Perwakilan Rakyat Daerah, DPRD, Regional People's Representative Assembly).[54] A striking element of the Novanto decision was the way in which the language of human rights was deployed to justify the dubious decision made in his favour.

One outcome of the recent spate of corruption suspects escaping charges through pretrial hearings is that it has sparked a broader conversation on the need for reform. Proposals for reform of the KUHAP have been around for almost as long as the KUHAP itself. The DPR has included the bill on revision of the KUHAP (known as the RUU KUHAP) in its list of priority bills for deliberation between 2015 and 2019, and it was included on the priority list of bills for discussion in 2018. As at March 2018, however, there had been no public deliberations on the bill and its status was listed as 'unknown' (Indonesia. Directorate General of Laws and Regulations, Ministry of Law and Human Rights 2018). The glacial pace of discussions meant a reformed KUHAP was not passed before this group of legislators' term in office expired in late 2019 and its fate under the new DPR remains uncertain.

Having said that, the most recent publicly available draft does appear to be a major improvement on the pretrial concept under the current KUHAP. Activists and legal scholars have placed considerable hope in the proposal to introduce investigating judges (*hakim pemeriksa pendahuluan*) to replace pretrial motions.[55] 'Investigating judges' are defined as officials with the authority to evaluate the process of investigation and prosecution (art. 1(7) of the RUU KUHAP). The draft bill elaborates this further, stating that they have the authority to rule and decide on the legality of arrest, detention, search, seizure of goods, and the tapping of communications. Investigating judges can also cancel or suspend detention and decide that: statements made by suspects violate their right not to incriminate themselves; evidence or testimony obtained illegally cannot be used as evidence; suspects or defendants must have legal representation; and an investigation or prosecution was conducted for an improper purpose. They can also determine whether a case should progress to prosecution (art. 111 of the RUU KUHAP).

Police investigators and prosecutors also have greatly reduced authority to order lengthy detention under the RUU KUHAP. Investigators can detain individuals for up to five days before they must be brought before the investigating judge, who can decide whether detention should be extended (see arts. 58–60).

It is necessary to point out again that these reforms, although meritorious, remain proposals only, and are likely to see major pushback from police investigators and prosecutors, who will no doubt feel that the new provisions would scale back their authority.

Reflecting on the language of the RUU KUHAP, it does appear that there is a genuine desire to right the errors of the 1981 KUHAP and ensure the rights of suspects are better protected. However, in a notoriously corrupt judicial system, there is real danger in providing investigating judges with so much authority. This does not mean that the progressive reforms proposed by the RUU KUHAP should be opposed; rather Indonesia may well find once again that the reforms designed to protect human rights again end up benefiting corrupt officials.

Notes

1 See General Elucidation to the KUHAP, para. 3(c).
2 A number of these rights had also been established through Law No. 14 of 1970 on Judicial Power. For example, art. 8 of this Law describes the presumption of innocence. The elucidation to art. 4(2) also talks in general terms about the need for the investigation process to not be convoluted or extend for years.
3 *Habeas corpus* allows a person to be brought before a court to determine whether there is legal authority to detain the person.
4 In March 2018, the Supreme Court issued a circular stating that people on the wanted persons list (DPO) could not file a pretrial application through their legal counsel or family (Supreme Court Circular 1 of 2018 on Prohibition on the Filing of Pretrial Applications by Suspects Who Have Fled or are on the Wanted Persons List). The circular was issued in response to a series of fugitives wanted for alleged corruption filing pretrial applications through others.
5 Police Chief Regulation No. 14 of 2014 on the Management of Criminal Investigations, art. 1(21). This definition of 'sufficient preliminary evidence' was also used in an earlier regulation, Police Chief Regulation No. Pol. Skep/1205/IX/2000 on Guidelines for the Administration of Criminal Investigation.
6 Constitutional Court Decision No. 21/PUU-XII/2014, 109.
7 The Criminal Code (KUHP) is largely unchanged from the Dutch Wetboek van Strafrecht (WvS) promulgated in 1918. The rupiah value of stolen goods under art. 364 is so low because it was last updated in 1960, through Government Regulation in Lieu of Law No. 16 of 1960 on Changes to the Criminal Code.
8 See also, for example: Detik (2015). These issues are discussed in more detail in Chapter 9 of this book by Rifqi Assegaf.
9 See also Constitutional Court Decision No. 21/PUU-XII/2014, p. 104.
10 In a recent example, from August 2017, the KPK arrested interim South Jakarta District Court clerk Tarmizi, for receiving a bribe of Rp. 300 million. He was arrested along with two lawyers and an 'office boy'. See Belarminus (2017a).
11 South Jakarta District Court Decision No. 04/Pid.Prap/2015/PN.Jkt.Sel.
12 In fact, in a previous pretrial hearing in 2012, Judge Suko Harsono ruled that a corruption suspect had been named a suspect illegally. South Jakarta District Court Decision No. 38/Pid.Prap/2012/PN.Jkt.Sel cancelled the suspect status of Bachtiar Abdul Fatah. Harsono refused, however, to grant the applicant's request to have his investigation terminated, stating that it was beyond the scope of pretrial hearings. Harsono was eventually reported to the Judicial Commission and Supreme Court, and received an ethical sanction for his decision, which was eventually overturned. See Rahmi (2015).
13 South Jakarta District Court Decision No. 04/Pid.Prap/2015/PN.Jkt.Sel, 237.
14 South Jakarta District Court Decision No. 04/Pid.Prap/2015/PN.Jkt.Sel, 239.

15 South Jakarta District Court Decision No. 04/Pid.Prap/2015/PN.Jkt.Sel, 242.
16 Constitutional Court Decision No. 21/PUU-XII/2014, 104.
17 Constitutional Court Decision No. 21/PUU-XII/2014, 102.
18 Constitutional Court Decision No. 21/PUU-XII/2014, 106.
19 South Jakarta District Court Decision No. 32/Pid.Prap/2015/PN.Jkt.Sel.
20 Included in these twenty-seven pretrial cases are four cases that were withdrawn and one case that was thrown out when the trial proper began (Novanto's second pretrial hearing).
21 Constitutional Court Decision No. 21/PUU-XII/2014, 107.
22 Constitutional Court Decision No. 21/PUU-XII/2014, 107.
23 The Attorney General's Office has the special authority to terminate investigations or prosecution 'for the public good' (art. 35 of Law No. 16 of 2004 on the Prosecutor's Office (*Kejaksaan*)).
24 Constitutional Court Decision 65/PUU-IX/2011, 29.
25 Supreme Court Regulation No. 4 of 2016 on Prohibition of Reconsideration Requests for Pretrial Decisions
26 Supreme Court Circular No. 4 of 2014.
27 Constitutional Court Decision No. 98/PUU-X/2012.
28 The Constitutional Court had, in fact, already considered the inclusion of civil society organisations as 'interested third parties' in Decision No. 76/PUU-X/2012. The challenge to art. 80 in this case involved an attempt to limit the meaning of the phrase 'concerned third parties' to exclude civil society. The Court rejected the case and said that it considered the phrase should include civil society organisations.
29 Supreme Court Chief Justice Decision No. 057/KMA/SK/IV/2009.
30 At the time of the Central Jakarta District Court decision, there was widespread speculation that Agusrin had bribed Central Jakarta District Court Judge Syarifuddin Umar. In 2012, Syarifuddin was convicted to four years in prison for corruption resulting in state losses of Rp. 20.16 billion, in relation to a different case.
31 'Other acts' refers to losses as a result of unlawful forced entry to property, body or property searches, and confiscation. Unlawful detention also includes detention for an extended period beyond that provided for by law (see elucidation to art. 95(1)).
32 See Government Regulation No. 27 of 1983.
33 Even Novanto's leadership of the DPR was somewhat controversial. Under the 2009 Law on Legislative Bodies (Law No. 27 of 2009 on the People's Consultative Assembly (MPR, Majelis Permusyawaratan Rakyat), People's Representative Assembly (DPR), Regional Representatives Assembly (DPD, Dewan Perwakilan Daerah) and Regional People's Representative Assembly (DPRD, Dewan Perwakilan Rakyat Daerah), the Speaker of the DPR was to come from the party with the largest proportion of seats in the DPR (art. 82(2)). Following the 2014 Legislative Election, this was the Indonesian Democratic Party of Struggle (PDI-P). But just days before the 2014 Presidential Election, the outgoing 2009–2014 DPR passed the revised Law No. 17 of 2014 on Legislative Bodies, which stated that the DPR leadership was to be selected by DPR members. This allowed members of the opposition 'Red and White Coalition' to secure all leadership positions, including that of the Speaker.

34 Constitutional Court Decision No. 20/PUU-XIV/2016, 97.

35 The pretrial hearing decision lists the occasions on which KPK investigators called Novanto for questioning (see Decision No. 97/Pid.Prap/2017/PN.Jkt.Sel, 45). Novanto did, however, attend KPK questioning on 13 December 2016 and 10 January 2017 as a witness in the case of Ministry of Home Affairs officials Irman and Sugiharto. On 6 April, he was interrogated in court as a witness in relation to their case. He was also questioned as a witness in the investigation into businessman Andi Agustinus [alias Andi Narogong] on 14 July 2017.

36 No. Sprin.Dik-56/01/07/2017.

37 Decision No. 97/Pid.Prap/2017/PN.Jkt.Sel, 5.

38 Decision No. 97/Pid.Prap/2017/PN.Jkt.Sel, 11.

39 Decision No. 41/PID.SUS/TPK/2017/PN.JKT.PST.

40 Novanto's name was, in fact, mentioned several times during the trial and the prosecutor's sentencing demand even mentioned him as having responsibility for determining the budget for the e-KTP project, but the judges' decision strangely did not mention him by name. This deeply suspicious omission prompted the Judicial Commission to form a team to investigate how Novanto's name could have gone missing. See Decision No. 97/Pid.Prap/2017/PN.Jkt.Sel, 6; Haryanto 2017; and Hakim 2017a.

41 Decision No. 97/Pid.Prap/2017/PN.Jkt.Sel, 8.

42 It is common for police and prosecutors to be 'loaned' to the KPK as investigators but, in accordance with art. 39(3) of the KPK Law, they should first be temporarily dismissed from their home institution. His pretrial hearing request stated that eleven police investigators were serving as KPK investigators without formal temporary leave from the police. See Decision No. 97/Pid.Prap/2017/PN.Jkt.Sel, 12.

43 Decision No. 97/Pid.Prap/2017/PN.Jkt.Sel, 16.

44 Decision No. 97/Pid.Prap/2017/PN.Jkt.Sel, 217. In fact, the Irman and Sugiharto case was relevant to the pretrial because it went to the question of whether there was sufficient evidence to justify Novanto's naming as a suspect.

45 Decision No. 97/Pid.Prap/2017/PN.Jkt.Sel, 219.

46 Decision No. 97/Pid.Prap/2017/PN.Jkt.Sel, 224.

47 Decision No. 97/Pid.Prap/2017/PN.Jkt.Sel, 223.

48 Decision No. 97/Pid.Prap/2017/PN.Jkt.Sel, 233.

49 Decision No. 97/Pid.Prap/2017/PN.Jkt.Sel, 231.

50 Decision No. 97/Pid.Prap/2017/PN.Jkt.Sel, 234.

51 Decision No. 97/Pid.Prap/2017/PN.Jkt.Sel, 215.

52 Decision No. 97/Pid.Prap/2017/PN.Jkt.Sel, 235.

53 Constitutional Court Decision No. 95/PUU-XV/2017.

54 Law No. 22 of 2014 on the Election of Governors, District Heads and Mayors. Following an enormous public outcry, then President Susilo Bambang Yudhoyono issued an emergency regulation, Government Regulation in Lieu of Law No. 1 of 2014 on the Election of Governors, District Heads and Mayors, to reinstate direct elections. This regulation was then passed into law by the national legislature (through Law No. 1 of 2015 on the Passage into Law of Government Regulation in Lieu of Law No. 1 of 2014 on Election of Governors, District Heads and Mayors, and revised as Law No. 8 of 2015 on the Revision of Law No. 1 of 2015).

55 In previous versions of the draft, the investigating judge was called a 'commissioner judge' (*hakim komisaris*).

References

ABC 2018. 'Setya Novanto, Indonesia's Former Speaker of Parliament, Jailed for 15 Years over Corruption Charges', 24 April www.abc.net.au/news/2018-04-24/indonesias-former-speaker-of-parliament-jailed-for-corruption/9693818

Aji, Wahyu 2017. 'KPK Kebut Limpahkan Perkara, Praperadilan Novanto Terancam Gugur', *Tribunnews.com*, 25 November www.tribunnews.com/nasional/2017/11/25/kpk-kebut-limpahkan-perkara-praperadilan-novanto-terancam-gugur

Aries, Albert 2017. 'Tren Praperadilan Baru', *Kompas*, 21 October

Arkhelaus, W. 2017. 'KPK to Reveal New Suspects in e-KTP Graft Case', *Tempo*, 13 March https://en.tempo.co/read/news/2017/03/13/055855477/KPK-to-Reveal-New-Suspects-in-e-KTP-Graft-Case

Aziz, Abdul 2017. 'Jeratan KPK yang Sering Kandas di Praperadilan', *Tirto.id*, 8 March https://tirto.id/jeratan-kpk-yang-sering-kandas-di-praperadilan-ckke

BBC Indonesia 2017. '"Dimana Benjolnya?" Reaksi Warganet terhadap "Drama Setnov": Dari Bakpao sampai Tiang Listrik', 17 November www.bbc.com/indonesia/trensosial-42021754

BBC Indonesia 2018. '"Tak Ada Benjol Bakpau" dan Lima Hal Lain yang Muncul Dari Rangkaian Sidang Setya Novanto', 29 March www.bbc.com/indonesia/amp/trensosial-43552229

Belarminus, Robertus 2017a. 'OTT KPK di PN Jaksel, Dugaan Suap Libatkan Panitera Kembali Terulang', *Kompas.com*, 22 August https://nasional.kompas.com/read/2017/08/22/07392341/ott-kpk-di-pn-jaksel-dugaan-suap-libatkan-panitera-kembali-terulang

Belarminus, Robertus 2017b. 'Novanto Mangkir Pemeriksaan KPK, Pengacara Beralasan Uji Materi di MK', *Kompas.com*, 15 November https://nasional.kompas.com/read/2017/11/15/12040721/novanto-mangkir-pemeriksaan-kpk-pengacara-beralasan-uji-materi-di-mk

Belarminus, Robertus 2017c. 'KPK Terbitkan Surat Perintah Penangkapan Terhadap Setya Novanto', *Kompas.com*, 16 November https://nasional.kompas.com/read/2017/11/16/01330181/kpk-terbitkan-surat-perintah-penangkapan-terhadap-setya-novanto

Belarminus, Robertus 2017d. 'KPK Tidak Hadir, Hakim Tunda Sidang Praperadilan Novanto hingga 7 Desember', *Kompas.com*, 30 November https://nasional.kompas.com/read/2017/11/30/12260781/kpk-tidak-hadir-hakim-tunda-sidang-praperadilan-novanto-hingga-7-desember

Belarminus, Robertus 2017e. 'Hakim Gugurkan Gugatan Praperadilan Setya Novanto', *Kompas.com*, 14 December https://nasional.kompas.com/read/2017/12/14/11150801/hakim-gugurkan-gugatan-praperadilan-setya-novanto

Budiarti, Rita Triana and Barus, Deni Muliya 2006. 'Kesaksian Nurdin Menyodok Novanto', *Gatra*, 10 August http://arsip.gatra.com/2006-08-10/majalah/artikel.php?pil=23&id=96955

Crouch, Harold A. 2010. *Political Reform in Indonesia after Soeharto*. Singapore: Institute of Southeast Asian Studies

Detik 2015. 'Kasus Pencurian Rp. 41 Ribu, Pelaku Dibui dan Jaksa Abaikan Perma', *Detik*, 13 May https://news.detik.com/berita/2914348/kasus-pencurian-rp-41-ribu-pelaku-dibui-dan-jaksa-abaikan-perma

Domingo, Pilar and Sudaryono, Leopold 2016. 'The Political Economy of Pre-trial Detention: Indonesia Case Study', *Overseas Development Institute*, September www.odi.org/sites/odi.org.uk/files/resource-documents/10911.pdf

Fatmawati, Nur Indah 2017. 'Novanto Tersangka Lagi, KPK Kirim SPDP 3 November Lalu', *Detik*, 10 November https://news.detik.com/berita/d-3722166/novanto-tersangka-lagi-kpk-kirim-spdp-3-november-lalu

Fitzpatrick, Daniel 2008. 'Culture, Ideology and Human Rights: The Case of Indonesia's Code of Criminal Procedure', in Tim Lindsey (ed.), *Indonesia: Law and Society*, 2nd edn.Sydney: Federation Press, pp. 499–515.

Gabrillin, Abba 2018. 'Dokter IGD Diberi Tahu Rawat Inap Novanto atas Persetujuan Direktur RS', *Kompas.com*, 23 March https://nasional.kompas.com/read/2018/03/23/13313681/dokter-igd-diberi-tahu-rawat-inap-novanto-atas-persetujuan-direktur-rs

Hakim, Rakhmat Nur 2017a. 'KY Bentuk Tim Investigasi soal Hilangnya Nama Setya Novanto dalam Berkas Putusan', *Kompas.com*, 12 August https://nasional.kompas.com/read/2017/08/12/23355141/ky-bentuk-tim-investigasi-soal-hilangnya-nama-setya-novanto-dalam-berkas

Hakim, Rakhmat Nur 2017b. 'Novanto Tak Ada, Pengacara Sebut Penyidik KPK Geledah Rumah', *Kompas.com*, 16 November https://nasional.kompas.com/read/2017/11/16/07182831/novanto-tak-ada-pengacara-sebut-penyidik-kpk-geledah-rumah

Hart, J't 1987. 'Aspects of Criminal Justice', in Hans Thoolen (ed.), *Indonesia and the Rule of Law: Twenty Years of New Order Government: A Study*. London: Frances Pinter, pp. 166–208

Haryanto, Alexander 2017. 'Nama Setya Novanto Kembali Disebut dalam Tuntutan e-KTP', *Tirto.id*, 22 June https://tirto.id/nama-setya-novanto-kembali-disebut-dalam-tuntutan-e-ktp-crmn

Hidayat, Faiq 2018. 'Tiba di Pengadilan, Novanto Siap Hadapi Sidang Tuntutan e-KTP', *Detik*, 29 March https://news.detik.com/berita/d-3942632/tiba-di-pengadilan-novanto-siap-hadapi-sidang-tuntutan-e-ktp

Hukumonline 2003. 'Buyung: Tidak Perlu Ada Hakim Komisaris', *Hukumonline*, 18 October www.hukumonline.com/berita/baca/hol9001/buyung-tidak-perlu-ada-hakim-komisaris

Hukumonline 2010. 'Lagi, Hakim Perluas Objek Praperadilan', *Hukumonline*, 4 November www.hukumonline.com/berita/baca/lt4cd2decce98cf/hakim-perluas-objek-praperadilan

Hukumonline 2012. 'MA Tolak PK Agusrin', *Hukumonline*, 27 November www.hukumonline.com/berita/baca/lt50b4bdec77368/ma-tolak-pk-agusrin

ICJR 2014. 'Pretrial Hearing in Indonesia: Theory, History and Practice in Indonesia'. Jakarta: Institute for Criminal Justice Reform

Indonesia. Directorate General of Laws and Regulations, Ministry of Law and Human Rights 2018. 'RUU tentang Hukum Acara Pidana', http://peraturan.go.id/ruu-tentang-hukum-acara-pidana.html

Ihsanuddin 2017. 'Direktur RSCM: Novanto Sudah Tak Perlu Rawat Inap', *Kompas.com*, 20 November https://nasional.kompas.com/read/2017/11/20/00332581/direktur-rscm-novanto-sudah-tak-perlu-rawat-inap

Indrayana, Denny 2017. 'Acid Attack Will Not Weaken Novel Baswedan or the KPK', *Indonesia at Melbourne*, 19 April http://indonesiaatmelbourne.unimelb.edu.au/acid-attack-will-not-weaken-novel-baswedan-or-the-kpk/

The Jakarta Post 2015. 'Former Makassar Mayor Wins Pretrial Court Decision', 12 May www.thejakartapost.com/news/2015/05/12/former-makassar-mayor-wins-pretrial-court-decision.html

Jensen, Fergus and Da Costa, Agustinus Beo 2015. 'Indonesia Minister Distances Government from Freeport Extortion Allegation', *Reuters*, 14 December https://uk.reuters.com/article/uk-indonesia-freeport/indonesia-minister-distances-government-from-freeport-extortion-allegation-idUKKBN0TX1C120151214

Kahfi, Kharishar 2017. 'Setya Cleared as Suspect after Winning Pretrial Motion against KPK', *Jakarta Post*, 29 September www.thejakartapost.com/news/2017/09/29/setya-cleared-as-suspect-after-winning-pretrial-motion-against-kpk.html

Kompas.com 2010. 'Serahkan Kasus Agusrin', *Kompas.com*, 5 November https://nasional.kompas.com/read/2010/11/05/05265966/serahkan.kasus.agusrin

KPK (Corruption Eradication Commission) 2016. *Annual Report 2015*. Jakarta: KPK www.kpk.go.id/images/Annual%20Report%202015%20low.pdf

KPK (Corruption Eradication Commission) 2017. *Annual Report 2016*. Jakarta: KPK www.kpk.go.id/images/Laporan%20Tahunan%20KPK%202016%20Bahasa%20Indonesia.pdf

KPK (Corruption Eradication Commission) 2018. *Annual Report 2017*. Jakarta: KPK www.kpk.go.id/nuweb/images/Laporan%20Tahunan%20KPK%202017.pdf

Kumparan 2017. '7 Kejanggalan Putusan Praperadilan Setya Novanto', 5 October https://kumparan.com/@kumparannews/7-kejanggalan-putusan-praperadilan-setya-novanto

Lev, Daniel S. 1985. 'Colonial Law and the Genesis of the Indonesian State', *Indonesia* 40, October, 57–74.

Lev, Daniel S. 2008. 'Between State and Society: Professional Lawyers and Reform in Indonesia', in Tim Lindsey (ed.), *Indonesia: Law and Society*. 2nd edn. Sydney: Federation Press, pp. 48–67

Liputan6 2005. 'Ribut-Ribut Pupuk Beracun Made in Singapura', *Liputan6*, 25 February http://news.liputan6.com/read/96346/ribut-ribut-pupuk-beracun-imade-ini-singapura

Liputan6 2013. 'Ruangan Digeledah KPK, Ini Dugaan Keterlibatan Setya Novanto', *Liputan6*, 20 March www.liputan6.com/news/read/539864/ruangan-digeledah-kpk-ini-dugaan-keterlibatan-setya-novanto

McBeth, John 2017a. 'Indonesia's Mr Teflon Goes Free Again', *Asia Times*, 5 October www.atimes.com/article/indonesias-mr-teflon-goes-free/

McBeth, John 2017b. 'Indonesia's Mr Teflon Finally in the Dock', *Asia Times*, 20 November www.atimes.com/article/indonesias-mr-teflon-finally-dock/

Medistiara, Yulida 2017. 'Setya Novanto Sempat Ajukan Praperadilan Lagi Sebelum "Hilang"', *Detik*, 16 November https://news.detik.com/berita/d-3729174/setya-novanto-sempat-ajukan-praperadilan-lagi-sebelum-hilang

Pakpahan, Vanroy 2011. 'KPK Analisis Dugaan Korupsi Pengadaan e-KTP', *Tribunnews.com*, 7 September www.tribunnews.com/nasional/2011/09/07/kpk-analisis-dugaan-korupsi-pengadaan-e-ktp

Putra, Muhammad Andika 2017. 'Sia-Sia Praperadilan Setya Novanto', *CNN Indonesia*, 8 December www.cnnindonesia.com/nasional/20171208083351-12-260984/sia-sia-praperadilan-setya-novanto

Rachman, Dylan Aprialdo 2018. 'Fredrich Yunadi Divonis 7 Tahun Penjara', *Kompas.com*, 28 June https://nasional.kompas.com/read/2018/06/28/17040681/fredrich-yunadi-divonis7tahun-penjara

Rahadian, Lalu 2016. 'Kasus Pemufakatan Jahat Setya Novanto Dihentikan Sementara', *CNN Indonesia*, 15 April www.cnnindonesia.com/nasional/20160415151743-12-124221/kasus-pemufakatan-jahat-setya-novanto-dihentikan-sementara

Rahmi, Novrieza 2015. 'Metamorphosis "Wajah" Praperadilan', *Hukumonline*, 5 June www.hukumonline.com/berita/baca/lt55716335453cd/metamorfosis-wajah-praperadilan

Republika 2016. 'Dari 57 Gugatan Praperadilan, KPK Kalah 4 Perkara', *Republika*, 15 June www.republika.co.id/berita/nasional/hukum/16/06/15/o8synp335-dari-57-gugatan-praperadilan-kpk-kalah-4-perkara

Reuters 2016. 'Indonesia's Parliament Reappoints Scandal-hit Speaker', *Reuters*, 30 November www.reuters.com/article/us-indonesia-parliament/indonesias-parliament-reappoints-scandal-hit-speaker-idUSKBN13P1CO

Saragih, Bagus BT 2015. 'Hadi's Pretrial Victory a "Disaster" for KPK', *Jakarta Post*, 26 May www.thejakartapost.com/news/2015/05/26/hadi-s-pretrial-victory-a-disaster-kpk.html

Sari, Dianing 2011. 'Isu Suap akim Syarifuddin Beredar Sejak Maret 2011', *Tempo*, 3 June https://nasional.tempo.co/read/338462/isu-suap-hakim-syarifuddin-beredar-sejak-maret-2011

Sheany 2018. 'Setya Novanto's Doctor Sentenced to 3 Years in Prison for Obstruction of Justice', *The Jakarta Globe*, 16 July https://jakartaglobe.id/news/setya-novantos-doctor-sentenced-to-3-years-in-prison-for-obstruction-of-justice

Sinaga, Eri Komar 2015. 'Budi Gunawan Ditetapkan Sebagai Tersangka Saat Menjabat Kabiro Pembinaan Karir', *Tribunnews.com*, 13 January www.tribunnews.com/nasional/2015/01/13/budi-gunawan-ditetapkan-sebagai-tersangka-saat-menjabat-kabiro-pembinaan-karir

Sundaryani, Fedina S 2015. 'Police Name Former Deputy Law Minister Suspect in Graft Case', *The Jakarta Post*, 26 March www.thejakartapost.com/news/2015/03/26/police-name-former-deputy-law-minister-suspect-graft-case.html

Syukur, M. 2014. 'Mantan Gubernur Riau Rusli Zainal Divonis 14 Tahun Penjara', *Liputan6*, 12 March www.liputan6.com/news/read/2021835/mantan-gubernur-riau-rusli-zainal-divonis-14-tahun-penjara

Taher, Andrian Pratama 2017. 'Alasan Sidang Praperadilan Setnov Ditunda 20 September 2017', *Tirto.id*, 12 September https://tirto.id/alasan-sidang-praperadilan-setnov-ditunda-20-september-2017-cwqM

Tashandra, Nabilla 2016. 'MKD Pulihkan Nama Baik Setya Novanto di Kasus "Papa Minta Saham"', *Kompas.com*, 28 September https://nasional.kompas.com/read/2016/09/28/15363421/mkd.pulihkan.nama.baik.setya.novanto.di.kasus.papa.minta.saham

Tashandra, Nabilla 2017. 'Pengacara: Pelipis Novanto Benjol Segede Bakpao', *Kompas.com*, 16 November https://nasional.kompas.com/read/2017/11/16/20145241/pengacara-pelipis-novanto-benjol-segede-bakpao

Tempo 2010. 'Aliran Janggal Rekening Jenderal', *Tempo*, 28 June

Tempo 2016. 'Setya Novanto Declares Golkar Support for the Government', *Tempo*, 17 May https://en.tempo.co/read/news/2016/05/17/055771592/Setya-Novanto-Declares-Golkar-Support-for-the-Government

Tempo 2017. 'Mangkir Panggilan KPK, Setya Novanto: Saya Mengabdi Rakyat Dulu', *Tempo*, 6 November https://nasional.tempo.co/read/1031331/mangkir-panggilan-kpk-setya-novanto-saya-mengabdi-rakyat-dulu

Tribunnews.com 2013. 'Ini Kronologi Rekayasa Proyek KTP Elektronik Versi Nazaruddin', *Tribunnews.com*, 25 September www.tribunnews.com/nasional/2013/09/25/ini-kronologi-rekayasa-proyek-ktp-elektronik-versi-nazaruddin?page=all

United Nations Human Rights Council 2008. 'Report of the Special Rapporteur on Torture and Other Cruel, Inhuman or Degrading Treatment or Punishment, Manfred Nowak: Addendum: Mission to Indonesia, 10 March, A/HRC/7/3/ Add.7

United States. Department of State 2016. 'Indonesia 2016 Human Rights Report', Country Reports on Human Rights Practices for 2016', www.state.gov/documents/ organization/265550.pdf

Waskita, Ferdinand 2011. 'Praperadilan Nazaruddin Ditolak Hakim Jaksel', *Tribunnews.com*, 14 November www.tribunnews.com/nasional/2011/11/14/ praperadilan-nazaruddin-ditolak-hakim-jaksel

Widianto, Willy 2010. 'Kejaksaan dan KPK Kalah di Sidang Praperadilan Gubernur Bengkulu', *Tribunnews.com*, 4 November www.tribunnews.com/nasional/2010/11/ 04/kejaksaan-dan-kpk-kalah-di-sidang-praperadilan-gubernur-bengkulu

Legislation

Herziene Inlandsch Reglement (HIR) colonial procedural law 1941, revised in 1926 – a revision of *Indisch Reglement*, 1848

Wetboek van Strafrecht (WvS)

Criminal Code (*Kitab Undang-Undang Hukum Pidana*, KUHP: Law No. 1 of 1946 as amended by Law No. 27 of 1999 on the Indonesian Criminal Code)Criminal Procedure Code (*Kitab Undang-Undang Hukum Pidana*, KUHAP)

Law No. 28 of 1999 on State Officials That Are Clean and Free from Corruption, Collusion and Nepotism

Law No. 31 of 1999 on Corruption (as revised by Law No. 20 of 2001)

Law No. 30 of 2002 on the Corruption Eradication Commission

Law No. 16 of 2004 on the Prosecutor's Office (*Kejaksaan*)

Law No. 14 of 1970 on Judicial Power

Law No. 22 of 2014 on the Election of Governors, District Heads and Mayors

Law No. 17 of 2014 on the People's Consultative Assembly (MPR), People's Representative Assembly (DPR), Regional Representative Assembly (DPD) and Regional People's Representative Assembly (DPRD) (2014 Law on Legislative Bodies)

Law No. 8 of 2015 on the Revision of Law No. 1 of 2015 on the Passage into Law of Government Regulation in Lieu of Law No. 1 of 2014 on Election of Governors, District Heads and Mayors

Law No. 1 of 2015 on the Passage into Law of Government Regulation in Lieu of Law No. 1 of 2014 on Election of Governors, District Heads and Mayors

Government Regulation in Lieu of Law No. 16 of 1960 on Changes to the Criminal Code

Government Regulation No. 27 of 1983 on the Implementation of the Criminal Procedure Code

Government Regulation in Lieu of Law No. 1 of 2014 on the Election of Governors, District Heads and Mayors

Police Chief Regulation No. 14 of 2014 on the Management of Criminal Investigations

Police Chief Regulation No. Pol. Skep/1205/IX/2000 on Guidelines for the Administration of Criminal Investigation

Supreme Court Regulation No. 4 of 2016 on Prohibition of Reconsideration Requests for Pretrial Decisions
Supreme Court Circular No. 4 of 2014
Supreme Court Circular No. 1 of 2018 on Prohibition on the Filing of Pretrial Applications by Suspects Who Have Fled or are on the Wanted Persons List
Corruption Eradication Commission Standard Operating Procedures for Investigation No. 01/23/2008

Decisions

Constitutional Court Decision No. 65/PUU-IX/2011
Constitutional Court Decision No. 76/PUU-X/2012
Constitutional Court Decision No. 98/PUU-X/2012
Constitutional Court Decision No. 21/PUU-XII/2014
Constitutional Court Decision No. 20/PUU-XIV/2016
Constitutional Court Decision No. 95/PUU-XV/2017
Central Jakarta District Court Decision No. 41/Pid.Sus/TPK/2017/PN.Jkt.Pst
South Jakarta District Court Decision No. 38/Pid.Prap/2012/PN.Jkt.Sel
South Jakarta District Court Decision No. 04/Pid.Prap/2015/PN.Jkt.Sel
South Jakarta District Court Decision No. 32/Pid.Prap/2015/PN.Jkt.Sel
South Jakarta District Court Decision No. 97/Pid.Prap/2017/PN.Jkt.Sel
South Jakarta District Court Decision No. 145/Pid.Pra/2017/PN Jkt.Sel
Supreme Court Chief Justice Decision No. 057/KMA/SK/IV/2009
Investigation Order No. Sprin.Dik-56/01/07/2017

6 Reconsidering reform

The Supreme Court, the Constitutional Court and Indonesia's 'Extraordinary Legal Measure'

Tim Lindsey[1]

In 1974, two men, Sengkon and Karta,[2] were accused of the murder in Bojongsari, Bekasi, of a food-stall vendor, Sulaiman, and his wife, Siti Haya, who was also raped. Sengkon and Karta were local farmers and, on some accounts, *preman* (gangsters). Sengkon's name was allegedly whispered by the dying man as he was taken to hospital, and a sandal supposedly belonging to him was found near the scene of the crime.

In detention, Sengkon and Karta were beaten by the police and they later said they had been forced to sign confessions. They were convicted in the Bekasi district court in October 1977; Sengkon received twelve years' imprisonment and Karta seven. Sengkon appealed unsuccessfully to the West Java High Court; Karta did not appeal.[3] Neither could afford cassation to Indonesia's final court of appeal, the Supreme Court (Mahkamah Agung, Indonesia's highest appeal court), and the time period to do so soon elapsed.

When the pair were six years into their sentences, another Bojongsari local in prison for theft, Gunel,[4] voluntarily confessed to the murders and the rape, acknowledging that Sengkon and Karta were innocent. Eventually, he was convicted and sentenced to twelve years' imprisonment. Sengkon and Karta thus found themselves serving lengthy prison sentences for crimes of which they claimed they were innocent and to which another man had confessed. However, because the time periods for appeal by the two men had expired, there seemed to be no obvious remedy available to them.[5]

There had previously been a form of final case review by the Supreme Court that might have assisted Sengkon and Karta. This was a colonial legacy, a process known under the Dutch as the *Herziening van Arresten en Vonnissen* or simply *herziening*. Pursuant to art. 37 of the *Reglement op de Strafvordering* (S.1847–40) it was a right both the convicted person and the prosecutor could exercise (Harahap 2008: 607–44).[6] This right had been confirmed by Law No. 19 of 1964 on Judicial Powers (Pompe 2005: 280; 244). Article 15 stated that a *peninjauan kembali* ('PK' or judicial reconsideration) review could be conducted by the Supreme Court of a decision that has acquired *kekuatan hukum tetap* ('binding or permanent legal force') that is, a decision in respect of which no further appeal is otherwise possible, such as the decisions in Sengkon and Karta's cases. Article 15 added, however, that this could only be done in circumstances that were to be regulated later by statute. As no such statute had been passed by the 1960s, the Supreme Court issued a series of regulations to establish a procedure for reconsideration (Regulation No. 1 of 1969 and Circular Letter (*surat edaran*, a form of practice note, issued by the Supreme Court) No. 18 of 1969). These 'caused quite an uproar', as the question of the circumstances in which such final judicial review was appropriate was thought by many to be a matter that was for the legislature to decide by statute, not the courts through their internal administration (Pompe 2005: 244–5).

In the following year, art. 21 of the latest version of the Law on Judicial Powers (Law No. 14 of 1970) confirmed the existence of the reconsideration review but still left its content to be determined by statute. According to Pompe (2005: 244), Subekti, then Chief Justice of the Supreme Court, expected the government to quickly issue further legislation to implement art. 21, and so responded to criticism of the regulations by suspending them with Supreme Court Regulation No. 1 of 1971. He then 'definitively repealed' reconsideration review by issuing Supreme Court Regulation No. 1 of 1976. This acknowledges in its preamble that, as a statute had not then been passed that specifically implemented art. 21, the court had no basis proceed to regulate judicial reconsideration. This meant that 'the one hundred review cases pending before the Supreme Court were simply dismissed' (Pompe 2005: 245). This is why by the time Gunel's confession became known, there was no judicial mechanism available to Sengkon and Karta to overturn their conviction.

Fortunately for them, Albert Hasibuan, a member of the national legislature, the DPR (Dewan Perwakilan Rakyat, Peoples' Representative Assembly), and then one of Indonesia's most prominent legal figures, decided to take up their case. He began to lobby the authorities to find a way to have them released. As a result, Sengkon and Karta's cases became widely publicised, and media attention turned it into a national controversy. The Supreme Court eventually gave way to the pressure this created to find a solution to the two men's plight by passing Regulation No. 1 of 1980 on Judicial Reconsideration. This revived reconsideration by the Supreme Court of judicial decisions that had acquired binding legal force. It did so even though there was still no statute in existence that specifically implemented art. 21 of the 1970 Law on Judicial Powers.

In January 1981, Sengkon and Karta were finally exonerated and released from prison after the reconsideration application they made under the new Regulation was upheld by the Supreme Court.[7] Unfortunately, they did not enjoy their freedom for long. Sengkon was ill with tuberculosis he had contracted in prison, and their land had been sold by their families to pay legal expenses and living costs. They both unsuccessfully sued the state for compensation,[8] but not long after release, Karta – who had twelve children – died after being run over by a truck, and Sengkon succumbed to his illness soon after that.

At the same time that Sengkon and Karta's cases were causing widespread controversy about the need for a remedy to be available to convicted persons who had suffered injustice but had no further avenue of appeal, the DPR was debating a bill for a new Criminal Procedure Code (*Kitab Undang-undang Hukum Acara Pidana,* KUHAP). This was eventually passed on 31 December 1981 as Law No. 8 of that year. Article 263 of this statute contained detailed provisions dealing with the requirements for judicial reconsideration in criminal cases, and remains the principal source of law in this area today. This chapter examines these provisions in light of the issues in Sengkon and Karta's cases that gave rise to them. In doing so, it uses judicial reconsideration as a case study to explore the politics of legal policy formation in Indonesia, including the problematic relationship between the judicial system's 'twin peaks', the Supreme Court, the apex appeal court, and the Constitutional Court, the sole authority on constitutional interpretation of statutes.

KUHAP and the revival of reconsideration

In KUHAP, judicial reconsideration is described as an 'extraordinary legal measure' (*upaya hukum luar biasa*).[9] Article 263(1) states that it can be sought by a convicted person or his or her heir from the Supreme Court in respect of any judgment that has acquired binding legal force, except an acquittal or dismissal. Although often described as a 'final appeal', judicial reconsideration is better understood as the reopening of a case (Butt and Lindsey 2018: 89). Using this power, the Supreme Court can reconsider almost all final and binding judgments of any Indonesian court, including its own cassation decisions, and it can, if necessary, re-decide them. To lodge a judicial reconsideration application and, ultimately, for it to succeed, art. 263(2) requires the applicant to demonstrate one of the following:

- a new circumstance or determinative evidence (*novum*) has come to light that, if known during the trial, would have probably resulted in a full acquittal, a dismissal of the prosecutor's case or the case being brought under a less serious charge (art. 263(2)a);
- a fact or situation established in one decision contradicts aspects of other cases 263(2)b; or
- an oversight or obvious mistake was made in the decision 263(2)c.

The Elucidation – the formal explanatory memorandum that accompanies all regulation in Indonesia – to art. 263 states that the provisions sets out grounds for judicial reconsideration that are *limitatif,* or limited or restricted, in nature. This is important, for reasons that are explained later.

If the defendant or prosecutor appeals to a High Court or to the Supreme Court on cassation, the court hearing the appeal can impose a higher criminal penalty than the penalty imposed by the decision being appealed. It can, therefore, sometimes be risky for defendants to lodge these appeals. By contrast, a defendant takes no such risk by submitting a request for judicial reconsideration. Article 266(3) provides that in a reconsideration decision, the Supreme Court may not increase the penalty imposed in the most recent decision relating to the case. Article 264(3) adds that, by contrast to civil cases, there is no time limit for lodging judicial reconsideration applications in criminal cases.

Reconsideration and the Supreme Court's caseload

These provisions have attracted controversy ever since KUHAP was first proposed. In part, this was because the revival of judicial reconsideration proved extremely popular with litigants. In fact, it became so commonplace that it effectively turned the Indonesian judicial structure from a 'three-layered structure into a four-layered one' (Pompe 2005: 246). One reason for this at the time was that although arts. 268(1) of KUHAP and 66(2) of Law No. 14 of 1985 on the Supreme Court were explicit that application for judicial reconsideration could not act as a stay on enforcement of the court order being challenged, in reality it often did. Although art. 268(1) of KUHAP states that 'an application for judicial reconsideration cannot delay or stop the enforcement of the judgment' in question, many 'lower court judges were afraid to enforce' judgments being reviewed by the Supreme Court (which can decide whether they are promoted and where they are posted). In addition, many judges, including some in the Supreme Court, took the view that, notwithstanding the statutory provisions, enforcement can be stayed for 'a good reason', such as judicial reconsideration (Pompe 2005: 246). The result was that judicial reconsideration soon became, and remains, a popular strategic weapon for many litigants.

This created significant caseload problems for the Supreme Court. One Supreme court judge told Pompe (2005: 284) in the early 1990s that 'half of all Supreme Court cases are decided in [reconsideration]'. The Supreme Court is not a trial court. Its caseload therefore consists mainly of cassation and reconsideration cases,[10] so this comment suggests many cassations were being routinely reheard at reconsideration level. While the claim that half the Supreme Court's cases were reconsiderations 'may be an exaggeration', by 1994, reconsiderations certainly 'generated more cases than the entire court docket in the 1950s', with around 650 reconsideration cases decided annually, and a backlog of 550 (Pompe 2005: 284). Pompe recounts the comment by Supreme Court judge Yahya Harahap that many of these cases were 'spurious' and that the ratio of 'well-founded' reconsideration applications to 'irrational' ones was 'one to a thousand' (Pompe 2005: 284).

Today, many of these problems remain. As the court's overall caseload has grown, so have reconsideration cases. Although the court had cut its reconsideration case backlog to just 99 by end-2019, it had to decide 6,672 such cases that year in order to do so (Mahkamah Agung 2020). This meant reconsiderations were around a third of the 20,058 cases decided that year. In the previous year, the situation was much the same. It decided a total of

5,558 reconsideration cases, with a backlog left of 136. The total number of decisions issued the court by in 2018 across all types of cases was 17,638, so reconsiderations again constituted around a third of the court's work in that year (Mahkamah Agung 2019).[11]

It is therefore not surprising that many Supreme Court judges still regard judicial reconsideration as an unnecessary burden, and that some of its judges, including successive chief justices, have made repeated efforts to restrict its availability.

Is more than one judicial reconsideration application allowed?

The best example of this relates to art. 268(3) of KUHAP, which states bluntly that 'a request for judicial reconsideration of decision can only be made once'. The 2009 Judicial Powers Law (art. 24(2)) and the 2009 Supreme Court Law (art. 66(1)) also imposed a blanket prohibition on lodging more than one judicial reconsideration in any case, reiterating that the Supreme Court cannot 'conduct a judicial reconsideration of a judicial reconsideration'. These provisions sit well with judicial concerns about the workload reconsideration creates, and the court was long firm in its application of the rule they established. However, the potential injustice created if new exculpatory evidence emerges after a first application for judicial reconsideration has failed is obvious. Consider the predicament Sengkon and Karta might have been in had Gunel confessed after they had filed a reconsideration application and had it rejected.

Constitutional Court decisions on multiple reconsiderations

Indonesia's Constitutional Court (*Mahkamah Konstitusi*) is not an appeal court. Its jurisdiction is strictly limited to determining the constitutionality of statutes, adjudicating impeachment proceedings, and resolving disputes between state institutions and about election results (Butt and Lindsey 2018, 101–8). It cannot directly alter the judgments of other courts and cannot conduct judicial reconsideration. Despite this, its power to strike out statutory provisions that it considers unconstitutional has made it an important actor in controversies over interpretation of the KUHAP, sometimes to the frustration of the Supreme Court.

In 2013, the former Chair of the Corruption Eradication Commission (KPK), Antasari Azhar, who was serving an eighteen-year sentence for murder, wanted to bring a second judicial reconsideration application to have his case reopened. The details of the case remain disputed but Antasari claimed he was framed because of the KPK's success in investigating corruption among law enforcement officials. He challenged the constitutionality of art. 268(3) of KUHAP before the Constitutional Court. He succeeded, and the Court invalidated art. 268(3). However, the Court's decision did not mention the Judicial Powers and Supreme Court Law provisions that also prohibited multiple applications for judicial reconsideration. In short, while the Constitutional court struck down a provision imposing the limitation in criminal cases, it left in force others that appeared to impose the very same limitation for all cases, including criminal ones.

This was the argument relied on by Supreme Court Chief Justice Hatta Ali when he defiantly issued Circular Letter No. 7 of 2014.[12] Cleaving to his court's longstanding desire to contain its workload, he stated that, despite the Constitutional Court's decision, application for judicial reconsideration could only be made on one occasion, and he specifically ordered lower courts not to pass on more than one judicial reconsideration application per case. This was a direct challenge to the Constitutional Court's authority, and it caused some consternation and uncertainty. It led the government to announce that it would convene meetings of the two courts to resolve their differences, and was preparing a Government Regulation on judicial reconsideration to clarify the situation, although this seems never to have eventuated (Adzikia 2015).

The Constitutional Court made more efforts to settle the debate in 2016 and 2017,[13] holding in a series of further decisions that, because the substance of arts. 24(2) of the Judicial Powers Law and 66(1) of the Supreme Court Law were the same as art. 268(3), these other provisions no longer had binding legal power so far as they related to criminal cases.[14] Using words that reflected the debate sparked by the Sengkon and Karta case in the 1980s, the Constitutional Court said that the right to more than one judicial reconsideration was necessary in criminal cases because the goal of reconsideration in criminal cases was to determine the 'material truth', to protect human rights and prevent arbitrary actions by the state.[15]

This seemed to resolve the matter, and according to its Registry, the Supreme Court heard 3,487 judicial reconsideration requests in 2016, 3.2 per cent of which were a 'PK of a PK decision' (Nursobah 2017). In other words, after much confusion, the Constitutional Court had forced a reluctant Supreme Court to a position on judicial reconsideration that, while contrary to the words of KUHAP, resembles its original purpose: to ensure that the right to re-open the case be available to persons convicted of a criminal offence to prevent them suffering injustice.

However, this is a story that may not yet be over. As explained below, the draft KUHAP bill currently before the DPR contains a provision that would again limit reconsideration applications to just one.

Can the prosecution apply for judicial reconsideration of an acquittal?

Another aspect of KUHAP's provisions on judicial reconsideration that has been extremely contentious is whether prosecutors may seek judicial reconsideration, particularly of an acquittal. This controversy reflects major differences among Supreme Court judges about the purpose of reconsideration, and, importantly, some profound disagreements in the wider law and policy community, including among prosecutors, lawyers, scholars, activists and politicians, about how the reconsideration provisions of KUHAP should be interpreted.

Understanding the debates in the DPR in the early 1980s regarding KUHAP, and, in particular, judicial reconsideration, is useful for understanding these disagreements. This is because of the principle that where there is ambiguity a statute should be interpreted in accordance with the intention of its original drafters. I will therefore discuss purposive interpretation at Indonesian law, and the DPR debates and their application to KUHAP, before turning to discuss the substantive law dealing with prosecutors' rights to seek reconsideration.

Purposive interpretation of KUHAP

The purposive interpretation of legislation is a notion long established in Indonesian law, and the Dutch phrase *wethistoirsche interpretatie* is sometimes used to refer to it. The principle is often cited by Indonesian legal scholars, and has been relied upon in recent decisions of both the Constitutional Court and Supreme Court.

For example, in a decision reviewing the statute establishing the Indonesian Judicial Commission,[16] Indonesia's Constitutional Court adopted a purposive approach to interpreting that statute, based on an historical assessment of the original intent of the drafters of the 1945 Constitution. Likewise, in a case dealing with the South Sulawesi Provincial Election Commission,[17] the Supreme Court referred to Dutch legal scholar Professor L. J. Van Apeldoorn (1886–1979) to hold that 'interpretation aims to find and apply the intention of the drafters of the law where that law is expressed ambiguously'. Similarly, in a case relating to the company PT. Perkebunan Nusantara XI Pasa Djatiroto,[18] the Supreme Court, upholding the applicant's reconsideration application, referred to the applicant's reliance on writing by Apeldoorn and Professor J. H. A. Logemann (1892–1969) to support the proposition that in interpreting a statute a lawyer must consider the intention and wishes of the legislators to understand what was intended by them. Logemann is, in fact, the standard reference cited in dozens of Supreme Court cases as authority for the principle that judges must seek to interpret ambiguity in a statute in accordance with the intention of those who drafted it.

It is therefore significant that in the course of debate on the KUHAP bill in the DPR, a shift took place in the provisions that dealt specifically with prosecutors' right to apply for judicial reconsideration. This shift has important implications for interpreting art. 263 as it was finally passed, and it appears to have been a direct response to public anger regarding the Sengkon and Karta case.

The DPR debates

KUHAP was welcomed by reformers as a progressive reform, and legislators were under some pressure to pass a new code of criminal procedure law that could provide stronger guarantees of the rights of defendants. As Lev says, 'a milestone in post-revolutionary legal history, it is Indonesia's first new major code, replacing at last the procedural regime of the HIR[19] Rules of criminal procedure to define the balance in relationships between state agencies and private citizens' (Lev 1996: 156)

In the first draft of KUHAP presented to the DPR by the government, judicial reconsideration was dealt with in art. 257(1). Reflecting the colonial model, this provided that the right to apply for judicial reconsideration was granted to the 'person convicted or interested parties or the *Jaksa Agung* [Chief Prosecutor/Attorney General]'. In the Law as passed, however, judicial reconsideration is dealt with in art. 263, which states that judicial reconsideration may be sought only by 'the person convicted and his/her heir'. The rights of 'interested parties' and the Chief Prosecutor to seek judicial reconsideration had been deleted. Moreover, art. 263(1) specifically excludes application for reconsideration in respect of 'an acquittal or dismissal'. The Elucidation to art. 263 had also been changed to make it clear that the right to apply for reconsideration is to be *limitatif* (limited).

The reasons for the deletion of 'interested parties', the Chief Prosecutor and the exclusion of acquittals and dismissals are clear from the debates in the DPR in relation to the KUHAP bill. The Development Faction (Fraksi Karya Pembangunan) was the largest faction in the DPR at the time, and it represented Golkar, the government's political vehicle, and thus Soeharto's administration. Its views were doubtless influenced by the fact that Albert Hasibuan, in addition to being Sengkon and Karta's lawyer, was also a member of this faction and it was, in fact, he who delivered its initial speech on the bill.[20] In its Final Opinion, the Development Faction stated that it 'is clear that [judicial reconsideration] ... is made precisely to protect the interests of the convicted person' (Direktorat Jenderal Hukum dan Perundang-undangan 1981: 213). Hasibuan's position was backed by the Armed Forces Faction (*Fraksi ABRI*), which can also be taken to represent the views of the military-backed New Order government. In fact, ABRI went further than Golkar and, in its Final Opinion, it identified the Sengkon and Karta case as the main reason for the introduction of the new art. 263:

> A basis was sought to free Sengkon and Karta ... discussion of [the judicial reconsideration provision in the Bill] only happened after the occurrence of the Sengkon and Karta incident, so ... all parties felt the necessity to regulate this problem in the KUHAP bill. Given [Sengkon and Karta] it was easy to reach agreement. All parties feel that the ability for a decision that has already acquired fixed legal force to be

> reconsidered constitutes a guarantee that a person punished because of an error can be free again.
>
> (Direktorat Jenderal Hukum dan Perundang-undangan 1981, 224)

In summary, the following seems clear from the DPR debates: first, the drafting of art. 263 was directly influenced by the Sengkon and Karta case and a consequent desire to ensure that the right to re-open the case be available to persons convicted of a criminal offence to prevent them suffering injustice; and second, that the government unambiguously supported this approach.

Indeed, the Elucidation to KUHAP as passed clearly reflects the general aspirations of the DPR members to create a statute that was protective of defendants and their rights. The preamble states, for example, that pre-existing procedural laws in Indonesia 'do not in fact guarantee and protect human rights [and] protection of human dignity' as should be the case in a nation that respects the rule of law (s. 1). Existing colonial procedural laws therefore needed to be repealed because they are 'no longer in accordance with the nation's legal aspirations' and need to be replaced with new procedural laws based on the *Pancascila* (the state ideology) and the Constitution. Section 2 of the preamble adds that 'respect for and implementation of human rights' is central to the new procedural laws and that they should enshrine a more 'modern' approach. More particularly, s. 4 adds that laws must now have a greater focus on the rights and obligations of the criminal defendant and, accordingly, '...this Code also contains the rights and obligations of those who are subject to the prosecution process...' Although, as Simon Butt and I show in Chapter 3 of this book, KUHAP has, in many ways failed to meet these aspirations, largely due to institutional resistance (Lev 1996: 157), the aims of the drafters are nonetheless unambiguous.

This explains why references in the original KUHAP bill to judicial reconsideration being available to the prosecutor and were rejected in the course of debate in favour of the right being a right 'limited' to the 'convicted person and his or her heirs' that cannot be used in respect of 'an acquittal or dismissal'. As mentioned, this issue has nonetheless since become a matter of great controversy. The question of whether prosecutors can use the reconsideration mechanism to re-open an acquittal despite the plain terms of art. 263(1) is an important one in terms of the rights of defendants, because if they can do so, no acquittal in any Indonesian court other than on reconsideration by the Supreme Court is final. This gives a significant advantage to prosecutors, who are better placed than most defendants to conduct further expensive and time-consuming litigation. It also creates additional opportunities for the corrupt behaviour – specifically, for the bribing or political suborning of prosecutors and judges, and for prosecutors and judges to extort defendants. Corruption is widely seen as pervasive in Indonesian's judicial system, including in the Supreme Court, as senior judges (including successive Chief Justices) and government officials readily acknowledge (Butt and Lindsey 2011: 189–216.

Other legislative provisions on reconsideration by prosecutors

As mentioned, KUHAP is not the only current legislation dealing with judicial reconsideration. In 2009, the DPR passed the latest version of the Law on Judicial Powers, No. 48 of that year (amending the 2004 Law). Article 24(1) of that statute deals with judicial reconsideration. Like its predecessor, art. 21 of Law No. 14 of 1970 on Judicial Powers, this article does not mention the prosecutor as among those entitled to apply for judicial reconsideration. Instead, using precisely the same wording as the 1970 statute, the 2009 Law leaves the question of who may seek reconsideration to regulation by another statute, stating:

> As regards a court decision that has acquired binding legal force, *parties involved* may bring an application for judicial reconsideration to the Supreme Court, whenever there is particular matter or situation *as provided for in statute*.
>
> [emphasis added]

This means that to determine when a 'party involved' may apply for judicial reconsideration, provisions of statutes other than the Judicial Powers Law (which is a statute of a general character and simply states the existence of the remedy) must be consulted. The relevant specific purpose statute is, of course, KUHAP. The provisions of art. 263(1) of KUHAP, which set out the 'restricted' right to judicial reconsideration, should therefore be read as authoritatively defining the application of art. 24(1) of the Judicial Powers Law by limiting it to convicted persons and their heirs, and making it unavailable for acquittals or dismissals.

Supreme Court regulations on reconsideration by prosecutors

This would seem clear and, as Indonesian criminal procedure scholar Chairul Huda has argued, because art. 263(1) is unambiguous, no further interpretation is necessary or, as he puts it, 'permitted' (Hukumonline 2016a). However, the Supreme Court has often taken an entirely different view. In fact, it has repeatedly sought to widen the right to seek a judicial reconsideration by expressly extending it to prosecutors in respect of acquittals and dismissals, and has done so both in regulation and through its judgments. In this, it has preferred the colonial model, in particular, art. 37 of *Reglement op de Strafvordering* (S.1847-40), over KUHAP.

The two regulations that the court issued to regulate judicial reconsideration before the passing of KUHAP in 1981 are an example of this. As mentioned, the Supreme Court had introduced Regulation No. 1 of 1969 to create a procedure for judicial reconsideration. This was later replaced by Supreme Court Regulation No. 1 of 1971, passed to implement the new Law on Judicial Powers, No. 14 of 1970. Both these regulations granted the right to not just the person convicted but also the 'parties involved' and the 'prosecutor'.

As also mentioned, the next Supreme Court Regulation dealing with judicial reconsideration, No. 1 of 1980, was introduced specifically to resolve the Sengkon and Karta cases. It therefore added new wording explicitly granting the right to convicted persons but, unlike KUHAP, the Law on Judicial Powers and the clear tenor of debate in the DPR described above, it again also gave the right to the prosecutor. Specifically, it reiterated the wording of the earlier Supreme Court Regulations, stating in art. 10(1) that applications for judicial reconsideration in respect of criminal decisions of binding legal force may be lodged by the prosecutor or a party involved, as well as the defendant.

In other words, since the early 1980s, the DPR and the Supreme Court have taken opposite positions on the question of whether prosecutors are entitled to apply for reconsideration, with the Supreme Court repeatedly undermining the intentions of the legislators. As Lev (1996: 157) says of KUHAP, its reforms have not 'worked according to promise, largely because of the resistance of the institutions responsible for them', in this case, prosecutors and the courts.

Supreme Court decisions on reconsideration by prosecutors

It is not surprising that the Supreme Court adopted the same approach it took in its regulations to its reading of KUHAP in a series of high-profile decisions that began in 1996, even though it required interpretative gymnastics to do so.[21] Although in these decisions it allowed prosecutors to apply to for judicial reconsideration in respect of acquittals and dismissals, there are other decisions in which it did not. Before discussing the reasoning in these decisions in more detail, it is useful to explain why this sort of inconsistency in interpretation is not unusual in the Supreme Court.

Absence of precedent

Indonesia's adoption of a colonial form of the civil law system from the Dutch means there is no formal system of precedent or independent body of judge-made law. Formally, Indonesian court decisions bind only the parties involved in the case relating to that decision (Isnaini 1971: 13; Sudarsono 2001: 87). While an Indonesian judge may follow a previous decision from a higher or equal level court with respect to the interpretation of any given provision, he or she is not usually required to do so. Certainly, Indonesian first instance and appeal courts do generally consider selected, prominent decisions of the Supreme Court (*yurisprudensi tetap* or 'fixed jurisprudence') to be highly persuasive and are often reluctant to depart from a line of consistent Supreme Court decisions on a particular point of law or interpretation (BPHN 1993; Lotulung 1997). However, most Indonesian judges – particularly those in the Supreme Court – maintain that they retain absolute freedom to depart from previous decisions (Sudarsono 2001: 87; Utrecht and Djindang 1983: 204). This freedom is also attractive to some judges because it creates opportunities for corruption, which, as mentioned, is a major problem across the Indonesian judicial system. In any event, the Supreme Court has long been notorious for inconsistent and unpredictable decision-making.

Article 263(3), KUHAP

Returning now to the question of the prosecutor's rights to apply for judicial reconsideration, Supreme Court judges who have permitted this – despite the unambiguous prohibition on reconsideration of acquittals or dismissals in art. 263(1) of KUHAP – often rely on a somewhat puzzling provision, art. 263(3) of KUHAP:

> As regards a court decision that has obtained binding legal force, a request for reconsideration may be brought ... if in that decision an act as charged was declared proved but was not followed by a punishment.

They argue that this provision must be intended for use by prosecutors, because only prosecutors would have an interest in changing a decision where no punishment was imposed. The accused or their heirs, on the other hand, the court has said, would not avail themselves of art. 263(3), because they would never want a decision to be changed to impose a punishment. According to this argument, art. 263(3) would be redundant unless it authorised a request for reconsideration by someone other than the accused, and this must be the prosecutor (Hukumonline 2016a). In the *Pollycarpus* case (2008), for example, the court said:

> It is not possible that [Art 263(3)] would be used by the Defendant personally or his or her heirs because it would result in loss to those involved, so logically it is the General Prosecutor who has the right to bring a [judicial reconsideration].[22]

This approach ignores the possibility that an accused found to have committed acts but who had received no punishment for them might still wish to seek judicial reconsideration of that decision – not to receive a punishment but to challenge the finding that he or she had committed those acts. This could be for reasons of reputation or because such acts might form the basis of other legal action against him or her, whether criminal or civil, for example for damages for an unlawful act under art. 1365 of the Civil Code.[23] There are certainly examples of reconsideration being used to restore a reputation.[24] In other words, art. 263(3) is necessary, because art. 263(1) only applies where a person has been convicted. Conviction is not a requirement for art. 263(3), because this provision only applies where no punishment has been imposed.

Further support for this view is found in the fact that the grounds in art. 262(2) that apply to an application for a judicial reconsideration under art. 263(1) are also clearly stated to apply to an application under art. 263(3). All these grounds might conceivably be relevant to person who has not been punished but whom a court has declared to have committed certain acts he or she did not, in fact commit. That person might wish to make application to seek a full acquittal or dismissal because: new evidence has arisen regarding the acts (art. 263(2)(a)); because other courts have made contrary findings regarding the acts (art. 263(2)(b)); or because the finding 'was a clear mistake' (263(2)(3)). By contrast, not all the grounds in art. 263(2) are consistent with an application for a judicial reconsideration by prosecutor where a person is found to have committed acts but is not punished. It is, for example, not apparent why a prosecutor would ever wish to apply under art. 263(2)(a) to a win an acquittal or dismissal or a lighter punishment. This suggests the drafters did not, in fact, have the prosecutor in mind when they drafted art. 263(2). That, in turn, explains why the prosecutor is not mentioned at all in art. 263(3).

Article 24(1), Law on Judicial Powers

In other decisions supporting the prosecutor's right to apply for judicial reconsideration, Supreme Court judges have also relied on art. 24(1) of Law No. 48 of 2009 on Judicial Powers:

> Concerning a court decision that has acquired binding legal force, parties involved may bring a reconsideration to the Supreme Court, whenever there is particular matter or situation as provided for in statute.

The court has interpreted the phrase 'parties involved' in this provision broadly to cover prosecutors. This, however, ignores the fact that art. 24(1) is expressed to apply only where the matter or situation is 'provided for in statute'. This, of course, includes art. 263 of the KUHAP, which makes no reference to prosecutors or 'parties involved' and gives the right only to defendants and heirs. This point is reinforced by art. 76 of Law No. 14 of 1985 on the Supreme Court, which, as mentioned, makes it clear that the KUHAP is the key reference point for judicial reconsideration in criminal cases. It states that:

> In deciding an application for a judicial reconsideration of a criminal case that has binding legal force the procedure for judicial reconsideration as provided for in the Code of Criminal Procedure shall be used.

The alternative approach

There is an alternative line of Supreme Court decisions from 2007[25] in which the court has held that prosecutors do not have a right to apply for judicial reconsideration, usually for the obvious reason that prosecutors are not mentioned in art. 263(1), and reconsideration of an acquittal or dismissal is prohibited.[26] These decisions are sometimes quite emphatic. In the *Achmad Trisana Marseda* case,[27] for example, the court said bluntly that while in some cases prosecutors have been allowed to apply for reconsideration this is 'very exceptional' because it 'greatly offends the sense of justice'. Likewise, in the *Mulyar bin Samsi* case,[28] it held that art. 263(1) is a component of 'due legal process' – a 'normative limitation of state power over citizens'. This limitation cannot be reinterpreted or set aside because to do so would violate the principles of justice and legal certainty. A prosecutor's application for judicial reconsideration is therefore a misapplication of procedural law.

It is also worth noting that even in some of the cases that affirmed the prosecutorial right to seek reconsideration, there was dissent among the judges, something is still relatively uncommon in the Supreme Court. In the *Syahril Sabirin* case,[29] for example, two judges of a bench of seven argued against a prosecutor's right to judicial review. Justice Imron Anwari said that it was prohibited in the interests of legal certainty. Justice Abdul Kadir Mappong agreed, adding that it was also in the interests of consistent decision-making, noting that the limitations on applicants for judicial reconsideration are set out decisively in art. 263(1). In the *Joko Tjandra* case, two of the bench of five dissented. Justice Prof. Dr. Komariah E. Sapardjaja reasoned that art. 263 was drafted with the explicit intention of protecting the rights of criminal defendants. She argued that a prosecutor's right for judicial appeal is in conflict with the general principle that the defence should have the last say, enshrined in other parts of the law criminal procedure. She also pointed out that the historic basis for limiting the prosecution's right to judicial review was the need to protect individual's rights against the arbitrary power of the regime. Justice Suwardi agreed, arguing that it is necessary to apply the most specific law (that is, KUHAP) and not the more general one (the Judicial Powers Law) and that art. 263(1) of KUHAP is clear that the right to judicial review is a limited right the prosecution does not enjoy.

The conflicted, unsettled and unpredictable nature of Supreme Court opinion on whether the prosecutor has the right to seek judicial reconsideration is well illustrated by the changing and unexplained positions taken on the issue by Justice Djoko Sarwoko. In the *Mulyar bin Samsi* case (2007),[30] he held that art. 263:

> … has already firmly and restrictively [*limitatif*] provided that those who may bring a judicial reconsideration are the defendant or his or her heirs. This means that those who are not the defendant or his or her heirs may not bring a judicial reconsideration. Given the existence of these firm and restrictive provisions, there is no further need for special provisions that provide that those who are not the defendant or his or her heirs may not bring a judicial reconsideration; … this 'due proses of law' [sic] functions as a limitation on the power of the state in its actions towards members of society, and has a normative character, so that it

> cannot be constructed or avoided, because that would violate justice and legal certainty... on the basis of these matters it can be concluded that the Prosecutor may not bring a request for a judicial reconsideration in respect of a criminal decision that has binding legal force ... [31]

In the following year, however, he completely reversed his position, holding in the *Pollycarpus* case (2008)[32] that:

> KUHAP must be used to the maximum to obtain material truth by carrying out extensive construction of its provisions, and in this matter especially as regards Article 263 of KUHAP by allowing the Prosecutor to bring a request for a judicial reconsideration of a decision that has obtained fixed legal force, in the form of a dismissal or acquittal on all charges.[33]

Sarwoko did not acknowledge in the *Pollycarpus* decision that he had completely changed his position, nor did he give any reason for doing so. In the majority decision in the *Tjandra* case,[34] two years later in 2009, he adopted precisely the same form of words (at pp. 90–1) as in *Pollycarpus*. The clear inconsistency in Sarwoko's position in these cases was directly raised in the submissions of the defendant in the *Syahril Sabirin* case[35] (also in 2009). The point was recited in the judgment as being among the submissions made but is otherwise ignored. It was not addressed at all by the judges in their decision.

In summary, although the reasoning used by the Supreme Court in decisions allowing prosecutors to seek judicial reconsideration is weak and inconsistent, this line of authority has been the one most often followed. The contrary, and far more convincing, view has been adopted in a smaller number of decisions, even though it takes a more coherent view of the relevant legislation. In other words, the Supreme Court has most often been willing to rely on questionable legal justifications to allow prosecutors to use reconsideration mechanism to challenge outcomes favourable to defendants, such as acquittals.

This raises the question of the causes of this 'institutional resistance' to the KUHAP reforms (Lev 1996: 156–7) that quite deliberately denied prosecutors the right to apply for judicial reconsideration of acquittals and dismissals. Why has the Supreme Court been so willing to go to such lengths to read down the clear words of art. 263(1) in order to return this right to them (even though it would, of course, increase the court's workload)? Why are 'useful procedural protections ... often enough simply swept aside, despite the protests of advocates, as judges either follow the lead of prosecutors or rule conveniently to complicate the defence or facilitate the prosecution' (Lev 1999: 188–9)?

Analysis of the decisions in which prosecutors were given the right to reconsideration suggests that much of the answer to this perhaps lies in the political context in which they were made.

Context of decisions

The first in the line of decisions supporting prosecutorial reconsideration is the *Muchtar Pakpahan* case (1996).[36] In 1994, Pakpahan was a well-known labour leader, the head of SBSI,[37] a dissident union organisation he had established to oppose the Soeharto government's repressive labour policies. He was arrested in Medan and charged with inciting workers to demonstrate and strike, and sowing hatred against the president. He was convicted of the latter offence and sentenced to three years, increased by the North Sumatra High Court on appeal to four. In October 1995, his application for cassation was upheld by the Supreme Court and he was acquitted. However, the Soeharto government, which saw Pakpahan as a political threat, had him re-arrested and detained on subversion charges related to other events in Jakarta. According to Huda (Hukumonline 2016a), it was Soeharto himself who then instructed the prosecution to seek judicial reconsideration of Pakpahan's acquittal on the Medan charges. Accordingly, in 1996, the court, under significant pressure from the palace, 're-convened with surprising speed and overturned its own previous decision. It proceeded to re-impose the four-year sentence' (Zifcak 1998: 363).

The court justified its actions by asserting, without much justification offered to support it, that

> the right of the public prosecutor to apply for judicial review is supported by the principle of legality and serves the aim of achieving a balance between the human rights of individuals and the interests of the public, the nation and the state.[38]

It is clear enough, however, that it was the political imperative of imprisoning a prominent government critic in the tense final years of the Soeharto regime (which finally collapsed in May 1998) that motivated the court to perform the interpretative contortions necessary to read KUHAP as allowing prosecutors to seek reconsideration of acquittals. It is testimony to this that Pakpahan was freed within days of Soeharto's fall, as part of wider release of political prisoners at the time.

This analysis rings true also for other cases that followed *Pakapahan*. Although they all took place after the fall of Soeharto, they also involved great pressure on the Supreme Court, albeit for different reasons. Four will suffice to demonstrate the pattern.

The *Ram Gulumal* case (2001)[39] involved a dispute over control of two prestigious Indian private schools in Jakarta. Gulumal was accused of falsifying documents and embezzling funds of the Gandhi Memorial School. At first instance and on cassation he was found innocent. Then an internal memorandum by a senior Supreme Court judge, Andi Andoyo Soetjipto, was leaked to press in which he alleged that the cassation decision had been obtained by corruption, and called for judicial reconsideration. The resulting scandal triggered a huge 'wave' of criticism of the court (Tempo 2002), turning Soetjipto into a hero and humiliating the then Chief Justice, Soerjono. Prosecutors duly followed Soetjipto's suggestion and the obviously reluctant court found Gulumal guilty, although it only sentenced him to twenty days, the time he had already spent in detention (Pompe 2005: 162–5; Tempo 2002).

The *Pollycarpus* case (2008)[40] related to the 2004 murder of Munir Said Thalib, a prominent Indonesian civil rights activist who was poisoned with arsenic on a Garuda Indonesia flight from Jakarta to Amsterdam by a pilot, Pollycarpus Budihari Priyanto, who was also a covert intelligence operative. Munir's horrible death caused national outrage. Pollycarpus was acquitted on cassation in 2006, which provoked widespread and angry criticism of the Supreme Court. Prosecutors then successfully sought judicial reconsideration and Pollycarpus received a prison sentence of twenty years.

The *Joko Tjandra* case (2009)[41] was equally controversial, although for different reasons. Tjandra was accused of corruptly extorting Indonesian Bank Restructuring Agency bail-out funds as part of the politically explosive Bank Bali scandal of 1999. This involved claims that funds were syphoned off to fund President B. J. Habibie's election campaign, leading to the collapse of that campaign. Tjandra's acquittal at first instance and on cassation to the Supreme Court in 2001 was part of a flood of enormously controversial litigation surrounding the scandal. In 2008, new corruption cases brought fresh evidence to light of criminal behaviour in relation to the bank bail-outs of the early post-Soeharto era. By 2009, popular pressure on the Supreme Court to convict Tjandra was immense (Tempo 2008a, 2008b). Indeed, he appears to have anticipated the reconsideration outcome, fleeing Indonesia the day before the decision was handed down.

The Supreme Court likely felt the same sort of pressure for the similar reasons in the *Syahril Sabirin* case (2009).[42] Sabirin had been Governor of Indonesia's central bank, Bank Indonesia, during the Bank Bali scandal and was accused of enabling the wider fraud for which Tjandra was convicted. Sabirin had been sentenced to four years' imprisonment at first instance before being acquitted by a high court and again on cassation by the Supreme Court. In the same year that Tjandra was convicted, prosecutors applied for judicial reconsideration in Sabirin's case. Sabirin was found guilty, and received a two-year prison sentence.

There may have been reasonable grounds for the decisions the Supreme Court made in each of these five reconsideration cases – I make no comment on that, either way. Rather, the point I seek to make is that the grounds the court gave for allowing prosecutors to apply to reopen these cases are, at best, incoherent and weak, and contrary to the plain words of KUHAP. That makes it hard to avoid the impression that in each case, the court was motivated less by legal principle and more by external pressures and, in particular, in the post-Soeharto era, fear of popular opprobrium.

Appealing acquittals as policy: Cassation

In fact, allowing acquittals to be appealed by prosecutors seems to have become a policy of the Supreme Court. It is not a practice confined to reconsideration but has also been adopted in relation to cassation. Article 244 of KUHAP states that:

> the accused or prosecutor may file a cassation appeal at the Supreme Court for all judgments on criminal cases handed down by a court other than the Supreme Court, *except for acquittals.*
>
> [emphasis added]

Despite this, the Court regularly hears such cassations.[43] To justify this, it used to cite the New Order *yurisprudensi* established by Supreme Court Decision No. 275/K/Pid/1983, which the court decided somehow overrode art. 244. On this basis, the court typically differentiated between 'pure (or full) acquittals' (*bebas murni*) – loosely, an acquittal on the merits – and 'qualified acquittals' (*bebas tidak murni*), which covered other forms of acquittals, for example, an acquittal because of a procedural error. The Supreme Court would usually reject cassation appeals on *bebas murni* acquittals, for example, when the offence with which the accused was charged was not supported by sufficient evidence. By contrast, an acquittal decision might be considered *tidak murni* if it were based on incorrect application of an offence in the indictment. This could be a very subtle technical distinction, and it caused much confusion in legal circles – even among judges. Many commentators suggested that it was, in fact, a fictional distinction that allowed the Court to hear appeals against any acquittal at its own discretion (Hukumonline 2013).

In 2013, the Constitutional Court confirmed the Supreme Court's power to hear cassation of acquittals. In response to an application by a former civil servant acquitted of corruption who argued that art. 244 of KUHAP created legal uncertainty, it rather surprisingly handed down a decision that removed the phrase 'except for acquittals' from that provision. Following this decision, the Supreme Court changed the format of cassation applications, no longer differentiating between *bebas murni* and *bebas tidak murni* acquittals, so that prosecutors may now bring cassations in respect any acquittal.

However, the Constitutional Court has been more protective of defendants' rights in its interpretation of the provisions of KUHAP relating to reconsideration, and this has put it at loggerheads with the Supreme Court.

Constitutional Court decisions on reconsideration by prosecutors

In May 2016, the Constitutional Court sought to finally resolve the controversy over whether a prosecutor could seek judicial reconsideration (including in respect of acquittals).[44] It ruled that Art 263(1) of KUHAP was constitutional only if understood to mean that a request for judicial reconsideration can only be made by the convicted person or his or her heir, and cannot be submitted for acquittals or dismissals. Interpretations different to this result in legal uncertainty and are unconstitutional, it held. In doing so, the Constitutional Court confirmed a previous decision[45] in which it had first said that the prosecution may not submit a request for a judicial reconsideration (Sahbani 2016).

This would seem to have been a definitive resolution of the matter, given Constitutional Court decisions are 'final and binding'[46] and the court has now followed its own precedent on this issue.[47] Unfortunately, Prasetyo, the Chief Prosecutor at the time, took a different view. His office, he said, would continue to submit reconsideration requests regardless of the Constitutional Court's decision. It was justified in doing so, he claimed, because there was *yurisprudensi* – that is, leading Supreme Court decisions – that allow it (Hakim 2016). Here, he was referring to the line of decisions beginning with Pakpahan's case, described above, thus implying that the Supreme Court's view of the matter was superior to that of the only Indonesian court constitutionally empowered to interpret the Constitution.

However, the Supreme Court has since said that the 2016 Constitutional Court decision is 'strict', so it will no longer accept judicial reconsideration requests from the prosecution, because the Constitutional Court has more authority than the Chief Prosecutor (Hukumonline 2016b). Unfortunately, the Supreme Court Spokesman, Suhadi, then confused things by saying it is up the panel of judges in each case to decide how to apply the Constitutional Court decision (Kompas 2017), effectively returning the court to its previous position where conflicted lines of authority exist on the issue. All that can be said with certainty now is that uncertainty still prevails on whether the Supreme Court will allow prosecutors to seek judicial reconsideration.

Prasetyo, pressing for the power to challenge acquittals at the fourth and final level of appeal, has requested the DPR give the prosecution an explicit right to submit a request for reconsideration when they draft a revised version of KUHAP (Kami 2016). In this he does not seem to have been successful, although the terminology in KUHAP that has been exploited in the past by the Supreme Court to allow prosecutorial reconsideration applications seems set to remain, as I now explain.

The draft KUHAP bill

In the draft bill to amend KUHAP currently before the DPR at the time of writing (February 2020), judicial reconsideration is dealt with in arts. 260 to 267. Many of these provisions simply reproduce existing provisions, but there are some important changes. Some of these are positive, for example, the introduction in art. 265(5) of compensation for wrongful punishment. This will apply specifically when judicial reconsideration results in acquittal or a lighter sentence, with procedures to be determined by government regulation (art. 265(6)). Likewise, art. 266(1) reiterates that while applications for judicial reconsideration generally do not act as a stay in relation to enforcement of the judgment challenged, they will for death sentences,[48] destruction orders and destruction of evidence.

However, there are also a number of regressive changes that seriously weaken the rights of defendants. For example, the third of the grounds on which reconsideration can be sought under art. 263(2) of KUHAP – judicial error – does not appear in its replacement, art. 260(2). This means that a defendant wrongly convicted by judge who makes a clear mistake has no remedy if this is discovered after the time for appeal has passed. Reconsideration would only be available on the basis of new evidence (*novum*) or inconsistent findings of fact in different decisions. These are grounds are much more limited in nature and much more difficult to establish, as they are external to the original judgment.

The most worrying change for the purposes of this chapter is art. 262, which, as mentioned earlier, purports to re-establish the prohibition on multiple reconsideration applications, despite the Constitutional Court's ruling to the contrary.

Likewise, there is no clarity in the draft bill about whether prosecutors are entitled to seek judicial reconsideration. Article 263(3), the provision that allows reconsideration where there is a finding of an act that is not followed by a punishment, is retained as art. 260(3). This preserves the argument the Supreme Court has sometimes used to very tenuously approve reconsideration by prosecutors.

More concerning still is the fact that the words 'except for acquittals and dismissals' that appear in art. 263(1) of KUHAP have been deleted from the equivalent provision in the draft. Article 260(1) now simply states that judicial reconsideration is available to convicted persons and heirs in relation to 'all criminal decisions' that have acquired binding legal force. While prosecutors have not been added to list of those entitled to apply, it is not hard to see how the inclusion of acquittals and dismissals in the ambit of judicial reconsideration, when read with art. 260(3), could well support future judicial efforts to justify prosecutorial application for judicial reconsideration (Akbari 2014).

Conclusion

It remains to be seen if and when a new version of KUHAP will be passed, and whether the provisions just described appear in it. It would be disturbing if a legislature in democratic Indonesia cannot create a new criminal procedure code that is less restrictive of defendant's rights than that passed by the puppet DPR under Soeharto's repressive regime, notorious for its general lack of interest in human rights. On the other hand, it probably needed a scandal of the magnitude of Sengkon and Karta to make that DPR give defendants and their rights serious consideration. There is no such scandal now.

If the single application limit is re-introduced, and the ambiguities regarding the prosecutor's capacity to bring a judicial reconsideration application remain intact, then it can be expected that these provisions may be seized upon by the Supreme Court to revert to its pattern of institutional resistance to reform, that is, its preferred interpretations of judicial reconsideration that restrict defendants' rights. If my argument above that the Supreme Court has been more motivated by external pressures than by legal principle in its approach to judicial reconsideration is correct, then this is likely – simply because allowing prosecutors to apply for judicial reconsideration gives the Supreme Court an easy way to 'fix' unpopular decisions.

If this happens, then both the issue of multiple reconsideration applications and prosecutors' rights to seek reconsideration will likely once more come before the Constitutional Court. The question then will be whether that court follows its own precedent and, if it does, whether the Supreme Court and prosecutors will respect its rulings. Sadly, at a time of generally declining quality in superior court decision-making in Indonesia,[49] uncertainty is, as I said earlier, the only certainty.

Notes

1 I am grateful to Sarah Rennie and Tim Mann for research on which this chapter is based. It also draws in part on material in Butt and Lindsey (2018).
2 Many Indonesians use just one name.
3 Bekasi District Court Decision *Sengkon Bin Yakin dan Karta alias Karung alias Encep Bin Salam* (*Sengkon dan Karta*) (No. 2/K.T.S/Bks/1977, 20 October 1977); Bandung High Court decision: *Sengkon Bin Yakin dan Karta alias Karung alias Encep Bin Salam (Sengkon dan Karta)* (No. 38/1978/Pid/PTB, 25 May 1978, *Karta*); Supreme Court Decision *Sengkon Bin Yakin dan Karta alias Karung alias Encep Bin Salam* (*Sengkon dan Karta*) (No. 6 PKK/Kr/1980, 31 January 1981).
4 His name is sometimes given as 'Genul'. On some accounts, Gunel was Sengkon's nephew.
5 There are differing accounts of Sengkon and Karta's cases. This description is compiled from a number of sources, including Hasan (2010). Pompe (2005: 244–6) relates their cases to the revival of judicial reconsideration in KUHAP and identifies other similar cases, but questions whether Gunel's confession was genuine. Yusran (2019) gives a more emotive account that is representative of common Indonesian views of the case.
6 The word *herziening* is still occasionally used by Indonesian scholars and lawyers to refer to the judicial reconsideration process that replaced it.
7 Supreme Court Decision No. 6 PKK/Kr/1980, 31 January 1981.
8 Their compensation claims were rejected by the Bekasi District Court and their cassation application to the Supreme Court was not accepted on the grounds that it was filed a day late (Hasan 2010).
9 The term appears in the title of Chapter XVII of KUHAP, which deals in Part One with a particular form of cassation brought by the prosecutor 'in the interests of law' (*demi kepentingan hukum*) and, in Part Two, (arts. 263–9) with judicial reconsideration.
10 Under art. 24A(1) of the Constitution, the Supreme Court also has jurisdiction to review regulatory instruments 'below' a statute to ensure that they comply with statutes.

11 Criminal reconsideration decisions numbered 396. The largest group of reconsiderations were tax cases (3,419), followed by civil cases (1,053) (Mahkamah Agung 2019).
12 Supreme Court Circular Letter No. 7 of 2014 on the Submission of Applications for Judicial Consideration in Criminal Cases.
13 Constitutional Court Decision Nos. 108/PUU-XIV/2016; 1/PUU-XV/2017; and 23/PUU-XV/2017.
14 Interestingly, the court added that in civil cases multiple judicial reconsideration requests would cause prolonged resolution of cases and result in legal uncertainty. It felt that multiple judicial reconsideration requests needed to be treated separately for criminal and civil matters.
15 Constitutional Court Decision No. 1/PUU-XV/2017, quoting the considerations (*pertimbangan*) from Decision No. 108/PUU-XIV/2016.
16 Constitutional Court Decision No. 05/PUU-IV/2006, at p. 31.
17 Supreme Court Decision No. 02 PK/KPUD/2008, at p. 79.
18 Supreme Court Decision No. 300/C/PK/PJK/2009, at p. 29.
19 *Herziene Indonesisch Reglement* (HIR). The Dutch introduced the HIR in 1926 to regulate procedural law, both civil and criminal, but applied only to the islands of Java and Madura. A further statute was enacted in 1927 to cover the areas outside Java and Madura, known as the (*Rechtsreglement Buitengewesten* or Rbg).
20 Although Hasibuan did not deal with judicial consideration in that speech, it is hard to imagine that he would not have supported the judicial reconsideration reforms, given his prominent role in the Sengkon and Karta case.
21 These Supreme Court decisions include: *Muchtar Pakpahan* (Decision No. 55 PK/Pid/1996, 25 October 1996, see pp. 362–66); *Ram Gulumal Alias Ram* (No. 3 PK/Pid/2001, 2 August 2001); *Dr. Eddy Linus and others* (No. 54 PK/Pid/2006); *Soetiyawati Alias Ahua Binti Kartaningsih* (No. 15 PK/Pid/2006, 19 June 2006, pp. 5–14); *Pollycarpus Budihari Priyanto* (No. 109 of 2008: PK/Pid/2007, 25 January 2008, pp. 17–26); *Dr Edhy Sudjono Muliadi* (No. 8 PK/Pid/2008, p. 13); 2009: *Joko Tjandra* (No. 12PK/Pid.Sus/2009, 11 June 2009, p. 126); *Syahril Sabirin* (No. 07 PK/Pid.Sus/2009, 8 June 2009, pp. 41–50); and *Ny. Nyayu Saodah bin (alm) KA Kosim* (No. 41 PK/Pid/2009, 13 October 2009, pp. 24–5).
22 Decision No. 109 2008: PK/Pid/2007, p. 20.
23 Article 1365 of the Civil Code (*Kitab Undang-Undang Hukum Perdata, KUHPerdata*) states that a person who causes loss to another person by means of an unlawful act must, because of his or her fault in causing the loss, compensate for that loss. Among other things, it enables plaintiffs to claim civil compensation for loss caused by the criminal acts of defendants (Fuady 2002).
24 An extraordinary example of why a convict might wish to use judicial reconsideration to restore his or her reputation (although in this case a conviction was imposed) is the infamous case of Risman Lakoro and Rostin Mahaji, in Gorontolo. Parents were convicted of murdering their daughter in 2002, only for her to turn up alive in 2007, after they had served out their full prison sentences of three years each. Their lawyer, Saluhiddin Pakaya, representing the couple in what he described as a 'Gorontalo Sengkon and Karta', said 'We will apply for [judicial reconsideration] to rehabilitate their reputation' (Antara 2007; Gatra 2007; Ismoyo 2007).
25 This alternative line of Supreme Court authority includes: *Sdr. Mulyar bin Samsi* (Supreme Court Decision No. 84/PK/Pid/2006, 2007, 18 July 2007, pp. 7–8);

Achmad Trisana Marseda (Supreme Court Decision No. 25 PK/Pid.Sus/2007, 11 February 2008); *Johan Imago al Guan Kabir* (Supreme Court Decision No. 69 PK/ Pid.Sus/2010); *Anggodo Widjojo v the Head of Police* (Supreme Court Decision No. 152 PK/Pid/2010, 7 October 2010, pp. 64–66); and *Zaki Toya Bawazir* (Supreme Court Decision No. 16 PK/Pid/2010, 29 November 2011, pp. 23–4).

26 See, for example, Supreme Court Decision No. 152 PK/Pid/2010, p. 66.

27 Supreme Court Decision No. 25 PK/Pid.Sus/2007, p. 8.

28 Supreme Court Decision No. 84 PK/Pid/2006.

29 Supreme Court Decision No. 167 PK/Pid.Sus/2009

30 Supreme Court Decision No. 84/PK/Pid/2006, 2007.

31 Supreme Court Decision No. 84/PK/Pid/2006, 2007, pp. 7–9.

32 Supreme Court Decision No. 109 2008: PK/Pid/2007.

33 Supreme Court Decision No. 109 2008: PK/Pid/2007, p. 24.

34 Supreme Court Decision No. 12PK/Pid.Sus/2009.

35 Supreme Court Decision No. 07 PK/Pid.Sus/2009.

36 Supreme Court Decision No. 55 PK/Pid/1996, 25 October 1996.

37 SBSI (Serikat Buruh Sejahtera Indonesia, Prosperous Workers Union of Indonesia).

38 Supreme Court Decision No. 55 PK/Pid/1996, p. 733.

39 Supreme Court Decision No. 3 PK/Pid/2001 2 August 2001.

40 Supreme Court Decision No. 109 2008: PK/Pid/2007, 25 January 2008.

41 Supreme Court Decision No. 12PK/Pid.Sus/2009, 11 June 2009.

42 Supreme Court Decision No. 07 PK/Pid.Sus/2009, 8 June 2009.

43 See, for example, Supreme Court Decision No. 1521K/PID/2002.

44 Constitutional Court Decision No. 33/PUU-XIV/2016.

45 Constitutional Court Decision 16/PUU-VI/2008 (the *Religious Courts* case).

46 Decisions of the Constitutional Court are final and binding as of the time they are pronounced; they are not subject to appeal: art. 10, Law No. 24 of 2003 on the Constitutional Court; and see the Elucidation to art. 10, Law No. 8 of 2011.

47 Decisions of the Constitutional Court are evolving into a form of precedent, as it will generally not reconsider an argument for striking down a provision in a statute on which it has previously ruled. Unfortunately, it is not consistent in this, and there are some cases where it declined to follow its own previous decisions in similar cases. See Afrianty (2019) and Butt (2006).

48 This is likely a reaction to the execution under President Joko Widodo of prisoners with pending reconsideration applications. See Gunawan and Pamintori (Chapter 11 of this book).

49 On this, see Hukumonline.com (2010).

References

Adzikia, Aghnia 2015. 'Peraturan Pemerintah tentang Peninjuan Kembali akan Dibuat', *CNN Indonesia*, 10 January www.cnnindonesia.com/nasional/20150109215316-12-23640/peraturan-pemerintah-tentang-peninjuan-kembali-akan-dibuat/

Afrianty, Dina 2019. 'Child Marriage: Constitutional Court Finally Ditches Religious Arguments', *Indonesia at Melbourne*, 24 January https://indonesiaatmelbourne.unimelb.edu.au/child-marriage-constitutional-court-finally-ditches-religious-arguments/

Akbari 2014. 'RKUHAP Perlu Pertegas Boleh Tidaknya Jaksa Ajukan PK', *Hukumonline*, 21 March www.hukumonline.com/berita/baca/lt532c448ba863f/rkuhap-perlu-pertegas-boleh-tidaknya-jaksa-ajukan-pk

Antara 2007. 'Tragedi 'Sengkon-Karta' Gorontalo, Kado Buruk HUT Bhayangkara', *Antara*, 10 July www.antaranews.com/berita/69586/tragedi-sengkon-karta-gorontalo-kado-buruk-hut-bhayangkara

BPHN 1993. *Laporan Penelitian Tentang Peningkatan Yurisprudensi Sebagai Sumber Hukum*. Jakarta: Badan Pembinaan Hukum Nasional, Departemen Kehakiman

Butt, Simon 2006. *Judicial Review in Indonesia: Between Civil Law and Accountability? A Study of Constitutional Court Decisions 2003–2005*. Doctoral dissertation, University of Melbourne

Butt, Simon and Lindsey, Tim 2011. 'Judicial Mafia: Corruption and the Courts in Indonesia', in E. Aspinall and G. Van Klinken (eds.), *The State and Illegality in Indonesia.* Leiden: KITLV Press, pp. 189–216

Butt, Simon and Lindsey, Tim 2018. *Indonesian Law*. Oxford University Press

Direktorat Jenderal Hukum dan Perundang-undangan 1981), S*ejarah Pembentukan Undang-Undang Republik Indonesia No. 8 Tahun 1981 Tentang Hukum Acara Pidana.* Jakarta: Direktorat Jenderal Hukum dan Perundang-undangan.

Fuady, M. 2002. *Perbuatan Melawan Hukum: Pendekatan Kontemporer*. Jakarta: Citra Aditya Bakti

Gatra 2007. 'Alta Pembuka Kotak Pandora', *Gatra*, 25 July http://arsip.gatra.com/2007-07-16/majalah/artikel.php?pil=23&id=106308

Hakim RN 2016. 'Jaksa Agung: Meski MK Nyatakan Kami Tetap Ajukan PK', *Kompas*, 6 June http://nasional.kompas.com/read/2016/06/06/19043121/jaksa.agung.meski.mk.nyatakan. tak.bisa.kami.tetap.ajukan.pk

Harahap, M. Yahya 2008. *'Upaya Hukum Luar Biasa': Pembahasan Permasalahan dan Penerapan KUHAP: Pemeriksaan Sidang Pengadilan, Banding, Kasasi, dan Peninjauan Kembali*. Jakarta: Sinar Grafika

Hasan, Usman 2010. 'Legenda Sengkon dan Karta', *Kompasiana*, 2 February www.kompasiana.com/234/54ff676ca33311494c50ff70/legenda-sengkon-dan-karta

Hukumonline 2010. 'Banyak Putusan Kasus Korupsi di MA Tanpa Pertimbangan Jelas', *Hukumonline*, 27 August www.hukumonline.com/berita/baca/lt4c76a39a345b5/banyak-putusan-kasus-korupsi-di-ma-tanpa-pertimbangan-jelas/

Hukumonline 2013. 'Bebas Murni Atau Tidak Murni Sudah Tak Relevan', *Hukumonline*, 28 October www.hukumonline.com/berita/baca/lt526dcda563378/bebas-murni-atau-tidak-murni-sudah-tak-relevan

Hukumonline 2016a. 'Chairul Huda: Kembalikan PK Sesuai Ruh KUHAP', *Hukumonline*, 24 May www.hukumonline.com/berita/baca/lt57438b6e09ed8/chairul-huda--kembalikan-pk-sesuai-ruh-kuhap/

Hukumonline 2016b. 'MA: Larangan Jaksa Ajukan PK Mingikat Kejaksaan', *Hukumonline*, 22 May www.hukumonline.com/berita/baca/lt57412b95477b5/ma--larangan-jaksa-ajukan-pk-mengikat-kejaksaan

Ismoyo, Jarot D. 2007. 'Peradilan Yang Berkualitas', *Jurnal UNIERA* 3(1): 95–104

Isnaini, M. 1971. *Hakim dan undang-undang*. Jakarta: Ikatan Hakim Indonesia

Kami, I. M. 2016. 'Dilarang MK Ajukan PK, Jaksa Agung: Kami Akan Tetap Ajukan', *detikNews*, 6 June https://news.detik.com/berita/3226703/dilarang-mk-ajukan-pk-jaksa-agung- kami-akan-tetap-ajukan

Kompas 2017. 'MA Diminta Terbitkan Fatwa tentang PK Jaksa', *Kompas*, 4 March

Lev, Daniel S. 1996. 'Between State and Society: Professional Lawyers and Reform in Indonesia', in Daniel S Lev and Ruth McVey (eds.), *Making Indonesia*. Ithaca: Cornell University Press, pp. 145–163

Lev, Daniel S. 1999. 'The Criminal Regime: Criminal Process in Indonesia', in Vincente L. Rafael (eds.), *Figures of Criminality in Indonesia, The Philippines, and Colonial Vietnam*. Ithaca: Cornell University Press, pp. 145–163

Lotulung Paulus E. 1997. *Peranan Yurisprudensi Sebagai Sumber Hukum*. Jakarta: Badan Pembinaan Hukum Nasional, Departemen Kehakiman

Mahkamah Agung 2019. *Laporan Tahunan 2018*. Jakarta: Mahkamah Agung

Mahkamah Agung 2020. *Laporan Tahunan 2019*. Jakarta: Mahkamah Agung

Nursobah, A. 2017. 'Inilah Putusan Yang Diajukan Peninjauan Kembali di Tahun 2016', *Kepaniteraan Mahkamah Agung RI*, 13 January https://kepaniteraan.mahkamahagung.go.id/index.php/kegiatan/1410-inilah-putusan-yang-diajukan-peninjauan-kembali-di-tahun-2016

Pompe, Sebastiaan 2005. *The Indonesian Supreme Court: A Study of Institutional Collapse*. Ithaca: Cornell University Press

Sahbani, Agus 2016. 'Akhirnya ...MK Larang Ajukan PK', *Hukumonline*, 12 May www.hukumonline.com/berita/baca/lt573471 1a1fc21/akhirnya-mk-larang-jaksa-ajukan-pk

Sudarsono 2001. *PengantarIlmu Hukum*. Jakarta: Bineka Cipta

Tempo 2002. 'Sengketa Tak Kunjung Padam', 9 June https://majalah.tempo.co/read/hukum/119929/sengketa-tak-kunjung-padam?

Tempo 2008a. 'Hukum: Setelah Si Mas Gagal Membantu', 22 June, pp. 91–3

Tempo 2008b. 'Hukum: Yang Masuk Pusaran Kasus Artalyta', *Tempo*, 22 June, pp. 94–5Yusran, Alwi 2019. 'Mata Luka Sengkon-Karta dan Hukum Peninjauan Kembali (PK) di Indonesia', *Medium*, 21 September https://medium.com/@alwiyusran/mata-luka-sengkon-karta-dan-hukum-peninjauan-kembali-pk-di-indonesia-c71ca8e9fe5c

Utrecht, E. and Djindang, M. S. 1983. *Pengantar dalam Hukum Indonesia*, 10th edn. Jakarta: Sinar Harapan

Zifcak, Spencer 1998. 'But a Shadow of Justice': Political Trials in Indonesia', in Tim Lindsey (ed.), *Indonesia: Law and Society*, 1st edn. Sydney: Federation Press

Laws

Civil Code (*Kitab Undang-Undang Hukum Perdata, KUHPerdata*)

Code of Criminal Procedure (*Kitab Undang-undang Hukum Acara Pidana,* KUHAP), Law No. 8 of 1981, passed on 31 December 1981

Herziene Inlandsch Reglement (colonial procedural laws), Staatsblad No. 44 of 1941, Law No. 1 of 1951 and related laws and regulations)

Reglement op de Strafvordering (S.1847-40), Civil Code for Europeans (colonial)

Law No. 24 of 2003 on the Constitutional Court

Law No. 8 of 2011.

Law No. 19 of 1964 on Judicial Powers

Law No. 14 of 1970 on Judicial Powers

Law No. 14 of 1985 on the Supreme Court

Law No. 48 of 2009 on Judicial Powers (amending the 2004 Law)

Law No. 3 of 2009 on the Supreme Court (amending Law No. 14 of 1985)

Supreme Court Regulation No. 1 of 1969

Supreme Court Circular Letter No. 18 of 1969 on the Suspension of Supreme Court Regulation No. 1 of 1969
Supreme Court Regulation No. 1 of 1971 on the Implementation of Law No. 14 of 1970 on Judicial Powers
Supreme Court Regulation No. 1 of 1976 on the Revocation of Supreme Court Regulation No. 1 of 1971
Supreme Court Circular Letter No. 7 of 2014 on the Submission of Applications for Judicial Consideration in Criminal Cases

Court decisions

Bandung High Court Decision No. 38/1978/Pid/PTB, 25 May 1978 (*Sengkon Bin Yakin dan Karta alias Karung alias Encep Bin Salam*)
Bekasi District Court Decision No. 2/K.T.S/Bks/1977, 20 October 1977 (*Sengkon Bin Yakin dan Karta alias Karung alias Encep Bin Salam (Sengkon dan Karta*)
Constitutional Court Decision No. 05/PUU-IV/2006 (*Judicial Commission* case)
Constitutional Court Decision No. 16/PUU-VI/2008 (*Religious Courts* case)
Constitutional Court Decision No. 33/PUU-XIV/2016 (*Prosecutorial Reconsideration* case)
Constitutional Court Decision No. 108/PUU-XIV/2016 (*Multiple Reconsideration* case)
Constitutional Court Decision No. 1/PUU-XV/2017 (*Multiple Reconsideration* case)
Constitutional Court Decision No. 23/PUU-XV/2017 (*Multiple Reconsideration* case)
Supreme Court Decision No. 6 PKK/Kr/1980, 31 January 1981 (*Sengkon Bin Yakin dan Karta alias Karung alias Encep Bin Salam*)
Supreme Court Decision No. 55 PK/Pid/1996, 25 October 1996 (*Muchtar Pakpahan*)
Supreme Court Decision No. 3 PK/Pid/2001, 2 August 2001 (*Ram Gulumal Alias Ram*)
Supreme Court Decision No. 1521K/PID/2002
Supreme Court Decision No. 15 PK/Pid/2006, 19 June 2006 (*Soetiyawati Alias Ahua Binti Kartaningsih*)
Supreme Court Decision No. 54 PK/Pid/2006 (*Dr. Eddy Linus and others*)
Supreme Court Decision No. 84/PK/Pid/2006, 2007, 18 July 2007 (*Sdr. Mulyar bin Samsi*)
Supreme Court Decision No. 25 PK/Pid.Sus/2007, 11 February 2008 (*Achmad Trisana Marseda*)
Supreme Court Decision No. 109 PK/Pid/2007, 25 January 2008 (*Pollycarpus Budihari Priyanto*)
Supreme Court Decision No. 02 PK/KPUD/2008
Supreme Court Decision No. 8 PK/Pid/2008 (*Dr. Edhy Sudjono Muliadi*)
Supreme Court Decision No. 07 PK/Pid.Sus/2009, 8 June 2009 (*Syahril Sabirin*)
Supreme Court Decision No. 12 PK/Pid.Sus/2009, 11 June 2009 (*Joko Tjandra*)
Supreme Court Decision No. 41 PK/Pid/2009, 13 October 2009 (*Ny. Nyayu Saodah bin (alm) KA Kosim*)
Supreme Court Decision No. 167 PK/Pid.Sus/2009
Supreme Court Decision No. 300/C/PK/PJK/2009
Supreme Court Decision No. 69 PK/Pid.Sus/2010 (*Johan Imago al Guan Kabir*)
Supreme Court Decision No. 152 PK/Pid/2010, 7 October 2010 (*Anggodo Widjojo v the Head of Police*)
Supreme Court Decision No. 16 PK/Pid/2010, 29 November 2011 (*Zaki Toya Bawazir*)

7 Rethinking Indonesian extradition law

*Apsari Dewi**

Hadi Ahmadi, a people smuggling offender sought by Australia, was arrested in Indonesia on 29 June 2008, and Indonesia received a formal request for his extradition from Australia on 30 July 2008.[1] Indonesian officials processed the request, and in less than two months, on 26 September 2008, the District Court of South Jakarta ruled that Ahmadi was extraditable.[2] Five months later, the then president of Indonesia, Susilo Bambang Yudhoyono, granted the extradition request.[3] In all, it took approximately eight months for Indonesia to approve Ahmadi's extradition.

On 8 June 2010, Australia sent Indonesia another extradition request for Sayed Abbas, another people smuggling offender.[4] This request did not proceed in as streamlined a fashion. Despite the fact that a South Jakarta District Court decision on Abbas' extradition was issued on 11 July 2013,[5] the Presidential Decision to extradite Abbas was issued only on 15 June 2015, five years after Indonesia received the request.

Italy sent an extradition request to Indonesia for Antonino Messicati Vitale on 27 December 2012, for organised crime, extortion and vandalism offences.[6] The required documents for his extradition were only submitted by Italy on 13 February 2013.[7] Indonesia and Italy do not have a bilateral extradition treaty, yet Indonesia processed the request anyway. It is important to note that an extradition request from a country with which Indonesia does not have a bilateral treaty requires two presidential decisions. First, the president must decide that the extradition request can be processed,[8] and, second, a final presidential decision on the request itself is required. The first approval was issued on 27 June 2013.[9] The request was then processed by the Indonesian police on the 21 August 2013 and, after one and half months, the extradition dossier was submitted to the Provincial Prosecution Office of Bali. The Prosecutor then submitted the case to the District Court of Denpasar on 12 November 2013, and the extradition hearing took place on 20 November 2013. The court ruled at the first hearing that Vitale was extraditable and issued the order on the same day, the 20 November 2013. Just twelve days later, Vitale's extradition to Italy was granted by the President.[10]

The discrepancy in the extradition time frame in these three cases raises questions about how Indonesia processes extradition requests from foreign countries. Ahmadi and Abbas were requested by Australia, while Vitale was requested by Italy. It took a little over eight months for Indonesia to surrender Ahmadi, while for Abbas it took more than five years. Interestingly, Vitale was extradited within nine months, even though Indonesia and Italy do not have an extradition treaty, while Indonesia does have one with Australia. How can these differences be explained?

An efficient extradition process became important as extradition increased in significance in the twentieth century. It is now the main tool for enforcing cross-border criminal law (Bassiouni 2014: 6–7; Boister 2012: 215–17; Shelley 1997). For Indonesia, the number of extradition requests, both sent and received,[11] has increased in recent years as a result of globalisation. However, the modern objectives of extradition have shifted from preservation of power and foreign affairs (Bassiouni 2014: 5–7; Epps 2003: 374–7; Shearer 1971: 6–7), to striking a balance between international cooperation, suppression of criminality and, at the same time, protection of the human rights of the person affected by extradition (De Felipe and Martin 2012: 604; Dugard and Wyngaert 1998: 187–8).

This chapter will examine the extent to which Indonesian extradition law supports the objectives of modern extradition. It concludes that Indonesian extradition law is old-fashioned and, while sufficient to maintain international cooperation, it is less effective as regards the suppression of criminality and the protection of human rights.

Outdated extradition law

Extradition has a long history, dating back to ancient times, with the first recorded extradition treaty made in 1280 BC, between Egyptian Pharaoh Ramses II and King Hattusili III of the Hittites (Bassiouni 2014: 4–5; Blakesley 1981: 41–7; Epps 2003: 374–5; Shearer 1971: 5). As mentioned, extradition gained greater significance in the twentieth century as a direct result of globalisation and the changing nature of crime. Crime is no longer a national phenomenon but increasingly has cross border elements. Because of this, the law enforcement officers of any given state can no longer adequately respond to crime on their own. Now they need to cooperate far more frequently than in the past with law enforcement officers of other states by using the methods of international crime cooperation, and these include extradition.

In Indonesia, extradition existed when it was the Dutch East Indies, that is, before independence in 1945, when part of the archipelago had been a colony of the Kingdom of the Netherlands for approximately 350 years. During the colonial period, the Netherlands issued a Royal Decree specifically regulating extradition arrangements in the Dutch East Indies, the *Koninklijk Besluit* of 8 May 1883 No. 26 (*Staatsblad*[12] 1883-188) on *Uitlevering van Vreemdelingen* (Extradition of Foreigners). This was similar to the extradition law in force in the Netherlands itself, Staatsblad No. 66 dated 6 April 1875.[13] During this period, the Dutch East Indies extradited two Malay marine deserters, two police officer deserters, and four Spanish sailor deserters to Singapore. According to the Dutch Colonial Report of 1883, these extraditions were conducted on the basis of an extradition treaty between the Kingdoms of the Netherlands and Great Britain, which was the colonial power in Singapore.[14]

After independence in 1945, extradition law developed only slowly in Indonesia, despite its long history. In fact, Indonesia has had only two extradition laws since 1945: Staatsblad 1883-188, which was repealed in 1979; and Law No. 1 of 1979 on Extradition, which is currently in force. Although many problems have arisen over the years,[15] Indonesian extradition law has not been amended since 1979.

Staatsblad 1883-188 Uitlevering van Vreemdelingen

As mentioned, the first extradition law to come into force in Indonesia was the Koninklijk Besluit of 1883 and it continued in force after the Dutch colonial era formally ended in 1945, as the Indonesian Constitution declared that all existing laws and institutions remained in force until replaced by laws and institutions made by the independent state, provided they were not contrary to the Constitution.[16] Indonesia thus inherited Dutch extradition law in the middle of the twentieth century, even though much of it dated back to the previous century, as is the case with a number of other laws from Indonesia's former colonial rulers that still remain valid today.[17]

The characteristic features of the Staatsblad 1883-188 reflect the traditional nature of the law. It was aimed was principally at preserving good relations with foreign states. It must be remembered that the Staatsblad 1883-188 was a product of its age, when extradition focused on military and political offenders and was intended to be a friendly gesture between nations to help other sovereigns to preserve their power. The Staatsblad 1883-188 therefore supported extradition for military offenders, and extradition of sailors who opposed their superiors was covered in the extraditable crime list.[18] It did not exempt political offences from extradition, although the nineteenth century extradition laws typically did so. The Staatsblad 1883-188 also covered extradition for common crimes but extradition was only be possible for foreigners charged with, or punished for, the twenty-seven crimes listed in it.

Several extradition principles derived from the eighteenth and nineteenth centuries were also incorporated into the Dutch law. Among its twenty-eight provisions, the Law included a number of exemptions from extradition, such as refusal due to pending prosecution[19] and non-extradition of nationals.[20] As its title suggests, the Dutch law was aimed strictly at extradition of foreigners, thus, citizens could never be extradited. Rules of specialty were also set by the Dutch law. [21] This basically means that the requesting state can only prosecute the person requested for extradition for the offence for which the person is surrendered by the requested state (Boister 2012: 215). The principle is intended to be a safeguard for the person extradited. According to

Bassiouni, the principle of speciality developed to benefit the requested state, to ensure that the requesting state does not abuse the extradition process by false pretences (Bassiouni 1974: 354).

In addition, the Dutch law included rules and procedures for extradition, mainly proceedings for an incoming extradition request to Indonesia. It required authentication in the form of an attached original or certified copy of the judgment or charge laid against the person requested for extradition,[22] and the sending of the extradition request through diplomatic channels.[23] The Staatsblad 1883-188 also established the bifurcated system of extradition mentioned earlier, by which both the executive and judicial organs were involved in making a decision to extradite.[24]

Staatsblad 1883-188 stood as the law on extradition in Indonesia for thirty-four years until repealed by Law No. 1 of 1979. Bassiouni claims that independent Indonesia did not use inherited Netherlands treaties to grant extradition requests from other countries (Bassiouni 1974: 17). This is wrong. In fact, Indonesia granted thirteen extradition requests on the basis of the 1883 Koninklijk Besluit law and Netherlands extradition treaties between 1945 and 1978 (Departemen Kehakiman 1979: 40). As noted in the Indonesian government's official *History of the Establishment of the Law No. 1 of 1979*, Fulun, an Indonesian legislative member of the military faction, stated that several extradition requests were granted under the Dutch law to the United States, the United Kingdom, France, Malaysia, and Singapore for a range of offences, including drug offences, kidnapping, forgery, murder, and the distribution of counterfeit currency (Departemen Kehakiman 1979: 40). In addition, he emphasised that the accomplishment of these extradition requests was for the purpose of sustaining good relations between Indonesia and the extradition countries (Departemen Kehakiman 1979: 40). Moreover, Indonesia used the Netherlands extradition treaty to request the extradition from Singapore of Turk Westerling, a Dutch soldier who led a failed rebellion against the new Indonesian government in 1945.[25]

Although the Dutch law led to the grant of extradition requests received from other states, there is no evidence that this conduct was reciprocal. In other words, there is no record that Indonesia received any person surrendered by another country through the colonial extradition process. It is also important to note that between 1945 and 1978 Indonesia signed three extradition treaties: with Malaysia,[26] the Philippines[27] and the Kingdom of Thailand.[28]

Law No. 1 of 1979 on Extradition

As mentioned, Staatsblad 1883-188 was in effect for almost 100 years before it was finally replaced by Law No. 1 of 1979 on Extradition. The process of replacing it began in 1978, when the government finally decided that Staatsblad 1883-188 was outdated (Departemen Kehakiman 1979). Proposing the Extradition Bill to the Indonesian legislature, the DPR (Dewan Perwakilan

Rakyat, Peoples' Representative Assembly), Mudjono, the Minister of Justice at the time, explained that the 1883 Koninklijk Besluit was intended for surrendering persons in relation to Netherlands East Indies territories (Departemen Kehakiman 1979). He noted that the GBHN (*Garis-garis Besar Haluan Negara* or Broad Outlines of State Policy), established in 1978 by the MPR (Majelis Permusyawaratan Rakyat, the highest national legislative body), called for reform to improve national law.[29] Another important argument raised by the government was that Indonesia needed a better national legal framework as a basis for extradition treaty-making (Suryokusumo 2010: 110). The Indonesian legislature duly passed the bill and Law No. 1 of 1979 on Extradition came into force on 18 January 1979.

The new Extradition Law contains a number of improvements on the Dutch law and covers the main principles and rules of extradition. Yet despite the progress it represented at the time, the 1979 Law now appears to have been left behind by recent developments, and new forms of criminality.

Legal framework

To achieve international cooperation in extradition, a formal procedure is necessary. Article 2 of the 1979 Law stipulates that extradition shall be granted on the basis of a treaty. However, Indonesia, as noted above, does not limit extradition to treaties. The 1979 Law provides that extradition in the absence of a treaty 'may be granted on the basis of good relations and if the interests of the Republic of Indonesia so require'.[30] Thus, reciprocity or comity play a significant role in the practice of extradition in Indonesia as the country may grant extradition to any country on these bases, so long as there is Indonesian interest in extraditing the person sought. The 1979 Law does not, however, determine the scope and the meaning of 'interests of the Republic of Indonesia'. As a result, in the absence of a treaty, extradition depends heavily on discretion.

The 1979 Law does not strictly require a reciprocal arrangement in the absence of treaty. In practice, however, a reciprocal declaration arrangement is usually involved.[31] There are a few instances where Indonesia has granted extradition to a requesting state in the absence of a treaty. For example, in 2008 it granted an extradition request from France for Christian Burger, accused of child molestation in France.[32] Another example is Popa Nicolae, requested for extradition by Romania for fraud in 2009 and extradited on 22 March 2011.[33] Indonesia also granted an extradition request from Hungary for Eva Hovart, who was accused of fraud, on 26 May 2011.[34] Czechoslovakia requested the extradition of Tomas Toman, who was accused of murder, which was granted in 2012.[35] Indonesia had no extradition treaties with France, Romania, Hungary and Czechoslovakia and the extradition offences involved were also not covered by a suppression convention.[36] Thus, these extraditions were made on the basis of reciprocity.

The dual criminality principle

There are two ways of interpreting dual criminality principles under the 1979 Law. The first is through the list of extradition offences, and art. 3(1) of the 1979 Law stipulates that 'extradition shall be granted in respect of the crimes mentioned in the list of crimes, which is affixed as an inseparable text to the Law'. As extradition may only be granted for crimes listed in the 1979 Law, it appears Indonesia applies a narrow interpretation of dual criminality principle. The Law, however, covers a wider range of extradition crimes (thirty-three extradition offences are listed) than the Dutch law (which covered only twenty-seven), and encompasses most serious non-political offences.

The second method of determining dual criminality under the 1979 Law is, again, by exercise of the discretion of the Indonesian government and art. 4 of the Law provides that extradition may be granted at the discretion of Indonesia in respect of a crime not listed in the Law.[37] Article 15 does allow for the possibility of adding to the list of the extradition offences in the 1979 Law through a government regulation. Unfortunately, there has never been such a regulation passed by an Indonesian government.

Principle of speciality

The principle of specialty is covered in art. 15 of the 1979 Law. It prevents the person requested for extradition being prosecuted for an offence other than an offence for which extradition was granted, without first being given the opportunity to leave Indonesia. However, art. 15 of the Law does not clearly determine what needs to be included in the assurances provided by the requesting state. There is no specific requirement for assurance in relation to the principle of speciality. Article 15 only establishes that

> a request for extradition shall be refused if the person requested for extradition will be prosecuted, sentenced, or detained on the account of the commission of another crime than that for which extradition has been requested, unless with the approval by the President.

The Law does not provide a means by which it can be ensured that the person requested for extradition will not be prosecuted, sentenced, or detained for an offence other than an offence for which extradition was granted.

The Law is also silent in relation to the mechanism for providing assurance for an outgoing extradition request from Indonesia. Currently, the assurance is provided by the Ministry of Law and Human Rights. In practice, however, the Ministry does not consult relevant domestic law enforcement agencies before giving assurances to other countries.[38] Consequently, unaware of such assurances, other authorities have occasionally breached them, thereby also breaching the trust of requested states.

The issue of different interpretations of the principle of speciality was evident in the case of Peter Dundas Walbran. The problems here arose due to the differences in the legal systems of Indonesia and Australia. This is not surprising. The application of the principle of speciality is closely related to the criminal law of the contracting states party to an extradition treaty. This easily creates misunderstandings, especially when the parties to an extradition treaty have very different legal systems, as is the case with Indonesia and Australia.

The request for the extradition for Walbran was made by Indonesia to Australia for indecent acts against five minors.[39] The request was granted by the Minister for Justice of Australia in 2011, on the basis of the Minister's determination that Walbran should be surrendered to Indonesia for five offences that violated Indonesian law.[40] An issue arose as to the application of the charges against Walbran in Indonesia. The prosecutor indicted him for five offences, as requested in the letter of surrender from the Minister for Justice of Australia, but added two additional victims. At the time the extradition request was sent to Australia, Walbran's case was still at the investigation stage with the Indonesian police, as stated in the case file submitted by the Indonesian police to the prosecutor. As the investigation developed, the Indonesian police identified additional victims. Although Indonesian prosecutors charged Walbran with the offences endorsed by the Minister of Justice of Australia, Australia still considered that Indonesia breached the principle of speciality by adding new indictments at trial that involved new victims, albeit for the same sort of offence.

Exemptions to Extradition

The 1979 Law[41] covers a broader scope of grounds for refusal of an extradition request, than the Dutch law if replaced. This matches the recommendation in the United Nations Model Law on Extradition,[42] although it does not cover all the relevant recommendations made in the Model Law, including only seven grounds of refusal of twelve. The provisions of the extradition law provide two types of grounds for refusal: mandatory and optional. The mandatory exemptions to extradition include: concurrent jurisdiction (art. 8); double jeopardy (arts. 10 and 11); lapse of time (art. 12); discriminatory treatment exemption (art. 14); extradition to the third state (art. 16); and pending prosecution (art. 17). In contrast to the 1883 Koninklijk Besluit, the 1979 Indonesian Extradition Law makes it mandatory to refuse extradition for political offences (art. 5). The optional exemptions, on the other hand, comprise: non-extradition of nationals (art. 7); the death penalty (art. 13); and exemption of military offences from extradition (art. 6). The 1979 Extradition Law therefore includes the standard extradition exemption rules developed during the nineteenth century but not those developed last century.

Procedural obscurity of Indonesian Extradition Law

This section will discuss extradition proceedings for incoming extradition requests to Indonesia, as the majority of provisions in the 1979 Law govern incoming requests. Extradition requests from Indonesia to other countries are either governed by a treaty between Indonesia and the requested country or, alternatively, by the law of the requested country. The 1979 Extradition Law only addresses this matter briefly, setting out that an outgoing extradition request from Indonesia may only be made by Ministry of Justice (art. 44).

In practice, the extradition proceedings and the roles of institutions involved in Indonesia can be summarised as set out below. Extradition procedures involve action in both the political and judicial sphere, so two branches of the government are engaged in the extradition process – the executive and the judiciary.

Executive

Within the executive, a number of different institutions are involved. These can be divided into three branches, based on their role. The first is the coordinating authority, currently the Minister of Law and Human Rights, who performs the role of the former Minister of Justice. As mentioned, its role is similar to a central authority, and includes sending and accepting extradition requests,[43] assessing extradition requests, communicating with counterpart country,[44] and maintaining coordination with the competent authorities. In practice the Ministry of Law and Human Rights also provides advice to the president in making decisions on extradition.[45]

The second branch is made up of competent authorities. The president is the only decision-making authority for incoming extradition requests.[46] The Ministry of Foreign Affairs is the 'diplomatic channel', to receive and send extradition requests, and provide advice to the president on the relationship between Indonesia and the requesting state. Interpol plays an important role in the commencement of the extradition process by locating fugitive criminals and providing secure and fast mechanisms for sending provisional arrest warrants, for both incoming and outgoing extradition requests. In addition, Interpol is responsible for building the case file on extradition on behalf of the Indonesian police before it is submitted to the Prosecutor. For incoming requests, the police are responsible for arresting the fugitive criminal. The chief of the Indonesian police will provide advice to the president in making the final decision on extradition. Additionally, for outgoing requests, the chief of the Indonesian police has authority to make an outgoing extradition requests.

The prosecution service examines the extradition request and presents the extradition case to the district court. The Jaksa Agung (combined Prosecutor General and Attorney General), who heads the prosecution service, also provides advice to the president after receiving the court order on extradition before the president arrives at a final decision regarding the extradition. He or she may also make outgoing extradition request.

The third branch comprises the administrative authority. The Ministry of the State Secretariat organises the final documents to be considered by the president in making an extradition decision and producing a Presidential Decision in relation to it.

The judiciary

A judge of the district court determines the identity of the criminals and assesses whether an extradition exemption should be applied to the request. The court order is intended only to advise the executive (the president) on the extradition. Importantly, there is no obligation for the president to follow the court's order. The role of the judiciary in extradition is, therefore, only to provide a form of limited administrative review.

As mentioned above, the 1979 Law establishes two different procedures for incoming extradition requests. The first is particularly intended for requests from states with which Indonesia has extradition treaties. A second, specific procedure applies to non-treaty states. The most significant difference between these two proceedings relates to the involvement of the Indonesian president in the procedures. In the absence of a treaty, an incoming extradition request will have to obtain a presidential decision twice. The first decision is at the commencement of the extradition proceeding, when Indonesia receives the incoming request from the non-treaty country. At this stage, before the request is sent to the police for a further proceeding in extradition, a Presidential Decision to agree to cooperate with the state is needed. A second Presidential Decision is needed at the final stage, to decide whether the request is granted or denied. Consequently, the time spent in the extradition process for non-treaty states is, in theory, longer than for treaty states. In practice there are three stages of incoming extradition proceedings to Indonesia: pre-extradition; the main process of extradition; and the surrender of the criminal.

Pre-extradition

The pre-extradition stage occurs before a country sends an extradition request to the country where the criminal is located. At this stage, the requesting country attempts to locate a fugitive criminal by sending a 'red notice' through the Interpol network. If the Indonesian Interpol representative locates the person sought in Indonesia, the official will issue a notice to the country that seeks the fugitive.[47] That country then must send a provisional arrest warrant to Indonesia.[48] After receiving the warrant, the fugitive should be arrested as quickly as possible, to prevent him or her from evading capture.

The main process of extradition

After the person sought has been arrested, Indonesia requires the country that seeks the fugitive to send a formal extradition request. The 1979 Extradition Law does not set a timeframe for Indonesia to receive an extradition request after the arrest. Some treaties do set a time frame, for example the Agreement between Indonesia and Hong Kong to Surrender Fugitive Offenders sets a time limit of sixty days for a requesting state to send an extradition request after an arrest,[49] whereas the Extradition Treaty between Indonesia and the Republic of Korea sets a forty-five-day limit.[50] In practice, however, unless otherwise provided by a treaty, the requesting state has twenty days to send a request that fulfils the requirements established by Indonesian extradition law through 'diplomatic channels'.[51] If Indonesia does not receive the request for extradition within this time, the person will be released from detention.[52]

The Ministry of Foreign Affairs, as the diplomatic channel, will then forward the request to the Ministry of Justice. The distinction in procedures for treaty states and non-treaty states begins at this stage. For non-treaty states, the Minister of Justice and the Minister of Foreign Affairs must report the request for extradition to the president and advise him or her on it (art. 39). Although the 1979 Extradition Law only provides that the advice from the Minister of Foreign Affairs should be about whether the request will be reciprocal (art. 39), in practice, the advice provided by the both ministries will include the state of Indonesia's relationship with the foreign country, the seriousness of the offence, and whether it is in the interests of Indonesia to extradite the person.[53] The president then decides whether Indonesia should continue with the extradition proceeding or decline the request (art. 39(3)).

At the next stage, the Ministry of Justice assesses the request to determine whether it meets all the requirements set by the Indonesian extradition law (arts. 22(3) and (4)). If the requirements of Indonesian extradition law are fulfilled, the extradition request is sent to the Indonesian police and the Attorney General's Office for examination (art. 24). The police will examine the request and build a case dossier on the basis of the request. The case dossier is then sent to the prosecution. The prosecutor has seven days to examine the case, issue a Prosecutor's Note (*Nota Pendapat*) and send it to the District Court (art. 27). The 1979 Extradition Law is silent on the content of the Prosecutor's Note, nor is it mentioned in the Indonesian Criminal Procedure Code (KUHAP, *Kitab Undang-undang Hukum Acara Pidana*) or Law No. 16 of 2004 on the Attorney General's Office. In practice, however, the Prosecutor's Note covers the identity of the criminal and provides a summary and review of the request, stating whether it has met the requirements established by the Indonesian extradition law including the dual criminality and exemption rules.[54]

A judge of the District Court then examines the identity of the person requested for extradition and whether any of the grounds for refusal provided by the 1979 Extradition Law (art. 32) apply to the request. The court will then produce an order on the extradition case, which is sent to the Minister of Justice (art. 33(2)). The Minister of Justice will then gather opinions on the case from the Attorney General, the chief of the Indonesian Police, and the Minister of Foreign Affairs to be sent to the president through the Minister of the State Secretariat. At the final stage, the president has the ultimate discretion on whether to grant or refuse the request, even if the court order and advice from the respective authorities are in favour of extradition.

Surrender of the criminal

This stage involves the administrative process of surrendering the criminal from Indonesian authorities to the requesting state. The Ministry of Justice is responsible for communicating and setting the date with the requesting state. The Law provides that the criminal may be released within fifteen days if he or she has not been collected by the requesting state by the set date (art. 40(2)).

Failure to meet the modern objectives of extradition

As mentioned above, modern extradition needs to strike a balance between the interests of international cooperation in the enforcement of criminal laws, human rights protection of individuals, and the suppression of criminality (Dugard and Wyngaert 1998: 187; Plachta 2000: 64). The 1979 Extradition Law does not meet this objective. It has, for example, failed to facilitate expeditious international cooperation. The process under the Law is unduly bureaucratic and complex, which makes it difficult to achieve the timely surrender of a person to the requested states. In some cases, the proceedings may take up to five years, as in Abbas' case.

The 1979 Extradition Law also lacks clarity about extradition procedures. It does not govern procedure systematically, so it is difficult to understand the stages of procedure. For example, art. 22 (2) of the 1979 Law stipulates that the initial 'request for extradition shall be sent in writing through diplomatic channels to the Minister of Justice of the Republic of Indonesia in order to be forwarded to the President', and art. 22(3) and (4) sets out the supporting documents that must be attached to the request. In addition, art. 24 stipulates that when the extradition requirements have been satisfied, the Minister of Justice shall send the request and the supporting documents to the Indonesian police and the Attorney General's Office for examination. It is unclear when, and, indeed, why, an extradition request should be forwarded to the president at this stage and, in practice, it never happens at this point in the process.[55]

The Law is also silent on the role of each institution involved in extradition, reflecting a wider lack of definitions and interpretative provisions for extradition procedures. For example, art. 19(1) of the 1979 Law provides that a provisional arrest warrant shall be sent through Indonesian Interpol or through 'diplomatic channels' without defining what is meant by 'diplomatic channels'. In practice, the role of Interpol is broader than is suggested by the Law. While the 1979 Law only refers to Interpol as the channel of communication, in practice it also compiles the extradition case before it is submitted to the prosecutor.[56] Additionally, in practice, the Minister of the State Secretariat has an administrative role in the extradition process, even though he or she does not appear anywhere in the Law.[57]

In fact, the most striking technical problem in the 1979 Extradition Law is the obscure nature of its procedural mechanisms. There are several reasons for this. First, the bilateral extradition treaties to which Indonesia is a party are generally silent on proceedings for extradition. Apart from the standard recourse to presentation of extradition requests through diplomatic channels,[58] and the requisitions and supporting documents that need to be submitted,[59] the treaty does not regulate the procedure for extradition requests. The practice of extradition is instead left to the laws of the requested countries, which must fill all gaps arising under the treaty.

This leads to a second problem, namely that Indonesia's 1979 Extradition Law does not, in fact, fill the many gaps in the existing extradition treaty, as it does not contain a comprehensive procedural mechanism for extradition, and neither does any other Indonesian law. Further, the large number of government institutions involved in extradition proceedings in Indonesia often becomes a complicating factor, as government officials manage proceedings without clear direction as to their responsibilities or the procedures to be followed.

The fact that the extradition procedure is unclear in Indonesia has resulted in several specific obstacles to extraditions in practice. The most obvious of these is confusion about extradition proceedings. This is because the 1979 Law fails to define the ambit of relevant institutions involved, or the steps for processing extradition requests at the national level. For instance, pursuant to art. 18 of the 1979 Law, the chief of the Indonesian police or the Attorney General may, in an urgent case, order the arrest of the person sought for extradition. Article 19 of the 1979 Law requires that a requesting state to send a provisional arrest request directly to the chief of Police or the Attorney General through Interpol or diplomatic channels. The chief of Police or the Attorney General may process the request promptly and communicate directly with the requesting state (art. 20). By contrast, art. 21 of the 1979 Law provides that:

> If the person concerned is detained, the said person shall be released by the Attorney general of the Republic of Indonesia or the Chief of the Indonesian Police if, within a reasonable period starting from the date of detention, the President, through the Minister of Justice, does not receive an extradition request accompanied by its supporting documents from the requesting state as required by article 22 of the Law.[60]

These provisions reflect dissonance in the inter-agency cooperation scheme between the institutions involved. Articles 18 and 19 of the 1979 Law seem to suggest that, in an urgent case, the requesting country does not have to communicate the extradition request to the Minister of Justice but can simply contact the Indonesian police or the Attorney General's Office directly. Article 21 of the 1979 law requires, however, that the person shall be released from detention if, within a reasonable period of time, the Minister of Justice does not receive an extradition request. Thus, the Minister of Justice is responsible for determining whether the person sought should be released from detention. In practice, however, given that the law does not require the Chief of Police or the Attorney General to give notice of arrest to the Minister of Justice, law enforcement officials have failed to do so in several extradition cases.[61] As a result, the reasonable time frame does not take into account that the person requested for extradition was, in fact, in detention until the Minister of Justice received the extradition request.

Turning to the second implication of the absence of clear procedural mechanisms in the 1979 Extradition Law, some agencies in Indonesia perform roles in extradition beyond what is prescribed in the Law. For example, the Law requires that the extradition process commences only if the Minister of Justice is satisfied with the substantive requirements of extradition, as well as the supporting documents (arts. 22 and 23). The Law also requires the Indonesian police to examine the person sought for extradition and to build an extradition brief (arts. 25 and 26(1)), to be referred to the prosecutor at a later stage (art. 26(2)). The 1979 Law, does not, however, require police and prosecutors to examine the substantive requirements provided for in art. 22 of the 1979 Law, even though in developing the extradition brief and extradition note, police and prosecutors to practically need to review substantive matters, such as dual criminality and grounds of exception to extradition.

This problem hindered extradition arrangements in the Amanulah Rezaie case, another person sought by Australia for people smuggling offences. In this case, the Minister of Law and Human Rights took the view that the extradition request had fulfilled the conditions of extradition and that extradition could not be denied.[62] When the request was received by the prosecutor, however, he decided that there was a question as to the identity of Rezaie, and so refused to take the extradition proceedings further.[63]

According to Indonesian police officials and prosecutors, it is difficult to carry out their tasks with respect to extradition proceedings solely by reference to the 1979 Law.[64] On a number of occasions, Indonesian officials have struggled to make sense of the Law and the majority I interviewed identified the unclear nature of the domestic extradition proceedings as a major complicating factor in extradition.[65] One Indonesian police official said:

> After arresting and examining the person requested for extradition, we (police officials) have to build an extradition brief to be submitted to the prosecutor. In the brief, we have to make a summary of the request,

> including whether the substantial and procedural requirements are met. If we think the requirements are not fulfilled yet, then we have to advise the Ministry of Law and Human Rights. We cannot process the request. The prosecutor may return the extradition dossier to the police if they think that it does not fulfil the requirements.[66]

Another police official added that they typically refer to the Criminal Procedure Code in performing their task because the 1979 Law is so unclear. According to this official, although the Criminal Procedure Code does not deal much with extradition proceedings, it does establish the central role of the police in Indonesian criminal justice system. This includes investigating criminal cases, gathering evidence to substantiate a charge and compiling it in a criminal case dossier.[67] Accordingly, because extradition procedure is similar to the course of investigation in a criminal case, to make the extradition brief the police must ensure that dual criminality is met and no exemption is available to the person requested for extradition. A similar response was provided by the prosecutor.[68] Since prosecutors are responsible for presenting the person requested for extradition before the court (art. 27), they should provide the court with reasons why the person requested should be surrendered to the requesting state. In doing so, the prosecutors must also assess dual criminality and the grounds of exemptions for extradition, and should refuse to proceed further if they think that the requirements of extradition are not met, even though, pursuant to the 1979 Law, this responsibility for this lies with the Minister of Justice (arts. 23 and 24). The result is that, in practice, three agencies – the police, prosecutors and the Ministry of Justice – compete for control of the extradition process.

The third gap in extradition procedure in Indonesia appears in the application of the principle of specialty. As mentioned, this principle appears in art. 15 of the 1979 Law which requires that:

> an extradition request shall be refused if the person sought for extradition will be prosecuted, sentenced or detained on account of a crime other than that for which his/her extradition has been requested, unless with the approval of the President.

The Law does not positively assign any institution to examine whether the assurances provided by the requesting state are sufficient nor does it deal with the scope of the assurances. Rather, the law focuses only on extradition requests that are excluded from the concept of specialty. This raises questions about the substantive and procedural approach to assurances. How should an assurance provided by the requesting country be weighed, and which institution is responsible to determine the reliability of this assurance? This answer to this question is uncertain. In practice, however, the Ministry of Law and Human Rights carries out the role. During interviews I held with the officials of the Ministry of Law and Human Rights, I found that this ministry applied no standard approach to evaluate the criteria of diplomatic assurances received by Indonesia. An official said that 'so long as the extradition request is accompanied by a letter of assurance, it will be regarded as sufficient to tick the box that the rule of specialty is met'.[69]

The 1979 Law is also silent as to who has the capacity to provide an assurance on behalf of Indonesia. In general terms, art. 44 of the 1979 Law only prescribes that the outgoing extradition request shall be made by the Minister of Justice. Accordingly, in practice, the Minister of Law and Human Rights issues the assurance if required by the requested state.[70] Two issues emerge with respect to assurances provided on behalf of Indonesia. First, as the 1979 Law does not regulate how assurances are given by Indonesia, the Ministry of Law of Human Rights does not consult with the relevant law enforcement agencies before giving an undertaking, nor does it provide advice to the agencies regarding the kind of undertaking given by the Minister on behalf of Indonesia. This problem has affected extradition cooperation, as is evident from the Walbran case, when the prosecutor detained and tried Walbran in Mataram West Nusa Tenggara because the prosecutor was unaware that Indonesia had provided a diplomatic assurance that Walbran would be detained and tried in Jakarta.[71] Nahan, Walbran's prosecutor, stated that the Ministry had never contacted him to discuss the case. He further claimed that 'I have never seen the diplomatic assurances provided by Indonesia for Walbran's extradition and I was confused when Walbran's lawyer objected to trial being conducted in Mataram'.[72] Similar cases will lead to similar breaches of the diplomatic assurances provided by Indonesia.

Extradition proceedings can also be delayed under art. 33(2) of the 1979 Law, which requires the court order regarding extradition, together with its supporting documents, to be submitted by the court to the Minister of Justice for consideration of extradition. However, according to art. 14(j) of the Indonesian Criminal Procedure Code, it is only the public prosecutor who is authorised to enforce a court order.[73] Thus, the fact that the 1979 Law requires the court to submit the court order to the Minister of Justice is confusing and may delay the proceeding, because the Minister cannot enforce a court order. This provision becomes more problematic when the court opposes extradition, as in Abbas extradition case, and orders the release of the person sought for extradition from detention. The prosecutor who handled Abbas case states that:

> The district court ordered to release Abbas from detention as his extradition was dismissed by the District Court of South Jakarta. We could not execute that order straight away because the court had to submit the court order to the Ministry of Law and Human Rights. In the end, the prosecutor was in difficult position, not able to release Abbas, while Abbas' lawyer demanded that he should be released from extradition detention right away.[74]

The consequence of this perplexing provision was a further delay in the extradition proceeding.

Regardless of the limitations of the extradition procedures provided by the 1979 Law, it can still be used as an important tool in managing foreign relations. Extradition is clearly an executive decision in Indonesia. Article 2(1) of the 1979 Extradition Law, provides:

> The decision concerning request for extradition is not a decision of the judicial body but is a decision of the executive body, therefore as a last instance the decision lies in the hands of the President after having received a judicial advice from the Minister of Justice based on an order of the court.[75]

As mentioned, the 1979 Extradition Law requires that extradition cases be submitted for judicial determination, but does not make judicial determination binding. The final decision to grant or deny an extradition request lies solely with the president, and other institutions, including the judiciary, merely serve advisory roles.

As Indonesia is executive-heavy in the process of making extradition decisions, there are many opportunities for politics and national interest to influence the outcome of an extradition request send to Indonesia. The president must consider not only the particular case before him or her, but also the consequences of the decision for Indonesian's foreign relationships. The president's duties are even heavier in the case of an extradition request from countries with which Indonesia has treaty obligations. In these cases, the president should aim for his or her decision to strike a balance between national and individual interest.

This is a double-edged sword. For example, on one hand, executive discretion has been conducive to speeding up the extradition process between Indonesia and Australia when the relationship between these two countries is good. On the other hand, executive dominance can be counterproductive when political relations get difficult, and discretion may be used to delay the process for bargaining and even to deny the request for extradition. So far, the Indonesian president has exercised his or her executive discretion to refuse an extradition request only once,[76] however, Indonesia has certainly used its discretion to delay extradition processes for political reasons, as is evident from the Sayed Abbas case with which this chapter opened.

I do not want to give the impression that all executive discretion in extradition is exercised on the basis of politics. However, political interactions between states are complex and there are moments of tension between states that may offer explanations for why some cases take longer than the others, even for similar offences. Take, for example, this comment from an Indonesian official describing the interface between extradition and bilateral politics.

> When the President said to pause the cooperation with Australia, we did that. We did not process any new incoming extradition request from Australia [...]. What for? The President said no to cooperation. In the end, it will end up on the President's desk.[77]

This answer was given in response to a question about what happened to the extradition cooperation when the bilateral relationship between Indonesia and Australia was in crisis due to a telephone interception scandal, when Australian intelligence was caught tapping President Susilo Bambang Yudhoyono and his inner circle's phones (Bachelard et al. 2013). This shows that when the bilateral relationship between the two countries is strained, extradition cooperation may be directly affected.

In relation to human rights protections, the 1979 Extradition Law generally fails to provide human rights safeguards for individuals involved in extradition cases. It is silent in relation to fair trial standards, which are not prerequisites for an extradition request. More importantly, there is a possibility that the individuals requested for extradition may be subject to torture, cruelty, inhuman and degrading punishment in the requesting state, as the Law does not consider these factors pertinent in considering an extradition request. This category of human rights exception is recommended by the Model Law on Extradition[78] and the United Nations Model Treaty on Extradition.[79]

This problem is acknowledged by Atmasasmita (2007), who argues that the 1979 Law is overly concerned with the effectiveness of international cooperation and disregards the human rights of the offenders. This limitation in the law was relied on Adrian Adamas, who was requested for extradition from Australia by Indonesia, in his objection to the request (Johnston 2014: 20).[80] The Federal Court[81] and the Full Court of the Federal Court[82] held that the Australian Minister of Justice incorrectly interpreted the extradition treaty and should apply Australian standards concerning what constitutes a fair trial. However, these decisions were overruled by the High Court of Australia, which held that in making a surrender determination, the Minister was not obliged to apply Australian standards concerning a fair trial, but instead held that the standard of 'unjust, oppressive or incompatible with humanitarian considerations' in the Extradition Treaty between the two countries 'encapsulated a single broad evaluative standard to be applied alike by Australia and Indonesia'.[83]

In this circumstance, it is debatable whether the 1979 Law is effective as a tool to suppress criminality. It seems clear that its objectives are more to maintain good relationships with other states than to suppress trans-border crimes. There are many provisions that rely on the discretion of the government, which make it difficult to predict the outcome of an extradition request. For example, the power to grant an extradition request on the basis of comity or reciprocity is a matter for executive discretion to determine whether it is in the interests of Indonesia to extradite the person.[84] However, again, it is unclear what constitutes the 'interests of Indonesia'. Extradition requests for offences not listed in the Law also depend on the discretion of the Minister of Justice, as does the invoking of several grounds of refusal. The fact that extradition is an executive process rather than a judicial one again reflects the fact that the main objectives of extradition in Indonesia are a long way from fighting criminal impunity.

Extradition treaties

International law does not appear in the formal hierarchy of Indonesian law so its status is unclear.[85] The question of whether Indonesia follows monism or dualism in relation to the domestic status of international law has been an issue of much scholarly debate. According to Juwana, Indonesia follows dualism, that is, treaties cannot be implemented without implementing legislation (Juwana 1991: 1–2). He says that what he means by 'implementing legislation' is that a treaty needs to be transformed into domestic law.[86] On the other hand, Kusumaatmadja, a former Foreign Minister as well as a leading scholar of international law in Indonesia, argues that Indonesia is monist due to its legal inheritance from the Netherlands, which is a monist jurisdiction (Kusumaatmaja and Agoes 2003). In addition, the Law No. 24 of 2000 on International Agreements provides that Indonesia is monist, as an international treaty is said to be binding after ratification and publication in the state gazette.[87] Butt argues, however, that even if Indonesia is formally monist, it is dualist in practice because, in reality, treaties are never implemented until domestic laws are in place (Butt 2014: 27–8). The relationship between international and domestic law therefore remains somewhat uncertain in Indonesia, but it seems that it is, at the very least, extremely difficult to apply international laws without domestic legislation.

Certainly, Indonesia is heavily dualist in relation to extradition treaties. Law No. 1 of 1979 on Extradition recognises a treaty *only* if it is ratified by a statute.[88] This provision is in line with the provisions of the 2000 International Agreements Law.

Indonesian bilateral extradition treaty practices also indicate the traditional approach of Indonesia towards extradition. First, it is evident from the number of extradition treaties concluded by Indonesia, which is relatively low – only twelve in the last seventy-two years. As noted above, three of these were concluded before the enactment of the 1979 Extradition Law (Malaysia,[89] the Philippines[90] and the Kingdom of Thailand).[91] These treaties remain valid. Since Indonesia passed the new Extradition Law, it has concluded further extradition treaties with just nine countries: Australia,[92] Hong Kong,[93] South Korea,[94] India,[95] Papua New Guinea,[96] Singapore,[97] China,[98] Vietnam,[99] and the United Arab Emirates. [100] Of these twelve treaties, only eight are applicable, as the last four have not yet been ratified by it. Without transformation into a domestic law, Indonesia's signature of these treaties does not give rise to any obligation to extradite.

To date, Indonesia has largely executed extradition treaties with neighbouring countries, or countries within the Asian region, reflecting a characteristic of conventional extradition practice, which often limited extradition treaties to nearby states. The earlier extradition treaties concluded by Indonesia, when Dutch extradition law still applied, were with the founding countries of the Association of South East Asian Nations (ASEAN), of which Indonesia is a leading member.[101] Australia, Malaysia and Singapore are close neighbours of Indonesia. The most distant state with which Indonesia has signed an extradition treaty is the United Arab Emirates, and this was only concluded recently, in 2014, and has still not been ratified. This practice is, in many ways, similar to the approach of the European countries in the eighteenth century (Bassiouni 2014: 4–5); it now seems somewhat old-fashioned, given the increasing importance of extradition as a remedy for globalised crime.

Conclusion

The chapter has surveyed Indonesian approaches to extradition including the legal framework and the procedures for extradition. The 1979 Extradition Law significantly improved on the provisions of the earlier *Staatsblad* 1883-188 on *Uitlevering van Vreemdelingen* (Extradition of Foreigners). It offers a range of new provisions on the rules of extradition such as the political offence exception and discriminatory treatment exemption. It also covers broadens the category of extradition offences to meet the dual criminality requirement.

However, the 1979 Law does not meet the contemporary standards of extradition for facilitating international crime cooperation, or balancing the suppression of criminality with the protection of human rights. After the establishment of the Law, Indonesia did expand its range of bilateral extradition treaties, although their geographical scope is still limited mainly to neighbouring countries. The Law, however, has not been amended by Indonesia since 1979. This has led to major gaps in the practice of extradition arrangements between Indonesia and other countries and reform is now urgently needed.

Notes

* This chapter is based on the author's 2018 PhD thesis, 'Extradition between Indonesia and Australia', at the University of Melbourne Law School.

1 Extradition Request for Hadi Ahmadi, Diplomatic Note No. P042/2008, 29 July 2008.

2 *Extradition Case of Hadi Ahmadi* [2008] The District Court of South Jakarta 02/Pid.c/2008/PN.Jkt.Sel (26 September 2008).

3 Presidential Decision No. 10 of 2009 on Extradition of Hadi Ahmadi to Australia, 20 April 2009.

4 Extradition Request for Sayed Abbas, Diplomatic Note No. P036/2010, 8 June 2010.
5 *Extradition Case of Sayed Abbas* [2013] The District Court of South Jakarta 01/ Pid.C/Ekst/2013/PN. Jkt.Sel (11 July 2013).
6 Receipt of Extradition Request for Antonino Messicati Vitale, No. AHU.5.AH.08.02-166, Ministry of Law and Human Rights of the Republic of Indonesia.
7 Receipt for Antonino Messicati Vitale Extradition Request Documents, No. 03269/HI/02/2013/59, Ministry of Foreign Affairs of the Republic Indonesia.
8 Law No. 1 of 1979 on Extradition (*Ekstradisi*), art. 39.
9 Approval for Processing the Extradition Request for Antonino Messicati Vitale, No. B-758/M.Sesneg/D-4/PU.03/06/2013, Ministry of State Secretariat.
10 Presidential Decision No. 30 of 2013 on the Extradition Request to Italy for Antonino Messicati Vitale, 2 December 2013.
11 Interview with Andi Geman Sinaga, Official at the International Law and Central Authority, Ministry of Law and Human Rights, 16 January 2016.
12 *Staatsblad*: Bulletin of Acts and Orders.
13 See the *Dutch East Indies Colonial Report* (Dutch East Indies Government 1883).
14 See the *Colonial Report* (Dutch East Indies Government 1883), www.statengeneraaldigitaal.nl.
15 Interview with Dr Jan Marinka, Head of Legal Bureau and International Cooperation of the Attorney General's Office of Indonesia, Jakarta, 4 November 2015; and interview with Professor Romli Kartasasmita, Chair of Indonesian Extradition Bill Drafters, 26 November 2015.
16 Indonesian Constitution of 1945 Transitional Provisions, Part II; Government Regulation No. 2 of 1945.
17 For example, Indonesian criminal law was adopted from the Dutch colonial laws. The *Wetboek van Strafrecht voor Indonesie* of 1918 is still in force. See Butt and Lindsey, Chapter 3, this volume; Hart 1987: 166–7; and Kartanegara 1980, vol. 1: 28–9.
18 Koninklijk Besluit van, 8 May 1883 No. 26 (Staatsblad 1883-188) on Uitlevering van Vreemdelingen [Extradition of Foreigners], Royal Decree of 8 May 1883 No. 26 2 (21).
19 Koninklijk Besluit, 8 May 1883 No. 26 (Staatsblad 1883-188) on Uitlevering van Vreemdelingen [Extradition of Foreigners], Royal Decree of 8 May 1883 No. 26: 6.
20 Koninklijk Besluit, 8 May 1883 No. 26: 17.
21 Koninklijk Besluit, 8 May 1883 No. 26: 7.
22 Koninklijk Besluit, 8 May 1883 No. 26: 11.
23 Koninklijk Besluit, 8 May 1883 No. 26: 8.
24 Koninklijk Besluit, 8 May 1883 No. 26: 8.
25 *Re Westerling*, 17 I.L.R. 82 (No. 21) (1950).
26 Treaty between the Government of the Republic of Indonesia and the Government of Malaysia Relating to Extradition, signed 7 June 1974, entered into force 26 December 1974. Ratified by Law No. 6 of 2015.
27 Extradition Treaty between the Republic of Indonesia and the Republic of Philippines, signed 10 February 1976, entered into force 26 July 1976.
28 Extradition Treaty between the Republic of Indonesia and the Kingdom of Thailand, signed 29 June 1976, entered into force 18 March 1978.
29 TAP MPR No. IV/MPR/1978.

30 Law No. 1 of 1979 on Extradition, art. 2(1).
31 Interview with Cahyo Rahadian Muzhar, Director of International Law and Central Authority, Ministry of Law and Human Rights, 19 November 2015.
32 Data obtained from the Ministry of the State Secretariat, 'Permintaan Ekstradisi 2015 [Outgoing Extradition Request 2015]'.
33 Ibid.
34 Ibid.
35 Ibid.
36 'Transnational criminal law' is 'the law that suppresses crime that transcends national frontiers'. Boister (2012: 13) describes it as 'the indirect suppression by international law through domestic penal law of criminal activities that have actual or potential trans-boundary effects'. Put simply, a transnational criminal law arises when there is a treaty in place between states that have an interest in dealing with the crime. A large number of these categories of treaty, including drug trafficking, human trafficking, terrorism, corruption, transnational organised crime and money laundering, are categorised as suppression conventions. States, in general, enter into agreements to criminalise such conduct and to assist each other in the prosecution of these crimes in order to suppress criminal activity. Examples of suppression conventions are the United Nations Conventions against Corruption (UNCAC) and the United Nations Convention on Transnational Organised Crime (UNCTOC).
37 Law No. 1 of 1979 on Extradition, art. 4(2).
38 Interview with Dr Jan Marinka, 4 November 2015.
39 Ministry of Law and Human Rights of the Republic of Indonesia Ref M.HH. AH.08.02-12, dated 15 March 2010.
40 Diplomatic Note No. PO93/2011, dated 24 August 2011.
41 Law No. 1 of 1979 on Extradition.
42 The Model Law on Extradition is complementary to the Model Treaty on Extradition. The Model Treaty was established by the United Nations in 1995 to assist states in their treaty negotiations and give states options to adjust the provisions according to their differing legal systems. The Model Law, on the other hand, is intended to provide a comprehensive guiding tool for legislators to improve their national law on extradition, while at the same time taking into account modern standards and developments in extradition law and practices. It offers significant assistance for states wishing to update and modernise their legislation on extradition. The Model Law on Extradition recommends twelve exemptions to extradition. See United Nations Office on Drugs and Crime 2004.
43 Law No. 1 of 1979 on Extradition, art. 22.
44 Interview with Henry Sulaiman, Directorate of Economic Law, Civil and International Institution, Ministry of Law and Human Rights, Jakarta, 11 August 2015.
45 Interview with Henry Sulaiman, 11 August 2015.
46 Law No. 1 of 1979 on Extradition, art. 36.
47 Interview with Dadang Sutrasno, Indonesian Interpol, Jakarta, 8 September 2015.
48 Law No. 1 of 1979 on Extradition, art. 19(1).
49 Agreement between the Government of Hong Kong and the Government of the Republic of Indonesia for the Surrender of Fugitive Offenders, signed 5 May 1997, entered into force 8 May 2001, s 14(4).

50 Extradition Treaty between the Republic of Indonesia and The Republic of South Korea, signed 28 November 2000, entered into force 23 October 2007, art. 10(4).
51 Interview with Henry Sulaiman, 11 August 2015.
52 Law No. 1 of 1979 on Extradition, art. 21.
53 Interview with Official 1 of the Ministry of Foreign Affairs of Indonesia, Jakarta, 13 August 2015; Interview with Henry Sulaiman, 11 August 2015.
54 Interview with Virgaliano Nahan, Jakarta, 11 November 2015.
55 Interview with Henry Sulaiman, 11 August 2015.
56 Interview with Dadang Sutrasno, 8 September 2015.
57 Interview with Rory Permadi, Extradition Section of the Ministry of the State Secretariat, Jakarta, 11 January 2016.
58 Extradition Treaty between Australia and the Republic of Indonesia, signed 22 April 1992, [1995] ATS 7, entered into force 21 January 1995: 11(1).
59 Ibid., 11(2) and 13.
60 The Law does not specify the 'reasonable period of time', although the Extradition Treaty between Indonesia and Australia provides that the time frame for sending the extradition request after provisional arrest is 45 days: Extradition Treaty between Australia and the Republic of Indonesia, signed 22 April 1992, [1995] ATS 7, entered into force 21 January 1995: 10 (4).
61 Interview with Dadang Sutrasno, 8 September 2015; and Interview with Official 1 of the Attorney General's Office of Indonesia, Jakarta, 11 September 2015.
62 Interview with Henry Sulaiman, 11 August 2015.
63 Interview with Official 2 of the Attorney General's Office of Indonesia, Jakarta, 9 November 2015.
64 Interview with Dadang Sutrasno from Indonesian Interpol, Jakarta, 8 September 2015; Interview with Jajang Ruhyat, Indonesian Interpol, Jakarta, 8 September 2015; and Interview with Official 2 of the Attorney General's Office of Indonesia, 9 November 2015, 1.
65 Interview with Dr Jan Marinka, 4 November 2015; Interview with Rory Permadi, 11 January 2016; Interview with Henry Sulaiman, 11 August 2015; Interview with Official 1 of the Coordinating Ministry of Politics, Legal and Security of Indonesia, 24 November 2015; Interview with Jajang Ruhat, 8 September 2015; Interview with Official 1 of the Ministry of Foreign Affairs of Indonesia, 13 August 2015; and Interview with Professor Romli Kartasasmita, 26 November 2015.
66 Interview with Dadang Sutrasno, 8 September 2015.
67 Interview with Jajang Ruhyat, Indonesian Interpol, Jakarta, 8 September 2015.
68 Interview with Virgaliano Nahan, Jakarta, 11 November 2015; Interview with Dr Jan Marinka, 4 November 2015.
69 Interview with Henry Sulaiman, 11 August 2015.
70 Interview with Henry Sulaiman, 11 August 2015.
71 Interview with Virgaliano Nahan, Jakarta, 11 November 2015.
72 Interview with Virgaliano Nahan, Jakarta, 11 November 2015.
73 Law No. 8 of 1981 on Criminal Code of Procedures, art. 14 (j). The authority of the public prosecutor to enforce a court order is also regulated by art. 30(1) (b) of Law No. 16 of 2004 on The Attorney General's Office of Indonesia.
74 Interview with the Prosecutor in the Sayed Abbas case, Jakarta, 11 November 2015.
75 Law No. 1 of 1979 on Extradition, Elucidation.

76 Indonesia refused to grant an extradition request from Germany for Hans Peter Naumann for drug trafficking because Naumann was tried in Indonesia for drug offences. (Interview with Rory Permadi, 11 January 2016.)
77 Interview with an official of the Ministry of Law and Human Rights.
78 'Model Law on Extradition, Distributed as a Conference Room Paper, *E/CN.15/ 2004/CRP.10, 13th Session of the Commission on Crime Prevention and Criminal Justice in Vienna (11–20 May 2004)*', s. 6.
79 The model treaty recommends torture, cruel, inhuman or degrading treatment or punishment and minimum guarantees in criminal proceedings as mandatory exemptions to extradition. See Model Treaty on Extradition, GA Res 52/88, UN Doc, 70th Plen Mtg, UN Doc A/RES/52/88 (12 December 1997) art. 3(f).
80 *Minister for Justice (Cth) v. Adamas* (2013) 253 CLR 43.
81 *Adamas v. O'Connor (No. 2)* (2012) 291 ALR 77.
82 *O'Connor v. Adamas* (2013) 210 FCR 364.
83 *Minister for Justice (Cth) v. Adamas* (2013) 253 CLR 43, 37. See also Johnston 2014: 20.
84 Law No. 1 of 1979 on Extradition. art. 2(2).
85 Law No. 12 of 2011 on Types and Hierarchy and Formation of Indonesian Legislation (*Jenis dan Hierarki dan Pembentukan Peraturan Perundang Undangan Republik Indonesia*) art. 7(1).
86 Ibid.
87 Law No. 24 of 2000 on International Agreements (*Perjanjian Internasional*), arts. 10 and 13.
88 Law No. 1 of 1979 on Extradition, elucidation of art. 2(1).
89 Extradition Treaty between the Republic of Indonesia and Malaysia, signed 26 December 1974 (Entered into force 7 June 1974, ratified by Law No. 9 of 1974.
90 Extradition Treaty between the Republic of Indonesia and the Republic of Philippines, signed 10 February 1976, entered into force 26 July 1976, ratified by Law No. 10 of 1976.
91 Extradition Treaty between the Republic of Indonesia and the Kingdom of Thailand, signed 29 June 1976, entered into force 18 March 1978, ratified by Law No. 2 of 1978.
92 Extradition Treaty between Australia and the Republic of Indonesia, signed 22 April 1992, [1995] ATS 7, entered into force 21 January 1995.
93 Agreement between the Government of Hong Kong and the Government of the Republic of Indonesia for the Surrender of Fugitive Offenders, signed 5 May 1997, entered into force 8 May 2001, ratified by Law No. 1 of 2011.
94 Extradition Treaty between the Republic of Indonesia and The Republic of South Korea, signed 28 November 2000, entered into force 23 October 2007, ratified by Law No. 10 of 1976.
95 Extradition Treaty between the Republic of Indonesia and India, signed 5 January 2011, entered into force 21 July 2014, ratified by Law No.13 of 2014.
96 Extradition Treaty between the Republic of Indonesia and Papua New Guinea, signed 17 June 2013, entered into force 10 March 2015, ratified by Law No. 6 of 2015.
97 Extradition Treaty between the Republic of Indonesia and Republic of Singapore, signed 27 April 2007.
98 Extradition Treaty between the Republic of Indonesia and the People's Republic of China, signed 1 July 2009.

99 Extradition Treaty between the Republic of Indonesia and the Socialist Republic of Vietnam, signed 27 June 2013.

100 Extradition Treaty between the Republic of Indonesia and the United Arab Emirates, signed 2 February 2014.

101 The Association of South East Asian Nations (ASEAN) was established in Bangkok in 1967 by five countries: Indonesia, Malaysia, Philippines, Singapore and Thailand. The other five countries, Brunei Darussalam, Vietnam, Lao PDR, Myanmar and Cambodia joined ASEAN during the 1980s and 1990s. See 'The Association of South East Asian Nations (ASEAN)' <http://asean.org/asean/about-asean/overview/>.

References

Atmasasmita, Romli 2007. 'Kebijakan Hukum Kerjasama Di Bidang Ekstradisi Dalam Era Globalisasi: Kemungkinan Perubahan Atas UU No. 1 Tahun 1979', 13 December www.tiarramon.wordpress.com/

Bachelard, Michael; Kenny, Mark; and Wroe, David (2013) 'Tony Abbott Refuses to Apologise for Indonesian Spying Program', *The Sydney Morning Herald*, 19 November www.smh.com.au/politics/federal/tony-abbott-refuses-to-apologise-for-indonesian-spying-program-20131119-2xsn4.html

Bassiouni, M. Cherif. 1974. *International Extradition and World Public Order*. Leyden: Sijthoff

Bassiouni, M. Cherif. 2014. *International Extradition: United States Law and Practice*, 6th edn. Oxford: Oxford University Press

Blakesley, Christopher L. 1981. 'The Practice of Extradition from Antiquity to Modern France and the United States: A Brief History', *Boston College International & Comparative Law Review* 4: 39

Boister, Neil 2012. *An Introduction to Transnational Criminal Law*, 1st edn. Oxford: Oxford University Press

Butt, Simon 2014. 'The Position of International Law within the Indonesian Legal System', *Emory International Law Review* 28: 1–28

De Felipe, Miguel Beltran and Martin, Adan Nieto 2012. 'Post 9/11 Trends in International Judicial Cooperation: Human Rights as a Constraint on Extradition in Death Penalty Cases', *Journal of International Criminal Justice* 10: 581

Departemen Kehakiman 1979. 'Sejarah Pembentukan Undang-Undang Republik Indonesia No. 1 Tahun 1979 tentang Ekstradisi'

Dugard, John and Wyngaert, Christine Van den 1998. 'Reconciling Extradition with Human Rights', *The American Society of International Law* 92(2): 187–212

Dutch East Indies Government 1883. 'Colonial Report' www.statengeneraaldigitaal.nl/document/tekst?id=sgd%3Ampeg21%3A18831884%3A0002033&pagina=56

Epps, Valerie 2003. 'The Development of the Conceptual Framework Supporting International Extradition', *Loyola of Los Angeles International & Comparative Law Review* 25: 369

Gautama, Sudargo 1991. *Hukum Dagang & Arbitrase Internasional*. Bandung: Citra Aditya Bakti

Hart, J't. 1987. 'Aspects of Criminal Justice', in Hans Thoolen (ed.), *Indonesia and the Rule of Law: Twenty Years of 'New Order' Government*. London: Frances Pinter pp. 166–208

Johnston, Peter 2014. 'The Incorporation of Human Rights Fair Trial Standards Into Australian Extradition Law', *AIAL Forum* 76: 20

Juwana, Hikmahanto 1991. 'Kewajiban Negara Mentransformasikan Ketentuan Perjanjian Internasional ke dalam Peraturan Perundang-undangan: Studi Kasus Kewajiban Indonesia Pasca Keikutsertaan dalam Cape Town Convention', in Sudargo Gautama (ed.), *Hukum Dagang & Arbitrase Internasional.* Bandung: Citra Aditya Bakti, pp. 1–2

Kartanegara, Satochid 1980. *Hukum Pidana*, vol. 1. [Jakarta]: Balai Lektur Mahasiswa.

Kusumaatmadja, Mochtar and Agoes, Etty R. 2003. Pengantar Hukum International

Plachta, Michael 2000. 'Contemporary Problems of Extradition: Human Rights, Grounds for Refusal and the Principle Aut Dedere Aut Judicare'. UNAFEI Annual Report for 1999, Resource Material Series No. 57

Shearer, Ivan A. 1971. *Extradition in International Law.* Manchester: University Press

Shelley, Louise 1997. 'Threat from International Organized Crime and Terrorism', Congressional Testimony before the House Committee on International Relations www.fas.org/irp/congress/1997_hr/h971001ls.htm

Suryokusumo, Sumaryo 2010, *Hukum Pidana Internasional (Ekstradisi).* Jakarta: Tatanusa

Thoolen, Hans 1987. *Indonesia and the Rule of Law: Twenty Years of 'New Order' Government.* London: Frances Pinter

United Nations Office on Drugs and Crime 2004. 'Model Law on Extradition', Distributed as a Conference Room Paper, E/CN.15/2004/CRP.10, 13th Session of the Commission on Crime Prevention and Criminal Justice in Vienna, 11–20 May

Interviews

Interview with Andi Geman Sinaga, Official at the International Law and Central Authority, Ministry of Law and Human Rights, 16 January 2016

Interview with Cahyo Rahadian Muzhar, Director of International Law and Central Authority, Ministry of Law and Human Rights, 19 November 2015

Interview with Dadang Sutrasno from Indonesian Interpol, Jakarta, 8 September 2015

Interview with Dr Jan Marinka, Head of Legal Bureau and International Cooperation of the Attorney General's Office of Indonesia, Jakarta, 4 November 2015

Interview with Henry Sulaiman, Directorate of Economic Law, Civil and International Institution, Ministry of Law and Human Rights, Jakarta, 11 August 2015

Interview with Jajang Ruhyat, Indonesian Interpol, Jakarta, 8 September 2015

Interview with Official 1 of the Attorney General's Office of Indonesia, Jakarta, 11 September 2015

Interview with Official 1 of the Coordinating Ministry of Political, Legal and Security of Indonesia, Jakarta, 24 November 2015

Interview with Official 1 of the Ministry of Foreign Affairs of Indonesia, Jakarta, 13 August 2015

Interview with Official 2 of the Attorney General's Office of Indonesia, Jakarta, 9 November 2015

Interview with Prosecutor for Sayed Abbas Case, Jakarta, 11 November 2015

Interview with Rory Permadi, Extradition Section at the Ministry of the State Secretariat, Jakarta, 11 January 2016

Interview with Virgaliano Nahan, Jakarta, 11 November 2015

Legislation

Undang-Undang Dasar Negara Republik Indonesia of 1945 [Constitution of 1945] (Indonesia)
Law No. 1 of 1979 on Extradition] (Indonesia)
Law No. 12 of 2011 on Types and Hierarchy and Formulation of Indonesian Legislation (Indonesia)
Law No. 24 of 2000 on International Agreement (Indonesia)
Law No. 8 of 1981 on Criminal Procedure Code (Indonesia)
Law No. 16 of 2004 on The Attorney General's Office of Indonesia (Indonesia)
Presidential Decision No. 10 of 2009 on Extradition of Hadi Ahmadi to Australia, 20 April 2009
Presidential Decision No. 30 of 2013 on Extradition Request to Italy for Antonino Messicati Vitale, 2 December 2013
Model Treaty on Extradition, GA Res 52/88, UN Doc, 70th Plen Mtg, UN Doc A/RES/52/88, 12 December 1997), Ratified by Law No. 6 of 2015
Koninklijk Besluit van 8 May 1883 No. 26 (Staatsblad 1883-188) on Uitlevering van Vreemdelingen [Extradition of Foreigners], Royal Decree of 8 May 1883 No. 26

Treaties

Agreement between the Government of Hong Kong and the Government of the Republic of Indonesia for the Surrender of Fugitive Offenders, signed 5 May 1997, entered into force 8 May 2001
Extradition Treaty between Australia and the Republic of Indonesia, signed 22 April 1992, [1995] ATS 7, entered into force 21 January 1995
Extradition Treaty between the Republic of Indonesia and India, signed 5 January 2011, entered into force 21 July 2014
Extradition Treaty between the Republic of Indonesia and Papua New Guinea, signed 17 June 2013, entered into force 10 March 2015
Extradition Treaty between the Republic of Indonesia and Republic of Singapore, signed 27 April 2007
Extradition Treaty between the Republic of Indonesia and The Kingdom of Thailand, signed 29 June 1976, entered into force 18 March 1978
Extradition Treaty between the Republic of Indonesia and the People's Republic of China, signed 1 July 2009
Extradition Treaty between the Republic of Indonesia and The Republic of Philippines, signed 10 February 1976, entered into force 26 July 1976
Extradition Treaty between the Republic of Indonesia and The Republic of South Korea, signed 28 November 2000, entered into force 23 October 2007
Extradition Treaty between the Republic of Indonesia and the Socialist Republic of Vietnam, signed 27 June 2013
Extradition Treaty between the Republic of Indonesia and the United Arab Emirates, signed 2 February 2014
Treaty between the Government of the Republic of Indonesia and the Government of Malaysia Relating to Extradition, signed 7 June 1974, entered into force 26 December 1974

Court cases

Extradition case of Hadi Ahmadi [2008] The District Court of South Jakarta 02/Pid.c/2008/PN.Jkt.Sel, 26 September 2008
Extradition Case of Sayed Abbas [2013] The District Court of South Jakarta 01/Pid.C/Ekst/2013/PN. Jkt.Sel, 11 July 2013)
Minister for Justice (Cth) v Adamas (2013) 253 CLR 43
Approval for Processing the Extradition Request for Antonino Messicati Vitale, No. B-758/M.Sesneg/D-4/PU.03/06/2013, Ministry of the State Secretariat

Diplomatic Notes

Extradition Request for Hadi Ahmadi, Diplomatic Note No. P042/2008, 29 July 2008
Extradition Request for Sayed Abbas, Diplomatic Note No. P036/2010, 8 June 2010

Part III

Penalties and sentencing

8 Drivers of prison overcrowding in Indonesia

Leopold (Leo) Sudaryono

> I was put in a *kamar* (room) with 12 other detainees, … at one point we had 15 people inside. The room was small and so muggy we named it the *keong* (snail shell). It was just …. around 3 x 4 meters, including a toilet. …. We could ask officers to unlock the room door (*buka keong*, *buka* means open), so we could get more space outside the *keong*, but we need to pay Rp. 150,000 (AUD 15) collectively per *piket* (shift of 8 hours).[1]

As early as 1990, Human Rights Watch reported that prisons in Indonesia were riddled with a multitude of problems (Human Rights Watch 1990) that included chronic corruption, imminent threats of violence, poor quality water and sanitation, and the absence of basic health and education services (Sudaryono 2011). The *Reformasi* (Reformation) movement that began in 1998, and transformed almost every aspect of life in Indonesia, did not bring improvement to conditions in prisons. On the contrary, they became worse. Figure 8.1 shows an unprecedented influx of new prisoners, which multiplied the number of inmates by 409.7 per cent from 65,427[2] to 267,315[3] between 2003 and 2019, exceeding the capacity of the prisons by 167 per cent nationally.

Indonesia has now emerged as one of the top ten countries in the world measured by prison population. In fact, in 2018 Indonesia ranked the seventh,[4] a jump from thirteenth position in 2009,[5] with total growth between 2000 and 2018 at 378.25 per cent. By contrast, the world prison population grew at an average of only 24 per cent over the same period (Walmsey 2019).

Beyond the figures, the impact of overcrowding is devastating on multiple levels and has been very well studied worldwide.[6] Not only does it paralyse prison officials' ability to provide order and security for inmates, let alone meaningful rehabilitation programmes, but it also leads to inhumane conditions and unjust suffering by prisoners.

Between 2010 and 2014, attempts were made by the government to relieve crowding by building 18 more prisons, providing additional space for 4,466 inmates. In 2009, prison authorities also expedited the early release of inmates by granting blanket parole and remissions (sentence reductions) (Directorate General of Corrections 2010). Around 24,000 inmates were subsequently released. In 2015, 118,000 prisoners were again granted remissions of up to

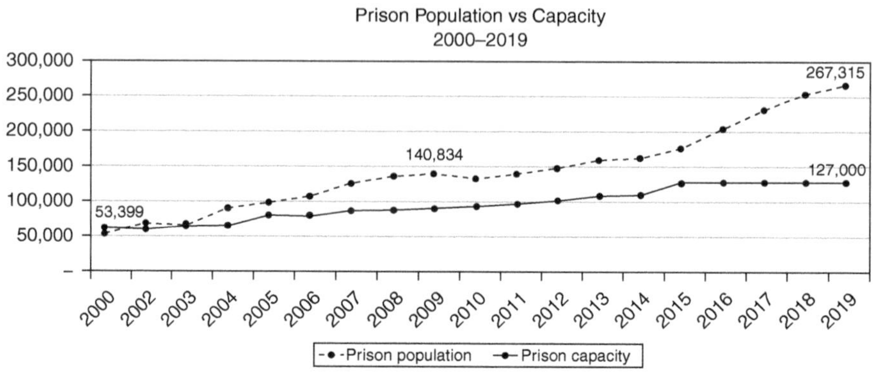

Figure 8.1 Prison Population vs Capacity from 2000 to 2018.[1]

[1] Data from 2010 onward are compiled from SDP (Corrections Database) http://smslap.ditjenpas.go.id, as at 28 August 2019. Data between 2008 to 2010 are based on the Directorate General of Corrections annual report on 2011. Data between 2000 to 2007 are based on report issued by the STADOK (statistic and documentation unit of the DGC) on 2005 and 2007. For less complete data covering a similar period see World Prison Brief Database by the Institute for Criminal Policy Research, www.prisonstudies.org/country/indonesia, as at 28 August 2019.

three months, which allowed 5,682 prisoners to be released (Jakarta Globe 2015). However, these measures were not enough to stop crowding – the number of inmates over this period continued to increase, reaching 188,585 on April 2016 (SDP v3 2018).[7] Despite this, the government continues to rely heavily on the construction of new prisons and the expedited early release of inmates to resolve problems.[8]

This chapter argues that Indonesia needs to acknowledge two major drivers of prison overcrowding: (i) harsh criminal policy that overly relies on imprisonment as the primary means of disciplining societies; and (ii) incentives within justice system that benefit from, and lead to, excessive, prolonged pre-trial detention. Understanding these underlying causes and dealing with them is essential if the government intends to control overcrowding, which is now growing uncontrollably.

The term ‘prison overcrowding’ is loosely and repeatedly used in many different reports and other publications (Bleich 1989: 1125), however, there is no consensus on its definition among scholars and practitioners (Kennedy 1985: 113–15). What constitutes a state of overcrowding may therefore vary across cultural context or countries (Christie 1994: 15). A rather simplistic, but possibly sufficient, meaning refers to a situation where the number of inmates exceeds the capacity of a facility to provide adequate ‘accommodation space’ and basic services (Mandela Rule 42).[9] Again, ‘adequate’ is an ‘extremely fluid’ and ‘very slippery concept’ (Bleich 1989), since there is no ‘internationally agreed set of criteria’ enforced by countries (Albrecht 2012: 67). Even the

United Nations (UN)-initiated Standard Minimum Rules for the Treatment of Prisoners only provides an ambiguous reference, stating 'All accommodation provided .... shall meet all requirements of ... minimum floor space' (art. 10), while the European Committee for the Prevention of Torture indicates a minimum of 4 metres square per prisoner.

The United States (US) Bureau of Justice Statistics views 'prison capacity' in three categories: design capacity, operational capacity, and rated capacity.[10] 'Design capacity' refers to the number of inmates that planners or architects intended for a facility, while 'operational capacity' is the number of inmates that can be accommodated based on a facility's staff, existing programmes, and services. 'Rated capacity', the level at which most prisons run, refers to the number of beds or inmates assigned by a rating official to institutions within a jurisdiction. In Indonesia, the Directorate General of Corrections lists the total prison capacity as the capacity reported by the warden and the Inspectorate General of the Ministry of Law and Human Rights, based on guidance provided by Ministerial Decision No. M.01.PL.01.01/2003 on Building Standards for Corrections Facilities (*Pola Bangunan Pemasyarakatan*). Therefore, Indonesia uses 'rated capacity' under the categories set by the USJS to determine the benchmark of overcrowding.[11]

Multiple impacts of prison overcrowding

There is a wealth of evidence-based knowledge about the impact of prison overcrowding on inmates, their families and prison staff. Cobb, a former inmate in America who initiated a series of campaigns and litigation against prison overcrowding, experienced increasing levels of prison violence which included rape, assault, murder or suicide in the three prisons in which he spent his thirty years of imprisonment (Cobb 1985: 81). Outsider accounts confirm his finding that overcrowding leads to increased levels of stress among prisoners and prison violence (Cox and Rhodes 1990: 126–7).

Inmates and families

An inmate previously detained in the South Jakarta Police office cells shared his experience of being put in 3 x 4-metre cell with 15 others.[12] The effect of overcrowding like this is damaging at various levels. The most direct impact is on prisoners' daily life. Due to a deterioration in the quality of basic services, such as food, clean water and sanitation, treatable illnesses like upper respiratory infections, scabies and other skin ailments become endemic (Sudaryono 2013). In fact, mortality in Indonesian prisons has reached an alarming rate. In 2008, the Directorate General of Corrections reported that 893 inmates died in Jakarta prisons, mostly of opportunistic infections caused by HIV/AIDS (Directorate General of Corrections 2009). Overcrowding also diverts prison resources originally allocated for rehabilitation programmes, which are necessary to assess and lower the inmates' risk of re-offending. As the quality of food and other basic services gets worse, prisoners also need to 'self-service' their own needs to reduce the additional suffering caused by overcrowding, for example by making illegal payments to prison officials or other inmates to win benefits or preferential treatment.

The punitive consequences of overcrowding are also devastating for families. In addition to loss of income (if the offenders are the main breadwinner, Cobb 1985: 77), families need to spend between US$ 40 and US$ 500 a month to support the basic needs of relatives in police detention (Domingo and Sudaryono 2016). The majority of families of offenders (67 per cent) experience damaging impact on their livelihood, including net loss of income, loss of assets, and significant debt, among others (Domingo and Sudaryono 2016). Further, research suggests that incarceration also puts enormous pressure on marital relationships. Forty-five per cent of inmates lost communication with their family and 22 per cent experienced divorce or separation (Salmon 2007). With families torn apart, the social bonds that can help keep potential offenders away from crime diminish (Rose and Clear 1998: 457). These severe impacts on inmate's families, most of whom are socially disadvantaged, contribute to an increased risk of perpetuating intergenerational cycles of poverty and crime (Breen 2008: 23).

Staff

As to prison staff, Vaughn and Cox found in their separate studies that overcrowding also has significant negative impact on the well-being of prison staff over the long term, as measured against work performance, stress levels and health (Vaughn 1993). Olson supports this, revealing growing disciplinary problems among both staff and inmates in a number of Texas prisons as overcrowding increased (Ekland-Olson and Cohen 1983: 163).

Budget

Furthermore, the strain on state budgets has been enormous to bear and difficult to justify, even in developed countries. In the US, United Kingdom (UK) and Australia, parliaments have questioned the soaring cost of imprisonment and requested less budget allocation for building prisons. (Brown 2010: 138). To accommodate 2.4 million inmates in the US, the National Association of State Budget Officers reports: 'State spending on prisons totalled US$ 53.3 billion in fiscal 2013'.[11] This represents '3.2 percent of total state spending and 6.9 percent of general fund spending'. There have been attempts to reduce the cost by contracting out more of the management of prison to private sectors, but corrections spending is still the fifth biggest public budget item in the US after primary, secondary and higher education, public assistance, and Medicaid.

Although the UK and Northern Ireland only host 92,400 inmates (Sturge 2019), a small fraction of the US prison population, the UK's National Offender Management Service reports that for 2017/2018 the operating cost of managing inmates directly was £37,543 per person or, in total, £3.46 billion.

The Secretary of State for Justice is therefore implementing a multi-year programme to further cut back costs by relying on more non-custodial treatment. Similarly, in Australia, the annual expenditure of the government of the state of Victoria to manage prisons housing 7,666 offenders (excluding community corrections) as at June 2018 had reached A$ 906 million, a large increase from A$ 593 million in 2011/12.[13]

Another neighbour of Indonesia, the Philippines, has also confronted problems of this kind. Under President Duterte, the Philippines hosts 135,168 inmates, 397 per cent above rated capacity (Philippines. Senate 2016a). The opposition, led by Senator Recto, has condemned the fact that annual prison spending is almost three times the spending of basic education spending, and the food budget for inmates per capita is ten times that for malnourished children (Philippines. Senate 2016b).

The Indonesian government faces similar challenges. It allocates A$ 472 million annually to host 226,000 inmates in 473 prisons across the archipelago, which is just A$ 5.72 per inmate per day (A$ 1.5 of which is for food).[16] Just to maintain the standard of living for prisoners, which is still poor, the government has to spend more on prisoners than it does on primary-junior high school students (A$ 2.05 per student per day: LaRocque 2015). More grants of parole and fewer custodial sentences would relieve the pressure on government resources. In 2017, for example, by discharging 23,653 inmates through an expedited parole scheme, A$ 16,441,573 was saved (Erdianto 2017).

Drivers of prison overcrowding

Given the seemingly uncontrollable growth of prison population and its multiple devastating impacts, the Indonesian government needs to consider whether its existing measures have sustainably addressed the driving factors of prison overcrowding – or if it even understands what the drivers are. There are a number of approaches that could be taken. An in-depth comparative analysis could be employed to identify the factors based on documented experience across nations dealing with similar situations. Alternatively, a rights-based approach could be used to register non-compliance and barriers to overcoming that. However, this author choses a political economy analysis to unpack structural incentives that contribute to the problem and help explain why the problem persists (Domingo and Denney 2013). More specifically, I seek to identify formal and informal rules derived from legislation, and the interplay between actors and their interests as a living, complex system. Using this approach, two main drivers of prison overcrowding are discussed below: criminal policy and pre-trial detention.

The first driver: Post-98 harsh criminal policy

In the mid 1990s, Indonesia experienced a period of anomie where communal violence erupted in seventeen provinces. Braithwaite (2010: 7) noted that 'very few, if any, nations experienced a higher density of armed conflict in the late 1990s and early 2000s than Indonesia'. Barron et al. (2016) calculated that around 21,495[14] people were killed during the conflicts and more than a million were displaced between 1996 and 2003.[15] This series of catastrophes, coupled with the devastating economic crisis of 1997, eventually gave way to political changes that began on May 1998 and saw Indonesia shift from an authoritarian rule under Soeharto to a more democratic system.

Restoring order and enforcing the rule of law were key and pressing objectives of the *Reformasi* (reform) movement. Shouted by protesters and raised up high on the banners since the first day of the occupation of the national legislature by students in late May 1998, the rule of law (*negara hukum*) became the primary foundation of legitimacy on which the new post-Soeharto system was to be built. Foreign agencies played a key role too. Rule of law was a key requirement prescribed by the Bretton Woods institutions, the IMF and the World Bank, to bail Indonesia out of crisis and ensure the economic and political stability needed for democratic rule.

However, the country chronically lacked experience of what rule of law is. Arief Budiman, a prominent Indonesian sociologist, stated that Indonesians were more familiar with the 'law of the ruler' than the 'rule of law', which had prevailed almost without interruption since colonial times (Lindsey 1999: v). People had longed for justice and legal certainty for decades, and this prompted the call by the 1998 reform movement for rule of law and impartial law enforcement. The public also believed that stricter law enforcement is necessary to stop violent conflict. Many of Indonesia's frequent communal conflicts have often been triggered by isolated incidents that were not properly brought to justice due to 'weak and inconsistent law enforcement' and the 'corruption of law enforcement officials' (Braithwaite et al. 2010: 134).

The People's Consultative Assembly, the MPR (Majelis Permusyawaratan Rakyat), which was then responsible for putting the demands of reform movement into law, believed that taking a harsher stance on crime was the *primum remedium* (first resort), instead of *ultimum remedium* (last resort), to restore order.[16] Its members saw this as marking a new era, representing a positive symbol of state willingness to use force, but this time to protect the public by whatever means necessary (Garland 2001: 138).

However, Indonesia followed a pattern that Shelley (1982: 64) has identified as the mistaken route of many post-colonial developing countries, simply reinforcing the criminal policy of colonial rulers in the past centuries: expanding police power; imposing new offences and longer mandatory sentences; and establishing more penal institutions. Post-1998 Indonesian governments sought to shape the new system and control the behaviour of society during the transition by adopting these harsher penal policies. Garland (2001) observed that many governments, like those in the United States, find penal solutions 'are immediate, (and) easy to implement'. Within a year of Soeharto's resignation in May 1998, the new administration therefore introduced dozens of new offences. There was little political resistance to 'tough on crime' policies in either the legislation or police.[17] It was considered a form of accountability toward their constituencies' and their concerns over the perceived escalation of crimes. This is known as the 'democracy-at-work' thesis (Beckett 1997: 15–16). Furthermore, some politicians found that taking a stricter stance against crime by imposing a policy of harsher sentences could attract a greater popular vote (penal populism) (Bottom 1995), and, increasingly, the greater goal was to 'win votes rather than to reduce crimes or to promote justice' (Pratt 2007: 3). All parties accepted that offenders, the 'source of social disorder', needed to be isolated from society, rather than striving to find deeper, possibly more disturbing, causes of crime. More stringent penal policy is attractive because it is less complex, and leaves 'fundamental social and economic arrangements untouched' (Garland 2001: 200), particularly in a post-conflict context. Harsh criminal policy is relied on to unify and reassure the general public, exhausted by years of conflict and decades of injustice, of the common purpose of the new regime. It represents a 'significant break' with the past (Garland 2001: 13).

This stance is also a convenient shortcut to meet the 'Rule of Law index' required by the World Bank, which includes 'perceptions of the incidence of both violent and non-violent crime, the effectiveness and predictability of the judiciary'.[18] While re-establishing justice and order may take longer and be a more costly route, improving public perceptions of security could be achieved relatively quickly by legislative measures and selective policing. There are, however, at least four negative consequences of this approach.

Large number of new offences

Akbari has found that between 1998 and 2014 Indonesia introduced 1,601 criminal offences, 716 of which are new (Akbari 2015, and see Figure 8.2). A significant number of the new offences were originally administrative ones but were then converted into criminal offences. 738 of the offences are punishable with five years of imprisonment or above, and thus further encourage pre-trial detention. (ICJR 2015a: 14). In fact, these changes actually doubled the total number of criminal offences in Indonesia. Akbari offers an example of the criminalisation of administrative action: a civil servant's failure to follow administrative procedure in rescinding documents is now punishable by ten years of imprisonment (Law No. 43 of 2009 art. 86).

Many of these offences seem to have been created without consideration of the incarceration rate and prison overcrowding. The most striking example of this relates to Indonesia's 'war against drugs'.

Indonesia, which had a population of more than 240 million in 1998, and is now approaching 270 million, is the biggest potential market for narcotics in its region. As early as the 1970s, Indonesia considered narcotics abuse one of six national priorities (Lindsey and Nicholson 2016: 47). However, the problem worsened toward the end of 1990s as a greater range of drug varieties became more available, with some domestically produced (Lindsey and Nicholson 2016: 46). The 'war on drugs' become a key theme globally.

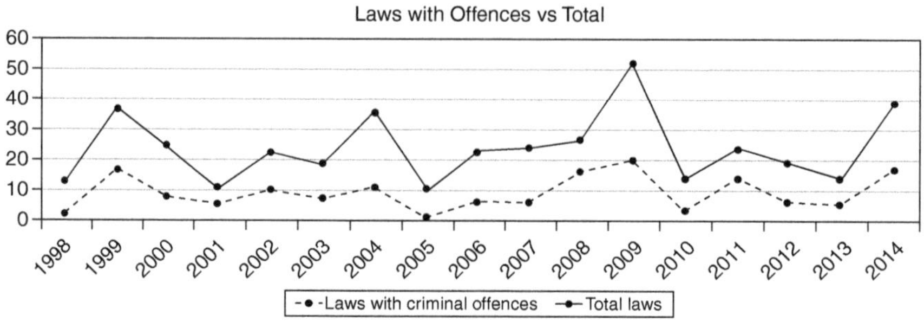

Figure 8.2 Comparison of total new legislation (solid line) and those with new Offences (broken line) in Indonesia.

Source: ICJR (2015a: 14)

Even the Netherlands, a country known for its 'tolerant, non-punitive' policy towards drug abuse, struggled with the problem.

In 2009, Indonesia revoked the 1997 Narcotics Law and put a new Law in its place. This introduced a very broad new range of drug offences, ranging from consumption, possession, and trafficking to producing. However, while the new Law provides for much heavier sentences, it contains much ambiguity in its formulation the offences. Some conduct may involve a number of different offences, which carry very different sentences. The selection of the charge or combination of charges used in a case depends solely on the discretion of the police and prosecutor. As discussed below, this generates uncertainty on the offender's side as well as facilitating corruption by law enforcers. The result has been a very significant increase in the number of drug convictions in Indonesia, as Figure 8.2 suggests.

Minimum mandatory sentences

A second source of negative consequences created by harsh penal policies is the increased number of minimum mandatory sentences in the new legislation, particularly as regards narcotics offences. Frase and Tonry (2001: 265) found that one major causal factor for global mass-incarceration is the 'substantial growth of drug offences' and severe penalties for such offences in many parts of the world. For example, Norway, another country that had previously had a considerably lenient penal policy, felt the need to 'buckle up' and accelerate its war against drugs as international concern about drug crime increased (Christie 1994: 65). Until 1964, a drugs offender in that country could only be sentenced to maximum six months of imprisonment. Twenty years later, the maximum sentence for drugs cases was twenty-one years of imprisonment. Some countries, including Malaysia and Mexico, even introduced mandatory minimum sentences, and Indonesia followed suit, imposing a minimum

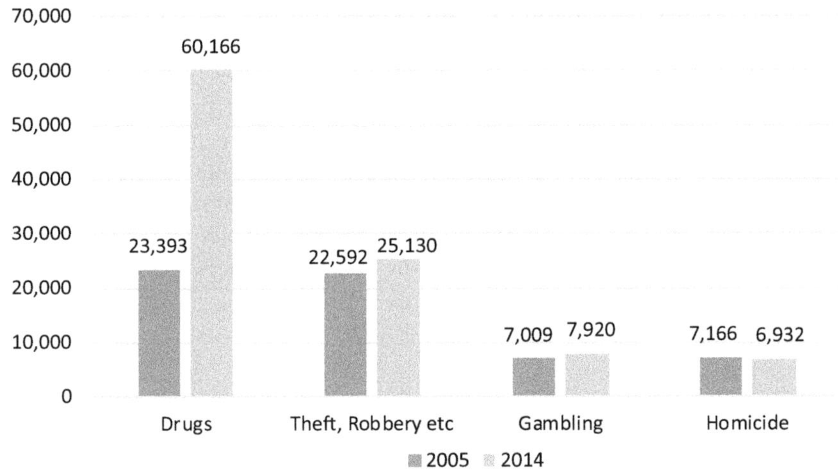

Figure 8.3 Comparison of top four crimes for which inmates received nine years' imprisonment.

Source: Information Request to DGC, 16 February 2015

of four years of imprisonment for the possession of any amount of illicit substances (category A) under the 2009 Narcotics Law.

As Figure 8.3 shows, although the number of convictions for theft, gambling and homicide have been relatively steady over the last nine years, the number of offenders imprisoned for drugs-related offences in Indonesia has increased three-fold since the mandatory sentence was introduced in 2009. Ninety-eight per cent of suspects of are now imprisoned regardless of their real risk of re-offending or causing harm to society. This has helped rapidly inflate the number of prisoners in Indonesia to a level way beyond the capacity of prisons.

Lack of sentencing options

Third, the new offences were introduced in the absence of alternative sentencing options. The Criminal Code (KUHP, *Kitab Undang-Undang Hukum Pidana*), which was enacted by the Dutch for *inlanders* (indigenous non-Europeans) in 1918, currently recognises only three types of sentence: the death sentence, imprisonment and fines.[19] Seventy-six per cent of sentences for the new offences rely on incarceration as the chief option. As Assegaf explains in Chapter 9 of this volume, this leaves judges with effectively no choice but to imprison offenders, regardless of the type of crime or offenders' personal profiles.

This obsolete sentencing policy does not reflect the contemporary socio-legal context of Indonesia and needs to be revised. The legislature should amend the Code and introduce a set of alternative sentencing options. For different crimes there should be different treatments to punish and rehabilitate the offenders. There are certain types of crimes for which imprisonment may not be appropriate – for example, victimless crimes like drug abuse, prostitution, and street gambling. Offenders who commit these crimes are often victims of the broader social problems and may require empowering intervention, not imprisonment (Losel 2007). Being shut in a cell full of other addicted drug users without receiving any meaningful rehabilitation programme will not address drug users' problems. In some cases, it actually leads to a new problem: drug circulation in the prisons due to high demand for drugs.

Local offences

A fourth consequence of the harsh penal policy applied since 1998 has been a proliferation of criminal laws created by local governments. The post-reform decentralisation policy (art. 18, Second Amendment to 1945 Constitution) grants local governments authority they share with the central government over all aspects of governance apart from seven key areas, which remain the central government's exclusive domain (foreign policy, security, defence, justice, national fiscal and monetary policy, and religion: art. 10(3), Law No. 32 of 2004 on Regional Administration). To exercise these broad responsibilities, local governments (executive and legislative) enact regional regulations (*perda*). To ensure adherence to perda, local governments have been given the power to impose criminal sanctions (art. 15(1), Law No. 12 of 2011 on Establishment of Laws and Regulations) of up to maximum six months *kurungan* (imprisonment for misdemeanours) or fines of up to A$ 5,000 (art. 238(2), Law No. 23 of 2014 on Regional Administration replacing the 2004 Law). There are three main problems arising from this. First, prior to Law No. 23/2014, perda had been used to impose excessive criminal sentences (Hukumonline 2015), disregarding the principle of proportionality (BPHN 2010: 1). Second, perda in a number of regions are based on the local majority religion and may be discriminatory. Third, many perda overlap, replicate or contradict existing national criminal laws. The enforcement of perda has also been very erratic (Priyangga 2017; Lowing 2017) but they have also contributed significantly to overcrowding in local detention centres.

The second driver: Excessive pre-trial detention

Pre-trial detention affects the population size of prison in two ways. First, because many districts and cities lack separate facilities for pre-trial detainees (such as a remand centre), they are held either in police cells or, more often, in prisons, mixed with convicts. Of the total number of prisoners in Indonesia in 2013 (241,000), 54.1 per cent were pre-trial detainees waiting for, or undergoing, trial (Correction Database System, SDP v2, 2013). Likewise, ICJR found 98 per cent of suspects were detained by the police (ICJR 2012, 2015b)

Second, excessive and prolong pre-trial detention, in practice, often indirectly determines the minimum length of sentence offenders must serve. Problems are created for prosecutors and judges should a court incarcerate an offender for a period shorter than the length of his or her detention prior to the time of sentencing. As an illustration, one judge has been recorded as considering fifteen days imprisonment adequate for a rickshaw driver convicted of street gambling but, because the offender had already been detained for 110 days, the sentence was adjusted to three months (Domingo and Sudaryono 2016: 29, and see Assegaf, Chapter 9)

Pre-trial detention refers to a period between the point of arrest and the point the court commences the hearing. It encompasses the investigation and prosecution stages, better known in Indonesian legal practice as the pre-adjudication stage:

1. Investigation: the investigator (usually police, but sometimes other investigators stipulated by law) can issue detention orders for up to 20 days for the purposes of investigation, extendible to 40, or, in total 60, days (art. 24, KUHAP). Should the investigation not completed by that period, the investigator must release the detainees.
2. Prosecution: the prosecutor has up to 50 days to detain offenders (art. 25, KUHAP). Within this period the district attorney will examine evidence presented by investigator and compile the indictment for court. Alternatively, the prosecutor may refer the case back to the investigator due to incomplete evidence or if the case does not constitute a criminal offence.

In other words, by the time trial commences, offenders may have been detained for as many as 110 days, regardless of the offence of which they are accused.

Judges in the district court have the power to detain offenders for up to a further ninety days during the trial (art. 26, KUHAP). Should the offender or the prosecutor file an appeal – and around 4.79 per cent of criminal cases are appealed to the provincial level High Courts, and 2.94 per cent to the Supreme Court (Supreme Court 2016: 17, 87–89) – offenders could be detained in total for 400 days (arts. 27–28, KUHP).

In practice, police discretion to detain a suspect at the investigation stage generally determines whether the person stays in custody until the end of justice chain. Prosecutors and judges admit they will almost automatically extend the detention status of offenders whose case appears before them since 'Judges and prosecutors feel that they do not have enough resources for risk assessment, for instance related to flight risk' (Domingo and Sudaryono 2016: 28). Likewise, if offenders are not under arrest, judges will not usually issue a detention order unless the decision at the first instance was to convict the offender. For all these reasons, I now look more closely at detention in the investigation stage.

Legal norms

The Criminal Procedure Code (KUHAP, *Kitab Undang-undang Hukum Acara Pidana*), enacted in 1981, sets criteria for detention, including the risk of the suspect escaping, destroying evidence or re-committing the crime (art. 21). Unfortunately, KUHAP adopts the model in the colonial HIR (*Herziene Inlandsch Reglement*), the criminal procedural code for non-Europeans, and so provides no accountability mechanism to scrutinise the grounds used to justify detention. As Lev (1985: 62) says 'HIR provided far fewer protections against government authority. It was easier, for example, to arrest, detain, and convict an Indonesian under the HIR than a Dutch subject under the *Strafvordering*' (the colonial criminal code applicable to Europeans).

After twenty-four hours of detention, the investigator only needs a detention warrant from his or her direct supervisor to extend the detention – not a warrant from the court, which is the norm in many other justice systems. Recently the Constitutional Court acknowledged that pre-trial hearings (*praperadilan*) can examine the grounds on which an investigator started a criminal case against a suspect, as well as whether the arrest has met formal requirements (as Mann discusses in more detail in Chapter 5). However, there is still no formal procedure by which a suspect can challenge his or her detention. KUHAP allows police to apply alternative forms of detention including city arrest, house arrest or suspension of detention. Although in many other jurisdictions, a suspect can request a variation to the form of detention, in Indonesia this is a matter that can only be resolved by the police unit that has detained the person.

Domingo and Sudaryono (2016) found that pre-trial detention in Indonesia is unduly prolonged and excessively used. Although interrogation takes place in the first two to three days, detention is often extended to the maximum period of two months, regardless of the crime alleged. This observation was supported by a series of interviews I conducted with fifty-six inmates in 2016.[20] Fifty-four were detained by the investigators (the other two were charged with corruption and not detained). Thirty-six were detained for between forty-five and sixty days for drug use (art. 127, Narcotics Law) or possession (art. 111), assault (art. 170, KUHP), or various crimes against property (fencing, stealing, etc). Twelve offenders were held for from three to six weeks for gambling and drug dealing. Only six offenders were detained for less than five days, three for gambling and three for assault.

Looking at the type of offence and the length of detention, the only correlation that can be made is in relation to corruption cases, where offenders were not detained by the investigator or the prosecutor until the district court delivered its verdict. Both interviewees, the treasurer of a Regency (*kabupaten*, or county) and the director of a BUMD (regional government owned enterprise), admitted 'recourse to alternatives to detention is a matter of negotiation' with the detaining authorities. As seen in Table 8.1, more than half

Table 8.1 Length of detention by police experienced by interviewee

No Inmates	*Length of Detention*	*%*
36	46 to 60 days	64.3%
12	21 to 45 days	21.4%
0	6 to 20 days	0.0%
6	1 to 5 days	10.7%
2	0	3.6%

Source: Author's research.

of the fifty-six interviewees were detained by police for the longer period of forty-six to sixty days.

Incentives

There are a number of incentives for police to detain suspects for unduly prolonged periods. The first is the broadly punitive sentiment common among the general population. The public expect the police to detain and incapacitate crime suspects. The presumption of innocence is not only weak in practice in the criminal justice system but not greatly valued in community attitudes toward alleged offenders. Therefore pre-trial detention is often 'considered part of punishment' (Domingo and Sudaryono 2016: 21). Police crime units raised concern that delays in arresting suspects, and decisions not to detain suspects, regardless of the complexity of the crime involved, are taken as an indication of low performance or even corruption on their part (Domingo and Sudaryono 2016: 28).

A second incentive relates to convenience or practicality. Regardless of the crime involved, ICJR found 98 per cent of crime suspects were detained (ICJR 2012). In a focus group discussion involving police crime units from several districts, officers admitted that it is much easier to simply detain suspects during the investigation stage. The suspect can easily be interrogated and confronted at any time. Police officers interviewed by ODI-TAF offered mixed responses about the use of violence during detention. Those who admitted knowing about the practice said they consider it necessary for the suspect to be in police custody so intimidation or torture can be used to extract key information (Domingo and Sudaryono 2016: 24). This was seconded by interviews with inmates in 2016. Of fifty-six inmates, nineteen admitted experiencing violence during police custody, as the following table (Table 8.2) shows.

Granting suspension of detention entails undertaking enormous responsibilities and risks – ensuring offenders will not run away, tamper with the evidence, or repeat the offence – that investigators prefer not to take (Art. 21 (1), KUHAP). Police district officers commented that they will not object to

Table 8.2 Violence experienced during police custody

Age	*Gender*	*City*	*Offence*	*Violence experienced*
22	M	Yogyakarta	111 – Possession	Beaten during investigation
21	F	Pontianak	112 – Possession + 114	Slapped by other inmates in police cell
26	F	Tangerang	112 – Possession + 127 Drug use	Boyfriend beaten by police
34	F	Yogyakarta	112 – Possession + 127 Drug use	Received smack on the head during arrest
25	M	Tangerang	112 – Possession + 127 Drug use	Beaten repeatedly in car on the way to the police office
26	M	Banjarmasin	127 – Drug use	Slapped in the face
25	M	Tangerang	127 – Drug use	Hit three times on the head
25	M	Tangerang	170 – 1st degree assault, led to death	Electrocuted with Taser gun during interrogation
22	M	Tangerang	170 – 1st degree assault, led to death	Beaten during arrest
32	M	Tangerang	170 – 1st degree assault, led to death	Face painted by police
32	M	Pontianak	170-2nd degree assault	Hit on the face during arrest
54	M	Banjarmasin	303 – Gambling	Beaten during arrest
54	M	Tangerang	303 – Gambling	Held in neck-lock during arrest
32	M	Pontianak	310 – Traffic accident	Violence by police and fellow inmates: not specified
35	M	Yogyakarta	363 – Burglary	Head stamped on and beaten during arrest.
25	M	Pontianak	363 – Fencing	Shot in the leg
21	M	Yogyakarta	363 – Theft	Beaten during arrest
21	M	Banjarmasin	365 – Snatch and grab	Repetitively beaten
23	M	Yogyakarta	365- Mugging – 5 cases	During arrest and investigation: beaten, threat to shoot

Source: Author's research.

suspension of detention as long as it is granted after interrogation is complete, and the decision is not theirs (Domingo and Sudaryono 2016: 28).

Performance metrics make up a third incentive. Since the police were formally separated from the military from April 1999 to enable them to carry out their exclusive responsibility of maintaining security and order, they have received enormous, if not unprecedented, institutional support. The police chief was upgraded by Yudhoyono to ministerial level in 2010,[21] and the police budget is now the third largest of all Indonesian government agencies, increased from Rp. 16.6 trillion in 2006 to Rp. 95 trillion in 2018 (Baker

2015: 118; Mei 2018). However, there are still discourses reflecting on poor public perceptions of police performance and lack of integrity, and whether the decision to grant autonomy to police was correct (Muradi 2014: 161). Several prominent politicians, including Ruhut Sitompul (Democrat Party), repeatedly question police ability to meet the reform expectations, arguing that their role should be shared with other agencies like the military. Challenged by this, former Police Chief Tito Karnivian has emphasised that the police have met performance indicators as verified by the Ministry of State Apparatus and Bureaucratic Reform (Menpan RB) and the National Development Planning Agency (Annur 2014). However, doubts remain.

Police performance is measured by three key functions: (i) *keamanan dan ketertiban* (security and order); (ii) *pelayanan masyarakat* (public service, like traffic or vehicle/driver registration); and (iii) *penegakan hukum* (law enforcement). The first function is the responsibility of police intelligence (*intelkam, intelijensi dan keamanan*), community policing (*binmas, bina masyarakat*), and the general security unit (*sabhara, samapta bhayangkara*, riot police and first dispatch for crimes). The second function is the responsibility of the traffic unit (*lantas, lalu lintas*), and the third function belongs to the criminal detective unit (*reserse*). Performance of the law enforcement function is measured by increased number of criminal cases successfully referred to, and accepted by, the prosecutor (P21 status). While there are incentives to handle more cases every year, this is not reflected in the budget. A study of the performance index conducted by Polri-Partnership for Good Governance shows that the annual budget can only cover the investigation costs of 36 per cent of the cases at the regional level (*Polda, polisi daerah*), and 51 per percent at the district level (*Polres, polisi resort*) (Biro Reformasi Birokrasi Polri 2016: 13).

The contradiction could not be more striking. On one hand, state budget allocated for the police is almost as high as that of the Ministry of Public Work and Public Housing (MenPUPERA, Menteri Pekerjaan Umum dan Perumahan Rakyat), the second largest in 2018. Teuku Taufiqulhadi, of the Badan Anggaran, the Budgetary Agency of the DPR (Dewan Perwakilan Rakyat, People's Representative Assembly, the national legislature), considers police complaints about the lack of budget for law enforcement to be inappropriate because the police budget is the highest of all non-ministry state institutions (Khadafi and Alum 2018). In a context where almost all ministries have experienced budget cuts due to, among other things, huge infrastructure programmes, the police have enjoyed a double increment, from Rp. 44 trillion in 2014, to Rp. 95 trillion in 2018 under the administration of President Joko Widodo (Jokowi) (Movanita 2017).

On the other hand, the performance indicators were set by the police themselves, who are the regulator and operator of security activities in Indonesia, reporting directly to the president; if the president lacks time to oversee them, they report to no one. Their target is based entirely on the previous year's records. In the modern criminal justice world, many police forces have adopted predictive policing. This model is new, and it helps policymakers calculate potential crimes in a territory based on various variables (socio-economic features, residential type, previous crimes, demographic information and so on), using mathematical models (Portland State University 2012). The current budget formulation the Indonesian police apply in allocating budget for investigating cases may not reflect actual security or crimes issues on the ground, and this creates a vicious cycle: improved performance leads to more cases handled, which leads to more budget allocation, which leads to improved performance – and still more cases.

The other problem is that by targeting, and therefore handling, more cases than budgeted, the police have to either split the budget – the budget for one case is used for two or three cases – or rely on non-budget financial resources, which are corrupt or of dubious legality. There are two immediate consequences of the first option. First, splitting the budget leads first to poor quality investigations, and overreliance on the use of torture to extract information or confessions. Second, police will pursue 'easy cases' that require minimum resources to solve but may not reflect what the public consider a priority or a security threat, such as street gambling.

As to the second consequence, Meliala has stated that there are three non-budget sources to help finance investigations: *Parman* or *Partisipasi Teman* (friends' contributions); *Parmas* or *Partisipasi Masyarakat* (victims' contribution); and *Parmin* or *Partisipasi Kriminil* (criminals' contribution, or bribes).[22] Of course, there are no means to verify the amount or use of these non-budget resources, and they undermine the integrity and the very purpose of criminal justice system. With the budgeting process as is, it will only become a greater driver of the use of detention as a tradable commodity, and that brings me to the fourth incentive for excessive pre-trial detention: rent-seeking.

Detention has monetary value, and this is particularly true of police cells, which were mostly designed only for temporary/short term detention. Inhumane living conditions creates demand for detainees to access items or services to ease the suffering. The police have fixed a standard cost for the daily rations (*standar biaya konsumsi tahanan*) for detainees of between Rp. 32 and 55,000 per day depending on provincial location (Finance Ministry 2016). This may provide sufficient nutrition for healthy living but all former police detainees said that the food they received was worth way less than that. Detainees typically receive two meals (lunch and dinner) of *nasi cadong* (poor quality steamed rice with tofu/tempe and stewed vegetables) and a morning snack every day in most cells. Detainees of Polda (regional level police) may receive better food than Polres (district level police) or Polsek (sub-district level police office) detainees. When inmates are asked how much they consider the value of the daily food allowance, all calculated the range between Rp 12,000 and Rp 15,000. Detainees may order 'outside food' or other items such as *nasi padang* (rice with decent spicy chicken or meat) or the more affordable *nasi goreng* (fried rice) for twice the normal price. For detainees who have families frequently visiting, durable and shareable food items like salted eggs or spicy, dried anchovies make the *nasi cadong* more bearable.

Drinking water is also another paid item. Three inmates (one female) previously detained in a Polsek prison in South Kalimantan needed to drink tap water in the toilet (which in Indonesia is undrinkable for health reasons), unless they collectively bought *galon* or bottled water.

Buka keong ('open the shell') is a practice experienced by a former detainee during his time in a Polres in Jakarta in 2016.[23] In this Polres, there were ten cells in a detention area. A cell each was allocated for women and juveniles, with the rest left for male adults. Eleven to fifteen detainees were put in 3 x 4 metre cells, which were always hot, humid and smelly. *Buka keong* is a request made to the guard to unlock the cell during the guard's shift (eight hours) to allow detainees to stretch their legs or sleep more freely within the locked detention area. The cost to *buka keong* is Rp. 150,000 per cell per shift or around Rp. 10,000 per inmate per shift. New inmates who appear to have good family or financial support to pay are always welcome. Another type of payment is *uang kebersamaan* (collective money), ranging between A$ 75 and A$ 200, paid once by new inmates in Yogyakarta and Pontianak. The money is used to cover basic expenses for those in the cell. Visiting family members are also required to pay between A$ 2 and A$ 5 per visit, or two packs of cigarettes. This occurred in all police prisons in which the inmates I interviewed were detained.

A second aspect of the monetary value of detention is payment for 'helping with the case'. Detention offers opportunities for many police officers (not necessarily the investigator in charge) to facilitate 'assistance' for the detainees. Twenty-six of fifty-six detainees interviewed admitted they were offered 'assistance with the case' by the investigator or other police officers. Five others were approached by the prosecutors. Eleven inmates refused to use the service. The type of assistance available includes: destroying or reducing the amount of evidence (for narcotics cases); changing offences (for narcotics, from possession to consumption); revising or creating new interrogation files (BAP); reduced sentences; deleting 'R' (recidivist) status on the detainee's record; suspension of detention (a form of conditional release); and granting the detainee' justice collaborator' status, which entitles him or her to a reduced sentence and other benefits. Like the services offered, the amount of payment sought also varies enormously, from A$ 200 to A$ 50,000.

Table 8.3 summarises the experiences of the twenty-six detainees interviewed.

Conclusion

Prison overcrowding is the 'grand result of thousands of decisions made by independent actors' in the three branches of government (police, prosecutor and judiciaries) (Kaufman 1985). To understand the overcrowding problem, criminal policy, the work of each state institution involved, and the complex interplay of interests in the justice chain must all be taken into account.

Table 8.3 Payment made by detainees during police detention

Age	*Sex*	*City*	*Charge*	*Represented by lawyer?*	*Payment*	
					Legal case	*Living Conditions*
34	F	Yogyakarta	127 – Drug use	Yes	Paid A$ 800 for a lenient sentence	No
23	M	Yogyakarta	365 Mugging – 5 cases	No	Asked forA$ 200, to delete 'R' (recidivist) status, detainee refused	No
25	M	Yogyakarta	170 – 1st degree assault leading to death	Yes	Asked for A$ 9K, refused	Yes, A$ 2 /visit, A$ 30 for water
22	M	Yogyakarta	111 – Drug possession	Yes, after interrogation	Paid A$ 30K to drop article charge 116.	Yes, A$ 80 for 'collective money'
21	M	Yogyakarta	127 – Drug use	No	Paid A$ 25K to change charge from possession to drug use	No
33	M	Yogyakarta	303 – Gambling	No	Asked for A$ 2K, refused	No
35	M	Yogyakarta	363 – Burglary	No	Paid A$ 15K for lower sentence, by police	Yes A$ 75 for collective money
25	M	Tangerang	127 – Drug use	Yes	Asked for A$ 15K, for assistance but police changed their mind	A$ 2/week for water, A$ 5/visit
26	M	Tangerang	127 – Drug use	No	Offered dropping of charge (art. 112). Family paid, do not know how much	No
54	M	Tangerang	303 – Gambling	No	Negotiating the value of evidence	No
35	M	Tangerang	170 – 2nd degree assault		Asked for A$ 10K for 3 offenders	

26	F	Tangerang	127 – Drug use	No	Asked for A$ 100K to destroy evidence, deal at A$ 4K,	No
61	F	Tangerang	303 – Gambling	No	Asked for A$ 4.5K to be freed, no deal	
43	F	Tangerang	303 – Gambling	No	Asked for A$ 2K to be freed, no deal	
29	F	Tangerang	372- Embezzlement	No	Offered 'assistance' but refused by detainee	No
22	F	Tangerang	112 – Drug possession	Yes	Asked for A$ 25K to be freed, or A$ 2K to change to lesser charge (use)	A$ 1/day for water, A$ 5/visit
26	F	Tangerang	112 – Drug possession	No	Asked for A$ 30K to change charge from art. 112 to 127. Offered suspension of detention if can give 'rich drug users' to police	
24	F	Pontianak	112 – Drug possession + 127- Drug user	No	Offered to change charge, detainee refused	No
21	F	Pontianak	112 – Drug possession + 114	No	Asked for A$ 1.500 to be freed, but refused, no guarantee	No
26	F	Pontianak	112 Drug possession 2 cases. Second case while in prison	Yes	Charge changed from art. 112 to 127 (use); boyfriend paid for it	No
45	F	Pontianak	351 – Assault leading to death	No	Offered assistance by prosecutor, refused	No
32	M	Pontianak	310 – Traffic accident	No	Offered assistance by prosecutor – A$ 500	A$ 5/visit, A$ 200 on one occasion to police via other inmates
30	F	Banjarmasin	112 – Drug possession + 127 – Drug use	Yes from LBH	Offered help via husband	No

(*continued*)

Table 8.3 Cont.

Age	*Sex*	*City*	*Charge*	*Represented by lawyer?*	*Payment*	
					Legal case	*Living Conditions*
26	M	Banjarmasin	127 – Drug use	Yes, from the university, after 15 days	Offered 'assistance' but refused by detainees	Drinking water from the tap in the toilet, must pay for bottled water
21	M	Banjarmasin	365 – Snatch and grab	No	Asked for A$ 5K to be freed. Lesser sentence offered by prosecutor, refused	Drinking water from the tap in the toilet, must pay for bottled water, A$ 2/visit
20	F	Banjarmasin	374 – Embezzlement	Yes, from family after 2 months	Offered A$ 5K for sentence below 2y, by prosecutor, family handled	Drinking water from the tap in the toilet, must pay for bottled water
51	M	Banjarmasin	Corruption	Yes, from family	Paid A$ 10K to prosecutor, but prosecutor moved to another office	No
35	M	Tangerang	114 – Drug dealing	No	Paid A$ 1K for justice collaborator status, offered A$ 6K to change to lighter charge	A$ 2.5/visit
25	M	Tangerang	112 – Drug possession and 127 – Drug use	No	Offered lesser charge for A$ 5K by police	No
46	M	Tangerang	Corruption	Yes, from family	Yes, but refused to share the details	No
38	M	Tangerang	310 – Traffic Accident leading to death	No	Police and the family of victims asked for A$50K to drop the case	No. Wife brings water and food every day

Source: Author's research.

This chapter has looked at how post-Soeharto law-makers have responded to public demands for the rule of law in Indonesia by introducing a harsh criminal policy that relies heavily on imprisonment, following the model of the Dutch colonial administration. Opportunities that emerged after 1998 to synthesise a justice model based upon the cultural and social context have been missed. To restore order, governments in transition opted simply for strong punitive criminal policy.

Romli Atmasasmita[24] and Awaluddin Djamin, two figures influential in constructing post-reform criminal policy, have admitted that correction or re-adjustment is acutely needed, and they believe the moment is ripe.[25] However, with the current administration facing continued challenge from its political opponents, a stricter approach to crime is preferred. This can be seen by Jokowi's uncompromising attitude towards narcotics and the death penalty, discussed by Gunawan and Pamintori later in this book (Chapter 11). In this environment, proposals to revise and decriminalise the current narcotics law struggle to get traction.

In 2012, the Supreme Court took the initiative to soften the criminal policy by using an internal regulation to increase the minimum threshold of arrestable offences from A$ 0.02 (set in the 1950s) to A$ 250.[26] Until then, the threshold was so low that every criminal suspect could validly be detained. Unfortunately, police and prosecutors adamantly disregard this regulation, claiming their powers in this regard are fixed by legislation and are beyond the Supreme Court's jurisdiction.

The other driver within the justice chain contributing to the prison overcrowding is excessive and unduly prolonged pre-trial detention, with police enjoying unchecked power to detain suspects for up to sixty days. This authority needs to be limited by shortening the detention period and placing the decision to detain beyond that period with a judge, who can carefully review the preliminary evidence presented, the re-offending risk, and the profiles of the offenders, an approach now common in many other countries.

Finally, there is a vicious cycle within Indonesian law enforcement which is administrative in origins but has multiplying impact on the prison overcrowding. To demonstrate constantly improved performance in law enforcement, police set an increased number of criminal cases successfully referred to, and accepted by, the prosecutor (P21 status) as an indicator (ITK *Indikator Tata Kelola*). However, this target is not fully reflected in the budget. This has multiple effects. First, it leads to poor quality investigation; second, it encourages persistent use of torture as an efficient means to extract information; third, it means police focus on chasing easy cases that require minimum resources; and fourth, it forces reliance on external resources to finance police operations, of which only 20 per cent are currently funded by the state. The performance indicators for law enforcement should instead be based on a more independent, objective model of predictive policing of the kind now common in many countries around the world.

The coercive criminal policy and the broad discretion of law enforcement agencies allowed by the Criminal Procedure Code have created enormous opportunities for arrest and detention to become commodities with monetary values. This can only drive Indonesia deeper into its severe prison overcrowding crisis, with all its many devastating impacts.

Notes

1 Interview by the author with anonymous, a former police detainee, on 3 March 2017 at Cipinang Prison Class 1A.
2 The 2005 STADOK (Statistics and Documentation) Report of the DGC. Until 2011, information from about 500 prisons was gathered and compiled manually in the Directorate General of Corrections' annual report.
3 May 2019, http://smslap.ditjenpas.go.id/public/grl/current/monthly/year/2019/month/5, as at 28 June 2019.
4 www.prisonstudies.org/highest-to-lowest/prison-population-total?field_region_taxonomy_tid=All, as at 28 August 2019.
5 See Walmsley 2009 and data from World Prison Brief 2009 (online database at www.prisonstudies.org/).
6 See, for example, Cobb 1985; Cox and Rhodes 1990; Ekland-Olson et al. 1983; Rose and Clear 1998; Vaughn 1993; and, in the Indonesian context, Domingo and Sudaryono 2016.
7 Annual remission and parole are granted every 27 April at the Directorate General of Corrections' anniversary ceremony.
8 Minister of Law and Human Rights Regulation No. 11 of 2017 on the Grand Strategy for Handling Prison Overcrowding. See Wijaya 2016.
9 *Rule 42* – 'General living conditions addressed in these rules, including those related to adequate personal space, shall apply to all prisoners without exception.'
10 Bureau of Justice Statistics, www.bjs.gov/index.cfm?ty=tp&tid=133, as at 21 April 2015.
11 Total rated capacity in 522 prisons in Indonesia was 127,113 but inmates numbered 262,985: http://smslap.ditjenpas.go.id/public/grl/current/monthly, as at 1 July 2019.
12 Interview with anonymous, a former police detainee, on 3 March 2017 at Cipinang Prison Class 1A.
13 See Victorian Corrections, Prisons & Parole webste: www.corrections.vic.gov.au/prison/corrections-statistics-quick-reference, as at 28 August 2019.
14 The figure includes communal violence and insurgencies.
15 The conflicts segregated areas into religion-based zones in the provinces of Maluku, North Maluku, and Central Sulawesi, and ethnic-based zones in Central Kalimantan and West Kalimantan, forcefully displacing many locals to new areas.
16 MPR Decision No. XI/MPR/1998 on Clean and Good Governance and the Eradication of Corruption/Nepotism/Collusion.
17 Interview with Prof. Romli Atmasasmita, 22 November 2016.
18 The World Bank Data Bank: http://databank.worldbank.org/data/databases/rule-of-law.
19 Article 10, Indonesian Criminal Code.

20 The interviews were conducted as part of my doctoral research at the Australian National University. They took place between June to November 2016, in eight prisons across five provinces (Banten, Jakarta, DIY, West Kalimantan, and South Kalimantan) and involved fifty-six respondents. The research focussed on finding the drivers of overcrowding, a cause which had full support from the Directorate General of Corrections. The respondent selection was based on gender and top ten crimes committed by convicts as registered in the sites. The focus of the interview was on offenders' experience during investigation, prosecution, and the trial. All respondents required full anonymity.

21 Presidential Regulation (Perpres) No. 52 of 2010 on the Organisational Structure and Management of the Indonesian National Police.

22 Interview with Adrianus Meliala, 17 January 2017.

23 Interview with a former police detainee, 3 March 2017.

24 Interview, Prof. Romli Atmasasmita, former Director General of Law and Regulations and Head of National Law Development Body, at his office in Jalan Brawidjaja, Jakarta, 23 November 2016.

25 Interview, Prof. Awaluddin Djamin, former Indonesian Police Chief, at his residence in Kebayoran Baru, 23 May 2017.

26 Supreme Court (Mahkamah Agung, Indonesia's highest appeal court) Regulation No. 2 of 2012 on the Readjustment of the Minimum Threshold for Misdemeanours and Fines.

References

Akbari, Anugerah Rizki and ICJR (Institute for Criminal Justice Reform) 2015, 'Potret Kriminalisasi Pasca Reformasi dan Urgensi Reklasifikasi Tindak Pidana di Indonesia' (The Post-reform Criminalization and the Urgency of the Criminal Reclassification in Indonesia), Report. ICJR, p 14

Albrecht, Hans-Joerg 2012. 'Prison Overcrowding – Finding Effective Solutions: Strategies and Best Practices against Overcrowding in Correctional Facilities'. Max-Planck-Institut für Ausländisches und Internationales Strafrecht, www.mpicc.de

Annur, Andika Dwi 2014. 'Ruhut: TNI-Polri Satu Atap Lagi Saja', *RimaNews*, 20 November http://archive.rimanews.com

Baker, Jacqui 2015. 'Professionalism without Reform: The Security Sector under Yudhoyono', in Edward Aspinall, Marcus Mietzner and Dirk Tomsa (eds.), *The Yudhoyono Presidency: Indonesia's Decade of Stability and Stagnation.* Singapore: Institute of Southeast Asian Studies, pp. 114–35

Barron, Patrick; Jaffrey, Sana; and Varshney, Ashutosh 2016. 'When Large Conflicts Subside: The Ebbs and Flows of Violence in Post-Suharto Indonesia', *Journal of East Asian Studies* 16: 191–217 10.1017/jea.2016.6

Beckett, Katherine. 1997. *Making Crime Pay: Law and Order in Contemporary American Politics*. New York: Oxford University Press

Biro Reformasi Birokrasi Polri (Bureaucratic Reform INP) 2016. Indeks Tata Kelola Kepolisian Negara Republik Indonesia (ITK) Tingkat Polres/Polresta/Polrestabes/Polres Metro (Governance Index of the Indonesian National Police at district level). Jakarta: POLRI – Partnership for Good Governance

Bleich, Jeff 1989. 'The Politics of Prison Crowding', *California Law Review* 77(5): 1125–80

Bottoms, Anthony E. 1995. 'The Philosophy and Politics of Punishment and Sentencing', in Chris Clarkson and Rod Morgan (eds.) *The Politics of Sentencing Reform*. Oxford: Clarendon, pp. 17–49

BPHN (National Law Development Body) 2010. *Perencanaan Pembangunan Hukum Nasional Politik Hukum Pidana dan Sistem Pemidanaan* (The development of national law, criminal and sentencing policy). Jakarta: Ministry of Law and Human Rights

Braithwaite, John; Braithwaite, Valerie; Cookson, Michael; and Dunn, Leah 2010. *Anomie and Violence: Non-truth and Reconciliation in Indonesian Peacebuilding*. Canberra: ANU Press

Breen, Jessica 2008. 'The Ripple Effects of Imprisonment on Prisoners' Families', *Jesuit Centre for Faith and Justice, Working Notes* 57: 19–24

Brown, D. 2010. 'The Limited Benefit of Prison in Controlling Crime', *Current Issues in Criminal Justice* 22(1): 137–48

Cavadino, Michael and Dignan, James 1992. *The Penal System: An Introduction*. London: Sage Publications

Cavadino, Michael and Dignan, James 2006. 'Penal Policy and Political Economy', *Criminology and Criminal Justice* 6(4): 435–56

Christie, Nils 1994. *Crime Control as Industry: Toward GULAGS, Western Style*, 2nd edn. Abingdon and New York: Routledge

Clarke, R. J. 2005. 'Research Models and Methodology', University of Auckland, business.uow.edu.au/research/UOW012042.html

Cobb, Alonzo 1985. 'Home Truths about Prison Overcrowding', *The ANNALS of the American Academy of Political and Social Science* 478(1): 73–85

Cox, George and Rhodes, Susan L. 1990. 'Managing Overcrowding: Corrections Administrators and the Prison Crisis', *Criminal Justice Policy Review* 4(195): 115–43

Directorate General of Corrections 2009. *Annual Report 2009*. Jakarta: Directorate General of Corrections

Directorate General of Corrections 2010. *Annual Report 2010*. Jakarta: Directorate General of Corrections

Domingo, Pilar and Denney, Lisa 2013. *The Political Economy of Pre-trial Detention*, Overseas Development Institute, February www.odi.org

Domingo, Pilar and Sudaryono, Leopold 2016, *The Political Economy of Pre-trial Detention: Indonesia Case Study*, Overseas Development Institute, October www.odi.org

Ekland-Olson, Sheldon; Barrick, Dennis M.; and Cohen, Lawrence E. 1983. 'Prison Overcrowding and Disciplinary Problems: An Analysis of the Texas Prison System', *Journal of Applied Behavioral Science* 19(2): 163–76

Erdianto, Kristian 'Sepanjang 2017, Ditjen PAS Hemat Biaya Makan 174 Miliar', *Kompas.com*, 20 December https://nasional.kompas.com

Farrington, David P. 1980. 'Prison Size, Overcrowding, Prison Violence, and Recidivism', *Journal of Criminal Justice* 8: 221–31

Finance Ministry 2016. 'Standar Biaya Masukan 2016', Attachment No. II. 10.

Foucault, Michel 1975. *Discipline and Punish: The Birth of the Prison*. Harmondsworth: Peregrine Books

Frase, Richard and Tonry, Michael 2001. *Sentencing and Sanctions in Western Countries*. Oxford University Press

Garland, David 2001. *The Culture of Control: Crime and Social Order in Contemporary Society*. Oxford University Press

Greenberg, David and West, Valerie 2001. 'State Prison Populations and Their Growth, 1971–1991', *Criminology* 39(3): 615–54

Haney, Craig 2012. 'Prison Effects in the Era of Mass Incarceration', *The Prison Journal* 20(10): 1–24

Hukumonline 2015 'Aturan Pemidanaan dalam Perda Mesti Tunduk terhadap RUU KHP', 14 September www.hukumonline.com/berita/baca/lt55f676656cccf/aturan-pemidanaan-dalam-perda-mesti-tunduk-terhadap-ruu-kuhp/

Human Rights Watch 1990. 'Prison Conditions in Indonesia', August www.hrw.org/

ICJR (Institute for Criminal Justice Reform) 2012, *Potret Penahanan Pra-Persidangan di Indonesia: Studi Tentang Kebijakan Penahan Pra-persidangan dalam Teori dan Praktek* [*Portrait of the Conditions of Pre-trial Detention in Indonesia: A Study on the Policy in Theory and Practice*]. Jakarta: ICJR

ICJR (Institute for Criminal Justice Reform) 2015a. *Potret Kriminalisasi Pasca Reformasi dan Urgensi Reklasifikasi Tindak Pidana di Indonesia* [*The Post-reformation Criminalisation and the Urgency of the Criminal Reclassification in Indonesia*]. Jakarta: ICJR

ICJR 2015b. 'Sepanjang Belum Naik Status Jadi Terdakwa, Tersangka Tidak Perlu Ditahan, Inilah Alasannya', 11 January http://icjr.or.id/sepanjang-belum-naik-status-jadi-terdakwa-tersangka-tidak-perlu-ditahan-inilah-alasannya/

Indonesia. Supreme Court (Mahkamah Agung) 2016. 'Laporan Tahunan Mahkamah Agung RI 2016' [The Supreme Court Annual Report]

Jakarta Globe 2015. 'Majority of Graft Inmates Get Independence Day Sentence Cuts', 18 August http://jakartaglobe.id/Karsted, Suzanne 2001. Comparing Cultures, Comparing Crime: Challenges, Prospects and Problems for a Global Criminology, *Crime, Law and Social Change* 36(3): 285–308

Kaufman, G. 1985. 'The National Prison Overcrowding Project: Policy Analysis and Politics, a New Approach', *The Annals of the American Academy of Political and Social Science* 478: 161–72

Kennedy, Edward M. 1985. Prison Overcrowding: The Law's Dilemma. *The Annals of the American Academy of Political and Social Science* 478(1): 113–22

Khadafi, Robbi and Alum, Reko 2018. 'Mengungkap Permainan Anggaran Penanganan Perkara di Polri', *Law Justice: Portal Berita dan Investigasi*, 5 January https://law-justice.co

Lacey, Nicola 2008. *The Prisoners' Dilemma: Political Economy and Punishment in Contemporary Democracies*. New York: Cambridge University Press

LaRocque, Norman I. A. 2015. 'Summary of Indonesia's Education Sector Assessment', ADB Papers on Indonesia, no. 5, October. Philippines: Asian Development Bank, www.adb.org/

Lev, Daniel S. 1985. *Colonial Law and the Genesis of the Indonesian State*. Ithaca: Southeast Asia Program Publication, Cornell University

Levitt, Steven D. 2004. 'Understanding Why Crime Fell in the 1990s: Four Factors that Explain the Decline and Six that Do Not', *Journal of Economic Perspectives* 18(1): 163–90

Lindsey, Timothy (ed.) 1999. *Indonesia: Law and Society*, 1st edn. Annandale, N.S.W.: The Federation Press

Lindsey, Tim and Nicholson, Pip 2016. *Drugs Law and Legal Practice in Southeast Asia: Indonesia, Singapore and Vietnam*. Oxford: Hart Publishing

Lösel, Friedrich 2007. 'Counterblast: The Prison Overcrowding Crisis and Some Constructive Perspectives for Crime Policy', *The Howard Journal* 46(5): 512–19

Lowing, Nixon S. 2017. 'Penerapan Sanksi Denda dalam Penegakan Hukum atas Peraturan Daerah Tentang Sampah di Kota Manado' (Implementation of Fine on the Enforcement of Regional Regulation on Waste Management in Manado Municipality), *Lex et Societatis* V(8), October https://ejournal.unsrat.ac.id/index.php/lexetsocietatis/article/view/18117

Mathiesen, Thomas 2000. *Prison on Trial*. 2nd edn. Winchester: Waterside Press

Mei, Amelia R. 2018. 'Polri Terima Anggaran Rp 95 Triliun di 2018', *Detik.com*, 19 January https://news.detik.com

Moore, Mick 2001. 'Types of Political Systems: A Practical Framework for DFID Staff'. Report to UK Dept for International Development (DFID) staff. (Version 2). October

Movanita, Ambaranie Nadia Kemala 2017. 'Anggaran Polri Naik Dua Kali Lipat Era Jokowi, Tito Berterima Kasih', *Kompas.com*, 10 July https://nasional.kompas.com

Mullen, Joan 1985. 'Prison Crowding and the Evolution of Public Policy: National Institute of Corrections: Our Crowded Prisons', *The Annals of the American Academy of Political and Social Science* 478(1): 31–46

Muradi 2014. *Politics and Governance in Indonesia: The Police in the Era of Reformasi*. Abingdon and New York: Routledge

Philippines. Senate 2016a. 'Press Release: PH Jails Packed 4 Times their Capacity; Digong Urged to Free Sick, Old Prisoners', 4 August www.senate.gov.ph/press_release/2016/0804_recto1.asp

Philippines. Senate 2016b. 'Press Release: Recto: P74K Yearly Budget per Prisoner is Thrice Bigger than Gov't Spending per Student', 30 August www.senate.gov.ph/press_release

Portland State University. Criminology and Criminal Justice Senior Capstone Project 2012. 'Predictive Policing: A Review of the Literature'. Paper 5. http://pdxscholar.library.pdx.edu/ccj_capstone/5

Pratt, John 2002. *Punishment and Civilization: Penal Tolerance and Intolerance in Modern Society*. London: Sage Publications

Pratt, John 2007. *Penal Populism: Key Ideas in Criminology*. London: Routledge

Priyangga, Satya W. 2017. *Penerapan Sanksi Pidana Dalam Peraturan Daerah Kota Metro No. 4 Tahun 2014 Tentang Kawasan Tanpa Rokok (Implementation of Criminal Offence in the Regional Regulation of Metro Municipality on the Smoke-Free Zone)*. Bandar Lampung: Lampung University

Roberts, Julian V.; Stalans, Loretta J.; Indermaur, David; and Hough, Mike 2003. *Penal Populism and Public Opinion: Lessons from Five Countries*. Oxford University Press

Rose, Dina. R. and Clear, Todd. R. 1998. 'Incarceration, Social Capital, and Crime: Implications for Social Disoganization Theory', *Criminology* 36(3): 441–80

Rusche, Georg and Kircheimer, Otto 1939. *Punishment and Social Structure*. New York: Columbia University Press

Rusche, Georg and Dinwiddie, Gerda 1978. 'Labor Market and Penal Sanction: Thoughts on the Sociology of Criminal Justice', *Crime and Social Justice* 10(fall-winter): 2–8

Salmon, Sarah. 2007. 'Memorandum Submitted by Action for Prisoners' Families. Selected Committee on Home Affairs', June www.publications.parliament.uk

Schwendinger, Herman and Schwendinger, Julia 2013. 'Looking Back: Reflecting on the Birth of Radical Criminology at Berkeley', *Journal of Crime and Justice* 36(2): 148–52

Shelley, Louise I. 1982. *Crime and Modernization: The Impact of Industrialization and Urbanization on Crime*. Southern Illinois University Press

Sturge, Georgina 2019. 'UK Prison Population Statistics', Briefing Paper No. CBP-04334, House of Commons Library, www.parliament.uk/commons-library

Sudaryono, Leopold 2011. 'Reform at the Doorstep of Prisons in Indonesia', The Asia Foundation, https://asiafoundation.org/2011/08/10/reform-at-the-doorstep-of-prisons-in-indonesia

Sudaryono, Leopold 2013. 'Overcrowding Crisis: A Disintegrating Justice System Is Causing Rampant Prison Overcrowding', *Inside Indonesia*, no. 113, July-September www.insideindonesia.org

Sykes, Gresham M. 1958. *The Society of Captives: A Study of a Maximum Security Prison*. Princeton University Press

UNODC (United Nations Office on Drugs and Crime) 2013. *Handbook on Strategies to Reduce Overcrowding in Prisons*, Criminal Justice Handbook Series in cooperation with the International Committee of the Red Cross, www.unodc.org/documents/justice-and-prison-reform/Overcrowding_in_prisons_Ebook.pdf

Vaughn, Michael S. 1993. 'Listening to the Experts: A National Study of Correctional Administrators: Responses to Prison Overcrowding', *Criminal Justice Review* 18(1): 12–25

Walmsey, Roy 2009. 'World Prison Population List', 8th edn., ICPR (Institute for Criminal Policy Reform) www.prisonpolicy.org/scans/wppl-8th_41.pdf

Walmsey, Roy 2019. 'World Prison Population List', 12th edn., ICPR (Institute for Criminal Policy Reform)

Weatherburn, Don and Bray, Rohen 1990. 'Non-Custodial Sanctions, Prison Costs and Prison Overcrowding', Australian Institute of Criminology www.aic.gov.au/media_library

Wijaya, Callistasia Anggun 2016. 'New Prison Facilities Planned to Resolve Overcapacity', *The Jakarta Post*, 14 June www.thejakartapost.com

Young, Jock 1999. *The Exclusive Society: Social Exclusion, Crime and Difference in Late Modernity*. London: Sage Publication

Legislation

MPR (Majelis Perwakilan Rakyat, People's Consultative Assembly) Decision No. XI/MPR/1998 on Clean and Good Governance and the Eradication of Corruption/Nepotism/Collusions

Criminal Code (*Kitab Undang-Undang Hukum Pidana*, KUHP: Law No. 1 of 1946 as amended by Law No. 27 of 1999 on the Indonesian Criminal Code)

Law No. 32 of 2004 on Regional Administration

Law No. 12 of 2011 on Establishment of Laws and Regulations

Law No. 23 of 2014 on Regional Administration

Presidential Regulation (Perpres) No. 52 of 2010 on the Organisational Structure and Management of the Indonesian National Police

Supreme Court Regulation (Peraturan) No. 2 of 2012 on the Readjustment of the Minimum Threshold for Misdemeanours and Fines

Minister for Law and Human Rights Regulation No. 11 of 2017 on the Grand Strategy for Handling Prison Overcrowding

Minister for Law and Human Rights Decision No. m.01-Pr.01.01 of 2003 on the Building Standard of Corrections Facilities

9 Injustice and inconsistency

Sentencing minor property offenders under Supreme Court Regulation No. 2 of 2012

Rifqi S. Assegaf[1]

In January 2012, the Supreme Court of Indonesia sentenced Rasminah,[2] a housemaid, who had been convicted of stealing a few plates and soup ingredients from her employer. She received four months and ten days of imprisonment. Although her sentence was identical to the length of her pre-trial detention (Solopos 2012), meaning she did not have to spend another day in prison, it was heavily criticised by the public who perceived it as a further example of the injustice common to the criminal justice system when dealing with petty offences by economically or socially-deprived offenders.[3] Criticisms also came from lawmakers. A member of the national legislature (DPR, Dewan Perwakilan Rakyat, Peoples' Representative Assembly) said that 'the Supreme Court Justices did not have souls when deciding that case', while also blaming law enforcement officers for allowing such a petty case to be brought to court in a first place (Viva 2012). Another member threatened to launch a formal inquiry into the matter (Tempo 2012). The Minister of Law and Human Rights, who is responsible for law-making and correction facilities, complained about the attitude of law enforcers in detaining alleged offenders and urged them to consider social justice in handling minor offences (Republika 2010). While there is some merit in the criticisms, what was absent from the discourse was acknowledgement that the lawmakers must also share some blame because these issues occurred, in part at least, because of shortcomings in the legislation.

The Indonesian Criminal Code (*Kitab Undang-undang Hukum Pidana* or KUHP) establishes different types and levels of punishment for property offences, such as theft and embezzlement, depending on the offences' seriousness. Before 2012, theft was punishable by a maximum of five years of imprisonment or, alternatively, a very low fine, Rp. 900 (US$ 0.06).[4] If the offence was considered a minor property offence, the penalties were very light, no more than three months of imprisonment or a Rp. 250 fine (US$ 0.07. However, the amount of loss necessary for theft to be classified as a minor offence was very low (as it is for fines in KUHP in general): Rp. 250 or less (US$ 0.017). This is because the last time the DPR and government adjusted the fines or standards of loss for minor offences was in 1960.[5] With such low standards of loss and small fines in general, judges never convicted offenders of minor property offences, choosing more serious offences instead, and were very reluctant to impose fines for any offences, preferring imprisonment.[6]

In response to the criticisms described earlier, as well as the flaws in KUHP just mentioned, "a few days after the Rasminah decision" the Supreme Court drafted a policy that might prevent such cases from reoccurring.[7] A month later, in February 2012, the Supreme Court passed Regulation No. 2 of 2012 on Adjustment of Standards for Minor Offences and Value of Fines in KUHP (Supreme Court Regulation No. 2 of 2012), which basically altered the amount of loss necessary for an offence to constitute a minor property offence under KUHP by increasing it to Rp. 2.5 million (US$ 167), as well as increasing the maximum fine for almost all offences.

This would seem a necessary reform and, indeed, a long overdue one, but within a few years of its enactment, anecdotal evidence suggested that the Regulation had not yet been widely implemented. In late 2013, for instance, the Supreme Court spokesperson stated that 'cassation appeals on minor property offence cases are still mounting on Supreme Court Justices' desks' (Hukumonline 2013). The media also reported a number of cases in which the regulation was not applied.[8]

This chapter examines the implementation of the Supreme Court Regulation No. 2 of 2012, using all published minor theft and embezzlement cases decisions in the Bandung, Tangerang and Central and South Jakarta District Courts between 2012 and 2015, along with selected decisions from other jurisdictions, including the Supreme Court, as comparisons. This chapter seeks to demonstrate that in many cases law enforcers and judges still fail to consistently implement the regulation, or wrongly interpret it. Further, there are also strong indications of deliberate avoidance of the regulation, such as by charging minor offenders under other laws or amplifying the actual amount of losses. I argue that these are caused by several interrelated factors: the mindsets of lawmakers, law enforcers and judges; pragmatic issues, such as the desire to avoid appeals and make case handling smoother; corruption; and, finally, a lack of seriousness on the part of the Supreme Court to implement its own reform initiative and check abuse of power by law enforcement officers.

Overview of Supreme Court Regulation No. 2 of 2012

While judges generally enjoy wide discretionary power in sentencing, they are influenced and limited by a range legal and extra-legal factors. Statutes and case laws provide a range of types and levels of maximum (and sometimes also minimum) penalties that can, or should be, imposed by judges, as well as guiding or instructing them to consider various aggravating and mitigating factors in sentencing. The severity of criminal sanctions is shaped by the gravity or seriousness of the offence, which is usually defined in two ways: the degree of offender's culpability and the level of harm caused by the offence.[9] 'Harm' refers to injury done or risked by the offence. In property-related offences, such as theft or burglary, the harm is typically determined by the level of financial loss[10] and, in the case of burglary, also by the degree of distress and fear or loss of confidence caused by the offences, as well as damage caused to buildings, if any (Simester and Sullivan 2005: 168, 168–95). 'Culpability' refers to issues such as offender's intentions in committing the offence, for example, the degree of planning or motivation for the offence and other circumstances that correlate to the degree of offenders' responsibility for their conduct.[11]

Studies in other jurisdictions also show that there are various extra-legal factors that can influence judges in sentencing: the background of offenders (for example, sex, age, social-economic condition, attitude or personality); the background of judges and their personal values, character, attitude toward the offence and punishment philosophies (Hogarth 1971); the role of other relevant actors, such as prosecutors, victims, clerks, legal assistants or local communities;[12] courts' organisational interests;[13] situational or local contexts (crime rate, local concern about certain crimes, etc.) (Johnson 2006: 290–2); and so forth.

In the Indonesian context, however, one of the factors that has caused injustice in sentencing minor property offences cases is, as indicated earlier, undoubtedly the substantive law, particularly the definition of minor property offences in KUHP, which had led to disproportionate responses from law enforcement officials and judges. In this regard, the enactment of Supreme Court Regulation No. 2 of 2012 was an appropriate response. The Regulation contains only four articles. Article 1 directly alters the amount of loss necessary for offences to constitute minor property offences in KUHP, such as petty theft and embezzlement,[14] by increasing it from Rp. 250 (US$ 0.017) to Rp. 2.5 million (US$ 167), while art. 3 adjusts the maximum fines for all offences, other than gambling,[15] by increasing them a thousand-fold. The maximum fine for any minor property offence is now Rp. 250,000 (US$ 17). As a side note, the logic of increasing the standard of loss by 10,000 times the original amount in KUHP to align it with the huge gold price increase between 1960 and 2012, but at the same time, only increasing the fines by 1,000 times, is problematic. It makes the cost of offending still significantly lower than the potential benefit to be won from the offence, and thus may not deter people from committing an offence, or, at least, may discourage the judges from imposing fines – both problems the reforms sought to address.[16]

The remaining provisions of the 2012 Regulation provide guidance for judges in applying it. Article 2(1) and (2) requires the chief judge of every court to closely examine the amount of loss in a case filed by the prosecutor and, if it is considered minor, to assign it to a single judge to be tried under the *hukum acara cepat* or 'fast or expedited legal process'. If the defendant is detained prior to the trial, he or she must immediately be released (art. 2(3)). It also advises judges to impose fines rather than imprisonment (art. 4).[17]

The main objectives of the enactment of Supreme Court Regulation No. 2 of 2012 are to deliver justice for petty offenders and restore the public image of the judiciary. The elucidation (explanatory memorandum) to the regulation is explicit about this:[18]

> The large volume of minor theft offences brought to, and tried in, courts has become a public concern. The public in general view take the view that it is very unjust for such minor cases to be brought under Article 362 of the KUHP, which has a maximum penalty up to five years despite the insignificant value of the stolen goods...which creates negative public perceptions of the judiciary. In general, the public does not understand how a case ends up on trial, who the stakeholders are who have authority in each stage of the criminal process ... thus [they] focus their attention on the court and demand that the court consider [their] sense of justice

It is very clear that one reason for the Supreme Court to issue this Regulation was that it does not want the judiciary alone to be blamed for injustice caused by the failures of first, lawmakers, who failed to provide sensible legal provisions to deal with minor offences, and second, the police and prosecutors, who processed and charged minor case offenders in the first place, leaving judges in a difficult position.[19]

The Regulation also aims to improve efficiency in law enforcement. According to the Criminal Procedural Code (*Kitab Undang-undang Hukum Acara Pidana*, KUHAP), minor offence cases should be tried by the 'fast procedure',[20] meaning such cases should be: (1) tried by single judge (art. 205(3)), not a panel of three as in normal proceeding; (2) prosecuted by the police (art. 205(2)), thus lessening the workload of the prosecutors; (3) tried in one day (art. 206) without a need for a lengthy decision or minutes of the court session (art. 209), and so forth. The 'fast procedure' saves courts and other law enforcement agencies time and resources. Besides, minor offence cases cannot be appealed to the Supreme Court,[21] thus easing its workload.

Supreme Court Regulation No. 2 of 2012 is also a response to the overcrowding of prisons and detention centres.[22] By increasing the level of fines, it is expected that judges will be encouraged to impose fines instead of imprisonment.[23] Furthermore, since the maximum penalties for minor property offences are less than five years, under the Criminal Procedure Code the offender cannot be detained before or during trial.[24] In the long run, these measures have the potential to reduce the prison and detention centre population, a problem discussed in Chapter 8 of this volume (Sudaryono).

The responses to Supreme Court Regulation No. 2 of 2012 were diverse. Activists and scholars generally supported the initiative.[25] The formal response from the Attorney General's Office (AGO) was also positive. The Deputy Attorney General, for instance, stated that the regulation was in line with the spirit of the law and his office would enforce it (Hukumonline 2012c). On the other hand, the police force had reservations. The Chief of National Police, while claiming to support the regulation, was concerned by its potential to increase the number of offences, particularly if the regulation was applied to repeat offenders (Hukumonline 2012c).

To strengthen the legal basis of the regulation, ensure the compliance of other law enforcement agencies, and respond to the police's concerns, the Supreme Court, the Ministry of Law and Human Rights, the AGO and the National Police signed a Joint Agreement (*Nota Kesepahaman Bersama*) in October 2012, which, in principle, adopts all provisions of Supreme Court Regulation No. 2 of 2012, with two additions: first, law enforcers and judges are authorised to settle minor property offence cases through restorative justice by mediating between offender and victim (art. 4); and second, minor offence provisions cannot be used in the case of reoffenders or recidivists (art. 5(4)) (a provision that is, in fact, inconsistent with KUHP).[26]

Not every property offence with a small loss and committed by a first-time offender is considered a minor offence. KUHP does not have distinct terms for different types of theft, such as burglary or robbery. Basically, these offences are all called 'theft' (*pencurian*) but with different elements and different maximum penalties, as shown in Table 9.1. Legal textbooks or court decisions, however, often distinguish between them by adding qualifications, such as 'theft with violence' (*pencurian dengan kekerasan*) for robbery, or 'aggravated theft' (*pencurian dengan pemberatan*) for types of theft other than simple theft.

As shown, some types of aggravated theft can be considered minor theft, depending on the amount of the stolen goods and where the act is done. On the other hand, burglary (regardless of the value of the stolen goods) and robbery, is outside the scope of the Regulation. Similarly, while (simple) embezzlement is punishable by four years of imprisonment or Rp. 900,000 fine (art. 372), if the value of the goods embezzled is Rp. 2.5 million or less, it is viewed as minor embezzlement (art. 373). However, embezzlement in respect of which the offender has some kind of working relationship, irrespective of its value of the funds stolen, is considered aggravated embezzlement (art. 374) and is not covered by the Regulation.

Four years of implementation

Evidence from district courts in and around Jakarta: Lack of compliance

To have a regulation is one thing but to implement effectively it is another entirely. Of approximately 890 theft and embezzlement cases decisions in the Bandung, Tangerang and Central and South Jakarta District Courts between 2012 and 2015 (except 2013) published online on the Supreme Court website, 45 cases (with 58 defendants) involve facts that meet the new definition of minor theft and embezzlement. However, all offenders were charged and punished under non-minor offence provisions.[27] None of the decisions even

Table 9.1 Classes of theft-related offences in KUHP (after 2012)

Type of offence	*KUHP's provision*	*Offence definition*	*Maximum penalty*
Theft (including day-time 'burglary'[1])	art. 362	Stealing property	Five years' imprisonment or Rp. 900,000 fine
Aggravated theft (including night-time burglary)	art. 363(1)	… 3: Theft by night in a 'dwelling or in an enclosed yard where a dwelling stands' (night-time burglary); 4: Theft by more than one offender; 5: Theft using force to enter the location of the crime or to get property (for example, breaking, entering, climbing, damaging or using counterfeit keys, false orders or false costume)	Seven years' imprisonment
Minor theft	art. 364	This is the same offence as in art. 362 and art. 363(1) 4 and 5 but the amount of the stolen goods here is not more than Rp. 2,500,000 and the offence is not committed inside a dwelling or in an enclosed yard where a dwelling stands (that is, it is not burglary)	Three months imprisonment or Rp. 250,000 fine
Theft with violence (robbery)	art. 365(1)	Theft preceded, accompanied or followed by force or threat of force against persons	Nine years' imprisonment

1 For the purposes of this chapter, the term 'burglary' is used to describe an act of theft by entering into 'a dwelling or an enclosed yard where a dwelling stands', by day or night, without an element of force when entering the property. According to art. 363(1) 3 of KUHP, only night-time burglary is considered aggravated theft. As a consequence, daytime burglary is (or should be) considered (simple) theft under art. 362. Soesilo, a commentator on KUHP, also implicitly classifies daytime burglary as theft under art. 362. See Soesilo 1981: 218.

mentioned Supreme Court Regulation No. 2 of 2012, as if it did not exist. However, according to these courts' (irregular) annual reports, there are around 30 minor offence cases decided each year in some of these courts,[28] none of which have been published and therefore cannot be assessed.

In general, the sentences imposed on the 58 defendants listed in the website were relatively harsh. All received imprisonment, with an average sentence of 7.6 months. Just three defendants were sentenced to three months or less of imprisonment, in accordance with the maximum penalty for minor

Table 9.2 Top five most severe and most lenient punishments

Sentence (months)	*Sentence recommendation by prosecutor (months)*	*Pre-trial detention (months)*	*Crime*	*Details of stolen goods*	
				Value (Rp)	*Goods*
18	18	4.2	Aggravated theft (art. 363(1) 5)	1,500,000	Bags, etc.
18	16	3.9	Embezzlement (art. 372)	750,000	Bed covers
14	12	3.2	Aggravated theft (art. 363(1) 4 and 5)	300,000	Gas tanks
14	16	3.4	Aggravated theft (art. 363(1) 5)	500,000	Cell phone and money
12	18	4.1	Aggravated theft (art. 363(1) 4)	2,000,000	Bags, etc.
2	4	1.9	Aggravated theft (art. 363(1) 4	1,100,000	Cell phone
3	5	2.8	Aggravated theft (art. 363(1) 4	1,000,000	Chickens
3.1	4	3.1	Aggravated theft (art. 363(1) 4	0	Money
4	6	2.5	Theft (art. 362)	200,000	Money
4	6	3.5	Theft (art. 362)	300,000	Tyres

offences. Others received just over three to twelve months (50 defendants) or over one year (five defendants). Table 9.2 lists the most severe and the most lenient punishments imposed by these courts.

While the overall data shows no nexus between the punishment severity and the amount of losses or type of the goods stolen, it does demonstrate a strong correlation between the punishment and the sentence recommendation filed by the prosecutor. The average length of prison sentences imposed by judges was almost four-fifths of the prosecutors' recommendation.[29] The recommendation also influenced differences in the severity of sentences between genders. Although on average female defendants received slightly shorter imprisonment terms (7.5 months) than males (7.7 months), the average length of prosecutor's sentencing recommendations for them were also shorter than for male defendants. This indicates that it was not necessarily the judges' attitude toward the different genders that the determined differences in their sentences.

Anecdotal evidence also indicates that punishment severity was not necessarily influenced by differences between individual judges.[30] The same panel of judges in Bandung District Court that sentenced a person who stole a Rp. 300,000 gas tank (US$ 20) to fourteen months in prison, which was two months above the prosecutor's recommendation,[31] meted out exactly the same punishment to a man who stole a car worth Rp. 170 million (about US$ 11,300).[32] Another panel of judges in Tangerang District Court sentenced a person stealing a half million rupiah (about US$ 33) of goods to fourteen months of imprisonment,[33] while only imposing a fifteen months prison sentence for the theft of a motorbike worth almost Rp. 15 million (US$ 1000).[34] In all these cases, there were no noticeable mitigating or aggravating factors that might have contributed to the vast disparity in sentences.

Examples from other jurisdictions

Although none of the published decisions from the above four courts applied the Regulation, that does not mean that Supreme Court Regulation No. 2 of 2012 is, overall, ineffective. As mentioned, data from the annual reports of some of these courts show that there were a number of minor offence cases that they decided according to the regulation each year. Furthermore, if a search is made for the Indonesian equivalent of the phrase 'Supreme Court Regulation No. 2 of 2012' in the Supreme Court website or media reports, decisions of other courts that do enforce the regulation can be found. However, cases where the regulation was deliberately not applied, misinterpreted, or inconsistently applied can also encountered.

Decisions that applied or mentioned the regulation: General

A purposive sampling of forty decisions from different district courts in the Supreme Court website that mention the phrase 'Supreme Court Regulation No. 2 of 2012' shows that in a majority of cases the regulation was applied mostly to convict (thirty decisions), but also in a few cases to dismiss charges, such as where minor theft was wrongly dealt with as theft. Some judges even used the regulation to lower penalties for non-minor offence cases. However, there were also a number of cases where the regulation was mentioned, usually in defence arguments, but not used by the courts.

Of the thirty decisions (with thirty-three defendants) in which the regulation was used to convict, all defendants were sentenced under the minor-theft or minor-embezzlement provisions, even though some had been charged under other provisions (see Table 9.3). In cases where the defendants were detained prior to the trial, the courts released them.[35] Further, the majority of the accused received only suspended sentences (twenty-two defendants), followed by imprisonment (nine defendants) and fines (two defendants), as shown in Chart 9.1. There was one case that was settled through mediation between victim and defendant and ratified by court decision.[36]

In almost all cases where the courts imposed imprisonment, the defendants had already been detained prior to the trial – mostly because they were initially charged with a non-minor offence. Further, the length of the imprisonment was usually closely linked, or even identical, to the duration of the pre-trial detention, as shown in Table 9.3.

Table 9.3 Correlation between imprisonment sentence, charge and pre-trial detention

Charge (article)	*Pre-trial detention (months)*	*Sentence*		*Decision*
		Article	*Months*	
364	Not clear	364	1.8	25/Pid.C/2015/PN.Sim
364	0	364	1	62/Pid.C/2015/PN.Rap
364	0	364	1	214/Pid.C/2014/PN.Rap
363(1) 4	2.1	363(1) 4 & Regulation No. 2 of 2012	3	235/Pid.B/2015/PN.Stb
363(1) 4	2.5	364	3	300/Pid.B/2015/PN.Stb
363(1) 4	2.2	363(1) 4 & Regulation No. 2 of 2012	3	340/Pid.B/2015/PN.Stb
364	0.3	364	0.3	3/Daf.Pid.C/2013/PN.Slk
362	2.3	364	3	33/Pid/C/2013/PN.Smd
363(1) 4	1.6	363(1) 4 & Regulation No. 2 of 2012	1.6	191/Pid.B/2015/PN.Stb.

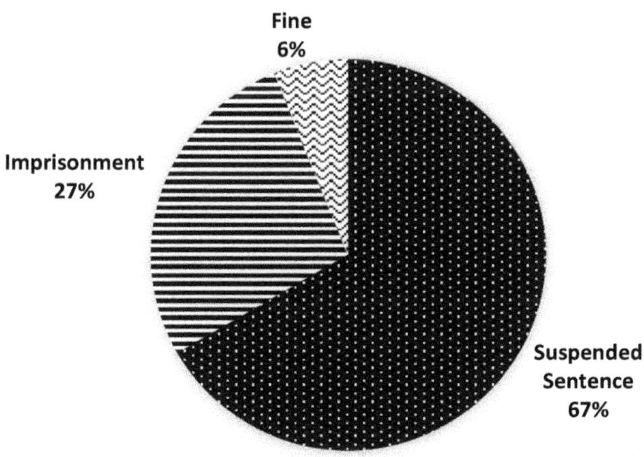

Chart 9.1 Types of punishment in cases that applied Supreme Court Regulation No. 2 of 2012.

This indicates that judges tend to avoid imprisonment but, at the same time, are also reluctant to impose fines as instructed by the Regulation, perhaps because they believe most of the accused cannot afford them, and so will eventually serve time in prison in lieu of paying a fine. As one judge told me, 'How can a petty thief pay a fine, when the motive for the offence is itself financial deprivation?'

Supreme Court Regulation No. 2 of 2012 was also used to reject or to dismiss minor offence cases that involved charges under other provisions. For example, in a case concerning embezzlement of approximately Rp. 2.3 million, the prosecutor charged the defendant with (simple) embezzlement (art. 372). On the defence lawyer's petition, the court dismissed the case due to wrong application of the law.[37] In another case, the prosecutor refused to process minor offence cases that had been brought under the wrong provisions by the police (Sinar Indonesia Baru 2014).

Judges also considered the *raison d'être* for the enactment of Supreme Court Regulation No. 2 of 2012 in determining the severity of punishment for small offences that did actually not fall under the regulation. For example, the Ranai District Court meted out a light sentence to a recidivist burglar that was significantly lower than the prosecutor's sentence recommendation, reasoning, among others, that, although the case was concerned with burglary and reoffending (and so could not be dealt with under the Regulation), the spirit of the Regulation should be taken into consideration, given the loss was only Rp 2.2 million. [38]

However, there were also cases that, while mentioning the Regulation, departed from it for various reasons, as shown in Table 9.4.

There are some similarities in all the cases in Table 9.4 in which the courts expressly refused to apply Supreme Court Regulation No. 2 of 2012. First, all cases were brought under non-minor offences provisions and the defendants were detained prior and during to the trial, most of them for far more than three months. Further, in the Karanganyar, Sekayu and Mungkid District Court decisions, although the judges departed from the Regulation, the lengths of the prison terms almost mirror the duration of the detention. In the Mungkid District Court decision, in particular, the judges clearly acknowledged and agreed that the defendant should be sentenced according to the minor theft provisions.[39] However, perhaps because the defendant was charged with theft, the judges seemed reluctant to depart from it but sentenced the defendant to just three months of imprisonment. This was far below the prosecutor's recommendation but still within the penalty range in the Regulation.

There were cases, however, where the courts did not apply the Regulation because of misinterpretation of it (Decision No. 106/Pid.B/2015/Sky), or different legal understandings between defence lawyers and the judges about whether or not the case should be considered a minor offence (Decision No. 52/Pid.B/2014/PN.Kray). Both issues are now discussed in more detail.

(Mis)interpretation and inconsistency

Four years after the enactment of Supreme Court Regulation No. 2 of 2012, law enforcement officials and judges still have different opinions about what is considered minor theft under art. 364 of KUHP. As mentioned, according to KUHP and the Regulation, (simple) theft (art. 362) and some aggravated thefts – those committed by more than one perpetrator (art. 363(1) 4) or done with some sort of force to enter the location of the crime or to get the property (art. 363(1) 5) – are considered minor theft, so long as the amount of the

Table 9.4 Decisions that deliberately departed from Supreme Court Regulation No. 2 of 2012

District court & case number	*Loss Rp)*	*Charge*		*Decision*		*Length of detention (month)*	*Reasons for departure*
		Ground (article)	*Recommended Sentence (month)*	*Ground (article)*	*Sentence (month)*		
Semarang District Court (Decision No. 525/ Pid.B.2014)	1,420,000	362	18	362	10	4	The court rejected the defence lawyer's argument that the case was a minor theft and so should be processed as a 'fast proceeding', stating that prosecutors were entitled to process the case under the theft provision (art. 362). It did not comment on the small nature of the loss in the case.
Solok District Court (Decision No. 11/ Pid.B/ 2012)	470,500		10	362	5	3.8	The majority of judges convicted the defendant of theft, with one dissenting opinion arguing the case should be tried under Supreme Court Regulation No. 2 of 2012.
Karanganyar District Court (Decision No. 52/Pid.B/2014)	250,000	363(1) 4	8	363(1) 4	4	3.8	The court rejected the defence lawyer's argument for applying the regulation, reasoning that since the offence was done in a mosque where the mosque's employee lives, it should be considered 'an enclosed yard where a dwelling stands'.

(continued)

Table 9.4 Cont.

District court & case number	*Loss Rp)*	*Charge*		*Decision*		*Length of detention (month)*	*Reasons for departure*
		Ground (article)	*Recommended Sentence (month)*	*Ground (article)*	*Sentence (month)*		
Sekayu District Court (Decision No. 106/ Pid.B/2015)	500,000		6	363(1) 4	4.5	4.3	The court rejected the defence lawyer's argument for applying the regulation, reasoning that it only applies to minor theft under art. 362, not aggravated theft (theft committed by multiple offenders (art. 363()] 4), as in the case at hand.
Mungkid District Court (Decision No. 120/ Pid.B/2014)	764,000	362	8	362	3	2.3	The court acknowledged that the case should be tried under Supreme Court Regulation No. 2 of 2012 but still convicted the defendant of theft, as charged by the prosecutor, without providing any reasoning for this.

stolen goods is less than Rp. 2.5 million and it is not done at a dwelling or an enclosed yard where a dwelling stands (not burglary).[40] However, not every judge comprehends this simple proposition.

Sekayu District Court, for example, rejected the defence lawyer's argument for applying Supreme Court Regulation No. 2 of 2012 with just one line of reasoning: that the Regulation is applicable only to petty theft under art. 362, not aggravated theft under art. 363(1) 4 (theft by multiple offenders), as in the case at hand.[41] Similar mistakes were also made by a Supreme Court Justice who was actually sympathetic to the accused, who was charged with aggravated theft for stealing 30 kg of rubber tree sap worth around Rp. 750,000. In the first instance court, the judges agreed with the charge but only punished the man with two months of imprisonment, instead of one year as recommended by the prosecutor, a sentence reinforced by the High Court on appeal.[42] When the prosecutors brought the case to the Supreme Court, it also affirmed the High Court decision. One judge dissented. He asserted that since the offender was young and still attending school, imprisoning him would jeopardise his future.[43] More importantly, he maintained that the loss caused by the offence was relatively small and still within the standards of Supreme Court Regulation No. 2 of 2012.[44] However, instead of dismissing the case for wrong application of the law, he only proposed a more lenient punishment, a suspended sentence, reasoning that:[45]

> the provision in art. 364 cannot be used in the case at hand because the defendant, in committing the offence, was not alone, but [acted] together with other defendants.... This makes the offence fall into the category of aggravated offence (*vide* art. 363(1) of the KUHP)

The boundary between minor theft and other theft-related offences is less clear when the act is done in 'a dwelling or in an enclosed yard where a dwelling stands' as in arts. 364 and 363(1) 3. Soesilo, a commentator of KUHP, defines the above phrase as follows.

> 'a dwelling' (*woning*) = a place that is used to rest (*berdiam*) day and night, meaning to eat, sleep, etc. A warehouse or a store that is not used to rest day and night is not considered 'a dwelling', while a shed, train cart or boat that is used, day and night, as a residence (*kediaman*) is included in a definition of a dwelling. An enclosed yard = a yard with clear marks that surround it, such as fence, plants, etc.
>
> (Soesilo 1981: 217)

Sugandhi, another KUHP commentator, includes 'room' (*petak kamar*) in the definition of 'dwelling', as long as it is used as a place to rest days and nights (Sugandhi 1981: 379). No firm Supreme Court case law (*yurisprudensi*) offers a definition of this term. All these examples indicate that the term 'dwelling' refers to a particular building that is primarily used to rest and sleep. The question is whether this is true of a building that is not mainly designed for resting and sleeping but can be used, or has facilities, for such use.

In 2014, the Karanganyar District Court convicted a man of night-time burglary for stealing a Rp. 250,000 bicycle parked in a mosque yard (art. 363(1) 3). The judges declined to apply Supreme Court Regulation No. 2 of 2012, reasoning that because the offence was done in a mosque yard where the mosque's employees live, it should be considered theft in 'an enclosed yard where a dwelling stands' (burglary).[46] On the other hand, the Surakarta District Court sentenced an offender who stole Rp. 64,000 cash from a mosque charity box for theft (art. 362) even though the prosecutor charged him primarily with aggravated theft (art. 363(1) 3) because the offence was done in a mosque and, prior to the offence, the offender stole the key of the charity box from the mosque employee's room, located within the mosque.[47] This decision was later affirmed on appeal by the local High Court.[48] It is not clear why these courts did not apply the Regulation if they were convinced that mosque employee's room or mosque is not regarded as a 'dwelling'. When the prosecutor brought this case to the Supreme Court, it rejected the appeal, simply stating that the offence was indeed a violation of art. 362 of KUHP and the lower court decisions were applying the law correctly.[49] In several other cases, also concerning charity box theft in mosques, the prosecutors were more concerned with the issue of the thieves breaking open the box to get the money, not where the offences were done, and so charged the thieves under art. 363(1) 5 – theft by force against the property – rather than burglary.[50] In each case, the courts accepted these charges.

Several law enforcers and judges also included petty theft on construction sites[51] and plantations[52] as burglary, probably because workers usually stay overnight in these locations. However, in many other theft cases involving plantations, the police and judges applied Supreme Court Regulation No. 2 of 2012[53] and/or interpreted plantations as not being a dwelling or an enclosed yard where a dwelling stands.[54] In some cases, the same judges have even made inconsistent interpretations in this regard. For example, a panel of judges in Rantau Prapat District Court convicted a man who had stolen approximately Rp. 500,000 worth of palm fruit from a private plantation of aggravated burglary (art. 363(1) 3 and 4), interpreting the plantation area to be 'an enclosed yard where a dwelling stands'.[55] However, in other cases, they applied Supreme Court Regulation No. 2 of 2012 to thefts in plantation area, suggesting that they did not view it as an enclosed yard.[56]

As a side remark, from a pragmatic legal reasoning perspective, it is 'understandable' that police, judges and victims (particularly corporations) would consider some kinds of palm oil fruit theft cases as not being petty crime, even where value of the stolen fruits is less than Rp. 2.5 million. This is not (only) for the reason, as discussed, that they occurred in an enclosed yard, but also because some of them were done in ways that indicate a high level of planning, including offenders bringing a truck to carry the stolen goods.[57]

Calculation of loss and potential mark-up

Another key legal issue in the implementation of Supreme Court Regulation No. 2 of 2012 is concerned with the calculation of loss. Usually, law enforcers and judges determine losses solely based on the testimony of the victim, without questioning its accuracy or reliability and the method by which it is calculated, hence creating the possibility of error. For example, in one case, the prosecutor calculated loss using the original or purchase price of the stolen goods – in this case, used cellular phones - and came to a total loss of Rp. 3.6 million, and therefore charged the offender with theft.[58] The court, correctly, argued that the loss should be calculated based on the current market price of the phones, which were below Rp. 2.5 million and, accordingly, dismissed the charge.[59]

There is also a possibility that a victim will mark-up loss, with or without the knowledge of law enforcers and judges, to exceed the threshold for minor property offence provisions. As an illustration, in a case tried by the Rantau Prapat District Court, the defendant was charged under a non-minor offence provision for stealing palm fruits, even though the market price of the fruit, as acknowledged by the prosecutor, was only Rp. 450,000.[60] Nevertheless on top of that price, the prosecutor, based on the victim's testimony, added the production cost of growing the fruit, such as fertiliser and maintenance – which should already be included in the market price – and so came up with a total loss of 'approximate Rp. 2.5 million',[61] allegedly to avoid applying Supreme Court Regulation No. 2 of 2012. Somehow the judges approved this without questioning the odd calculation, and did so despite the fact that a Rp. 2.5 million loss is still within the threshold of loss for minor offence. Two of the judges in the above panel also agreed to what is seen as odd calculation of losses in other palm oil fruit theft cases, as shown in Table 9.5.

The total value of losses in each case in Table 9.5 was held by the judges involved to be just above the loss criterion in the Regulation. However, the range of the actual amount of the palm fruit bunches that were stolen in each case is relatively wide, from just 47 to 166 bunches. Since all the offences were done in similar areas and decided by similar judges in the same court, there are only three possible explanations: there was fluctuation of price over the time; there were different quantities and qualities of fruits in each bunch; and/or, the losses – particularly the weight in each bunches and the market price of the fruit – were arbitrarily determined by the victims, including to avoid the application of the regulation. One cannot tell the actual losses from the text of the decisions alone because, as in most other decisions, the text usually only states the total losses and the weight and/or the volume of the losses, without elaborating on the market price of the stolen fruits.[62]

Some judges in the Simalungun District Court seem to be aware of these problems and tried to minimise them by ordering the prosecutors to bring the higher-level management of the company to testify about the actual losses from the offence (Hetanews 2018). However, the Head of the District

Table 9.5 Value v. amount and weight of stolen palm fruit

Stolen goods details			*Year*	*Decision*
Value (Rp)	*Quantity (bunch)*	*Weight (kg)*		
2,538,000	47	1,410	2016	594/2016/PN Rap
2,625,000	70	1,750	2016	498/2016/PN Rap
2,700,000	90	N/A	2015	446/2015/PN Rap
2,652,000	120	N/A	2015	464/2015/PN Rap
2,611,200	136	N/A	2016	07/2016/PN Rap
2,650,000	151	2,039	2015	111/2015/PN Rap
2,655,400	166	1,870	2015	512/2015/PN Rap

Court, at the request of the heads of the local police and prosecutor's office (who argued such an order created difficulties for their officers), agreed to only request them to bring the 'field supervisor', a lower-level management figure.[63] Interestingly, the heads of the local police and prosecutor office also requested the Head of the District Court to apply Law No. 39 of 2014 on Plantations in deciding palm oil theft cases (Hetanews 2018). This is another important issue in the enforcement of Supreme Court Regulation No. 2 of 2012, and it is discussed in the next section.

Charging minor offences under special statutes

Criminal penalties are stipulated not only in KUHP, but also in numerous 'special' statutes. The main objective of enacting special criminal statutes is to create new offences that are not yet covered or penalised by KUHP. However, some statutes also criminalise acts that are similar to what is already prohibited in KUHP, or at least define the offences in a broad and vague manner that can apply to offences also proscribed in KUHP, such as minor theft, but which impose a more severe penalty. As a consequence, police and prosecutors can use, and in several cases have used, special statutes to avoid implementing Supreme Court Regulation No. 2 of 2012.

As an illustration, art. 107 d of Law No. 39 of 2014 on Plantations states that any person who, without right, 'harvests and/or picks up crops' can be given a maximum of four years' imprisonment or a four billion rupiah fine. In one case, the Stabat Prosecutors Office charged a man with 'stealing' Rp. 150,000 worth of palm fruits under the above provision and recommended ten months of imprisonment. The prosecutor described the offence as follows.[64]

> [T]he defendant, together with Zulpandi and Fajar Nugraha...took palm fruits belonging to Sewangi Sejati Ltd...by entering their plantation with a sickle and when they were on the site, the defendant...started to look for the ripe fruits and then Fajar Nugraha harvested six bunches of fruit

with his sickle, which were then collected by the defendant…and carried […] away

Clearly, the act was identical to (minor) theft and, in most cases, judges would consider it as such. However, since the prosecutor only charged the defendant under art. 107 d of the Plantation Law, and the act met all elements of that crime, the judges perhaps felt they did not have any option but to apply that Law. It might have been different if the prosecutor had charged the offender with alternative offences. For example, in a petty illegal logging case that caused Rp. 691,000 loss, the prosecutor charged the defendant with illegal logging (under Law No. 18 of 2013 on the Prevention and Eradication of Illegal Logging) or theft. Regardless of this, the district court sentenced the man under art. 364 of KUHP, since the loss was within the definition of minor theft, which decision was then modified by the High Court, which convicted him of theft.[65] The Supreme Court affirmed the High Court decision without offering substantial reasoning.[66] While it is unclear why the Supreme Court did not sentence the defendant for minor theft, at least this decision can guide lower court judges to consider minor illegal logging as theft, where applicable.

The media has reported other incidents where minor offences resulted in charges under the Prevention and Eradication of Illegal Logging Law or the Management of Coastal Zones and Small Islands Law (Law No. 27 of 2007),[67] which have led to criticism from the Supreme Court, the DPR, and the general public (Republika 2015).

Explaining the data

The data show that the way a case is processed prior to trial significantly influences the enforcement, or lack of enforcement, of Supreme Court Regulation No. 2 of 2012. All cases that involved minor offence charges and were registered as such, were always decided according to the regulation. The reverse was also true, with few exceptions.[68] The question is: why were the majority of minor offence cases not treated in this way in the first place? More importantly, why are most judges, regardless how the cases were handled before trial, not applying the regulation?

Issues in registration and distribution of cases

According to court internal procedures, the registration and distribution of criminal cases should be done in the following manner. When the prosecutor submits an indictment letter to the court, the Head of Clerks for Criminal Cases (*Panitera Muda Pidana*) should review it and register it in a register book (Mahkamah Agung 2007: 228). If the case involves a minor offence, and should be tried by 'fast procedure', the clerk should register it as 'Pid.C' (*Pidana Cepat*, fast-tracked criminal case, expedited hearing).[69] On the other hand, if it involves other offences, like theft or aggravated theft, it should be registered it as 'Pid.B' (*Pidana Biasa*, regular criminal case), and must be tried under the normal procedure. Next, the clerk sends the list of cases to the head of the district court to be distributed to either a single judge or a panel of judges, depending on the type of procedure (Mahkamah Agung 2007: 228). The problem is that all minor offence cases that were not tried under Supreme Court Regulation No. 2 of 2012 were registered as non-minor offence cases.

A possible explanation, as one prosecutor suggested to me, is that the losses stated in the indictment letters submitted by the prosecutors to the courts (which are solely based on the police report or BAP (*Berita Acara Pemeriksaan*)), were above Rp. 2.5 million, and so were registered as normal proceedings (as non-minor offences cases) by the courts.[70] Only later in the hearings did the prosecutors and judges become aware of the actual losses in the cases. If that were the case, however, why did prosecutors not recommend lenient sentences, equal to, or less than, three months imprisonment as the maximum penalty for those offences? A more plausible explanation is that the prosecutors knew that the losses were Rp. 2.5 million or less but still charged the offenders with non-minor offences and the court clerks simply registered them without thoroughly screening the indictment letters to check the actual losses, or mistakenly assumed them to be non-minor cases.

Despite all that, judges could still have processed those cases as normal proceedings but departed from the charges in the sentencing process in order to apply the Regulation. While according to the Criminal Procedural Code (KUHAP) judges should base their decisions on the provisions used in the indictment,[71] in firm jurisprudence (693/K/Pid/1980), the Supreme Court has allowed courts to depart from a charge as long as they apply a similar provision to that used by the prosecutor, but with a lower penalty.[72] Further, even without relying on this Supreme Court decision, judges could have accepted the charge but sentenced the defendant to three months or less to match the maximum penalty in the Regulation, which was not the case.[73] In short, although there were issues about how the cases were registered and distributed, there must be other, more influential factors, causing judges to disregard Supreme Court Regulation No. 2 of 2012. This will be discussed next.

Pragmatic reasons: Preventing appeal and smoothing investigation

Preventing an appeal

Studies in other countries show that judges are fallible and subject to cognitive biases in making judgments, including in sentencing. One of the biases is called the 'anchoring effect', a tendency to heavily rely on the first piece of information offered (the 'anchor') in making subsequent judgments.[74] In the context of sentencing, it is argued that the prosecutor's recommended sentence commonly becomes an 'anchor', making the severity of the punishment imposed by judges often the same as the prosecutor's recommendation (Englich, Mussweiler and Strack 2006: 192–3).

An important finding of this research is that the sentences imposed by Indonesian judges were usually close to the prosecutors' recommendation. Of all of the studied Bandung, Tangerang and Central and South Jakarta District Courts decisions, only in one case was the sentence less than half of the prosecutor's recommended sentences, and two sentences were exactly half of them. However, while the anchoring effect thesis should be taken seriously, it is my view that the judges in these cases very likely consciously sentenced as they did to prevent appeals.

To explain, judges are fully aware that according to the AGO's internal guidelines, prosecutors must appeal any sentence that is less than half of what is recommended by the prosecutors.[75] For their decisions to be appealed is problematic for judges, because, as admitted by several judges, it creates additional workload for them. It means that they have to spend more time to prepare the decision to make it presentable for evaluation by the higher courts. It also means that they have to assure all relevant evidence is included and accurately cited in the minutes of the court session (*Berita Acara Persidangan*). Due to poor support from the court clerks, however, sometimes judges need to basically rewrite them. As one judge told me, 'Why should judges bear the burden of departing from the prosecutors' sentence recommendation unless there is a very strong reason to do so, when they have other important tasks to attend to?' Some judges also asserted that the defendant is better off if the decision is not appealed by the prosecutor, especially if he or she was, and is still, detained, because the appeal process could take months. It would only prolong the defendant's time behind bars, not to mention the possibility of receiving heavier punishment.

Judges need not worry about their decisions being appealed by defendants because most were detained prior and during the trial and will, usually, not take the risk of appealing for the reasons just stated. Besides, most are neither aware of the Regulation nor represented by lawyers.[76] As the Head of Rantau Prapat District Court said when asked by a journalist about his decisions to detain minor theft cases offenders and assign the cases to be tried in normal proceedings 'I will not comment on these matters. What is your capacity to complain when the accused persons themselves did not object?' (Medansatu 2016). Some judges also 'persuaded' defendants or their families to accept the decision.[77] Furthermore, even if the defendant does appeal, judges know that the High Court or the Supreme Court will take their side in most cases, as will be shown later.

Smoothing the investigation and trial

In principle, KUHAP only allows police and other law enforcement agencies to detain an offender charged with committing a crime punishable by five years of imprisonment and above when certain conditions are met. Accordingly, if the police are to implement Supreme Court Regulation No. 2 of 2012, they cannot detain offenders, which means that they need to use extra personnel and expend additional funds (neither of which are usually available) to process a case, including bringing suspects in for interrogation and trial.[78] Being unable to detain offenders also diminishes their opportunity to extract illegal payments from the potential detainee, as explained below. Besides, there are sometimes legitimate reasons to detain petty offenders, such as preventing public retaliation (lynching) (Maduracorner 2014). In short, it is often more practical and beneficial to charge an offender with non-minor offence provisions.[79] Alternatively, as has happened in several cases, police sometimes simply release or discharge the accused, hence frustrating the public and victims (Haluan 2017; Tempo 2015a). Not all police take such shortcuts, of course. Some process the cases under the minor offence provisions, as shown earlier, or even resolve them through mediation between the offender and the victim (Kompas 2013).

Corruption in the criminal justice system

Discussion of injustice or poor law enforcement in Indonesia cannot escape the issue of endemic corruption in the criminal justice system, which has been demonstrated by numerous studies.[80] These practices can take various forms. The most common are a negotiation between offenders and law enforcement officers, including judges, to 'avoid' the case being processed in the first place, or to 'buy' lenient charges and sentences or even an acquittal.[81] Charging and sentencing offenders with non-minor offences that carry more severe sanctions, creates an opportunity for higher 'settlement'. It also allows law enforcers to detain offenders, which is another source of 'income'.[82]

In a broader context, judicial reluctance to acquit minor theft or embezzlement offenders mischarged under other provisions is also, perhaps, influenced by their interest in maintaining 'good relationships' with the police and, in particular, prosecutors. It is a well-known fact that corrupt prosecutors can 'request' who will hear a case, to receive a favourable outcome in cases, including lenient (or severe) sentences for offenders. So, judges who strictly apply the law will lose the opportunity to sit in such cases and extract illegal rents from prosecutors or defendants.

It is also not uncommon for victims to actively influence how a case is handled, for instance, by giving 'incentives' to law enforcers and judges to assure that the offender is detained, charged and punished severely for retaliation (Satgas PMH 2010: 13–19), or to create deterrence, particularly if the victim is a corporation that frequently suffers minor property offences. Sometimes, this is done for a different motive. A former Head of a District Court mentioned to me that he was once offered a monthly payment by a palm oil plantation's head of security to impose relatively severe punishment, above a year, on petty palm fruit thieves, because the security head wanted to scapegoat them so that he could 'steal' the fruits on a large scale and blame the losses on others. The judge refused, although the briber informed him that some of his fellow judges had already taken the offer. It is safe to say that the briber also paid the police and the prosecutor for the same purpose. This, together with the company's interest in creating deterrence, might be one of the explanations for issues in the palm fruit theft cases discussed above, such as apparent mark-up of losses, charging an offender under special statutes, and inconsistency in legal interpretation.

Disagreement with the regulation, mindset issues and draconian laws

Not every law enforcer and judge is pleased with Supreme Court Regulation No. 2 of 2012 for various, sometimes interrelated, reasons: the standard of losses is too high; it increases the crime rate; and it reduces opportunities for corruption. Several judges and prosecutors, for example, are of the opinion that the standard of loss for an offence to be considered minor is too high, and so is unjust for the majority of victims, who are not well-off. One prosecutor even challenged the Regulation in the open court hearing, arguing that:[83]

> The prosecutor does not agree with the absolute implementation of Article 1 of the Supreme Court Regulation 2 of 2012 ... it should be applied on a case to case basis, since individual victims' response to (financial) loss is relative (from one victim to another), on one hand, a Rp. 1,420,000 loss is big for someone, but on the other hand, for others, it is not.

There is also a link between prosecutors and judges as regards a pro-victim mindset. Judges, for example, tend to consider the impact of offences on victims far more than, or disproportionately to, the impact of, for instance, imprisonment, on petty offenders (and their families).[84] This is partly related to judges' view that petty offenders, who are mostly of lower social status, will not suffer much from imprisonment (Assegaf 2018). The only exceptions that lead judges to seriously consider meting out lenient sentences are if the victim forgives the offenders or if the offence was done merely for survival.[85]

There is also concern about the impact of implementing Supreme Court Regulation No. 2 of 2012 on levels of crime. Generally, law enforcers, like lawmakers and the public, believe that the level of criminal sanction and punishment severity are closely related to the level of crime deterrence (Detik 2012b Hukumonline 2012c), despite lack of strong evidence supporting this conclusion.[86] They also view theft as a serious offence that disturbs the public peace (*meresahkan masyarakat*) and disrupts business (*mengganggu usaha/bisnis*), in addition to harming individual victims. Thus, applying the regulation, with its light penalties, will, on this perception, induce, or, at least, not deter, offending or reoffending (Hukumonline 2012c).

This is worsening with the enactment of various draconian special statutes, such as the Plantation Law or the Prevention and Eradication of Illegal Logging Law, mentioned earlier. With their strong 'deterrence paradigm' to protect business interests, these laws disregard the objectives of Supreme

Court Regulation No. 2 of 2012 by creating offences that can be applied (and indeed are applied) to minor property offences.[87]

Lack of seriousness of the Supreme Court

These massive levels of non-compliance can only occur due to a lack of accountability mechanisms. The Supreme Court is aware of some of the problems in the enforcement of Supreme Court Regulation No. 2 of 2012 but seems to blame them entirely on other law enforcement agencies (Hukumonline 2013). More concerningly, Supreme Court judges themselves also ignore the regulation. As shown earlier, they do not correct lower court decisions that sentence minor offences cases under other provisions nor do they respond to the objections made by the defendants.[88] The Supreme Court has also failed to provide guidance to assure consistent legal interpretation. It has not answered important legal questions, such as the definition of 'dwelling', and has even wrongly interpreted simple clauses in the Regulation.

Conclusion

This chapter has shown that justice for petty offenders is not simply an issue of weak regulation. Four years after the enactment of Supreme Court Regulation No. 2 of 2012, many minor theft and embezzlement cases tried by Bandung, Tangerang and Central and South Jakarta District Courts, and in other jurisdictions (including the Supreme Court), were still conducted under non-minor offence provisions. Most of the defendants were detained prior and during to the trial. There were also issues concerning wrong and inconsistent legal interpretation, as well as avoidance of the Regulation by aggravating the losses caused by the offences or charging offenders under special statutes. On the positive side, this study also demonstrates that judges tended to impose a lenient punishment (suspended sentences) for petty offenders in cases where the Regulation was applied. Only when defendants are detained prior to the trial do judges usually impose imprisonment.

What really matters in sentencing minor property cases are complex interrelated extra-legal and legal factors, from whether the cases were wrongly registered to law enforcers' to judges' pragmatic interests in easing their workload - sentencing defendants in accordance with prosecutor's charge and sentence recommendations to avoid the decisions of being appealed, and the common practice of detaining defendants to smooth the investigation and trial process. Other factors that lead to non-compliance with the Regulation include: corruption in the criminal justice system; the perception of law enforcers and judges that applying minor offence provisions, with their light sanctions, will neither deliver justice for the victim nor deter potential offenders from committing crime; and lack of proper supervision and guidance from the Supreme Court.

Sentencing in palm fruit theft cases represents an excellent example of the complexity and interrelated factors. Law enforcers, judges and lawmakers face a high level of theft in palm oil plantations, which has been seen as serious threat to the business.[89] Many of these cases involve syndicates and reoffending (Kompas 2016). Pragmatic interests, (illegal) financial incentives, and deterrence and pro-victim perceptions have induced law enforcers and judges to avoid the application of Supreme Court Regulation No. 2 of 2012. Lawmakers have now offered legal grounds for them to do so by inserting provisions on minor theft in plantation areas in the Plantation Law. Judges need not worry about relying on these provisions, due to lack of certainty about whether theft in the plantation should be categorised as theft or burglary (because of the Supreme Court's failure to provide guidance), and lack of supervision and inconsistent application of its own Regulation by the Supreme Court.

From another perspective, this chapter also reveals the courts' failure to enforce their own reform initiative to ensure justice and check abuse of the power by law enforcement officers. Instead of judges checking the power of police and prosecutors in processing criminal cases, they are 'dictated' to, particularly by prosecutors, through sentence recommendations. This practice is, to some extent, similar to what occurred during Guided Democracy between 1955 and 1966 (when the judiciary was under overt government control). Then, judges were instructed to discuss sentences they might impose with prosecutors before the prosecutors proposed sentence recommendations, so as to close the potentially wide gap between them.[90] Today, judges do it voluntarily, for pragmatic reasons but the consequences are just as concerning.

Most of these problems are structural, and so need long-term efforts to address them, including, perhaps, by changing the procedural law to authorise the police to detain offenders only a short period of time, where necessary, just enough to allow them to prepare cases and bring them to court.[91] Another short-term remedial measure would be to ensure that all Chief Judges in district courts and their staff register minor offence cases according to the Regulation and impose disciplinary sanctions on those who fail to do so. The Supreme Court could also easily clarify, either by case law or circular letter, what constitutes 'a dwelling or an enclosed yard where a dwelling stands' in art. 364 of KUHP, as this has also contributed to the inconsistent application of Supreme Court Regulation No. 2 of 2012.

Notes

1 This article is based on part of the author's PhD research. I thank Professor Tim Lindsey, my supervisor, for his valuable input and comments, particularly in relation to earlier drafts of this article.

2 Many Indonesians have only one name.

3 In the same month as the Rasminah decision, the Palu District Court convicted a youth, 'AAL', for stealing a pair of sandals belonging to a police officer, before

releasing him into his parents' custody without any other penalty. A few years earlier Minah, who stole three cacao fruits, and Basar and Kholil, convicted for stealing a watermelon, were sentenced to 1.5 month and 15 day suspended sentences, respectively. In 2010, a married couple, Supriyono and Sulastri, were both sentenced to 3.5 months of imprisonment for stealing a cluster of bananas, while Manisih, charged with theft of two kilograms of cotton, received a twenty-four-day prison sentence. Some of them had been detained prior and during to the trial. The list could go on, but see Hukumonline 2012a; Okezone 2010; and Solopos 2010.

4 The figure amount used in this chapter are based on the late 2018 exchange rate of US$ 1.00 = Rp. 15,000.

5 See Government Regulation in Lieu of Law No. 16 of 1960 on Several Adjustments to the Criminal Code, subsequently validated by Law No. 1 of 1961. The value of fines for all offences, except gambling, was also adjusted in the same year but by Government Regulation in Lieu of Law No. 18 of 1960, later validated as Law No. 1 of 1961.

6 See, for example, Suhariyono 2012: 225; Suparni 2007: 65. Some published versions of KUHP even misprint or inconsistently state the amount of loss in provisions concerning minor offences, as well as the value of fines.

7 Lembaga Kajian dan Advokasi untuk Independensi Peradilan (LeIP) assisted the Supreme Court in preparing this Regulation. LeIP is an NGO focusing on legal and judicial reform in Indonesia.

8 See, for example, Detik 2015a, 2015b.

9 See von Hirsch, and Jareborg 1991: 2–3; and von Hirsch 1985: 71–3.

10 These may include the substantial value of the loss to the victims, regardless of monetary worth, as well as the level of inconvenience caused by, and the consequential financial harm of, the offence. Thus, courts also need to assess the impact of the offence according to individual victim circumstances. See, for example, Warner 2002: 341.

11 Such as whether or not there are excuses, for example duress or necessity: von Hirsch 1985: 71–3.

12 See, for example, Kim, Spohn and Hedberg 2015: 597–9.

13 This refers to the interest of courts in disposing of cases with minimum effort or to ensure efficiency (particularly when their caseload is high), such as by reducing the sentences for pleas of guilty: Dixon 1995: 1162–3.

14 Other offences that are included in this category are certain types of minor frauds (arts. 379 and 384), damaging property (art. 407) and minor fencing, receiving stolen property (art. 482).

15 The fine for gambling was increased earlier by Law No. 7 of 1974 on Gambling Control.

16 In the 1960s adjustment, the law increased the standard of loss from Rp. 25 to Rp. 250 (ten times) and increased the value of the fines from Rp. 60 to Rp. 900 (fifteen times), and thus did not create problems like those created by the current adjustment. One of the drafters of the Regulation (who requested anonymity) told me that several judges in the team did not agree to adjust the fine by a factor of 10,000 because they believed it would make them too severe.

17 Paragraph 9 of the Elucidation to Supreme Court Regulation No. 2 of 2012.

18 Paragraph 1 and 3 of the Elucidation of the Supreme Court Regulation No. 2 of 2012.

19 Some judges are frustrated by having to deal with minor cases, particularly if the offence is trivial. See Putro 2010: 227–8.

20 Article 205(1) of Law No. 8 of 1981 on the Criminal Procedural Code.
21 Article 45A(2)b of Law No. 5 of 2014 on Supreme Court (as amended). The defendant can appeal to the provincial-level High Court, but only if he or she receives an imprisonment sentence (art. 205(3) of the Criminal Procedural Code).
22 Paragraph 9 of the Elucidation to Supreme Court Regulation No. 2 of 2012.
23 Paragraph 9 of the Elucidation to Supreme Court Regulation No. 2 of 2012.
24 Article 21(4) of Law No. 8 of 1981. There are only a few offences punishable by less than five years of imprisonment that are exempted from this provision, not including minor theft or minor embezzlement.
25 See, for example, Detik 2012a; Hukumonline 2012b; Kompas 2012a.
26 Although KUHP allows additional, heavier, maximum penalties for reoffenders, they are only applicable to particular offences that do not include minor property offences (arts. 486, 487 and 489 of KUHP). Thus if judges were to properly apply them, a recidivist committing minor offences would also be tried under art. 364.
27 This study only assesses decisions that can clearly be categorised as minor theft or minor embezzlement.
28 The only data available are in the annual reports of the Central Jakarta District Court (year 2016) and Bandung District Court (year 2015). According to these reports, Jakarta District Court decided 29 minor offence cases in 2016, while the Bandung District Court decided 22, 43 and 24 cases in 2013, 2014 and 2015 respectively. See Bandung Jakarta District Court 2016: 25. For Central Jakarta District Court annual report, see http://pn-jakartapusat.go.id/library/344581489394700.pdf.
29 The average length of imprisonment recommended by the prosecutors was 10.5 months, while the average length of imprisonment imposed by the judges was 7.6 months.
30 Due to limited information on the background and personal values or views of the judges, as well as the fact that all the cases were tried by panel of three judges, it is difficult to assess individual judges' sentencing patterns.
31 Decision No. 1059/Pid.B/2015/PN.Bdg.
32 Decision No. 1330/Pid.B/2015/PN.Bdg.
33 Decision No. 2337/Pid.B/2014/PN.Tng.
34 Decision No. 1838/Pid.B/2014/PN.Tng.
35 See, for example, Stabat District Court Decision No. 235/Pid.B/2015/PN.Stb; Stabat District Court Decision No. 300/PID.B/2015/PN.Stb; and Solok District Court Decision No. 03 /Daf.Pid.C/2013/PN.Slk.
36 Solok District Court Decision No. 02/Pid.R/2013/PN.Slk.
37 Wates District Court Decision No. 114/Pid.B/2014/PN.Wat. The Yogyakarta High Court affirmed the decision (Decision No. 2/PID.PLW/2015/PT.Yyk). For a similar decision, see Yogyakarta District Court Decision No. 85/Pid.B/2016/PN.Yyk.
38 Decision No. 6/Pid.B/2014/PN.Rni [17]. The defendants were sentenced to between four and five months of imprisonment, far below the recommended sentences, which were one and a half years and two years. The court also took the fact that the nature of the losses did not hinder the victims in conducting their daily activities, and that the victim was out of town during the offence, as reasons for imposing lenient sentences.
39 Decision No. 120/ Pid.B/2014/Pn.Mkd [21].
40 Soesilo states that daytime burglary, as long as the amount of loss is still within the definition of minor theft, should be considered minor theft. See Soesilo 1981: 218.

However, this interpretation is in conflict with art. 343 of KUHP, which clearly excludes petty theft in a dwelling from being considered minor theft.

41 Decision No. 106/ Pid.B/2015/PN.Sky [22].

42 Tebing Tinggi District Court Decision No. 403/Pid.B/2012/PN.Ttd and Medan High Court Decision No. 435/PID/2012/ PT.Mdn, as quoted in the Supreme Court Decision No. 1410 K/Pid.Sus/ 2013 [3–4].

43 Supreme Court Decision No. 1410 K/Pid.Sus/2013 [7].

44 Supreme Court Decision No. 1410 K/Pid.Sus/2013 [6].

45 Supreme Court Decision No. 1410 K/Pid.Sus/2013 [6].

46 Decision No. 52/Pid.B/2014/PN.Kray [18].

47 Surakarta District Court Decision No. 248/Pid.B/2012/PN.Ska, as quoted in Supreme Court Decision No. 702 K/Pid/2013.

48 Semarang High Court Decision No. 364/Pid/2012, as quoted in Supreme Court Decision No. 702 K/Pid/2013.

49 Supreme Court Decision No. 702 K/Pid/2013 [9].

50 See, for example, South Jakarta District Court Decision No. 1326/Pid.B/2012/PN.Jkt.Sel; Tangerang District Court Decision No. 1945/Pid.B/2014/PN.Tng; Central Jakarta District Court Decision No. 86/Pid.B/2014/PN.Jkt.Pst; and Bandung District Court Decision No. 50/Pid.B/2015/PN.Bdg.

51 Tangerang District Court Decision No. 2512/Pid.B/2014/PN.Tng.

52 See, for example, Rantau Prapat District Court Decision No. 179/Pid.B/2015/PN.Rap; Tebing Tinggi District Court Decision No. 348/Pid.B/2015/PN.Tbt; and Lubuk Basung District Court Decision No. 06/Pid.B/2015/PN.Lbb.

53 There are approximately twenty theft cases in plantations in the studied sample that were tried under the minor theft provisions.

54 Stabat District Court Decision No. 191/Pid.B/2015/PN.Stb [12].

55 Rantau Prapat District Court Decision No. 242/Pid.B/2015/PN.Rap.

56 See, for example, Rantau Prapat District Court Decision No. 98/Pid.C/2015/PN.Rap; Rantau Prapat District Court Decision No. 176/Pid.C/2015/PN.Rap; and Rantau Prapat District Court Decision No. 59/Pid.C/2015/PN.Rap.

57 See, for example, Pasaman Barat District Court Decision No. 62/Pid.B/2016/PN-Psb. In this case, the defendants were charged with aggravated theft even though the amount of stolen palm fruits was only Rp. 2,400,000. Despite that, the offence was well-planned and the offenders well-equipped. For instance, the offenders knew where the company left its harvest before transferring it to another place. They also brought a truck to carry the fruit (Decision No. 62/Pid.B/2016/PN-Psb [3–4]).

58 Yogyakarta District Court Decision No. 85/PID.B/2016/PN.Yyk [3], in conjunction with Supreme Court Decision No. 963 K/Pid/2016 [4].

59 Yogyakarta District Court Decision No. 85/PID.B/2016/PN.Yyk [3], in conjunction with Supreme Court Decision No. 963 K/Pid/2016 [4].

60 Decision No. 986/Pid.B/2015/PN.Rap.

61 Decision No. 986/Pid.B/2015/PN.Rap [4–5].

62 In several cases, the judges even mention the type of goods without stating their value: Central Jakarta District Court Decision No. 1493/Pid.B/2014/PN.Jkt.Pst; Bandung District Court Decision No. 772/Pid.B/2015/PN.Bdg; and South Jakarta District Court Decision No. 1329/Pid.B/2012/PN.Jkt.Sel. The only case concerning palm fruit theft that I came across that assessed the actual loss in a great detail was Muaro District Court Decision No. 72/Pid.B/2015/PN.Mrj.

63 See Hetanews 2018. As explained by Li (2017: 4), field supervisors usually are part of the so-called 'mafia system' of bribery and corruption in palm oil plantations.
64 Stabat District Court Decision No. 698/Pid.Sus/2015/PN.Stb [11].
65 Sumenep District Court Decision No. 307/Pid.Sus/2015/PN.Smp, and Surabaya High Court Decision No. 02/PID/2016/PT.Sby, as quoted in Supreme Court Decision No. 725 K/PID/2016 [2–5].
66 Supreme Court Decision No. 725 K/PID/2016 [7–8].
67 See, for example, Tempo 2015b; and Tempo 2013.
68 As shown in Table 3, there were only a few cases found where the judges departed from non-minor theft or embezzlement charges and applied the regulation. See, for example, Stabat District Court Decision No. 235/Pid.B/2015/PN.Stb; Stabat District Court Decision No. 300/Pid.B/2015/PN.Stb; and Stabat District Court Decision No. 340/Pid.B/2015/PN.Stb.
69 See attachment to Chief Justice Decision No. 44/KMA/SK/III/SK/2014 on the Template of Decisions and Standards of Case Registration.
70 A public prosecutor interviewed told me that the prosecutors prepare their case solely based on information gathered by the police during the investigation and presented by the police in the BAP. They are basically not involved in the investigation process, let alone the interviewing of suspects or witnesses. According to KUHAP, only the investigator (the police) has the power to call upon and interview a suspect or a witness (art. 7(1)g). Law No. of 2004 on the Prosecutor's Office gives a new power to a prosecutor to conduct a 'pre-charge' (*prapenuntutan*) process, that is an addition to 'investigation' (*pemeriksaan tambahan*), which in practice may include interviewing witnesses. However, this power can only be exercised in complex cases, or cases involving serious public and state concerns (see Elucidation to art. 30(1) e).
71 Article 182(3) and (4) of the Criminal Procedural Code.
72 This principle was drawn from a case where the Supreme Court found that the evidence presented in this case only showed that the defendant committed an aggravated theft (art. 363(1)), even though the prosecutor charged him with robbery [art. 353(1) and (2)).
73 As mentioned, only six out of seventy-seven defendants received three months imprisonment or less in Bandung, Tangerang and Central and South Jakarta District Court decisions.
74 As argued in Guthrie, Rachlinski and Wistrich (2000: 787): 'Anchors induce people to consider seriously the possibility that the real value is similar to the anchor, thereby leading them to envision circumstances under which the anchor would be correct. Even when people conclude that an anchor provides no useful information, mentally testing the validity of the anchor causes people to adjust their estimates upward or downward toward that anchor.'
75 Attorney General Circular Letter No. 013/A/JA/12/2011. This guideline only applies to cases that are considered general offences, such as theft, murder and the like. For 'special offence' cases, for instance, corruption or drug offence cases, the bar is higher.
76 There was only one defendant represented by a lawyer in the Bandung, Tangerang, Central Jakarta, and South Jakarta District Court cases referred to in this study.
77 In informal discussions, several judges mentioned to me that they sometimes informally advised the defendants or their family, before or immediately after reaching the verdict, not to appeal the decision, reasoning, among others, that the

decisions already took into account the defendants' best interests (presumably by comparing them with more severe penalty recommendation of the prosecutors and in light of the nature of the offences and the victims interest), and the cost of the appeal might be worse for them than the existing sentence.

78 It is commonly argued that many petty offenders do not have a permanent residence or any type of identification that would enable the law enforcement officers and judges to locate them for investigation or trial purposes. See, for example, Okezone 2012.

79 Commenting on how the police and prosecutors dealt with the Asyani case, a member of the DPR suspected that law enforcers were intentionally avoiding application of Supreme Court Regulation No. 2 of 2012 so they could detain the suspect (Republika 2015). In this case, Asyani, a sixty-three-year-old woman, was charged with 'stealing' several logs owned by the state-own enterprise. The value of the stolen logs was not clear, but some argued they were less than Rp. 2.5 million. Instead of charging the woman with theft (or possible minor theft) under KUHP, the police and prosecutor charged her with violating arts. 12(d) and 83(1) of Law 18 of 2013 on Prevention and Eradication of Forest Destruction (which carry a minimum of one year of imprisonment and a fine of Rp. 500 million (US$ 33,300)) for possessing (*menguasai*) or owning (*memiliki*) illegal logs. See also Tempo 2015c).

80 See, generally, for example, Asmara 2011; Assegaf 2007; Butt and Lindsey 2011; ICW, 2002; Pompe 2005.

81 See, for example, and Asmara 2011; ICW 2002; Satgas PMH 2010: 13–19.

82 Domingo and Sudaryono 2016.

83 Semarang District Court Decision No. 525/Pid.B/2014/PN.Smg. See similar comments from the Head of Pematangsiantar Prosecution Office made during a media interview: Tribunnews 2014.

84 Of the 16 District Court and Supreme Court judges I interviewed on general issues of sentencing, almost all considered the impact of the offence on the victim to be the most important factor in determining the level of punishment to be imposed.

85 One judge interviewed gave examples of what might be considered as theft motivated by survival: stealing rice, a chicken, fish or other basic foods.

86 While there is evidence that severe punishment (not criminal sanction) does seem to deter some types of offences, there are much stronger links between the likelihood of being punished (certainty of criminal enforcement) and deterrence. See Antunes and Hunt 1974: 486; Durlauf and Nagin 2011: 13–54; Grogger 1991: 297, 308; Klepper and Nagin 1989: 721; Paternoster 2010: 765.

87 The 'theft provision' in the Plantations Law, for example, was intended to respond to the many theft cases that have disrupted the business. See, for example, Surambo et al. 2010: 17. I argue that this law, which was enacted two years after the issuance of Supreme Court Regulation No. 2 of 2012, was deliberately intended to prevent the application of the Regulation in minor palm fruit theft cases. This is evident from the fact that it provides shorter maximum penalty stipulated for 'plantation theft' (four years of imprisonment) than the five years maximum penalty for 'general theft' in KUHP. Had the drafters been seriously concerned to deter offences, they would have prescribed longer imprisonment terms. This shows that their real interest was mainly to ensure that minor palm fruit theft cases are processed under this special, more punitive, law, not Supreme Court Regulation No. 2 of 2012. After all, lawmakers know that judges very seldom impose maximum imprisonment penalties anyhow.

88 See previous part for some of the examples of the above issues. For other Supreme Court Decisions that also did not enforce the regulation, see Decision No. 133 K/PID/2013; Decision No. 1042 K/Pid/2015; Decision No. 272 K/Pid/2016; Decision No. 402 K/Pid/2016; and Decision No. 3 K/PID/2017.

89 See, for example, BBC 2017; and Li 2017.

90 Supreme Court Circular Letter No. 8 of 1964. A few years later, this policy was revoked by Circular Letter No. 11 of 1969, for the reason that the practice was contrary to judicial independence. See also Lev 2000: 178–9.

91 Under the current law (art. 19(1) of KUHAP), the police can only arrest and lock-up a minor offence suspect for a day, however, they need more time than this to prepare and bring the case to the court.

References

Antunes, George and Hunt, A. Lee 1974. 'The Impact of Certainty and Severity of Punishment on Levels of Crime in American States: An Extended Analysis', *Journal of Criminal Law and Criminology* 64(4): 486

Asmara, Teddy 2011. *Budaya Ekonomi Hukum Hakim*. Semarang: Fasindo

Assegaf, Rifqi S. 2007. 'Judicial Reform in Indonesia: 1998–2006', in Naoyki Sakumoto and Hikmawanto Juwana (eds), *Reforming Laws and Institutions in Indonesia: an Assessment*. Japan: Institute of Developing Economies (IDE)/Japan External Trade Organization, pp. 11–44

Assegaf, Rifqi S. 2018. 'Sentencing Guidance in the Indonesia's Criminal Code Reform Bill: For Whose Benefit?', *Australian Journal of Asian Law* 19(1): 1

Bandung Jakarta District Court 2016 *Yearly Report of Bandung Jakarta District Court 2015*

BBC 2017. 'Penambahan Pengaman di Kelapa Sawit: Mencegah Pencurian atau Intimidasi Warga?', 11 August www.bbc.com

Butt, Simon and Lindsey, Tim 2011. 'Judicial Mafia: The Courts and State Illegality Indonesia', in Edward Aspinall and Gerry van Klinken (eds), *The State and Illegality in Indonesia*. Leiden: KITLV Press, pp. 189–213

Detik 2012a. 'MA Putuskan Pencurian di Bawah Rp. 2,5 Juta Tidak Bisa Ditahan', 28 February www.detik.com

Detik 2012b. 'Maling Minyak Tak Pernah Jera Karena Dihukum Ringan', 13 November www.detik.com

Detik 2015a. 'Kasus Pencurian Rp 41 Ribu, Pelaku Dibui dan Jaksa. Abaikan Perma', 13 May www.detik.com

Detik 2015b. 'Lagi, Jaksa Bui Terdakwa Kasus Pencurian Rp 75 Ribu dan Abaikan Perma', 15 May www.detik.com

Dixon, Jo 1995. 'The Organizational Context of Criminal Sentencing', *American Journal of Sociology* 100(5): 1157

Domingo, Pilar and Sudaryono, Leopold 2016. 'The Political Economy of Pre-trial Detention: Indonesia Case Study'. Overseas Development Institute Report

Durlauf, Steven N. and Nagin, Daniel S. 2011. 'Imprisonment and Crime: Can Both Be Reduced?', *Criminology and Public Policy* 10(1): 1

Englich, Birte; Mussweiler, Thomas; and Strack, Fritz 2006. 'Playing Dice with Criminal Sentences: The Influence of Irrelevant Anchors on Experts' Judicial Decision Making', *Personality and Social Psychology Bulletin* 32(2): 188

Grogger, Jeffrey 1991. 'Certainty vs. Severity of Punishment', *Economic Inquiry* 29(2): 297

Guthrie, Chris; Rachlinski, Jeffrey J.; and Wistrich, Andrew J. 2000. 'Inside the Judicial Mind', *Cornell Law Review* 86: 777

Haluan 2017. 'Parah, Dilepaskan Polisi, Terduga Maling di Padang Serang Balik Warga', 15 July www.harianhaluan.com

Hetanews 2018. 'Polisi Minta Tidak Berlakukan Perma Tapi UU Perkebunan', 26 February www.hetanews

Hogarth, John 1971. *Sentencing as a Human Process*. University of Toronto Press

Hukumonline 2012a. 'Terdakwa Anak Pencuri Sandal Divonis Bersalah', 5 January www.hukumonline.com

Hukumonline 2012b. 'Batasan Nilai Tipiring Naik 10.000 Kali Lipat', 29 February www.hukumonline.com

Hukumonline 2012c. 'Respon Kejaksaan dan Polri atas Perma Tipiring, 4 March www.hukumonline.com

Hukumonline 2013. 'MA Keluhkan Pelaksanaan Perma Tipiring', 23 September www.hukumonline.com

ICW (Indonesian Corruption Watch) 2002. *Menyingkap Tabir Mafia Peradilan*. Jakarta: ICW

Johnson, Brian D. 2006. 'The Multilevel Context of Criminal Sentencing: Integrating Judge-and County-Level Influences', *Criminology* 44(2): 259

Kim, Byungbae, Spohn, Cassia and Hedberg, E. C. 2015. 'Federal Sentencing as a Complex Collaborative Process: Judges, Prosecutors, Judge Prosecutor Dyads, and Disparity in Sentencing', *Criminology* 53(4): 597

Klepper, Steven and Nagin, Daniel 1989. 'The Deterrent Effect of Perceived Certainty and Severity of Punishment Revisited', *Criminology* 27: 721

Kompas 2012a. 'Di Bawah 2,5 Juta Tidak Bisa Ditahan', 29 February www.kompas.com

Kompas 2012b. 'Pencuri Semangka Divonis 15 Hari Penjara', 16 December www.kompas.com

Kompas 2013. 'Bocah yang Mencuri Susu Demi Gizi Adiknya Akhirnya Dibebaskan', 3 December www.kompas.com

Kompas 2016. '14 Tersangka Sindikat Pencuri Sawit Diserahkan ke Kejari Simalungun', 14 October https://regional.kompas.com

Lev, Daniel S. 2000. 'Judicial Institution and Legal Culture', in *Legal Evolution and Political Evolution and Political Authority in Indonesia: Selected Essays.* Boston: Kluwer Law International, pp. 161–214

Li, Tania Murray 2017. 'After the Land Grab: Infrastructural Violence and the "Mafia System" in Indonesia's Oil Palm Plantation Zones', *Geoforum* 96: 328–37

Maduracorner 2014. 'Terduga Maling Dilepas, Warga Kompak Datangi Mapolsek Manding', 4 June www.maduracorner

Mahkamah Agung 2007. *Pedoman Teknis Pelaksanaan Administasi dan Teknis Peradilan (Buku II Mahkamah Agung RI)*. Jakarta: Mahkamah Agung

Medansatu 2016. 'Menyoal Sidang Kasus Pencurian Senilai Rp. 98 Ribu di PN Rantau Prapat…', 17 March www.medansatu.com

Okezone 2010. 'Pencuri Pisang Divonis 3,5 Bulan Penjara', 28 October www.okezone.com

Okezone 2012. 'Perma Tipiring Soal Hapus Penahanan Sulit Diterapkan', 3 March www.okezone.com

Paternoster, Raymond 2010. 'How Much Do We Really Know about Criminal Deterrence?', *Criminal Law and Criminology* 100(3): 765

Pengadilan Negeri Bandung 2015. *Laporan Akuntabilitas Kinerja Pemerintah Pengadilan Negeri Bandung Kelas 1A Khusus 2015*. PN Bandung

Pengadilan Negeri Jakarta Pusat 2016. *Laporan Tahunan 2016*. PN Jakarta Pusat

Pompe, Sebastian 2005. *The Indonesian Supreme Court: A Study of Institutional Collapse*. Cornell Southeast Asia Program

Putro, Widodo Dwi 2010. 'Mencari Kebenaran Materiil Dalam "Hard Case" Pencurian Tiga Buah Kakao', *Yudisial* 4(3): 220

Republika 2010. 'Menkumham Minta Polisi Jangan Sembarangan Tahan Rasminah', 12 October www.republika.co.id

Republika 2015. 'Kasus Tipiring Tetap Diproses Polri Menyatakan Sudah Melakukan Mediasi antara Perhutani dengan Nenek Asyani', 19 March www.republika.co.id

Satgas PMH (Satuan Tugas Pemberantasan Mafia Hukum) 2010. *Mafia Hukum: Modus Operandi, Akar Permasalahan dan Strategi Penanggulangan*. Jakarta: Satgas PMH

Simester A. P and Sullivan, G. R. 2005. 'On the Nature and Rationale of Property Offences', in R. A. Duff and Stuart Green (eds), *Defining Crimes: Essays on the Special Part of the Criminal Law*. Oxford University Press, pp. 168–95

Sinar Indonesia Baru 2014. 'Kejari Medan Tolak 11 SPDP dari Penyidik Polri Terkait Tipiring', 14 February www.hariansib.co

Soesilo, R. 1981. *Kitab Undang-undang Hukum Pidana (KUHP) serta Komentar-komentarnya Lengkap Pasal Demi Pasal*. Jakarta: Politeia

Solopos 2010. 'Kasus Pencurian Buah Randu, Hakim Jatuhi Vonis Hukuman 24 Hari Penjara', 2 February www.solopos.com

Solopos 2012. 'Tidak Layak Pencuri 6 Piring dihukum 130 Hari Penjara', 1 February www.solopos.com

Sugandhi, R. 1981. *Kitab Undang-undang Hukum Pidana (K.U.H.P.) dengan Penjelasannya*. Jakarta: Usaha Nasional

Suhariyono, A. R. 2012. *Pembaruan Pidana Denda di Indonesia*. Jakarta: Papas Sinar Sinanti

Suparni, Niniek 2007. *Eksistensi Pidana Denda dalam Sistem Pidana dan Pemidanaan*, 2nd edn. Jakarta: Sinar Grafika

Surambo, Achmad; Susanti, Elsa; Herdianti, Endang; Hasibuan, Fatilda; Fatinaware, Inda; Safira, Maya; Dewy, Puspa; Winarni, R. Retno and Sastra, Tini 2010. 'The Oil Palm Plantation System Weakens the Position of Women'. Research Report, Sawit Watch & Women's Solidarity for Human Rights

Tempo 2012. 'Ketua MA Pertanyakan Rencana DPR Bentuk Panja', 2 February www.tempo.co

Tempo 2013. 'Tiga Petani Ditahan Gara-gata Ranting Mahoni', 16 January www.tempo.co

Tempo 2015a. 'Copet di Komuter: Percuma Saja Diserahkan Polisi 4', 6 July www.tempo.co

Tempo 2015b. 'Penebang Mangrove Didenda Rp 2 Miliar Jalani PK', 12 March www.tempo.co

Tempo 2015c. 'Sidang Kasus Pencurian Jati Nenek Asyani Menangis Histeris', 12 March www.tempo.co 2015

Tribunnews 2014. 'Kajari Pematangsiantar Nilai Dalam Perma 2 Tahun 2012 Terlalu Tinggi', 28 March www.medantribunnews

Viva 2012. 'Yani: Hukum Rasminah, Hakim MA Tak Bernurani', 1 February www.viva.co.id

von Hirsch, Andrew 1985. *Past or Future Crime: Deservedness and Dangerousness in the Sentencing of Criminals*. New Brunswick, N. J.: Rutgers University Press

von Hirsch, Andrew and Jareborg, Nils 1991. 'Gauging Criminal Harm: A Living-standard Analysis', *Oxford Journal of Legal Studies* 11(1): 1

Warner, Kate 2002. *Sentencing in Tasmania*, 2nd edn. Federation Press

Legislation

Criminal Code (*Kitab Undang-Undang Hukum Pidana*, KUHP: Law No. 1 of 1946
Criminal Procedural Code (*Kitab Undang-Undang Hukum Acara Pidana*, KUHAP: Law No. 8 of 1981)
Law No. 27 of 2007 on Management of Coastal Zones and Small Islands
Law No. 39 of 2014 on Plantation
Law No. 18 of 2013 on Prevention and Eradication of Forest Destruction
Law No. 7 of 1974 on Gambling
Law No. 5 of 2014 on Supreme Court
Government Regulation in Lieu of Law No. 16 of 1960
Government Regulation in Lieu of Law No. 18 of 1960
Supreme Court Regulation No. 2 of 2012
Attorney General Circular Letter No. 013/A/JA/12/2011
Chief Justice Decree No. 44/KMA/SK/III/SK/2014 on Template of Decision and Standards of Case Registration

Court Decision

Supreme Court

Decision No. 693 K/Pid/1980
Decision No. 1042 K/Pid/2015
Decision No. 133 K/Pid/2013
Decision No. 1410 K/Pid.Sus/2013
Decision No. 272 K/Pid/2016
Decision No. 3 K/Pid/2017
Decision No. 402 K/Pid/2016
Decision No. 702 K/Pid /2013
Decision No. 725 K/Pid/2016
Decision No. 963 K/Pid/2016

High Court

Jogjakarta High Court Decision No. 2/PID.PLW/2015/PT.Yyk

District Court

Decision No. 50/Pid.B/2015/PN.Bdg
Decision No. 772/Pid.B/2015/PN.Bdg

Decision No. 1493/Pid.B/2014/PN.Jkt.Pst
Decision No. 86/Pid.B/2014/PN.Jkt.Pst
Decision No. 1059/PID.B/2015/PN.Bdg
Decision No. 106/ Pid.B/2015/PN.Sky
Decision No. 120/ Pid.B/2014/PN.Mkd
Decision No. 1330/Pid.B/2015/PN.Bdg
Decision No. 1838/Pid.B/2014/PN.Tng
Decision No. 2337/Pid.B/2014/PN.Tng
Decision No. 52/Pid.B/2014/PN.Kray
Decision No. 6/Pid.B/2014/PN.Rni
Decision No. 986/Pid.B/2015/PN.Rap
Decision No. 06/Pid.B/2015/PN.Lbb
Decision No. 62/Pid.B/2016/PN.Psb
Decision No. 72/Pid.B/2015/PN.Mrj
Decision No. 03 /Daf.Pid.C/2013/PN.Slk
Decision No. 02/Pid.R/2013/PN.Slk
Decision No. 1329/Pid.B/2012/PN.Jkt.Sel
Decision No. 1326/Pid.B/2012/PN.Jkt.Sel
Decision No. 191/Pid.B/2015/PN.Stb
Decision No. 235/Pid.B/2015/PN.Stb
Decision No. 300/PID.B/2015/PN.Stb
Decision No. 340/Pid.B/2015/PN.Stb
Decision No. 698/Pid.Sus/2015/PN.Stb
Decision No. 59/Pid.C/2015/PN.Rap
Decision No. 176/Pid.C/2015/PN.Rap
Decision No. 179/Pid.B/2015/PN.Rap
Decision No. 242/Pid.B/2015/PN.Rap
Decision No. 98/Pid.C/2015/PN.Rap
Decision No. 525/Pid.B/2014/PN.Smg
Decision No. 1945/Pid.B/2014/PN.Tng
Decision No. 2512/Pid.B/2014/PN.Tng
Decision No. 348/Pid.B/2015/PN.Tbt
Decision No. 114/Pid.B/2014/PN.Wat
Decision No. 85/Pid.B/2016/PN.Yyk

10 Manoeuvring mandatory minimum sentences

Judicial decisions on corruption

Rifqi S. Assegaf[1]

In recent decades, jurisdictions across the world have reintroduced mandatory minimum sentences to their criminal codes. A mandatory minimum sentence[2] is a fixed minimum penalty prescribed by law to be imposed by judges for an offence, in contrast to, for example, structured discretion, where the law only fixes maximum penalties and otherwise leaves judges with a discretion to sentence, so long as they do not exceed them (Hoel and Gelb 2008: 7). Mandatory minimum penalties are not a new phenomenon. During the sixteenth to eighteenth centuries, the 'Bloody Code' in England progressively required the mandatory death penalty for all felonies (McLynn 2002: xi). This explosion of capital offences was caused by the view that fear of the gallows was the only way to deter serious offences (Greenblatt 2008: 1, 2–3; McLynn 2002: xi). In France, the Napoleonic Criminal Code (1810), while abolishing fixed punishments, introduced mandatory minimum and maximum sentences, whereby judges only enjoyed sentencing discretion within the penalty range provided (Lobingier 1918: 114, 128). This limitation was made as a response to the corrupt, arbitrary, feudal and often inhuman practices of the French judicial system before the Revolution (Canals 1960: 541, 542–3; Cappelletti 1985: 1, 11–16).

The comeback of mandatory minimum sentences in modern times is mainly grounded on the crime prevention justification. However, in many cases, it is also motivated by politics, because promising to introduce mandatory minimum laws, as a symbol of 'tough on crime platforms' during campaigns, has proven a successful tactic for winning electoral support (Tonry 2009: 100–1). Minimum penalty laws are also sometimes claimed to satisfy the objectives of international legal protocols (Trotter and Garozzo 2012: 553, 582).

Studies have challenged the association of minimum penalties with crime prevention.[3] Evidence suggests that in the US, for example, where many statutes require a very severe minimum sentence, not only have those laws failed to deter crimes but they have also created severe injustice (particularly for minority defendants), overcrowding of the prison population, and increased appeal rates (Greenblatt 2008: 1, 4; Tonry 2009: 65). Further, it is well established that, in the US at least, law enforcers, judges and juries altered their behavior to avoid imposing harsh statutory minimum penalties, such as in drugs-related cases or for reoffenders.[4] The police, for example, became more selective processing offences or searching potential offenders (Tonry 2009: 65, 76–8). Prosecutors were inclined to look for plea bargains to avoid trials or were reluctant to prosecute some violations. Others even attempted to evade minimum penalties by 'undercharging', that is, only charging offenders with lesser offences, or by departing from the mandatory minimum, as is possible in some, limited circumstances in the US (Greenblatt 2008: 1, 30; Tonry 2009: 65, 72). Judges, too, tried to escape imposing minimum penalties 'by using their own power, as well as by harnessing the powers of the jury and prosecutor' (Greenblatt 2008: 1, 2). They interpreted statutes in certain ways, limited the introduction of evidence, or adopted narrow interpretations of procedural and evidentiary rules that would trigger minimum sentences (Greenblatt 2008: 1, 26; Tonry 2009: 65, 72–3). The judges also informed jurors of the harsh punishment the defendant would receive, expecting they would not convict or would find the defendant guilty of a lesser offence (Greenblatt 2008: 1, 26; Tonry 2009: 65, 72–3). Some judges have even resigned or refused to impose mandatory sentences in protest (Greenblatt 2008: 1, 33).

In Indonesia, there is an increasing trend for the government and the legislature to enact so-called 'special criminal statutes'[5] with mandatory minimum penalties. From 1997 to 2014, for example, there have been 219 new offences introduced that impose minimum sentences (Akbari 2015: 22–3), although they are, in general, not as severe as, for instance, those in the US. Despite this, there are studies and anecdotal evidence that shows that in a number of cases, Indonesian law enforcement officials, particularly judges, have refused to impose the minimum penalties required.

The purpose of the chapter is to assess how law enforcers in Indonesia, particularly judges, have responded to mandatory minimum provisions in the Corruption Eradication Law.[6] Studying the application of minimum penalties in corruption offences is appealing because the public generally expect the courts to impose severe sentences in these cases, in line with the spirit of the law, but, at the same time, the gravity of the offence and the culpabilities of the offenders are diverse. Offenders, for example, range from low-level officials who received only small profits for assisting an offence, to high ranking officials and business persons who obtained huge profits and caused significant loss to state finances.

This assessment has been done by reviewing court decisions, and the author's analysis of those decisions was assisted by interviews conducted with two Supreme Court judges, seven first instance Anti-corruption Court (ACC) judges and one prosecutor in a district prosecutor's office in Jakarta. The court decisions are 205 corruption cases decided by the first instance Jakarta and Bandung ACC between 2012 and 2015 (excluding 2013). This sample comprises all these courts' online-published decisions that used either art. 2(1) or art. 3 of the Corruption Eradication Law as the basis of their rulings. As a comparison, I also reviewed all theft and embezzlement cases (280 cases, arts. 362, 372 and 374 of the Criminal Code)[7] decided in the same periods by four district courts in Central and South Jakarta, Bandung and Tangerang.[8] The term 'case' here needs clarification. In practice, prosecutors can charge several offenders committing a collective offence in a single trial or separately. In this chapter, I treat each offender as a single case.

This chapter reveals that while judges generally complied with the minimum penalties in the Corruption Eradication Law, they strategically avoided convicting the defendants under art. 2(1), which carries severe minimum penalties, preferring to instead sentence them under art. 3, which carries much lower minimum penalties. This is done, mainly, by deliberately misinterpreting both provisions. I argue that the driving factors for this 'manoeuvre' are to avoid injustice (for example, to avoid imposing severe punishment for minor corruption offences) and, mainly, because of paradigmatic issues and the weakness of cases brought by the prosecutors. I also consider the possibility that judicial corruption plays a role.

This chapter is organised as follows. It begins with a discussion of growing trends to incorporate minimum penalties in special statutes in recent decades; problems in the design of the statutes, particularly concerning the elements of crimes and the range of minimum and maximum penalties; and general observations about how law enforcers and judges respond to these issues. This part also assesses the Supreme Court's stand on the binding nature of minimum penalties, particularly in corruption cases. The second part of the chapter provides analysis of how and why the selected courts navigate the requirement to impose minimum penalties in the law.

An overview of minimum penalties in special statutes, issues surrounding them, and law enforcers and courts' responses

Before 1997, the principal offences and sanctions in Indonesian criminal law were mainly stipulated in the Criminal Code or *Kitab Undang-undang Hukum Pidana*. This Code originated from the Netherlands where there was (and is) generally trust in the judiciary (Tak 2008: 27). It does not recognise the notion of a minimum sentence. The minimum duration of imprisonment is just one day, with Rp. 3,750 for fines (less than US$ 1).[9] The first mandatory minimum penalty law was introduced in 1997 for drug-related offences[10] and numbers grew rapidly after that, with an increasing trend to stipulate new offences in special statutes. Between 1998 and 2014, of approximately 154 statutes that impose criminal sanctions (with a total of 716 offences), around 30 per cent of them (219 offences) impose minimum penalties, as shown in Graph 10.1. [11]

The formal and most common reason given by lawmakers for introducing minimum penalties is to create a stronger deterrent. The Elucidation (*penjelasan* or explanatory memorandum) to Law No. 31 of 1999 on Corruption Eradication, for example, reads:[12]

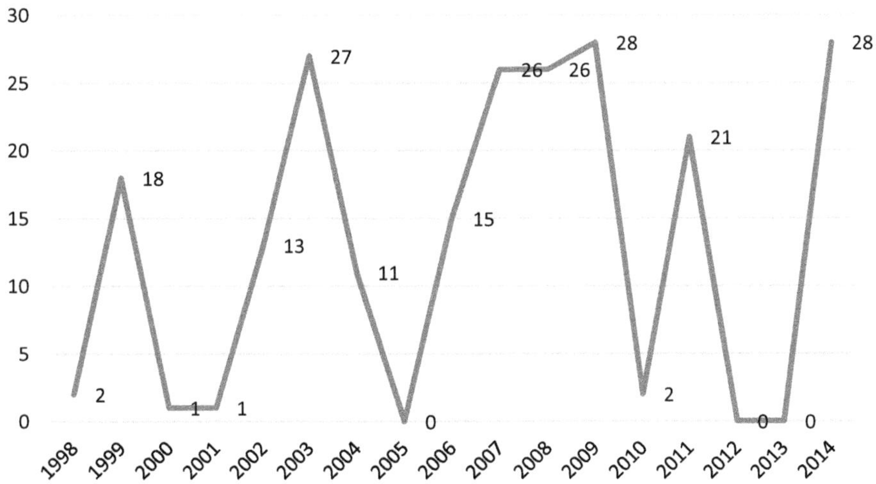

Graph 10.1 Number of statutes imposing mandatory minimum penalties, by year (1998–2014).

Source: Akbari 2015: 22–3.

> To effectively achieve the objective of corruption prevention and eradication, this Law contains different provisions to the earlier Law, including prescribing minimum mandatory sentences, more severe fines and the death penalty

Another connected justification is to minimise 'disparity of sentences', which, in the Indonesian context, refers to light charges and punishments for those who have committed serious offences,[13] as a result of judicial corruption or other factors. As in other jurisdictions, this is sometimes motivated by politics,[14] or is a response to what is understood to be the demands of international laws.[15]

The severity of minimum penalties in the special statutes, as well as their distance from the maximum penalties varies: from just one month to ten years of imprisonment, and from merely Rp. 2 million (US$ 133) to Rp. 5 trillion (US$ 333 million) of fines (Table 10.1). Furthermore, the ratio between the level of imprisonment penalties vis à vis the level of fines in various statutes is confusing.[16]

On the positive side, there is no extreme minimum penalty statute, such as the 'three strike laws' that apply in some jurisdictions.[17]

The very low minimum penalties and the wide margin between the minimum and the maximum penalties in some of the statutes presented in Table 10.1 raises questions about the standards used to formulate them, and how they can bring about deterrence or minimise sentencing disparity. Arief, a

Table 10.1 Examples of the minimum and maximum sentences in some special statutes

Statutes & crimes/offences	*Sanctions/penalties*			
	Imprisonment		*Fines (thousand Rp.)*	
	Min	*Max*	*Min*	*Max*
Central Bank (Law No. 23 of 1999) Unlawfully use foreign money for financial transaction or payment contrary to the law (art. 65 in conjunction with art. 2(3))	1 month	3 months	2,000	6,000 [(b)]
Labour (Law No. 13 of 2003) Employer fails to pay salary to an employee who does not come to work due to lawful reasons, such as sickness, leave, etc. (art. 186(1), in conjunction with art. 93(2))	1 month	4 years	10,000	400,000 [(a)]
Corruption eradication (Law No. 31 of 1999 as amended) Abuse of power to benefit him/herself or another (art. 3)	1 year	Life or 20 years	100,000	1,000,000 [(a)]
Child protection (Law No. 23 of 2002 as amended) Rape of children – not by parent, guardian or educator (art. 81(1))	5 years	15 years	N/A	500,000 [(b)]
Narcotic (Law No. 35 of 2009) Own, keep, provide non-plant narcotics in group I (for example, opium) contrary to the law (art. 112(1))	4 years	12 years	80,000	8,000,000 [(b)]
Banking (Law No. 7 of 1992 as amended) A shareholder who instructs a bank's commissioner, director or employee to do/not do things resulting in the bank not taking the necessary measures to ensure its adherence to the applicable law (art. 50A)	7 years	15 years	10,000,000	200,000,000 [(b)]
Human Rights Court (Law No. 26 of 2000) Genocide (art. 36)	10 years	Death, life or 25 years	N/A	N/A

Notes:
(a) the imposition of the fine is optional.
(b) the imposition of the fine is compulsory in addition to imprisonment.

leading Indonesian criminal law scholar, has criticised these practices (2007). He also warns that the minimum penalties should only be used for serious offences, such as those that incur more than seven years' imprisonment (Arief 2002: 128).

These issues aside, the most troubling matter is the ambiguity of some statutes in describing the elements of the offences. This has allowed minimum penalties to be misused by law enforcers and judges to charge and sentence offenders committing lesser offences, thus causing injustice. As an illustration, arts. 111(1) and 112(1) of the Narcotics Law provides a minimum of four years' imprisonment for those who 'plant', 'grow' 'own', 'keep' or 'possess' certain types of drugs. The minimum penalty increases to five years for 'offering', 'selling', 'buying' or 'receiving' drugs (art. 114(1)). These stringent provisions are aiming at drugs producers, sellers or traffickers. However, due to ambiguous wording, they are frequently abused to charge drug users, regardless of the fact that the Law contains other provisions intended specifically for users,[18] by extorting higher payments to stop prosecution or alter the charge or recommend a lighter one.[19] With approximately 44,000 drug-related cases decided by the lower courts each year (Mahkamah Agung 2018b: 49), the majority of which concern drug users, these practices have not only caused overcrowding of prisons (Sindonews 2017 and see Sudaryono, this volume) but also, in many cases, massive injustice.

In 2012, the Constitutional Court ruled on the constitutionality of minimum penalties when reviewing a Corruption Eradication Law case. The review was lodged by Herlina Koibur, a convict who received four years of imprisonment for assisting corruption that benefited her to the value of Rp. 3 million (US$ 200) (Detiknews 2012), arguing that the minimum penalties in art. 2(1) of the Law violated the right of legal certainty provided by art. 28D of the 1945 Constitution. However, the Court disagreed. It maintained that the adoption of statutory minimum penalties is a matter of legal policy within the constitutional power of lawmakers because corruption is an extraordinary crime and the Law aims to achieve crime deterrence for the general public.[20]

Nevertheless, due to criticism of mandatory minimum penalties, lawmakers recently removed them from some statutes, or provided different levels of minimum penalties for different types of offenders in new statutes. For example, the minimum and maximum penalties for certain illegal logging offences for members of local communities (who live near or in the forest and whose livelihood depends on it) in the 2013 Prevention and Eradication of Forest Destruction Law are significantly lower than for other types of offenders – between three months and two years for the former, and one year to five years for the later.[21] It seems that the drafters tried to balance the need for minimum sentences against the need to minimise their negative consequences. The newer Local Government Law, the Election Law and Money Laundering Law, for instance, completely removed minimum penalties. However, in the latter case, the motive was perhaps more to do with assisting political and government elites, since many of them had fallen 'victim' to the minimum penalties in the earlier Money Laundering Law.

Furthermore, since 2012, the Juvenile Criminal Justice System Law prohibits the application of minimum penalties to underage offenders.[22] Before that, the Supreme Court frequently ruled that the top minimum penalties to be imposed on child offenders were only half of those are mandated in the statutes, following the logic of half maximum penalty discount rules for them already recognised in the earlier law (Arsil 2012a, 2012b).

Law enforcers' and courts' response to minimum sentences: General picture

The responses of law enforcers and judges to mandatory minimum statutes are not uniform. In general, police and prosecutors appear to have no hesitation in applying them, while judges have shown more restraint. As an example, in people smuggling cases between 2011 and 2015, of ninety-nine defendants, most of whom were of low economic status, the majority were charged under art. 120 of Law No. 6 of 2011 on Immigration Law, which carries a five-year minimum sentence (Missbach 2016: 8). However, 21 per cent of them were sentenced to terms of imprisonment below the minimum (Missbach 2016: 12). Part of the reason for judges to ignore the minimum penalties was that the roles of the defendants in the offences were minimal and their motive was mainly economic necessity (Palmer and Missbach 2018: 11–15). Judges also argued that the minimum sentences in the Immigration Law were too severe compared to other statutes, such as the Corruption Eradication Law or the Narcotics Law, and were thus discriminatory and unjust (Palmer and Missbach 2018: 13–14).

Police and prosecutors also seem to respond to statutory minimum penalties in the statutes on drug offences enthusiastically. There are indications that since the enactment of the new Narcotics Law in 2007, the number of drug offence cases has skyrocketed (Detiknews 2008). As mentioned, most of the victims were drug-users and were inappropriately charged with provisions designed for drug producers, sellers or traffickers, which carry severe minimum penalties. Judges' responses to this problem were varied. Many imposed sentences according to the law, while others sentenced below the minimum penalties or convicted the defendants under more appropriate provisions, even though the offenders were not charged by the prosecutors under these provisions (Assegaf 2019). As explained in the next section, this is, in fact, contrary to procedural law.

In the case of corruption, some judges also sentenced below the minimum penalties required, including by imposing suspended sentences (Rumadan, Wijaya and Mulyani 2013). In 2008 alone, both lower courts and the Supreme Court imposed suspended sentences on at least thirteen defendants who had caused billions of rupiahs of state losses (Indonesian Corruption Watch 2009). Their motives for avoiding imposing the minimum penalty are not always honourable, as is explained in the next section. There were also several cases where the prosecutor also sought sentences below the minimum, but usually only in petty corruption cases (Indonesian Corruption Watch 2018: 16).

There are, however, instances where both law enforcers and judges were pressured to apply minimum penalties. This particularly occurs in sex-related offences, where the culpability of the offender is ambiguous. An example of this is when an adult and an under-age person, or two under-age persons, have consensual sex, but later the 'victim' or her or his families press charges for involuntary sex or even rape, which carry heavy minimum penalties. In some cases, judges have chosen to ignore the law in order to achieve what is, in their eyes, a more just outcome. In one case, for example, the judges imposed a penalty below the three years mandatory sentence on a young man for unwanted fondling and fingering of his sixteen-year-old girlfriend's genitals (although the evidence suggested she consented), stating that the severe penalty was unjust in this case because, among others, there was no intention on the part of the man to break the law, and the defendant 'showed responsibility' in agreeing to marry his girlfriend (although her parents rejected the proposal).[23]

The Supreme Court's position on minimum penalties

Before 2012, the Supreme Court had not yet taken a firm position on how to deal with the problematic issues concerning minimum penalties. In a leading 2005 decision (*yurisprudensi tetap*)[24] concerning minimum sentences in Law No. 39 of 1999 on Human Rights, the Court annulled a High Court decision that departed from the minimum sentence by imposing five years' imprisonment on Eurico Guterres, a key human rights offender in violations in East Timor, and increased it to ten years, in line with the law. The Supreme Court began by stating that, 'according to legal principles and judicial practice, the boundary of judicial sentencing discretion is the minimum and minimum penalties in the statutes'.[25] Then, it further declared:[26]

> Judges cannot impose a sentence under or above the statutory minimum/maximum penalties...since it will create bad precedent ...and hinder the achievement of the punishment objectives, which are to be beneficial, bring about justice and maintain legal certainty.

However, in the *Kardono* case (2010), which concerned the Corruption Eradication Law, the Supreme Court changed its position. Kardono received Rp. 2.9 million (US$ 193) for allowing his company to be used by Erwin (the main perpetrator) in a project tender. However, Erwin never completed the project, causing the state losses of approximately Rp. 61 million (US$ 4,066), which triggered a criminal process. The prosecutor charged Kardono under art. 2(1) of the Corruption Eradication Law, which carries a minimum of four years' prison and a Rp. 200 million (US$ 13,333) fine. The Supreme Court, however, only imposed a single year's imprisonment, without fines, reasoning that[27]

1. ...the fact that the prosecutor only charged the defendant with Article 2(1) ...puts the panel in a dilemma in seeking to impose a just punishment and enforce the law at the same time...
2. ... the application of a mandatory minimum penalty... can harm the sense of justice because it is disproportionate to the culpability of the offender and the state's financial loss and also the gain that the defendant received from the offence, that is Rp. 2,900,000;
3. ...corruption should not be responded to permissively, regardless of the amount of the state loss, but at the same time, imposing sentences that disturb the sense of justice should also be avoided;
4. In very particular cases, the Supreme Court...can interpret and apply the law in a way that not fully in line with the spirit and the intention of the drafter of the law, to ensure justice

While this decision could be helpful for lower court judges in deciding future similar cases, there is an issue. The choice of the words 'in very particular cases, the Supreme Court...can interpret and apply the law...' seems to indicate that it has reserved for itself permission to depart from minimum sentences. Further, the Supreme Court is, in any case, inconsistent in applying these rules. Just a few months later, it gave Herlina Koibur four years' imprisonment for assisting corruption, even though she received only Rp. 100,000 (less than US$ 7.00) more than Kardono (Detiknews 2012). This raises an issue about the binding nature of the *Kardono* case, particularly for lower courts.

The Supreme Court has also addressed the issue of the binding status of the mandatory minimum sentence in several circular letters (*surat edaran*). A circular letter is a policy document circulated to all courts that serves as a guideline, including on how to apply the law. It must be followed by all judges. The first guidance issued was in Circular Letter No. 7 of 2012, in which the Court prohibited judges from sentencing below the required penalties when dealing with corruption cases.[28] The circular letter also prohibited judges from imposing a suspended sentence (probation) in such cases.[29]

In Circular Letter No. 3 of 2015, however, the Court allowed judges to step aside from the minimum penalty in certain drug-related cases, that is, when a drug user is incorrectly charged with non-drug user provisions.[30] This measure was taken as an alternative to a practice where judges sentence defendants in such cases under other, more correct, provisions that were not included in the prosecutors' charges, which is (also) against the law.[31]

Later, in Circular Letter No. 1 of 2017, the Supreme Court expanded its permission to depart from minimum penalties in the Child Protection Law. This permission is only applicable in cases where an adult defendant has committed sexual offences against under-age persons in specific contexts, such as when the matter has been settled outside the court between the defendant and the victim (including their families), including if both later marry, or the act was consensual in nature and not done by a father to his child, or by a teacher to his or her student.[32]

To conclude, the only well-defined guidance from the Supreme Court on minimum penalties, based on *yurispudensi* and the circular letters, is that lower court judges can sentence below minimum penalties only in certain drugs and sexual offences cases. In other cases, including corruption cases, they must apply the minimum sentences in the laws.

Manoeuvring the mandatory minimum in sentencing corruption cases

The problematic articles 2(1) and 3 of the Corruption Eradication Law and light sentences: The Supreme Court's solutions

As discussed earlier, there are a number of cases where both lower courts and the Supreme Court sentenced corruption defendants to punishments below the mandatory minimum, including suspended sentences. What is more, the average sentence was relatively lenient. Part of the reason for this is that, like the Narcotics Law, some clauses in the Corruption Eradication Law are multi-interpretable, particularly arts. 2(1) and 3, the most common provisions used to charge corruption offences. Article 2(1) reads:

> Any person who illegally (*secara melawan hukum*) enriches (*memperkaya*) him or herself, another person or a corporation in a way that could damage the state finances and economy is punishable by imprisonment for life, or between a minimum of four years and a maximum of 20 years imprisonment, and fines between a minimum of Rp. 200,000,000 (two hundred million rupiahs, or US$ 13,333) and a maximum of Rp. 1,000,000,000 (one billion rupiah, or US$ 66,666).

Article 3 defines the element of the crimes in a fairly similar manner:

> Any person, who, with the aim of profiting (*menguntungkan*) him or herself, another person or a corporation, misuses his or her authority, opportunities, or means at his or her disposal which arise because of the office and the position he or she holds (*kedudukan dan jabatan*), and by doing so could damage state finances and the economy, is punishable by imprisonment for life, or between a minimum of one year and a maximum of 20 years imprisonment and/or fines between a minimum of Rp. 50,000,000 (fifty million rupiahs, or US$ 3,333) and a maximum of Rp. 1,000,000,000 (one billion rupiah).

The critical difference between the two clauses (aside from the level of minimum penalties) is the meaning of 'illegally enriching' (*secara melawan hukum memperkaya*) and aims of 'profiting' (*menguntungkan*) by 'misusing authority, opportunities, or means arising from one's office and position'. However, the Law does not define 'enriching' and 'profiting'. Assuming that both share a similar meaning, actions that fall under art. 3 will also meet the elements of crime in art. 2(1), but will result in a much less severe minimum sentence, which is troubling. More importantly, since art. 3 highlights the element of abuse of power, it can be interpreted as a specific clause to charge power holders (or at least public officials), which is troubling. According to general sentencing principles in the Criminal Code, if offences are committed by a public official, this is considered an aggravating factor that deserves higher penalties.[33]

These issues become more relevant in sentencing because in most corruption cases the prosecutors charge the defendants with a 'subsidiary charge' – with art. 2(1) as the primary and art. 3 as subsidiary. This gives judges options about which charge is most suited to the case before them. According to internal guidelines issued by the Attorney General's Office[34] and general practice, prosecutors can construct their charges in five ways. The first is the 'single charge', that is, where a prosecutor only accuses the defendant of a solitary or single offence, with one charge. Where a defendant commits a single offence but the prosecutor is not sure yet what is the most appropriate charge to be used, they will use either an 'alternative' or 'subsidiary charge'. In both approaches, the prosecutor would include two (or more) offences in their initial indictment letter (*surat dakwaan*), which is submitted before the trial and, as mentioned, read out at the first hearing. At the end of the hearing, the prosecutor recommends what he or she believes is the proven offence (and also the recommended sentence) by reading out the formal charge (*surat tuntutan*) in closing submissions, but lets the judges decide the most fitting one, with freedom to choose an offence from the indictment letter or the formal charge. The only difference between the two approaches is that in the subsidiary model, the offence would be set out in priority order (primary, subsidiary and so forth) and the judges should consider them in that order. If judges choose to sentence for the subsidiary offence (usually the lesser offence), they have to give reasons why the first offence is not proven. As for the alternative model, the judges can choose the most appropriate offence without having to consider the other(s). The fourth type, 'cumulative charges', is used in a case where a defendant has committed more than one offence (multiple offences). There is also a combination of these four types of charges.

To guide judges in determining what provision is to be used in the above context, the Supreme Court issued Circular Letter No. 7 of 2012, which clarifies the subject (addressee) and the object (action) of the two provisions. Concerning the subject, it maintains that 'arts. 2(1) and 3 are designed for any person…[thus] both are applicable for civil servant and non-civil servant (private individuals)'.[35] On the issue of the object, the Court requests judges to consider the harm of the offence. It states that:[36]

> If the element of illegal enriching him or herself, another person or a corporation in Article 2 is not satisfied, then [judges should] impose

> [a punishment under] Article 3, with a minimum threshold of Rp. 100 million [US$ 6,666]. It is not just to impose Article 2 with a minimum of four years of imprisonment and fine for the defendant who only damages state finances to the extent of Rp. 100 million

The Supreme Court also maintains that when a defendant causes severe financial state loss, but he or she is only charged under art. 3 (with a single charge), judges should impose 'proportional punishment', meaning judges should not simply apply the minimum penalties in that provision.[37]

The use of the amount of the state loss as a standard to differentiate between the objects of the two clauses is reasonable to prevent the possible injustice of a relatively large minimum sentence for petty corruption, and the other way around. However, it is not clear why judges are asked to assess first whether or not the element of illegal enriching is satisfied before applying art. 2(1). Furthermore, the Letter does not provide a definition of 'illegal enrichment', which, as discussed next, allows for multiple interpretations.

Aside from the issue of the application of arts. 2(1) and 3 of the Corruption Eradication Law, the Supreme Court has also demanded, in several circular letters, that judges inflict 'proportional punishment' for large corruption cases as a deterrent,[38] to respond to public criticism of the many lenient punishments imposed by courts. In Circular Letter No. 12 of 2010, for example, the Supreme Court requested judges to take extra effort to ensure that the criminal process can bring about deterrence, including by not imposing marginal sentences.

After the 2012 Supreme Court guidelines: Almost one hundred per cent compliance with minimum penalties but light punishment

Of 205 cases decided in the Jakarta and Bandung ACC between 2012 and 2015, almost all defendants were sentenced at or above the mandatory minimums. In nine cases where prosecutors recommended fines between Rp. 50 and 100 million when charging under art. 2(1), which is below the Rp. 200 million minimum fine,[39] the judges adjusted them. The only case where judges sentenced below the mandatory minimum was the *Hendra Saputra* case.[40]

The justification for judges not applying minimum sentence in this case was 'to do justice', given the background of the offender, as well as his motive and role in the offence. Saputra, a primary school dropout, worked as an office boy at a company owned by Riefan Avrian, a son of a former government minister. In 2012, Avrian borrowed Saputra's name to set up a phony company, PT Imaji Media, and made him the CEO to bid for a Rp. 24.5 billion project in his father's office. The company won the project, which was then subcontracted to Avrian's own company. Saputra agreed to all of the actions, to secure his job, and received a Rp. 19 million (US$ 1,266) 'bonus' after the project was completed. However, there was a problem with the execution of the project, and the state suffered an almost Rp. 5 billion loss

Table 10.2 Average sentence for corruption cases (arts. 2(1) and 3) by range of state loss caused (2014–15)

Range of state loss (Rp)	*Av. charge (month)*	*Av. sentence (month)*	*Av. illicit gain (Rp)*	*Av. state loss (Rp)*	*Total cases*
1–25 million	18	12	12,215,155	12,215,155	2
> 25–100 million	24.92	19.69	50,848,346	60,609,994	13
> 100 million-1 billion	29.60	20.83	167,750,275	378,010,592	109
> 1–10 billion	45.63	32.66	590,232,198	2,702,466,190	59
Above 10 billion	92.18	58.5	5,111,796,512	104,129,746,929	22
Average	40.76	28.12*	810,992,496	12,333,258,793	205

Notes: * Approximately two years and four months of imprisonment.
As mentioned, the sample used in this study is actually court decisions between 2012 and 2015 (excluding 2013). However, there are only four decisions for the year 2012 published on the court's website.

(US$ 333,333), which led to criminal charges. The prosecutors charged Saputra with art. 3 and recommended two years and six months imprisonment and a Rp. 50 million fine. The majority of judges in the panel, however, found him guilty of violating art. 2(1), the primary charge, but sentenced him to just one year in prison and Rp. 50 million fine, below the mandatory minimum. They reasoned that he was merely used and manipulated by Avrian, the main perpetrator (who was tried separately).[41] The judges also took the limited intellectual capacity of the defendant into account to mitigate the sentence.[42] One judge dissented and found Saputra not guilty, using similar reasoning.[43] It is not clear, however, why the judges did not simply apply Circular Letter No. 7 of 2012 to come to the same judgment without having to violate the law.

While judges generally observed the minimum penalties in the Corruption Eradication Law, the average prison sentence imposed is relatively light: two years and four months (Table 10.2). This is very close to the average sentences across Indonesia according to other studies, about two years and eight months (in 2014), or two years and two months (in 2016) (Indonesian Corruption Watch 2014, Indonesian Corruption Watch 2016). The lowest sentence was one year of imprisonment (85 cases), while the highest was nine years (three cases).

Moreover, 58 per cent of defendants received only between 12 and 18 months or less,[44] while 25 per cent received a significantly longer imprisonment, between 48 and 108 months. This means that the relative severe average sentence for corruptors was influenced by the quarter of 'outlier' cases. Furthermore, except for very big corruption cases (above Rp. 10 billion of loss), the average sentence imposed by judges was close to the average charge (sentence recommendation) proposed by prosecutor, as shown in Table 10.2.

The level of punishment severity (and also charges) changes if ranked by the range of the amount of illicit profits received by the offenders, instead of state loss, as in Table 10.2 (see Table 10.3). The average sentence for the defendants receiving higher illicit profits appeared more severe, particularly for the large-scale cases (above Rp. 1 billion),[45] although, of course, the average lenient sentence is the same.

Beside the lenient prison terms, the average fine was also light, approximately Rp. 101.5 million (US$ 6,766): just above one-tenth of the maximum fines. Most defendants (143 persons or 70 per cent) received the minimum fine in the law, Rp. 50 million, while only 15 defendants received between Rp. 250 million and Rp. 1 billion. The highest fine was imposed on a middle-ranking local government official who caused state loss below Rp. 6 billion.[46]

At face value, corruptors were punished more severely than thieves and embezzlers, especially if the amount of illicit gain received by the offenders is used as a reference of the comparison, as shown in Table 10.4.

Table 10.3 Average sentence for corruption cases (arts. 2(1) and 3) by range of illicit gain obtained by the offender

Range of illicit gain (Rp)	*Av. charge (month)*	*Av. sentence (month)*	*Av. illicit gain (Rp)*	*Av. state losses (Rp)*	*Total cases*
0	42,16	25.73	0	12,821,403,342	60
1–25 million	32.14	23.57	15,411,986	43,162,261,983	14
> 25–100 million	30.21	20.49	62,852,161	914,275,390	41
> 100 million-1 billion	37.37	27.29	318,413,655	9,758,935,977	73
> 1–10 billion	73.29	56.79	2,357,309,049	14,721,891,298	14
Above 10 billion	128	88	70,636,029,522	35,738,077,031	3
Average	**40.76**	**28.12**	**810,992,496**	**12,333,258,793**	**205**

Table 10.4 Average sentence for theft and embezzlement (Arts. 362, 373 and 374 of the Criminal Code)

Range of victim loss (Rp.)	*Av. charge (month)*	*Av. sentence (month)*	*Av. value of stolen goods/ victim loss (Rp.)*	*Total cases*
1–25 million	12.86	9.87	7,701,706	147
25–100 million	19.54	15.79	57,877,919	48
100 million – 1 billion	21.79	17.84	227,714,948	75
1–10 billion	27.4	20.7	2,859,717,247	10
Above 1 billion	N/A	N/A	N/A	0
Average	**16.92**	**13.41**	**184,980,406**	**280**

Table 10.5 Comparison between numbers of defendants sentenced under art. 2(1) and 3 and punishment severity

Article	*Total cases*	*Sentences*		
		Average (month)	*Below 4 years (total case)*	*4 years-above (total case)*
2 (1)	40	62	1	39
3	165	20	152	13

However, the use of illicit gain as a reference to compare corruption cases with theft and embezzlement is misleading. Unlike in corruption cases, the amount of 'illegal gain' received by thieves and embezzlers is also the 'total loss' of the victim (the actual harm of the offences).[47] If both groups of offence are compared according to the level of the harm (the loss they caused to the victim or state), the disparity of punishment severity between them is much narrower, especially for offences involving smaller loss (below Rp. 1 billion).

Further, if the differences between the minimum and maximum penalties for those offences – as an expression of seriousness of an offence – are included in the equation, corruptors were arguably punished far lighter than thieves and embezzlers. The prison terms for theft and aggravated embezzlement are much lower: a maximum of only five years' imprisonment (with the exception of embezzlement, which is only four years) and no minimum. There is also the possibility of the imposition of a suspended sentence. The minimum and maximum imprisonment sentences for corruption under arts. 2(1) and 3 are from one to twenty years for the former, and four to twenty years for the latter. In contrast, the prison terms for theft and aggravated embezzlement are much lower: a maximum of only five years' imprisonment (with the exception of embezzlement, which is only four years) and no minimum. There is also the possibility of the imposition of a suspended sentence.

Escaping the severe minimum sentence: Deliberately misinterpreting the Corruption Eradication Law and the Circular Letter

The reason for the lenient sentences for corruption is that in most the cases judges deliberately chose to convict defendants under art. 3, which carries only a one-year minimum imprisonment. Of 205 defendants, 165 of them (80 per cent) were sentenced under that provision, as presented in Table 10.5.

Of the 152 cases in which the defendants were sentenced to less than four years' imprisonment, most (139 cases or 91.4 per cent) involved more than Rp. 100 million of state loss.

This practice is related to the type of charges used and recommended by the prosecutors. In the majority of cases, the prosecutor indicted the defendants with a subsidiary charge, with art. 2(1) as the primary and art. 3 as the secondary. At the end of the proceedings, however, the prosecutor recommended that judges sentence under art. 3 (77 per cent of cases). In most cases, judges accepted the prosecutor's recommendations, although, as shown below, many of the cases actually satisfied the elements of the primary charge, art. 2(1).

To justify the primary charges as not proven, there are several strategies commonly used by judges (and also by the prosecutors). They include: deliberately misinterpreting the elements of crimes in art. 2(1) of the Corruption Eradication Law (particularly the element of 'any person' and 'enriching'), as well as the Rp. 100 million threshold in the Circular Letter No. 7 of 2012; and reading the subsidiary charge as an alternative charge.

Enriching v. profiting

As mentioned, art. 2(1) uses the term 'enriching' (*memperkaya*) while art. 3 uses 'profiting' (*menguntungkan*). To avoid applying art. 2(1), in the majority of cases judges interpreted 'enrichment' as 'an act to make someone become rich or richer'. They then claimed this element of crime was not established because the wealth of the defendant or another pre- and post-offence, was never proven to establish it had increased, despite the fact that he or she or the other party gained profits from the offence.[48] Meanwhile these judges used a lower threshold to establish the element of 'profiting', that is, whether the defendant or others received some profit from the offence. Some judges claimed, referring to Circular Letter No. 7 of 2012, that the element of enrichment was not established in cases where the defendants only received less than Rp. 100 million, or, when parts or all of the unlawful gains were recovered.[49] This is because they see the Rp. 100 million threshold in the letter as referring to the profit won from the offence, not the state loss. This can also work the other way around. In one case, the judges claimed that 'because the [stolen] money is still kept safe in the desk in the defendants' office and has not been used…we cannot conclude that he became rich because of the offence'.[50]

On the other hand, other judges interpreted 'enrichment' in a broader manner, and were more relaxed in imposing art. 2(1). Some defined it as 'a change or increase of one's wealth, measured by the gains received'[51] or simply as 'increase of wealth, either money or valuable assets'.[52] A few, referring to *yurisprudensi* and other Supreme Court decisions, defined it as a condition where 'a defendant or other party or a corporation received some money or asset illegally'.[53]

'Any person': General and specific

Another, equally common, strategy to escape convicting defendants under art. 2(1) is to interpret the element of 'any person' in this clause as general in nature, while seeing art. 3 as more specific, applying to those with position and authority, either in public office or a private entity, despite the clear directive on this matter in the Circular Letter No. 7 of 2012. Worse, in one case, judges indicated that art. 3 was intended to apply only to public officials, but still convicted a private individual under this provision, because he committed the offence together with public officials.[54] By contrast, judges who applied art. 2(1) interpreted the phrase generically, with or without referring to the Circular Letter No. 7 of 2012 and other Supreme Court decisions.[55]

Some judges also maintained that 'any person' in art. 2(1) should be read in conjunction with the term, 'illegally', which is also general in nature, compared with a more specific phrase in art. 3 – '...misuse his or her authority, opportunities, or means at his or her disposal which arise because of the office he or she holds...'. Thus, they claimed it is 'more correct' to apply art. 3 to those who commit the offences by abusing power or authority.[56]

Reading a subsidiary charge as an alternative charge

As discussed, if prosecutors use a subsidiary charge, judges should decide first whether or not the primary charge is proven before examining the second charge. However, there are cases where the judges read the subsidiary charge as an alternative charge. For example, in a case where the defendant obtained almost Rp. 645 million, or US$ 43,000 (and did not return it), the judges immediately convicted him under the second charge, art. 3, without giving substantial reasons for this.[57] Some judges also employed a similar approach but justified their decisions by referring to similar practices of the Supreme Court.[58]

Interpreting the Rp. 100 million threshold as illicit gain obtained

The majority of the decisions did not cite Circular Letter No. 7 of 2012, which should guide them in applying arts. 2(1) and 3 of the Corruption Eradication Law. In cases where judges did refer to that guideline, most, as mentioned earlier, referred to the Rp. 100 threshold not as the state loss but as gain the defendant personally received. Even when the illegal gains acquired were above Rp. 100 million, but the defendant had returned it entirely (or an amount equal to or below Rp. 100 million), judges claimed that art. 2(1) should not be applied.[59] However, there are some exceptions.

In one case, the judges explicitly interpreted the Rp. 100 million threshold as being the total state loss. They found the defendant, who gained, and caused loss of, precisely Rp. 100 million, guilty of violating art. 2(1) and sentenced him to four years.[60] In a few other cases, judges interpreted threshold as the total profit received by all defendants in an offence, not what an individual defendant gained.[61] A panel of judges in the Bandung ACC, for instance, convicted a woman who only received Rp. 20 million (US$ 1,333) illegal profit (and had already returned it all) under art. 2(1), reasoning that the offence had also enriched other defendants to a total value that exceeded the Rp. 100 million threshold.[62]

Self-contradicting interpretations

Most judges interpreted arts. 2(1) and 3 inconsistently, depending on what clause they wished to use. In some cases, this was also true of the Circular

Letter No. 7 of 2012. For example, when a panel of judges in the Bandung ACC sentenced a man under art. 2(1), they concluded that the term 'any person' in this provision is identical to the phrase 'whoever' (*barang siapa*) in the Criminal Code, which refers to any individual who can bear criminal responsibility.[63] In fact, those same judges also used a similar interpretation when enforcing art. 3 and further clarified (by reference to several Supreme Court decisions and not Circular Letter No. 7 of 2012), that 'the meaning of [the term] "any person" in corruption offences does not refer only to public servants, but also private individuals, businesspersons and corporations'.[64] However, in other cases, where they wished to apply art. 3, they argued that 'any person' in art. 2(1) is aimed at those who do not have authority, opportunity, or means to commit corruption.[65] As mentioned, similar inconsistent interpretation also arises in the interpretation of 'enrichment'.[66] Also, all judges who argued that subsidiary charges can be read as alternative charges did not apply this interpretation in most of their other decisions.

Worse, some judges even used different interpretations to support the same conclusion, some of which were inherently contradictory, as shown in Table 10.6.

In conclusion, the only consistent pattern in the cases described above is that judges tried to sentence according to the prosecutors' charges, including their sentence recommendations. However, this does not explain why it is necessary for them to engage in such acrobatic interpretations.

Understanding the practices

As shown in above, judges deliberately avoid imposing the relatively severe minimum penalties in art. 2(1) of the Corruption Eradication Law by misinterpreting the elements of crimes in this provision and Circular Letter No. 7 of 2012, as well as the procedural law (in the case of treating a subsidiary charge as an alternative charge) to impose more lenient minimum penalties under art. 3. Some of these strategies are similar to the strategies used by the US judges presented earlier. Also, although these approaches are less confrontational compared to what other judges did in sentencing people smugglers and drug users, the essence is the same: avoiding the severe mandatory minimum penalties. As discussed below, part of the motive of the ACC judges in finding ways to impose less severe minimum penalties was also similar, that is, to avoid what they see as injustice. However, in many cases, they were driven by other factors: paradigmatic issues; the weaknesses of the charges; and, possibly, judicial corruption.

Doing justice to petty corruptors

As mentioned, one of the reasons judges avoided imposing art. 2(1) was to prevent injustice, mainly when the harm caused by the offence or the culpability of the defendant was relatively minimal. Of 152 cases where the judges employed art. 3 and imposed imprisonment under four years, seven cases

Table 10.6 Conflicting interpretations by the same panel of judges of Bandung ACC

State loss (Rp-thousand)	*Illicit gain acquired (thousand)*	*Charge*		*Sentence*		*Interpretation*
		Art	*Prison (month)*	*Art*	*Prison (month)*	
Inconsistent interpretation of 'any persons' and 'illegally'						
4,647,751	None	2(1)	90	3	48	• The element of 'any person' in art 2(1) was established because the defendant can bear criminal responsibility for his/her offence (Decision No. 2 of 15; 208). The defendant was a public servant. • The element of 'illegally' in art 2(1) was not met because the defendant committed the offence by reason of his power and position (Decision No. 2 of 15; 211–12).
1,568,551	Unclear	3	42	3	36	• The 'element of 'illegally' in art 2(1) was proven because the defendant failed to observe his duty (which relates to his power and position) (Decision No. 96 of 15; 167–70). The judges, however, argued that the element of 'enriching' was not met, and so applied art 3 [171–2].
2,444,033.5	90,000 (fully returned)	3	24	3	16	The judge used a similar argument to Decision No. 2 of 15 (see above) for a private individual defendant (Decision No. 69 of 14; 162–3). Note: the illicit gains were less than Rp. 100 million and the defendant had already returned them in full.
Inconsistent interpretation of 'enrichment'						
1,568,551	Unclear	3	42	3	36	The element of 'enriching' was not met because the amount of money that the defendant received was small, and it was thus more appropriate to define it as 'profiting' under art 3 (Decision No. 96 of 15; 171–2).

750,000	641,330 (fully returned)	3	18	3	12	The element of 'enriching' was not established because all the state loss has been voluntarily repaid by the defendants (Decision No. 95 of 15; 160).
390,786.6 (fully recovered)	122,339. 8	3	24	3	16	The element of enrichment was not proven because the stolen money was still safe in the desk in the defendants' office and had not been used (Decision No. 58 of 15; 83). Note: unlike Decision No. 95 of 15, the judges did not use the argument that the state loss had been fully recovered in this case to argue that the element of enrichment was not proven.
131,780	131,780	3	48	3	36	The element of 'enriching' was not met because, 'although the defendant admitted that he spent all the money that he received from the offence, the court did not find any evidence of an increase of the defendant's wealth' (Decision No. 80 of 15; 184)
300,000	300,000	2(1)	54	2(1)	48	The element of 'enriching' was met because the defendant received money from the offence (although his pre- and post-wealth was never verified) (Decision No. 121 of 14; 49).

concerned small corruption (ranging from Rp. 4.4 million to Rp. 49 million of state loss), or 13 cases, if Rp. 100 million is used as the threshold. The numbers increase to approximately 63 cases if more significant state losses are included, where the amount of illicit gain received by the defendants were still relatively small (below Rp. 50 million). This may indicate that the role of the defendants was relatively minimal, or that the real motive of the corrupt acts involved was not greed.

For judges, it is safer to sentence using art. 3 in such cases, even if that means they have to 'misinterpret' the law, than to impose penalties below the minimum penalty in art. 2(1). Several judges interviewed admitted that they are afraid of being reported, reviewed or even sanctioned by the Supreme Court or the Judicial Commission if they sentence below the mandatory sentences. Another judge also said that they could be suspected of taking bribes by doing so. In short, by applying art. 3 in small corruption cases, they can balance the interests of justice and protect their career at the same time.

However, the justice-seeking argument can only explain the legal manoeuvrers and lenient punishments in small-scale corruption cases. The majority of cases were not in this category. As shown earlier, seventy-three defendants who received between Rp. 100 million and Rp. 1 billion of the money stolen were sentenced, on average, to only approximately two years and three months (or just below just twenty months, if only those who were sentenced under art. 3 are counted). There were also a few small corruption cases where judges also imposed relatively stiff sentences.[67] Further explanation is needed.

Paradigm issues: Returning state loss and light punishment are enough

There is a tendency for judges to only impose lenient sentences when the state losses were already recovered, wholly or partially, either voluntarily by the defendants or due to confiscation by law enforcers. As an illustration, 45 defendants who received illegal gains between Rp. 50 million and Rp. 5.5 billion (with an average of Rp. 326 million, or US$ 21,733) and had returned them entirely were only sentenced to, on average, approximately 14.6 months.[68] More than half of them (26 defendants) who also repaid all state losses (with an average loss of Rp. 1.34 billion, or US$ 89,333) received a few days' additional imprisonment reduction.[69]

These practices strongly relate to the judges' conception of corruption offences and the role of asset recovery in sentencing. All judges and the prosecutors interviewed argued that recovery of state loss is the most important factor to be considered in sentencing corruption offences, like any other economic crime. Some referred to Posner's economic approach to law thesis. As a consequence, the amount of losses recovered, whether repaid voluntarily or confiscated, becomes one of the decisive mitigating factors. In fact, as mentioned above, by merely returning all the illegal profit – not the state losses – defendants could win a generous sentencing reduction. Two judges even claimed that as long as the loss is fully recovered, it is not important to seek a prison sentence. One of them reasoned that a voluntary payback is a sign of remorse and further said to me:

> it is not fair, actually, to imprison [the defendant]. If the law permits [judges] not to impose the criminal penalty on those who already return the illicit gain, I will not do so, or at least will sentence the defendant lightly or to the same duration as his or her pre-trial detention

Another judge admitted that she used to give a huge sentencing discount to defendants who returned all the state losses but now limits the discount because she is afraid the practice will not create enough deterrence.

These paradigms and approaches are problematic because, as correctly pointed out by one of the judges, if the maximum risk in performing an act of corruption is just the return of the illicit gain or a light punishment, people will commit the offence because of the huge potential benefit. Besides, the probability of detection or prosecution for committing corruption in Indonesia is still low. The reference to Posner's thesis on 'economic approach to law' is also false, or at least, misleading. What Posner advocates is not asset recovery as the goal of sentencing but the use monetary penalties, fines or (civil) treble-damages (if adequate or appropriate) as opposed to imprisonment in sentencing white-collar crimes.[70] This is not what happened in these cases. As previously shown, the levels of fines inflicted by judges were also lenient, usually around Rp. 50 million (US$ 3,333). Although judges also ordered the defendants to pay restitution (*uang pengganti*), this is not a monetary penalty like Posner's 'treble-damages' because it only requires repayment of the illicit profits obtained from the offence.[71] Aside from this argument, the philosophical basis of Posner's thesis is not without its own problems.[72]

More troubling, there are indications that some judges did not consider whether the recovery of losses were the result of voluntary payment by the defendant or due to confiscation in giving the sentencing discount. There were some cases in which they imposed a light punishment (between twelve and sixteen months) in cases where state losses (ranging from Rp. 250 million to Rp. 10 billion, or from US$ 16,666 to 666,666) were recovered, chiefly or entirely, due to confiscation by the investigators.[73] In fact, in justifying a one-year imprisonment sentence for an offender who caused an almost Rp. 10 billion state loss (which was recovered), the judges explicitly stated that the reason they mitigated the sentence was that the loss had already been recovered by law enforcers through confiscation.[74]

My interviews with judges also shows that the practice of imposing light punishment on corruptors is also related to how they view the seriousness of corruption offences, as well as what they see as just punishment for corruptors, considering their social status. One judge, for example, confessed that he treated theft cases differently to corruption because the first offence harms individual victims while the latter (only?) harms the state. Many also justified their light sentences with what Bentham called the 'individual sensitivity of punishment' argument: that the corruptor, who usually comes from middle or higher social status, will suffer more than, for instance, thieves, if both were to receive the same level of imprisonments, which is thus unfair.[75] One judge made the argument that one year in prison for a corruptor who used to have a pleasant life might be harsher than five years' imprisonment for an ordinary thief. Some also reasoned that those who are convicted of corruption suffered shame and fines, as well as orders to return the profit of the offences, in addition to the imposition of imprisonment, in contrast to blue-collar convicts. Another judge sees corruption offenders as being of more benefit to the public outside a prison cell, perhaps because many of them are public officials or business persons. The last two justifications resonate with the issue of 'status shield' in the white-collar crimes sentencing literature, that is, how the high status of offenders protects them from severe sanctions (Van Slyke and Bales 2012: 217, 220–1).

These paradigms, perhaps, also explain the disparity of sentences between theft and embezzlement cases and corruption cases discussed earlier. All the ACC judges, aside from the ad hoc judges, also served as judges in the Central and South Jakarta or Bandung District Courts.

Lack of robustness of the case

Another issue that drove judges impose lenient sentences, or even in some cases, acquittals, is the lack of robustness of the cases. In a number of cases, police and prosecutors seemed to fail to establish the culpability of the offenders, including whether or not they received illicit gains. For example, sixty co-defendants in the cases studied were said to have not received any profit from the offences. This seems odd, because some of them were high-level officials,[76] so that they were unlikely to be involved in committing offences (or being used or forced to commit them) without any benefit. In some cases where the offences were done in concert between the public officials and private individuals, prosecutors claimed that only the private individuals received the illegal profit of the offence,[77] which is also unlikely.

Similar issues occur in proving the degree of a defendant's culpability. In a number of cases where the defendants (government officials) had fully paid private contractors for works that had then not been completed, they were only proved to be negligent, for instance, failing to monitor the projects or recheck them before making payment, and so received only a year of imprisonment.[78] Nevertheless, judges sentenced equally lightly for those whose wrong-doing was obvious.[79] Judges also complained to me that many of the defendants brought to trial were not the 'mastermind' behind the offences.

In contrast, in at least from six cases assessed that were investigated that involved charges brought by the Corruption Eradication Commission (Komisi Pemberantasan Korupsi or 'KPK'), the agency could demonstrate the detailed role of each defendant and the illicit profit they received. This

Table 10.7 Sentences of the Jakarta ACC in cases brought by the KPK

Charge		*State loss (Rp)*	*Illicit gain (Rp)*	*Sentence*	
Article	*Prison (month)*			*Article*	*Prison (month)*
2(1)	144	121,830,768,863	17,136,912,198	2(1)	96
2(1)	144	80,002,814,755	1,030,000,000	3	108
2(1)	60	36,484,670,450	770,291,375	3	48
2(1)	48	80,002,814,755	550,000,000	3	48
3	108	463,668,000,000	300,000,000	3	72
3	60	13,071,468,264	20,000,000	3	30
Average	**94**	**132,510,089,514**	**3,301,200,595**		**67**

Note: See Jakarta ACC Decisions: No. 48/Pid.Sus/TPK/2013/PN.Jkt.Pst; No. 59/Pid.Sus/TPK/2012/PN.Jkt.Pst; No. 36/Pid.Sus/TPK/2013/PN.Jkt.Pst; No. 62/Pid.Sus/TPK/2014/PN.Jkt.Pst; and No. 65/ Pid.Sus/TPK/2014/PN.Jkt.Pst.

gave confidence to, or even 'compelled', judges to inflict tougher punishments, even when they sentenced the defendants under art. 3, as shown in Table 10.7. The severe punishments were imposed not only because these cases involved big loses. A senior judge, comparing the conventional law enforcement agencies to the KPK, said to me:

> When the KPK is the prosecutor [and investigator of the case], the evidence [in the case] is very strong…everything, even the amount [each defendant received]. Who did what, the money went where …the culpability [of the defendant] is crystal clear.

Improper influence: The usual suspect

Another plausible factor that motivated judges to manoeuvre the law and inflict lenient minimum punishments is to do with improper influence. As argued elsewhere, two among many of the modus operandi of judicial corruption in Indonesia are to 'buy and sell' lower punishment and favourable charges (for the same goal).[80] Furthermore, the Jakarta ACC, and, in particular, the Bandung ACC, are notorious for these practices (Asmara 2011). In fact, a few years back, two of the Bandung first instance ACC judges and one Bandung high court judge assigned to hear corruption cases were convicted of receiving bribes from defendants (CNN 2016).

Conclusion

This chapter has shown that, overall, judges in the Jakarta and Bandung ACCs observed the minimum penalties in art. 2(1) and art. 3 of the Corruption Eradication Law. Only in one case did the judges ignore the four-year minimum sentence under art. 2(1), because the culpability of the defendant was minimal. However, judges intentionally circumvent the mandatory minimum in the Corruption Eradication Law, by convicting most defendants under art. 3 (which carries a minimum prison sentence of only a year). This was done by deliberately misinterpreting some elements of crimes in arts. 2(1) and 3. Judges also ignored provisions of the Criminal Procedure Code and Supreme Court guidelines for the same purpose. As a result, the overall sentence was low – around just two years and four months.

Part of the judges' intention in seeking lesser minimum penalties was to avoid injustice in cases involving minimal harm (such as when the state losses were small), or where the offenders' culpability was nominal (for instance, their roles in the offences were marginal, or they only received small profits). However, such cases comprise only a small percentage of cases. There is substantial evidence that in the majority of cases, the middle and large-scale corruption offences, the legal manoeuvres were driven by other factors: paradigmatic issues; the lack of robustness of the cases; and, possibly, judicial corruption. Concerning the issue of paradigm, most judges seem to believe that the recovery of state loss is the critical factor in sentencing, and, in a number of cases, regardless of the gravity of the offences, the culpability of the offenders, or whether the recovery was due to voluntary repayment from the defendants or because of forfeiture by the law enforcers. Judges also showed class-bias in sentencing, arguing that lenient punishment for a corruptor with high social status is equal to a more severe punishment for a thief from a lower social status.

The statutory minimum penalty is a double-edge sword. On one hand, it can certainly cause grave injustice. However, at the same time, it serves some legitimate purposes – not deterring crimes, as claimed (because there is no strong correlation between the severe threat of punishment and fewer crimes, except for several types of offences), but ensuring proportionality in punishment between the harm of the offence and the culpability of the offenders. Many of the critics of statutory minimum penalties in other jurisdictions are concerned with the injustice they cause when the mandatory minimum is too severe or is required in less serious offences, particularly offences that are usually committed by socially disadvantage offenders. This problem usually arises when the introduction of the statutory minimum penalties are driven simply by the crime prevention objective or are motivated by non-legal considerations.

In the case of Indonesia, the source of the injustice is generally not the severity of the minimum penalties, but rather weaknesses in the drafting of the statutes, which are then exploited by law enforcers and, to some extent, judges. The Narcotics Law, for instance, does not define offences in a precise manner. Likewise, the drafter of the Immigration Law did not anticipate that many of those involved in people smuggling would be merely small players, and so did not differentiate penalty levels between offenders with different level of culpability. More importantly, the lawmakers did not anticipate (or perhaps ignored) potential abuses in the application of the laws, that is applying minimum penalties for illegitimate purposes. At the same time, without mandatory minimum penalties for serious offences, particularly white-collar crimes (like corruption), where the perpetrators usually have political influence and financial power to 'buy justice', law enforcers and judges can effortlessly impose overly-lenient punishments. In addition, overly-wide discretion also can lead to serious unwarranted sentencing disparity, as this chapter shows, and this is also a form of injustice.

What is the solution? The current draft Criminal Code Bill now before the Indonesian national legislature seeks to limit the use of minimum penalties to serious offences. This is positive. In the provisions concerning corruption offences, however, the Bill lowers the minimum penalties for the offence now stipulated in art. 2(1) of the Corruption Eradication Law, from four to two years, although it increases the minimum penalties in art. 3 to two years (Detiknews 2018; Hukumonline 2018). Worse, it does not change the problematic element of crimes in those provisions. Moreover, the Bill provides a much wider sentencing discretion than the current Criminal Code, and also introduces new class-biased mitigating consideration clauses on sentencing (Assegaf 2018: 1).

If there are no modifications to the final draft of the Bill, we can envisage that average penalties for middle and large-scale corruption offences might become even lower than they are now. What is needed are mandatory minimum penalties for serious offences with clearer definition of the element of crimes. Such laws should also provide limited and well-defined exemptions that allow judges to depart from the mandatory minimum in certain cases particularly when dealing with minor offences. This will prevent potential abuse by law enforcers and judges and simultaneously give room for them to impose proportional punishments.

Notes

1 PhD candidate, Melbourne Law School. This article is based on part of the author's PhD research. I thank Professor Tim Lindsey, my supervisor, for his valuable input and comments, particularly in relation to earlier drafts of this article.

2 In this chapter, the terms 'mandatory minimum sentence', 'mandatory minimum penalty', 'statutory minimum penalty', 'minimum penalty', and 'minimum sentence' are used interchangeably, since all share the same meaning.

3 See, for example, Tonry 2009: 65, 67–8; Vincent Schiraldi, 'Digging Out: As US States Begin to Reduce Prison Use, Can America Turn the Corner on its Imprisonment Binge?' (2004); and 'United States Sentencing Commission, Special Report to the Congress: Mandatory Minimum Penalties in the Federal Criminal Justice System' (1991), cited in Greenblatt 2008: 1, 4. In general, there is no strong evidence that the severity of punishment or, in particular, threat of punishment, deters crime. This is because there are many variables that might influence the increase or decrease in crime rates. There is evidence that severe punishment does seem to deter some types of offences, such as traffic violation and drink driving. There are much stronger

links between the likelihood of being punished (certainty of criminal enforcement) and deterrence. See Antunes and Hunt 1974: 486; Durlauf and Nagin 2011: 13–54; Grogger 1991: 297, 308; Klepper and Nagin 1989: 721.

4 For example, minimum five years' imprisonment for selling ten grams of crack cocaine or twenty-five years or a mandatory life sentence for a person guilty of committing a severe violent felony who has two previous convictions (the 'three-strike law') (Turner et al. 1995: 16).

5 The terms 'special criminal statute' (*undang-undang tindak pidana khusus*) refers to a Law that criminalise particular actions not been dealt with, or not sufficiently dealt with, in the general criminal provisions in the Criminal Code, which applies to all persons and in all times and places (not just to particular reasons or classes of persons, or in a particular place and time). This type of statute may provide specific provisions that differ from the general principles stipulated in the Criminal Code and the Criminal Procedural Code. Examples of these statutes include Law No. 31 of 1999 on Corruption Eradication and Law No. 35 of 2009 on Narcotics.

6 Law No. 31 of 1999, as amended by Law No. 20 of 2001.

7 Article 362 is concerned with (simple) theft offences, art. 372 with embezzlement and art. 374 with aggravated embezzlement conducted by people with a work relationship with the property owner. The reason for choosing these offences is that they share similar types of harms (but not seriousness), loss of property and breach of trust, with corruption cases. Of the 280 cases studied, the majority (99 cases) were concerned with aggravated embezzlement (art. 374), followed by theft (95 cases) and embezzlement (86 cases).

8 The majority of Jakarta and Bandung ACC judges, except ad hoc judges (who are specially appointed from other branches of the legal profession to hear corruption cases), also heard the theft and embezzlement cases from Central Jakarta and Bandung District Courts.

9 The currency equivalents used in this chapter are based on the late 2018 exchange rate of US$ 1.00 = Rp. 15,000.

10 Law No. 5 of 1997 on Psychotropic Substances.

11 Although not all new statutes prescribe minimum penalties, they still generally impose severe penalties. Of 154 special statutes, almost all (91.34%) incorporated imprisonment as a type of punishment. Further, unlike the Criminal Code, most special statutes impose severe penalties, including accumulation of sanctions for a single offence (usually imprisonment *and* fines) or give the option to judges to impose more than one type of principal punishment. See Akbari 2015: 10–12 and 20–2; Wahyudi 2004: 88.

12 See also, for example: Elucidation (explanatory memorandum) to Law No. 18 of 2013 on the Prevention and Eradication of Forest Destruction; Elucidation to Law No. 23 of 2004 on the Elimination of Domestic Violence; and Elucidation to Law No. 9 of 2013 on the Prevention and Eradication of Terrorist Financing.

13 See, for example, government responses to the constitutional review of minimum penalties provisions in the Corruption Eradication Law in Constitutional Court Decision No. 39/PUU-X/2012 [17–18]. See also Hukumonline 2011.

14 For example, the allegations of political motives behind the introduction of severe minimum penalties and chemical castration for offenders committing sexual abuse of children. See Institute for Criminal Justice Reform 2016.

15 See, for example, government responses to the constitutional review of the minimum penalties in the Corruption Eradication Law in Constitutional Court Decision No. 39/PUU-X/2012 [17–18].

16 See further assessment on these issues in Arief 2007.

17 A number of countries, and some states in the US, recognise what is often referred to as the 'three strikes, you're out' legislation. These laws allow severe mandatory minimum penalties, sometimes fixed penalties, for offenders who commit offences for the third time. In some cases, the first (or some of the earlier offences) must be considered serious, for example, must be a felony. The range of minimum penalties for these re-offenders varies, between five to twenty years. Some even prescribe a lifetime sentence without parole. See Turner et al. 1995: 16.

18 See, for instance, arts. 103 and 127 of Law No. 35 of 2009 on Narcotics.

19 For further discussion of this, see Assegaf 2019.

20 Constitutional Court Decision No. 39/PUU-X/2012; 33–4.

21 Article 82(1) and (2) of Law No. 18 of 2013 on Prevention and Eradication of Forest Destruction. See similar provisions in arts. 83(3), 84(3), 87(3). The Fisheries Law also introduces a lower maximum penalty for offences committed by traditional and small-scale fishers compared to others.

22 Article 79(3) of Law No. 11 of 2012 on the Juvenile Criminal Justice System.

23 Mempawah District Court Decision No. 86/Pid.Sus/2013/PN.Mpw [35–6]. The defendant was charged with using force, threat, false information, or persuasion to commit indecent conduct with an under-age person (art. 82 of Law No. 23 of 2002 on Child Protection). The judges found the defendant only guilty of persuading the victim to commit the act, by, among others, saying that he loved her and promised to marry her.

24 *Yurispudensi Tetap* refers to a series of Supreme Court decisions on a particular legal issue that, in theory, acquire strong 'persuasive' authority. (Supreme Court decisions are usually not seen as binding.) The Court annually publishes collections of this type of case law.

25 Supreme Court Decision No. 06 K/Pid.HAM.AD HOC/2005 in Mahkamah Agung 2008a: 418.

26 Supreme Court Decision No. 06 K/Pid.HAM.AD HOC/2005 in Mahkamah Agung 2008a: 415.

27 Supreme Court Decision No. 2399 K/Pid.Sus/2010 in Mahkamah Agung 2011: 488–9.

28 Supreme Court Circular Letter No. 7 of 2012 [23 and 27].

29 Supreme Court Circular Letter No. 7 of 2012 [23].

30 Supreme Court Circular Letter No. 7 of 2012 [attachment].

31 According to the Criminal Procedure Code, judges must decide a case based on the basis of charges used by the prosecutors in the indictment letter (art. 182(3) and (4) of Law No. 8 of 1981 on the Criminal Procedure Code, *Kitab Undang-undang Hukum Acara Pidana*, KUHAP). The Supreme Court had previously strictly maintained this rule. The only exception is when the charge involves an aggravated offence, such as robbery, but the court finds that the offender has only committed a similar but lesser offence, such as theft or burglary. Supreme Court Decision No. 693/K/Pid/1986.

32 Supreme Court Circular Letter No. 1 of 2017 [6]. Actually, this circular letter does not refer to Child Protection Law nor mention 'sexual offences', but simply 'offences.' However, from the context given in the circular letter, it is safe to assume that it was meant to be applied to offences stipulated in the Child Protection Law.

33 Article 52 of the Criminal Code provides that the sentence for public officials who abuse their power to commit an offence can be increased by up to one-third of the

maximum penalty of the offence. Similar sentence aggravation applies to private individuals (see, for example, arts. 307, 374, 375 and 349 of the Criminal Code).

34 Attorney General Circular Letter No. SE-004/J.A/11/1993.

35 Supreme Court Circular Letter No. 7 of 2012 [21].

36 Supreme Court Circular Letter No. 7 of 2012 [21]. The words in brackets are added by the author. Note also that in Supreme Court Circular Letter No. 3 of 2018, the Court increases the threshold and indicates that the guidance is not compulsory by stating '[If] the state loss is above Rp. 200,000 [US$ 13,333] [the judge] can impose Article 2(1) …'. Further, when justifying the new rules, the Court implicitly states that previous guidance (Circular Letter No. 7 of 2012) is also meant to be optional, which is strange, given the wording used, and given that the whole purpose of the Letter was to help judges to differentiate between the two problematic provisions. In addition, no judge interviewed perceived it as optional.

37 Supreme Court Circular Letter No. 7 of 2012 [21–2].

38 See, for example: Supreme Court Circular Letters: No. 1 of 2000; No. 3 of 2001; and No. 12 of 2010.

39 See, for example, Bandung ACC Decisions: No. 2/Pid.Sus/TPK/2014/PN.Bdg; 64/Pid.Sus/TPK/2014/PN.Bdg; No. 65/Pid.Sus/TPK/2014/PN.Bdg; and No. 84/Pid.Sus/TPK/2015/PN.Bdg.

40 There was another case where the Jakarta ACC sentenced a defendant below the minimum penalty in art. 2(1). However, it seemed that the judges misquoted the Article because they concluded in the judgment that the defendant had violated art. 3. See Jakarta ACC Decision No. 85/Pid.Sus/TPK /2015/PN.Jkt.Pst [96–105].

41 Jakarta ACC Decision No. 36/Pid.Sus/TPK/2014/PN.Jkt.Pst [184–5].

42 Jakarta ACC Decision No. 36/Pid.Sus/TPK/2014/PN.Jkt.Pst [185].

43 Jakarta ACC Decision No. 36/Pid.Sus/TPK/2014/PN.Jkt.Pst [173–83].

44 Of 117 defendants in this category, the majority, eighty-five (73%) caused above Rp. 250 million in state loss. Forty-four of them also obtained between Rp. 100 million and 5.5 billion in illicit profit.

45 This does not necessarily mean that the judges gave more weight to the level of illicit gains than state loss. As shown in Table 10.3, when the judges imposed stiffer sentences on those receiving higher illicit gains in the fifth group (illicit gain range from > Rp. 1 to 10 billion), that is 56.79 months (compared to 32.66 months of average sentences imposed on those that caused the same amount of state loss, as shown in Table 10.2), the average of state losses is also bigger (Rp. 14,721,891,298, in contrast with just Rp. 2,702,466,190). As for the last group (illicit gain above Rp. 10 billion), the severe sentence is an exception because it only involved three defendants, so cannot be used a reference to justify such a conclusion.

46 Bandung ACC Decision No. 31/Pid. Sus/TPK/2014/PN.Bdg.

47 In fact, unlike in corruption cases, the actual profit received by a thief from selling the stolen goods is usually smaller than the value of the goods itself.

48 See, for example, Bandung ACC Decisions: No. 150/Pid.Sus/TPK/2013/PN.Bdg; No. 79/Pid.Sus/TPK/2014/PN.Bdg; No. 24/Pid.Sus/TPK/2015/PN.Bdg; No. 90/Pid.Sus/TPK/2014/PN.Bdg; and No. 127/Pid.Sus/TPK/2013/PN.Bdg.

49 Bandung ACC Decisions: No. 24/Pid.Sus/TPK/2015/PN.Bdg; No. 48/Pid.Sus/TPK/2015/PN.Bdg; No. 77/Pid.Sus/TPK/2014/PN.Bdg; No. 75/Pid.Sus/TPK/2015/PN.Bdg; No. 103/Pid.Sus/TPK/2015/PN.Bdg; and No. 77/Pid.Sus/TPK/2014/PN.Bdg.

50 Bandung ACC Decision No. 58/ Pid.Sus/TPK/2015/PN.Bdg [83].

51 Jakarta ACC Decision No. 78/Pid.Sus/TPK/2014/PN.Jkt.Pst [238].
52 Jakarta ACC Decision No. 79/Pid.Sus/TPK/2014/PN.Jkt.Pst [538].
53 Jakarta ACC Decision No. 58/Pid.Sus/TPK/2013/PN.Jkt.Pst [237]. The decision referred to the Supreme Court Decisions 275 K/Pid/1983; 577 K/Kr/1980; and 951 K/Pid/1982. The judges relied on a similar interpretation in another decision, but without citing any case law (See Jakarta ACC Decision No. 77/Pid.Sus/TPK/2013/PN.Jkt.Pst [237]).
54 Bandung ACC Decision No. 114/Pid.Sus/TPK/2014/PN.Bdg [117].
55 See, for example, Bandung ACC Decisions: No. 17/Pid.Sus/TPK/2015/PN.Bdg [158–9]; 8/Pid.Sus/TPK/2015/PN.Bdg [159–60]; and No. 63/Pid.Sus/TPK/2015/PN.Bdg [106–8].
56 Jakarta ACC Decisions: No. 69/Pid.Sus/TPK/2013/PN.Jkt.Pst; No. 1/ Pid.Sus/TPK/2014/PN.Jkt.Pst; No. 38/Pid.Sus/TPK/2014/PN.Jkt.Pst. Bandung ACC Decisions: No. 16/Pid.Sus/TPK/2015/PN.Bdg; No. 35/Pid.Sus/TPK/2014/PN.Bdg; and No. 48/Pid.Sus/TPK/2014/PN.Bdg.
57 Bandung ACC Decision No. 12/Pid.Sus/TPK/2014/PN.Bdg.
58 Jakarta ACC Decision No. 85/Pid.Sus/TPK/2015/PN.Jkt.Pst [96], referring to Supreme Court Decisions: No. 606 K/Pid/1984 and Decision No. 112 K/Pid/2006.
59 Bandung ACC Decisions: No. 76/Pid.Sus/TPK/2014/PN.Bdg; No. 103/Pid.Sus/TPK/2015/PN.Bdg; and No. 48/Pid.Sus/TPK/2015/PN.Bdg.
60 Bandung ACC Decision No. 78/Pid.Sus/TPK/2015/PN.Bdg [106]. However, in other cases, the same panel interpreted the Rp. 100 million threshold as the profit gained by the offender. See, for example, Bandung ACC Decisions: No. 111/Pid.Sus/TPK/2014/PN.Bdg; No. 77/Pid.Sus/TPK/2014/PN.Bdg; and No. 82/ Pid.Sus/TPK/2014/PN.Bdg.
61 Bandung ACC Decisions: No. 65/Pid.Sus/TPK/2015/PN.Bdg; No. 64/Pid.Sus/TPK/2014/PN.Bdg; No. 84/Pid.Sus/TPK/2015/PN.Bdg; and No. 135/ Pid.Sus/TPK/2015/PN.Bdg.
62 Bandung ACC Decision No. 90/ Pid.Sus/TPK/2015 [230]. For a similar interpretation by the same judges but not referring to the Criminal Code, see 20/Pid.Sus/TPK/2014/PN.Bdg.
63 Bandung ACC Decision No. 74/Pid.Sus/TPK/2014/PN.Bdg [100].
64 Bandung ACC Decision No. 50/Pid.Sus/TPK/2014/PN.Bdg [90]. For a similar interpretation, see Bandung ACC Decision No. 20/Pid.Sus/TPK/2014/PN.Bdg [114], although in the latter case, the judges did not quote the case law.
65 Bandung ACC Decisions: No. 35/Pid.Sus/TPK/2014/PN.Bdg [116–17]; and No. 47/Pid.Sus/TPK/2014/PN.Bdg.
66 See Table 10.6.
67 See Bandung ACC Decisions: No. 78/Pid.Sus/TPK/2014/PN.Bdg; No. 3/Pid.Sus/TPK/2014/PN.Bdg; and No. 133/Pid.Sus/TPK/2014/PN.Bdg.
68 The person who obtained the biggest illicit gain, Rp. 5.5 billion, and returned it entirely, received only 18 months of prison (Jakarta ACC Decision No. 85/Pid.Sus/TPK/2014/PN.Jkt.Pst).
69 The total amount of state loss that was recovered used here is an estimation, because there is the possibility that other offenders already returned the losses in separate trials but these decisions were not published on the website, and so could not be assessed for this study.
70 In his 1980 article on 'Optimal Sentences for White-Collar Criminals', Posner argues for the adequacy of using optimal monetary penalties, particularly fines as

the alternative to imprisonment of offenders with the financial ability to pay them (Posner 1979: 409, 410–16). A fine is considered optimal if it creates a relatively similar deterrent to imprisonment. Similarly, he maintained that where the statute recognised the concept of 'treble-damage' (that the offender can be ordered to pay more than the actual damage or losses, usually tripled), it is sufficient to impose such penalty [417]. See also Landes and Posner 1975: 1.

71 In addition to imprisonment and fines, the courts should also have ordered the defendants to pay restitution (*uang pengganti)* to the value of the amount of illicit profits they received (art. 18(1) b of Law No. 31 of 1999 on Corruption Eradication). In some cases, however, judges wrongly interpret this as repayment of the state loss. Even on this interpretation, however, it is not considered monetary penalty, but merely compensation or 'simple damages'.

72 For a discussion of this issue see: Malloy 1989: 147; Von Hirsch 1992: 55.

73 See, for example, Bandung ACC Decisions: No. 19/Pid.Sus/TPK/2015/PN.Bdg; No. 39/Pid.Sus/TPK/2015/PN.Bdg; No. 50/Pid.Sus/TPK/2014/PN.Bdg; No. 136/Pid.Sus/TPK/2014/PN.Bdg; and No. 26/Pid.Sus/TPK/2014/PN.Bdg.

74 Bandung ACC Decision No. 75/Pid.Sus/TPK/2015/PN.Bdg [365].

75 See Bentham 1823: 51–62, 182. For a revival of Bentham's argument, see Kolber 2009: 1565.

76 Such as the: President of a university (Bandung ACC Decision No. 87/Pid.Sus/TPK/2015/PN.Bdg); the heads of state-owned companies (Bandung ACC Decision No. 76/Pid.Sus/TPK/2015/PN.Bdg; Jakarta ACC Decision No. 15/Pid.Sus/TPK/2015/PN.Jkt.Pst); and the heads of regional offices of central government agencies (Jakarta ACC Decisions: 58/Pid.Sus/TPK/2014/PN.Jkt.Pst and 58/Pid.Sus/TPK/2014/PN.Jkt.Pst)

77 Compare, for example, Bandung ACC Decisions: No. 83/Pid.Sus/TPK/2014/PN.Bdg; No. 4/Pid.Sus/TPK/2015/PN.Bdg; No. 5/Pid.Sus/TPK/2015/PN.Bdg; No. 71/Pid.Sus/TPK/2015/PN.Bdg; No. 77/Pid.Sus/TPK/2015/PN.Bdg; and No. 76/Pid.Sus/TPK/2015/PN.Bdg.

78 Jakarta ACC Decision No. 1/Pid.B/TPK/2012/PN.Jkt.Pst [133]. Bandung ACC Decisions: No. 41/Pid.Sus/TPK/2014/PN.Bdg [205]; and No. 108/Pid.Sus/TPK/2013/PN.Bdg [111].

79 Bandung ACC Decisions: No. 27/Pid.Sus/TPK/2014/PN.Bdg [150]; No. 45/Pid.Sus/TPK/2014/PN.Bdg [117]; and No. 116/ Pid.Sus/TPK/2014/PN.Bdg [118]. Jakarta ACC Decision No. 69/Pid.Sus/TPK/2013/PN.Jkt.Pst [104–8].

80 See, for example, Indonesian Corruption Watch 2002; Satuan Tugas Pemberantasan Mafia Hukum 2010: 13–19; and Asmara 2011.

References

Akbari, Anugerah Rizki 2015. *Potret Kriminalisasi Pasca Reformasi dan Urgensi Reklasifikasi Tindak Pidana di Indonesia*. Jakarta: Institute for Criminal Justice Reform

Antunes, George and Hunt, A. Lee 1974. 'The Impact of Certainty and Severity of Punishment on Levels of Crime in American States: An Extended Analysis', *Journal of Criminal Law and Criminology* 64(4): 486

Arief, Barda Nawawi 2002. *Bunga Rampai Kebijakan Hukum Pidana*. Bandung: Citra Aditya Bakti

Arief, Barda Nawawi 2007. 'Tinjauan terhadap Pengenaan Sanksi Pidana Minimal Khusus'. Unknown presentation.

Arsil 2012a. 'Pengurangan Ancaman Pidana Minimum dalam Pengadilan Anak sebagai Yurisprudensi?', 26 March www.krupukulit.com

Arsil 2012b. 'Ancaman Pidana Minimum Tidak Mengikat Bagi Terdakwa Anak', 20 June www.krupukulit.com

Asmara, Teddy 2011. *Budaya Ekonomi Hukum Hakim*. Jakarta: Fasindo

Assegaf, Rifqi S 2018. 'Sentencing Guidance in the Indonesia's Criminal Code Reform Bill: For Whose Benefit?', *Australian Journal of Asian Law* 19(1): 1

Assegaf, Rifqi S. 2019. 'The Supreme Court: *Reformasi*, Independence and the Failure to Ensure Legal Certainty', in Melissa Crouch (ed.), *The Politics of Court Reform: Judicial Change and Legal Culture in Indonesia*. Cambridge University Press, pp. 31–58

Assegaf, Rifqi S. (2020.). 'Injustice and Inconsistency: Sentencing Minor Property Offences Post Supreme Court Regulation 2 of 2012', in Tim Lindsey and Helen Pausacker (eds.), *Crime and Punishment in Indonesian Law*. New York: Routledge

Bentham, Jeremy 1823. *An Introduction to the Principles of Morals and Legislation*. Oxford: Clarendon Press

Canals, José M. 1960. 'Classicism, Positivism and Social Defense', *Journal of Criminal Law, Criminology, and Policy Science* 50(6): 541

Cappelletti, Mauro 1985. 'Repudiating Montesquieu? The Expansion and Legitimacy of Constitutional Justice', *Catholic University Law Review* 35(1): 1

CNN 2016. 'Deretan Hakim Tersangkut Kasus Suap', 26 May www.cnnindonesia.com

Detiknews 2008. 'BNN: Lapas Overload Bukan Alasan Maraknya Narkoba', 11 March www.detiknews.com

Detiknews 2012. 'Korupsi Rp. 3 Juta Dipenjara 4 Tahun, Herlina Menggugat ke MK', 11 May www.detiknews.com

Detiknews 2018. 'Hukuman Pidana hingga Denda Koruptor Lebih Rendah di RKUHP', 12 March www.detiknews.com

Durlauf, Steven N. and Nagin, Daniel S. 2011. 'Imprisonment and Crime: Can Both Be Reduced?', *Criminology and Public Policy* 10(1): 1

Greenblatt, Nathan 2008. 'How Mandatory Are Mandatory Minimums: How Judges Can Avoid Imposing Mandatory Minimum Sentences', *American Journal of Criminal Law* 36: 1

Grogger, Jeffrey 1991. 'Certainty vs. Severity of Punishment', *Economic Inquiry* 29(2): 297

Hoel, Adrian and Gelb, Karen 2008. 'Sentencing Matters: Mandatory Sentencing', Research Paper, Victoria Sentencing Advisory Council

Hukumonline 2011. 'Sanksi Berat Disiapkan untuk Pembalak Liar', 17 June www.hukumonline.com

Hukumonline 2018. 'Duplikasi Pengaturan Delik Tipikor dalam RKUHP Potensi Transaksional', 11 June www.hukumonline.com

Indonesian Corruption Watch 2002. *Menyingkap Tabir Mafia Peradilan*. Jakarta: ICW

Indonesian Corruption Watch 2009. *'Vonis Percobaan Bagi Terdakwa Korupsi Telah Jadi "Jurisprudensi"?'*, Media Release. Jakarta: ICW

Indonesian Corruption Watch 2014. *Catatan Pemantauan Perkara Korupsi yang Divonis oleh Pengadilan Selama Tahun 2014: Koruptor Masih Dihukum Ringan*. Jakarta: ICW

Indonesian Corruption Watch 2016. *Catatan Pemantauan Perkara Korupsi yang Divonis oleh Pengadilan Selama Tahun 2016: Vonis Tanpa Menjerakan Koruptor.* Jakarta: ICW

Indonesian Corruption Watch 2018. *'Catatan Pemantauan Perkara Korupsi yang Divonis oleh Pengadilan Selama 2017: Vonis Pengadilan Untungkan Koruptor'.* Report. Jakarta: ICW

Institute for Criminal Justice Reform 2016. *'Legalkan Hukum Kebiri (Chemical Castration), Upaya "Balas Dendam" Pemerintah Atas Nama Kepentingan Korban'.* Press Statement, 15 January. Jakarta: ICJR

Klepper, Steven and Nagin, Daniel 1989. 'The Deterrent Effect of Perceived Certainty and Severity of Punishment Revisited', *Criminology* 27: 721

Kolber, Adam. J 2009. 'The Comparative Nature of Punishment', Buffalo University Law Review 89: 1565

Landes, William and Posner, Richard 1975. 'The Private Enforcement of Law', *Journal of Legal Studies* 4(1): 1

Lobingier, Charles Sumner 1918. 'Napoleon and His Code', *Harvard Law Review* 32(2): 114

Mahkamah Agung 2008a. *Yurisprudensi Mahkamah Agung RI 2008*. Jakarta: MA

Mahkamah Agung 2018b. *Laporan Tahunan 2017*. Jakarta: MA

Mahkamah Agung 2011. *Yurisprudensi Mahkamah Agung RI 2011*. Jakarta: MA

Malloy, Robin Paul 1989. 'Is Law and Economics Moral-Humanistic Economics and a Classical Liberal Critique of Posner's Economic Analysis', *Valparaiso University Law Review* 24: 147

McLynn, Frank 2002. *Crime and Punishment in Eighteenth Century England.* London: Routledge

Missbach, Antje 2016. 'Sentencing People-Smuggling Offenders in Indonesia', CILIS Policy Paper 12. Centre for Indonesian Law, Islam and Society, the University of Melbourne

Palmer, Wayne and Missbach, Antje 2018. 'Judicial Discretion and the Minimum Statutory Sentence for Migrant Smuggling through Indonesia', *Asian Journal of Law and Society* 1–19, doi: 10.1017/als.2018.7

Posner, Richard 1979. 'Optimal Sentences for White-collar Criminals', *American Criminal Law Review* 19: 409

Rumadan, Ismail, Wijaya, Johanes Brata and Mulyani, Tri 2013. *Penafsiran Hakim terhadap Pidana Minimum Khusus dalam Undang-Undang Nomor 31 Tahun 1999 Jo Undang-Undang Nomor 20 Tahun 2001 tentang Tindak Pidana Korupsi: Suatu Kajian Asas, Teori, Norma dan Praktik Penerapannya.* Jakarta: Puslitbang Mahkamah Agung

Satuan Tugas Pemberantasan Mafia Hukum 2010. *Mafia Hukum: Modus Operandi, Akar Permasalahan dan Strategi Penanggulangan.* Jakarta: Satgas PMH

Sindonews 2017. 'Penghuni Lapas di Indonesia Didominasi Napi Kasus Narkoba Rabu', 17 May www.sindonews.com

Tak, P. J. P 2008. *The Dutch Criminal Justice System.* Nijmegen: Wolf

Tonry, Michael 2009. 'The Mostly Unintended Effects of Mandatory Penalties: Two Centuries of Consistent Findings', *Crime and Justice* 38(1): 65

Trotter, Andrew and Garozzo, Matt 2012. 'Mandatory Sentencing for People Smuggling: Issues of Law and Policy', *Melbourne University Law Review* 36: 553

Turner, M. G., Stundt, J. L., Applegate, B. K. and Cullen, F. T. 1995. 'Three Strikes and You're Out legislation: A National Assessment', *Federal Probation* 59: 16

Van Slyke, Shanna and Bales, William D. 2012. 'A Contemporary Study of the Decision to Incarcerate White-Collar and Street Property Offenders', *Punishment & Society* 14(2): 21

Von Hirsch, Andrew 1992. 'Proportionality in the Philosophy of Punishment', *Crime and Justice* 16: 55

Wahyudi 2004. *Kebijakan Legislatif dalam Rangka Mengefektifkan Pelaksanaan Sanksi Pidana Denda*. LLM Thesis. Semarang, Indonesia: Diponegoro University

Laws and regulations

Criminal Code (*Kitab Undang-Undang Hukum Pidana*, KUHP: Law No. 1 of 1946)

Criminal Procedural Code Law (*Kitab Undang-Undang Hukum Acara Pidana*, KUHAP: Law No. 8 of 1981)

Law No. 5 of 1997 on Psychotropic Substances

Law No. 31 of 1999 on the Eradication of Corruption (amended by Law No. 20 of 2001)

Law No. 20 of 2001 amending Law No. 31 of 1999 on the Eradication of Corruption

Law No. 35 of 2009 on Narcotics

Law No. 11 of 2012 on Juvenile Criminal Justice System

Law No. 18 of 2013 on Prevention and Eradication of Forest Destruction

Supreme Court Circular Letter No. 1 of 2000

Supreme Court Circular Letter No. 3 of 2001

Supreme Court Circular Letter No. 12 of 2010

Supreme Court Circular Letter No. 7 of 2012

Supreme Court Circular Letter No. 1 of 2017

Attorney General Circular Letter No. SE-004/J.A/11/1993

Court decisions

Supreme Court decisions

Decision No. 693/K/Pid/1986

Decision No. 06 K/Pid.HAM.AD HOC/2005

Decision No. 2399 K/Pid.Sus/2010

Constitutional Court decision

Decision No. 39/PUU-X/2012

Jakarta Anti-corruption Court decisions

Decision No. 1/Pid.B/TPK/2012/PN.Jkt.Pst

Decision No. 59/Pid.Sus/TPK/2012/PN.Jkt.Pst

Decision No. 36/Pid.Sus/TPK/2013/PN.Jkt.Pst

Decision No. 48/Pid.Sus/TPK/2013/PN.Jkt.Pst

Decision No. 58/Pid.Sus/TPK/2013/PN.Jkt.Pst

Decision No. 69/Pid.Sus/TPK/2013/PN.Jkt.Pst

Decision No. 77/Pid.Sus/TPK/2013/PN.Jkt.Pst

Decision No. 1/Pid.Sus/TPK/2014/PN.Jkt.Pst
Decision No. 36/Pid.Sus/TPK/2014/PN.Jkt.Pst
Decision No. 38/Pid.Sus/TPK/2014/PN.Jkt.Pst
Decision No. 58/Pid.Sus/TPK/2014/PN.Jkt.Pst
Decision No. 62/Pid.Sus/TPK/2014/PN.Jkt.Pst
Decision No. 65/ Pid.Sus/TPK/2014/PN.Jkt.Pst
Decision No. 79/Pid.Sus/TPK/2014/PN.Jkt.Pst
Decision No. 85/Pid.Sus/TPK/2014/PN.Jkt.Pst
Decision No. 15/Pid.Sus/TPK/2015/PN.Jkt.Pst
Decision No. 85/Pid.Sus/TPK/2015/PN.Jkt.Pst

Bandung Anti-corruption Court decisions

Decision No. 103/Pid.Sus/TPK/2015/PN.Bdg
Decision No. 108/Pid.Sus/TPK/2013/PN.Bdg
Decision No. 111/Pid.Sus/TPK/2014/PN.Bdg
Decision No. 114/Pid.Sus/TPK/2014/PN.Bdg
Decision No. 116/Pid.Sus/TPK/2014/PN.Bdg
Decision No. 12/Pid.Sus/TPK/2014/PN.Bdg
Decision No. 127/Pid.Sus/TPK/2013/PN.Bdg
Decision No. 133/Pid.Sus/TPK/2014/PN.Bdg
Decision No. 135/Pid.Sus/TPK/2015/PN.Bdg
Decision No. 136/Pid.Sus/TPK/2014/PN.Bdg
Decision No. 150/Pid.Sus/TPK/2013/PN.Bdg
Decision No. 16/Pid.Sus/TPK/2015/PN.Bdg
Decision No. 17/Pid.Sus/TPK/2015/PN.Bdg
Decision No. 19/Pid.Sus/TPK/2015/PN.Bdg
Decision No. 2/Pid.Sus/TPK/2014/PN.Bdg
Decision No. 20/Pid.Sus/TPK/2014/PN.Bdg
Decision No. 24/Pid.Sus/TPK/2015/PN.Bdg
Decision No. 26/Pid.Sus/TPK/2014/PN.Bdg
Decision No. 27/Pid.Sus/TPK/2014/PN.Bdg
Decision No. 3/Pid.Sus/TPK/2014/PN.Bdg
Decision No. 31/Pid.Sus/TPK/2014/PN.Bdg
Decision No. 35/Pid.Sus/TPK/2014/PN.Bdg
Decision No. 39/Pid.Sus/TPK/2015/PN.Bdg
Decision No. 4/Pid.Sus/TPK/2015/PN.Bdg
Decision No. 41/Pid.Sus/TPK/2014/PN.Bdg
Decision No. 45/Pid.Sus/TPK/2014/PN.Bdg
Decision No. 47/Pid.Sus/TPK/2014/PN.Bdg
Decision No. 48/Pid.Sus/TPK/2014/PN.Bdg
Decision No. 48/Pid.Sus/TPK/2015/PN.Bdg
Decision No. 5/Pid.Sus/TPK/2015/PN.Bdg
Decision No. 50/Pid.Sus/TPK/2014/PN.Bdg
Decision No. 58/Pid.Sus/TPK/2015/PN.Bdg
Decision No. 63/Pid.Sus/TPK/2015/PN.Bdg
Decision No. 64/Pid.Sus/TPK/2014/PN.Bdg
Decision No. 65/Pid.Sus/TPK/2014/PN.Bdg

Decision No. 65/Pid.Sus/TPK/2015/PN.Bdg
Decision No. 71/Pid.Sus/TPK/2015/PN.Bdg
Decision No. 74/Pid.Sus/TPK/2014/PN.Bdg
Decision No. 75/Pid.Sus/TPK/2015/PN.Bdg
Decision No. 76/Pid.Sus/TPK/2014/PN.Bdg
Decision No. 76/Pid.Sus/TPK/2015/PN.Bdg
Decision No. 77/Pid.Sus/TPK/2014/PN.Bdg
Decision No. 77/Pid.Sus/TPK/2015/PN.Bdg
Decision No. 78/Pid.Sus/TPK/2014/PN.Bdg
Decision No. 78/Pid.Sus/TPK/2015/PN.Bdg
Decision No. 79/Pid.Sus/TPK/2014/PN.Bdg
Decision No. 8/Pid.Sus/TPK/2015/PN.Bdg
Decision No. 82/Pid.Sus/TPK/2014/PN.Bdg
Decision No. 83/Pid.Sus/TPK/2014/PN.Bdg
Decision No. 84/Pid.Sus/TPK/2015/PN.Bdg
Decision No. 87/Pid.Sus/TPK/2015/PN.Bdg
Decision No. 90/Pid.Sus/TPK /2015 /PN.Bdg
Decision No. 90/Pid.Sus/TPK/2014/PN.Bdg

Other court decision

Mempawah District Court Decision No. 86/Pid.Sus/2013/PN.Mpw

11 The death penalty in Indonesia

Developments and prospects

Ricky Gunawan and Raynov T. Pamintori

When Joko Widodo (Jokowi) was inaugurated as the seventh President of the Republic of Indonesia on 20 October 2014, many applauded him, domestically and internationally, including the human rights community. President Jokowi was seen as a fresh leader who did not have a bleak human rights record and promised to move Indonesia forward to become a stronger democratic country with a better human rights protection agenda. His campaign platform included a pledge that he would uphold respect for human rights and resolve past human rights abuses in a just manner. When he began to carry out executions of drug offenders in January 2015, many were therefore in disbelief. His promise of improved human rights suddenly seemed in peril. He then continued the executions for another two rounds, in April 2015 and July 2016, confirming the fears of many that his election promises about human rights had little meaning. Jokowi's decision to undertake executions is actually no surprise for those who had followed his anti-drugs rhetoric during his 2014 electoral campaign, although it was entirely at odd with his human rights promises.

This chapter seeks to provide a legal and political analysis of the current state of the death penalty in Indonesia. To understand the magnitude of the problem, we begin with an outline of the legal framework in relation to the death penalty as a background, along with statistics on executions in Indonesia since *Reformasi* (Reform) began in 1998. We will then delve into four key events under Jokowi's administration: first, the executions in January 2015 and the two batches of executions that followed afterwards; second, the third round of executions in July 2016, which perhaps served as a turning point; third, 2017, a year of what we would call 'calm anomaly' that paved the way for a fragile de-facto moratorium in the years that followed; and, fourth, relevant legislation and court judgments from 2014 until the present. By looking at these four key themes, we hope to better understand the legal and political context surrounding the intensified use of the death penalty under Jokowi. We conclude in the final section by offering an assessment of progress towards abolition of the death penalty in Indonesia, which is not hopeless but certainly very vulnerable.

Legal framework of the death penalty in Indonesia

The death penalty was first applied as a national law in what is now Indonesia by a compilation of laws issued by the Dutch colonial regime in 1810. At that time, every execution of a death sentence had to receive a warrant from the Governor-General (Utrecht 1994: 18–19). In 1946, the Indonesian government adopted the Criminal Code the Dutch colonial government had enacted in 1918, with some amendments (see Butt and Lindsey, Chapter 2, this volume). This amended Criminal Code still prevails and, as shown in Table 11.1, it provides for a number of offences that carry the death penalty.

In addition to the Criminal Code, there are other Indonesian laws that apply capital punishment. The number of these laws has risen over the course of seventy-five years since the country gained its independence, with the most recent law being enacted in 2016. As of November 2017, there are now at least twelve laws that provide for capital punishment.

Constitutional provisions

Despite these provisions, art. 28A of the 1945 Constitution of the Republic of Indonesia provides that 'every person shall have the right to life and to defend his/her life and existence'. Further, art. 28I of the Constitution states that:

> the right to life, freedom from torture, freedom of thought and conscience, freedom of religion, freedom from enslavement, recognition as a person before the law, and the right not to be tried under a law with retrospective effect are all human rights that cannot be limited under any circumstances.

In 2007, the Constitutional Court attempted to resolve the contradictions between these Constitutional provisions and the many Indonesian laws that allow the death penalty in deciding a constitutional challenge to death penalty provisions in the 2009 Narcotics Law. The Court found that the imposition of capital punishment is not contrary to the norms of the Constitution and that the right to life is not an absolute right but can be limited, provided that is done in accordance with prevailing laws. The Court based its argument on art. 28J of the Constitution and the fact that there is no explicit prohibition on the use of the death penalty in international law. Article 28J(2) provides as follows:

> The rights set out above may be limited by legislation directed at protecting the rights and freedoms of others, and which accords with moral considerations, religious values security and public order in a democratic society.

Table 11.1 Capital punishment in Indonesian laws

No.	*Law*	*Death penalty – eligible offences*
1	Criminal Code	Treason, treason towards heads of neighbouring states, premeditated murder, aggravated robbery, and aggravated extortion.
2	Military Penal Code	Military treachery, military revolt in times of war, espionage, acts of violence towards injured civilians or military personnel in times of war, and desertion to the enemy's side.
3	Emergency Law No. 12 of 1951 on Firearms	Illegally producing, receiving, handing over, possessing, carrying, keeping, transporting, concealing, using, or exporting from Indonesia a firearm, ammunition, or explosives.
4	Presidential Decision No. 5 of 1959 on the Authority of the Attorney General / Military Attorney General with regard to Increasing Sentences against Crimes that Jeopardise Implementation of Food and Clothing Provision	Committing economic crimes that impede the implementation of government programmes to provide food and clothing, administer security for people and the state, and combat political and economic imperialism.
5	Government Regulation in Lieu of Law No. 21 of 1959 on the Aggravation of Sentence for Economic-related Crimes	Committing economic crimes that result in economic turmoil.
6	Law No. 4 of 1976 on the Amendment and Addition of Several articles under the Criminal Code that relate to Expansion of Enforceability of Provisions on Crimes against Aviation and Aviation Facilities	Hijacking of an airplane causing death or damage to an airplane, acts of violence towards a person in a plane or defacement of a plane causing death or damage to the plane.
7	Law No. 5 of 1997 on Psychotropic drugs	Using, producing, trafficking, importing, or possessing psychotropic drugs listed in the 1st schedule to the Law.
8	Law No. 31 of 1999 in conjunction with Law No. 20 of 2001 on Eradication of Corruption	Committing corruption in respect of state funds available to counteract emergency situations, natural disasters, widespread riots, or economic crises, in addition to repeated corruption.
9	Law No. 26 of 2000 on Human Rights Court	Genocide, crimes against humanity.
10	Government Regulation in Lieu of Law No. 1 of 2002 on Eradication of Terrorism	Committing any form of terrorism including planning, instructing someone, assisting, or conspiring to carry out an act of terrorism and/or an attempted terrorism.

Table 11.1 Cont.

No.	*Law*	*Death penalty – eligible offences*
11	Law No. 35 of 2009 on Narcotics	Illegally producing, importing, exporting, trafficking, receiving, exchanging, or delivering drugs in the 1st and 2nd schedules to the Law, weighing more than 1 kg (plants) or 5 grams (non-plants).
12	Government Regulation in Lieu of Law No. 1 of 2016 on the Second Amendment of Law No. 23 of 2002 on Child Protection	Committing sexual violence against a child that causes serious injury, mental illness, infectious disease, damage to reproductive function, or the death of the victim.

Butt and Lindsey (2018: 253) comment:

> Despite the explicit language of Article 28I(1), it appears that these rights are subject to limitation under Article 28J(2) of the Constitution, just as are other constitutional rights. This is because a majority of the Constitutional Court has, relatively consistently, decided that Article 28I(1) should not be viewed or interpreted in isolation, but rather should be read alongside Article 28J(2). In this way, the Court has refused to accord any special status to Article 28I(1) rights, contrary to what appears to be the clear intent of the Constitution drafters, expressed in Article 28I(1) with the words 'cannot be limited under any circumstances'.

Criminal procedure

The Indonesian Criminal Procedure Code regulates all aspects of criminal proceedings in criminal courts. This means that a suspect who is charged with an offence that may incur the death penalty will go through the same criminal proceedings as those who are not. The suspect will be investigated by police and the case will be brought before the court by a prosecutor. There are three stages at which judicial authorities can examine the case: district court, the provincial high court, and the Supreme Court. The suspect is entitled to appeal if he or she is not satisfied with the court's judgment. A Supreme Court judgment in a criminal case is deemed final and binding, that is, it has immediate, permanent legal force. Theoretically, whatever sentence is imposed, a prosecutor is allowed to execute that sentence.[1] In practice, however, prosecutors usually take a more cautious approach when the death penalty is involved. Although they are allowed to execute death row prisoners after the Supreme Court has reached a final and binding decision, they will usually wait until all legal avenues available are exhausted.

These avenues include an extraordinary appeal, the case review or *peninjauan kembali* (PK). One of the grounds for a PK is that an applicant prisoner can present new evidence that may result in acquittal or reduce his or her sentence.[2] A prisoner is also entitled to submit a clemency petition to the president, and here death row prisoners have rights that differ from those who are not sentenced to death. According to art. 3 of the Law No. 22 of 2002 on Clemency,[3] if a person has been sentenced to death, his or her execution must be postponed until the president issues a decision on any clemency request that person has lodged.

The procedure for execution is regulated by Presidential Decision No. 2 of 1964 on Procedures for Execution of the Death Sentence in the Criminal Court and Military Court. In summary, this states that execution is carried out by a firing squad, with the prisoner being shot to death.

A new draft Criminal Code is currently being deliberated in the People's Representative Assembly (DPR, Dewan Perwakilan Rakyat) and there is a revision proposed to the provisions on capital punishment in the current draft. While the Criminal Code currently rules that the death penalty is a primary punishment, in the draft code it is an alternative punishment. The draft code states that judges can impose death sentence with ten years' suspension if: the defendant shows remorse and there is hope for transformation; his or her role in the criminal act is minor; and there are mitigating factors. After the ten year suspension or probation period is complete, the convict's death sentence can be commuted to life in prison if he or she has demonstrated good behaviour.

Death penalty and execution by numbers

In the first three years of the rule of President Joko Widodo (Jokowi), eighteen death row prisoners were executed. All were drug offenders. This is an egregious achievement for Jokowi. Since the authoritarian Soeharto regime was overthrown by the Reformasi movement in 1998, the state had never seen such a number of executions in a short period. The following paragraphs will offer a comparison between the numbers of people executed during the era from Soeharto's fall in 1998 to October 2014, when Jokowi took office, and those executed during Jokowi's first term (2014–2019).

President Megawati Soekarnoputri's presidency marked the first executions after the New Order (1966–1998) ended. She was inaugurated in July 2001 and left office in October 2004. Under her rule, five people were executed, in three different groups. This means the execution rate under Megawati was around two people per year. The first were Gerson Pande and Fredrik Soru, two Indonesian nationals, convicted of premeditated murder. They were executed in 2001. Then, Ayodhya Prasad Chaubey, from India, was executed on 5 August 2004, after being found guilty of a drug-related offence. Before Megawati ended her tenure, two more people were executed, on 1 October 2004: Saelow Prasert and Namsong Sirilak, both Thai nationals who were sentenced to death for smuggling heroin into Indonesia.

Table 11.2 Executions under Yudhoyono

Name	*Nationality*	*Case*	*Execution Date*
1. Astini	Indonesia	Premeditated murder	20 March 2005
2. Turmudi	Indonesia	Premeditated murder	13 May 2005
3. Fabianus Tibo	Indonesia	Premeditated murder	22 September 2006
4. Marinus Riwu	Indonesia	Premeditated murder	
5. Dominggus Da Silva	Indonesia	Premeditated murder	
6. Ayub Bululbili	Indonesia	Premeditated murder	28 April 2007
7. Hansen Anthony Nwaolisa	Nigeria	Drug offence	26 June 2008
8. Samuel Iwuchukwu Okoye	Nigeria	Drug offence	
9. Ahmad Suraji	Indonesia	Premeditated murder	10 July 2008
10. Usep alias Tubagus Yusuf Maulana	Indonesia	Premeditated murder	18 July 2008
11. Sugeng	Indonesia	Premeditated murder	19 July 2008
12. Sumiarsih	Indonesia	Premeditated murder	
13. Rio Alex Bullo	Indonesia	Premeditated murder	8 August 2008
14. Imam Samudra	Indonesia	Terrorism	9 November 2008
15. Ali Ghufron (Muklas)	Indonesia	Terrorism	
16. Amrozi	Indonesia	Terrorism	
17. Adami Wilson	Nigeria	Drug offence	14 March 2013
18. Suryadi Swabuana	Indonesia	Premeditated murder	17 May 2013
19. Jurit	Indonesia	Premeditated murder	
20. Ibrahim	Indonesia	Premeditated murder	
21. Mohammad Abdul Hafeez	Pakistan	Drug offence	17 November 2013

Source: Amnesty International (2015).

President Susilo Bambang Yudhoyono (SBY) executed twenty-one people over the ten years of his leadership, which also amounts to an execution rate of around two individuals per year. There was a pause, which most people referred as an 'unofficial moratorium', from 2009 to 2012, but in 2013 Yudhoyono resumed executions (Table 11.2).
President Jokowi executed more people in his first year than his predecessors, almost matching the total of executions carried out during Yudhoyono's ten years. With eighteen people already executed less than two years into his administration, Jokowi's execution rate had reached six per year. Two distinctive features of the executions under Jokowi are an increasing number of foreign nationals executed, and the sole targeting of drug offenders for execution (Table 11.3).

The increasing trend is reflected not only in the rate of executions, but also the number of death sentences imposed by the courts. In September 2016, for example, Reprieve's database recorded 178 people on death row, of whom 105 were drug offenders. By December 2018 the number had increased to 298, with 186 drug offenders. Meanwhile, information provided by the Prisons

Table 11.3 Executions under Jokowi

Name	*Nationality*	*Case*	*Execution date*
1. Tran Thi Bich Hanh	Vietnam	Drug offences	18 January 2015
2. Daniel Enemuo	Nigeria		
3. Namaona Dennis alias Solomon Chibuke Okafer	Nigeria		
4. Ang Kim Soei	Netherlands		
5. Marco Archer	Brazil		
6. Rani Andriani	Indonesia		
7. Okwudili Oyatanze	Nigeria	Drug offences	29 April 2015
8. Sylvester Obiekwe Nwolise	Nigeria		
9. Martin Anderson	Nigeria		
10. Raheem Agbaje Salami	Nigeria		
11. Rodrigo Gularte	Brazil		
12. Andrew Chan	Australia		
13. Myuran Sukumaran	Australia		
14. Zainal Abidin	Indonesia		
15. Humphrey Jefferson Ejike	Nigeria	Drug offences	29 July 2016
16. Seck Osmane alias Cajetan Uchena Onyeworo	Nigeria		
17. Michael Titus Igweh alias Izuchukwu F. Ezimoha	Nigeria		
18. Freddy Budiman	Indonesia		

Source: Amnesty International (2015).

Department of the Ministry of Law and Human Rights stated that in April 2015 there were 121 people on death row, with fifty-three of them there for drugs offences. By October 2017, there were 165 death row prisoners, with seventy-three of them drug offenders.[4]

In the last three years of Jokowi's first term, legal and political developments resulted in fewer executions being carried out. The decision to increase the amount of capital punishment sentences and executions could be seen as a spur-of-the-moment decision, but it can also be linked to wider problems with drug policy in Indonesia. In the following sections, we chronicle developments in the application of the death penalty in Indonesia from Jokowi's first months as President, until 2019.

Developments in the death penalty in Indonesia: Legal and political analysis

The rise in mass executions

When Jokowi was running for president, he included a long list of human rights promises in his presidential platform – the *Nawacita*.[5] In it, he said that one of the main issues Indonesia was facing was declining state authority, as indicated by ongoing, unresolved human rights violations and feeble law enforcement. As a priority, Jokowi and his 2014 vice-presidential running mate, Jusuf Kalla, promised to continue law reform programmes that were 'free from corruption' and 'carried out in a dignified and reliable manner'. This would include respect for human rights and the addressing of past human right abuses.[6] This promise, together with the fact that Jokowi does not have a military background and was not a member of the established political elite or an oligarch, meant that his candidacy attracted support from many human rights groups in Indonesia. Jokowi's first wave of executions in January 2015 therefore shocked many, particularly human rights communities – both domestic and foreign. So how did this happen?

We have argued elsewhere that Jokowi's lacklustre first hundred days contributed, in part, to what appeared to be his sudden decision to escalate executions (Gunawan and Pamintori 2017). This was a time of 'rising public disappointment and slipping popularity' (Kwok 2015), rather than a promising start to a human rights and democracy agenda.

In November 2014, Jokowi appointed HM Prasetyo as the Attorney General. As part of the executive body, the Attorney General's Office (AGO) should have spearheaded Jokowi's campaign to uphold the rule of law and protect human rights. However, it failed to substantially advance the government's anti-corruption and human rights agenda. A number of past cases of human rights abuses faced a dead-end, as the AGO did not want to pursue their investigation for political reasons, leaving victims with very little hope for justice. Also, while there have been many prosecutors implicated in corruption cases, there seemed to be no fundamental reform within the AGO to address this acute problem. Therefore, many argued that the AGO needed a leader from outside the institution who had a demonstrated leadership in anti-corruption efforts and a true commitment to human rights. Prasetyo, however, is a former prosecutor with no experience of human rights cases; he was also a member of the Nasdem political party, which strongly supports Jokowi. Prasetyo's appointment was therefore slammed by human rights groups (Widhiarto and Perdana 2014), who argued that the leadership of the AGO should be impartial and have no political interests – and that, furthermore, Prasetyo was, in any case, an inappropriate appointment, because he had no track record in human rights protection at all.

In December 2014, Jokowi also declared a so-called drug emergency, quoting faulty statistics to justify his claims that: 40–50 people die every day in Indonesia because of drugs (Stoicescu 2015); 4.5 million people are drug-dependent; and 1.2 million people can no longer be rehabilitated because their addiction is so severe.[7] He added that he would therefore not grant any clemency petitions filed by drug prisoners, stating, 'Let me be clear, the death penalty does not come from the president, it comes from the court's judgment. But if they seek pardon, I will not give it' (Indonesia. Sekretariat Kabinet 2014a).

Jokowi's message quickly gained momentum and plans for execution accelerated, with Yasonna Laoly, then Minister of Law and Human Rights, visiting Nusakambangan Island, where executions usually take place, and where there are four maximum security prisons. His visit was part of the wider preparation of Nusakambangan, given that the prisons department fell under his authority (Zakaria 2014). Yasonna's visit, combined with recurring statements from Prasetyo that the AGO was preparing for executions (without mentioning any dates), attracted media attention, which continuously raised the issue of impending executions. For about two weeks from mid-December 2014, Prasetyo repeatedly issued statements that the AGO would carry out executions 'before the first sunrise in 2015'. Names of death row prisoners to be executed circulated in the media but these kept changing, resulting in uncertainty for the prisoners named.

The media reports ignited considerable public debate, and Jokowi visited the two largest Islamic mass organisations in Indonesia, Nahdlatul Ulama (NU)[8] and Muhammadiyah to seek advice – or perhaps, 'blessing' – on major policy issues, including the death sentence for drug traffickers and terrorists (Sekretariat Kabinet 2014b).[9] Leaders from both organisations agreed to the execution of drug offenders. Although it appeared that Jokowi still intended to carry out executions towards the end of 2014, Prasetyo announced not long after the President's visit to NU and Muhammadiyah that the executions had been delayed because the AGO wished to ensure that the prisoners concerned had no legal avenues left.[10]

Early in January 2015, preparations for execution continued as the AGO and Ministry of Law and Human Rights had more meetings to finalise the technicalities of who would be executed, where and when; as well informing the families of prisoners to be executed (and their representatives, if they were foreign nationals). During the same period, another political glitch arose when Jokowi picked Budi Gunawan as his sole candidate for Chief of Indonesian National Police. This decision was heavily criticised, as Budi Gunawan was implicated in a previous corruption case and was once an adjutant of the then President, Megawati Soekarnoputri, who was now Chair of PDI Perjuangan, the political party that nominated Jokowi for the presidency. Many people therefore surmised that Jokowi's decision was influenced by Megawati instead of being his own. A few days later, Indonesia's Anti-Corruption Agency (KPK, Komisi Pemberantasan Korupsi) named Budi Gunawan as a suspect in a corruption case that in relation to events that had taken place in 2003–6.

The resulting scandal gripped the country for two reasons. First, it occurred within the first one hundred days of his presidency, and Jokowi was already seen as a weak leader under the influence of Megawati, an issue raised by his opponents during the presidential campaign. Second, because Jokowi was seen as being aligned with Budi Gunawan rather than the KPK, Jokowi was perceived as breaching his anti-corruption promises. This scandal meant Jokowi was under fire from both his political rivals and the public. He needed to show he was a tough leader and could exercise political power effectively.

Likewise, Prasetyo, whose appointment was met with much disapproval, held his new post in a country where the majority are in favour of the death penalty. This provided a textbook opportunity to show that he, too, was a strong and capable figure. Against this backdrop, executions became the perfect political tool for Jokowi's regime to re-establish its authority.

As a result, on 18 January 2015, Jokowi executed six people:

Marco Archer Cardoso Mareira	Male	Brazil
Daniel Enemoa	Male	Nigeria
Ang Kim Soei	Male	The Netherlands
Denis Namaona	Male	Nigeria
Rani Andriani	Female	Indonesia
Tran Thi Bich Hanh	Female	Vietnam

The first five were executed in Nusakambangan, while Tran Thi Bich Hanh was executed in Boyolali, Central Java.

A number of records were broken with this first wave of executions. It was the first time since *Reformasi* that an execution killed more than five people at the same time. Not only that, it was the first time – perhaps, in Indonesian modern history – that foreign nationals from abolitionist countries (Brazil and the Netherlands) were executed. In response, Brazil and the Netherlands summoned their ambassadors (BBC Indonesia 2015b) back to their countries, resulting in diplomatic tensions with Indonesia.

Many human rights advocates in Indonesia and abroad condemned the executions and called for a moratorium[11] but Jokowi did not heed the protests. After the first wave of executions, Jokowi's human rights stance suddenly became ugly. His actions attracted a lot of support from both the Indonesian media and the Indonesian public, making it even harder for the human rights communities to be heard.

The second batch of execution followed sooner than many had imagined. On 29 April 2015, Jokowi executed eight prisoners.

Andrew Chan	Male	Australia
Myuran Sukumaran	Male	Australia
Raheem Agbaje Salami	Male	Nigeria
Sylvester Obiekwe Nwolise	Male	Nigeria
Okwudili Oyatanze	Male	Nigeria
Martin Anderson	Male	Nigeria
Rodrigo Gularte[12]	Male	Brazil
Zainal Abidin	Male	Indonesia

One person was reprieved at the very last minute: Mary Jane Veloso, from the Philippines, following intense behind-closed-door lobbying and a final plea to Jokowi from Benigno Aquino III, the then President of the Philippines.[13] Another individual was originally included in the list, Serge Atloui (France), but because he had a pending administrative court decision challenging the Presidential Decision that had rejected his clemency petition, his name was removed one day before the execution.

The second batch of executions placed Indonesia under the international spotlight like never before. Australian 'megaphone diplomacy',[14] another fierce protest from Brazil, vigorous demands from Indonesian civil society,[15] and mounting pressure from international communities (BBC Indonesia 2015c), including UN leaders,[16] all thrust Indonesia into the headlines of major international news outlets.[17]

As with the first batch of execution, the second batch broke another record. With eight more people executed in April 2015, fourteen people had been executed in just four months. Jokowi's stubborn and bloody presidency continued to defend the use of executions, arguing that Indonesia was in the midst of a drug emergency and executions were needed to deter drug offenders.

Jokowi prepared to resume executions, with the third batch taking place on 29 July 2016. This time Jokowi was prepared to break more records, with fourteen people listed for execution. However, eventually only four were executed.

Executed		
Freddy Budiman	Male	Indonesia
Seck Osmane	Male	Nigeria
Michael Titus Igweh	Male	Nigeria
Humphrey Ejike Jefferson[18]	Male	Nigeria
Listed for execution, and not executed		
Ozias Sibanda	Male	Nigeria
Fredderik Luttar	Male	Nigeria
Okonkwo Nongso Kingsley	Male	Nigeria
Eugene Ape	Male	Nigeria
Obina Nwajagu	Male	Nigeria
Zulfiqar Ali	Male	Pakistan
Gurdip Singh	Male	India
Agus Hadi	Male	Indonesia
Pujo Lestari	Male	Indonesia
Merri Utami	Female	Indonesia

There was no official, proper or clear information provided by the AGO to the families and lawyers of the deceased as to why only four prisoners were eventually executed. The only information that was given by the AGO was that the four prisoners were involved in large-scale drug trafficking and the other ten death row prisoners were spared at the last minute, for 'judicial and non-judicial reasons' (Waluyo 2016).

With these four people shot in July 2016, Jokowi's regime had executed eighteen people in total within roughly eighteen months (January 2015–July 2016). Since Reformasi, no regime had ever carried out executions at such a prolific rate, within so a short period of time. With all eighteen prisoners executed being drug offenders, Jokowi seemed determined to pursue his objective of addressing Indonesia's 'drug emergency'. But is this justification really valid?

Justification for the executors

Human rights groups were very critical when the first round of executions was carried out. They argued that the death penalty violates the right to life enshrined in the Constitution, where, as mentioned, it is stated to be a non-derogable right. Protests also came from drug user groups. More than twenty organisations working on drug treatment, harm reduction programmes, and drug policy reform sent an open letter to Jokowi (Kompas 2015). They argued that the death penalty does not solve drug trafficking problems. Worse, the lure of drug trafficking, which offers large sums of money for people willing to carry drugs, have pushed many poor people to undertake that work out of desperation. Many people involved in the illicit drug trade are just 'mules', manipulated by syndicates, who exploit their vulnerabilities. The drug user support groups demanded that Jokowi evaluate his drug policy and introduce more humane policies to address Indonesia's drug problems.

Unfortunately, this criticism – from both human rights and drug user support organisations – fell on deaf ears. For Jokowi, the rights of so-called 'victims of drugs scourge' outweighed the rights of the offenders and he continued to rely on his favourite statistics: forty to fifty Indonesians die every day, so the death penalty is needed to curtail drug crimes. However, as Claudia Stoicescu, a public health researcher, points out, the data used to justify the use of the death penalty for drug offences and other punitive measures is problematic (Stoicescu 2015). For example, the 4.5 million people who use drugs, and who are in need of rehabilitation, is not an estimation of an actual number but rather a projection. The figure of forty to fifty people dying every day from drugs results from research that used dubious methodology to measure drug mortality. Her timely analysis, regrettably, did not seem to reach Jokowi and his inner circle. Human rights groups, public health experts and prominent academics from Indonesia and abroad then joined forces to issue a public letter to Jokowi to amplify the criticism (Irwanto, et al. 2015). Irwanto et al.'s article in *The Lancet*, one of the world's most influential international medical journals, argued that the statistics Jokowi used were not reliable and that, as a public policy matter, he should support his decision with credible evidence. This was not, however, reported by major Indonesian media outlets and Jokowi's administration seemed to pay no attention to the rebuttals.

Another rationalisation for the use of the death penalty for drug offences is state sovereignty. The argument runs in two ways. First, executing drug offenders is a matter of upholding domestic law, because the law states that persons committing illicit drug trafficking can be sentenced to death. Further, because judges have sentenced the traffickers to death, the government is just implementing the court's decisions. Any protest to the Indonesian government is deemed an attempt to interfere with the domestic law. Second, drug problems are seen as a 'proxy war' led from outside Indonesia, an effort by foreigners destroy the country.[19] Therefore, executing drug offenders serves as a kind of defence mechanism to protect Indonesia from external threats.

The 'state sovereignty' defence argument may also explain why the majority of people executed under Jokowi have been foreigners. To date, fifteen of the eighteen executed drug prisoners have been foreigners, and only three Indonesians were executed. Foreigners are probably intentionally on the list because it provides double protection for Jokowi. Drugs are already widely seen as evil, a social hatred that is now firmly embedded in society. The public therefore considers that executing drug offenders is a social good, and the state receives 'rewards' for doing this. Executing foreign drug traffickers, who are portrayed as threatening Indonesian integrity, also invokes a sense of nationalism in the general public, which helps shield Jokowi from criticisms by human rights groups and international community.

If we look at Indonesia's Criminal Code from a historical view, however, it appears the state sovereignty argument is unfounded. As mentioned, Indonesia inherited its Criminal Code largely intact from the Dutch. The Dutch code included the death sentence as a primary punishment, as a political weapon for colonial rulers to maintain public order.[20] If Indonesia wants to uphold state sovereignty and break its colonial ties, it would make more sense to remove the colonial-era death penalty from its penal system. This is actually one of the stated political rationales for Indonesia to revise its criminal code: the current one is inherited from the Dutch and Indonesia wants its own modern, national criminal code. In our view, it is inconsistent for Indonesia to be revising its criminal code, while at the same time maintaining one of the methods of punishment used by the Dutch to perpetuate colonialism.

The executions of July 2016: A personal account of a turning point

The executions of April 2015 can be seen as the most dramatic round of executions in modern Indonesian history. There were eight foreign nationals executed at the same time, including Australians, with Australia being Indonesia's close neighbour. This drew forceful pressure from international communities. However, the third round involved perhaps the most chaotic official executions Indonesia has ever organised (Daily Mail 2016).

To explain what we mean, it is useful to offer a narration of events leading up to these executions. LBH Masyarakat (Community Legal Aid Institute) and Reprieve were the legal team for Humphrey Ejike Jefferson ('Jeff') and Meri Utami. The authors, who work with LBH Masyarakat and Reprieve, were present at the executions in April 2015 and July 2016, and the following section comprises their personal observations. The chronological description that follows has not previously been shared beyond the membership of LBH Masyarakat and Reprieve.

On Saturday, 23 July 2016, LBH Masyarakat received news from the Embassy of Nigeria that the Indonesian Ministry of Foreign Affairs had sent a letter to it on Friday, 22 July 2016. The letter from Foreign Affairs to the Embassy advised that there were four Nigerian nationals who would be executed in the near future, without mentioning the exact date. On Sunday, 24 July 2016, LBH Masyarakat also heard news that Utami's family had also been asked to come to Nusakambangan for execution, without any information about when and where the execution would take place.

On the morning of Monday, 25 July 2016, LBH Masyarakat filed a clemency petition on behalf of Jeff at the Central Jakarta District Court. In the afternoon, LBH Masyarakat contacted the Nigerian Embassy again to get an update and were told that the Embassy had been asked to come to the Cilacap District Prosecutor's office on Tuesday at 1.00 p.m., while Utami's family had been asked to arrive at the office at 8.00 a.m. on the same day. Given the uncertainty, Ricky Gunawan (one of the authors) and his colleagues left Jakarta and arrived at the Cilacap District Prosecutor's office on Tuesday morning, around 8.00 a.m.

Their attempts to find out what was happening from the many prosecutors who were present in the building were to no avail. Although the prosecutors held a closed meeting from 9.00 to 10.30 a.m., Gunawan and his colleagues were given no further information from other officials. Families of death row prisoners started arriving and were asked to stay in certain rooms. At about 11.00 a.m., two members of the LBH Masyarakat legal team met with Tangerang District Prosecutor's team[21] inside the building and provided identity documents, but were not asked to hand over their mobile phones. Fifteen minutes later Gunawan and associates also met the Central Jakarta District Prosecutor,[22] submitted their documents, and their mobile phones were taken from them.

At about midday, Raynov Pamintori (the other author) and Utami's family left the Cilacap District Prosecutor's office together with the families of Gurdip Singh and Zulfiqar Ali, for Nusakambangan, using a minibus provided by Tangerang District Prosecutor. When they arrived in Nusakambangan, however, Raynov was told that he could not meet Utami. Only her family and a Catholic pastor (Utami's religious counsellor) were allowed to go to Batu Prison to meet Utami. One hour later, Gunawan and Muhammad Afif (also of LBH Masyarakat) left the Cilacap District Prosecutor's office for Nusakambangan, using a car provided by the Central Jakarta District Prosecutor. Afif and Gunawan arrived in Nusakambangan at 2.00 p.m., and both were allowed to go to Batu Prison to meet Jeff, but only after being made to wait for about an hour outside the prison.

At around 3.40 p.m., Jeff, accompanied by Afif and Gunawan, met the prosecutor in-charge from the Central Jakarta District Prosecutor office, who handed Jeff a notification of execution. This notification report is the official notification of intended execution from the AGO. After consulting with Afif and Gunawan, Jeff decided to refuse signing the notification report because he had a pending clemency decision. Jeff also said to the prosecutor, 'I oppose the death penalty and want to continue to live'.

Inside Batu Prison, Gunawan and Afif were able, with Jeff's help, to identify fourteen people who had been isolated for execution. This included Zulfiqar Ali, who was in a wheelchair with a small oxygen tube behind his wheelchair. Gunawan and Afif left Batu Prison at about 4.30 p.m. and were taken to the Cilacap District Prosecutor's office. They were not allowed to leave Wijayapura Pier in Cilacap unguarded, as many journalists were waiting outside. Afif and Gunawan then arrived at their hotel at about 6.00 p.m. The AGO had still not made any press statements about the executions. There was no information available to the public or in any media as to who was isolated, ready for execution. It was kept secret, despite many journalists being present in Cilacap. Given this situation, LBH Masyarakat decided to issue information on its Facebook page about the fourteen death row prisoners who were isolated. News reports followed.

On Wednesday, 27 July 2016, Gunawan and Afif arrived at the Cilacap District Prosecutor's office around 9 a.m. and went through registration again to visit Jeff and Utami. This time they tried to register other members of their legal team too. One hour later, a few prosecutors approached them separately asking them to visit Jeff and Utami individually, without other team members. They had some time to debate this with the prosecutors, but given that the prosecutors kept insisting and had power to control the visitors, it was decided that Gunawan would visit Jeff and Afif would meet Utami. Meanwhile other team members would wait in Cilacap. It took some time for them to arrive in Batu Prison. Along the way from the Cilacap District Prosecutor's office to Batu Prison, Gunawan tried to get more information about the executions from the prosecutors but none was given.

Afif and Gunawan arrived at the prison around 2 p.m. and were told that their time with the prisoners was limited, despite there being signs saying that visiting hours are from 9 a.m. to 4 p.m. Once inside, Gunawan met with Jeff, while Afif briefed Utami and her family members. Gunawan also had a brief conversation with Zulfikar Ali. He said to him, 'Please tell the world that I am innocent. I genuinely did not know about the drugs that they had accused me of'.

On Thursday, 28 July 2016, Afif and Gunawan again went to the Cilacap District Prosecutor's office in the morning for visiting registration. Things were quite different this day. The security was tighter and there were many police officers around the building. They saw a few high-ranking government officials, possibly from the AGO, but could not clearly identify them. More and more journalists were now coming to the Cilacap District Prosecutor's office – and, like the previous two days, they were not allowed to come into the building or even the parking area. While waiting for the prosecutors to take them from the Cilacap District Prosecutor's office to Wijayapura, Afif and Gunawan were given special ID tags with 'Family' written on them. They then became suspicious that the executions might occur that evening, even though, as they calculated, the 72 hours after notification would not have expired by then. Indonesia's law on procedure of execution provides that a notification of execution must be conveyed at least 72 hours before the execution is carried out.[23] Would the AGO be bold – or maybe arrogant – enough to carry out the execution that night? On the way to Batu Prison, the prosecutors who were with them kept saying, 'Please be prepared tonight. Don't turn off your phone, okay?' Gunawan asked what that meant, even specifically asking whether the execution would take place that night. But the prosecutors did not respond, other than repeating, 'Just be ready'.

Inside his isolation cell, Freddy Budiman received visits from a large number of prison officials. They prayed and sang together. A few prison officials recorded that moment on their mobile phones. Everyone – male and female, old and young prison officials – cried and said goodbye to him. Doctors checked Utami's condition, to see whether she was pregnant. Zulfiqar Ali did not use his wheelchair any more. Prison guards walked him from his cell to the prison hall area where his family, who had come all the way from Pakistan, were waiting. Gurdip Singh, also a prisoner, bowed his head to Ali's mother, when she walked in, begging for her forgiveness. Gurdip had 'set up' Zulfiqar and at Zulfiqar's trial, Gurdip revoked his earlier statement that the narcotics belonged to Zulfiqar. Jeff and other African nationals were talking with their families back home on mobile phones provided by the AGO. Some of them could make connection, while others had signal problems. Obviously, it was the final moment for every prisoner with their families – at least for those who could reach them. It was a heart-breaking time for all.

Gunawan and Afif left Batu Prison around 3.30 p.m. Before leaving, Gunawan apologised to Jeff for failing to save him and asked whether he had any final words. Jeff replied, 'Please tell Jokowi, may God protect him'. Jeff asked Gunawan to take care of his glasses, watch, diary and books, which contained his songs and praises to God.

At about 7.30 p.m., Gunawan received a call from the prosecutor in-charge asking him to get ready because the prosecutor would pick him up at the hotel in half an hour. At around 8.00 p.m., Gunawan, together with the prosecutors from Central Jakarta District Prosecutor's Office, left the hotel and went to Nusakambangan. When he arrived, Gunawan saw family members, including relatives of Agus Hadi and Pujo Lestari (who were among those scheduled for execution on drug smuggling charges but were eventually not executed). More family members kept arriving until 10 p.m. There was a storm in progress, with strong wind and lightning. The tent, which had been put up for family members waiting for the executions, collapsed. The family members then waited in the security post near the pier in Nusakambangan.

At about 1 a.m., national television broadcast the news that the AGO had conducted the executions. Family members watched it on a television in the security post but no one could confirm what had happened at midnight. A number of prosecutors talked to each other and cracked jokes, while the families of Zulfiqar Ali and Gurdip Singh consoled each other. It was a painful moment for all family members.

At about 1.30 a.m., representatives of the AGO, other government officials and a few religious counsellors arrived at the pier area in Nusakambangan from the execution site. Gunawan spoke to one religious counsellor who told him, 'They only executed four. Our sons[24] were included. Your friend was too'.

At about 2 a.m., the AGO's Deputy Attorney General for General Crimes, Noor Rachmad, held a press conference in Wijayapura and advised that they had executed four prisoners. At 3.00 a.m., four ambulances came down from the execution site, with the prosecutors in charge of each of the prisoners in the ambulance. They then met with the relatives of the prisoners – or, in Jeff's case, Gunawan. The prosecutor only handed him Jeff's glasses. Gunawan asked, 'Where's Jeff's watch? He asked me to take care of it'. The prosecutor replied, 'I don't know'.

At about 4 a.m., the four ambulances, along with family members of the deceased, arrived in Wijayapura and went to their designated burial places. Jeff's body went to a crematorium in Banyumas, where it was cremated. His ashes were sent to Nigeria a couple of weeks later.

For those who had been present at the second batch of executions in April 2015, this third batch was clearly much more disorganised. First, there was no clear and official information provided by the prosecutor, leading to legal teams and family members being confused about procedures. Unlike the second batch, there was no formal convening to notify about the executions, nor was there a technical meeting prior the executions. Second, the visiting procedure was disorganised and differed from one district prosecutor to another. Third, the AGO gave no information to the public about the executions. It was obvious that the government wanted to carry out the executions discreetly. Fourth, Indonesia has regulations on executions but not on what to do if an execution is postponed – especially if it is postponed at the last minute. Utami is still in the Cilacap Correctional Facility. A few months after her execution was postponed, LBH Masyarakat requested that the AGO transfer her back to Tangerang Correctional Facility. The AGO disregarded this request and did not provide adequate information. When the same request was conveyed to the Ministry of Law and Human Rights and its Prisons Department, the Ministry responded that this was not under their jurisdiction, because the AGO had transferred Utami from Tangerang to Cilacap/Nusakambangan for execution. Neither agency had any idea about what to do if an execution is cancelled, because, as mentioned, there are no rules or regulations about this matter. Fifth, and most fundamentally, the Indonesian government disrespected and violated their own laws. For example, Jeff had a pending clemency decision and his execution was carried out less than seventy-two hours after notification.

The third batch of executions also saw many elements of unfair trials of those who were executed or faced execution.[25] Therefore, although there were no prisoners from abolitionist or European countries executed, Indonesia remained under the international spotlight.[26]

Despite the muddled processes and blatant breaches of law in the July 2016 executions, there appear to be hopeful signs post-execution. The international press conducted two key interviews with Jokowi after July 2016. One was in November 2016, ahead of Jokowi's planned visit to Australia, although this visit was cancelled by him due to other urgent domestic matters. When asked by ABC News Australia about Indonesia's use of the executions, Jokowi said, 'We are very open to options'.[27] His statement may have been made out of diplomatic courtesy, given that he was about to visit Australia. Nevertheless, given how adamant Jokowi had been from October 2014 to July 2016 on continuing to use executions to address Indonesia's drug problems, his statement to ABC News was particularly significant. In the past, when the media asked Jokowi about this issue, he would respond that he would not hesitate to carry out executions to save Indonesia's future generations from the drugs menace.

Jokowi made further hints in an interview with Agence France-Presse (AFP), this time before the French President, Francois Hollande, visited Indonesia in March 2017 (Daily Mail 2017). When the AFP asked Jokowi whether he would consider a moratorium, he said, 'Why not? But I must first ask my people. If my people say OK, if they say yes, I will start to prepare'. This statement contains a number of possible meanings. First, like Jokowi's previous statement, it may have been a diplomatic courtesy to show respect for France as an abolitionist country. Second, throughout the period of executions, Jokowi never backed off at all; he showed no mercy to drug traffickers. While there are a number of prisoners who received last-minute reprieve in the second and third round of executions, it remains unclear on what basis he postponed their executions. So, it was encouraging that he said that he was open to a moratorium. It was, at least, a small shift. The danger in Jokowi's statement, however, is the proviso about public opinion. In many retentionist countries, even abolitionist ones, public opinion tends to favour the death penalty. A public opinion survey could result in support for maintaining the use of the death penalty. Yet, as in the case of Malaysia[28] and Japan,[29] if there is careful consideration about the questions asked, a public opinion survey may result in the public questioning the purpose of the death penalty, or even shifting from supporting the death penalty to opposing it. Whether or not the Indonesian public is ready for such a public opinion survey, and how it might respond, is an issue beyond the scope of this chapter.

A calm anomaly

The years 2017 and 2019 were much calmer. No executions took place and plans for the next round of executions slowly disappeared from public discourse. As discussed below, there are at least three key developments that have apparently helped create this tranquil atmosphere: first, the Ombudsman of

Indonesia's findings on the third batch of executions; second, the Supreme Court's ruling on a PK petition; and, third, Indonesia's candidacy for the non-permanent seat at the UN Security Council (SC). At the international level, criticisms of the previous rounds of executions by United Nations (UN) member states have also had an impact.

Towards the end of 2016, Attorney General Prasetyo showed no sign of stopping executions. During a legislative hearing, he declared that the fourth round of executions would be carried out in the near future and it would still target drug offenders (Irmasari 2016). He issued similar statements in February (Movanita 2017), May (Purnama 2017), and June 2017 (Iskandar 2017). However, on each occasion, he did not give dates for the executions and commented that there was an ongoing 'review' of prisoners' legal status and available avenues. Prasetyo also complained about a Constitutional Court judgment, No. 107/PUU-XIII/2015, which dealt with a constitutional challenge to an article in the Clemency Law that restricts the use of a prisoner's right to clemency to within one year after the prisoner's final court decision (discussed in more detail below). The Constitutional Court decided to annul the article, removing the time limit to bring a clemency application, and Prasetyo claimed this has been used by death row prisoners to stall their executions.

On 31 January 2017, the Supreme Court commuted the death sentence of Yusman Telaumbanua to five years' imprisonment. Yusman, through his lawyer, a member of KontraS, a leading Indonesian human rights NGO, had submitted a PK petition to the Supreme Court on 23 June 2016. The basis of the PK was new evidence that Yusman was underage when a district court in Nias, North Sumatra, had sentenced him to death in 2013 (Tempo.co 2016). The PK petition was successful and the Supreme Court decided to commute the sentence (Nias Satu 2017), because under Indonesian law the death sentence cannot be imposed on a minor. There is also evidence that Yusman was tortured by police in the investigation stage and was allegedly innocent (KontraS 2015). KontraS issued a media briefing on this case, which was widely reported domestically. Yusman was released on 17 August 2017 after serving five years in prison.

On 3 May 2017, the UN Universal Periodic Review (UPR) of Indonesia was held. In that session, at least 28 of 107 UN member states made recommendations on the issue of the death penalty in Indonesia, with most urging that a moratorium be imposed. According to LBH Masyarakat's monitoring, this is over nine times more than the total of states who had made recommendations to Indonesia on the same issue in the previous cycle of the UPR.[30]

Another important event occurred on 28 July 2017, when the Ombudsman published its findings about alleged maladministration prior to, and during, the July 2016 executions, particularly as regards the execution of Humphrey Jefferson (Jeff). In August 2016, LBH Masyarakat submitted a complaint to the Ombudsman regarding his execution. LBH Masyarakat argued that Jeff's execution violated the Clemency Law and the Law on Procedures of

Execution (Wijaya 2016). The Ombudsman later found that violations of Jeff's rights had, indeed, occurred. The Ombudsman argued that the execution did not comply with regulations and the AGO and the Supreme Court had been negligent and discriminated against Jeff (Ompusunggu 2017).

After these three key events, the government, particularly the AGO, has rarely spoken about further executions. The last time Prasetyo spoke about another round of executions was in August 2017, when he said twelve people would be included in next round of executions (Poskota News 2017), but that remains the only statement he has made on executions since the Ombudsman's findings were released.

In September 2017, Indonesia made a final decision on recommendations it had received in the May 2017 UPR session. In the report of the Working Group on the UPR of Indonesia, it is understood that Indonesia accepts or supports at least three recommendations that encourage the state to consider imposing a moratorium of execution (UN General Assembly 2017, Add.1).

In February 2018, Prasetyo was asked by the DPR's Law Commission in a public hearing why the execution of drug convicts had not continued. Prasetyo replied that Indonesia was facing an urgent matter that needs priority. 'We want to become a non-permanent member of the UN Security Council', he added. Prasetyo explained that, because of this, the AGO had to postpone any plans for executions. Looking at his statement, it seems obvious that Indonesia is aware if they carry out executions that would create international headlines that would be damaging for its candidacy.

Together, these events may indicate that the Indonesian government is thinking about the imposition of a *de-facto* moratorium but does not intend to take concrete action in case there is a domestic political backlash against Jokowi's administration.

Although there have been no executions since 2017, Indonesia's drug war has simultaneously turned bloodier. There are more frequent reports of drug suspects being shot dead on the streets, with police claiming that drug trafficking suspects have resisted arrest. Rights activists (Kompas 2018) have observed that this phenomenon is influenced by President Rodrigo Duterte's policy in the Philippines and, indeed, Jokowi has encouraged police to use tougher approaches against drug traffickers, sometimes specifically referring to Duterte's approach. Between January and June 2017, police reported that twenty-seven drug traffickers were shot dead (Batubara 2017); in each case, the claim was that they had resisted arrest. Police also mentioned that this approach has effectively reduced the rate of drug trafficking, although there is no plausible evidence to support that claim. Amnesty International Indonesia has reported that from January to September 2017, as many as eighty drug trafficking suspects were shot dead. This is a striking increase compared to the rate of 'only' eighteen people in 2016 (Utama 2017). Amnesty claimed this increase had been influenced by Jokowi's statements, which seemed to encourage a severe approach (Belarminus 2017). In January 2017, twelve people were shot dead, an increase from two in December 2016. In December

2016 Jokowi had declared an even more massive war on drugs and asked a rhetorical question about how many drug offenders had died, compared to 'thousands' of Indonesia's young generation killed by drug use (Agung 2016). The same pattern occurred in August 2017, when another increase of shoot-to-kill incidents occurred after a statement by the president in July 2017 that law enforcers should shoot drug offenders if they offer even the slightest resistance, and show them no mercy (Kuwado 2017).

These are not the only times the President has publicly encouraged police and the National Narcotic Body (BNN) to shoot drug offenders. On 26 June 2016, on the commemoration of the International Day against Drug Abuse and Illicit Trafficking, Jokowi asked law enforcers to 'pursue, arrest, beat, slam, and shoot drug traffickers on sight' if the law allows it (Hermawan 2016). He stated that this was required because of the increasing rate of drug users in 2015 and because the drug mortality rate had reached thirty to forty people every day.

The president's message was re-issued by the heads of the National Narcotics Agency (BNN, Badan Narkoba Nasional) and the Police. The Head of the BNN, Budi Waseso, said his officers had been equipped with new firearms to carry out their duty and could do what the Philippines has done in their war on drugs (Rakhmatulloh 2016). The Head of National Police, Tito Karnavian, also instructed the police to shoot drug offenders, especially foreigners, to show that Indonesia is not weak in enforcing its laws (Gual 2017). There was even a specific suggestion from a member of the legislature, Nasir Djamil,[31] that Indonesia should follow the Philippines' extrajudicial killings in eradicating drug problems (Kompas 2016).

A public opinion survey on recent killings of drug offenders is yet to be carried out but there are no signs that Indonesian citizens object to this approach. Indonesian human rights groups, however, take the issue seriously and have raised it with the Ombudsman, which has warned the police and BNN (Sopia 2017).

The events of 2017 therefore showed a slightly positive trend but, simultaneously, worsening developments. The executions may have temporarily stopped but extrajudicial killings have led to an increased number of drug suspects being shot dead. While it is difficult to prove a direct link, it seems that the shift to extrajudicial killings is less risky politically for the government than conducting executions. A harsh law enforcement approach and noticeably tougher regime is preferable and more popular in the government's view.

At the international level, Indonesia's de-facto moratorium appears to feed into its stance on the UN General Assembly resolutions on a moratorium on the use of the death penalty. In December 2016 and December 2018, Indonesia abstained from voting for the two UN resolutions. This reflects Indonesia's hesitation on abolition. On the one hand, it indicates that the Indonesia government is not yet comfortable about moving beyond its unstated moratorium. This is not because respect for the right to life has become a matter of principle; rather it is a political decision contingent upon the government's domestic situation. On the other hand, Indonesia cannot easily retreat from moratorium, given abolition of the death penalty is a global trend, and Indonesia seems to want to follow this norm.

Legislation and court judgment developments

Indonesia is becoming increasingly dependent on criminal sanctions to maintain law and order (see Sudaryono, Chapter 8, this volume). Between 1998 and 2014, 716 new offences were introduced for which criminal sanctions that vary from fines and temporary imprisonment, to life imprisonment and death are available. Sixty-two per cent of the crimes are perceived as infringement-level offences, or misdemeanours, of lesser severity than the other 38 per cent (Akbari 2015).

This increase has brought with it the idea that criminal sanctions are the solution to crime. There is a growing idea that the harsher the sanction, the more effective it is to solve the problem. The demand to impose or introduce more severe sanctions, including capital punishment, for some criminal offences is usually accompanied by the narrative of an 'emergency' – for example, a drug emergency (Waskita 2015), a corruption emergency (Fajardin 2016), or a sexual violence emergency (BBC Indonesia 2016). The latter 'emergency', for example, influenced the issuing by Jokowi of Government Regulation in Lieu of Law No. 1 of 2016 on the Second Amendment of Law No. 23 of 2002 on Child Protection. This took place following pressure from public, which was concerned about intensive media reports of cases of sexual violence against children. The Regulation mentions the increasing incidence of sexual violence against children and that the prevailing law and sanctions had failed to prevent these crimes or create a deterrent effect.[32] It then introduces the death penalty into the Child Protection Law as the maximum sanction for sexual violence against children, along with additional sanctions, such as publication of the offender's identity, the fitting of electronic tracking devices to the offender, and even chemical castration.

However, there have also been some more encouraging developments. At least two key court decisions now benefit people in conflict with law, particularly those facing the death penalty. Both were made by the Constitutional Court. Under Law No. 24 of 2003 on the Constitutional Court, Indonesian citizens are entitled to file a constitutional challenge to laws deemed to violate, or potentially violate, their constitutional rights. The Constitutional Court is the judicial body that has the competence to decide whether provisions in a law contradict norms in the Indonesian constitution.[33]

The first key decision was made in 2014, when Antasari Azhar, a former commissioner of Indonesia's Anti-Corruption Commission (KPK), filed a constitutional challenge against art. 268(3) of the Criminal Procedure Code that limits the use of the PK. Previously, the Criminal Procedure Code had provided that a PK petition can only be filed once. Azhar, who at that time, had received a guilty verdict in a murder case, felt the limitation violated his right to justice, so asked the Court to annul the article. The Court, on 6 March 2014, granted his request.[34] As a result, PK petitions in criminal cases can now be submitted more than once (for more on the PK, see Lindsey, Chapter 6, this volume).

The logical implication of the Court decision is that all prisoners, including death row prisoners, are entitled to file a PK petition more than once if they wish. However, the Supreme Court made a contradictory move against the Constitutional Court decision. On 31 December 2014, it issued Supreme Court Circular Decision No. 7 of 2014 on Submission of Peninjauan Kembali Petitions in Criminal Cases. The Decision ignored the Constitutional Court judgment and emphasises that PK petitions may only be filed once, referring to provisions of the Supreme Court Law and Judicial Authority Law,[35] which also regulate limitations in filing a PK petition but which were not challenged by Azhar in his constitutional review petition. The Supreme Court argued that the Constitutional Court judgment could be used by drug offenders on death row to postpone their executions (Sahbani 2015) and hence would obstruct law enforcement. The Supreme Court therefore instructed courts under its jurisdiction to follow the provisions of the said laws.

This Supreme Court Decision has created problems for death row prisoners who have filed a second PK. Courts have shown inconsistencies in implementing the Supreme Court Decision: some have accepted second PK petitions, but others have rejected them. In Jeff's case, the Central Jakarta District Court refused to forward his second PK petition to the Supreme Court. The same court, however, received and forwarded a second PK petition from Eugene Ape, another death row inmate (Irmansyah 2017).

The second key decision made by the Constitutional Court was when it annulled the time limit for the filing of a clemency petition. Article 7(2) of the Clemency Law stated that a clemency petition can only be filed within a year of a final and binding court judgment.[36] On 15 June 2016, after a constitutional challenge by Suud Rusli, a death row prisoner convicted of murder, the Constitutional Court, in judgment No. 107/PUU-XIII/2015, declared the provision to be contrary to the Constitution and revoked it. Thus, death row prisoners can now submit a clemency petition at any time. This protects the rights of people facing the death penalty, because the Indonesian Law on Clemency already provides that a death row prisoner cannot be executed if he or she is in the process of submitting a clemency petition to the President.[37]

However, the AGO has disregarded this decision. When the July 2016 executions were carried out, some of the executed prisoners had submitted clemency petitions and the president was yet to make decisions on their petitions. Attorney General Prasetyo argued that the decision cannot be applied to death row prisoners who were convicted before the Constitutional Court decision was issued in June 2016. Human rights activists disagree with the Attorney General's interpretation (Fachrudin 2017a). Debate on this issue is still ongoing and the Attorney General was forced to request guidance from the Supreme Court (Fachrudin 2017b). It was reported that the Supreme Court had replied to the request with letter No. 7/WK.MAY/III/2017 dated 29 March 2017 (Taher 2017). In it, the Supreme Court states that it is of the opinion that scheduling an execution falls within the authority of the executer, in this case the AGO. The Supreme Court suggested the Attorney General first question the prisoner about his or her plan for the clemency process before determining the execution schedule. At the same time, the letter does not prohibit prisoners from submitting a clemency petition more than a year after a final and binding court judgment.

Another important development to note is that, as mentioned, the DPR is currently deliberating amendment of the Criminal Code. The draft of the revised Criminal Code still allows for capital punishment, but it is categorised as an 'alternative' punishment. The draft also provides for a ten-year probationary period for death row prisoners. If, over the ten years the prisoner has served since they were sentenced to death, he or she has shown good behaviour, the sentence may be commuted to life sentence or imprisonment by Presidential Decision. According to reports, this formulation was agreed by both the government and the legislature as a compromise to accommodate the views of both those who support the death penalty and those who oppose it (Hakim 2017). The draft Criminal Code does not show overt movement towards abolition of the death penalty in Indonesia but it should be seen as a slightly positive step to limit the imposition of the death penalty and reduce the number of executions.

In fact, legislative developments in recent years show some small steps towards protection of the rights of those facing the death penalty. At the very least, judicial institutions and the legislature have now become aware that reform in criminal justice is needed and that the rights of those accused of breaking laws, including those who are facing the death penalty, need protection. The abolitionist movement needs to maintain this momentum by continuing to advocate for reform in the criminal justice system and promoting safeguards for the protection of the rights of people facing the death penalty.[38] At the very least, this might lead to less use of the death penalty and fewer executions.

Conclusion

In the first three years of Jokowi's administration, frequent implementation of the death penalty was disturbing but there are now signs of some promising progress. First, the way executions are carried out in Indonesia and its use of the death penalty is highly politicised. The selection of death row prisoners to be executed is contingent upon political dynamics at the time. Under Yudhoyono's rule, terrorism was the most pressing law and order issue, so there was momentum for the execution of terrorists. During Jokowi's administration, drug problems emerged as the primary social issue to be addressed to ensure his political standing. It is therefore essential to understanding the complexity of political sensitivities surrounding law and order issues to assess the likelihood of the use of the death penalty under a given presidential administration. The fact that Indonesia's drug policy is not evidence-based, and that Jokowi's decision to undertake executions is not supported by credible evidence, strengthens the idea that the use of the death penalty and execution is primarily political.

Second, when Jokowi was running for president, he was seen as a 'down-to-earth' leader, close to the grassroots, who took advice from many people. This image changed after his administration carried out three rounds of executions within just eighteen months. The third batch of executions, in particular, was conducted in the face of much criticism. The fact that only four of the fourteen people on the list of executions were executed indicates that Jokowi probably did listen to criticism but it may have been politically difficult for him to cancel all the executions. Thus, four people were executed and ten remain in limbo. Never before has any post-Soeharto president carried out so many executions in such a short period of time. But also, never before has a president offered reprieves to so many death row prisoners, some just seconds away from the firing squad. The fact that there are death row prisoners whose executions are now postponed indefinitely suggest that Indonesia's regulations on the implementation of execution require further specificity.

Third, after couple of years of inward-looking governing, Jokowi seems to have realised that, as president, he needs to understand which issues are favourable for him internationally, and which are not. This helped him to grasp human rights debates in international diplomacy. As a country that boasts it is the fourth largest democratic country in the world, where Islam and democracy can go hand-in-hand, Indonesia must continue to maintain its positive image. Three batches of executions obviously tarnished the human rights façade Indonesia has been trying to build internationally. However, Jokowi seems to understand that domestically Indonesia is not ready to abolish the death penalty. If Indonesia made significant moves towards a moratorium or abolition at UN forums like the Human Rights Council's Universal Periodic Review (UPR), it could result in a domestic backlash. This perhaps explains why Indonesia wants to be seen in international community as hinting towards moratorium, without being explicit.

Fourth, precisely because the death penalty is a highly politicised subject, the current temporary 'moratorium' on executions in Indonesia is very vulnerable. It is dependent upon the domestic political situation. People who follow Indonesian politics may be aware that Jokowi has been busy addressing fundamental national issues, such as dealing with the rise of religious intolerance and its connection with the Ahok case (see Peterson, this volume). He has sought to maintain close relations with some Islamic groups, while trying to distance others, for example by disbanding Islamist group Hizbut Tahrir Indonesia as he worked towards the 2019 elections (La Batu 2017). However, it is hard to predict what will happen in the future now he has been re-elected to his second, and constitutionally final, term.

Some small progress has been made and further steps towards moratorium and abolition must be secured. This means that those who oppose the death penalty must be determined and work hard. In many countries, the abolition of the death penalty has been the result of strong leadership. This does not seem to be the formula in Indonesia – at least not in the near future. A realistic possible win for the abolition movement in Indonesia would be a *de facto* moratorium, with detailed safeguards to protect death row prisoners robustly enhanced, to limit and restrict the use of the death penalty and executions in the future.

Notes

1 For example, if the judgment says the suspect is sentenced to imprisonment, the prosecutor should transfer the suspect to a prison. See Criminal Procedure Code, art. 270.

2 Law No. 8 of 1981 on the Code of Criminal Procedure, art. 263(2). Apart from presenting new evidence, a PK application may also be made on the basis that a judgment clearly displays a judicial mistake or when in various judgments something is stated to have been proven but the matters which form the basis for this are mutually contradictory. For more detail, see Lindsey (Chapter 6, this volume).

3 Some provisions of this Law were revised by Law No. 5 of 2010 on Amendment of Law No. 22 of 2002 on Clemency.

4 Two remarks must be made here. First, Reprieve's database counts all persons facing the death penalty, including those whose trials are still ongoing. On the other hand, statistics provided by the Prison Department include only prisoners whose cases are final and binding or which have permanent legal force status. Second, the Prison Department made the data we rely on here available through a freedom of information request and it is not available on their website, which provides only general information about prison populations.

5 *Nawacita* is a Sanskrit word that literally translates as 'nine dreams/hopes'. It set out Jokowi and Jusuf Kalla's formal vision, mission and plan of action, if elected as President and Vice President of the Republic of Indonesia. The full document can be accessed at (http://kpu.go.id/koleksigambar/VISI_MISI_Jokowi-JK.pdf).

6 Details of achievement indicators of the *Nawacita* on human rights issues can be found at the following link: https://referensi.elsam.or.id/wp-content/uploads/2015/07/Policy-Brief-Kebijakan-HAM-1.pdf.

7 See for example, Praditya 2014; Rahman 2014.

8 Nahdlatul Ulama literally means 'Awakening of Ulama' (*ulama* are Muslim religious scholars). It is the largest Muslim non-government organisation in Indonesia.

9 Said Aqil Siraj, Chairman of Nahdlatul Ulama, said that 'those who do damage on this earth must be killed, crucified, and that is in accordance with the Constitution, art. 28'. See Republika 2014.

10 See for example, DetikNews 2014; Okezone 2014; Tempo.co 2014.

11 See for example, BBC Indonesia 2015a; Guardian 2015a; Tempo.co 2015a.

12 Rodrigo Gularte had suffered paranoid schizophrenia and bipolar disorder since he was ten years old. An Indonesian hospital verified that Rodrigo had mental

illness and required mental health treatment. Rodrigo's legal team (consisting of LBH Masyarakat and KontraS, among others) had filed a guardianship petition in Cilacap District Court on 22 April 2015, seven days before he was executed, and had been notified by the court regarding the first hearing. The legal team then informed the AGO and the Ministry of Law and Human Rights of this, asking for postponement. However, the government ignored this information and the request. The AGO instead conducted their own medical examination of Rodrigo. He was deemed mentally fine, although this second opinion medical report was never disclosed to Rodrigo's family, the Brazilian Embassy, or the legal team. In the end, Rodrigo was executed without being aware of his situation. See Safi 2015.

13 Just few hours before execution was carried out, a woman in the Philippines surrendered herself to the police claiming that she had recruited Veloso to traffic the drugs. The allegation that Veloso was a victim of human trafficking and her testimony would be needed for investigation is one of the reasons Benigno Aquino III's plea was accepted by Jokowi. See Holmes 2015.

14 See, for example, Tempo.co 2015b; and Lee 2015.

15 See, for example, BBC Indonesia 2015d; and BBC 2015a.

16 See, for example, Al Jazeera 2015a; The Guardian 2015b; UN News 2015.

17 See, for example, Al Jazeera 2015b; Bachelard 2015; BBC 2015b; Cochrane 2015; Dixon 2015; Kapoor 2015; Phipps 2015; Ritzen 2015; Topsfield 2015.

18 Also known as 'Jeff', Jefferson was a client of LBH Masyarakat since 2008. Jeff's case was fabricated and he was tortured to confess a crime he did not commit. A brief summary in English of his case can be found at the following link: https://adpandotnet.files.wordpress.com/2013/09/adpan-appeal-case-indonesia-humphrey-eleweke-final.pdf.

19 See, for example, Iradat 2017.

20 See Sahetapy 1979; Saleh 1978: 22.

21 Merri Utami was convicted in Tangerang District Court, so she was under authority of Tangerang District Prosecutor.

22 Jeff was convicted in Central Jakarta District Court, so he was under the authority of Central Jakarta District Court.

23 Presidential Decision No. 2 of 1964 on Procedures for Execution of the Death Sentence in the Criminal Court and the Military Court, art. 6(1).

24 This was a reference to the three Christian prisoners among the four who were executed.

25 See, for example, Amnesty International 2016; Lamb 2016; Ramadhani and Aritonang 2016; Topsfield, Rosa and Rompies 2016.

26 See, for example, BBC 2016; Cochrane 2016; Lamb and Phipps 2016; Quiano 2016.

27 Hawley 2016. See also The Guardian 2016.

28 In 2013, the Death Penalty Project in association with the Malaysian Bar Council, under the supervision of Prof. Roger Hood of the Centre for Criminology University of Oxford, conducted a public opinion survey on the death penalty in Malaysia. The full report can be downloaded here: http://portfolio.cpl.co.uk/DPP/Malaysia-report/2/ See also Koshy 2013.

29 Similarly, in 2015, the Death Penalty Project in collaboration with Mai Sato and Paul Bacon, conducted a public opinion survey on the death penalty in Japan. The full report is available here: www.deathpenaltyproject.org/news/2193/the-public-opinion-myth-why-japan-retains-the-death-penalty/. See also Hirano 2015.

30 In the previous cycle of UPR of Indonesia, only three states made recommendations on the issue of the death penalty. See, for example, LBH Masyarakat 2017; UN General Assembly 2012, 2017.

31 Nasir Djamil was a representative of PKS (Partai Keadilan Sejahtera, the Prosperous Justice Party), an Islamic party.

32 Government Regulation in Lieu of Law No. 1 of 2016 on Second Amendment of Law No. 23 of 2002 on Child Protection, General Elucidation (explanatory memorandum), paragraph 4.

33 See art. 24C(1) of the 1945 Constitution of the Republic of Indonesia; art. 10(1) of Law No. 24 of 2003 on the Constitutional Court; art. 29(1)(a) of Law No. 48 of 2009 on Judicial Authority; and art. 9(1) of Law No. 12 of 2011 on the Making of Laws and Regulations.

34 Constitutional Court Decision No. 34/PUU-XI/2013, dated 6 March 2014, p. 89.

35 Article 24(2) of Law No. 48 of 2009 on Judicial Power provides that 'Against a case review decision, another case review petition cannot be submitted'. In addition, art. 66(1) of Law No. 14 of 1985 on the Supreme Court says that 'A case review petition can only be submitted once'. Both articles became a justification for the Supreme Court to maintain the prohibition on more than one PK petition.

36 A final and binding status of a court judgment is achieved when a defendant does not file an appeal against a decision made by a district court or high court, or when the Supreme Court has made a decision in his or her case. See Law No. 22 of 2002 on Clemency, Elucidation to art. 2(1).

37 Law No. 22 of 2002, art. 13.

38 See Gunawan, Pamintori and Bajammal (2019), for further discussion of strengthening safeguard mechanisms for persons facing the death penalty in Indonesia.

References

Agung, D. H. 2016. 'Presiden: Kita Nyatakan Perang Besar pada Narkoba', *Tirto*, 6 December https://tirto.id

Akbari, Anugerah Rizki 2015. *Potret Kriminalisasi Pasca Reformasi dan Urgensi Reklasifikasi Tindak Pidana di Indonesia*. Jakarta: Institute for Criminal Justice Reform

Al Jazeera 2015a. 'UN Chief Asks Indonesia Not to Execute Drug Convicts', *Aljazeera*, 26 April www.aljazeera.com

Al Jazeera 2015b. 'Indonesia Executes Drug Smugglers by Firing Squad', *Aljazeera*, 29 April www.aljazeera.com

Amnesty International 2015. *Flawed Justice Unfair Trials and the Death Penalty in Indonesia*. United Kingdom: Amnesty International, International Secretariat

Amnesty International 2016. 'Indonesia: Jokowi Should Not Become the Most Prolific Executioner in Recent History', 28 July www.amnesty.org/

Bachelard, Michael 2015. 'Chan and Sukumaran Execution "Illegal", but Indonesia Ignores Australia Again', *Sydney Morning Herald*, 2 May www.smh.com.au

Batubara, Puteranegara 2017. 'Sepanjang Tahun 2017, 27 Pengedar Narkotika Ditembak Mati Polisi', *Okezone*, 14 June https://news.okezone.com

BBC 2015a. 'Indonesia Executions: Joko Widodo Stands Firm', 28 April www.bbc.com

BBC 2015b. 'Indonesia Executes Eight Prisoners for Drug Offences', 29 April www.bbc.com

BBC 2016. 'Indonesia to Execute 14 Drug Convicts Despite Protests', 27 July www.bbc.com

BBC Indonesia 2015a. 'Pegiat HAM Kecam Eksekusi Hukuman Mati Narkoba', 16 January www.bbc.com/indonesia

BBC Indonesia 2015b. 'Pasca Eksekusi Mati, Brasil Tarik Duta Besar di Jakarta', 18 January www.bbc.com/indonesia

BBC Indonesia 2015c. 'Eksekusi akan "Ganggu Kredibilitas" Indonesia', 27 April www.bbc.com/indonesia/

BBC Indonesia 2015d. 'Terus Disampaikan Seruan Pembatalan Eksekusi', 28 April www.bbc.com/indonesia

BBC Indonesia 2016. '"Murka" dan Tuntutan Hukuman Mati untuk Pemerkosa Yuyun', 4 May www.bbc.com/indonesia

Belarminus, Robertus 2017. 'Amnesty Duga Ada Korelasi Pernyataan Jokowi dengan Naiknya Kasus Tembak Mati Pengedar Narkoba', *Kompas*, 19 September http://nasional.kompas.com

Butt, Simon and Lindsey, Tim 2018. *Indonesian Law*. Oxford: Oxford University Press.

Cochrane, Joe 2015. 'Despite Protests, Indonesia Moves Forward to Execute Drug Convicts', *New York Times*, 25 April www.nytimes.com

Cochrane, Joe 2016. 'Indonesia Executes 4 Prisoners Convicted of Drug Crimes', *New York Times*, 28 July www.nytimes.com

Daily Mail 2016. 'Indonesian Executions a "Complete Mess": Lawyer', 29 July www.dailymail.co.uk

Daily Mail 2017. 'Indonesia's President Says Open to Death Penalty Review', 28 March www.dailymail.co.uk

DetikNews 2014. 'Indonesia Darurat Narkoba: Soal Eksekusi Mati, Rakyat Indonesia Akhirnya Di-PHP-in Jaksa Agung', 31 December https://news.detik.com

Dixon, Robyn 2015. 'Indonesia Set to Execute Prisoners Convicted of Drug Crimes', *LA Times*, 27 April http://beta.latimes.com

Fachrudin, Fachri 2017a. 'LBH Masyarakat Minta Pemerintah Hentikan Persiapan Eksekusi Mati', *Kompas*, 23 February http://nasional.kompas.com

Fachrudin, Fachri. 2017b. 'Jaksa Agung Minta MA dan MK Terbitkan Fatwa Terkait Pengajuan Grasi', *Kompas*, 18 August http://nasional.kompas.com

Fajardin, Mohammad Atik 2016. 'Hukuman Mati Koruptor, KPK Minta Dukungan Jaksa dan Hakim', *Sindonews*, 22 August https://nasional.sindonews.com

Gual, Marselinus 2017. 'Kapolri Perintahkan Tembak Mati Bandar Narkoba Asing', *CNN*, 20 July www.cnnindonesia.com

The Guardian 2015a. 'Six Drug Convicts Executed in Indonesia, Including Five Foreigners', 18 January www.theguardian.com

The Guardian 2015b. 'Ban Ki-Moon Makes Pleas to Indonesia over Executions', 14 February www.theguardian.com

The Guardian 2016. 'Indonesia's President Joko Widodo Hints at Abolishing Death Penalty', 5 November www.theguardian.com

Gunawan, Ricky and Pamintori, Raynov T. 2017. 'New Hope for Abolition of the Death Penalty', *Indonesia at Melbourne*, 2 May http://indonesiaatmelbourne.unimelb.edu.au

Gunawan, Ricky; Pamintori, Raynov T.; and Bajammal, Ma'ruf 2019. *Memperkuat Perlindungan Hak Orang Berhadapan dengan Hukuman Mati/Eksekusi*. Jakarta: LBH

Masyarakat, March https://lbhmasyarakat.org/laporan-kebijakan-memperkuat-perlindungan-hak-orang-berhadapan-dengan-hukuman-mati-eksekusi/
Hakim, Rakhmat Nur 2017. 'DPR dan Pemerintah Sepakat Hukuman Mati Tetap Diberlakukan', *Kompas,* 10 October http://nasional.kompas.com
Hawley, Samantha 2016. 'Joko Widodo: Indonesian President on Trust and Abolishing the Death Penalty Ahead of Australia Visit', *Australian Broadcasting Commission News*, 5 November www.abc.net.au
Hermawan, Fajar W. 2016. 'Presiden Jokowi Ingin Pengedar Narkoba Ditembak di Tempat', *Beritagar*, 27 June https://beritagar.id
Hirano, Keiji 2015. 'Public Support for Death Penalty Not Overwhelming, Researchers Say', *Japan Times*, 16 September www.japantimes.co.jp
Holmes, Oliver 2015. 'Mary Jane Veloso: What Happened to the Woman Who Escaped Execution in Indonesia?', *The Guardian*, 28 April www.theguardian.com
Indonesia. Sekretariat Kabinet 2014a. 'Sudah Darurat, Presiden Jokowi Tegaskan Tidak Ada Pengampunan untuk Kasus Narkoba', 18 December http://setkab.go.id
Indonesia. Sekretariat Kabinet 2014b. 'Dikunjungi Presiden Jokowi, NU dan Muhammadiyah Dukung Hukuman Mati Bagi Pengedar Narkoba', 24 December http://setkab.go.id
Iradat, Damar 2017. 'BNN: Narkotika Senjata Proxy War', *Metrotvnews*, 13 July http://news.metrotvnews.com
Irmansyah, Ade 2017. 'Ombudsman RI Pastikan Terjadi Maladministrasi dalam Eksekusi Mati Humphrey Ejike', 28 July http://kbr.id
Irmasari, Dewi 2016. 'Eksekusi Mati Gelombang IV, Jaksa Agung: Mayoritas Kasus Narkoba', *Detik*.com, 6 December https://news.detik.com
Irwanto; Wirawan, Dewa N.; Praptoraharjo, Ignatius; Irianto, Sulistyowati; Mulia, Siti Musdah; et al. 2015. 'Evidence-Informed Response to Illicit Drugs in Indonesia', *The Lancet* 385(9984): 2249–50, 6 June www.thelancet.com
Iskandar, Rezki Apriliya 2017. 'Jaksa Agung Kantongi Nama Terpidana Yang Dieksekusi Mati Jilid IV', *Liputan6*, 5 June http://news.liputan6.com
Kapoor, Kanupriya 2015. 'Indonesia Executed Drug Convicts, Sparks Anger from Australia, Brazil', *Reuters*, 28 April www.reuters.com
Kompas 2015 'Eksekusi Mati Bukan Jawaban untuk Menekan Angka Kejahatan Narkotika', 17 January http://nasional.kompas.com
Kompas 2016. 'Politisi PKS Ingin Pemerintah Indonesia Tiru Cara Filipina Berantas Narkoba', 8 September http://nasional.kompas.com
Kompas 2018. 'Banyak Tembak Mati Pengedar Narkoba, Indonesia Dinilai Mulai Ikuti Langkah Duterte', 5 March https://nasional.kompas.com/read/2018/03/05/19565001/banyak-tembak-mati-pengedar-narkoba-indonesia-dinilai-mulai-ikuti-langkah
KontraS 2015. 'Rekayasa Kasus Berujung pada Vonis Hukuman Mati Terhadap Yusman Telaumbanua dan Rasula Hia', 16 March www.kontras.org
Koshy, Shaila 2013. 'Malaysians Believe in Death Penalty, but Not Willing to Mete It Out, Survey Shows', *The Star*, 1 December www.thestar.com.my
Kuwado, Fabian Januarius 2017. 'Jokowi: Saya Sudah Katakan, Tembak di Tempat Saja…', *Kompas*, 21 July http://nasional.kompas.com
Kwok, Yenni 2015. 'Indonesia's Jokowi Marks 100 Days of Presidency with Scandal, Falling Support', *Time*, 28 January http://time.com
La Batu, Safrin 2017. 'Jokowi Signs Regulation Banning Hizbut Tahrir', *The Jakarta Post*, 11 July www.thejakartapost.com

Lamb, Kate 2016. 'Indonesia Ready to Execute 14 This Week Despite Doubts over Prisoners' Guilt', *The Guardian*, 27 July www.theguardian.com

Lamb, Kate and Phipps, Claire 2016. 'Indonesia Executions: 14 People Who Could Face the Firing Squad This Week', *The Guardian*, 27 July www.theguardian.com

LBH Masyarakat 2017. 'Evaluasi Situasi HAM Indonesia di Universal Periodic Review (UPR) Yang Ke-3: 28 Negara Merekomendasikan Moratorium Hukuman Mati', 4 May http://lbhmasyarakat.org

Lee, John 2015. 'Indonesia Executions: Why Australian Anger Will Outlive Political Fallout', *CNN*, 29 April http://edition.cnn.com

Movanita, Ambaranie Nadia Kemala 2017. 'Kejagung Tengah Persiapkan Eksekusi Mati Jilid IV', *Kompas*, 22 February http://nasional.kompas.com

Nias Satu 2017. 'PK Dikabulkan, Mahkamah Agung Batalkan Vonis Mati atas Yusman Telaumbanua', 25 February http://niassatu.com

Okezone 2014. 'Kejagung Dikabarkan Batal Eksekusi Mati Gembong Narkoba', 24 December https://news.okezone.com

Ompusunggu, Moses 2017. 'Indonesian State 'Negligent' in Execution of Nigerian', *The Jakarta Post*, 28 July www.thejakartapost.com

Phipps, Claire 2015. 'Who Were the Eight People Executed by Indonesia', *The Guardian*, 28 April www.theguardian.com

Poskota News 2017. 'Kejaksaan Agung Agendakan Eksekusi Mati 12 Napi', 26 August http://poskotanews.com

Praditya, Ilyas Istianur 2014. 'Jokowi Tegaskan Indonesia Darurat Narkoba', *Liputan6.com*, 18 December http://news.liputan6.com

Purnama, Dara 2017. 'Kejagung Siapkan Nama-Nama Terpidana Yang Akan Dieksekusi Mati Pada Gelombang IV', *Okezone*.com, 19 May https://news.okezone.com

Quiano, Kathy 2016. 'Indonesia Executed Four Convicted Drug Offenders', *CNN*, 29 July http://edition.cnn.com

Rahman, Muhammad Razi 2014. 'Presiden Jokowi: Indonesia Sudah Darurat Narkoba', *Antara News*, 9 December www.antaranews.com

Rakhmatulloh 2016. 'Buwas Akan Tembak di Tempat Bandar Narkoba', *Sindonews*, 6 December https://nasional.sindonews.com

Ramadhani, Nurul Fitri and Aritonang, Margarteh S. 2016. 'Injustice Victims May Be Executed', *The Jakarta Post*, 27 July www.thejakartapost.com

Republika 2014. 'NU dan Muhammadiyah Dukung Eksekusi Mati', *Republika*, 29 December www.republika.co.id

Ritzen, Yarno 2015. 'The Death Penalty: A Wave of Execution in Indonesia', *Aljezeera*, 28 April www.aljazeera.com

Safi, Michael 2015. ' "Am I Being Executed?" Brazilian Killed by Indonesia Unaware until End, Says Priest', 30 April www.theguardian.com

Sahbani, Agus 2015. 'MA Kukuhkan PK Hanya Sekali', *Hukumonline*, 2 January www.hukumonline.com

Sahetapy, J. E. 1979. *Ancaman Pidana Mati Terhadap Pembunuhan Berencana.* Bandung: Alumni

Saleh, Roeslan 1978. *Masalah Pidana Mati,* 2nd edn. Jakarta: Aksara Baru.

Sopia, Santi 2017. 'Ombudsman Ingatkan Polri Soal Tembak Mati Terduga Narkotika', *Republika*, 19 September http://nasional.republika.co.id

Stoicescu, Claudia 2015. 'Indonesia Uses Faulty Stats on 'Drug Crisis' to Justify Death Penalty', *The Conversation*, 5 February https://theconversation.com

Taher, Andrian Pratama 2017. 'MA Sudah Beri Fatwa Soal Batasan Waktu Grasi Terpidana Mati', *Tirto.id*, 31 August https://tirto.id/ma-sudah-beri-fatwa-soal-batasan-waktu-grasi-terpidana-mati-cvHm

Tempo.co 2014. 'Eksekusi Mati Bandar Narkoba Ditunda', 24 December https://nasional.tempo.co

Tempo.co 2015a. 'Dunia Desak RI Batalkan Hukuman Mati', 17 January https://nasional.tempo.co

Tempo.co 2015b. 'Australia Asks Jokowi to Cancel Execution', 19 January https://en.tempo.co

Tempo.co 2016. 'Kontras Ajukan PK Kasus Terpidana Mati Yusman', 23 July https://nasional.tempo.co

Topsfield, Jewel 2015. 'Bali 9 Executions: Andrew Chan and Myuran Sukumaran Shot Dead in Indonesia', *Sydney Morning Herald*, 29 April www.smh.com.au

Topsfield, Jewel; Rosa, Amilia; and Rompies, Karuni 2016. '"They Electrocuted Me" Says Indonesia's Death Row Prisoners Nearing Execution', *Sydney Morning Herald*, 24 April www.smh.com.au

UN General Assembly 2012. 'Report of the Working Group on the Universal Periodic Review: Indonesia', 5 July, A/HRC/21/7

UN General Assembly 2017. 'Report of the Working Group on the Universal Periodic Review: Indonesia', 14 July, A/HRC/36/7

UN News 2015. UN Chief Expresses '"Deep Regret" about Execution of Eight People in Indonesia', 29 April www.un.org/

Utama, Abraham 2017. 'Tembak di Tempat Kasus Narkoba "Meningkat Empat Kali Lipat" pada 2017', *BBC Indonesia*, 20 September www.bbc.com

Utrecht, E. 1994. *Rangkaian Sari Kuliah Hukum Pidana I*. Surabaya: Pustaka Tinta Mas

Waluyo, Andylala 2016. 'Pemerintah Eksekusi 4 Terpidana Kasus Narkoba', *VOA Indonesia*, 29 July www.voaindonesia.com

Waskita, Ferdinand 2015. 'Indonesia Darurat Narkoba, Ketua MPR Dukung Hukuman Mati', *Tribun News*, 28 April www.tribunnews.com

Widhiarto, Hasyim and Perdana, Yuliasri 2014. 'Jokowi's AG Choice Slammed', *The Jakarta Post*, 21 November www.thejakartapost.com/news/2014/11/21/jokowi-s-ag-choice-slammed.html

Wijaya, Randyka 2016. 'Dugaan Maladministrasi Eksekusi Mati, Jaksa Agung Dilaporkan ke Ombudsman', *KBR.id*, 8 August

Zakaria, Idhad 2014. 'Menkum HAM: Nusakambangan Siap Jadi Lokasi Eksekusi Eati', *Liputan6*, 12 December http://news.liputan6.com

Legislation

Criminal Code (*Kitab Undang-Undang Hukum Pidana*, KUHP: Law No. 1 of 1946 as amended by Law No. 27 of 1999 on the Indonesian Criminal Code)

Criminal Procedure Code of 1981 (Kitab Undang-undang Hukum Acara Pidana, KUHAP)

Emergency Law No. 12 of 1951 on Firearms

Law No. 4 of 1976 on the Amendment and Addition of Several Articles under the Criminal Code, which Relate to the Expansion of Enforceability of Provisions on Crimes against Aviation and Aviation Facilities

Law No. 5 of 1997 on Psychotropic drugs

Law No. 31 of 1999 in conjunction with Law No. 20 of 2001 on Eradication of Corruption
Law No. 26 of 2000 on Human Rights Court
Law No. 22 of 2002 on Clemency
Law No. 35 of 2009 on Narcotics
Presidential Decision No. 5 of 1959 on the Authority of Attorney General/Military Attorney General with regards to Increasing Sentences against Crimes that Jeopardise the Implementation of Food and Clothing Provision
Presidential Decision No. 2 of 1964 on Procedures of Execution of Death Sentence in Criminal Court and Military Court
Government Regulation in Lieu of Law No. 21 of 1959 on the Aggravation of Sentence against Economic-related Crimes
Government Regulation in Lieu of Law No. 1 of 2002 on Eradication of Terrorism
Government Regulation in Lieu of Law No. 1 of 2016 on Second Amendment of Law No. 23 of 2002 on Child Protection
Government Regulation in Lieu of Law No. 1 of 2016 on Second Amendment of Law No. 23 of 2002 on Child Protection, General Elucidation

Court decision

Constitutional Court Decision No. 34/PUU-XI/2013, dated 6 March 2014, p. 89

Part IV

Crime and the environment

12 Corporate environmental criminal liability in Indonesia

Mas Achmad Santosa and Stephanie Juwana

Indonesia is one of the most resource-rich countries in the world. It is blessed with over 120 million hectares of forest, around 6.4 million square kilometres of ocean, and numerous mining areas. Indonesia's forests are among the most extensive and valuable in the world. Its production forests alone cover an area of 68.8 million hectares (Ministry of Environment and Forestry of the Republic of Indonesia 2018: 113). No less valuable, Indonesian waters are inhabited by an abundance of the most commercially-valued fishes. The Ministry of Marine Affairs and Fisheries in 2017 reported fish resources potential of 12.5 million tons per year. In terms of mining, Indonesia is rich in mineral resources, including coal, copper, gold, nickel and tin. In fact, Indonesia is ranked among the world's top ten countries for the production of gold and natural gas.

This naturally attracts major companies investing in the forestry, fisheries and mining sectors to Indonesia. However, while they have contributed to national economic growth and national development, major companies have also committed numerous crimes. As Soedjono Dirdjosisworo (Dirdjosisworo 1991: 1) says:

> economic growth leads to new forms of crimes that are not less dangerous and also cause significant loss. Indonesia today faces challenges from contemporary crimes that threaten the environment [and] energy sources.

This chapter has six parts. The first provides an explanation of the goals that corporate criminal liability serves. The next two parts provide an overview of the historical development of corporate criminal liability in Indonesia and how Indonesian laws regulate this concept. The fourth part presents four environmental cases in which corporations were tried and punished. The third and fourth parts also explore different conceptions of corporate criminal liability and how law enforcement does not have a shared common understanding of what constitutes corporate crime, differences that drive discrepancies in the application of corporate criminal liability. The fifth part provides an analysis of problems with corporate criminal liability regulation and implementation in Indonesia. Overall, this chapter concludes that, although Indonesian law has tried to conceptualise corporate criminal liability, the application of corporate criminal liability has not yet developed as it should.

Why corporate criminal liability is important

The traditional view of criminal law, which focuses on individual liability, is inadequate to counter corporate crime. As mentioned, many of the most economically and socially dangerous crimes in Indonesia originate from corporate business activities and so stricter control of corporate activities is needed, along with harsher punishments.

There are at least three goals of corporate criminal liability: retribution, deterrence and rehabilitation (Maglie 2005: 563). According to the first goal, punishment should reflect the seriousness and the severity of the moral violation. It should be proportional to the crime committed (Brodowski 2014: 35). Corporate wealth, which is commonly much greater than that of individuals, enables corporations to pay greater fines. Corporate offences are normally extreme and considered widely damaging crimes; they are therefore better compensated for by the corporation than by an individual. Just punishment for corporate crime also helps encourage public confidence in, and respect for, the law.

The second goal of punishment is deterrence, that is, that punishment is needed in order to deter corporations from committing future violations. Deterrence plays an important role in corporate crime cases. Corporations are naturally formed for the goal of seeking maximum profit. Therefore, corporations are more likely to commit an offence when the profits from an offence exceed the cost of punishment.

Third, corporate criminal liability also allows criminal punishment to meet the goal of rehabilitation. This goal aims to change the personal values and behaviour of persons convicted of crime. In the context of a corporate criminal liability, criminal sanctions aim to create changes to the corporation to prevent future offences. Imposing sanctions on a corporation can correct the corporate culture of the organisation. This can result in complete reform of a corporation's practices (Maglie 2005: 564).

The justifications for imposing criminal punishment on individuals can also apply to the punishment of corporations. According to Wells, there are six requirements of imposing criminal punishment (Wells 2001: 18):

1. There is a body of rules capable of guiding action (primary rules)
2. There are beings (persons) capable of following these rules or not as they choose, capable of choosing on the basis of reasons, and capable of treating the prospect of suffering specified evils as a reason against doing an act (to be weighed with other reasons for and against),
3. There is a procedure (authority) for inflicting types of evil (penalties) upon a person if he or she does not follow the rules,

4. There are (secondary) rules connecting failure to follow primary rules (crimes or offences) with certain penalties,
5. Both the primary and secondary rules are supposed to be known to the persons subject to them (in general, at least), and
6. Imposition of the penalty is (in general, at least) justified by the person's not having followed the appropriate rule when he could have.

There is one other justification for corporate criminal liability, which derives from social and political perspectives: society's perception that corporations deserve to be criminally punished allows corporations to be the subject of criminal punishments within the laws (Maradona 2018: 26).

The historical development of the recognition of corporate criminal liability in Indonesia

The Indonesian Criminal Code is a legacy of the colonial Dutch Penal Code (*Wetboek van Strafrecht*), which did not recognise the concept of corporate criminal liability. It came into force in 1918. The Indonesian Constitution of 1945 contains a transitional provision that states that all laws in existence shall remain applicable unless replaced by new laws. This applied to the Dutch Criminal Code. Law No 1 of 1946 made several limited adjustments to this Code to suit the conditions in Indonesia after Independence. However, no fundamental changes have ever been made regarding corporate criminal liability. Prosecutions under the Criminal Code focused primarily on individual actors and legal persons were excluded as a subject of criminal law. This understanding was influenced by the classical thinking of German scholars.[1]

In 1951, Dutch legislators introduced the liability of corporations for economic crimes in the Economic Offences Law, leading to the amendment of art. 51 of the Dutch Criminal Code, which now stipulates the following:

1. Offences can be committed by natural persons and legal persons.
2. If an offence has been committed by a legal person, prosecution can be instituted and the punishments and measures provided by law can be imposed, if applicable, on:
   a. the legal person, or
   b. those who have ordered the offence, as well as on those who have actually controlled the forbidden act, or
   c. the persons mentioned under (a) and (b) together.
3. For the application of the former subsections, equal status as a legal person applies to a company without legal personality, a partnership, a firm of ship owners, and a separate capital sum assembled for a special purpose.

This amendment was a significant change of position. Previously, the Dutch Penal Code had stated that no punishment could be imposed on the director of a corporation who evidently took no part in the commission of an offence.

Despite the Dutch Criminal Code amendment, the Indonesian Criminal Code remains unchanged. Recognition of corporate criminal liability in Indonesia does now exist but only in various specific-purpose criminal laws outside the Indonesian Criminal Code, despite the fact that the Code is supposed to serve as the basic source of substantive criminal law.

Being aware that corporations can be used as vehicles for criminal activities, Indonesia first recognised the concept of corporate criminal liability in 1951 through Emergency Law No. 17 of 1951 on Stockpiling. After Independence, Indonesia faced numerous challenges, including stockpiling. The imposition of corporate criminal liability was quite revolutionary at that time. It recognised the attribution of liability to the corporation itself and to persons acting on behalf of the corporation, and it enabled both liabilities at the same time. Article 11 stipulates:

1. If an offence punishable according to this law is done by a legal entity, the prosecution and punishment shall be imposed to such legal entity or persons considered in paragraph 2 below, or both.
2. An offence punishable according to this law is considered done by a legal entity if it is committed by one or more persons acting individually or collectively on behalf of such legal entity.

Unfortunately, this newly-introduced concept was not easily implemented by the law enforcers at that time, as the Emergency Law failed to provide further guidance on how to establish the criminal liability of corporations.

Law No. 7 of 1955 on Economic Crimes was the next law to recognise the concept of corporate criminal liability. The attribution of liability is similar to art. 11(1) of the Stockpiling Law but a longer explanation was provided on how to determine when an offence is committed by a corporation. Article 15(2) provides that an economic offence could be deemed an act of the corporation if the offence was committed by a natural person who acted within the scope of the corporation, based on employment or other relationships, regardless of whether the offence was committed individually or collectively.

These two Laws marked the initial stage of the development of corporate criminal liability in Indonesia but it soon became a common arrangement. It was followed, for example, by the Law on Subversion (1963);[2] the Law on Narcotics (1976);[3] the Law on the Post (1984);[4] the Law on Industry (1984);[5] the Law on Psychotropics (1997);[6] the Law on Environment Protection and Management (1997);[7] the Law on the Prohibition on Monopolistic Practices (1999);[8] the Law on Consumer Protection (1999);[9] the Law on the Eradication of Corruption (1999);[10] the Law on the Prevention and Eradication of Money Laundering (2002);[11] and the Law on Fisheries (2004).[12] In fact, by 2017, more than 120 Laws had recognised the corporation as a criminal law subject (Priyatno 2017: 29). However, there are significant conceptual dissimilarities between these laws. This is a consequence of the different understandings endorsed by law-makers regarding the concept of a corporation as a perpetrator and liability for its conduct, which will be discussed further below.

Law No. 8 of 1981 on the Criminal Procedural Code, replaced the prevailing law on criminal procedure during colonial period, the *Herziene Inlandsch Reglement* (HIR). Like the Indonesian Criminal Code, the Indonesian Criminal Procedural Code also does not recognise corporations as legal subjects. To provide practical guidance for procedure in prosecuting corporations, the Attorney General of Indonesia issued Regulation PER-028/A/JA/1-/2014 on Guidance for the Handling of Criminal Cases with Corporations as the Legal Subject in October 2014. Two years later, the Supreme Court also made a significant move by issuing Supreme Court Regulation No. 13 of 2016 on Guidance for the Handling of Crimes Committed by Corporations.

How Indonesian laws regulate corporate criminal liability

Corporation as a legal subject

For decades, prosecutions in Indonesia tended to focus on individual liability for all wrongdoings, even where wrongdoing was done to advance the interests of a corporation. The Indonesian Criminal Code confines criminal liability to 'persons', which was traditionally interpreted as encompassing only natural persons, and this perception dominates practice.[13]

However, as just explained, a number of regulations have been introduced since 1951 that expressly identify the corporation as a legal subject of criminal law. For example, Law No. 31 of 1999 specifically defined the term 'persons' as not just compassing natural persons but also corporations as legal persons. Another example is Law No. 32 of 2009, which defined 'persons' as individuals and corporations, whether incorporated or not. Law No. 31 of 1999, Law No. 8 of 2010, Supreme Court Regulation 13 of 2016, and the Attorney General's Regulation, mentioned above, all offered a similar definition: 'A corporation is an organised collection of people and/or wealth, both legal and non-legal entities'. Based on this, the term 'corporation' now applies to any type of corporation and both legal and non-legal entities, including limited liability partnerships Commanditaire Vennootschap (CV) firms and partnerships.

Moreover, the Supreme Court Regulation has the effect that criminal liability is not limited to a single corporation but can also be applied to a group of corporations. It also governs the liability of a corporation after a restructuring, merger, consolidation, spin-off or liquidation, as Table 12.1 explains.

Corporate crime

Supreme Court Regulation No. 13 of 2016 defines 'corporate crime' as an act committed by one or more persons based on a relationship of employment or other relationship, where such act is committed on behalf of the corporation, whether within the corporation of outside it.[14] The 'persons' referred in the

Table 12.1 Supreme Court Regulation 13 of 2016

Matter/condition	*How Supreme Court Regulation regulates the matter*
In relation to parent and subsidiary company	In a situation where a parent and/or subsidiary company is involved in a crime, each corporation is held liable separately depending on its share of involvement in such crime.[1]
When restructuring happens after the crime	Restructuring will not free a corporation from its liability; the liability will be borne by the successor or surviving corporation.
When merger or acquisition happens after the crime	The liability is limited to the value of assets that are placed in the new corporation.
When separation/spin-off of the corporation happens after the crime	The liability is imposed on each separated company depending on its share of involvement in the crime.
When the corporation is in liquidation	The liability still lies with the corporation. Thus, initiating liquidation does not free a corporation from its criminal liability. Criminal liability is only lifted if the corporation has been effectively dissolved. However, this does not stop the state from going after the liquidated assets. Assets which are alleged to have been used to conduct a crime or are the result of a crime can be recovered. The claim for these assets is filed against the former management, heirs, or third parties who control the assets of the liquidated corporation.[2]
When the corporation is closed after the crime	There are two possibilities: 1. When the investigation/prosecution is conducted during the winding up process, the investigators/prosecutors can ask the court to delay the closing process so that the corporation can still be processed for criminal proceedings. 2. However, a corporation that has been closed is immune from criminal proceedings. There are other channels to pursue the liability of corporation, such as a civil lawsuit against directors.

1 Article 16 of Supreme Court Regulation No. 13 of 2016.
2 Article 8(2) of Supreme Court Regulation No. 13 of 2016

definition may also be other individuals who, while not officially authorised to make decisions, are nevertheless in a position to control the corporation, influence its policies, or participate in policy-making.

Defining **mens rea** *and* **actus reus** *within the context of corporate criminal liability*

Acknowledging the concept of corporate criminal liability gives rise to two essential questions. First, how to establish a corporation as the doer of the *actus reus* (criminal act)? Second, how to determine the *mens rea* (intention to commit the crime) of a corporation. One of the theories that can be applied to address these questions is the *respondeat superior* theory (the doctrine that a party is responsible for acts of their agents). This theory adopts the principles governing vicarious liability, that is, where the *actus reus* and the *mens rea* of the individuals who act on behalf of a corporation are automatically attributed to the corporation (Maglie 2005: 560). The theory states that the *actus reus* and *mens rea* of the individuals who act on behalf of a corporation are automatically attributed to the corporation. However, those two aspects do not have to be attributable only to a single person. This means that the person who commits the *actus reus* does not need to have the *mens rea* which is the basis of such *actus reus*, provided that the person who commits the *actus reus* is carrying out the instruction or order of another person, who has the directing mind to desire the conduct performed by the person who is instructed. By the combination of the *actus reus* committed by the doer not having *mens rea* and *mens rea* possessed by the person who instructs or orders, in aggregate, the two aspects can be satisfied (*actus reus* and *mens rea*) in order to impose criminal liability on a corporation. This opens the possibility that the *actus reus* doer commits his act based solely on the directing mind of doing his superior's instruction without knowing the real background of the criminal act committed. This person should not have to bear the burden of criminal liability for the *actus reus* committed by him or her because he or she does not possess the *mens rea* required. The corporation, however, is liable for the criminal act because it meets the requirement of *actus reus* and *mens rea* as the aggregation of the actors' behaviour.

The Dutch Supreme Court in 2003 provided a basis to resolve the matter. It ruled that an owner could be held criminally liable for the conduct of his employee if the conduct was at his or her 'disposal' (or if the owner was able to intervene in the conduct), and if, with regard to the course of events, it could be said that the owner had 'accepted' the conduct. These criteria (disposal and acceptance) were applied by the Dutch Supreme Court to establish corporate criminal liability in several cases (Keulen 2010: 5).[15]

The Dutch Supreme Court also ruled that corporation can only be held criminally liable if there is a 'reasonable attribution' of the act to the corporation. The 'reasonable attribution' basis states that the attribution of certain illegal conduct to the corporation may, under certain circumstances, be reasonable if the illegal conduct took place within the scope of the corporation.[16] To make it more comprehensive, the Court also identified four situations where the conduct will be within the scope of corporation (Keulen 2010: 3)

a. where the case concerns an act or an omission of someone who works for the corporation, whether or not under a formal contract of employment;
b. the conduct concerned fits the everyday 'normal business' of the corporation;
c. the corporation gained profit from the conduct concerned; and

d. the course of action was at the 'disposal' of the corporation, and the corporation has 'accepted' the conduct – acceptance including the failure to take reasonable care to prevent the conduct from being performed.

However, these categories are limited to the *actus reus* part of the liability test. With regard to establishing *mens rea,* the Court proposed two approaches. The first is by attributing the *means rea* of a natural person to the corporation. The second is by deriving the *mens rea* from other circumstances that are closely related to the corporation, such as its policy and decisions (Keulen 2010: 6).

Another approach relating to *actus reus* and *mens rea* attribution was introduced by Fisse and Braithwaite (1993). They propose the model of reactive corporate fault that suggests that the attribution of liability occurs when a corporation fails to react satisfactorily to the *actus reus* of an offence (Maglie 2005: 559). 'Reactive corporate fault' may be broadly defined as unreasonable corporate failure to devise and undertake satisfactory preventive or corrective measures in response to the commission of the *actus reus* of an offence by personnel acting on behalf of the organisation (Fisse and Brathwaite 1993: 48).

In Indonesia, an approach is proposed by Sjahdeini that derives from identification theory, whereby the *actus reus* and *mens rea* of corporation is ascribed to the directing mind of the corporation (Sjahdeini 2017: 201). On this view, the offence must give benefit to the corporation and be committed within the scope of corporation. If the misconduct is committed by other than the directing mind of corporation, that misconduct must be based on the order or the approval of the directing mind of corporation in order for the corporation to be criminally liable (Sjahdeini 2017: 199).

To establish the *actus reus* and *mens rea* of corporations, the Attorney General and Supreme Court of Indonesia have established a set of criteria, which will be discussed in the next section. The approach of the Dutch, Fisse and Braithwaite, and Sjahdeini are endorsed by the two regulations. However, it should be noted that before relying on the Attorney General's guidelines and the Supreme Court regulation, law enforcement officers should refer to the laws they are using to process the case. Only if those laws do not regulate this issue can they refer to the Attorney General's guidelines and the Supreme Court regulation.

Finally, it should be noted that the requirement to prove the *mens rea* element does not apply to strict liability offences. Strict liability is liability without fault, which is explained in the European Commission's Green Paper on Remedying Environmental Damage in 1993 as:

> Strict liability, or liability without fault, eases the burden of establishing liability because fault need not be established. However, the injured party must still prove that the damage was caused by someone's act. Strict liability provides an incentive for taking measures to prevent damage from occurring in the first place.

An example of the application of this doctrine in Indonesia is found in art. 88 of Law No. 32 of 2009 on Environmental Protection and Management Law,[17] which stipulates the following:

> Any person whose actions, efforts, and/or activities using B3,[18] producing and/or managing the B3 waste, and/or who pose a serious threat to the environment shall have strict liability for damages that occur without proving the fault element.

Criteria for corporate liability

Attorney General's Regulation PER-028/A/JA/1-/2014 on Guidance for the Handling of Criminal Cases with Corporations as Legal Subject

According to this regulation, prosecutors can use the following criteria to identify corporate criminal liability:

1. the criteria of offence that can give rise to corporate criminal liability are according to prevailing laws.
2. the other criteria besides the aforementioned are the following:
   a. the misconduct is committed based on the decision of the organ of the corporation that committed or participated in the crime;
   b. the misconduct is actively or passively committed by people who, based on work and other relations, act within the sphere of the corporation;
   c. the misconduct involves the human resources, capital resources, and/or other facilities or support of the corporation;
   d. the misconduct is committed by a third party based on an order of the corporation and/or the organ of the corporation;
   e. the misconduct is committed within the sphere of the daily business activities of the corporation;
   f. the misconduct benefits the corporation;
   g. the misconduct is accepted or normally accepted by the corporation;
   h. the corporation possesses the proceeds of crimes; and/or
   i. other acts that may be imputed to the corporation based on the law.

Supreme Court Regulation No. 13 of 2016 on Guidance for the Handling of Crimes Committed by Corporation

To determine the *actus reus* of the corporation, the Supreme Court Regulation defines corporate crime as an act committed by one or more persons based on a relationship of employment or other relationship, where such act is committed on behalf of the corporation, whether within the corporation of outside it. The Regulation also provides definitions of 'relationship of employment', 'other relationship' and 'within the scope of the corporation', as follows:

1. Relationship of employment: the relationship between corporation and its employees based on an agreement that has elements of work, wages and/or duties/commands.
2. Other relationship: a relationship between the directors of the corporation and/or corporations and people and/or other corporations to make the other parties act on behalf of the first party based on an agreement, written or unwritten.
3. Within the scope of corporation: the business scope of the corporation or the scope of work of corporation which includes and/or supports the business activities of corporation, directly or indirectly.

Although the term 'outside the scope of corporation' is not defined in the Regulation, it can be assumed that it is defined as all corporate activities outside the scope of business of daily activities of the corporation. It is possible that a corporation can commit criminal acts when conducting activities that are totally different from its usual daily activities (Maradona 2018: 157).

The Supreme Court Regulation does not limit the notion of 'persons' to the directors or managers of the corporation.[19] The broad definition of 'persons' in this sense includes all individuals who are employed by the corporation and also those who have a relationship with the corporation other than through employment. Thus, the corporation can still be held liable for offences committed by persons situated at the lowest or most marginal level of the organisation.

Further, the Supreme Court Regulation provides that in determining the *mens rea* of the offence, judges can use three criteria.[20] These are formulated alternatively, not cumulatively:

1. whether the corporation obtained any benefit from the crime or whether the crime was done in the interests of the corporation;
2. whether the corporation acquiesced in the crime; or
3. whether the corporation took the necessary measures to prevent or mitigate adverse effects and ensure compliance with the law to prevent the crime.

There are significant similarities between the criteria in the Supreme Court Regulation and the four circumstances provided by the Dutch Supreme Court (HR 21 October 2003 (Drijfmest)), namely:

1. where the case concerns an act or an omission by someone who works for the corporation, whether or not under a formal contract of employment;
2. the conduct concerned fits the everyday 'normal business' of the corporation;

3. the corporation gained profit from the conduct concerned;
4. the course of action was at the 'disposal' of the corporation, and the corporation has 'accepted' the conduct – acceptance including the failure to take reasonable care to prevent the conduct from being performed (Keulen 2010: 5).

Models of corporate criminal liability found in Indonesian laws

Regulating corporate criminal liability in several different laws, when the Indonesian Criminal Code has not yet formally recognised such liability, causes inconsistency and a lack of uniformity among laws in Indonesia. According to Mardjono Reksodiputro,[21] there are three models of corporate criminal liability in Indonesian law in terms of how the law sees the corporation as the perpetrator of a wrongdoing and bearer of the liability. Sutan Remy Sjahdeini (2006: 58) has added a fourth model. We now briefly describe these models.

First model: the corporate officer is the perpetrator and should be held liable for his or her action. This traditional approach is based on the *universitas delinquere non potest* principle, which held that imposing criminal liability on a legal entity was impossible, as it did not have the capacity to act. The fundamental notion underpinning this principle was that legal persons (*rechtspersoonlijkeid*) were not recognised in criminal law. Friedrich Carl von Savigny stated:

> Criminal law has to do with natural persons as thinking and feeling persons exercising their free will. A legal person however is not such a person, but merely a property-owning being, ... with its reality based on the representative will of certain individual persons, which, by way of fiction, is attributed to its own will.
>
> (Möhrenschlager 1998: 1)

This model is found in the Indonesian Criminal Code, which, as mentioned, is based on the Dutch Criminal Code. In the Elucidation (explanatory memorandum) to the 1886 Dutch Criminal Code, it was stated that an action could only be committed by individuals (*natuurlijke persoon*). Accordingly, the Indonesian Criminal Code does not recognise legal entities as a subject of criminal law. This can be seen in arts. 169 and 392 of the Code. Article 169 regulates participation in an offence committed within the scope of an association. However, only sanctions against its founders and directors are mentioned.[22] Similarly, art. 392 only regulates punishment for business owner, directors and commissioner for offences committed within the scope of a limited liability company (private company) and cooperative.[23] Consequently, those who are not involved in the criminal act but hold a significant part in the corporation's management cannot be prosecuted (Maradona 2018: 67).

Second model: The corporation is the perpetrator and the corporate officer should be held liable for the action. This is based on the notion that a corporation is the perpetrator of a crime but the corporation is not itself liable. Instead, the corporate officer should bear the liability. This model is based on the understanding that senior officers of the corporation are responsible for actions committed by a person or persons in the corporation, without considering whether the senior officer knows about the actions or not. This is due to the basic duties and obligations that attach to senior officers (Muladi 2009: 88). This model appears in the Fisheries Law in art. 101:[24]

> In the event criminal acts set out in Article 84(1), 85, 86, 87, 88, 89, 90, 91, 92, 93, 94, 95 and 96 are committed by a corporation, prosecution and criminal sanctions will be imposed on its managers and the fine will be increased by 1/3 of the fine imposed.

Third Model: The Corporation is the perpetrator and the corporation should be held liable for the action. According to this model, the corporation is acknowledged as a criminal legal subject and can be liable for a crime. Imposing liability on corporate officers fails to advance the goals of corporate criminal liability itself. It fails to create a deterrent effect for the corporation, prevent future offences by it, or correct corporate culture. Punishment of the corporation is provided for in several laws, including the Environmental Protection and Management Law, particularly in arts. 116–20.

To create maximum deterrent effect, other sanctions are also imposed in art. 119 of the Environmental Protection and Management Law:

> Besides the penalty as referred to in this law, business entities shall be liable to additional penalty of disciplinary measures in the form of:
> a. seizure of profits earned from the crime;
> b. closure of business and/or activity, entirely or partly;
> c. corrective measures regarding the impacts of the crime;
> d. an order for performing any neglected obligation; and/or
> e. placement of companies under probation for a maximum of 3 (three) years.

Fourth model: The corporation and its officer are the perpetrators and both should be held liable. Corporate criminal liability should not displace individual liability if the individual is also the perpetrator of the conduct. This concept of liability is based on three arguments. First, society must perceive criminal justice as a just system, so a person who commits an offence should be responsible for it. Second, corporations will always be vehicles for individuals to commit crimes. This will enable the corporate officer to free him or herself from liability by claiming that the impugned action is not for personal benefit, but for that of the corporation. Third, as a legal institution, it is impossible for a corporation to operate without human intervention. Its actions and legal mind are attached to individuals.

Along these lines, art. 116 of the Environmental Protection and Management Law provides that individual actors may also be prosecuted along with the corporation:

(1) In the event of environmental crime being committed by, for and on behalf of a business entity, the prosecution and punishment shall be imposed on:
  a. the said business entity; and/or
  b. any person who instructed the crime or person who is responsible for the conduct.
(2) In the event of the environmental crime as referred to in paragraph (1) being committed by a person acting within the scope of business entity on the basis of working relations or other relations, the penalty shall be imposed on the person without regard to whether the crime is committed individually or collectively.

The provision is adopted from art. 51 of the Dutch Criminal Code, and allows for secondary liability. The liability covers both legal persons (corporation) and natural persons (individuals) who order the commission of an offence, and persons who 'actually control' the commission of the offence. This secondary liability is not limited to the 'formal' officers of a legal person (for example, its directors), nor to persons who act as though they hold an official position within the legal person. As a result, employees without any authority may be held criminally liable within the framework of Article 51 of the Dutch Criminal Code, which states:

1. Offences can be committed by natural persons and legal persons.
2. If an offence has been committed by a legal person, prosecution can be instituted and the punishments and measures provided by law can be imposed, if applicable, on:
   a. the legal person, or
   b. those who have ordered the offence, as well as on those who have actually controlled the forbidden act, or
   c. the persons mentioned under (1) and (2) together.
3. For the application of the former subsections, equal status as a legal person applies to a company without legal personality, a partnership, a firm of ship owners, and a separate capital sum assembled for a special purpose.

Sanctions against corporations

There are two categories of corporate sanction: financial and non-financial (Wells 2001: 32). Financial sanctions are considered the main sanctions for corporations. Legal theorists consider deterrence as a main goal of corporate criminal liability, hence fines for corporation should be much higher than individual fines. However, the effectiveness of fines to serve deterrent and retributive purposes is debated. Therefore, non-financial sanctions are also needed to complement the financial sanction. Brent Fisse (1990: 220) stated:

> Fines do not emphatically convey the message that serious corporate offences are socially intolerable. Rather they create the impression that corporate crime is permissible provided the offender merely pays the going price.

Financial sanctions do not always make a contribution to reforming the corporation's internal regulation and procedures. Additionally, they do not necessarily ensure that individuals within the company are disciplined. For this reason, legislators have introduced a variety of non-financial sanctions, such as probation, adverse publicity, community service, director compensation orders, and punitive injunctions.

The stipulations on corporate punishment in different Indonesian laws vary greatly. Here we focus on laws regulating environment crimes (Table 12.2).

Liability of natural persons within the corporation

As stipulated in the Attorney General's Regulation, discussed earlier, prosecutors can file charges against the corporation itself, corporate officers, or both. It also provides that corporate officers should be the subject of prosecution if the law does not recognise the corporation as a legal subject. Corporate officers are corporate officers according to the prevailing law, and include: controllers of the corporation; persons who give orders; and leaders who, whether within or outside the organisational structure of the corporation, have effective control.

The criteria to establish the criminal liability of corporate officers under the Attorney General's Regulation are as follows:

1. a person who commits an offence individually, commits an offence with others, gives an order to another person to commit an offence, provokes another person to commit an offence, or aids in the commission of an offence;
2. a person who has the control and authority to take measures in preventing the offence, does not take any action to prevent the offence, and is aware of the risk resulting from the offence;
3. a person who understands the significant risk of the offence and is aware of the commission of the offence; and/or
4. other actions that can impute liability to corporate officers according to the laws.

Table 12.2 Fines and imprisonment (sanctions imposed on corporate officers)

Fines and imprisonment (sanctions imposed on corporate officers)	
Article 101, Law No. 45 of 2009, on Fisheries	In the event the criminal acts detailed in arts. 84(1), 85, 86, 87, 88, 89, 90, 91, 92, 93 94, 95 and 96 are committed by a corporation, prosecution and criminal sanctions will be imposed on its managers and the fine will be increased by 1/3 of the fine imposed.
Regulates fines imposed to the corporation	
Article 113, Law No. 39 of 2014 on Plantations	(1) In the event the criminal acts detailed in arts. 103, 104, 105, 106, 107, 108 and 109 are committed by a corporation, in addition to the conviction of its officers under these articles, the corporation is liable to the maximum fine plus an additional 1/3 of the fine applicable to an individual.
Regulates fines imposed on corporations and also other penalties	
Article 119, Law No. 32 of 2009 on Environmental Protection and Management Law	Besides the penalty referred to in this law, the business entities shall be liable to an additional penalty of disciplinary measures in the form of: a. seizure of profits earned from the crime; b. closure of business and/or activity entirely or partly; c. corrective measures in relation to the impacts of the crime; d. an order to perform the obligation neglected; and/or e. placement of companies under probation for 3 (three) years at the maximum.
Article 21, Supreme Court Regulation No. 13 of 2016	Upon conviction, both primary and supplemental penalties may be imposed. Primary penalties consist of fines, while supplemental penalties are as provided for in the relevant legislation. Should a fine not be paid within the prescribed period, assets of the corporation may be confiscated by the prosecution service and subsequently auctioned, with the proceeds being used to pay the fine.

Also, like the Netherlands, Indonesia recognises secondary liability, which allows prosecution and punishment to be imposed on all of: legal persons; the natural person who ordered the offence; and the natural person who actually controlled the offence. This is found in art. 116 of the Environmental Protection and Management Law and follows art. 51 of the Dutch Penal Code. Regarding secondary liability in art. 51 of the Dutch Penal Code, Nico Keijzer explains that:

> Art. 51 of the Criminal Code is structured in such a way that, if it is established that a corporation has committed an offence, there are three

> possibilities for punishment. The corporation may be punished, or the person who was in control of the offence being committed may be punished, or both may be punished. Accordingly, the public prosecutor may prosecute the corporation, or the person in control of the committed offence, or both. For prosecuting a corporation, it is not a requirement that a natural person in control of the commission of the offence is identified. If the person in control is being prosecuted, it must first be established that the corporation has committed the offence, and second that the accused was the natural person in control of the commission of the offence.
>
> (Keijzer 2013: 3)

However, the regulation of corporate officers' liability under Law No. 18 of 2013 on the Prevention and Eradication of Forestry Degradation is quite different. In the Elucidation to art. 109 (3), it is stated that the corporate officers who can be held liable are only those who have a functional position in the organisational structure of the corporation. Once again, this shows how corporate criminal liability in Indonesia is regulated quite differently in different laws.

Criminal procedural system in Indonesia relating to corporate criminal liability

As mentioned, Law No. 8 of 1981 on the Criminal Procedure Code replaced the criminal procedural law introduced in the colonial period, the *Herzeine Inlandsch Reglement* (HIR). Like the Indonesian Criminal Code, the Indonesian Criminal Procedural Code does not recognise the corporation as a legal subject.

This has created problems, one of them arising when the prosecutors and judge have to provide the full name, place of birth, date of birth, gender, nationality, address, religion, and occupation of the defendant in the bill of indictment and the verdict. That information does not exist where the corporation is the defendant. On the other hand, the Indonesian Criminal Procedural Code provides that the bill of indictment[25] and verdict[26] will be void if those requirements are not satisfied.

In practice, law enforcement officers refer to the Law used to process the case to find a legal basis for the procedural law (Pramono 2012: 308). For example, the Corruption Law deals with the procedural law related to the criminal liability of corporation in the following way:

> Article 20
>
> …
>
> (3) If the prosecution is processed against the corporation, then its board represents the corporation.

(4) The board representing the corporation as mentioned in paragraph (3) can be represented by another person.
(5) The judge can by order summon the board of the corporation to the court and can also order the board brought to the court.
(6) If the prosecution is against the corporation, then the court submits the letter of summons to the residence of the board or the office of the board.

However, there are several laws that recognise corporate criminal liability but do not contain any provisions on criminal procedure, including the Fisheries Law. To avoid a vacuum in procedural arrangements and provide practical guidance for prosecuting corporations, the Attorney General of Indonesia issued Regulation PER-028/A/JA/1-/2014 on Guidance for the Handling of Criminal Cases with Corporations as Legal Subjects in October 2014. Two years later, the Supreme Court also made a significant move by issuing Supreme Court Regulation No. 13 of 2016, discussed earlier.

Attorney General's Regulation

The Attorney General's Regulation adopts several provisions from the Attorney General's Letter to Provincial Public Prosecutor Office Chairs on Corporations as Suspects and Defendants in Criminal Corruption Cases, from five years earlier (B-036/A/Ft.1/06/2009). In general, it provides thorough guidelines on the criteria for an offence, the investigation process, the prosecution process, the execution of verdict, and assets handling.

It also provided a model of the initial Indictment Letter (*Surat Dakwaan*) and Prosecution Letter (*Surat Tuntutan*) for corporations. To end the debate on how to meet the requirements stipulated in the Indonesian Criminal Procedural Code to specify identity information about the defendant in the Bill of Indictment, the Attorney General's regulation stated the following:

1. A Bill of Indictment against corporation contains the following information about the corporation:
   a. Name of corporation.
   b. Number and date of the Corporation's Deed of Establishment and its amendment.
   c. Number and date of Articles of Association when the offence occured.
   d. Place of residence.
   e. Nationality of corporation.
   f. Line of business.
   g. Taxpayer Registration Number.
   h. Identity of person representing the corporation in accordance with Article 143 paragraph (2) letter (a) of the Criminal Procedural Code.
2. If the requirements specified in paragraph (1) letter a, b, c, d, e, f, h, i, j, k and l in this article are not met, the verdict is deemed void. …

This provision resolves the confusion that has sometimes led to significant debate in court. It does not contradict the Indonesian Criminal Procedural Code but adds adjustments, and its provisions will be discussed further below. However, this regulation is an internal technical guideline, and was made only for prosecutors, and applies only to them. Consequently, this regulation can only be used to address problems in relation to prosecution and not the larger problems in the Indonesian criminal law system as a whole.

Supreme Court Regulation

The Supreme Court Regulation of 2016 focuses on verdicts and judicial process. It acknowledges the lack of detailed procedural law arrangements relating to corporate criminal liability, as it states in the preamble:

> c. There are many laws in Indonesia that recognise corporations as a legal subject that can be held liable, but cases being processed with corporations as legal subject are still very limited in number, [and] one of the reasons behind this is the fact that there is ambiguity in procedure on how to make corporations criminal offenders, therefore it is considered necessary to have a guidance for law enforcement officers in handling criminal cases against corporations.

The identification information for corporations as defendants that should be included in verdicts is similar to what appears in the Attorney General's Regulation, although the Supreme Court regulation provides more comprehensive provisions on the nature of corporate criminal liability, investigation and trial, and penalties (again, further detail is provided below). However, as a Supreme Court regulation, this instrument does not create new legal norms nor does it codify the prevailing laws. That being so, it is still necessary to amend the Indonesian Criminal Code to accommodate the codification of the conceptual provisions on crimes committed by corporations.

Comparison of laws

As mentioned, the regulation of corporate criminal liability in a range of different laws outside the Criminal Code has become a common pattern in Indonesia, causing a serious lack of uniformity among the laws including regarding environmental liability. Table 12.3 shows how several environment-related laws in Indonesia adopt different concepts and make different stipulations.

Environmental corporate criminal liability cases in Indonesia

Muladi and Dwija Priyatno commented in their research in 1991 that corporate criminal liability decisions are very hard to find in Indonesian courts,

Table 12.3 Concepts and stipulations concerning the environment in laws

Law	*Definition of corporation*	*Stipulation on the corporate crime*	*Who is held liable*	*Sanction*
Environmental Protection and Management Law	'Persons' is defined as individuals and corporations, whether incorporated and not.	Crime is committed by, for and on behalf, of the corporation.	1. The corporation; and/or 2. the person who instructed the crime or the person who is responsible for the conduct.	Besides the penalty referred to in the law, the business entity shall be liable to an additional penalty of disciplinary measures in the form of: a. seizure of profits earned from the crime; b. closure of business and/or place of activity, entirely or partly; c. corrective measures regarding the impact of the crime; d. an order to perform an obligation neglected; and/or placement of companies under probation for 3 (three) years at the maximum.
Fisheries Law	'Persons' is defined as individuals and corporations.	Not provided.	The corporate officer	Prosecution and criminal sanctions will be imposed on the corporate officers and the fine will be increased by a third.
Plantations Law	'Persons' is defined as individuals and corporations, whether incorporated and not.	Crime is committed by the corporation.	1. The corporation; 2. the corporate officer	The corporation will be liable for a maximum fine penalty plus 1/3 of the criminal penalties applicable to individuals.

(continued)

Table 12.3 Cont.

Law	*Definition of corporation*	*Stipulation on the corporate crime*	*Who is held liable*	*Sanction*
Prevention and Eradication of Forest Degradation Law	A corporation is an organised collection of people and/ or wealth, both legal and non-legal entities.	Crime is committed by individuals, based on work or other relationship, acting within the scope of the corporation, personally or collectively.	1. The corporation; and/or 2. the corporate officer	If the prosecution is against the corporation, then the sanction will be fines. The corporation can also be liable for other sanctions, such as full or partial closure (art. 109(6)).
Corruption Law	A corporation as an organised collection of people and/ or wealth, both in form of a legal entity or non-legal entity.	Crime is committed by people who are, based on work and other relations, acting in the corporate environment, both personally and collectively.	1. The corporation; and/or 2. the corporate officer	The corporation is liable for a maximum fine penalty plus 1/ 3 of the criminal penalties for individuals.

despite the fact that the research was conducted almost half of century after Indonesia established a legal basis to prosecute and punish corporations (Muladi and Priyatno 1991: 128). The prosecution of PT Newmont Minahasa Raya[27] was the first environmental case to position a corporation as a defendant. It overcame the traditional reluctance of the authorities to prosecute corporations for environmental crime. The case was brought in August 2005. However, the court ruled that PT Newmont Minahasa Raya and its president, Richard Ness, were acquitted of all charges. The judges argued that it had not been proven that the pollution in issue was caused by the company's activities.

In this section we analyse four cases where corporate criminal liability has been applied and corporations are punished. They are: PT Dongwoo Environmental Indonesia; PT Kallista Alam; PT Indominco Mandiri; and PT Baruna Segara Mandiri. The first two cases were decided before the issue of Attorney General's Regulation PER-028/A/JA/1-/2014 and Supreme Court Regulation No. 13 of 2016, whereas the third case was decided afterwards. The fourth case is a case on fisheries. As explained, the Fisheries Law endorsed the second model of corporate criminal liability, where the corporate officer is the one held liable.

PT Dongwoo Environmental Indonesia

Awing, a worker of the company, disposed of a total of 410.2 tons of hazardous and toxic waste produced by the company's business activity in an open area at Pasir Gombong, Bekasi. This caused health problems for people in the neighbourhood. Awing was paid for Rp. 300,000 for every disposal and received a total of Rp. 18,000,000. The money paid to Awing was approved by the director of the corporation, Kim Young Woo.

The indictment was brought against PT Dongwoo Environmental Indonesia under art. 41(1), in conjunction with arts. 45 and 47 of Law No. 23 of 1997 on Environmental Protection and Management. The defendant was identified as Kim Young Woo, not PT Dongwoo Environmental Indonesia.

The judges at first instance returned a guilty verdict[28] against PT Dongwoo Environmental Indonesia. The company received a Rp. 325,000,000 fine and six months imprisonment in the event of default of payment. Additionally, the financial benefits obtained from the disposal of 410.2 tons of waste were seized. The judges also ordered the company's closure. The appeal court upheld the first court's conviction.[29]

The Supreme Court, however, rendered the following verdict:[30]

1. The first two judgments should be annulled;
2. PT Dongwoo Environmental Indonesia, represented by its CEO Kim Young Woo, found guilty of environmental pollution;
3. PT Dongwoo Environmental Indonesia liable to fine of Rp. 650,000,000 and six months imprisonment in default of payment;

4. financial benefits obtained from the disposal of 410.2 tons to be seized; and
5. PT Dongwoo Environmental Indonesia be closed.

In parallel, Kim Young Woo was also convicted of ordering a crime of environmental pollution. The original judgment was upheld by the High Court judgment,[31] and Kim Young Woo was sentenced to six months imprisonment, a Rp. 100,000,000 fine, and three months imprisonment in the event of default in payment.

Analysis

Our analysis of the PT Dongwoo Environmental Indonesia cases is three-pronged. First, Kim Young Woo was identified as the defendant. The case was brought by the prosecutors against PT Dongwoo Environmental Indonesia but, due to their lack of understanding of corporate criminal liability, the indictment identified Kim Young Woo as the defendant. This made the indictment inconsistent, as the accusation of environmental pollution was against PT Dongwoo Environmental Indonesia.

This misinterpretation could lead to a violation of art. 182 of the Indonesian Criminal Procedural Law, which states that the judge's decision must be based on the prosecutor's indictment. The guilty verdict against PT Dongwoo Environmental Indonesia could therefore be said to be a ruling beyond of the scope of the indictment. This case was brought before the issue of the Attorney General's Regulation, so there was no guidance on the form for court documents for a case against a corporation at the time. However, the Indonesian Supreme Court did not do anything about the inconsistency in the identity of the defendant, and still followed the form of the lower court's decision.

Second, the court order for imprisonment in default of payment is problematic because it is impossible for corporations to be threatened with imprisonment in default of payment (Wells 2001: 34). Further, the imprisonment of a director of the company for an offence for which the company was tried could be said to be a punishment of an individual without trial. This is in violation of the presumption of innocence principle and the principle that there should be no criminal punishment without trial. If the fine sanction was not satisfied, then Kim Young Woo would undergo double punishment: his own and that imposed on PT Dongwoo Environmental Indonesia. However, the Environmental Protection and Management Law does not include a provision on a subsidiary punishment in default of payment. If this proceeding had occurred after the Supreme Court Regulation was issued, the judges would have been able to refer to that regulation, which provides that should a fine not be paid within the prescribed period, assets of the corporation may be confiscated by prosecutors and subsequently auctioned, with the proceeds being used to pay the fine.

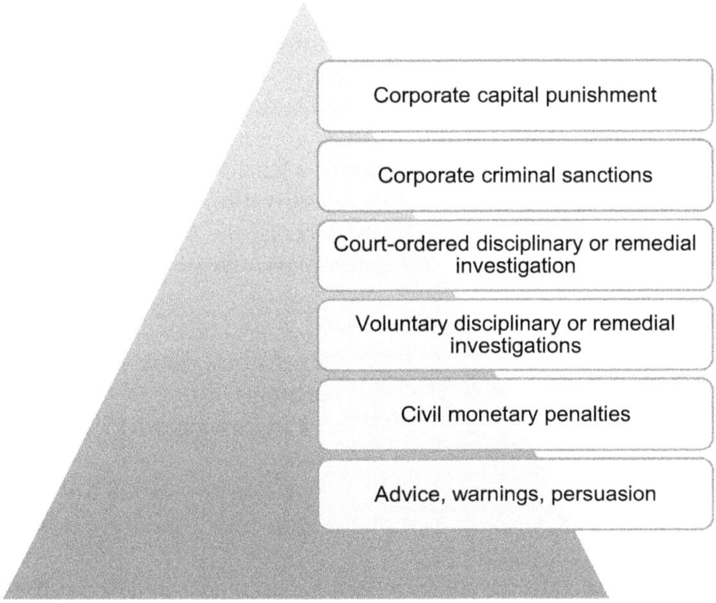

Figure 12.1 Effect of Supreme Court Regulation on Criminal Liability.

The third issue that arises relates to the order for company closure. This is the most drastic non-financial sanction against corporations; some experts even argue that it is equal to the human death penalty. Braithwaite (1993: 142), for example, developed an enforcement pyramid, with company closure categorised as corporate capital punishment (Figure 12.1).

This drastic form of punishment is occasionally needed to deal with the most extreme forms of corporate intransigence. In some jurisdictions in the US, for example, company closure is used against corporations formed for an illegal purpose (Wells 2001: 37). Accordingly, there should be sentencing guidelines to identify in what circumstances prosecutors should decide to seek corporate capital punishment. According to Gruner (2005), sentencing guidelines for prosecutors and courts should at least meet three requirements:

1. The guidelines must provide sufficient sentences but not greater sentences than necessary. They should provide just punishment. It should be noted that sanctions imposed may also have an impact on innocent parties such as employees, shareholders and consumers.
2. The guidelines must provide certainty and fairness in sentencing, so as not to create sentencing disparities among defendants with similar records committing similar offences.
3. The guidelines must reflect advances in knowledge of human behaviour as that knowledge relates to the criminal justice process. (Gruner 2005: 60)

PT Kallista Alam

The PT Kallista Alam case is one of a number of environmental cases in Indonesia that received a lot of public attention. The company was processed through three channels of legal action in a 'multi-door' approach that involved criminal law, administrative law, and civil law actions.

PT Kallista Alam is a palm oil company located in Aceh. It conducted land clearing, using fire, to enable palm oil cultivation in 2012. The misconduct resulted in serious air pollution as an effect of the illegal burning, which affected Singapore and Malaysia. The company was prosecuted under the following provisions:

a. Article 69 of Law No. 32 of 2009 on Environmental Protection and Management for the offence of illegal burning;
b. Article 108 of Law No. 32 of 2009 on Environmental Protection and Management, which stipulates the sanction;
c. Article 116, Article 118 and Article 119 of the Law No. 32 of 2009 on Environmental Protection and Management, which provides regulations on corporate criminal liability; and
d. Article 64 of the Indonesian Criminal Code in relation to 'continuing act'.

The judges of the Meulaboh District Court found PT Kallista Alam guilty and sentenced it to pay a Rp. 3 billion fine.[32] The company then filed an appeal with the Banda Aceh High Court, resulting in a verdict restating the District Court verdict.[33] After that, it filed a cassation appeal and the Supreme Court upheld the two previous verdicts.[34]

Analysis

The interesting thing about this case is that the prosecutor's office prosecuted both a natural person (Subianto Rusid, Director of PT Kallista Alam) and a legal person (PT Kallista Alam) in separate cases. Although the case against PT Kalista Alam led to a positive conviction, the case against Subianto Rusid was dismissed by the Banda Aceh High Court and the Supreme Court. The courts viewed the criminal act as proven but did not find Subianto Rusid to be criminally liable for the act. This obviously implied that the corporation's fault in this case did not depend on whether the director of the corporation was proven guilty.

Another interesting fact is that the prosecutors relied on art. 64 of the Indonesian Criminal Code, despite that fact that the Indonesian Criminal Code does not recognise the corporation as a legal subject. This decision was also endorsed by the judges of the District Court, High Court and Supreme Court, although no reasoning was given to explain why the Criminal Code was appropriate for prosecuting a corporation.

PT Indominco Mandiri

Indominco Mandiri is a large thermal coal surface mine located in the regencies of Bontang, Kutai Kertanegara and East Kutai, near the city of Bontang.

PT Indominco Mandiri owns a temporary storage area for hazardous and toxic waste to store fly ash and bottom ash.[35] However, the area is not big enough to store all the waste. As a result, fly and bottom ash wastes are also placed in an open area near a paving block production site, which can turn the ash waste into pavers. However, PT Indominco Mandiri has only one paving block machine. This resulted in a huge pile of fly ash and bottom ash, amounting to around 4,000 tons.

PT Indominco Mandiri was indicted for violations of art. 103[36] or, alternatively, art. 104 of the Environmental Protection and Management Law,[37] both in conjunction with art. 116.[38] It is clearly stated in the indictment that the defendant was PT Indominco Mandiri, based on the model indictment provided in the Attorney General's Regulation.

One of the arguments presented in his defence by the director of the company was that the company was not aware that its actions were a violation of the Law. Accordingly, the company lacked the requisite intent to commit the violation.

The judges acknowledged that corporations are indeed a legal subject under criminal law. Five theories were mentioned by them in their decision, as follows.

Strict liability theory: Based on this theory, proof of *mens rea* in relation to the *actus reus* is not required. Violation of art. 104 is in fact a strict liability crime according to art. 88[39] of the Environmental Protection and Management Law. Therefore, establishing corporate criminal liability is feasible without establishing the *mens rea* and *actus reus* elements.

Vicarious liability theory: This theory is used to justify the corporation being held liable for the acts of its employees.

Doctrine of delegation: This doctrine justifies the delegation of part of the management function by corporate leaders to the employee; therefore, the employee may act on behalf of the corporation.

Identification theory: This theory argues that legal or illegal acts committed by high-level managers can be properly identified as the acts of the corporations.

Corporate organ theory: A company may in many ways be likened to a human body. It has a brain and nerve centre that controls what it does. It also has hands, which hold the tools and act in accordance with directions from the centre. Some of the people in the company are mere servants and agents who are nothing more than hands to do the work and cannot be said to represent the mind or will. Others are directors and managers who represent the directing mind and will

> of the company and control what it does. The state of mind of these managers is the state of mind of the company and is treated by the law as such.

The judges rendered the following verdict:[40]

1. PT Indominco Mandiri found guilty of committing illegal dumping;
2. PT Indominco Mandiri fined Rp. 2,000,000,000 on the condition that if the fine is not paid within a period of one month after the judgment becomes legally binding, then PT Indominco Mandiri's properties will be confiscated and auctioned to pay the fine; and
3. PT Indominco Mandiri ordered to treat or use the pile of fly ash and bottom ash waste.

Analysis

The PT Indominco Mandiri verdict shows a far more sophisticated understanding of corporate criminal liability. The court no longer imposed imprisonment in the event of default of payment. The confiscation and auction of the company's properties as a subsidiary punishment was imposed on the basis of art. 28(3)[41] of the Supreme Court Regulation.

In addition to the fine, the judges ruled that PT Indominco Mandiri must manage the waste. This remedial order serves to also satisfy the rehabilitation goal of corporate criminal liability. PT Indominco Mandiri is forced to improve its machinery so that it can manage the waste without causing pollution. This punishment is based on art. 33 of the Supreme Court Regulation.[42] In relation to the rehabilitative goal mentioned before, this punishment has the potential to correct the culture of the corporation, so it is more aware of the problems of environmental pollution.

In addressing corporate criminal liability, the judges used a range of doctrines to attribute the liability to PT Indominco Mandiri. Unfortunately, the criteria set out in the Supreme Court Regulations were not elaborated in the judges' considerations. Likewise, there is no comprehensive explanation of how those doctrines were translated into the context of the case. The doctrines were simply listed without explanation.

PT Baruna Segara Mandiri

PT Baruna Segara Mandiri runs a fishing business. It owns six fishing vessels, including KM Fransiska and PT Tuna Jaya 111. In early 2016, KM Fransiska was damaged by fire, but its licence remained valid. At the same time, KM Tuna Jaya 111's licence had expired.

To maintain the business, the president director of the company instructed one of the Directors to operate KM Tuna Jaya 111 but using the licence belonging to KM Fransiska. Accordingly, the director gave an order to staff to change the name on the body of KM Tuna Jaya 111 to 'KM Fransiska', with the result that KM Tuna Jaya 111 was involved in fishing activity without a valid licence.

The defendants stipulated in the indictment were the director and president director of the company. The prosecutors and judges relied on art. 101[43] of the Fisheries Law, a provision imposing corporate criminal liability.

The defendants were declared liable and punished with a year's imprisonment and a Rp. 500,000,000 fine, along with a 'subsidiary punishment'[44] of three months imprisonment.[45]

Analysis

As discussed above, the provision of corporate criminal liability in the Fisheries Law falls within the second model: 'the corporation is the perpetrator and the corporate officer should be held liable for the action'. Consequently, although PT Baruna Segara Mandiri may be considered liable, the prosecution and punishment were directed at the corporate officers, in this case the director and president director. This second model has imprisonment as principal punishment.

Although the Attorney General's Regulation and the Supreme Court Regulation have attempted to provide comprehensive guidelines for prosecuting companies, the Fisheries Law creates confusion because it endorses the notion that prosecution of corporate entities should involve the attribution of liability only to the personnel responsible.

Problems with corporate criminal liability regulation and implementation in Indonesia

In our analysis above, five problems have been identified. First, not all laws in Indonesia recognise corporate criminal liability. Corporate criminal liability in Indonesia has developed by recognising such concepts in laws outside the Indonesian Criminal Code. Therefore, implementing corporate criminal liability in Indonesia will depend on whether or not the applicable statute recognises the concept. For example, the Fisheries Law (which regulates fishery activities within Indonesia's territorial waters and Exclusive Economic Zone) recognises the concept of corporate criminal liability, while Law No. 1 of 1973 on Continental Shelf (which regulates activities within the continental shelf) does not, although both statutes regulate marine activities. The fact that corporations committing offences in territorial waters and Exclusive Economic Zone can be held liable, but not if the offences happen in the continental shelf waters, shows how inconsistent criminal law enforcement is in Indonesia.

Second, the laws recognising corporate criminal liability in Indonesia endorse different approaches. The lack of uniformity in corporate criminal liability stipulations in various Indonesian laws is very clear and Mardjono

Reksodiputro and Sutan Remy Sjahdeini have described four different models of corporate criminal liability recognised in them. This inconsistency is caused by the fact that the Indonesian Criminal Code has not yet recognised the concept, and lawmakers use the Indonesian Criminal Code as a main reference in legal drafting. The result is that there is an absence of consensus about a single system of corporate criminal liability that lawmakers can use.

Third, the Indonesian Criminal Procedural Law has not yet provided procedures for the implementation of corporate criminal liability. There are some laws that provide stipulations on criminal procedure in implementing corporate criminal liability but, because other laws do not include such stipulations, law enforcement officers often encounter confusion and procedural problems. The Attorney General's Regulation and the Supreme Court Regulation have helped law enforcement officers develop a better understanding of how to deal with corporate criminal liability, but they are not a complete solution,

Fourth, there is not much *yurisprudensi* (jurisprudence, leading Supreme Court decisions) providing guidance on how to interpret the regulations because corporate criminal liability cases in Indonesia, are still very few, compared to many other countries. In the Netherlands, the Dutch Supreme Court provided clarifying rulings on how corporate criminal liability should be established by introducing the 'disposal and acceptance' and 'reasonable attribution' concepts. In the PT Indominco Mandiri case, however, the judges did not elaborate on how the criteria set forth in the Supreme Court Regulations and the doctrines on corporate criminal liability applied to the context of the case.

Fifth, corporate criminal liability is implemented differently in different contexts. As a result of the four problems just described, there are discrepancies and inconsistency in the application of corporate criminal liability. The cases presented in the previous section show how the application of corporate criminal liability has varied enormously from case to case (Table 12.4).

Conclusion

The development of the corporate criminal liability concept in Indonesia has been highly influenced by the Netherlands. However, unlike the Netherlands, which introduced the corporate criminal liability concept in its Penal Code, Indonesia has developed its recognition of corporate criminal liability concept through a range of laws outside Criminal Code. As a consequence, significant dissimilarities between laws have arisen. These are most apparent in terms of how liability is attributed, who is held responsible, and what sanctions are imposed.

As just explained, there are now at least five problems with the corporate criminal liability regulation and implementation in Indonesia. First, not all laws in Indonesia recognise corporate criminal liability. Second, the

Table 12.4 Application of corporate criminal liability in different cases

	PT Dongwoo Environmental Indonesia	*PT Kalista Alam*	*PT Indominco Mandiri*	*PT Baruna Segara Mandiri*
Year of first level case	2008	2013	2013	2017
The defendant stipulated in the Bill of Indictment	The director	The corporation	The corporation	The director
The sanction	1. Fines imposed on the corporation, but the director should be imprisoned in default of payment; and 2. company closure.	Fines	1. Fines; and 2. ordered other action.	1. Fines; and 2. imprisonment

laws recognising corporate criminal liability in Indonesia endorse different approaches. Third, the Indonesian Criminal Procedural Law has not yet provided procedures for the implementation of corporate criminal liability. Fourth, there is not much jurisprudence providing guidance on how to interpret the regulations, because corporate criminal liability cases in Indonesia are still very few. Fifth, corporate criminal liability is implemented quite differently in different cases.

An example of the lack of uniformity of understanding among the laws in Indonesia is the debate about whether the prosecution of corporate entities will automatically result in attribution of liability to the responsible personnel, and vice versa. In some cases, prosecution of the director of the company is considered an application of corporate criminal liability, for example, in fisheries cases and cases, where the director is punished after a trial of the corporation. On the other hand, with corporations being the prime target of prosecution in some violations, prosecutors often undermine individual accountability. Individual accountability is frequently displaced by corporate liability. There is thus an undermining of individual accountability at the level of public enforcement measures, with corporations rather than individual personnel typically being the prime targets of prosecution.

However, the PT Indominco Mandiri case is an excellent example of how corporate criminal liability can be applied. Here, the Attorney General's Regulation helped prosecutors compose a proper indictment that did not create confusion. Moreover, in this case, the judges used the Supreme Court Regulation to impose a more suitable punishment.

However, it remains necessary to amend the Indonesian Criminal Code and the Criminal Procedural Code so that there is a single and clear system of corporate criminal liability that lawmakers and law enforcement officers can agree upon. Although provisions in Indonesian Criminal Code and Indonesian Criminal Procedural Code do not necessarily replace provisions that already exist in other laws, amendment of these Codes to recognise and facilitate corporate liability will be a great encouragement for lawmakers to make adjustments to other laws. Otherwise, the application of corporate criminal liability in Indonesia will remain ineffective, inconsistent, and confusing.

Notes

1 In Germany (and countries and countries inspired by German doctrines such as Italy, Spain, Portugal, Greece, and Poland) the principle *societas delinquere non potest* has often dominated legal theory. This principle holds that a corporation, as an entity, is not capable of committing a crime. See Diskant 2008: 144; Wells 2001: 139.
2 Law No. 11/PNPS/1963 on Subversion, revoked by Law No. 26 of 1999.
3 Law No. 9 of 1976 on Narcotics, amended by Law No. 22 of 1997 and, most recently, by Law No. 35 of 2009.
4 Law No. 6 of 1984 on the Post, amended by Law No. 38 of 2009.
5 Law No. 5 of 1984 on Industry, amended by Law No. 3 of 2014.
6 Law No. 5 of 1997 on Psychotropics.
7 Law No. 23 of 1997 on Environmental Protection and Management Law, amended by Law No. 32 of 2009.
8 Law No. 5 of 1999 on the Ban of Monopolistic Practices.
9 Law No. 8 of 1999 on Consumer Protection.
10 Law No. 31 of 1999 on the Eradication of Corruption, amended by Law No. 20 of 2001.
11 Law No. 15 of 2002 on the Prevention and Eradication of Money Laundering, amended by Law No. 25 of 2003 and, most recently, by Law No. 8 of 2010.
12 Law No. 31 of 2004 on Fisheries, amended by Law No. 45 of 2009.
13 Article 2 stipulates that 'The Indonesian statutory penal provisions are applicable to any person who is guilty of a punishable act within Indonesia', but does not provide any explanation of whether the term 'persons' covers legal persons, not just natural persons.
14 Article 3 of Supreme Court Regulation No. 13 of 2016.
15 See HR 21 October 2003 NJ 2006, 328 (Drijfmest).
16 See HR 21 October 2003, NJ 2006, 328 (Drijfmest).
17 Law No. 23 of 1997 on Environmental Protection and Management Law, amended by Law No. 32 of 2009.
18 B3 is the Indonesian abbreviation for 'hazardous and toxic waste', which means any waste containing dangerous and/or toxic material that, due to its characteristics and/or concentration and/or amount, directly or indirectly, may damage and/or pollute the living environment and/or endanger human health.
19 Article 3, Supreme Court Regulation No. 13 of 2016.
20 Article 4, Supreme Court Regulation No. 13 of 2016.
21 See Priyatno 2004: 53.

22 Article 169:
(1) Participation in an association that has intent to commit crimes or in another association prohibited by general regulations, shall be punished by a maximum imprisonment of six years.
(2) Participation in an association that has the intent to commit misdemeanours shall be punished with a maximum imprisonment of nine months or a maximum fine of three hundred Rupiahs.
(3) In respect of the founders or directors said punishments may be increased by one third,

23 Article 392: 'Any business owner, any executive or any commissioner of a limited liability company, any Indonesian limited liability company or any cooperative society, who, with deliberate intent publishes an untrue statement of accounts or balance sheet, shall be punished by a maximum imprisonment of one year and four months'.

24 Law No. 31 of 2004 on Fisheries, amended by Law No. 45 of 2009.

25 Article 143 of the Indonesian Criminal Procedural Code:
'... Prosecutors must provide date, signature and the following information to the bill of indictment. ...
(2) A bill of indictment that does not fulfill the requirements specified in paragraph (2) shall be deemed void. ...'

26 Article 197 of the Indonesian Procedural Code:
'(1) A verdict contains the following:
a. ...
b. full name, place of birth, age or date of birth, gender, nationality, address, religion and occupation of the defendant;
c. ...'

27 *The Republic of Indonesia v. PT Newmont Minahasa Raya,* No. 284/Pid.B/2005/PN.Mdo.

28 *The Republic of Indonesia v. PT Dongwoo Environmental Indonesia*, No. 458/Pid.B/2008.PN.Bks.

29 *The Republic of Indonesia v. PT Dongwoo Environmental Indonesia*, No. 456/Pid/2009/PT.Bdg.

30 *The Republic of Indonesia v. PT Dongwoo Environmental Indonesia*, No. 862 K/Pid.Sus/2010.

31 The original judgment was No. 457/Pid.B/2008/PN.Bks, and the High Court judgment was No. 157/Pid/2009/PT.Bdg.

32 Meulaboh District Court Decision Number 131/Pid.B/2013/PN.MBO.

33 Banda Aceh High Court Decision Number 201/Pid/2014/PT BNA.

34 Supreme Court Decision Number 1554 K/Pid.Sus/2015.

35 Fly ash and bottom ash are considered hazardous and toxic waste, according to Government Regulation No. 101 of 2015 on Hazardous and Toxic Waste Management.

36 Article 103: 'Any person producing B3 waste and not conducting the treatment required set forth in Article 59, shall be subject to imprisonment for one year at the minimum and 3 (three) years at the maximum and a fine amounting to Rp. 1,000,000,000 (one billion rupiah) at the minimum and Rp. 3,000,000,000 (three billion) at the maximum'.

37 Article 104: 'Any person performing dumping of waste and/or materials into environmental media in relation to Article 60, shall be subject to imprisonment

for 3 (three) years at the maximum and a fine amounting to Rp. 3,000,000,000 (three billion) at the maximum'.

38 Article 116: (1) In the event of environmental crime being committed by, for, and on behalf of, a business entity, the prosecution and punishment shall be imposed on:

the said business entity; and/or person who instructed the crime or person who is responsible for the conduct.

(2) In the event of the environmental crime as referred to in paragraph (1) being committed by a person acting within the scope of business entity on the basis of working relations or other relations, the penalty shall be imposed on the person without regards to whether the crime is committed individually or collectively.

39 Article 88: 'Any person whose actions, efforts, and/or activities using B3, produce and/or manage the B3 waste, and/or who pose a serious threat to the environment is subject to strict liability for damages that occur without proving the fault element'.

40 *The Republic of Indonesia v. PT Indominco Mandiri,* No. 562/Pid.Sus-Lh/2017/Pn.Trg.

41 Article 28(3): 'If the defendant fails to complete the payment of fine, then the corporation's properties may be confiscated by prosecutor for auction to pay the fine'.

42 Article 33: 'An additional punishment to recover the damages caused by a corporate crime may be imposed on the related corporation and its implementation should be based upon the prevailing laws'.

43 Article 101: 'In the event of the criminal acts set forth in Article 84(1), 85, 86, 87, 88, 89, 90, 91, 92, 93 94, 95 and 96 are committed by a corporation, the prosecution and criminal sanction will be imposed on its managers and the fine is added with 1/3 of the fine imposed'.

44 The subsidiary punishment applies only if the fine is not paid.

45 *The Republic of Indonesia v. I Komand Redana,* No. 794/Pid.Sus/2016/PN.Dps.

References

Brodowski, Dominik; Vogel, Joachim et al. (eds.) 2014. *Regulating Corporate Criminal Liability.* New York: Springer

Dirdjosisworo, Soedjono 1991. 'Hukum Pidana Indonesia dan Gelagat Kriminalitas Masyarakat Pasca Industri', presented as Professorial Inauguration Speech at the Faculty of Law, University Parahyangan

Diskant, Edward B. 2008. 'Comparative Corporate Criminal Liability: Exploring the Uniquely American Doctrine through Comparative Criminal Procedure', *The Yale Law Journal* 118(126): 126–76

European Commission. *Green Paper on Remedying Environmental Damage.* Com (93)47. Brussels: EC

Fisse, Brent 1990. 'Sentencing Options against Corporations', *Criminal Law Forum* 1(2): 211–58

Fisse, Brent and Braithwaite, John 1993. *Corporations, Crime and Accountability.* Cambridge University Press

Gruner, Richard S. 2005. *Corporate Criminal Liability and Prevention.* New York: Law Journal Press

Husein, Yunus 2014. 'Combating Environmental Crime with Anti-money Laundering Initiatives', in Gregory Rose (ed.), *Following the Proceeds of Environmental Crime: Forests, Fish and Filthy Lucre.* New York: Routledge, pp. 71–80

Jonge, Alice De 2011. *Transnational Corporations and International Law: Accountability in the Global Business Environment.* Cheltenham: Edward Elgar Publishing Limited

Keijzer, Nico 2013. 'Corporate Criminal Liability', paper presented at the meeting of Satgas REDD UKP4, Jakarta, 20 May

Keulen, Berend F. and Gritter, Erik 2010. 'Corporate Criminal Liability in the Netherlands', *Electronic Journal of Comparative Law* 14(3): 1–12

Maglie, Cristina de 2005. 'Models of Corporate Criminal Liability in Comparative Law', *Washington University Global Studies Law Review* 4(3): 547–66

Maradoa 2018. 'Corporate Criminal Liability in Indonesia: Regulation, Implementation and Comparison with the Netherlands'. Doctorate Thesis. Rotterdam: Erasmus University Rotterdam

Ministry of Environment and Forestry of the Republic of Indonesia 2018. *The State of Indonesia's Forests 2018.* Jakarta: Ministry of Environment and Forestry of the Republic of Indonesia

Möhrenschlager, Manfred 1998. 'Development on an International Level', paper presented at the International Colloquium on Criminal Responsibility of Legal and Collective Entities, Berlin, Germany, 4–6 May

Muladi and Priyatno, Dwija 1991. *Pertanggungjawaban Pidana Korporasi* (*Corporate Criminal Liability*). Bandung: Sekolah Tinggi Bandung

Muladi and Priyatno, Dwidja 2009. *Pertanggungjawaban Pidana Korporasi.* Jakarta: Kencana

Muladi 2013. 'Pertanggungjawaban Pidana Korporasi (Corporate Criminal Liability) dalam Kerangka "The Legal Environment of Business"'. Jakarta

Pramono, Widyo 2012. *Pertanggungjawaban Pidana Korporasi Hak Cipta.* Bandung: Alumni

Priyatno, Dwidja 2004. *Kebijakan Legislasi tentang Pertanggungjawaban Pidana Korporasi di Indonesia.* Bandung: Utomo

Priyatno, Dwidja 2017. Kebijakan Formulasi Sistem Pertanggungjawaban Pidana Korporasi dalam Peraturan Perundang-undangan Khusus di Luar KUHP di Indonesia. Jakarta: Sinar Grafika

Sjahdeini, Sutan Remy 2006. *Pertanggungjawaban Pidana Korporasi.* Jakarta: Grafiti Pers

Sjahdeini, Sutan Remy 2017. *Ajaran Pemidanaan: Tindak Pidana Korporasi dan Seluk-Beluknya.* Depok: Kencana

Wells, Celia 2001. *Corporations and Criminal Responsibility.* Oxford University Press

Legislation

Herziene *Inlandsch Reglement* (HIR) of 1926, Dutch Colonial Civil Procedure Code

Criminal Code (*Kitab Undang-Undang Hukum Pidana*, KUHP: Law No. 1 of 1946 as amended by Law No. 27 of 1999 on the Indonesian Criminal Code)

Criminal Procedure Code of 1981 (Kitab Undang-undang Hukum Acara Pidana, KUHAP)

Law No. 7 Drt of 1955 on Economic Crimes

Law No. 11/PNPS/1963 on Subversion, revoked by Law No. 26 of 1999.

Law No. 9 of 1976 on Narcotics, which was amended by Law No. 22 of 1997 and most recently by Law No. 35 of 2009.
Law No. 6 of 1984 on Post, which was amended by Law No. 38 of 2009.
Law No. 5 of 1984 on Industry, which was amended by Law No. 3 of 2014.
Law No. 5 of 1997 on Psychotropics.
Law No. 23 of 1997 on Environmental Protection and Management Law, which was amended by Law No. 32 of 2009.
Law No. 5 of 1999 on the Ban of Monopolistic Practices.
Law No. 8 of 1999 on Consumer Protection.
Law No. 31 of 1999 on the Eradication of Corruption, which was amended by Law No. 20 of 2001
Law No. 41 of 1999 on Forestry
Law No. 15 of 2002 on the Prevention and Eradication of Money Laundering, which was amended by Law No. 25 of 2003 and most recently by Law No. 8 of 2010.
Law No. 31 of 2004 on Fisheries, which was amended by Law No. 45 of 2009.
Law No. 39 of 2014 on Plantations
Supreme Court Regulation No. 13 of 2016
Attorney General Regulation PER-028/A/JA/1-/2014
Decree of the Ministry of Marine Affairs and Fisheries of the Republic of Indonesia No. 50/KEPMEN-KP/2017 on Potential, Allowable Catch and Level of Exploitation of Fisheries Resources in the Fisheries Management Area of Indonesia

Court cases and decisions

The Republic of Indonesia v. PT Dongwoo Environmental Indonesia, No. 458/Pid.B/2008.PN.Bks.
The Republic of Indonesia v. PT Dongwoo Environmental Indonesia, No. 456/Pid/2009/PT.Bdg.
The Republic of Indonesia v. PT Dongwoo Environmental Indonesia, No. 862 K/Pid.Sus/2010
The Republic of Indonesia v. PT Indominco Mandiri, No. 562/Pid.Sus-Lh/2017/Pn.Trg.
The Republic of Indonesia v. I Komand Redana, No. 794/Pid.Sus/2016/PN.Dps.
The Republic of Indonesia v. PT Newmont Minahasa Raya, No. 284/Pid.B/2005/PN.Mdo.

13 Explaining the failure of palm oil licensing in Indonesia

Josi Khatarina

(Corruption) usually occurs in regions with high natural resources ... (such as) mining and plantations.

Jusuf Kalla[1]

The Indonesian vice-president made this statement in response to a case in which a head of local government was caught red-handed by the Anti-Corruption Commission (KPK, Komisi Pemberantasan Korupsi) in February 2018. Not long before this, The Gecko Project[2] published the first part of an investigative report detailing the interplay between money, power, and politics in the issuance of palm oil plantation licences in Seruyan, Central Kalimantan (The Gecko Project 2017). This report made public the modus operandi of palm oil licensing corruption, something that advocacy groups working on forestry and palm oil issues were already familiar with. In fact, the vice-president's comment simply reflects the general public's perception that local governments tend to be corrupt in issuing palm oil licences.

While corruption is probably the main motive for elites in local governments to issue licences using incorrect legal procedures, anti-corruption law is not the only law that can be used to discourage such practices. Environment and natural resources laws, including Law No. 39 of 2014 on Plantations, also contain criminal sanctions that can be applied to such violations. Using the punishment framework introduced by Mandiberg and Faure (2009), criminal provisions in environmental and natural resources laws can be categorised as 'abstract endangerment crimes'. A criminal provision is categorised as abstract endangerment crime when the harm is not mentioned explicitly (Voorde, 2014: 166) because the conduct itself is dangerous, so there is no need to link it to actual harm caused by the crime (see Duff and Marshall, 2015).

One of the characteristics of this crime category is that it is usually easy to prosecute (Mandiberg and Faure 2009: 497). Yet, my preliminary research shows that there has been a very little prosecution using such provisions in Indonesia. This chapter seeks to answer the question of why there is an absence of punishment while violations are prevalent, even though the law has introduced a low burden of proof for prosecutions? To answer this question, I will focus on the implementation of criminal law sanctions in the 2014 Plantation Law that target licence issuers who violate laws and regulations when issuing licences.

This chapter is structured as follows. The first section discusses the problem of proliferation of problematic licences after decentralisation in the post-Soeharto era (2000–15). This part will also show that issues faced by palm oil licensing are not unique and are shared by other sectors. Next, it will explain how different laws in natural resource management area approach common problems in different ways and discuss their similarities and differences. The comparison is needed to judge the Plantation Law's approach by comparison to other similar laws. The fourth section discusses the weak implementation of the laws thus far, with judicial decisions as a case study. As there is an absence of enforcement under the Plantation Law, I widen my research into other sectors and find similar patterns, which offer some explanation for the phenomenon. The last section seeks explanation of the factors that impede the proper implementation of the Plantation Law. The discussion in this part will be divided into three factors; adequacy of written legal rules; adequacy of institutional capacity; and, lastly, the extent of political support for consistent implementation of the law.

The proliferation of licences and their irregularities

Decentralisation is claimed to be the key 'answer' to improve democracy, security, and development as it promises to bring government 'closer' to the public (see for example Eaton, Smoke, and Connerley 2010). Embedded in this concept is a more inclusive and responsive decision-making process. Thus, in the context of natural resources management, democratic decentralisation is argued to improve fairness in the distribution of benefits as well as the sustainability of natural resources, as locals have more concern for, and knowledge of, the place in which they live (Agrawal and Ribot 1999; Carney 1995; Larson 2003; Resosudarmo 2007). This is one of the arguments for the Post-Soeharto transfer after 1998 of natural resources management authority, including in relation to plantations, to district level governments.

The environmental effect, however, has not been as expected. Motivated by personal gain as well as an interest in boosting local revenues, local governments have issued unprecedented numbers of licences to exploit natural resources in a manner that at times violates laws and regulations (Hadiz 2004; Khatarina 2018; Resosudarmo 2007;). Wide non-compliance in issuing licences, discussed in more detail below, is exacerbated by the absence of consistent enforcement, as many illegal activities can continue without legal consequences. The combination of the improper licensing with the absence of enforcement has led to multi-dimensional social, economic and environmental problems, such as licence overlaps, conflict over land ownership, untraceable revenues, and a high level of environmental destruction such as deforestation (Bullinger and Haug 2012; Indrarto et al. 2012; Suwarno and Hein 2015).

The evidence of widespread irregular licensing was revealed by an audit conducted under the leadership of the President's Delivery Unit in cooperation with local governments in three provinces (UKP4 2013). The main purpose of this audit was to obtain complete and clear evidence of the non-compliance in land-based licensing in order to develop evidence-based policy. In other words, it was not developed to assist law enforcement. The audit was conducted in 2013–14 and covered mining and plantation licences in eight districts. It covered the entire licensing process, from company establishment to the production stage. The audit relied mainly on documents, but also conducted selective fieldwork based on purposive sampling.

Common irregularities revealed by the audit can be divided into two stages. The first is during the licensing process or before a plantation permit is received; the second is after licences are issued, for example, not submitting a report on plantation operations. This research focuses on the first part of irregularities because penalties for local governments in the Plantation Law are directed at local government conduct when issuing licences, not conduct after licences have been issued. For palm oil, Table 13.1 shows some of the findings that indicate the level of irregularities before plantation licences are issued.

The data shows that none of the licensees involved submitted a complete set of all the documents legally required for the issue of a plantation licence. The documents missing vary, for example, some licensees do not have a tax number, while others do not have a location permit, and some do not have environmental licences.

The absence of these basic documents is a sign that the administrative procedure that should have taken place to issue the documents or licences was not properly followed. For example, to obtain a location permit or environmental licence, local communities must be informed and their concerns must be considered.[3] The absence of these documents shows these processes have not taken place.

Table 13.1 Findings on non-compliance before plantation permits are issued

Issues	*8 districts*
Total plantation licences	229
Do not have all the basic documents for conducting business (for example, NPWP, SIUP)[1]	229 (100%)
Do not have all the requirements to apply for a plantation licence (for example, a recommendation on compliance with spatial plans, known as a location permit)	229 (100%)
Plantation licences issued without environmental licences	115 (50%)

[1] NPWP (*Nomor Pokok Wajib Pajak*, Tax File Number); SIUP (*Surat Izin Usaha Perdagangan*, Trading Permit).

This can have serious and multi-dimensional effects. For example, regarding the fact that many companies do not have the obligatory tax number, the KPK has found that company tax compliance in the palm oil sector is very poor, only around 46 per cent (Perkasa 2017). This means that in 2015, for example, when state revenue from palm oil was Rp. 22.27 trillion (A$ 2.2 billion), Indonesia was losing about the same amount from tax in this sector. This situation is common in other areas of the natural resources industry. In mining, for example, the KPK has confirmed that around 30 per cent (4,000 of 12,000 companies working on mining) do not have the required tax number, which means the state is losing around Rp. 20 trillion from this sector each year (Chandra 2017; Friana 2017; Rastika 2014).

Regarding social impacts, the failure to follow proper procedure, particularly the failure to obtain environmental licences, has resulted in many conflicts with local communities (Levang, Riva, and Orth 2016) and many environmental problems including deforestation. For example, location and environmental permits are the administrative safeguard to ensure plantation locations accord with government spatial planning. As Table 13.1, above, shows, these permits are very often ignored. As a result, some plantation licences are issued in forest areas, some even in the protected forest areas. This is obviously a serious impediment to efforts to keep standing forests intact.

Theoretically speaking, licences or permits are legal instruments intended to ensure economic activities can achieve maximum benefit with the very minimal impact, be it social or environmental. The absence of documents and the presence of irregular licensing processes is a sign that local governments perceive the process as a mere formality, instead of serving the purpose of minimising risks from economic activities. The reasons for this may be various. It could be because local governments disagree with the process or because they are simply not aware of it, or it could be because the process has been captured.

In the next section, I will evaluate the central government's response to these problems by analysing regulatory provisions related to the central government's authority to impose administrative and criminal sanctions on local governments that fail to follow licensing procedures for palm oil plantations.

Sanctions in the environmental and natural resource management legal framework

There have been plenty of environmental and natural resource management laws enacted after 1999, but the laws that will be investigated are only those have introduced administrative and criminal sanctions to address problematic behaviour by licence issuers. Some experts consider laws that govern the use of natural resources to be part of the environmental legal framework, either categorising them as 'sectoral environmental laws' (Santosa 2001),or seeing them as environmental in 'the widest sense of environmental law'

(Bedner 2008: 195). Adopting this understanding, the scope of laws that will be covered in the analysis in this chapter include those related to the environment, forestry, spatial planning, mining, forestry, and plantations.

Table 13.2 shows a summary of comparison of approaches (administrative and criminal sanctions) in natural resources and environmental law, both before and after decentralisation.

Table 13.2 Comparison of natural resources legal framework for administrative and criminal sanctions

No.	*Law before decentralisation*	*Law after decentralisation*
1.	**Spatial Planning** Law No. 24 of 1992 on Spatial Planning a. This law **does not** introduce specific criminal sanctions, but article 18 of the Law does mention that control (*penertiban*) over the use of space not in accordance with spatial plans will incur sanctions. b. The Elucidation (explanatory memorandum) to art. 18 states that sanctions includes criminal, civil and administrative sanctions, which apply based on laws and regulations, even though the law itself does not specify the type of sanctions.	Law No. 26 of 2007 on Spatial Planning a. Article 73 of the law **states** that (1) 'any government officials who issue licences not in accordance with spatial plans as mentioned in art. 37(7), shall be liable to a maximum imprisonment of five years **and a maximum** fine of Rp. 500 Million'. (2) The punishment can also include dishonourable dismissal.
2.	**Environment** Law No. 23 of 1997 on Environmental Management a. This law **does not** introduce sanctions for officials who issue licences or have authority to conduct supervision and monitoring to licence holders. b. The law does not introduce a clause that allows higher levels of government to step in, in the absence of action from the licence issuers (known as second line enforcement).	Law No. 32 of 2009 on Environmental Protection and Management c. Article 77 introduces **second line enforcement**, by which the central government (the responsible ministry) is given authority to issue administrative sanctions when local governments as licence issuers are considered to have intentionally not applied administrative sanctions for serious violations. d. Articles 111 and 112 of the Law **introduce criminal sanctions** for officials who have authority to issue licences, as well as officials who have authority to conduct supervision and monitoring of licence holders.

(*continued*)

Table 13.2 Cont.

No.	*Law before decentralisation*	*Law after decentralisation*
		e. Article 111 introduces sanctions for: • officials who issue environmental licences without EIA. They will be liable to maximum imprisonment of three years **and** a maximum fine of Rp. 3 billion. • Officials who issue business licences (such as plantation licences) without environmental licences. They will be liable to maximum imprisonment of three years of **and** a maximum fine of Rp. 3 billion. f. Article 112 introduces sanctions for: i. Officials who do not exercise oversight of compliance of businesses to environmental licences and laws and regulations in general, resulting in pollution and/or environmental destruction and the loss of human life. They will be liable to a maximum imprisonment of 1 year and/or a maximum fine of Rp. 500 Million.
3.	**Mining** Law No. 11 of 1967 on Mining The law does not introduce sanctions for licence issuers.	Law No. 4 of 2009 on Mining The law does not introduce criminal sanctions, but takes administrative approach by introducing **second line enforcement**, which grants authority to the central government to withdraw a licence issued by local government, preceded by an evaluation of the licence.
4.	**Forestry** Law No. 41 of 1999 on Forestry The Law does not introduce sanctions for licence issuers.	Law No. 18 of 2013 on Prevention and Eradication of Forest Degradation This Law does not replace the Law No. 41 of 1999 but complements it. It introduces the heaviest sanctions compared to other natural resources laws. It expands and elaborates **crimes by public officials** in relation to illegal logging or illegal use of forest area. It now includes: a. officials who issue licences without authority or not in accordance with laws/regulations;

Table 13.2 Cont.

No.	*Law before decentralisation*	*Law after decentralisation*
		b. officials who protect illegal loggers or illegal users of forest areas; and c. officials who intentionally do not observe their duty and cause illegal logging or illegal use of forest areas. The penalty has a maximum of ten years and fine of Rp. 10 billion.
5.	**Plantation** Law No. 18 of 2004 of on Plantations The Law does not introduce sanctions for licence issuers.	Law No. 39 of 2014 on Plantations This law introduces criminal sanction for licence issuers who issue plantation licences contrary to spatial plans or laws and regulations in general. The maximum penalty is five years of imprisonment and a maximum fine of Rp. 5 billion.

The criminal sanctions in these laws not only target local governments but also cover all official actors involved in licensing, including central government officials. For example, the central government is authorised to issue licences for activities that are located between two provinces (see art. 48(2) 2014 Plantation Law) or when a project is considered to have a strategic national value (arts. 28 and 74 of the 2009 Mining Law). Nevertheless, after 1999, most of the power to issue licences in the environment and natural resources field has been transferred to local governments. In other words, under decentralisation, the main culprits for environmental and social harms caused by improper licensing are local government officials. Thus, this chapter will look at the application of the coercive approaches in the context of local governments. However, this is not intended to imply that the central government has behaved in a manner utterly consistent with the national legislation.

A non-unified approach

As Table 13.1 above shows, different laws use different regulatory approaches; some take a combination of administrative and criminal sanctions, while some alternate between the two. Despite these differences, there is a general tendency for all laws to introduce heavier sanctions to discourage violations. This shows that lawmakers acknowledge problems with local government power to issue licences and rely on sanctions to prevent them.

The 2009 Environmental Protection and Management Law is an example of a law that combines the administrative approach with criminal sanctions. The offences introduced are varied, and they apply not only to licence issuers but also officials responsible for conducting supervision or monitoring, the failure to do which causes severe harm to the environment or human beings. In terms of the administrative approach, the Law not only introduces administrative sanctions but also 'second line enforcement', by which the central government is authorised to revoke licences issued by local governments when certain conditions are met.

On the other hand, the 2009 Law on Mining uses only an administrative approach. This is a completely different path to the 2007 Spatial Planning Law, which introduces criminal sanctions. There are two aspects of the administrative approach that are worth attention: first, it uses the concept of second-line enforcement, whereby the central government is granted the authority to withdraw licences issued by local governments in certain situations. Second, the Law also requires the central government to evaluate mining licences issued by local governments as a condition for the revocation. This prescription serves two functions: first, it allows the central government to conduct assessment of mining licences issued by local governments; and, second, it ensures revocation of licences is based on objective considerations.

The last approach, the main concern of this chapter, involves the use only of criminal sanctions. For example, the 2007 Spatial Planning Law introduces criminal sanctions for government officials who issue licences that are not in accord with spatial plans. Another example is 2013 Prevention and Eradication of Forest Degradation Law. This Law introduces the heaviest sanctions of all the laws considered, and it expands and elaborates the type of criminal offences relevant to public officials involved in illegal logging or illegal use of forest areas. In fact, it covers not only officials who issue licences without authority or not in accordance with laws and regulations, but also officials who protect illegal loggers or illegal users of forest areas. Further it also sanctions officials who intentionally do not carry out their duties and, because of that, illegal logging or illegal use of forest area takes place. The penalties in the Law include a maximum of ten years and a fine of Rp. 10 billion (cumulatively).

Likewise, the 2014 Plantation Law also introduces criminal sanctions for public officials who do not obey the regulatory framework in issuing licences, and omits the administrative approach. As with the other Laws, the elements of the criminal sanctions are relatively easy to establish, as the sanctions aim to deter perpetrators from violating administrative procedures. Thus, it does not require causality between the offence in certain situation, such as death or environmental destruction. As mentioned, the idea behind criminalising such violations of laws and regulations is that 'adherence to the regulatory scheme is the most effective way to prevent serious environmental harm' (Mandiberg and Faure 2009: 454) and criminalising such conduct can generate a deterrent effect (494).

The tendency toward a coercive approach

While different laws take different approaches, there is a general inclination to resort to the coercive strategy to curb the problematic behaviour. All the sanctions introduced are relatively heavy, imposing imprisonment of three, five or ten years. In addition, all laws but the 2014 Plantation Law also impose cumulative penalties in the form of imprisonment and a fine. The 2014 Plantation Law allows the alternative of five years' imprisonment or Rp. 5 billion in fines. This coercive tendency also applies to administrative sanctions, by which the Law allows the central government to withdraw licences issued by local governments in certain circumstances.

This tendency to resort to a coercion in environment and natural resources laws is not unusual; in fact, it is in line with the general inclination of Indonesian lawmakers in the post-Soeharto era. Akbari (2015: 31), for example, finds that from 1998 to 2014 there were 274 newly-introduced penalties for conduct that can be categorised as criminal (*kejahatan*), while 442 were introduced for violations of laws or 'misdemeanours' (*pelanggaran*). The research further suggests that the Indonesian government has the view that (newly) introduced rules will not be obeyed if not accompanied by criminal sanctions. This phenomenon is not unique to Indonesia. Mandiberg and Faure (2009: 510) have shown that this approach is the most common one taken in environmental statues in the United States and the European Union.

It has been discussed above how widespread violations of administrative procedures in issuing licences have resulted in serious harm, not only to the environment but also to society in general. Given the repetitive nature of these kinds of violation, enforcement of procedural provisions is very important to deter defendants (specific deterrence) or others who might attempt the same crime (general deterrence). Regrettably, as the next section shows, enforcement of criminal sanctions is largely absent, not only in the 2014 Plantation Law but across all environment and natural resources laws.

The absence of enforcement

Investigation of the Supreme Court judgment database shows that there are very few cases that have applied the laws discussed above, even though breaches are widespread, as the audit has indicated, and the offences are relatively easy to prove. As at 29 November 2017, my search of the Supreme Court decision database showed only four relevant cases: one under Law No. 26 of 2007 on Spatial Planning and three under Law No. 41 of 1999 on Forestry. There were none under the 2014 Plantation Law.

2007 Spatial Planning Law

There are many allegations that a large number of plantation licences are situated outside areas allocated for plantation activities in national and regional spatial plans, and are even located in forbidden areas, such as protected forest or conservation areas (Indrarto et al. 2012: 6, 32). As mentioned, the 2007 Spatial Planning Law imposes criminal sanctions for issuing licences that do not comply with spatial plans. Nevertheless, I found almost no cases in which licence issuers were penalised for issuing such irregular licences. There is only one case in the Supreme Court database in which criminal sanctions in the 2007 Spatial Plan Law were used to deal with a forestry-type licence issued outside the designated area for the activity.

This case concerns a head of the Forestry Agency at the District Level in Simalungun (Amran Sinaga), who was convicted for his actions in issuing a recommendation[4] for harvesting logs in a conservation area (as per Provincial Government Regulation No. 7 of 2003 on the Spatial Plan for North Sumatera Province).[5] Sinaga was charged under three different Laws: the 1999 Forestry Law; the Criminal Code (art. 263(1) on forgery); and the 2007 Spatial Planning Law (art. 71 in relation to art. 61; and art. 73(1)). In the first instance, Sinaga was acquitted of all charges (*dibebaskan dari seluruh dakwaan*). At the cassation level, however, the Supreme Court imposed four years' imprisonment (Decision No. 194 K/Pid.Sus/2012). Sinaga was considered 'an authoritative official who intentionally co-operated to issue a licence contrary to the spatial plan' (under art. 73 of the 2007 Spatial Plan Law). The Court stated that the accused had failed to consider that the area was inside 'protected forests and other protected areas' as prescribed in the relevant local government spatial planning regulation. Unfortunately, this judgment was reversed by the Supreme Court on judicial review (PK, *peninjauan kembali*) (Akbar 2017), and on 2 February 2017, Sinaga was elected Deputy Mayor of Simalungun.

2013 Law on Eradication of Forest Degradation

Similarly, compared to the many allegations of wrongdoing in forestry licences, the criminal provisions of the 2013 Eradication of Forest Degradation Law are rarely used, and only three cases could be found in the Supreme Court database. All targeted low-level officials.

The first case was decided in 2014, in Riau.[6] In this case, the accused was the local village head, Syamsir, known as a *penghulu* by the indigenous community in Riau (Parsudi 1995: 221). He was charged with four alternative charges under the1999 Forestry Law, Law No. 18 of 2013 on Prevention and Eradication of Forest Degradation, and the Criminal Code. Syamsir was convicted because the court found him to be an 'official who committed, ordered or participated in a conspiracy to conduct illegal logging and/or illegal use of forest area as referred to in art. 28(e) of the 2013 Law on Eradication of Forest Degradation'. The Court found that Syamsir's crime was to issue a land certificate without first checking whether the area was part of the forest area, resulting in logging in a conversion forest area. In his defence, Syamsir stated that in issuing the land title, he never checked with the forest authority as he claimed that he did not know that the area was part of the forest. He received punishment of two years' imprisonment and a fine of Rp. 1 billion.

The next case also involved a village head, Salim Samat, the head of Belang-belang village in South Halmahera,[7] who issued a blank Certificate of Validity of Forest Product (SKSHH, *Surat Keterangan Sahnya Hasil Hutan*), adding his signature and an official stamp, it so it could be used to transport illegally harvested logs. He was charged under art. 105(f) in relation to art. 28(f) of the 2013 Law on Eradication of Forest Degradation, with a subsidiary/secondary charge under art. 83(1) in relation to art. 55 of the 2013 Law. The Court found the first charge proved, and he was convicted for being an official who issued an SKSHH without a rightful process (*tanpa hak*). The Court stated in the decision that 'procedure used in issuing the certificate ... was not in accordance to laws and regulations' because 'it was issued in blank and only been signed and stamped by the offender' (2015: 38).

The last case involved a civil servant at the Forestry Agency of Parigi Moutong District, Rio Hendra.[8] Hendra was convicted because he issued a certificate of validity of forest product while not in a proper site (he was in a car, on the side of a road, not in the actual area of logging), without first conducting an administrative and physical checking. As a consequence, the harvested logs transported using the certificate were not sourced from private forest as claimed by the certificate holder. The Supreme Court further stated that, therefore, the certificate was invalid (2016: 14–15). The Court found Hendra's conduct satisfied art. 28(d) of 2013 Eradication of Forest Degradation Law, because he was an 'official who was participating or assisting to commit illegal logging and/or illegal use of forest area as referred to in art. 28(d)'. He was sentenced to two years of imprisonment and a fine of Rp. 1 billion under art. 105(d) of the 2013 Law.

Others

My search of the Supreme Court database also reveals that criminal provisions for licence issuers are considered by the Court to be a sign of the seriousness of lawmakers' intention to discourage certain practices. This is found in a Supreme Court decision assessing the legality of Presidential Regulation No. 18 of 2016 on the Acceleration of Development of Waste-Based Electricity Generators in Jakarta, Tangerang Bandung, Semarang, Surakarta, Surabaya, and Makassar.[9]

In this case, the applicants (a group of individuals and NGOs), argued before the Supreme Court that the 'acceleration' part of the regulation, particularly art. 6(2), contradicts art. 40(1) of Law No. 32 of 2009 on Environmental Protection and Management. Article 6(2) of the Regulation allows construction of electricity generators to take place in parallel with the process for obtaining construction licences and environmental licences, while art.

40(1) of the 2009 Environmental Law prohibits business licences being issued without environmental licences. To support their argument, the applicants argued that the introduction of criminal sanctions for relevant officials who issue business licences without environmental licences (art. 111(2) of the 2009 Environmental Law) shows that lawmakers intended to prohibit issuance of business licences, such as the construction of electricity generators, without careful consideration of their impact on the environment, represented by the issuance of environmental licences.

The Supreme Court granted the plaintiff's petition and took the view that the Presidential Regulation was contrary to art. 40(1) of the 2009 Environment Law, and art. 111(2) as well. The Court stated in its judgment that the combination of the two articles in the Law clearly shows that environmental licences must be obtained before business licences could be issued. This, it said, was in line with the 'paradigm of supervision and management of the environment, which made environmental licences part of a procedure for an activity' (2016: 136). The 2016 Presidential Regulation was therefore annulled by the Supreme Court.

Analysis

Several observations can be made about the use of criminal provisions to enforce licensing laws. First, such provisions are very little used, as there are very few convictions, despite the many sanctions now available in the many environment and natural resources laws. My interview with civil servant investigators in the Directorate General of Estate Crops and the Ministry of Environment and Forestry also indicates that they have not processed any cases on criminal sanctions for licence issuers such as local governments. One informant from the Ministry of Environment and Forestry said that this is not because there are no offenders, but because the office lacked 'political will' and preferred to ignore or to discontinue such cases. The absence of political will is even more obvious in the plantation sector, as can be seen from the absence of institutional capacity among civil servant investigators, which will be discussed separately in the next section.

Second, the cases show that when the rare prosecutions do take place, they target less important actors, while ignoring higher level official violations. In the Amran Sinaga case, for example, there was a more powerful actor, – the Mayor, who signed the licence (and not just the mere recommendation signed by Sinaga). However, the mayor has never been convicted.[10] Those convicted in the three cases under the 2013 Eradication of Forest Degradation Law were also low-level officials and no cases concerning high level officials have ever been processed under this Law. This does not mean that no such cases have ever come to the attention of law enforcers. One high-level official from the Ministry of Environment and Forestry mentioned that 'Yes, there are cases concerning heads of local government who violate the law [in issuing licences], but we get no green light to continue these cases'. Again, the absence of political will to prosecute such crimes hinders the use of the sanctions.

This finding is an obvious example of the widely accepted cynical view of the condition of law enforcement in Indonesia: '*tajam ke bawah, tumpul ke atas*', sharp at 'the bottom' and blunt at 'the top'. Even Presidents Yudhoyono and Jokowi have acknowledged this chronic problem of Indonesian law enforcement (Belarminus 2017; Romadoni 2016).

Third, despite this kind of 'discriminatory' law enforcement, there are signs that the existence of criminal sanctions does have the intended effect of providing stronger back-up for the administrative procedure outlined by the laws and regulations. The case of the use of criminal sanctions in the Supreme Court review of the presidential regulation is evidence of this. As shown, the provision was used to demonstrate lawmakers' intention to strengthen the administrative procedure. Thus, licences such as environmental licences are meant to be taken seriously - they are not a mere formality to pave the way for development.

There are too few decisions to draw a settled conclusion, but the three cases suggest that, despite its potential, the absence of convictions in the face of the many allegations, the tendency of the cases to target low-level officials, and the 'misuse' of discretion to discontinue investigations, are clear signs that the coercive approach has not been optimised to eradicate the problematic behaviour of local governments. In other words, there is still a big gap between intention of the law and its implementation.

Reasons for the absence of enforcement

It has been suggested that there are at least three factors contributing to the problematic implementation of legal rules in Indonesia (Khatarina 2020): inadequate legal rules; an absence of supportive institutional set-up; and an absence of consistent political will. The indicators of the absence of the political will have been shown above; below I assess the two other factors in relation to the implementation of art. 106 of the 2014 Plantation Law.

Inadequate legal rules

Waddell (2004: 159) argues that having unambiguous and applicable rules is crucial to ensuring effective law enforcement. I do not find the absence of rigorous use of the sanctions to be rooted in the drafting issues, mostly because other, more basic, reasons intervene. Nevertheless, that does not mean that problematic drafting is not a problem.

There are several drafting problems in the 2014 Plantation Law that could potentially hamper its implementation, even if adequate political will was present: the drafting of art. 106; and drafting in regard to the plantation PPNS (*Penyidik Pegawai Negeri Sipil,* Civil Servant Investigator).

Article 106 of the Law reads:

> Ministers, Governors, and Mayors who hold authority to issue plantation licenses who:
>
> a. Issue a license against spatial function; and/or
> b. Issue a license against rules and regulations;
>
> as mentioned in Article 50 shall be liable to maximum imprisonment of five years or a maximum fine of Rp. 5 billion.

According to the category of criminal provisions introduced by Mandiberg and Faure stated (2009: 497), art. 106 can be categorised as an 'abstract endangerment crime'. In the wording of art. 106, there is no requirement to prove *mens rea* (criminal intent), or the impact of the conduct, or causality between the conduct and the impact. Nevertheless, there are several aspects of the drafting of art. 106 that make it difficult to enforce: the article is vague, not far-reaching, and potentially conflicts with other laws.

The first problem is the limited definition of 'perpetrator' in art. 106, as the crime can only be committed by ministers, governors or mayors holding the authority to issue plantation licences. On one hand, this limitation to the licence issuers shows the clear intention of the lawmakers to hold the ultimate decision-makers accountable for their actions. On the other hand, this limited application potentially prohibits wider use of the Law. For example, under a different regulation, heads of local government are obliged to delegate their power to issue licences to the head of the office of One-Stop Integrated Service or *Perizinan Terpadu Satu Pintu* or PTSP (art. 11(4) Presidential Regulation No. 97 of 2014 on Implementation of the One-Stop Integrated Service). While some heads of local government still hold onto their authority for several types of licences, such as plantation licences or location permits (see for example art. 3(1) Mayor of Ogan Komering Ilir District Regulation No. 2 of 2017 on Delegation in the Permits and Non-Permits to Head of PTSP Agency District of Ogan Komering Ilir), most have duly transferred their power to the PTSP (Tarigan 2015). In the case of a head of PTSP committing a misdemeanour, he or she will escape the scope of art. 106 because it only applies to governors or mayors. In this context, art. 106 is thus potentially ineffective in curbing all actors involved in the problematic behaviour.

In the same context, there are also indications that even though formal authority has been transferred to a head of PTSP, heads of local government are often still practically involved and, in reality, hold the ultimate decision on licence issuance. In this situation, the limited scope of art. 106 could also hinder the effective use of the article to actually catch the real perpetrators – governors and mayors who have formally transferred their authority to the head of PTSP.

To avoid these problems, the Law should have considered approaches used in other previously enacted laws such as the 2013 Environmental Law or the

2013 Eradication of Forest Degradation Law. Both cover different type of offenders – not just licence issuers but also officials responsible for monitoring and any officials who protect offenders. This approach would ensure the 2014 Plantation Law the range of different actors whose disobedience contributes to the problems. If this approach had been taken, a delegation of authority to another agency, such as PTSP, would not interrupt application of the Law to all relevant perpetrators.

The second problem with art. 106 is a conflict in rules between the 2014 Plantation Law and the 2007 Spatial Planning Law. Both laws introduce sanctions for the same offence, but the sanctions do not correspond. The 2007 Spatial Planning Law introduces a lower sanction for both imprisonment and fines, but it uses a cumulative approach to the two. It also allows for an additional sanction of dishonourable dismissal from office. The 2014 Plantation Law, on the other hand, introduces higher imprisonment and higher fines, but makes them alternative. It also does not introduce the additional sanction of dismissal. These unnecessary differences not only reconfirm a poor law-making process (see Khatarina 2018) but potentially creates problems at the implementation level, as they give discretion to law enforcement agencies to choose which law will be applied, which can easily be abused.

Lastly, some parts of art. 106 are very broad, and vagueness provides room for misuse. A particular problem is with the qualification of the crime, which is 'not in accordance with rules and regulations'. The concept of 'rules and regulations' has a very broad scope; it can encompass many different aspects of licensing, such as the format of licences. Arguably, the degree of fault in having a different format for a licence that could be categorised as 'not in accordance to regulations' is a totally different degree of wrongdoing in comparison to not having the required licence at all. Thus, the use of this very broad term could undermine the actual intention of the lawmakers, which is presumably to discourage substantive violation of the laws and regulations. This problem also gives unnecessary discretion to already problematic law enforcement agencies and, in the end, will further weaken the credibility of the Law and the criminal sanctions it introduces.

Failure to introduce a comprehensive approach

A minute from the national legislature's deliberation of the 2014 Plantation Bill shows that discussion of the non-compliance of local governments in plantation licensing was non-existent, which means discussion of how to comprehensively deter perpetrators was also absent. The lawmakers did not, for example, discuss different approaches taken by previous laws on the environment and natural resources that faced similar problems. The relative success of the administrative approach taken by Law No. 4 of 2009 on Mining, for example, was not considered at all.

The administrative approach introduced in that 2009 Law has allowed the Ministry of Energy and Mineral Resources to introduce a 'Clean and

Clear Program', widely known as 'C&C'. The program was basically designed to ensure all mining licences follow applicable laws and regulations, at least administratively (Resosudarmo et al. 2014: 277–8). Through this programme, the ministry has successfully centralised data on mining licences issued by local governments, which can be used for many purposes. Based on evaluation, many licences that are administratively incorrect are revoked. This evaluation also helps improve tax compliance (Dewi 2017). The complementary use of the two approaches, criminal and administrative, has been proven to lead to higher compliance in some European countries (Faure and Svatikova 2012). The absence of an administrative approach in the 2014 Plantation Law is evidence of the lawmakers' failure to introduce – or even consider – a comprehensive approach to curb non-compliance by licence issuers.

While it is not uncommon for laws to 'borrow' principles across national borders and adapt them to their own issues (Bedner 2008), this case shows that lawmakers have even failed to make use of lessons readily available within Indonesia's borders.

PPNS and National Police

As with the substantive aspects of its criminal provisions, the 2014 Plantation Law also failed to strengthen the authority of civil servant plantation investigators (Plantation PPNS). While the 2004 and 2014 Plantation Laws require the Ministry of Agriculture to use civil servant investigators (PPNS) to help ensure effective implementation of the criminal sanctions, they are less progressive than other Laws such as the 2009 Environmental Law. For example, under the 2014 Plantation Law, plantation PPNS are required to closely coordinate with the police in carrying out their duties, including in conducting arrests and detention to suspects (arts. 102(3), 2014 Plantation Law). It is widely known that coordination with the police is, in many cases, problematic, primarily due to the vulnerable position of the PPNS, who can easily be manipulated by corrupt police and prosecutors (Santosa 2001: 253–4; Syarif 2010: 16; Yserhan, Herlambang and Adyan 2017: 35). Other reasons include the fact that dependence on the police makes it difficult for the PPNS to mount a quick response or use flexibility, for example when conducting arrest and detention. This is why several other agencies, such as the environmental ministry or the tax office, introduced PPNS who are more 'independent' of the national police. The 2009 Environmental Law even goes further by allowing PPNS to directly coordinate with prosecutors in preparing an indictment, thus bypassing the police, who usually perform this role (art. 94(6), 2009 Environmental Law).

The signs of failure become even stronger when the 2014 Plantation Law is compared to the 2004 Plantation Law, as the 2014 Law actually increases the dependence of the PPNS on the police. In the 2004 Law, there is no provision that obliges PPNS to coordinate with the police in conducting detention and confiscation. In the 2014 Law, however, this duty is clearly mentioned in art. 102(3). This contradicts the direction of other, more progressive, laws that try to create greater independence from the police. To explain this situation, I looked at the minutes of deliberation of the 2014 Plantation Law in the national legislature, the DPR (Dewan Perwakilan Rakyat, People's Representative Assembly), but there was no discussion of this issue in particular, nor of the regulatory approach to deter local governments in violating laws and regulations in the licensing process. This shows the absence of attention to this issue, probably due to PPNS not being in a central position within the Directorate General of Estate Crops, as will be explained below. Thus, those who represented the government during the discussion in the legislature did not realise the impact on plantation PPNS of imposing a duty to coordinate with the police.

Issues relating to the criminal provisions and the PPNS are not the only problems in the 2014 Plantation Law (Khatarina 2018). These weaknesses are rooted in a law-making process that has been captured by political interests, and the absence of a transparent and participatory evidence-based legislative process (Khatarina 2018). As a result, the 2014 Plantation Law has failed to create a comprehensive and unambiguous legal framework to curb the problematic behaviour of local governments in plantation licensing. Thus, while art. 106 provides more opportunity for compliance by national legislation in licensing, the aforementioned problems in the 2014 Law make it harder for law enforcement agencies (particularly the Directorate General of Estate Crops) to successfully enforce it.

These problems in the Plantation Law are made worse by the very weak capacity of the Directorate General of Estate Crops as the motor for implementation of the law, particularly in relation to criminal enforcement.

Weak institutional capacity

The implementing agency obviously has a very important role in ensuring effective implementation of a law. The capacity and integrity of an implementing agency is as important, if not more important, than the legal mandate itself, as it defines convention or legal culture regarding implementation of a law (Davis and Trebilcock 1999: 8–9, 108–9).

In this sense, the plantation PPNS have a crucial role to ensure effective implementation of the criminal provisions on the Plantation Law. The criminal law in their jurisdiction is distinctive to their sector and they need special knowledge to develop successful cases (Hardjasoemantri 2006: 433). The integrity and professionality of the PPNS is therefore important, as they are the spearhead in investigating violations of their sectoral law. The quality of their work should define the worth of the larger police force as the main authority in investigations of crimes. When the PPNS has strong presence and capacity, as do those in the Ministry of Environment and Forestry, for example cases brought by them carry more weight with the police and are more likely to continue to court.

To develop a capable and effective enforcement agency, there is a set of required abilities, such as to detect and respond (Santosa 2014). In the case of the Directorate General of Estate Crops as the host of plantation PPNS, these two abilities are very weak. This can be seen from the absence of a supportive organisational structure for the PPNS, the absence of resources, and the absence of mechanisms detect violations and respond to them.

The Directorate General of Estate Crops has no special unit to house the PPNS (Munandar 2014). An interview with the secretary of the Directorate General of the Estate Crops also reveals how insignificant the role of the PPNS is to the general functions of the Directorate General. When asked about PPNS, the official responded that 'we [the Directorate General of Estate Crops] do not have PPNS, PPNS are with the regional [government] as they are within their authority'. The official, whose task includes giving administrative and technical services to all units in the directorate (art. 511 Minister of Agriculture Regulation No. 45 of 2015 on Organisation and Scope of Works), was simply not aware of the role of the Directorate General of Estate Crops as the coordinator of local plantation PPNS and the fact that the Ministry of Agriculture also has PPNS, despite their less significant number.

Her mistake is understandable, as the Minister of Agriculture Regulation on the organisational structure of the Directorate General of Estate Crops shows it does not even have a specific unit for law enforcement. A simple search of the term 'PPNS' on the Minister of Agriculture's official website also does not show any result at all.[11] In comparison, other ministries such as the Ministry of Environment and the Ministry of Forestry (in 2014 merged into the Ministry of Environment and Forestry), always have a special unit on enforcement, situated at the high Echelon I level (a Directorate General for Enforcement), a clear sign of a greater attention to enforcement.

The absence of a special unit in the Directorate General of Estate Crops undermines the role of PPNS, as is obvious from the low number of staff and the budget allocation for investigations. As at 2015, the Directorate General of Estate Crops had just six PPNS at the central level[12] and, as Munandar (2014) reports, 72 altogether, with 68 at the local level, all with very broad responsibilities.[13] As there is no data on who are PPNS in the Directorate General of Estate Crops, I found through interviews that the six PPNS hold structural positions as high as a director general and some are at the level of director. The structural position would make it difficult, if not impossible, for them to actually conduct investigations. By comparison, there are 1,426 PPNS in forestry at the central level, most of whom do not hold structural positions and exclusively conduct investigations into crimes under their jurisdiction (Ministry of Environment and Forestry 2015: 239).[14] To be sure, there is a far greater area to cover for forestry compared to plantations. Nevertheless, the few plantation PPNS could not possibly cover eight provinces (with more than 100 districts), which each host more than 100,000 ha of private plantations of palm oil. This means there are districts that have no PPNS. For example, in South Sumatra, which has around 250,000 ha plantations, no districts had PPNS (Kompas 2015, see also Wakker, 2014). In more recent developments, however, there are now thirty staff members of Directorate General of Estate Crops being trained to be PPNS. The focus of their work is, however, still conventional crimes, such as fraud in relation to seed, fertilisers and pesticides.[15]

Finally, the absence of adequate detection and response mechanisms is another indicator of the weak institutional capacity of the Ministry of Agriculture in exercising its authority to enforce criminal provisions. There are several signs: first the Directorate General of Estate Crops does not have a system to ensure reporting of licensing issued by local governments. Despite being local governments being required by the national regulation on licensing to report licences they issue,[16] this is rarely done. The Directorate General of Estate Crops does not even have a mechanism in place to ensure this obligation is met. Further, the licence reports that were received were not managed or archived in a meaningful way until very recently, with the launch of the SIPERIBUN (Sistem Informasi Perizinan Perkebunan, Information System for the Licensing of Plantations).[17] SIPERIBUN is an initiative of the Presidential Office in 2014, and it took time and effort from outside institutions such as the Anti-Corruption Commission to ensure adoption by the Directorate General of Estate Crops. Before this, my observation of the sub-directorate of Standardisation, Quality and Business Monitoring (SQBM (*Standarisasi, Mutu dan Pembinaan Usaha*), the echelon III entity that stores reports from local governments on issued licences) was that the copied licences were manually stored and there was no system to manage them. They were treated as ordinary letters and there was no classification based on plantation location, size, name, or anything. In other words, because the central government did not have any system to manage information about plantation licences issued by local governments, it therefore also had no system to detect irregularities in these licences.

The weak institutional capacity of the Ministry of Agriculture in criminal enforcement influences the absence of enforcement of offences related to licences in the larger enforcement environment. This is obvious in the case of the absence of criminal sanctions under the 2004 Plantation Law. Under the 2004 Law, an offence for licence issuers had not been introduced, but a criminal sanction did exist for plantation owners who operate without licences. Unfortunately, there was no use of this provision for almost ten years until it was encouraged by the President's Office under the Improvement of Law Enforcement Programme of REDD+ (Satgas REDD+, 2013). The many police officials and prosecutors who work on natural resources-related crimes in their respective agencies and joined the programme admitted that they never previously had experience of applying this criminal sanction for plantation owners. Thus, they were not familiar with it, and never independently pursued it. On the other hand, prosecutions for similar matters under forestry or environmental law handled by the police were many, because they are more familiar with environmental law and forestry law. This is because PPNS from these two other ministries have previously cooperated with the police on many occasions to follow up their investigations on of crimes related to licences. It is clear from this finding that the role of the PPNS is crucial to secure police' and prosecutors' interest in continuing a case. As the motor of criminal law enforcement of the plantation law, the plantation PPNS have failed to do so.

Conclusion

Among the worst excesses of decentralisation are irregular licences created as a result of the ignorance of head of local governments about national laws and regulations relevant to issuing licences. This has happened in many areas, including forestry, mining and plantation. A survey of environment and natural resources law shows that, in response, a variety of administrative and criminal sanctions have been introduced into the law. For the plantation sector, art. 106 of the 2014 Plantation Law introduces criminal sanctions for heads of local government who issue licences in a manner contrary to the laws and regulations. This sanction appears to be the only significant attempt taken in the plantation sector to change local government attitudes to take national guidelines on licensing mechanisms more seriously.

However, issues with the drafting of the law and the institutional capacity of the Ministry of Agriculture are likely to stymie this attempt. The drafting of the law is problematic as it is too limited, so it could miss the real perpetrators. At the same time, it is vague and therefore provides loopholes for misuse. As for the institution, the Directorate General of Estate Crops has no special unit to administer criminal enforcement, and understanding of the importance of such a unit is largely absent. Until recently, the number of Plantation PPNS in the Directorate General of Estate Crops was very limited, and most of them have structural positions that make it difficult for them to carry their task of investigating crimes.

As the role of the sectoral PPNS is important to instigate the involvement of the larger enforcement forces, the absence of investigations conducted by the national police is to be expected. Consequently, my finding that art. 106 is not being used is not a surprising one.

In summary, my research found that no investigation of the many reports of irregular licences is taking place using the newly introduced criminal sanctions. As far as I am aware, the criminal sanctions in art. 106 of the 2014 Plantation Law are basically unused. With the absence of enforcement, the opportunity to improve local government compliance has been wasted.

Notes

1 Jusuf Kalla was Vice-President of the Republic of Indonesia, from to 2004 to 2019 and, again, from 2014 to 2019. See Taufiqurrahaman 2017.

2 The Gecko Project is an investigative journalism that is designed to report on land deals and corruption that lead to the loss of rainforest, see https://thegeckoproject.org/about.
3 Article 6(5) Ministry of Agriculture and Spatial Planning/Head of National Land Agency Regulation No. 2 of 1999 on Location Permits; arts. 10 and 11; Ministry of Agriculture and Spatial Planning/Head of National Land Agency Regulation No. 5 of 2015 on Location Permits.
4 The recommendation was based on actual measurement on the ground conducted by Sinaga's staff (known as *surat pengukuran*), as well as recommendations from other officials.
5 The defendant argued that the area is outside the forest area prescribed in SK Menhut No. 44/2005 on Forest Area Designation in North Sumatra Province.
6 Decision No. 236/Pid.Sus/2014/PN RHL, Pengadilan Negeri Rokan Hilir, Riau.
7 Decision No. 100/Pid.Sus/2015/PN Lbh, Pengadilan Negeri Labuha, South Halmahera.
8 Court of First Instance Decision No. 204/Pid.Sus/2015/PN. Prg; High Court Decision No. 35/Pid.Sus/2016/PT PALA; Supreme Court Cassation Decision No. 1247 K/Pid.Sus/2016.
9 Supreme Court Decision No. 27/P/HUM/2016.
10 The cassation judgment does mention (at p. 69) that there was a separate prosecution (*berkas terpisah*) initiated in respect of the mayor but his case never reached court. The mayor was finally convicted, but in different circumstances, see Gorganews 2017.
11 The search was conducted on 5 October 2018 in the official website of the Ministry of Agriculture www.pertanian.go.id.
12 According to Dudi Gunadi, coordinator of PPNS at the Directorate General of Estate Crops (Kompas 2015). Numbers have increased, but only very slowly. In December 2009, the Director General of Estate Crops had sixty-eight plantation PPNS: six at the central level and sixty-two at the regional level, see DitjenBun Kementerian Pertanian 2009.
13 The scope of jurisdiction for PPNS includes Law No. 12 of 1992 on Crop Cultivation Systems (*Sistem Budidaya Tanaman*); Law No. 29 of 2000 on the Protection of PlantVarieties (*Perlindungan Varietas Tanaman*); and Law No. 18 of 2004, as amended by Law No. 39 of 2014 on Plantations.
14 While for the environment, there are 96 PPNS at the central level and 320 at regional level. This does not include other law enforcement-related officials, such as forest police (totalling more than 8,000) or officials tasked with monitoring of administrative obligations who do not hold power to investigate crimes (known as PPLH, Pejabat Pengawas Lingkungan Hidup, Environmental Protection Supervision Officials).
15 These are some of the crimes mentioned in the opening speech of a recent PPNS training course, see Humas Polri 2018.
16 Article 33 of the Ministry of Agriculture Regulation No. 26/Permentan/OT.140/2/2007 on Licensing Guidelines for Plantation Businesses; and art. 45(2) of the Ministry of Agriculture No. 98/Permentan/OT.140/9/2013 on Licencing Guidelines for Plantation Businesses.
17 A newly introduced national database system on plantation licensing, see http://sip.ditjenbun.pertanian.go.id.

References

Agrawal, Arun and Ribot, Jesse C. 1999. 'Accountability in Decentralisation: A Framework with South Asian and West African Cases', *Journal of Developing Areas* 33: 473–502

Akbar 2017. 'Perjalanan "Pahit" Amran Sinaga yang Berujung Manis', *Tribun News Medan*, 2 February http://medan.tribunnews.com/2017/02/02/perjalanan-pahit-amran-sinaga-yang-berujung-manis?page=4

Akbari, Anugerah Rizki 2015. *Potret Kriminalisasi Pasca Reformasi dan Urgensi Reklasifikasi Tindak Pidana di Indonesia.* Jakarta: ICJR

Bedner, Adriaan 2008. 'Amalgamating Environmental Law in Indonesia', in J. Arnscheidt, B. van Rooi and J. M. Otto (eds.), *Law Making for Development; Exploration into the Theory and Practice of International Legislative Projects.* Leiden: Leiden University Press, pp. 171–98

Belarminus, Robertus 2017. 'SBY Tak Ingin Penyakit Masa Lalu Menghinggapi Indonesia', *Kompas*, 9 September https://nasional.kompas.com/read/2017/09/09/10040501/sby-tak-ingin-penyakit-masa-lalu-menghinggapi-indonesia

Bernadetta, Dewi and Prayogo, Dody 2013. 'Mining and Development in Indonesia: An Overview of the Regulatory Framework and Policies', IM4DC Action Research Report, Queensland: The Centre for Social Responsibility in Mining, Sustainable Mineral Institute, the University of Queensland

Bullinger, Cathrin and Haug, Michaela 2012. 'In and Out of the Forest: Decentralisation and Recentralisation of Forest Governance in East Kalimantan, Indonesia', *Austrian Journal of South-East Asia Studies* 5(2): 243–62

Burgess, Robin; Hansen, Matthew; Olken, Benjamin A.; Potapov, Peter; and Sieber, Stefanie 2011. 'The Political Economy of Deforestation in the Tropics', *The Quarterly Journal of Economics* 127(4): 1707–54

Carney, Diana 1995. 'Management and Supply in Agriculture and Natural Resources: Is Decentralisation the Answer?', *ODI Natural Resource Perspective*, 4 June, Overseas Development Institute

Chandra, Arda Ardi 2017. 'KPK: 3.202 Perusahaan Tambang di RI Tak Punya NPWP' *detik.com,* 8 June https://finance.detik.com/energi/d-3524710/kpk-3202-perusahaan-tambang-di-ri-tak-punya-npwp

Curran, L. M.; Trigg, S. N.; McDonald, A. K.; Astiani, D.; Hardiono, Y. M.; Siregar, P.; Caniago, I.; and Kasischke, E. 'Lowland Forest Loss in Protected Areas in Indonesian Borneo', *Science* 303: 1000–3

Davis, Kevin and Trebilcock, Michael J. 1999. *What Role do Legal Institutions Play in Development?*, Draft Prepared for the IMF Conference on Second Generation Reforms, 8–9 November www.imf.org/external/pubs/ft/seminar/1999/reforms/trebil.pdf

Dewi, Hanum Kusuma 2017. '30% IUP Tambang Belum Clean and Clear, KPK Siap Blokir', *Bareksa*, 6 December www.bareksa.com/id/text/2017/12/06/30-persen-iup-tambang-belum-clear-and-clean-kpk-siap-blokir/17673/news

DitjenBun Kementerian Pertanian 2009. 'Peranan PPNS Perkebunan Dalam Menyelesaiakn Berbagai Permasalahan di Lapangan', 16 December http://ditjenbun.pertanian.go.id/berita-176-peranan-ppns-perkebunan-dalam-menyelesaikan-berbagai-permasalahan-di-lapangan.html

Duff, R. A. and Marshall, S. E. 2015. 'Abstract Endangerment, Two Harm Principles, and Two Routes to Criminalization', *Minnesota Legal Study Research Paper* No. 15–1.

Eaton, Kent; Smoke, Paul; and Connerley, Ed 2010. 'Democracy, Development, and Security as Objectives of Decentralization', in Kent Eaton, Paul Smoke and Ed Connerley (eds.), *Making Decentralization Work: Democracy, Development and Security*. Boulder, CO: Lynne Rienner, pp. 1–24

Faure, Michael and Svatikova, Katarina 2012. 'Criminal or Administrative Law to Protect the Environment? Evidence from Western Europe', *Journal of Environmental Law* 242(24): 253–86

Friana, Hendra 2017. 'KPK Catat Ribuan Perusahaan Tambang Tak Bayar Pajak', *Tirto.id*, 9 October https://tirto.id/kpk-catat-ribuan-perusahaan-tambang-tak-bayar-pajak-cx6A

The Gecko Project 2017. 'The Making of Palm Oil Fiefdom', https://thegeckoproject.org/the-making-of-a-palm-oil-fiefdom-7e1014e8c342

Gorganews 2017. 'Mantan Bupati Simalungun Zulkarnain Damanik Akan Ajukan PK', 13 December http://gorganews.com/2017/10/10/mantan-bupati-simalungun-zulkarnain-damanik-akan-ajukan-pk/

Hadiz, Vedi 2004. 'Decentralisation and Democracy in Indonesia: A Critique of Neo-Institutionalist Perspectives', *Development and Change* 35(4): 697–718

Hardjasoemantri, Koesnadi 2006. *Hukum Tata Lingkungan*. Yogyakarta: Gadjah Mada University Press

Humas Polri 2018. '30 Pegawai Ditjen Perkebunan Ikuti Diklat PPNS di Diklat Reserse Polri di Megamendung Bogor', 19 March https://humas.polri.go.id/2018/03/30-pegawai-ditjen-perkebunan-perkebunan-ikuti-diklat-ppns-di-diklat-reserse-polri-megamendung-bogor/

ICEL, MoE and AECEN 2008. *Environmental Compliance and Enforcement in Indonesia; Rapid Assessment*. Jakarta: USAID, UNEP, AECEN

Indrarto, Giorgio Budi; Muharjanti, Prayekti; Khatarina, Josi; Pulungan, Irvan; Ivalerina, Feby; Rahman, Justitia; Prana, Muhar Nala ; Resosudarmo, Ida Aju Pradnja; and Muharrom, Efrian 2012. *The Context of REDD+ in Indonesia; Drivers, Agents and Institutions*. Bogor: CIFOR

Kementerian Lingkungan Hidup dan Kehutanan 2015. *Statistik KLHK 2015*. Jakarta: KLHK.

Khatarina, Josi 2018. 'Palm Oil in Indonesia and Natural Resources Management: Why the Lack of a Legal Framework', *Australian Journal of Asian Law* 19(1): 1–17

Khatarina, Josi 2020. 'Decentralisation, Law, and The Failure of Palm Oil Licensing'. PhD Thesis. Melbourne Law School, The University of Melbourne

Kompas 2015. 'Penegakan Hukum Libatkan PPNS Perkebunan', 9 September http://tataruangpertanahan.com/kliping-2015-penegakan-hukum-libatkan-ppns-perkebunan.html

KPK n.d. Infografis: 'Jejak Rasuah Kepala Daerah' https://acch.kpk.go.id/images/tema/ragam/infografis/Jeja-kasus-rasuah-kepala-daerah.jpg

Larson Anne, M. 2003. 'Decentralisation and Forest Management in Latin America: Towards a Working Model', *Public Administration and Development* 23: 211–226

Levang, Patrice; Riva, Wahyu F.; and Orth, Meri G. 2016. 'Oil Palm Plantations and Conflict in Indonesia', in Robert Cramb and John F. McCarthy (eds.), *Oil Palm Complex; Smallholders, Agribusiness and the State in Indonesia and Malaysia*. Singapore: NUS Press, pp. 283–300

Mandiberg, Susan and Faure, Michael 2009. 'A Graduated Punishment Approach to Environmental Crimes: Beyond Vindication of Administrative Authority in the United States and Europe', *Columbian Journal of Environmental Law* 34(2): 447–511

Munandar, Acep 2014. 'Pertemuan Koordinasi dan Evaluasi Pelaksanaan Tugas PPNS Perkebunan Tahun 2014', *Disbun Jabar*, 27 November www.disbun.jabarprov.go.id/index.php/berita/detailberita/367

Perkasa, Anugerah 2017. 'KPK Temukan 63 Ribu Wajib Pajak Industri Sawit Kemplang Pajak', *CNN Indonesia,* 4 May www.cnnindonesia.com/nasional/20170503174824-12-212023/kpk-temukan-63-ribu-wajib-pajak-industri-sawit-kemplang-pajak

Rastika, Icha 2014. 'KPK Temukan Potensi Hilangnya Penerimaan Pajak Sektor Minerba', *Kompas*, 23 April https://nasional.kompas.com/read/2014/04/23/2308186/KPK.Temukan.Potensi.Hilangnya.Penerimaan.Pajak.Sektor.Minerba

Ratnasari, Yulia 2016. 'KPK Catat Piutang 23 Triliun Berasal dari Suap Tambang', *Tirto.id,* 31 August https://tirto.id/kpk-catat-piutang-rp23-triliun-berasal-dari-suap-tambang-bFhP

Resosudarmo, Ida, A. P.; Ngakan, Putu Oka; Mardiah, Sofi; and Utomo, Nugroho, A. 2014. 'Governing Fragile Ecologies: A Perspective of Forest and Land-Based Management in the Regions', in Hall Hill (ed.), *Regional Dynamics in a Decentralized Indonesia*. Singapore: ISEAS, pp. 260–84

Resosudarmo, Ida, A. P. 2007. 'Has Indonesia's Decentralisation Led to Improved Forestry Governance? A Case Study of Bulungan and Kutai Barat Districts, East Kalimantan'. PhD Dissertation. Canberra, Australia: The Australian National University

Romadoni, Ahmad 2016. 'Jokowi: Hukum di Indonesia Masih Tajam ke Bawah, Tumpul ke Atas', *Liputan6*, 11 October www.liputan6.com/news/read/2623426/jokowi-hukum-di-indonesia-masih-tajam-ke-bawah-tumpul-ke-atas

Santosa, Mas Achmad 2001. *Good Governance dan Hukum Lingkungan*. Jakarta: Indonesian Centre for Environmental Law

Santosa, Mas Achmad 2014. 'Efektivitas Penegakan Hukum Administrasi Dalam Perlindungan dan Pengelolaan Lingkungan Hidup: Studi Kasus di Propinsi Jawa Tengah'. Disertasi Doktoral. Jakarta, Indonesia: Fakultas Hukum, Universitas Indonesia

Satgas REDD+ 2013. *Ringkasan Penegakan Hukum Terpadu dengan Pendekatan Multidoor Dalam Penanganan Perkara Tindak Pidana Sumber Daya Alam dan Lingkungan Hidup Di Atas Hutan dan Lahan Gambut. Jakarta*: Satgas REDD+

Suparlan, Parsudi 1995. *Orang Sakai di Riau; Masyarakat Terasing dalam Masyararakat Indonesia*. Jakarta: Yayasan Obor Indonesia

Suwarno, Aritta and Hein, Lars 2015. 'Governance, Decentralisation and Deforestation: The Case of Central Kalimantan Province, Indonesia', *Quarterly Journal of International Agriculture* 54(1): 77–100

Syarif, Laode, M. 2010. 'Current Development of Indonesian Environmental Law', *IUCN Academy of Environmental Law E-Journal* 1: 1–18 www2.ecolex.org/server2.php/libcat/docs/LI/MON-085540.pdf

Tarigan, Antonius 2015. 'Dilema Birokrasi Satu Pintu', *Kompas.com*, 8 January https://nasional.kompas.com/read/2015/01/08/19033681/Dilema.Birokrasi.Satu.Pintu

Taufiqurrahaman, Muhammad 2017. 'Korupsi Kepala Daerah: JK Jangan Merasa Tidak Diawasi', *Kompas*, 27 September https://news.detik.com/berita/d-3660177/korupsi-kepala-daerah-jk-jangan-merasa-tidak-diawasi

UKP4 (Unit Kerja Presiden untuk Pengawasan dan Pengendalian Pembangunan) 2013. *Laporan Penataan Perizinan*. Jakarta: UKP4

Voorde, Jeroen ten 2014. 'Prohibiting Remote Harms: On Endangerment, Citizenship and Control', *Utrecht Law Review* 10(1): 163–179.

Waddell, Sarah 2004. 'The Role of the "Legal Rule" in Indonesian Law: Environmental Law and Reformasi of Water Quality Management'. PhD Dissertation. Sydney: The University of Sydney

Wakker, Erick 2014. *Illegalities in Forest Clearance for Large-Scale Commercial Plantations,* AideEnvironment Asia, www.aidenvironment.org/media/uploads/documents/projects/Illegalities_in_Forest_Clearance.pdf

Yaserhan, Mindri; Herlambang; and Adyan, Antory R. 2017. 'Obstacles or Barriers Factors to the Roles of Police Investigators of Republic of Indonesia in Preventing and Eradicating Forest Destruction Against Illegal Logging in Lebong Regency', *Bengkoelen Justice* 7(1): 26–36 https://ejournal.unib.ac.id/index.php/bengkoelenjustice/article/viewFile/2980/1465

Court decisions

Decision No. 194 K/Pid.Sus/2012
Decision No. 27/P/HUM/2016
Decision No. 100/Pid.Sus/2015/PN Lbh
Decision No. 1247 K/Pid.Sus/2016
Decision No. 35/Pid.Sus/2016/PT PAL
Decision No. 204/Pid.Sus/2015/PN. Prg

Laws and regulations

Criminal Code (*Kitab Undang-Undang Hukum Pidana*, KUHP: Law No. 1 of 1946 as amended by Law No. 27 of 1999 on the Indonesian Criminal Code)
Law No. 11 of 1967 on Mining
Law No. 24 of 1992 on Spatial Planning
Law No. 23 of 1997 on Environmental Management
Law No. 41 of 1999 on Forestry
Law No. 18 of 2004 on Plantation
Law No. 26 of 2007 on Spatial Planning
Law No. 4 of 2009 on Mining
Law No. 32 of 2009 on Environmental Protection and Management
Law No. 18 of 2013 on Prevention and Eradication of Forest Degradation
Law No. 39 of 2014 on Plantation
Government Regulation No. 43 of 2012 on Procedures for Coordination, Supervision, and Technical Development on Special Police, Civil Servants Investigators, and other Security Forms
Presidential Regulation No. 18 of 2016 on the Acceleration of Development of Waste-Based Electricity Generators in Jakarta, Tangerang Bandung, Semarang, Surakarta, Surabaya, and Makassar
Ministry of Agriculture and Spatial Planning/Head of National Land Agency Regulation No. 2 of 1999 on Location Permits
Ministry of Agriculture and Spatial Planning/Head of National Land Agency Regulation No. 5 of 2015 on Location Permits
Ministry of Agriculture Regulation No. 26/Permentan/OT.140/2/2007 on Licensing Guidelines for Plantation Businesses

Ministry of Agriculture Regulation No. 61 of 2010 on Organisation and Scope of Work

Ministry of Agriculture No. 98/Permentan/OT.140/9/2013 on Licencing Guidelines for Plantation Businesses

Ministry of Environment and Forestry Regulation No. P.18/MenLHK-II/ 2015 on Organisation and Scope of Work

Ministry of Agriculture Regulation No. 45 of 2015 on Organisation and Scope of Work

Ministry of Forestry Decree No. 44 of 2005 on Forest Area Designation in North Sumatra Province

North Sumatra Provincial Government Regulation No. 7 of 2003 on the Spatial Plan of North Sumatra Province

14 Criminal injustice and agrarian conflict in Indonesia

Lilis Mulyani

Since *Reformasi*, the period after President Soeharto stepped down in 1998, there have been many conflicts over natural resources or agrarian conflicts in Indonesia, sometimes accompanied by significant violence. Most are continuations of tensions that already existed under Soeharto's New Order.[1] His centralised government prevented these conflicts from escalating because the state controlled national and local security through top-down use of military force. When the central government's power was reduced by decentralisation in 1999,[2] this created weaker control of regional areas, and long-latent agrarian conflicts began to emerge again. From 1998 to 2000 there were numerous incidents involving local people attempting to reclaim or occupy land.[3] Most of this happened in areas where they had been evicted for state development purposes.

There are two main types of agrarian conflicts in Indonesia. The first involves disputes over land claims, that is objections to legal and formally registered land right documents. For development reasons, the government favours business entities using land for economic extraction, sometimes giving them licences and formal land title without the proper processes being followed (see Khatarina, Chapter 13, this volume). In practice, this has often led to local people being dispossessed of their customary lands. Companies holding formal and registered land title may use the state to evict people from these lands, regardless of the fact that local people have occupied them for generations.

The second type of conflict occurs after land claims are resolved. Here, conflict mostly derives from the creation of property rights borders that create new criminal conduct, such as trespass or unauthorised collecting of property. In these cases, local people are prosecuted for accessing land that was previously accessible freely, or was under community control or even ownership.

This chapter discusses the uses (and misuses) of criminal law to punish farmers, local people or traditional customary (*adat*) communities in Indonesia for conduct that was permissible before agrarian conflict began. The use of criminal law is problematic because local people commonly become victims of land confiscation by the state but they are, in fact, rarely perpetrators of criminal acts, despite being punished as if they are.

The use of criminal law as a way to enforce property rights under dispute raises the main question discussed in this chapter: Why are people criminalised for conduct or actions previously allowed under the law? This chapter will first describe the typology of agrarian conflicts, including the actors and the use of statutes to punish certain conduct, before reflecting on injustices occurring in agrarian conflicts and how they relate to moral theory and the grounds of punishment (Husak 2007, 2010; Melissaris 2015), asking questions such as: What is a crime? What does it mean to be responsible for a crime? Lastly, this chapter discusses to what extent criminal law should be used to resolve agrarian conflicts in Indonesia.

Criminal law and agrarian conflicts

There has recently been a significant increase in criminal cases in areas where there is conflict over land. The KPA (Konsorsium Pembaruan Agraria, Consortium for Agrarian Reform)[4] recorded that the number of agrarian conflicts has increased every year since 2000, with plantation, forestry and infrastructure development areas showing the highest levels. Criminal cases relating to these conflicts increased from 156 in 2012 to 239 cases in 2013; 255 cases in 2014; 455 cases in both 2015 and 2016; and 659 in 2017. Farmers and local villagers are most likely to be charged with criminal offences of trespass and petty crimes, such as stealing seeds or tree branches, but they sometimes face more severe charges, such as inciting or plotting riots, destruction of plantations, and the use of sharp weapons. A summary of the cases appears in Table 14.1.

Although at first instance these cases may appear similar to other cases in the Indonesian criminal justice system, if looked at individually it becomes clear they are different, because in each there is a history of prolonged conflict surrounding the 'offence', which is the main reason for its commission. Most cases brought to court by public or private companies in areas where there are land conflicts are problematic in terms of the law used and the punishment imposed. Many involve 'criminalisation',[5] which I define as the use of criminal law where it is not morally justifiable. In Indonesia, the term 'criminalisation' is now widely used to suggest the misuse of criminal law to punish farmers and local people who try to defend their rights to land, or who do not understand the implications of government decisions that grant concessions over their customary lands to companies.

The following case studies provide examples of this. The first involves Minah,[6] an elderly woman, who was sentenced to three months' prison for 'stealing' from a plantation company property by taking three ripened cacao pods from the concession area. The plantation company, PT Rumpun Sari Antan, is a cacao company in the Banyumas District of Central Java. Although in some areas local villagers are permitted to plant under their cacao trees, this company imposed strict rules on local villagers, limiting their ability to harvest their plants. One day, Minah picked three ripened cacao

Table 14.1 Criminal cases involving local villagers, farmers and agrarian activists 2012–19

No.	*Common offences*	*Cases*
1	Trespass	Surokonto farmers, Kendal, Central Java (2017); Jolotigo, Pekalongan, Central Java (2005)
2	Theft	Samirin, Simalungun, North Sumatra (2019); Syafrudin Madili, Banggai, Central Sulawesi (2017); 11 farmers of Bungku Village Batanghari, Jambi (2010); Minah, Banyumas, Central Java (2009)
3	Incitement	Okih, Indramayu (2016); Ujang and Sukandi, Indramayu (2015); Tulang Bawang Farmers, Lampung (2016); Slamet Daroini, Blitar, East Java (2017)
4	Use of sharp weapons	Tulang Bawang Lampung (2016)
5	Destruction of property	Yasman, Bengkulu (2016); Rismaluddin, Muara Enim, South Sumatra (2015)
6	Unauthorised seed reproduction	Tukirin, Suprapto, Budi Purwo Utomo, Jumidi, Dawam, Kusen, Slamet, Burhana, Maman Nurrohman and Juwito Muhamma, Kediri, East Java (2004–2007); Munirwan, North Aceh (2019)
7	Harm to plantation business[1]	Nasihin and Bisri, Pekalongan, Central Java (2005); *adat* community of Entebang Sekadau, Central Kalimantan (2005); Busrah and Jamal, Tapanuli Selatan, North Sumatra (2010)
8	Plotting riot and incitement	Salim Kancil of Lumajang East Java (2015)
9	Arbitrary arrest without clear reasons	18 villagers, Paring Baru, Seluma, Bengkulu (2010); 24 farmers, Banggai, Central Sulawesi (2010)
10	Forest destruction and unauthorised logging	Agusri Masnefi and Ergi Datuk Samiak, Nagari Koto Malintang, Lubuk Basung, West Sumatra (2017)

Source: compiled from PILNET[2] 2010, KPA 2017 and interview with Rona, LBH Padang.

1 *Gangguan Usaha Perkebunan* (disruption of plantation business). Constitutional Court Decision No. 122/PUU-VIII/2015 repealed the article in Law No. 39 of 2014 on Plantations (*Gangguan Usaha Perkebunan*) that established this offence. However, the revised Law on Plantations, No. 39 of 2014, included criminal sanctions for individuals who cultivate, use, or occupy legal plantation concession areas, or cut down trees, or harvest without concession holder authorisation (arts. 55 and 107).

2 PILNET (Public Interest Lawyers Network) is a group of lawyers who helps farmers and local villagers at their criminal trials.

pods; once company staff found out, she returned them. The company, nonetheless, reported the case to the police as stealing, using the three cacao pods as evidence. In 2009, Minah was sentenced to a month and fifteen days imprisonment[7] for theft, pursuant to art. 362 of the Criminal Code. The case was highlighted in the media as 'a scar on society's sense of justice',[8] because the amount of loss suffered by the powerful company was seen as insignificant, yet it forced the case through the criminal courts. The case gained widespread attention across Indonesia. Legal moralists considered it wrong to convict Minah because there was no real harm caused by her actions. The case was also used by agrarian activists to show how concession holder companies use legal avenues to threaten local villagers to keep off the land.

Other common cases involving farmers and agrarian activists include people being arrested for protesting about company actions that disregard local villagers' plantings or cultivated gardens. Any protest by farmers or local villagers, with or without violence, is usually reported to police as incitement. If violent acts are involved, companies also report other offences, such as destruction of property. These tactics can be seen in cases such as the Tulang Bawang, Okih, and Juwito cases, as I will now explain.

In the Tulang Bawang case, the national government gave concessions to private companies in Lampung in 1986. The concession area included the gardens of seven transmigrant villages. The company and local authorities began to evict people from their lands in the 1990s, saying that the plantation companies now controlled in the area. Some of the villagers were forced to sign a letter formally transferring their land to the company after pressure by the military in 1993, while others continued to work as plasma-farmers[9] for the companies. In 2015, however, the villagers retaliated by occupying the land and closing the company's plantation. The company and the local police arrested four villagers for company property destruction.

In another case, Okih (an activist in a local peasant union) was arrested and convicted for stealing seven teak logs in 2005 from a forest area in Indramayu West Java, belonging to PT Perhutani.[10] Okih's defence was that he had been granted permission to take the logs after they fell naturally, due to bad weather. However, PT Perhutani denied it had given him this permission and reported him to the police. In 2013, the District Court (*Pengadilan Negeri*) found Okih guilty and sentenced him to seven months imprisonment with a fine of Rp. 500,000 (approximately A$ 50–55).[11] Prior to reporting him to police, PT Perhutani had approached Okih and asked him to stop his activism against the company.

Another notable case in Nagari Koto Malintang, West Sumatra, typified the use of forestry laws, particularly Law No. 18 of 2013 the Prevention and Combating of Forest Destruction, against traditional customary (*adat*) community members. In September 2017, Agusri Masnefi logged two trees on land which he considered to be his wife's clan's customary land (*ulayat kaum*). This land has been held for generations by his wife's family line as communally owned land (*ulayat*). Before he logged the trees, he asked permission from the *adat* elder, and a letter agreeing to this request was signed on 19 September 2017. Agusri asked the elder, Datuk Samiak, to help cut two trees to build a small shop for his family's livelihood. In 27 September 2017, officers from BKSDA (Balai Konservasi Sumber Daya Alam, Natural

Resource Conservation Council), an institution under the Provincial Forestry Office, reported Agusri and Datuk Samiak to the local police. They were detained from that date. Despite criticism, the prosecutor indicted them under art. 82(2) of Law No. 18 of 2013 and art. 55(1) of the Criminal Code. The maximum punishment for these crimes is ten months' imprisonment and a fine of Rp. 500,000. In the end, the Court found Agusri and Datuk Samiak guilty under Law No. 18 of 2013, but the length of the punishment handed down was equivalent to the number of days they had already spent in prison. The Court deducted the period of pre-trial detention as time served from their sentences, so that as soon as the judges read the verdict both were released from prison.

One of the most extreme cases of agrarian conflict involved Salim Kancil, who died on 26 September 2015, defending his farmland against mining companies supported by the head of Selok Awar-awar village, in the Lumajang district of East Java. Before the conflict, Salim was a farmer, cultivating small plots of land for his family's livelihood. The expansion of sand mining company activities into his village began to destroy his small farm and his income, as farming productivity decreased due to crop failure. He then tried to become a fisherman but his livelihood as a fisherman also suffered from insecurity. Salim then started to organise his fellow villagers, who were also affected by the expansion of the mining companies, to learn how to defend and reclaim their lands and livelihoods. He began to send letters to authorities, learning from agrarian-based NGOs about how he and his friends could reclaim rights to the land in their village. Once mining companies heard of his actions, he received many threats, including one from his own village head, who was the owner of one of the mining companies, as well as being, at the same time, the local authority giving permits for mining activities in Selok Awar-awar. Salim reported the intimidation and threats to the local police but received no response. He and his fellow agrarian activists then organised themselves in a local NGO called 'Forum' and began conducting non-violent acts of resistance, such as stopping trucks carrying sand from entering their villages. On 25 September 2015, he received a death threat, which he believed had been sent by one of the mining companies with the approval of the head of the village. On 26 September 2015, Forum advertised its plans for another action against the mining companies. At noon on the same day, Salim was dragged out of his house by scores of men and violently beaten to death.

Salim's death greatly angered the agrarian movement across Indonesia but his case was not the first of its kind and – unless there is drastic change – it will not be the last. Farmers, *adat* (traditional or customary) communities, and other local community members are vulnerable to eviction from their land and impacts on their livelihood. They are also vulnerable to being criminalised and even killed for defending their lands and livelihoods.

In 2015, a network of non-government organisations[12] involved with agrarian rights and justice created the 'Farmers' Criminalisation Emergency Fund' for farmers or agrarian activists facing court. This fund is used to pay lawyers and advocates for the farmers and activists in court. The fund is also used to create safe housing for victims of agrarian or land conflicts in a number of Indonesian cities, and to provide medical treatment for those in need.

These few examples are the product of increasing intensity in agrarian conflicts throughout Indonesia. A nation-wide increase in natural resource extraction (in particular palm oil and coal) and infrastructure development are seen as the main reasons for escalation of agrarian conflicts (KPA 2017, 2018). Such development processes require massive expanses of land, so the appropriation of the land of local villagers and farmers is inevitable under the current approach. Unfortunately, at present, state and company responses to such appropriation almost always result in the criminalisation of farmers or local villagers. Criminal actions are perpetrated by companies, and sometimes the state, against those unwilling to comply with the land appropriation process.

Cases involving the criminalisation of farmers, local villagers, and agrarian activists (as discussed above) all have commonalities, which are analysed in further detail below.

Actors and patterns

Franco and Carranza (2014: 43–4) have analysed agrarian conflict and the criminalisation of farmers in the Philippines. They see criminalisation as an indicator of an ongoing political battle between three broadly contending social-regulatory orders: fragmented and contradictory state law; law that serves economically powerful persons; and the vision of what the rule of law should mean according to equity and social justice-oriented peasant movements. This also true in the Indonesian context. The fragmented nature of state institutions and inconsistent laws on natural resources have created loopholes that have prevented the establishment of an effective mechanism for conflict resolution. Powerful actors have used this situation to maintain their interests at local and national levels. Further, the criminal justice system has been used to strengthen the position of those in power by creating fear among anyone (particularly farmers and agrarian activists), who attempts to resist.

A common pattern in agrarian conflict involves the same opposing actors: farmers or local villagers against concession companies (forestry or plantation – public or private companies). Farmers and local villagers have typically lived in the area for generations, whether they are people whose indigeneity can be traced through their communities' history as traditional customary or *adat* communities, or people who arrived through transmigration or other forms of migration more recently. Prior to the grant of concessions, these people had relationships with the land, whether formally documented or based only on their land tenure activities on the claimed lands.

Farmers or local villagers in most conflict areas are typically characterised by: low levels of education and knowledge; minimal or no formal legal documents for the land they claim; low institutional support; and a lack of alternative options for livelihood. Most of the villages or areas where agrarian or land conflict exists also suffer from poverty. Peluso and Watts (2001), for example, have commented that people living in areas surrounding natural resources-rich areas in Java mostly live in poverty. Many local villagers and farmers have been denied access to their cultivated lands, and many traditional customary (*adat*) communities have been evicted from their traditional customary (*ulayat*) lands. This has closed off many opportunities for them, including to earn a livelihood. Although they are surrounded by rich natural resources that were once open to them they now have little or no access to the land.

The second group of actors are concession holders, often natural resource extraction companies, including both public and private companies. These companies usually have legal documents to legitimate their claims. They also have other sources of power, such as financial capital and the technology needed for more efficient natural resource extraction. For example, palm oil companies usually hold the knowledge and technology necessary to establish modern palm oil factories or refineries – knowledge that is absent among most local communities. These big companies, therefore, usually monopolise the production chain of most important local commodities.

Some of the concession holders are public companies, being state-owned corporations or BUMN (*Badan Usaha Milik Negara,* State owned companies). Two of the most prominent state-owned companies involved in agrarian conflicts are Perum Perhutani, which dominates the forest industry, and PTPN (PT Perkebunan Nusantara, the Indonesian Plantation Company), which is very influential in the plantation sector. Perum Perhutani can be traced back to Dutch colonial history and forest management in Java and Madura from 1897 (BUMN Perhutani n.d.). It is currently the holding company for all state-owned forestry enterprises, which include PT Inhutani (PT Inhutani I-V, PT Hijau Lestari, PT Palawi Risorsis, and PT Perhutani Anugerah Kimia).[13] It covers a total area of 2.4 million hectares in Java and Madura alone, and total of 3.7 million hectares across Indonesia (Perum Perhutani 2016). PTPN, or PT Perkebunan Nusantara, is the major state-owned holding company for plantation activities in Java and other islands. It currently holds 1,181,751 hectares of land across Indonesia.[14]

Private companies are companies established according to Law No. 40 of 2007 on Limited Liability Companies (*Perusahaan Terbatas* or PT). These companies can have a national and even global network and are often linked to large multinational corporations. In the 1980s, private companies mostly worked in the oil or forestry industries. After 2000, many major private companies moved into coal mining and palm oil plantations (Garnaut 2015: 194).

Another continuing pattern in many agrarian or land conflicts is the involvement of the Indonesian police and army. Unfortunately, the part they play in the conflict is usually not to resolve conflicts but to maintain 'order' in local areas, which often means using force to prevent local movements from reclaiming lands. State-backed forces commonly create close relationships with companies. In many cases, corrupt practices are used by the companies, which provide regular 'security money' to the police and army, particularly at the local level (Lucas and Warren 2013: 24). A recent study by SOMO (Stichting Onderzoek Multinationale Ondernemingen) and Inkrispena in 2017 analysed the role of security forces in Indonesian palm oil plantation conflicts (SOMO and Inkrispena 2017), drawing conclusions reflected in an article in the Jakarta Post (2015) that stated:

> The general public is also concerned about civilian authorities 'inviting' military personnel to help secure their assets and provide security for them, particularly on issues or policies that are controversial and prone to unrest or security disturbance. It has become a trend for these civilian authorities or ministries to sign memorandums of understanding (MOUs) with military units on these matters.
>
> (Afrida 2015)

Further, the Consortium for Agrarian Reform found that of 659 agrarian conflict cases, 21 involved violence by the Indonesian police, including the unlawful arrest of farmers trying to defend their lands (Suryowati 2017). The involvement of Indonesian security forces (the army and the police) is usually based on who has the legal documents to the disputed land, but the research by SOMO and the Consortium also illustrates that, in some cases, state forces engage in the unethical practice of providing security to private entities. In 2019, the national human rights commission, Komnas HAM (Komisi Nasional Hak Asasi Manusia, National Commission for Human Rights) urged security forces to be neutral in any conflict, as they were then the government agencies most often reported for human rights misconduct and abuses (CNN Indonesia 2019).

Why and when certain acts are punishable: Differences between state and popular perspectives

Indonesia does not have a particular mechanism to resolve agrarian conflicts but criminal sanctions are often used against peasants and agrarian activists to obstruct their efforts to claim rights to land. The common pattern is to use selected crimes in the Criminal Code and other, more specific, laws, and then impose the highest possible sanction to provide a deterrent to other 'possible perpetrators', creating fear among other local actors in order to prevent them pursuing similar actions (Arrsa 2014: 58).

In the Indonesian legal system, there are general laws (*undang-undang umum*) and special laws (*undang-undang khusus*) (Butt and Lindsey 2018: 186–7). 'General laws' refer to laws that regulate general legal norms, for example, the Criminal Code (*Kitab Undang-Undang Hukum Pidana* or KUHP). 'Special laws' are laws made specifically for certain acts or crimes, for example

Table 14.2 Criminal offence types commonly used to prosecute farmers and local villagers

Types of offences	*Sanctions*
The Indonesian Criminal Code (KUHP)	
Articles 161(1), 161(2) and 406(1): incitement, violent action against a public authority, or any other disobedience; taking property belonging to other unlawfully or theft; and a deliberate act that unlawfully destroys, damages, renders useless or mislays property which wholly or partially belongs to another.	Maximum imprisonment of two to five years or a maximum fine of 4,500 rupiah.[1]
Law No. 8 of 2004 as amended by Law No. 39 of 2014 on Plantations	
Articles 55 and 107: unlawfully cultivating, using, occupying or controlling plantation land that falls under another person's title, or under the *ulayat* rights of an *adat* community.	Maximum imprisonment of four years or a maximum fine of 4 billion rupiah.
Law No. 18 of 2013 on Preventing and Combating Forest Destruction	
Articles 12, 13 and 17: any offences that are considered to cause forest destruction such as illegal tree cutting, illegal use of forest zones, also assisting offences.	Imprisonment from one to five years or a maximum fine between 500 million rupiah and 2.5 billion rupiah.
Law No. 12 of 1992 on Crop Cultivation Systems	
Articles 60 and 61: intentionally reproducing and distributing uncertified and unauthorised seed.	Imprisonment from three to twelve years or a fine from 50 million to 250 million rupiah.

[1] According to Supreme Court Regulation No. 2 of 2012 on Adjustment of Standards for Minor Offences and Value of Fines in the Criminal Code, the sum of fines provided for in the Criminal Code is to be multiplied to 25 times. This is intended to respond to major changes in the value of currency since the Criminal Code was first stipulated in 1946, as a re-enactment of the colonial statute of 1918. For a detailed discussion of this regulation and its effect, See Assegaf, Chapter 9, this volume.

environmental crimes and corruption. Certain laws, such as the Forestry and Plantation Laws can also contain types of offences or actions that are punishable but are more specific compared to offences in the Criminal Code. According to Indonesian law, if a legal norm appears in both special law and general law, the special law prevails over the general law (Manan 2004).[15] Prosecutors can choose which legal norm is more specific to the offence but, in practice, both types of law (general and special) are usually used simultaneously to prosecute farmers or peasants in agrarian conflict cases.

Table 14.2 shows the types of criminal offences most commonly used against claimants in agrarian conflicts. These are mostly derived from the Criminal Code Law, No. 39 of 2014 on Plantations, and Law No. 18 of 2013 on Preventing and Combating Forest Destruction.

Criminal Code

As indicated earlier, the Criminal Code prohibitions on trespassing and theft are two of the most commonly-used criminal offences in agrarian conflicts. Trespassing charges are usually based on formal state documents granting concessions to companies, which create 'invisible borders' (Dekker 2017) that did not previously exist in local understandings. As mentioned, villagers or local farmers typically have abundant access to the forest or plantation areas prior to the concessions being granted, but state legal documents then create 'property borders' that prevent villagers and farmers from accessing them (Li 2016). Using these documents, concession companies are able to use state force (police and military) to evict local villagers and farmers from land that has been accessible to them for generations. Companies then build fences in and around the concession zones, with signs warning that trespass is a punishable offence. Local villagers usually have no experience with this kind of situation and therefore continue to enter these areas (despite the warnings) because the land has always been accessible to them and they have no other option to secure their livelihoods. They cannot easily understand that they are no longer allowed to access this land because there is a widespread lack of consultation with local people on national policy and legal changes.

In addition to trespassing, taking things from within the concession areas is considered theft from the company's perspective, and so punishable according to Indonesian criminal law.[16] Prosecution under such provisions does not take into account the history of the local people in relation to the forest or plantation areas. The companies' arguments also do not fit with the local villagers' logic and experience. Before the companies came to the area, gathering from the forest was, for many of them, their chief means of livelihood. After the companies arrive, it becomes a punishable offence.

Plantations Law

The two statutes that are most often used as the legal foundation for punishable acts in relation to agrarian or land conflicts are, as mentioned, the Plantations Law and the Forestry Law. Many companies use Law No. 18 of 2004 on Plantations, as amended by Law No. 39 of 2014, to 'punish' local villagers for actions that, from the company's perspective, 'bring harm' to the business' operations. This Law not only prohibits trespassing or theft, but also punishes individuals who develop their own seeds from the products of the company. Information about the granting of new forest or plantation licences, said to be based on state land law, is hardly comprehensible to local people. One reason for this is that traditional customary (*adat*) land still exists in many areas. State law tends to negate the existence these of customary land interests, creating another dimension for land conflicts at the local level (Warman 2010).

As mentioned above, Law No. 18 of 2004 on Plantations was brought to the Constitutional Court for review, particularly arts. 21 and 47 on harm to plantation business. These articles are known as 'rubber articles' (*pasal karet*) because they are very broad and are often been used strategically to punish farmers, local villagers and agrarian activists who enter plantation concession zones. These provisions have also been used by many concession companies to make false accusations to police of theft, including inciting plantation destruction. The Court repealed these two articles in Decision No. 55/PUU-VIII/2010. Following that decision, an amended Plantation Law was passed in 2014 without these provisions.

Further, there are other cases, not related to land conflict, that have also criminalised farmers for being involved in unauthorised seed reproduction and distribution, conduct that was permitted before 1992. The most notable case involved the company PT BISI (Benih Inti Subur Intani). PT BISI reported Juwito and some fellow farmers for theft and unauthorised reproduction of corn seeds. In 2010, another farmer, Kunoto or Kuncoro, was also reported and convicted in May 2010 for offences under arts. 60–61 of Law No. 12 of 1992 on Crop Cultivation Systems, receiving seven months' imprisonment and a fine of Rp. 500,000.[17]

The cases of Kunoto and Juwito and his fellow farmers between 2004 and 2007 led to outcry across Indonesia, as farmers developing corn seeds were convicted. This and other similar cases led to agrarian activists forming a Farmers Seed Sovereignty Coalition (Koalisi untuk Kedaulatan Benih Petani)[18] to seek constitutional review of Law No. 12 of 1992 on Crop Cultivation Systems, challenging the licences required under that statute to develop seeds. In Decision No. 99/PUU-X/2012, the Constitutional Court ruled that smallholder farmers do not need approval from the Ministry of Agriculture, under art. 9(3) of the Law, to develop their own seeds, and it was not a criminal offence for them to do so. The decision was, among other things, intended as a response to the injustice created by the criminalisation of farmers developing their own seeds. Despite the Constitutional Court's decision, similar cases of seed criminalisation still occur. In 2019, for example, Munirwan of North Aceh, was imprisoned – although later released – for uncertified IF8 paddy seed reproduction and distribution (Tempo 2019).

Forestry Law

Articles 12 and 13 of Law No. 18 of 2013 on the Prevention and Combating of Forest Destruction are frequently used by forest concession companies, including state-owned forestry companies, to bring local villagers to court to face charges of forest destruction. These provisions are a double-edged sword. On one hand, they have been quite effective in sentencing those responsible for the destructive forest fires that sweep Indonesia each year – often set by concessionary companies to clear land. On the other hand, it has also been used to stamp out legitimate resistance from local villagers to forestry companies' incursions into their lands.

In the Nagari Koto Malindang *adat* community case, discussed earlier, a prominent academic from Andalas University, Kurnia Warman, testified in court for the defendants, Agusri and Datuk Samiak, stating that the Nagari Koto Malintang people had *ulayat* rights to the lands in question as their ancestral land. Two other academics, Hariadi Kartodiharjo, from Bogor Agricultural University, and Abdul Fickar Hadjar, a national law practitioner, also stepped in as *amicus curiae*[19] for the defendants (Vonilia and Saturi 2018). Like Warman, Kartodiharjo and Hadjar, many agrarian and *adat* movement activists have criticised the court process. According to the defence lawyers and academics, the forest belongs to the Nagari Koto Malintang community and the designation of the forest as a Conservation Forest has not been formalised, which means it has not been formally established by the Ministry as a state forest.[20]

Forest land issues are procedurally complicated. Under the Forestry Law, an area is established as a forest through a number of bureaucratic steps. First, the national Ministry of Forestry will select which areas are 'designated' as having a forest function based on the forest coverage of the area, in coordination with regional governments through a mechanism called 'coherency-compatibility' (*padu-serasi*) (see Epistema 2015). Second, the national and provincial forestry offices will begin to mark forest boundaries. This is followed by the third step of mapping the area as a 'state forest zone'. Lastly, a final forest map will be issued by the Ministry to declare the specified forest to be 'state forest' through the 'forest establishment' mechanism. Any disputes with local communities are meant to be settled during the forest boundary allocation (the second stage).

In the Nagari Koto Malintang case, the second stage of this process is yet to be completed. The only document that has been finalised is the forest area designation – 'designated' by a Ministry of Forestry Decision (the first stage of forest establishment).[21] This first stage is generally a top-down process. The local communities have not yet been involved via public consultation; and, as such, they have not had any real opportunity to raise any objections to the forest designation. Therefore, in the local communities' opinion, the Ministry of Forestry has no strong legal ground to say that the forest at Koto Malintang is state forest. Further, since the forest is part of the customary land, the Koto Malintang *adat* community and its members have customary rights to access the forest land.[22] The Koto Malintang *adat* community also dispute the process of forest establishment, arguing this can provide proof that the territory in question is part of their inter-generational ancestral lands. However, the *adat* community have not yet been given this opportunity, as community consultation only occurs at stage two of the process.

On the other hand, the Provincial Ministry of Forestry argues that the designation of forest zone function (*penetapan fungsi hutan* or stage one of forest establishment) provides sufficient legal ground to classify the forest as 'state forest' to the exclusion of local people. Following the logic of the State's argument, the Ministry could declare any area as having a 'forest function' and immediately apply forestry rules in the area.[23] In the Ministry's argument, there is no need at all for consultation with the local people. The court in this case upheld the reasoning of the Ministry of Forestry regarding the designation of forest function. It decided that the forest area did belong to the state, and Agusri and Datuk Samiak were therefore found guilty of stealing two logs from state forest.

This case illustrates different interpretations of forest designation and establishment processes. Cases such as this have also occurred elsewhere, with top-down forest designation causing local land and forest conflicts. This shows the vulnerability of local *adat* communities, who do not understand the consequences of the process, both due to legal uncertainty and a lack of community consultation. In effect, the forest designation process creates unseen property boundaries.[24] Combined with a lack of local community involvement and understanding, it is clear how these communities can very easily become vulnerable to prosecution under criminal provisions for 'trespassing' and 'stealing' from the state forest area – especially if they believe the disputed land to be their *ulayat* lands.

All these are among the reasons why so many of the provisions that criminalise farmers and local people have now been revoked by the Indonesian Constitutional Court, as shown in Table 14.3.

However, these Decisions are not enough on their own. The revoked provisions are still too often used by local officials to threaten local farmers or villagers at the behest of companies. The government must further steps to ensure that this stops.

Rethinking crime and punishment

Having briefly discussed the main types of cases and criminal offences used by actors in agrarian conflicts in Indonesia, three questions remain: Why should land conflicts be treated differently to general criminal offences? How is 'crime' defined? And why is the use of 'punishment' problematic in land conflict areas?

In resolving agrarian conflicts, careful analysis is needed, for three reasons. First, because of the nature of the conflict; second, because agrarian or land conflicts usually involve a series of events, not just a single one; and third, because the state, which is supposed to mediate land conflicts between local farmers and villagers with companies, has, instead, become the supporter of companies, and sometimes even the main actor in many agrarian or land conflicts.

The historical context is also important. Land claims or occupation are rarely one-sided actions. In most conflict areas, claiming or occupying land is a response to forced land appropriation by the state, or a company exploiting government grant of licences and concessions. Trespass or theft in relation to

Table 14.3 Statutory Provisions on agrarian issues repealed by the Constitutional Court

Statutory Provisions	*Constitutional Court Decision*
Law No. 41 of 1999 on Forestry	(1) Decision No. 35/PUU-X/2012 deemed article 1(6) unconstitutional as regards the words 'the State' and the article is revised to read 'Customary forest is a forest under the territory of customary or *adat* community'. It also deemed article 4(3) deemed unconstitutional and held that state control over forest must acknowledge *adat* communities. Article 5(1) and (2) held to no longer have binding legal force. (2) Decision 95/PUU-XII/2014 deemed article 50(3) (e) and (i) unconstitutional, and must exclude communities living for generations in the forest who collect forest resources for non-commercial uses.
Law No. 18 of 2004 on Plantations	Decision No. 55/PUU-VIII/2010 deemed articles 21 and 47(1) and (2) unconstitutional. Article 21 has no binding legal force as the word 'every person' is too wide and vague.
Law No. 12 of 1992 on Crop Cultivation Systems	Decision No. 99/PUU-X/2012 deemed articles 9(3) and 12(1) unconstitutional as the word 'individual' must exclude plant breeding by individual farmers. It also deemed the provisions to have no binding legal force.
Law No. 39 of 2014 on Plantation	Decision No. 138/PUU-XIII/2015 deemed articles 27(3), 29 and 30(1) unconstitutional, and held that the word 'individual' shall not include individual small farmers engaged in plant breeding activity for own community purposes.

plantations or forestry property must likewise be seen in its historical context, namely, that, in the recent past these areas were freely accessible and forest product gathering was not understood as a crime. Similar reasoning applies to seed reproduction and distribution among farmers. Before 1992, it was very common for local farmers to develop and exchange seeds among themselves. The aim was to find a seed that better resisted pests and produced better crops. However, since the enactment of Law No. 12 of 1992, farmers have been criminalised for this conduct. In theory, this ended when the Constitutional Court reinterpreted this Law in 2012 (see above) but in reality, farmers remain vulnerable to abuse of the Law.

In thinking about what is a crime and when the state can treat an act as a punishable crime, it is useful to revisit two important questions concerning crime and punishment: first, whether a particular act is harmful to another person or entity; and second, whether the act is morally, socially and/or culturally wrong. Husak in his book, *Overcriminalisation* (2007: 36), offers a list of requirements for conduct to be prohibited and punishable by the state. He argues that:

(1) the conduct prohibited must involve harm or evil;
(2) the conduct must be a wrongful act;
(3) punishment is justified when it is deserved, meaning that the person who does the act deserves to be punished;
(4) the liability of punishment shall be with those who initiate it. This also means that the burden of proof lies with the party that initiates the case;
(5) there is substantial state interest in pursuing the purpose of punishment to uphold justice through the criminal justice system;
(6) the law must advance the state's interest; and
(7) the law must not be more extensive than necessary to achieve the purpose of punishment.[25]

Kleinig, in his review of Husak's work, categorised these requirements in two groups: internal constraints and external constraints (2009: 27). Internal constraints are questions to check the importance of punishment according to criminal law (requirements 1–4), while external constraints are questions to check the importance of punishment from the point of view of the interests of the state (requirements 5–7).

Conduct is considered harmful if it will cause impairment or damage to another person. The law can also consider any potential impairment or damage to another person as 'a harm'. Simester and Von Hirsch (2011) provide a comprehensive discussion of the conditions that can satisfy the definition of 'harm to another person'. The definition of 'harm to another' becomes justification or legitimation for the state to validate punishment for a citizen. In theory, no person would want harm to happen to his or her body or property, and when another person acts in a way that causes obstruction to this ideal condition, he or she may pursue justice, for example, through criminal law. This impairment of the ideal condition is what Simester and Von Hirsch (2011: 37) call 'adverse effects that count as harm'. An adverse effect is when the ideal condition is obstructed. In terms of property damage, before a potential victim can argue there is harm to his or her property, the victim must be able to show the legitimacy of his or her ownership of the relevant property. Only if the victim can prove the legitimacy of his or her possession can the perpetrator can be held responsible for causing harm.

A legitimate claim over one's property or resource can be used as a key basis to determine whether there has been harm. A person or entity must legitimately own the property to be able to accuse another people of harming what is his or hers. But what happens in a situation where legitimacy is disputed and needs to be resolved? This problem arises in most agrarian conflicts. Land is often disputed between the parties, even where one party has legal documentation to support its claims. There is therefore a real need to understand the historical and social context of the land ownership to be able to correctly identify legitimate claims over the land, not just those that have a documentary base, so claims over legitimation of the land must be traced back through often-complex histories of land possession and dispossession.

In fact, a significant number of agrarian conflicts are related to claims about the formality and legitimacy of land documents, or lack thereof. These documents are often based on previous government documents (including those from the colonial period), or recent government decisions granting concessions to companies. Land documents are typically issued centrally by state ministries[26] without local approval or informed decisions from the community affected by the decision. This is largely because, in practice, companies with such land documents have the power to exclude and evict people from the concession zones.

In discussing damage or potential damage, another question is posed: Can damage be calculated purely in terms of capital damage? It is very difficult to calculate emotional damage, such as trauma,[27] but damage to property can usually be calculated as economic loss to the owner. Destruction of a building can be calculated on the basis of the cost to construct a similar building. The loss of a tree or a hundred trees can be calculated based on the purchasing value of the seed and maintenance costs to grow the tree(s) to the exact age or height of the tree(s) at the time they were destroyed. There are two different situations where destruction to property occurs in agrarian conflicts. The first is where villagers 'destroy' company 'property'. For this type of case, although company property has been damaged, the judge needs to acknowledge the situational context and the reasons for destruction. In this sort of case, the damage or economic loss to companies is clearly visible and this kind of act might become grounds for criminal proceedings

The second situation where destruction commonly occurs to property in agrarian conflicts is where the economic loss to the company – the 'victim' of wrongful act – is not significant. If this is the case, should the company pursue justice through the criminal justice system? For example, the company as the victim of 'theft' will not be affected economically by the stealing of three pods of cacao, or a single branch of a tree. This was the argument in the Minah and the Okih cases. The harm to the company in the Minah case was negligible – the three cacao pods taken had hardly any monetary value. In Okih's case, the teak logs he collected fell naturally, and he claimed he had permission from the company assistant to collect these. Arguably, the company brought these cases to court to create a 'fear effect' and keep other villagers away from the company's property. In my opinion, there was no real harm caused to the company in either case and therefore there were no grounds for punishment. Many of the local land conflict cases involving customary law and practices fall in this second category and could easily be resolved through mediation. Such cases do not need to be processed through the criminal justice system at all.

In terms of determining whether an act is morally wrong, the debate on criminalisation proposed by Edwards (2017); Husak (2010); and Moore (2009) can be drawn upon. This derives from Husak's basic question on criminalisation, 'for what conduct may the state subject persons to punishment?' Edwards

(2017: 71) responds to Husak's question by posing two main requirements. The first focuses on 'the act'. A punishment is permissible if the act is morally wrong. This means that 'only morally wrongful conduct is permissibly punished' (Moore in Edwards 2017: 70). For example, stealing is morally wrong conduct; there is no argument about that proposition. However, state prosecutors or judges should use their discretion when considering whether the 'taking of property' should be treated as theft, by situating the act in the broader context.

The second requirement focuses on 'the subject or the person'. A punishment is permissible if the person who commits a wrongful act deserves punishment. According to Edwards (2017: 71), 'not all wrongful actions make one deserving of punishment'. Applying this to situations when agrarian conflict exists, the people who are positioned as the 'perpetrators' are, in fact, usually also the victims of prolonged conflict. 'Perpetrators' of minor criminal offences have often been marginalised, evicted from their lands, had their access to livelihood restricted, and suffer from poverty as a result of a lack of options for livelihood once their lands have been sealed off by borders and made inaccessible by concessions. Local villagers therefore do not morally deserve punishment for accessing lands that were accessible to them for generations. It is the state and companies that locked them out of their lands that must provide alternative solutions to the situation, in particular by mediating the conflict.

The same argument can be applied to the 'gathering' of fruits, tree branches, or other resources that are required for local villagers' daily livelihood. The gathering of resources may involve economic activity, for example, gathering fruit to be sold for extra money. However, it is unclear what amount of 'gathering' of forest or plantation resources is permissible and should not be regarded as a 'theft'. Should the cutting down of a tree branch, cutting down of a tree or cutting down of a hundred trees be punished similarly? In the case of Minah, the judge who read the verdict said her case was 'small but it has hurt many people',[28] meaning that injustice to Minah had offended many members of the public. This indicates that the judge fully understood that Minah did not deserve punishment. It was not just a matter of her receiving a light punishment but that by punishing someone who does not deserve to be punished the justice system itself is damaged. The same is true in Okih's case. Taking seven teak logs cannot be considered a crime similar to those of illegal loggers stealing hundreds of thousands of trees from the Kalimantan forests. Okih was a peasant union activist fighting against a company that appropriated village lands, and he was convicted of theft based on the company's report. The company had the option to resolve the case through mediation, but it instead chose the criminal law route.

In addition to the requirements that a punishment be moral and deserved, I suggest that there should be a third condition before the state can impose a punishment: the wrongful act should be understood in its wider social context. This is what Melissaris (2015) calls the 'situated theory'. Melissaris (2015: 358) criticises the ideal theory of criminal law for separating a wrongful act from the real setting of the people, the community they live in, the historical context, their beliefs, and the way they interact with other people, including those who think the accused person has committed a wrongful act. Melissaris (2015: 360) proposes a 'situated theory' of crime and punishment, which views:

> the person-bearer of criminal responsibility not as an abstraction but as a participant in a complex scheme of institutional relations, which have a direct and necessary impact on the reasons determining the way in which the criminal law ought to treat people.

Melissaris' idea is important for understanding agrarian conflict and the criminal offences arising from incidents during conflicts. Each incident should be situated in its own context, which would include: the history of the conflict; the history of the relationships between the local people and the land; the process by which local people were dispossessed; and whether the dispute over land possession or ownership has been settled. This would extend the state's discretion in cases arising from agrarian conflict, for example by requiring it to ask questions including: Why did local villagers trespass in the concession areas? Did local custom or *adat* law allow resource gathering prior to the concession being granted?

Further, Moore (2009: 29) discusses the real costs of criminalisation by the state. Among these costs are: (1) enforcement costs; (2) disrespect towards the law for over-criminalising behaviour that probably does not need to be punished; and (3) discriminatory and arbitrary law enforcement, which means that law could be selectively enforced. In many land conflicts, the cost of conducting criminal prosecution for petty criminal offences committed by locals is not comparable to the total damage the offence caused. Cases that could be settled through mediation waste a lot of effort and resources if the court system is forced to process them. This can also lead to people losing respect for the law.

In the end it is the state's obligation to help mediate and resolve agrarian conflict. Prolonged conflict not only creates marginalisation and discrimination, but makes it more difficult to find solutions, as issues become increasingly complex over time. In Indonesia, where many high-profile corruption cases escape punishment, punishing poor villagers for trespassing or picking up fruits 'scars' the sense of justice of millions of people, not least because these sorts of cases remain common, and are often widely reported in the mass media. Lastly, and most importantly, discriminatory and arbitrary law enforcement is clearly visible in agrarian conflicts, as wealthy and powerful companies 'drag' people to court for minor offences, while corporations' crimes of taking away people's land forcefully, or through corrupt collision with government officials, are almost never brought to justice.

Conclusion

In agrarian or land conflicts, crime and punishment can be used by powerful actors to show 'who has the power' (Franco and Carranza 2012). This power is derived not only from capital but also from state law, which gives these actors a legal basis for their actions, rendering them 'lawful', and seeing any action against these decisions as 'unlawful'. The criminalisation of actions related to agrarian conflicts is largely directed towards controlling the conduct of local actors, rather than punishing state and corporate actors who actually deserve to be punished (morally if not legally). Influencing the behaviour of local actors is achieved by creating fear of performing particular actions, such as entering concession areas without permission or collecting produce from those areas without authorisation.

Most writers who have discussed the grounds of criminalisation – including Husak 2007; Melissaris 2015; Moore 2009; Simester and Von Hirsch 2011 – agree on the constraints of permissible punishment, namely that: harm should be significant; the perpetrator should deserve the punishment; and the conduct should be morally wrong. I also agree with Melissaris' contention that the social context should also be taken into consideration through 'situated theory'. Situated theory can be used to mitigate or reject punishment for particular actions, even if harm can be proven and the conduct is considered a morally wrongful act. Consideration of the broader social context is especially important in places where agrarian or land conflicts exist. Scrutinising these requirements before punishing the conduct of local villagers, farmers or agrarian activists in agrarian conflict areas could help prevent discrimination against, and over-criminalisation of, the true victims of agrarian conflicts.

Notes

1 An early draft of this chapter was presented at the Roundtable Discussion on 'Crime and Punishment in Indonesia', hosted by the Centre for Indonesian Law, Islam and Society at the University of Melbourne, 29 November 2018. I would like to thank all the workshop participants for their valuable input.
2 See Law No. 22 of 1999 on Regional Autonomy.
3 The term used depends on the perspective taken. Local peasants and villagers claim they are 'reclaiming' lands that were appropriated by the state or state-backed corporations. The state and corporations prefer to use the term 'land occupation' because they hold the formal documents to the lands, including plantation or forestry concessions. See Bachriadi and Lucas 2001; Lucas and Warren 2003: 87–126; Rachman 2017.
4 KPA is a non-government organisation concerned with agrarian justice issues.
5 Husak (2007) and Moore (2009) give guidance on the kinds of acts that can be regarded as 'crimes' punishable by the state, in what situations a common act becomes forbidden and punishable, and to what extent the concept of 'harm to others' can be applied.
6 Many Indonesians use only one name.

7 As Minah had already spent that an amount of time in police custody, she was immediately released after the verdict was read.

8 See Detik 2010; Kompas 2009. Even a former Constitutional Court Chief Justcie, Mahfud MD, raised concerns that the police, prosecutor, and the judges relied only on formal procedural law and were not concerned with issues of substantive justice.

9 A 'plasma' farmer is a smallholder farmer bound by a farming contract to a plantation company. In one common form of contract farming, smallholders contract with the company, which is the 'nucleus estate', and plasma farmers are bound to sell their produce to it.

10 PT Perhutani is a state-owned forestry company.

11 Indramayu District Court Decision No. 534/Pid.B/Sus/2013/PN.IM.

12 The so-called *Dana Darurat Kriminalisasi Petani* (Farmers' Criminalisation Emergency Fund) was established in 2015 by the KNPA (Komite Nasional Pembaruan Agraria, National Committee for Agrarian Reform) and NGOs including: KPA; AMAN (Aliansi Masyarakat Adat Nusantara, Adat Communities Alliance in Nusantara); KontraS (Komisi Untuk Orang Hilang dan Korban Tindak Kekerasan, Commission for the Disappeared and Victims of Violence); Walhi (Wahana Lingkungan Hidup Indonesia, Indonesian Forum for the Environment); Solidaritas Perempuan (Women's Solidarity); Kiara (Koalisi Rakyat Untuk Keadilan Perikanan, The People's Coalition for Fisheries Justice); SPI (Serikat Petani Indonesia, Indonesian Peasant Union); API (Aliansi Petani Indonesia, Indonesian Peasant Alliance); Pusaka (heirloom, bequest (forest people's programme in Indonesia); Sawit Watch (*sawit*: palm oil); Bina Desa (Village Development); Sajogyo Institute; Agra (Aliansi Gerakan Reforma Agraria, Alliance of Agrarian Reform Movement); IHCS (Indonesian Human Rights Committee for Social Justice); JKPP (Jaringan Kerja untuk Pemetaan Partisipatif, Working Network for Participatory Mapping); and the Rights and Resources Initiative.

13 PT Inhutani I was established under Government Regulation No. 21 of 1971 in East Kalimantan; PT Inhutani II under Regulation No. 32 of 1974 in South Kalimantan; PT Inhutani III under Regulation No. 31 of 1974 in Central Kalimantan; PT Inhutani IV under Regulation No. 22 of 1991 in North Sumatra; and PT Inhutani V under Regulation No. 23 of 1991 in South Sumatra. See Ministry of State-Owned Companies 2019.

14 PT Perkebunan Nusantara, 'Profil', www.holding-perkebunan.com.

15 In Indonesian legal doctrine, it is accepted that a law that contains content on a more specific matter will overrule a law that only contains rules on general matters based on the principle '*lex specialis derogate legi generalis*'. Some examples of the implementation of this principle can be seen in art. 63(2) of the Criminal Code and art. 1 of the Commercial Code (*Kitab Undang-Undang Hukum Dagang*).

16 Assegaf (Chapter 9, this volume) discusses in more detail petty crimes, including theft in which economic loss does not equal the punishment given, as in Minah's case, above.

17 This information was provided by KIBAR (Kediri Bersama Rakyat, Kediri Stands with the People) an NGO advocating for farmers' rights in Kediri, East Java. See KIBAR 2010.

18 Members of the coalition are: IHCS; API; FIELD (Farmers Initiative for Ecological Livelihood and Democracy); Bina Desa; Koalisi Rakyat untuk Kedaulatan Pangan (People's Coalition for Food Sovereignty); IPPHTI (Ikatan Petani Pengendalian

Hama Terpadu Indonesia, Indonesian Farmers Association for Pest Control); SPSI (Serikat Petani Kelapa Sawit, Palm-oil Farmers Association); Sawit Watch; SPI; and AGRA.

19 An *amicus curiae* is someone who is not a party to a case and may or may not have been solicited by a party and who assists a court by offering information, expertise, or insight that has a bearing on the issues in the case.

20 Case No. 129/Pid.B/LH/2017/PN Pbb District Court of Lubuk Basung, Agam, West Sumatra.

21 Based on Ministry of Forestry Decree No. 35/Menhut.11/2013 on 15 January 2013; and Ministry Decree No. 598/Menlhk/Setjen/PLA.2/8/2016 on the establishment of conservation forest function in Maninjau area.

22 Kurnia Warman testimony, *Koto Malintang Case*, n. 32, 61–3.

23 See testimony by Jony Akbar, *Koto Malintang Case*, 32.

24 Dekker (2017) provides an in-depth explanation of the invisible borders created by formal property right establishment. See also Blomley (2003) to understand how property borders include and exclude people from legal and geographical perspectives.

25 On this point, see also Tadros (2009: 75).

26 The ministry involved depends on the type of concession given. The Ministry of Forestry deals with forest concessions, the Ministry of Agriculture with plantations concessions, and the Ministry of Energy and Mineral Resources with mining concessions.

27 Compensation or restitution can be calculated based on the value of the loss, not only for physical lost (bodily harm, mental illness), but also non-physical loss, such as the trauma or the length of time victims (or family) needs to heal from trauma, grief, distress, or shock. Indonesian legislation and government regulations regulating kinds of compensation include Regulation No. 43 of 2017 on Restitution for Child Victims of Crime, and art. 35 of Law No. 26 of 2000 on the Human Rights Court.

28 '*Kasus ini kecil, namun sudah melukai banyak orang*', Muslih Bambang Lukmono was the Chair of the Panel of Judges, who sentenced Minah on 19 November 2009. See Fitri 2009 and Detik.com 2009.

References

Afrida, Nani 2015. 'Are Indonesian Soldiers Professional Enough?', *The Jakarta Post*, 10 May www.thejakartapost.com

Arrsa, Ria Casmi 2014. 'An Indication of Criminalization to Human Rights Defenders in Agrarian Disputes: An Analysis of Decision Number 250.Pid.B.2013/PN.PLG and Number 76/PID/2013/PT.PLG'. Malang: Universitas Brawijaya

Bachriadi, Dianto and Lucas, Anton 2001. *Merampas Tanah Rakyat: Kasus Tapos dan Cimacan.* Jakarta: Gramedia, Yayasan Adikarya IKAPI and Ford Foundation

Blomley, Nicholas 2003. 'Law, Property, and the Geography of Violence: The Frontier, the Survey, and the Grid', *Annals of the Association of American Geographers* 93(1): 121

BUMN (Ministry of State-Owned Companies), Perhutani n.d. 'Sejarah Perusahaan', www.bumn.go.id/perhutani/halaman/47

Butt, Simon and Lindsey, Tim 2018. *Indonesian Law.* Oxford University Press.

CNN Indonesia 2019. 'KOMNAS HAM: Polri Paling Banyak Diadukan Periode Januari-Maret 2019', *CNN Indonesia*, 16 July www.cnnindonesia.com

Dekker, Henri A. L. 2017. *The Invisible Line: Land Reform, Land Tenure Security and Land Registration.* Abingdon: Routledge

Detik.com 2009. 'Mencuri 3 Buah Kakao, Nenek Minah Dihukum 1 Bulan 15 Hari', 19 November www.news.detik.com

Detik 2010, 'Mahfud: Penegak Hukum terikat Pasal Formal Rasa Keadilan Bermasalah', 14 February www.news.detik.com

Edwards, James 2017. 'Criminalisation without Punishment', *Legal Theory* 23: 69–95

Epistema, Rimbawan Muda Indonesia (RMI) and Betang Borneo Foundation 2015. *Legality and Justice in the Establishment of Forest Zones in Indonesia. Policy Paper*. Jakarta: Epistema

Fitri, Emmy 2009. 'Indonesia Moved by Case of Grandmother Who Stole 3 Cocoa Pods', *Jakarta Globe*, 10 December www.jakartaglobe.id

Franco, Jennifer and Carranza, Danilo Tanael 2014. 'Backlash and Beyond: The Criminalisation of Agrarian Reform and Peasant Response in the Phillipines', *Oñati Socio-Legal Series* 4(1): 35–62

Garnaut, Ross 2015. 'Indonesia's Resources Boom in International Perspective: Policy Dilemmas and Options for Continued Strong Growth', *Bulletin of Indonesia's Economic Studies* 51(2) 189–212

Husak, Douglas 2007. *Overcriminalisation: The Limits of the Criminal Law.* Oxford University Press

Husak, Douglas 2010. *The Philosophy of Criminal Law: Selected Essays.* Oxford University Press

Husak, Douglas 2011. 'Reservations about Overcriminalization', *New Criminal Law Review* 14(1): 97–107

KIBAR 2010. 'Kriminalisasi Pak Kunoto alias Kuncoro', 8 February www.kibar-kediri.blogspot.com

KPA (Konsorsium Pembaruan Agraria, Consortium for Agrarian Reform) 2017. 'Annual Report 2017' www.kpa.or.id

KPA 2018. 'Annual Report 2018' www.kpa.or.id

Kleinig, John 2009. 'Douglas Husak, Overcriminalization: The Limits of the Criminal Law', *Criminal Justice Ethics* 28(1): 25–26

Kompas 2009. 'Tiga Buah Kakao Menyeret Minah ke Meja Hijau', 19 November www.regional.kompas.com

Li, Tania-Murray 2016. *Land's End: Capitalist Relations on an Indigenous Frontier.* Durham NC: Duke University Press

Lucas, Anton and Warren, Carol 2003. 'The State, the People, and Their Mediators: The Struggle over Agrarian Law Reform in Post-New Order Indonesia', *Indonesia* 76: 87–126

Lucas, Anton and Warren, Carol 2013. 'The Land, the Law and the People', in Anton Lucas and Carol Warren (eds.), *Land for the People: The State and Agrarian Conflict in Indonesia*. Athens: Ohio University, pp. 1–39

Manan, Bagir 2004. *Hukum Positif Indonesia.* Yogyakarta: Fakultas Hukum Universitas Islam Indonesia (FH UII)

Melissaris, Emmanuel 2015. (online version). 'Theories of Crime and Punishment', in Markus D. Dubber and Tatjana Hörnie (eds.), *The Oxford Handbook of Criminal Law.* Oxford University Press

Moore, Michael S. 2009. 'A Tale of Two Theories', *Criminal Justice Ethics* 28(1): 27–48

Peluso, Nancy and Watts, Michael (eds.) 2001. *Violent Environment*. Ithaca: Cornell University Press

Perum Perhutani 2016. 'Annual Report 2016'. www.bumn.go.id/perhutani.

Rachman, Noer Fauzi 2012. *Land Reform dari Masa ke Masa*. Jakarta: STPN (Sekolah Tinggi Pertanahan Nasional) Press

Rachman, Noer Fauzi 2017. *Land Reform dan Gerakan Agraria Indonesia*. Yogyakarta: Insist Press

Simester, A. P. and Von Hirsch, Andreas 2011. *Crimes, Harms and Wrongs: The Principles of Criminalisation*. Oxford: Hart

SOMO (Stichting Onderzoek Multinationale Ondernemingen) and Inkrispena 2017. 'The Two Hats of Public Security Actors in Indonesia Protecting Human Rights or Preserving Business Interests? Case Research in the Palm Oil and Logging Sector', 13 June www.somo.nl

Suryowati, Estu 2017. 'KPA: Polisi, Pelaku Kekerasan Terbanyak dalam Konflik Agraria', *KOMPAS.com*, 27 December www. nasional.kompas.com

Tadros, Victor 2009. 'The Architecture of Criminalization', *Criminal Justice Ethics* 28(1): 74–88

Tempo 2019. 'Kades di Aceh Utara Dipolisikan karena Kembangkan Benih Padi Unggul', 30 July www.tempo.co

Vonilia and Sapariah Saturi 2018. 'Pandangan Para Ahli soal Warga Nagari Terjerat Hukum Perusak Hutan Walau Berizin Adat', *Mongabay*, 12 March www. mongabay.co.id

Warman, Kurnia 2010. *Hukum Agraria Dalam Masyarakat Majemuk: Dinamika Interaksi Hukum Adat dan Hukum Negara di Sumatera Barat*. HUMA, Van Vollenhoven Institute and KITLV

Interview

Wendra Putra Rona, Padang Legal Aid (LBH, Lembaga Bantuan Hukum Padang), 15 August 2018

Legislation

Criminal Code (*Kitab Undang-Undang Hukum Pidana*, KUHP: Law No. 1 of 1946 as amended by Law No. 27 of 1999 on the Indonesian Criminal Code)

Commercial Code (Kitab Undang-Undang Hukum Dagang, KUHD: *Wetboek van Koophandel voor Indonesië*, 1847).

Law No. 12 of 1992 on Crop Cultivation Systems

Law No. 22 of 1999 on Regional Autonomy

Law No. 41 of 1999 on Forestry

Law No. 26 of 2000 on Human Rights Court

Law No. 8 of 2004 as Amended by Law No. 39 of 2014 on Plantations

Law No. 40 of 2007 on Limited Liability Companies

Law No. 18 of 2013 on the Prevention and Combating of Forest Destruction

Regulations

Government Regulation No. 21 of 1971 on the Establishment of PT Inhutani I, East Kalimantan

Government Regulation No. 32 of 1974 on the Establishment of PT Inhutani II, South Kalimantan
Government Regulation No. 31 of 1974 on the Establishment of PT Inhutani III, in Central Kalimantan
Government Regulation No. 22 of 1991 on the Establishment of PT Inhutani IV, North Sumatra
Government Regulation No. 23 of 1991 on the Establishment of PT Inhutani V, South Sumatra
Government Regulation No. 43 of 2017 on Restitution for Child Victims of Crime
Supreme Court Regulation No. 2 of 2012 on Adjustment of Standards for Minor Offences and Value of Fines in the Criminal Code

Court cases

Supreme Court Decision No. 534/Pid.B/Sus/2013/PN.IM Indramayu District Court, Okih bin Iyan
Constitutional Court Decision No. 55/PUU-VIII/2010 on Plantation Law
Constitutional Court Decision No. 35/PUU-X/2012 on Forestry Law
Constitutional Court Decision No. 99/PUU-X/2012 on Crop Cultivation Systems Law
Constitutional Court Decision No. 122/PUU-VIII/2015 on Plantation Law
Constitutional Court Decision No. 138/PUU-VIII/2015 on Plantation Law
Lubuk Basung District Court Decision No. 129/Pid.B/LH/2017/PN LBB, Ergi Dt. Samiak and Agusri Masnefi

Part V

Crime and religion

15 Blasphemy prosecutions in Indonesia and the Ahok case

Majoritarianism versus liberalism

Daniel Peterson

In November 1998, six months after President Soeharto resigned, a Special Session of the MPR (Majelis Permusyawaratan Rakyat, the People's Consultative Assembly) was convened in Jakarta. The session resulted in the promulgation of MPR Decree No. 17 of 1998 on Human Rights, which facilitated the enactment of Law No. 39 of 1999 on Human Rights and the incorporation of Chapter XA on Human Rights into the 1945 Constitution (Salim 2008: 108). Both contain a raft of ostensibly inalienable liberal democratic human rights guarantees that derive from the Universal Declaration of Human Rights (Lindsey 2002: 254).

In April 2010, however, a decision of Indonesia's Constitutional Court (Mahkamah Konstitusi) to uphold the country's 'Blasphemy Law' – Law No. 1/PNPS/1965 on the Prevention of the Abuse/Sullying of Religion – effectively subordinated many of those human rights to the protection of religious orthodoxy and the religious sensibilities of Indonesia's Muslim majority.[1] The decision also endorsed the role of Indonesia's religious scholars (*ulama*) and 'religious parent organisations' as the arbiters of religious orthodoxy, the protection of which the Constitutional Court saw as necessary to maintain public order in Indonesia.[2] As Lindsey writes, this was 'an obvious reference to [the Majelis Ulama Indonesia, MUI]' – the quasi-autonomous non-governmental organisation that is Indonesia's Council of Ulama and peak Islamic body (Lindsey 2012: 132 and 430), and whose religious edicts (*fatwa*) have come to serve as definitive articulations of what is considered 'true' Islam in contemporary Indonesia.

From a legal viewpoint, these two developments encapsulate a tension that exists in contemporary Indonesia between growing religious conservatism and majoritarianism on one hand, and liberalism on the other. Nowhere has this tension been played out on such a grand scale as it did with the conviction under the Blasphemy Law of Basuki 'Ahok' Tjahaja Purnama, Jakarta's former governor. Before I discuss the detail of Ahok's prosecution, however, I commence with a summary of what it was that Ahok did that was ultimately deemed blasphemous by the North Jakarta State Court.

Ahok's remarks

On 27 September 2016, Ahok, then governor of Jakarta, visited Pramuka Island in the Thousand Islands district (Kepulauan Seribu) off the coast of Jakarta. Speaking with a group of fishermen, Ahok, an ethnic Chinese Christian, made an off-the-cuff remark cautioning his audience against people who use the Qur'anic verse *Surah Al-Ma'ida* 51 to discourage Muslims from electing a non-Muslim candidate to public office. With the February 2017 gubernatorial election on the horizon, Ahok said:

> So don't believe people – it's possible that in your heart of hearts [you] can't choose me, you know, misled using *Surah Al-Ma'ida* 51, and suchlike. That is [your] right, so if [you] feel you can't choose me because you're afraid you'll go to hell because you've been fooled, that doesn't matter, because that is your own call ...[3]

The meaning of *Surah Al-Ma'ida* 51 is contestable. According to the Arabic version of the verse, Muslims are not to take Jews and Christians as their '*auliya*'. The official translation of the verse, endorsed by Indonesia's Ministry of Religion, translates 'auliya' as 'leader' (*pemimpin*) (North Jakarta Attorney-General 2016a: 3). However, a previous translation made between 1998 and 2002, and issued by Indonesia's Department of Religion (as it then was), defined auliya as 'loyal friend' (*teman setia*) (Tempo 2016).

On 6 October 2016, Buni Yani, a former lecturer at the London School of Public Relations Jakarta, posted a half-minute video excerpt of Ahok's speech to his personal Facebook page. The video was accompanied by a caption that Yani himself had written, which suggested that Ahok was saying that Muslims could be misled by the Qur'an. It was subsequently seized upon by certain conservative Islamic groups, including FPI (Front Pembela Islam, Islamic Defenders Front)[4] and MUI (Amnesty International 2016). Members of FPI and other groups sympathetic to FPI's Islamist cause then reported Ahok to the police on the basis of his remarks, alleging that the governor had blasphemed the Qur'an (Tim Advokasi BTI BTP 2017: 8).[5] Frustrated by a lack of response from law enforcement officials, on 14 October 2016, FPI and others initiated the first of four mass demonstrations conducted under the moniker of *Aksi Bela Islam* (Action to Defend Islam). While that first demonstration was primarily attended by hardliners, subsequent demonstrations on 4 November 2016 (*Aksi 411*), 2 December 2016 (*Aksi 212*), and 11 February 2017 (*Aksi 112*) comprised a much grander and broader section of Indonesia's Muslim population (Fauzi 2016).[6]

On 16 November 2016, Ahok was charged by police with blasphemy and, on 1 December 2016, the North Jakarta Prosecutor filed an indictment with the North Jakarta State Court alleging that Ahok had blasphemed the Qur'an (*penodaan terhadap Al-Qur'an*) or, in the alternative, insulted a group of Indonesian people (*penghinaan terhadap satu golongan rakyat Indonesia*). As persuasive authority, the indictment cited a 'Religious Opinion and Stance' (*Pendapat dan Sikap Keagamaan*) that had been issued by MUI on 11 October 2016. The religious opinion condemned Ahok's remarks, declaring them to be both blasphemous and antagonistic (North Jakarta Attorney-General 2016a).

Prior to the court's final deliberation, the prosecution requested that Ahok receive a one-year sentence suspended over a period of two years for the lesser offence of inciting hatred towards a group, as the prosecution had already conceded that blasphemy had not been established. The court, however, ruled that a suspended sentence would be 'inappropriate' (*tidak tepat*) based on the allegations contained in the prosecution's indictment. On 9 May 2017, Ahok was found guilty of blasphemy and sentenced to two years' imprisonment.[7]

My aim in this chapter is to analyse the arguments contained in Ahok's legal team's final pleading, the Notice of Defence (*Nota Pembelaan*), as a way to investigate the wider problematic relationship between Islam, law and human rights in Indonesia. The Notice comprises 634 pages and seven chapters. It was issued in court, both orally and in writing, on 25 April 2017, in the course of the penultimate trial session before the court issued its judgment. While the defence mounted by Ahok's legal team was unsuccessful, it nevertheless contained a number of legitimate legal arguments that received little to no acknowledgment by the court in its judgment.

I organise this chapter into three main sections. They are:

1. 'Fact-based defence': the fact-based defence presented by Ahok's legal team refuting the allegations of inciting hatred against a group and blasphemy;
2. 'Multiple interpretations': the claim Ahok's legal team made that the Blasphemy Law should not be applied on the grounds that it is open to multiple interpretations and therefore violates the principle and constitutional guarantee of legal certainty; and
3. 'Human rights': Ahok's defence based on constitutional human rights guarantees and statutory procedural guarantees, which I treat collectively as human rights.

I then conclude with a brief discussion of the court's very sparse reasoning for rejecting these defences. As mentioned, the court failed to engage with the defence's submissions to any significant degree in its judgment. Rather, it simply found that Ahok had, in fact, blasphemed because he had 'used [*Surah Al-Ma'ida* 51] in connection with the concept of deception, which had a negative connotation (Butt 2017). The court went no further in its engagement with the defence's submissions, stating simply that its opinion was 'in line and in accordance with the opinions of the experts submitted by the general prosecutor …'.[8]

The overarching issue that emerges from the discussion that follows is consistent with that which emerges from the raft of blasphemy cases[9] that preceded Ahok's trial, including the Constitutional Court's 2010 decision to uphold the Blasphemy Law: the subordination of the constitutional and statutory human rights of a member of a religious minority to the religious orthodoxy and sensibilities of the Muslim majority, as defined by MUI.

Fact-based defences

Having explained the facts of the case, I now turn to Ahok's defences based on allegations of fact.

Inciting hatred against a group

As mentioned, aside from being charged with blasphemy, Ahok was also charged, in the alternative, with the lesser offence of inciting hatred against a group. Article 156 of the KUHP (Kitab Undang-Undang Hukum Pidana, Indonesian Criminal Code) states:

> Whoever, in public, expresses feelings of enmity, hatred or insult toward a group or groups of Indonesian people, is liable to a maximum prison sentence of four years or a maximum fine of Rp. 4,500. The word 'group' in this article and the following articles means each and every group of Indonesian people that differs from one or several other groups because of race, country of origin, religion, place, origin, ancestry, nationality, or status according to state administrative law.

The defence's primary objection to this lesser charge was that Ahok's remarks about people who used *Surah Al-Ma'ida* 51 to mislead the *umma* (Muslim community) included no reference to a particular group that could be defined along lines prescribed in art. 156, namely race, country of origin, religion, place, origin, ancestry, nationality, or status according to state administrative law (Tim Advokasi BTI BTP 2017: 19). The defence had already posited this objection on 13 December 2016 in its Notice of Objection (*Nota Keberatan*) (Tim Advokasi BTI BTP 2016: 28), which it issued in response to Ahok's indictment. Here, it went further, noting that arts. 310 and 311 of the KUHP require that it be clear about to whom the insult is directed (Tim Advokasi BTI BTP 2017: 20).

Article 310 states:

1) Whoever, intentionally, attacks someone's honour or good name by accusing them of something, the intent of which is to make that publicly known, because of that defamation, faces up to nine months' imprisonment or a fine of up to Rp. 4,500.

Article 311 states:

1) If the person committing defamation or written defamation is permitted to prove the truth of the accusation, and is not able to prove it, and the accusation contradicts what is known, then s/he has committed slander and faces up to four years' imprisonment.

The defence argued that the court should not punish Ahok for the incorrect interpretation of what he had actually said that appeared in the very short, edited video of his speech posted by Buni Yani. Referencing Ahok's 2008 autobiography *Merubah Indonesia* [Changing Indonesia]*: The Story of Basuki Tjahaja Purnama*, in which Ahok writes about his experiences in politics dealing with political elites who used *Surah Al-Ma'ida* 51 to encourage Muslim voters not to elect him (Purnama 2008: 40), the defence submitted:

> [I]t is clear to whom [Ahok] was actually referring, [and that] the people to whom [he had] referred were his political opponents, not the Islamic umma, let alone the ulama.
>
> (Tim Advokasi BTI BTP 2017: 20)

Ahok's lawyers' argument was plain: their client's remarks were in reference to politicians in general. Ahok had not identified any politician based on race, country of origin, religion, place, origin, ancestry, nationality, or status according to state administrative law. Furthermore, given that the publication of Ahok's book in 2008, despite its best-seller status, never generated the same furore as his remarks in September 2016, nor resulted in Ahok or the book's publisher being charged with blasphemy, it made no sense that the same comments were now said to be blasphemous. The allegation, they argued, was therefore groundless.

Blasphemy

With regard to the blasphemy charge, Ahok's lawyers offered two defences. The first was that Ahok had not offended anyone's religious sensibilities. The true offender, rather, was Buni Yani, who had edited and posted the video of Ahok's speech. In his Facebook post, Yani had included his own caption containing an edited portion of Ahok's speech. The caption read:

> DEFAMATION OF RELIGION?
>
> 'Ladies and gentlemen [Muslim voters] … misled by *Surah Al-Ma'ida* 51' … [and] 'going to hell [also, ladies and gentlemen] fooled'.
>
> It seems that, with this video, something bad will happen.[10]

Crucially, Yani's Facebook post omitted the word 'use' (*pakai*), which had been part of Ahok's remarks at the Pramuka Island meeting. As mentioned, this gave the false impression that Ahok had claimed people were being misled and fooled by *Surah Al-Ma'ida* 51 itself, rather than those who, Ahok claimed, used the verse for misleading purposes (Lindsey 2016). In any case, the video, as mentioned, quickly went viral. The apparent disorder it created resulted in Yani himself being sentenced to one and half years' imprisonment for spreading hate speech, contrary to art. 32 of Law No. 11 of 2008 on Electronic Information and Transactions, on 14 November 2017.

In an attempt to shift the blame to Yani, Ahok's lawyers stressed that no one who had attended Ahok's speech on 27 September 2016 had reported Ahok to the police. Furthermore, the mass demonstrations began only after Yani edited and uploaded the video to social media (Tim Advokasi BTI BTP 2017: 5–6 and 15). Crucially, the defence also argued that Yani's decision to omit the word 'use' from his post misrepresented the meaning of Ahok's comments. The defence went further still, submitting that because Yani himself had been prosecuted, Ahok should be exonerated (Tim Advokasi BTI BTP 2017: 6). The court, however, appeared to ignore the charges against Yani and found that none of the witnesses produced by the prosecution believed that Buni Yani's decision to upload the video was blasphemous, or that his omission of the word 'use' was blasphemous. Rather, it found that it was Ahok's comments that had created unrest in the community, as alleged in the prosecution's indictment.[11]

Intent

The second fact-based defence was that Ahok had not exhibited any intent to blaspheme. Article 156a(a) states:

> Punishable by up to five years' imprisonment is whoever, *intentionally* [emphasis added], in public, expresses a feeling or conducts themselves in a way that:
>
> a. is principally of a nature of enmity toward, abusive, or sullying of a religion followed in Indonesia …

The defence produced evidence from several experts, all whom believed Ahok had no intention to blaspheme. The Notice of Defence, for example, refers to an article entitled 'Head of Police: Not in Defence, Ahok did not Intend to Defame Religion' (Romadoni 2016), in which Indonesian police chief Tito Karnavian is quoted as saying that Ahok's use of the word 'use' (*pakai*) in his statement 'So don't believe people … who use *Surah Al-Ma'ida* 51 …' was conclusive evidence that Ahok had not intended to insult Islam or the ulama (Tim Advokasi BTI BTP 2017: 207). As mentioned, it was only Buni Yani's decision to omit the term from his Facebook post that suggested that Ahok was claiming that people could be misled by the verse alone, not by people who use it.

The defence also argued that Ahok's reference to 'don't believe people who …' was the same claim Ahok had made on page 40, para 4, of his 2008 autobiography, under the heading 'Sheltering Behind a Holy Verse'. This paragraph was inspired by Ahok's experience campaigning for the 2007 Bangka Belitung gubernatorial election, throughout which Ahok had encountered certain elite public figures whose inability, Ahok wrote in his autobiography, to convince the public of their own suitability for the office of governor had forced them to use Qur'anic scripture to undermine Ahok's campaign. Ahok's reference to 'people who' was, therefore, directed at his rivals in the election, not at the ulama or the wider umma (Tim Advokasi BTI BTP 2017: 275).

Several of the prosecution's witnesses who had reported Ahok to the police, including Novel Bamukmin, Hj. Irena Handono and Ibnu Baskoro, were also aware of Ahok's autobiography and its reference to *Surah Al-Ma'ida* 51. Despite this, they did not report Ahok to the police until his remarks on Pramuka Island were reported (Tim Advokasi BTI BTP 2017: 276–7).

With regard to Ahok's reference in his Pramuka Island comments to 'suchlike' (*macem-macem itu*) who mislead using *Surah Al-Ma'ida* 51, the defence submitted that this was a reference not to ulama but to the flyers circulated during Ahok's campaigns for both the regency of Belitung and the governorship of Bangka Belitung. These flyers claimed that *Surah Al-Ma'ida* 51 was a reason not to vote for the Christian Ahok (Tim Advokasi BTI BTP 2017: 282). Ahok's lawyers submitted that it was established at trial that, aside from including their own translation of *Surah Al-Ma'ida* 51, the flyers also stated that the verse prohibited the election of a non-Muslim governor and suggested that previous violations of that prohibition had resulted in the Aceh tsunami (Tim Advokasi BTI BTP 2017: 15 and 282–83).

As well as using the content of Ahok's remarks to refute the allegation of intent to blaspheme, the defence also submitted that Ahok's lifelong respect for, deference to, and knowledge of, the Islamic faith was evidence that he could never have intended to 'sully the Qur'an or insult the ulama or umma' (Tim Advokasi BTI BTP 2017: 480). The detail of this claim is explained below, and it was relevant, the defence submitted, by virtue of arts. 184(1) and 185(6)(a) and (b) of the KUHAP (Kitab Undang-Undang Hukum Acara Pidana, Criminal Procedure Code).[12]

More specifically, the Notice of Defence stated:

> What the general prosecutor neglected to convey at trial, however, is that before [Ahok] became governor, THERE HAD NEVER BEEN a previous governor of the Islamic faith who […] cared as much [as Ahok] about the Islamic population. We are, moreover, convinced that if [Ahok] had truly intended to antagonise or insult the Islamic population or the Islamic religion, then surely it would have been reflected in [his] programmes, [that is, programmes] that did not side with the Islamic population or Islamic religion. This was not found to be the case. In this

> case it was established that many of [Ahok's] programmes as Governor of Jakarta sided with the Islamic population and Islamic religion.
>
> (Tim Advokasi BTI BTP 2017: 18)

The defence noted thirteen separate initiatives Ahok's government had undertaken in order to advance Jakarta's umma. These were many and varied and included, among others, the construction of new mosques, such as Masjid Fatahillah at the Jakarta Town Hall. As Ahok's lawyers stressed, after many years and countless governors, Masjid Fatahillah marked the first time the Jakarta provincial government's central office had its own mosque. Another first was the construction of Jakarta's first grand provincial mosque, Masjid Raya Jakarta, in West Jakarta, which cost the capital city Rp. 170 billion (Tim Advokasi BTI BTP 2017: 16–17).

Other initiatives included the transformation of the Jakarta Islamic Center in North Jakarta into a religious site and source of Islamic knowledge. Since the beginning of 2016, Ahok's government had also, at a cost of Rp. 2.5 trillion, issued Muslim students at Islamic schools and madrasah with a *Kartu Jakarta Pintar* (Smart Jakarta Card) – holders of which were offered discounts on nine basic food staples (*sembako – sembilan bahan pokok*)[13] during Lebaran. Since being elevated to the governorship in 2014, Ahok had also sent more than 200 mosque and *musholla* (prayer room) attendants on the *umrah*[14] and, pursuant to Gubernatorial Decree 2589 of 2015, provided between Rp. 15 and 75 million in financial assistance to 118 different musholla, mosques and *majelis taklim* (non-formal Islamic education) sites. Furthermore, in 2016, during Ramadhan, Ahok ensured that public servants could return home at 2 p.m. to be home with their families in time to break the fast at dusk. That same year, Ahok also paid Rp. 55 million of his own money in *zakat* (religious alms) and arranged for the slaughter of fifty-five cows to then be sent to state housing complexes, mosques, musholla, and majelis taklim sites (Tim Advokasi BTI BTP 2017: 17–18).

On 17 October 2016, as reported by *Liputan 6* (Putra 2016), both Ahok and Deputy Governor H. Djarot Saiful Hidayat had also signed a memorandum of understanding with the United Development Party (Partai Persatuan Pembangunan, PPP), a political party that identifies as Islamic, as a sign of their commitment to establishing employment programmes that would assist the umma (Tim Advokasi BTI BTP 2017: 490–1).[15]

The defence emphasised that Ahok's close affinity with the umma, and strong working relationship with it, was not limited to his time as Governor of Jakarta. While Regent of Belitung, the defence noted, Ahok had made similar efforts, which they said established that Ahok had enjoyed a close affinity with the Indonesian umma for more than a decade (Tim Advokasi BTI BTP 2017: 19).

Ahok's upbringing

In fact, the defence did not stop at a decade, citing Ahok's upbringing as evidence of their client's lifelong affinity with both the umma and the Islamic faith. It noted that although Ahok was a Christian, he had been raised by both his own biological parents and his Muslim foster parents, Andi Baso Amier and Hajjah Misribu (Tim Advokasi BTI BTP 2017: 19). This arrangement was the result of a close friendship between Ahok's biological father, Indra Tjahaja Purnama (Tjoeng Kiem Nam), and his foster father, Amier (Faqih 2016).

Ahok had grown up on the island of Belitung, a Muslim-majority island, without ever having experienced problems of a religious or racially-charged nature, the defence claimed (Tim Advokasi BTI BTP 2017: 19 and 478). Ahok also stated in court that, in his childhood village of Gantung, the Qur'an, and even the Arabic language, were considered sacred. Ahok was afraid to open the Qur'an on his own without the assistance of a Muslim companion because he feared doing so would be considered blasphemous (Tim Advokasi BTI BTP 2017: 480). The defence's argument was plain: someone who revered Islam to the extent Ahok did could surely not have intended to blaspheme that same religion.

Ahok's understanding of Surah Al-Ma'ida 51

The defence also countered the allegation that Ahok had misappropriated *Surah Al-Ma'ida* 51 by arguing that it was those who had used the verse for the purposes of political expediency who were the true blasphemers. The defence explained that Ahok's view was informed by his own understanding of the verse, which had been conveyed to him by Muslim friends and colleagues. The Notice of Defence stated:

> [Ahok] had also been informed by friends of his who [he] considered to be knowledgable of Islamic teachings, one of those being the former Indonesian President Abdurrahman Wahid, alias Gus Dur, that *Surah Al-Ma'ida* 51 is not a guideline to be used in the context of state leadership elections because *Surah Al-Ma'ida* 51 was revealed at a time when there were Muslims who wished to murder the Prophet (*Nabi Besar*) Muhammad SAW by forming a coalition with a Christian group and Jewish group.
>
> (Tim Advokasi BTI BTP 2017: 276)

In further defence of their client, Ahok's lawyers cited expert evidence provided in court by H. Hamka Haq. Haq is a member of the MUI Advisory Council (*Dewan Pertimbangan Majelis Ulama Indonesia*) (Mardiastuti 2017), the DPR (Dewan Perwakilan Rakyat, People's Representative Assembly, Indonesia's national legislature), and the Indonesian Democracy

Party – Struggle (Partai Demokrasi Indonesia – Perjuangan, PDI-P), the latter being the political party of which President Widodo is a member. In court, Haq acknowledged that *Surah Al-Ma'ida* 51 was susceptible to multiple interpretations. Haq explained, however, that the context of the verse was one of war, noting that if Indonesia were today at war with another nation that sought to subjugate the archipelago, then, by virtue of Indonesia's Muslim majority, a correct application of the verse would prohibit the Indonesian people from appointing a 'Christian wartime military commander' (Tim Advokasi BTI BTP 2017: 161 and 401). Because Indonesia is not currently at war, Haq argued that the verse was inapplicable. Haq also told the court that the verse, more importantly, is not applicable to political elections (Tim Advokasi BTI BTP 2017: 401).

Having addressed the defence's response to the factual aspects of the charges Ahok faced, I will now discuss another aspect of the defence submitted by Ahok's legal team, namely that the legislative provisions that prohibit blasphemy are susceptible to multiple interpretations.

Multiple interpretations

The defence's concern with the wording of art. 156a ('expressing a feeling or behaving in such a way that is, in principle, of a nature of enmity, abuse or sullying of a religion adhered to in Indonesia') was that it is susceptible to 'multiple interpretations' (*multitafsir*), which violates the principle of *lex certa* (legal certainty) (Tim Advokasi BTI BTP 2017: 628–9). The defence submitted that it was unclear what in actual fact constituted the sullying or dishonouring of religion. It therefore requested that the court rely on lex certa and not apply art. 156a. It also included a request from LBH (Lembaga Bantuan Hukum, Legal Aid) Jakarta[16] that the government and DPR immediately review the 'anti-democratic policies' contained in the Blasphemy Law and art. 156a of the KUHP (Tim Advokasi BTI BTP 2017: 629).

For the court to have acceded to this argument, however, it would have had to ignore the clear majority judgment of the Constitutional Court in its 2010 constitutional review of the Blasphemy Law (that is, art. 156a of the KUHP, incorporated therein by art. 4 of the 'Blasphemy Law'), upholding that Law.[17] The defence even acknowledged the authority of that Constitutional Court judgment in its Notice of Objection (Tim Advokasi BTI BTP 2016: 21) but, in discussion with me, Humphrey Djemat, one of Ahok's chief legal counsel, told me that the defence's position was that the North Jakarta State Court was not necessarily bound by the Constitutional Court's judgment.[18] Notwithstanding art. 24C(1) of the 1945 Constitution, which declares Constitutional Court decisions to be first and final, that is, not reviewable, it is a peculiarity of the Indonesian judicial system that the lower courts are not the implementing agencies for Constitutional Court decisions, as they are for Supreme Court decisions. Rather, it is for the government and DPR to pass or amend laws based on Constitutional Court decisions, which both the Supreme Court and lower courts then interpret. Indeed, in theory, in a civil law country such as Indonesia, court-made law is merely persuasive and courts are not bound by the doctrine of precedent, as they are in Anglo common law countries. As mentioned, the court in Ahok's case never addressed this argument in its judgment.

I now move to a discussion of the constitutional and statutory human rights guarantees cited in the Notice of Defence. For the purposes of this section, I treat the procedural guarantees contained in the KUHAP as human rights guarantees. I do this on the grounds that procedural fairness guarantees pertain to the constitutional and human right to procedural fairness and equal treatment before the law, as guaranteed by art. 28D(1) of the Constitution, which states:

> Every person is entitled to fair legal recognition, guarantee, protection, and certainty, as well as equal treatment before the law.

As noted earlier, the court's judgment failed to engage with any of the legal arguments I now discuss.

Human rights

Freedom of expression

Human rights provisions, particularly those guaranteeing the right to freedom of expression, were far more prominent in the Notice of Defence than the Notice of Objection. Indeed, the Notice of Defence commences and concludes by citing expert evidence on human rights law given in court on 15 April 2017 by Alghiffari Aqsa. Aqsa is Director of LBH Jakarta and nominated himself to the court as an *amicus curiae* (friend of the court) in order to be able to provide specific expert evidence with regard to Ahok's human rights.

Aqsa submitted that Ahok had been made 'a victim' of the 'anti-democratic' art. 156a during an election campaign, the democratic nature of which had been thoroughly compromised. Furthermore, it was the position of Aqsa and LBH Jakarta that Ahok's arrest was inappropriate given that, although art. 156a was current law, both the DPR and government had failed to observe the recommendation of the Constitutional Court, in its review of the blasphemy provisions of the KUHP, that art 156a should be revised and redrafted (Tim Advokasi BTI BTP 2017: 8–9 and 626–7).

With regard to Ahok's right to freedom of expression, Aqsa told the court:

> Ahok's statement at Pramuka Island, Kepulauan Seribu (27/09/16), was unequivocally not an act of religious interpretation. Ahok, in actual fact, had criticised a legal subject (a person) or parties who use religious verses from the Qur'an to trick the public for political gain. Ahok's statement also failed to meet the *mens rea* [criminal intent] requirement that must

> be established to fulfil the elements of art. 156a of the KUHP. Ahok's statement, in this instance, is protected by the [right to] freedom of opinion and expression, which is guaranteed by art. 28E of the Constitution, Law No. 9 of 1998 [on the Freedom to Express Opinions in Public], the International Covenant on Civil and Political Rights [ICCPR], and the Universal Declaration of Human Rights.
>
> (Tim Advokasi BTI BTP 2017: 9 and 627)

The defence argued that the ICCPR had been a part of Indonesian law from the time Indonesia acceded to the covenant.[19] It followed that the ICCPR not only provides standards for civil and political rights law in Indonesia, but that Indonesia is obliged by art. 2 of the ICCPR to adopt the laws necessary to nationally enact the rights contained therein (Tim Advokasi BTI BTP 2017: 9). The defence also submitted that Ahok's right to freedom of expression, as contained in art. 19(2) of the ICCPR, applied in this case. It cited the UN Human Rights Committee, which declared the right to freedom of expression, as guaranteed by art. 19, to include 'political discourse', 'religious discourse', and 'even expressions considered very offensive'. The defence submitted that 'art 156a(a) of the KUHP clearly limits the type of expression protected by the ICCPR' (Tim Advokasi BTI BTP 2017: 10), the implication being that art. 156a(a) should be ignored in favour of the ICCPR. The court did not deal with these submissions in its judgment.

Procedural fairness

Perhaps the defence's most significant argument was in relation to what it said was the denial of Ahok's rights to procedural fairness and legal certainty. The Notice of Defence cited art. 17 of Law No. 39 of 1999 on Human Rights, which states:

> Every person, without discrimination, has the right to access justice by submitting an application, complaint, and claim, whether in a criminal case, civil suit, or administrative case, and to be adjudicated through a free and impartial judicial process, in accordance with legal procedures, which guarantee an objective investigation conducted by a judge who is honest and fair in obtaining a decision that is fair and true.

Here, I focus on four specific issues that the defence submitted had compromised Ahok's right to procedural fairness, namely: the use of hearsay evidence; problems with witness expertise and prejudice; public order arguments; and reliance on MUI's Religious Opinion and Stance.

Hearsay

Of the fourteen 'reporting witnesses' (*saksi pelapor*, that is, witnesses who reported Ahok to the police for his remarks), twelve were treated by the court as 'factual witnesses' (*saksi fakta*). The defence challenged the relevance of the evidence of those twelve on the ground that none had been in attendance when Ahok delivered his remarks. Rather, all twelve had merely viewed Buni Yani's half-minute video excerpt of Ahok's speech online. While the religious sensibilities of these twelve witnesses had allegedly been offended by viewing the video, the defence submitted that to accept their evidence as factual evidence would constitute a violation of art. 1(26) and (27) of the KUHAP, as well as the principle prohibiting *testimonium de auditu* (hearsay) that appears in the elucidation to art. 185(1) of the KUHAP.

To explain these two arguments, art. 1(26) of the KUHAP defines a witness as:

> [A] person who provides information for the purposes of investigating, prosecuting and adjudicating a criminal case that s/he has heard themselves, seen themselves and experienced themselves.

Article 1(27) adds:

> Witness information is one type of evidence in a criminal case that is information from a witness concerning a criminal incident that s/he hears, sees and experiences on his/her own and states a reason from that knowledge.

Meanwhile, the elucidation to art. 185(1) states:

> Witness information does not include information obtained from other people or hearsay.

Conversely, none of the five witnesses who had actually been in attendance at Ahok's speech,[20] all of whom were Muslim, had expressed any concern with Ahok's remarks when they gave evidence in court (Tim Advokasi BTI BTP 2017: 298). The defence therefore submitted:

> THERE WERE NO FACTUAL WITNESSES in this case, just a few EXPERTS produced by the General Prosecutor … who declared there to be 'culpability' on the part of [Ahok] …
>
> (Tim Advokasi BTI BTP 2017: 7)

As the defence believed there to be no factual witnesses, it followed that the evidence heard in court from the prosecution's expert witnesses, which I discuss next, was inadmissible. If there was no factual evidence, the evidence submitted by the prosecution's expert witnesses was immaterial to the case.

Witness prejudice and expertise

The defence objected to the admissibility of evidence provided by twenty of the prosecution's twenty-two witnesses on the grounds that, as well as being hearsay, their evidence violated the procedural requirement that witness evidence be impartial in nature. Of the seven witnesses called to give expert evidence on Islam, the defence objected to all four expert witnesses with MUI affiliations on the grounds that MUI had issued what the defence said was a prejudicial religious opinion.[21] In the interests of brevity, however, here I address only those objections made with regard to the most well-known and controversial witness: Muhammad Rizieq Shihab, the founder and leader of FPI.

Muhammad Rizieq Shihab

MUI requested that the court allow Shihab, by reason of his academic credentials in Islamic studies and shari'a (Tim Advokasi BTI BTP 2017: 100),[22] to give expert evidence at trial.[23] It was Shihab's opinion that Ahok's remarks could be divided into six separate parts, all of which were problematic:

1. 'so, don't believe people' (*jadi, jangan percaya sama orang*);
2. 'don't pick Ahok' (*enggak pilih BTP*);
3. 'misled using *Surah Al-Ma'ida* 51' (*dibohongi pake surah al-Maidah 51*);
4. 'suchlike' (*macam-macam itu*);
5. 'because I'm worried I'll go to hell' (*karena saya takut masuk neraka*); and
6. 'fooled' (*dibodohin gitu*) (Tim Advokasi BTI BTP 2017: 96).

Shihab told the court that these remarks had the effect, respectively, of:

1. encouraging the people of the Thousand Islands district not to believe in people who used *Surah Al-Ma'ida* 51 to prohibit Muslims from electing a Jewish or Christian leader;
2. referencing the upcoming gubernatorial election, because Ahok's remarks were unrelated to fishing and fisheries;
3. portraying those Muslims in attendance as having been misled and *Surah Al-Ma'ida* 51 as a 'tool of deception', if not a 'source of deception', rendering the Qur'an itself a tool and source of deception;
4. unethically abusing those people who had conveyed the meaning of *Surah Al-Ma'ida* 51 to others, as well as abusing *Surah Al-Ma'ida* 51 itself;
5. emphasising the context of his remarks as being in reference to the gubernatorial election; and
6. emphasising the fact that Ahok's remarks were blasphemous because 'fooled' (*dibodohi*) is a stronger word than 'misled' (*dibohongi*) (Tim Advokasi BTI BTP 2017: 96–9).

Shihab then went further, declaring that Ahok's remarks not only dishonoured the Qur'an, but also dishonoured and insulted all who have conveyed the meaning of *Surah Al-Ma'ida* 51, including the Prophet Muhammad himself, the Prophet's *sahaba* (companions), *tabiin* (followers of the Prophet born after his passing), and all ulama (Tim Advokasi BTI BTP 2017: 99).

The defence objected to Shihab's evidence because, as indicated above, he had only learned of Ahok's remarks after being shown a video of Ahok's speech during an interview with police (Tim Advokasi BTI BTP 2017: 95). Aside from this, the defence also argued that Shihab would be unable to provide expert evidence in an objective manner, primarily due to his evident protracted hatred of Ahok (Tim Advokasi BTI BTP 2017: 93). In support, the defence cited art. 179(1) of the KUHAP, which states:

> Every person requested to give their opinion as an expert of medicine, the judiciary or a doctor or another expert, must, in the interests of justice, provide information regarding their expertise.

The defence explained its interpretation of this provision:

> [E]xpert information is heard at trial for the sake of attaining justice, which is essential, and for the sake of locating the material truth. For this, in determining someone's appropriateness as an expert, aside from considering their relevant expertise, it is first necessary to evaluate the subjectivity of the expert, as well as his/her background and political stance. It is inconceivable (*mustahil*) that the expert's opinion could assist in the attainment of essential justice [if] the aforementioned opinion is obtained from an expert who is partial and whose attitude to life is poor.
> (Tim Advokasi BTI BTP 2017: 92)

The defence also recalled Shihab's police report, in which he stipulated certain criteria that a person must apparently meet before they may interpret the Qur'an. The defence then used that against Shihab to impugn his own character and remind the court of the witness' criminal record. The defence stated:

> Muhammad Rizieq Shihab, in his police report, stated firmly that the interpreter [of Qur'anic scripture] needs to meet certain criteria, those being, among others, sound morals, a sound purpose and aim, and [that he] puts into practice the content of the Qur'an. Surely then this should apply to Muhammad Rizieq Shihab.
> (Tim Advokasi BTI BTP 2017: 92)

After expressing its respect and admiration for the ulama in general, the defence listed the following as examples of why Shihab was neither fit (*tidak patut*) to provide expert evidence nor to interpret the Qur'an according to his own self-imposed standards (Tim Advokasi BTI BTP 2017: 92 and 94):

1. Shihab had already, for a long period of time, participated 'in activities that showed very strong contempt for … Ahok';

2. Shihab is a recidivist, having already been convicted of violent conduct towards people or property on 1 June 2008, during the violent attack on the National Alliance for Religious Freedom (Aliansi Kebangsaan untuk Kebebasan Beragama dan Berkeyakinan),[24] and for expressing feelings of enmity, hatred, or insult towards the Indonesian government;
3. Shihab was a suspect in a criminal case for defaming the *Pancasila*;[25]
4. Shihab was being investigated for defaming Christianity during a lecture he gave in Pondok Kelapa on 25 December 2016[26] (the defence understood that three reports had been made regarding Shihab's conduct in this instance);
5. Shihab, as chairman of the National Movement to Safeguard the MUI Fatwa (Gerakan Nasional Pengawal Fatwa MUI), had been involved in the Aksi Bela Islam demonstrations on 14 October, 4 November, and 2 December 2016; and
6. Shihab was being investigated by the police for sending lewd images via electronic media to Firza Husein[27] (Tim Advokasi BTI BTP 2017: 93–4).

The court ignored the defence's objection to Shihab providing expert evidence, as it did with the defence's other objections to other religious expert witnesses produced by the prosecution. The court simply stated:

> [T]hat the opinion of the court is in line and in accordance with the opinions of the experts submitted by the General Prosecutor, those being, [among others], Religious Expert Muhammad Rizieq Syihab ...[28]

Why it did not respond to any of the defence's concerns regarding Shihab's fitness to provide evidence is unclear. Although it could have been out of fear of reprisal, given the scale of the 'Action to Defend Islam' demonstrations, as Djemat told me,[29] it is also possible that its decision was informed by its own bias. Indeed, as several 'netizens' noted following Ahok's conviction, the personal Facebook account of one of the presiding judges, Abdul Rosyad, displayed support for conservative and anti-Ahok Islamist groups and preachers, including Felix Siauw and KH. Abdullah Gymnastiar (aka Aa Gym), as well as Irena Handono, one of the prosecution's witnesses, who had reported Ahok to police in October 2016 (Han 2017).

I now discuss the defence's argument that the public disorder caused by Ahok's remarks was actually engineered in order to compel law enforcement officials to prosecute Ahok.

Public order and political engineering

The defence maintained that the decision of the relevant authorities to charge and then indict Ahok had been the result of public pressure, which had been engineered by organisations intent on removing Ahok from public office. In support of this argument, Ahok's team submitted a raft of media articles, all of which claimed that Ahok had been brought to trial by law enforcement authorities in order to appease demonstrators.

It also posed two questions, neither of which appeared to rely on any explicit legal authority, but which implicitly relied on the right to freedom from discriminatory treatment and the right to equal treatment before the law. These two rights are guaranteed respectively by arts. 28I(2) and 28D(1) of the 1945 Constitution. First, the defence submitted:

> That concerning *Surah Al-Ma'ida* 51, it is regrettable that we can say that *Surah Al-Ma'ida* 51 (in this case) has only been used for [Ahok]. Why do we say this? Because many non-Muslim gubernatorial/regental/mayoral candidates have been nominated by Muslim-based parties and [yet] not one of [those parties] has [ever] explicitly requested that they not elect a non-Muslim leader. Is that not ironic?
>
> (Tim Advokasi BTI BTP 2017: 7)

Secondly, the defence asked:

> Would [Ahok] still have been tried if [he] had not nominated himself as governor? Would [Ahok] still have been tried if he adhered to [Indonesia's] majority religion?
>
> (Tim Advokasi BTI BTP 2017: 11)

The defence's first question suggests that this trial was a 'witch-hunt' designed to undermine Ahok, while the second question suggests that Ahok had been targeted by these groups in order to remove a member of a religious minority from public office.

The defence also argued at trial that public pressure had indeed played a role in Ahok's swift indictment. What Ahok's case and the grand scale of the 'Action to Defend Islam' rallies demonstrate, however, is the perilous reality of the Constitutional Court's majoritarian reasoning. Public pressure can be engineered through public demonstrations in order to pressure law enforcement authorities to charge and indict a supposed blasphemer. It is often the case, however, that orthodoxy is not apparent until after MUI has issued an edict of its own condemning the religious expression of a particular individual, individuals or group. It is therefore to the MUI religious opinion regarding *Surah Al-Ma'ida* 51 that I now turn. As with most of the defence's other submissions, however, the court once again failed to acknowledge this particular submission in its ruling.

The MUI religious opinion – drafting, effect, and use

The discussion that follows is primarily based on the Notice of Defence, and information provided in court by of MUI Chairman Ma'ruf Amin

(Vice-President of Indonesia since October 2019). I begin by discussing the drafting of the religious opinion and the reasons the opinion was issued, at least according to Amin. I then discuss the fact that the MUI opinion is, in theory, of no more than persuasive value at law. Finally, I argue that it did not enjoy the full support of all relevant MUI figures and that, moreover, the timing of its drafting is controversial.

The drafting

Amin told the court that the MUI religious opinion resulted from a discussion and investigation conducted by MUI's central branch. That investigation commenced on 1 October 2016 and culminated in the issuance of the religious opinion on 11 October 2016.[30] Amin also told the court that, as early as 28 September 2016, MUI Central had received a significant number of reports from the public expressing concern and anger with Ahok's remarks.[31] Amin conceded that he did not have the necessary documentary evidence with him in court to establish this claim, but told the court he could produce that evidence if necessary.[32] Neither the court's judgment nor the Notice of Defence, however, mention Amin having been ordered to do so, and Djemat assured me that the court never compelled Amin to produce that evidence.[33] Indeed, the Notice of Defence states that Amin 'was unable to establish the results of the 1 October investigation' and that there was no evidence to suggest that the people of the Thousand Islands district had complained or demonstrated in response to Ahok's remarks (Tim Advokasi BTI BTP 2017: 438).

Amin explained that MUI's investigation commenced with the formation of a team comprising four of MUI's commissions: its Fatwa Commission, Appraisal Commission, Information and Communications Commission, and Law and Legislation Commission (Tim Advokasi BTI BTP 2017: 116). The entire membership of the Law and Legislation Commission, which, Amin explained, comprises more than sixty lawyers,[34] believed that Ahok had blasphemed (Tim Advokasi BTI BTP 2017: 138). The findings of the meeting were then conveyed in writing to the MUI Central Executive, which discussed the findings before determining to issue the religious opinion (Tim Advokasi BTI BTP 2017: 117).[35]

Amin explained that the religious opinion itself was drafted quickly because it was a simple problem: the meaning of *Surah Al-Ma'ida* 51 was clear, meaning that the team only needed to ascertain whether or not Ahok had said what he had said, which the video had already established.[36] Indeed, Amin conceded that when the MUI executive met with the four commissions to discuss Ahok's speech, the parties only discussed the sentence 'misled using *Surah Al-Ma'ida* 51'. They did not discuss the actual meaning of *Surah Al-Ma'ida* 51,[37] nor did they seek clarification from Ahok as to what his intent was.[38] Amin submitted that:

> [I]n this case we considered it unnecessary to seek clarification from the accused because we discussed his statement, and, in principle, we did not

> need to know [his] intent and meaning because we hold on to the principle of only punishing the physical (*yang zohir*), thereby leaving the spiritual to the concern of Allah SWT.[39]

Amin also stated:

> That if there is a request for a fatwa, if that indeed requires appraisal, as, for example, [in the case] of deviant sects, then an appraisal needs to be conducted first, but if matters do not require one and are very clear, then an appraisal is unnecessary, meaning a fatwa merely needs to be issued.[40]

For Amin to concede that MUI was not interested in Ahok's intent is significant. Indeed, that all sixty lawyers of MUI's Law and Legislation Commission were similarly disinterested is puzzling. As the defence noted, it also reflects poorly on their credentials as ulama because such disinterest constituted a failure to adhere to the Islamic teaching of *tabayyun* (seeking clarification) (Tim Advokasi BTI BTP 2017: 448). Hamka Haq told the court that tabayyun was an 'absolute' (*mutlak*) requirement 'because it is a directive from the Qur'an' (Tim Advokasi BTI BTP 2017: 451). Haq also believed that MUI, as a respected Islamic organisation, and in accordance with *Surah Al-Anfal*,[41] should not bow to public pressure (Tim Advokasi BTI BTP 2017: 441). Haq told the court that this surah, in principle, states: 'If you bow to the pressure of many people, then you are led astray by them from God's path'.

KH. Ahmad Ishomuddin, Advisory Leader of the executive board of Indonesia's largest Islamic social organisation, NU (Nahdlatul Ulama, literally, the 'Awakening of the Ulama'), and then-Deputy Chairman of the MUI Fatwa Commission, told the court that it is a principle of Islam to enquire as to what a person's 'actual intent' is; indeed, a failure to do so is 'contrary to Islamic teachings' (Tim Advokasi BTI BTP 2017: 449–50). Ishomuddin believed that simply watching the video of Ahok's speech did not constitute tabayyun and that any assertion that Ahok's status as a non-Muslim rendered tabayyun unnecessary was 'contrary to the spirit of Islam because Islam is a religion of justice'. Indeed, the fact that Islam is a just religion, Ishomuddin submitted, means that any feelings of hatred toward Ahok should not preclude justice being done and tabayyun is one way of attaining that justice (Tim Advokasi BTI BTP 2017: 450). Ishomuddin also told the court that, from his own research based on thirty[42] exegesis manuscripts (*kitab tafsir*), not one scholar had concluded that the word 'auliya' means 'leader'.[43] Conspicuously, on 21 March 2017, after giving evidence in court, the media reported that Ishomuddin was informed that his position as deputy chairman of the MUI Fatwa Commission had been made redundant. Amin subsequently qualified that Ishomuddin had not been dismissed as deputy chairman of that commission and that he would remain a member of MUI (Prastiwi 2017). In July 2018, Ishomuddin confirmed to me at the time that he remained deputy chair of the Fatwa Commission. He said, however, that Amin had made that announcement in order to appease those who opposed Ishomuddin and the evidence he provided in Ahok's favour.[44]

The defence also noted that MUI's treasurer, Fahmi Darmawansyah, who was tried for corruption in 2016, had been granted the right to tabayyun, with Zainut Tauhid, MUI Central's deputy chairman, having stated that MUI was obliged to conduct tabayyun (Kolid 2016). The defence concluded, therefore, that Ahok was 'a victim of injustice and double standards on the part of MUI' (Tim Advokasi BTI BTP 2017: 457). It followed that the MUI Central religious opinion was contrary to both the Qur'an and MUI's own Organisational Coordination Guidelines (Tim Advokasi BTI BTP 2017: 453).

Amin also acknowledged that, while MUI Jakarta, on 9 October 2016, had issued Ahok with a reprimand (*surat teguran*), MUI Central was compelled to issue its religious opinion, because people had continued to report Ahok to the police after the reprimand had been issued. 'Society's demands', Amin stated, had made the issue 'take on a national dimension' (Tim Advokasi BTI BTP 2017: 130), which compelled MUI Central to issue the religious opinion because the MUI Jakarta reprimand was no longer sufficient to respond to those demands (Tim Advokasi BTI BTP 2017: 128–9 and 135). Of all the apparent complainants, Amin, however, was only able to recall the Anti-Religious Defamation Forum (Forum Anti Penistaan Agama).[45] He could not recall the names of the 'many others' (*masih banyak lagi*) who, he claimed, had made similar demands (Tim Advokasi BTI BTP 2017: 116).

Recalling Amin's statement that MUI's investigation commenced on 1 October 2016, Amin also told the court that MUI Central had been made aware of complaints about Ahok's remarks just one day after he had made them. Amin's statement is at odds, however, with the defence's argument that no one had objected to, let alone knew about, Ahok's remarks until Buni Yani's Facebook post on 6 October 2016. The drafting period, 1 to 11 October, also contradicts Amin's subsequent statement that MUI had only issued its religious opinion in response to overwhelming public demand, given that it began well before Yani's post.[46] It also contradicts an interview Amin gave on 9 October 2016 with media outlet *Liputan 6*, where he stated:

> MUI does not want to comment indiscriminately or issue a fatwa for this case. But publishing an opinion, MUI will do so later after obtaining input and listening directly to the video in its entirety. We are yet to hold a meeting and are yet to hear the video recording in its entirety.[47]

The defence therefore concluded that Amin's submission to the court that MUI Central had commenced the drafting and investigatory process on 1 October 2016 was spurious. Rather, based on Amin's remarks on 9 October 2016, MUI Central had concluded in just two days that Ahok had dishonoured the Qur'an and/or the ulama (Tim Advokasi BTI BTP 2017: 444).

Amin also told the court that MUI had never in its history issued a document entitled 'religious opinion'. He explained, however, that a religious opinion and fatwa have the same effect.[48] Hamka Haq, however, told the court that MUI's own book of administrative guidelines (*Buku Pedoman Penyelenggaran Organisasi*) makes no mention of 'religious opinions' (Tim Advokasi BTI BTP 2017: 470).

Amin argued that MUI Central's decision to issue this religious opinion, as with a fatwa, constituted sufficient grounds for law enforcers to commence a criminal investigation into Ahok's remarks. Indeed, Amin told the court that the police had even told complainants that they needed to first request that MUI issue a fatwa or opinion before the police could commence an investigation into Ahok's remarks (Tim Advokasi BTI BTP 2017: 119–20). Amin stated:

> [T]he religious opinion and stance was directed at law enforcers ... in order that societal discord did not give rise to anarchic conduct, but could be controlled so it could be processed by law enforcers, those being first by the police and so on.[49]

Amin qualified that MUI did not have the authority to ensure that law enforcement officials implemented its fatwas.[50] While fatwas are binding on the umma, Amin clarified, they are not binding on the state.[51] Amin continued:

> Fatwas issued collectively by an authorised and competent institute, the fatwas that have been declared necessary by the state, both through legislation and requests from government ministries or state entities, means that MUI fatwas have two functions: first, they are binding on the umma from a shari'a perspective, and secondly, they are legally (*secara tanjidli*) binding if they later become state provisions.[52]

Amin's logic here differed significantly from his reasoning not to issue a fatwa in the subsequent case of Sukmawati Soekarnoputri, the third daughter of Indonesia's first president, Soekarno, who, on 30 March 2018 read a poem at Indonesian Fashion Week in Jakarta in which she expressed her preference for Indonesian song and dress over the Islamic call to prayer (*adzan*) and *niqab*.[53] Sukmawati's recitation moved people, including Amron Asyhari, chairman of the Hanura party, lawyer Denny Andrian Kusdayat, the East Java branch of Nahdlatul Ulama, the Anti-Defamation of Religion Forum, and the 212 Alumni Brotherhood, to report her to the police for blasphemy. In Sukmawati's case, however, charges were never laid. Amin, rather, stated that to perpetuate the controversy surrounding Sukmawati's comments would only give rise to societal unrest, a seeming admission that MUI fatwas have the opposite effect to what Amin said at trial (Peterson 2018).

Amin's explanation at trial is, however, easily reconciled with the Constitutional Court's 2010 Blasphemy Law review mentioned above. That is because the religious opinion was simply an articulation of the idea that religious orthodoxy must be protected from public criticism and doctrinal disagreement for the sake of maintaining public order. That said, why the court was unconcerned about the contradictions in Amin's evidence and the concerns raised by Haq and Ishomuddin is unclear. Again, nothing in its judgment addressed or engaged with any of the issues discussed above.

The use

The defence's primary objection to the MUI religious opinion was that, notwithstanding the fact that it is not an official source of positive law in Indonesia, both its content and issuance compromised Ahok's right to a fair trial. It did this by influencing public opinion and eliciting a public response, making it appear conclusive that Ahok had insulted both the Qur'an and the ulama (Tim Advokasi BTI BTP 2017: 462 and 466). The defence cited four positive legal sources in support of the fact that an MUI edict is not a source of positive law.

First, it referred to art. 1(3) of the 1945 Constitution, which declares Indonesia to be a *negara hukum*, a term that translates literally into English as a 'law state' but is usually understood in Indonesia to refer to the idea of 'rule of law'. Second, it cited art. 7(1) of Law No. 12 of 2011 on Lawmaking, which sets out the legislative and regulatory hierarchy in Indonesia. According to art. 7(1), that hierarchy is as follows:

a. 1945 Constitution;
b. Stipulations of the People's Consultative Assembly;
c. statutes/government regulation replacement statutes;
d. government regulations;
e. presidential regulations;
f. provincial regulations; and
g. regency/municipal regulations.

The defence also noted that art. 1(2) of Law No. 12 of 2011 defines laws as 'written regulations that cover generally-binding legal norms', enacted by 'authorised state institutions or officials through a procedure stipulated in law' (Tim Advokasi BTI BTP 2017: 430). Crucially, neither art. 7(1) nor art. 1(2) include fatwas, and MUI is not a state institution, but, as mentioned, a quasi-autonomous non-governmental organisation (Lindsey 2012: 132), that is, a non-governmental body that is partially funded by taxpayer money but subject to 'little or no democratic oversight' (Mounk 2018: 102).

Third and fourth, it cited both the elucidation of the KUHAP (third point, letter c), as well as art. 8 of Law No. 4 of 2004 on Judicial Authority, both of which state:

> Every person, suspected, arrested, detained, prosecuted and or brought to trial, shall be considered not guilty until a court decision declares guilt and is legally binding.

The defence's argument was as follows:

> We must understand that, in Indonesia, it can only be established that a person is guilty of having committed a criminal offence after [the issuance of] a legally-binding court decision. Meanwhile, an MUI opinion has already effectively sentenced [Ahok] by declaring that what [Ahok] said insulted the Qur'an and/or the ulama. This has evidently preceded the legally binding court decision, notwithstanding that the judicial process is currently on foot.
>
> (Tim Advokasi BTI BTP 2017: 20)

The religious opinion appeared to be cited in both Ahok's indictment and the court's judgment as if it were an authoritative source. The judgment read:

> [T]he opinion of the court is in line and in accordance with the opinions of the experts submitted by the general prosecutor ... and also in accordance with the Majelis Ulama Indonesia Religious Opinion and Stance No. Kep-981-a /MUI/X/2016, dated 11 October 2016, all of which, in general, declared that the statements of the accused were of the nature of sullying religion.[54]

The defence, perhaps out of a feeling of necessity, contested the validity of the MUI opinion itself. In the opening remarks of its Notice of Defence, the defence submitted:

> At trial it was also apparent that there were religious experts present, who occupied positions such as Deputy Chairman of the MUI Fatwa Commission and the MUI Advisory Council, who stated that they were not involved in the drafting process of the MUI Opinion and who were of the view that Ahok's speech did not sully religion. This also established that MUI itself was still conflicted as to whether or not Ahok had committed blasphemy. As a result, it affirmed [the point] that the MUI Opinion, juridically, formally and materially, must indeed be set aside.
>
> (Tim Advokasi BTI BTP 2017: 21)

The defence also submitted that the MUI opinion itself was 'baseless' (*tidak berdasar*) because it was based on one interpretation of the verse, which, as mentioned for the purposes of establishing blasphemy pursuant to art. 156a, 'did not constitute an absolute truth' (Tim Advokasi BTI BTP 2017: 476). The court again ignored this argument, possibly for the same reasons that I speculated above led it to ignore the defence's objections to the admissibility of the evidence of Rizieq Shihab.

The verdict

Before concluding, I briefly summarise the court's verdict. The court's decision to convict Ahok rested on four findings about:

1. the meaning of 'auliya';
2. the admissibility of the half-minute video excerpt of Ahok's speech;
3. why the court considered Ahok's remarks blasphemous; and
4. Ahok's intent.

As mentioned, nowhere in its judgment did the court acknowledge any of the human rights-based legal arguments submitted by the defence. It ignored crucial submissions based on Ahok's right to freedom of expression, as guaranteed by art. 28E of the 1945 Constitution and Law 9 of 1998 on the Right to Express Opinions in Public, as well as art. 19(2) of the International Covenant on Civil and Political Rights (ICCPR). The court also ignored all but one of the defence's submissions based on the KUHAP, which I note below.

The meaning of Auliya

The court conceded that the term 'auliya' had conflicting meanings:

> There is a difference of meaning or even interpretation of the word auliya which is found in *Surah Al-Ma'ida* 51 – there are those that interpret the word auliya as meaning leader and those that interpret the word auliya as meaning close friend. Differences of opinion such as this in the Islamic community are common. In the Islamic community itself, however, one may not find fault with another, one may not state that one opinion is true and another is false, moreover, that that other opinion is a falsehood. One must continue to respect the opinions of others. It is precisely this difference that is a blessing.[55]

Were criticism of a difference of opinion on religious orthodoxy within the Islamic community actually prohibited, however, as this passage suggests it should be, this would essentially prevent all exegesis and *ijtihad*,[56] thereby rendering Islamic religious scholarship effectively impermissible. Furthermore, notwithstanding the fact that Ahok is Christian, the very conduct the court found to be prohibited within the Islamic community, namely finding fault with another's religious interpretation, is the same thing MUI does whenever it issues an edict on a point of Islamic law such as, for example, the lawfulness of Ahok's statement referencing *Surah Al-Ma'ida* 51or the practices and beliefs of the Ahmadiyya. Ironically, the court itself cited the MUI religious opinion, thereby endorsing one opinion held in the Islamic community to the exclusion of all others.

Video evidence

The issue here was whether or not the edited video was admissible as evidence for the purposes of meeting the 'in public' requirement in art. 156a of the KUHP. The court found that Ahok's remarks had indeed been delivered in public because people, including witnesses, had learned about them through social media, news broadcasts, from their mosques, and/or from friends. They then obtained clarification of those remarks by searching for the video on YouTube, before discerning that the video had been uploaded by the Jakarta provincial government. When they subsequently filed complaints with the police, they were also able to submit the video as supporting evidence, the authenticity of which had been verified by the central forensic laboratory at Indonesian police headquarters.[57]

The court's finding, however, appears to contradict art. 1(26) of the KUHAP, which requires a witness to have heard, seen or experienced something themselves. However, in a discussion of this issue with Dian Rositawati from the Indonesian Institute for an Independent Judiciary (Lembaga Kajian dan Advokasi Independensi Peradilan), she argued that judges in blasphemy cases often interpret the 'in public' requirement as being satisfied if something has become public knowledge.[58]

Ahok's blasphemous remarks

Recalling Buni Yani's omission of the word 'use' (*pakai*), the court ultimately found it immaterial whether or not Ahok had said that *Surah Al-Ma'ida* 51 had been 'used to mislead' or that it was 'misleading of itself'. Rather, 'it was sufficient that Ahok had used the verse in connection with the concept of deception, which had a negative connotation' (Butt 2017). The court therefore found that Ahok's comments had 'degraded' (*merendahkan*), 'abused' (*melecehkan*), and 'insulted' (*menghina*) the Qur'an.[59]

The court also distinguished its findings from the opinions of the prosecution and defence, both of which concurred prior to the court's final deliberation that it was Buni Yani's decision to upload the half-minute video excerpt that resulted in societal unrest (*keresahan di masyarakat*). The court found that none of the witnesses produced by the prosecution believed that Buni Yani's decision to upload the video was blasphemous, nor that Yani's omission of the word 'use' (*pakai*) was blasphemous. Rather, it was Ahok's comments that had created unrest in the community, as alleged in the prosecution's indictment.[60]

The court also rejected the defence's submission that Ahok's indictment was political and motivated by the 2017 Jakarta gubernatorial election. While the court conceded that some parties may endeavour to exploit the case for political purposes, it found 'the case to be purely a case of blasphemy' (*kasus ini adalah murni kasus penodaan agama*).[61] It reasoned that many of the witnesses were not involved in politics and did not even live in Jakarta. The fact that certain reporting witnesses were from outside Jakarta does not, of course, mean that the case was not politically-charged. It simply means that these witnesses were not Jakarta residents. Indeed, the fact that non-Jakarta residents attended the demonstrations arguably suggests that the Aksi Bela Islam demonstrations, particularly those held on 4 November 2016 and 2 December 2016, were, in fact, orchestrated to create a sense of moral panic. As Charles Honoris, Treasurer of Ahok's Campaign Team, told me, 'This was purely a highly political case'.[62] Honoris also told me that the degree of mobilisation required to assemble as many as 500,000 people at once was 'unfeasible' without 'everything having been coordinated and with a not insignificant budget'.[63] The court's reasoning and finding that Ahok's prosecution was purely about blasphemy appears to be at odds with the political reality at the time.

Intent

As evidence of Ahok's intent to blaspheme, the court cited the following:

1. Ahok's remarks made on 27 September 2016 at Pramuka Island;
2. the section of Ahok's 2008 autobiography in which he mentions *Surah Al-Ma'ida* 51 by saying, 'From elites who take shelter behind an Islamic holy verse, they use *Surah Al-Ma'ida* 51';
3. Ahok's experience campaigning for the governorship of Bangka Belitung in 2007, when he found flyers citing *Surah Al-Ma'ida* 51 as Qur'anic justification for advocating a prohibition on non-Muslim leadership;
4. while conducting a briefing at the Jakarta Town Hall in 2015, Ahok, recalling a demonstration in opposition to his governorship because of his Christian faith, joked that he would tease those demonstrators by installing wifi in a mosque, then under construction, with the username 'Al Maidah 51' and the password '*kafir*' (person who does not believe in Islam); and
5. Ahok had already registered for the Jakarta governorship for the period 2017 to 2022 and had talked about the upcoming election.[64]

With regard to Ahok's intent, the court found that Ahok's remarks met the definition of intention to insult, as prescribed in the elucidation of art. 4(a) of the Blasphemy Law. That definition states:

> Criminal conduct intended here is that which, in principle, heads toward the intent to antagonise or insult.
>
> Therefore, written and oral descriptions conducted objectively, pragmatically and naturally, regarding a religion, which are accompanied by efforts to avoid the presence of words or an arrangement of words of a nature of enmity or insult, are not criminal conduct according to this article.

The court reasoned that in order to ascertain whether or not Ahok had intended to insult *Surah Al-Ma'ida* 51 or not, it needed to view and assess the overall conditions at the time Ahok delivered those remarks. Considering that Ahok, as governor of Jakarta, was a public official, the court found that he was well aware that issues relating to religion are sensitive and can give rise to inter-religious conflict. Ahok, therefore, should have avoided using words or sentences that 'degraded', 'abused' or 'insulted' a religion, as prescribed in the elucidation of art. 4(a) of the Blasphemy Law.[65] The court specifically objected to Ahok's use of the words 'misled, lied to' (*dibohongi*) and 'fooled' (*dibodohi*), both of which it found had negative connotations and 'displayed [Ahok's] deliberate intent to 'degrade or despise or insult the holiness of *Surah Al-Ma'ida* 51 as a section of Islamic holy scripture'.[66]

Notwithstanding the fact that the court was prepared to consider separate instances where it believed Ahok had displayed antagonism towards Islam and *Surah Al-Ma'ida* 51, nowhere in its ruling does it acknowledge any of the separate examples of initiatives undertaken by Ahok as governor to advance the umma, as submitted by the defence to refute the allegation that Ahok had intended to blaspheme. Indeed, as Djemat told me, Ahok was shocked and deeply saddened to learn that he had been accused of blaspheming Islam.[67]

Conclusion

My account of Ahok's trial shows that the liberal democratic human rights contained in Chapter XA of Indonesia's 1945 Constitution have, at least in this case, been rendered ineffective by the Constitutional Court's 2010 decision to uphold the Blasphemy Law. It also reveals how moral panic can be engineered under the banner of Indonesia's majority religion, and how Indonesian law enforcement authorities and the judiciary perceive such a moral panic as a threat to public order, and as something that they must consider while making decisions to charge, indict, and convict. Ahok's case also reinforces the de facto authority of MUI and its religious edicts in essentially predetermining the outcome of blasphemy cases. Indeed, that a public official could be found guilty of insulting the Qur'an in such circumstances reveals the extent to which both MUI's institutionalisation and the general politicisation of Islam have compromised Indonesian democracy.

Ahok's case does not, however, provide a comprehensive and conclusive understanding of the status of constitutional human rights guarantees in contemporary Indonesia because these issues remain the site of contestation. What Ahok's case does show is that the liberal democratic aspirations of 1999 and 2000 have been, at the very least, compromised by growing Muslim majoritarian sentiment that can be manipulated for political purposes. Indeed, rather than framing human rights as a liberal democratic discourse, as it is generally seen in the Western world, both the North Jakarta State Court in Ahok's case, and the Constitutional Court in its 2010 decision to uphold the Blasphemy Law, viewed human rights through a Muslim majoritarian frame, namely one that prioritises the religious sensibilities of the Sunni Muslim majority over the fundamental rights of Indonesia's religious minority groups.

Notes

1 Constitutional Court Decision No. 140 of 2009 [3.34.7].
2 Ibid. [3.58].
3 *[J]adi jangan percaya sama orang, kan bisa aja dalam hati kecil bapak ibu ga bisa pilih saya, ya kan dibohongi pakai surat Al Maidah 51 macem-macem itu, itu hak bapak ibu ya jadi kalo bapak ibu perasaan gak bisa kepilih nih karena saya takut masuk neraka dibodohin gitu ya ngga papa, karena ini kan panggilan pribadi bapak ibu …*
4 FPI seeks 'to carry out the Qur'anic edict of *amar ma'ruf nahi mungkar* – commanding good and preventing evil'. FPI does not challenge the existence of the Indonesian state but does promote adherence to the shari'a. It comprises two divisions: the *Jamaah* (congregation, group) division, which seeks to enjoin good, and Laskar Pembela Islam (FPI's militia), which seeks to prevent evil. FPI has become notorious for its often-violent vigilante activities. See Wilson 2008 and Pausacker, Chapter 17, this volume.
5 Tim Advokasi Bhinneka Tunggal Ika Basuki Tjahaja Purnama.
6 For a detailed account of the *Aksi Bela Islam* demonstrations, particularly the 2 December 2016 demonstration, see Fealy 2016.
7 North Jakarta State Court Decision No. 1537/Pid.B/2016/PN.Jkt Utr., 611–12. While it made no reference to the relevant provision in its judgment, art. 144(2) of Law No. 8 of 1981 on Criminal Procedure (KUHAP) states: 'Amendments to an indictment can only be made once, at the latest seven days before trial commences'.
8 North Jakarta State Court Decision No. 1537/Pid.B/2016/PN.Jkt Utr., 605–06. Those witnesses were: Hamdan Rasyid, H. Muhammad Amin Suma, KH. Miftakhul Akhyar, Yunahar Ilyas, Habib Muhammad Rizieq Syihab, H. Mahyuni, Mudzakkir, and H. Abdul Chair Ramadhan.
9 For comprehensive coverage of blasphemy cases in Indonesia (and around the world), see Human Rights First 2012.
10 Net.Z 2016. The parentheses included in this quote were used by Buni Yani in his Facebook post.
11 North Jakarta State Court Decision No. 1537/Pid.B/2016/PN.Jkt Utr., 611.
12 Article 184(1) defines 'lawful evidence' (*alat bukti yang sah*) as: witness information; expert information; documents; instructions; information from the accused. Article 185(6) states that in evaluating the truth of a witness' information, the judge must properly pay attention to: the ability to reconcile (*persesuaian*) the information of one witness with another; and the ability to reconcile the information of a witness with other evidence.
13 The nine basic household needs have been defined as: rice, sugar, cooking oil (or margarine), beef/chicken, eggs, milk, kerosene and salt.
14 The umrah is 'the lesser pilgrimage to Mecca at a time other than during the *hajj*' (Lindsey 2012: 508).
15 The United Development Party is an Islamic political party that was formed in 1973 as a result of Soeharto's decision to amalgamate the country's then Muslim parties – Nahdlatul Ulama, the Association of Islamic Education (Persatuan Tarbiyah Islamiyah), the Indonesian Muslims Party (Persaudaraan Muslimin

Indonesia), and the Indonesian Islamic Union Party (Partai Sarekat Islam Indonesia) – to form a single political party. See Porter 2002: 43–4.

16 LBH Jakarta, according to its website (www.bantuanhukum.or.id/web/) is a non-governmental organisation that provides impartial legal services, free of charge, to Indonesia's poor and victims of injustice.

17 For a discussion of this case see Lindsey and Butt 2016.

18 Interview with Humphrey Djemat, 20 July 2018, Jakarta.

19 Indonesia acceded to the ICCPR on 23 February 2006. While Indonesian law is unclear on the status of international law, it does appear that Indonesia is a 'dualist' state in practice, that is, it only recognises international law to the extent that international law has been transformed into domestic legislation and regulations. See Butt 2014.

20 These witnesses' names were: Nurkholis Majid; Jaenudin alias Panel bin Adim; Sahbudin alias Deni; Yuli Hardi; and Bambang Waluyo Wahab.

21 Those witnesses were: Dr H. Muhammad Hamdan Rasyid (MUI Central Fatwa Commission); Prof. Dr Muhammad Amin Suma (MUI Central Fatwa Commission); Prof. Dr Yunahar Ilyas (MUI Central Deputy Chairman, 2015–20); and H. Abdul Chair Ramadhan (MUI Law and Legislation Commission). See Tim Advokasi Bhinneka Tunggal Ika BTP 2017: 80–104 and 466–9.

22 Shihab completed his undergraduate studies in *Usul al-Fiqh* and education at King Saud University and his MA in shari'a at the International Islamic University Malaysia. He is currently completing his PhD at Universiti Sains Islam Malaysia, although Ma'ruf Amin told the court at trial that Rizieq had already completed his PhD, referring to him as 'Doktor'. See North Jakarta State Court Decision No. 1537/Pid.B/2016/PN.Jkt Utr., 133.

23 North Jakarta State Court Decision No. 1537/Pid.B/2016/PN.Jkt Utr., 133.

24 Referred to as the 'Monas Incident' (*Insiden Monas*) on 1 June 2008, the birthday of Indonesia's state ideology (the *Pancasila*), members of the AKKBB (Aliansi Kebangsaan untuk Kebebasan Beragama dan Berkeyakinan, National Alliance for the Freedom of Religion and Beliefs), while conducting a peaceful march from Gambir Station to the Hotel Indonesia roundabout, were violently attacked by members of FPI at the National Monument (*Monumen Nasional* – Monas) in Jakarta. While AKKBB claimed it marched in the name of religious freedom, seeking to put an end to violence within religion, FPI, led by former human rights lawyer turned 'born again' Muslim and *Hizbut Tahrir* member, Munarman, had heard that members of AKKBB were marching in support of the maligned, unorthodox Islamic sect Ahmadiyya. This, according to members of FPI and certain other Islamic groups assembled nearby to protest the increase in fuel prices, provided them sufficient reason to attack the AKKBB protestors.

25 The *Pancasila* (Sanskrit: five principles) is the five principles that constitute Indonesia's state ideology: Belief in Almighty God; a Just and Civilised Humanity; the Unity of Indonesia; Democracy led by the wisdom of the representatives of the people; and Social justice for all Indonesians.

26 While giving this lecture, Shihab rhetorically asked: 'If God had a child, then who was the midwife?' (*Kalau Tuhan beranak, terus bidannya siapa?*).

27 In January 2017, Shihab and a female student of his, Firza Husein, were investigated for sending each other WhatsApp messages containing pornographic content, contrary to Indonesia's anti-pornography statute, Law No. 44 of 2008. See also Pausacker, Chapter 17, this volume.

28 North Jakarta State Court Decision No. 1537/Pid.B/2016/PN.Jkt Utr., 605.
29 Interview with Humphrey Djemat, 20 July 2018, Jakarta.
30 North Jakarta State Court Decision No. 1537/Pid.B/2016/PN.Jkt Utr., 118.
31 North Jakarta State Court Decision No. 1537/Pid.B/2016/PN.Jkt Utr., 137.
32 North Jakarta State Court Decision No. 1537/Pid.B/2016/PN.Jkt Utr., 136.
33 Interview with Humphrey Djemat, 20 July 2018, Jakarta.
34 North Jakarta State Court Decision No. 1537/Pid.B/2016/PN.Jkt Utr., 331.
35 Amin conceded that MUI's Religious Communities Harmony Commission (*Komisi Kerukunan Umat Beragama*) was not included in the process (Tim Advokasi BTI BTP 2017: 436), although neither the judgment nor the Notice of Defence explain what its role in the drafting process might have been.
36 North Jakarta State Court Decision No. 1537/Pid.B/2016/PN.Jkt Utr., 137.
37 North Jakarta State Court Decision No. 1537/Pid.B/2016/PN.Jkt Utr., 121.
38 North Jakarta State Court Decision No. 1537/Pid.B/2016/PN.Jkt Utr., 122.
39 North Jakarta State Court Decision No. 1537/Pid.B/2016/PN.Jkt Utr., 127.
40 North Jakarta State Court Decision No. 1537/Pid.B/2016/PN.Jkt Utr., 131.
41 Chapter 8 of the Qur'an (Battle Gains).
42 In fact, KH. Ahmad Ishomuddin, Ishomuddin told me that he had read 32 (not 30) separate exegesis manuscripts, none of which concluded that 'auliya' meant 'leader'.
43 North Jakarta State Court Decision No. 1537/Pid.B/2016/PN.Jkt Utr., 407.
44 Interview, KH. Ahmad Ishomuddin, Jakarta, 24 July 2018.
45 This is a group comprising: the North Sumatra Muhammadiyah University Alumni Family Alliance (Ikatan Keluarga Alumni Universitas Muhammadiyah Sumatera Utara) of the greater Jakarta-Bogor-Depok-Tanggerang-Bekasi area; the National Muhammadiyah University Alumni Family (Keluarga Alumni Universitas Muhammadiyah seNusantara); the Jakarta Muhammadiyah University Alumni Alliance (Ikatan Alumni Universitas Muhammadiyah Jakarta) (Nailufar 2016); and the Indonesian Muslim Consumers Advocacy Institute (Lembaga Advokasi Konsumen Muslim Indonesia).
46 North Jakarta State Court Decision No. 1537/Pid.B/2016/PN.Jkt Utr., 199.
47 See Rimadi 2016; Tim Advokasi Bhinneka Tunggal Ika BTP 2017: 441.
48 North Jakarta State Court Decision No. 1537/Pid.B/2016/PN.Jkt Utr., 117.
49 North Jakarta State Court Decision No. 1537/Pid.B/2016/PN.Jkt Utr., 118.
50 North Jakarta State Court Decision No. 1537/Pid.B/2016/PN.Jkt Utr., 142.
51 North Jakarta State Court Decision No. 1537/Pid.B/2016/PN.Jkt Utr., 135.
52 North Jakarta State Court Decision No. 1537/Pid.B/2016/PN.Jkt Utr., 135.
53 The niqab is a form of clothing worn by some Muslim women, which covers the face.
54 North Jakarta State Court Decision No. 1537/Pid.B/2016/PN.Jkt Utr., 605–6.
55 North Jakarta State Court Decision No. 1537/Pid.B/2016/PN.Jkt Utr., 603–4.
56 'Ijtihad' is 'literally striving, intellectual exertion by a qualified scholar of Islamic law; the process of making a legal decision by independent interpretation of Islamic legal sources; legal reasoning and interpretation of shari'a' (Lindsey 2012: 499).
57 North Jakarta State Court Decision No. 1537/Pid.B/2016/PN.Jkt Utr., 600.
58 Interview, Dian Rositawati, 26 July 2018, Jakarta.
59 North Jakarta State Court Decision No. 1537/Pid.B/2016/PN.Jkt Utr., 604.
60 North Jakarta State Court Decision No. 1537/Pid.B/2016/PN.Jkt Utr., 611.

61 North Jakarta State Court Decision No. 1537/Pid.B/2016/PN.Jkt Utr., 612.
62 Interview, Charles Honoris, 20 July 2018, Jakarta.
63 Interview, Charles Honoris, 20 July 2018, Jakarta.
64 North Jakarta State Court Decision No. 1537/Pid.B/2016/PN.Jkt Utr., 607–8.
65 North Jakarta State Court Decision No. 1537/Pid.B/2016/PN.Jkt Utr., 609.
66 North Jakarta State Court Decision No. 1537/Pid.B/2016/PN.Jkt Utr., 610.
67 Interview with Humphrey Djemat, 20 July 2018, Jakarta.

References

Amnesty International 2016. 'Indonesia: Drop Blasphemy Case against Jakarta Governor', 16 November www.amnesty.org

Butt, Simon 2014 'The Position of International Law Within the Indonesian Legal System', *Emory International Law Review*: 28(1) law.emory.edu

Butt, Simon 2017. 'Why is Ahok in Prison? A Legal Analysis of the Decision', *Indonesia at Melbourne*, 6 June indonesiaatmelbourne.unimelb.edu.au

Cochrane, Joe 2016. 'Jakarta Protest, Tied to Faith, May Have Deeper Links to Secular Politics', *The New York Times*, 13 November

Faqih, Fikri 2016. 'Ahok Ceritakan Asal Muasal Jadi Anak Angkat Keluarga Muslim', *Merdeka*, 14 December www.merdeka.com

Fauzi, Ihsan Ali 2016. 'Mobocracy? Counting the Cost of the Rallies to "Defend Islam"', *Indonesia at Melbourne*, 9 December indonesiaatmelbourne.unimelb.edu.au

Fealy, Greg 2016. 'Bigger than Ahok: Explaining the 2 December Mass Rally', *Indonesia at Melbourne*, 7 December indonesiaatmelbourne.unimelb.edu.au

Han, Mister 2017. 'Abdul Rosyad, Hakim Yang Vonis Ahok Bersalah Ternyata Pemuja Hati', *Berita 168*, 9 May www.berita168.com/abdul-rosyad-hakim-yang-vonis-ahok-bersalah-ternyata-pemuja-hti/

Human Rights First 2012. 'Blasphemy Law Exposed: The Consequences of Criminalizing "Defamation of Religions"', 29 February (updated March 2012) www.humanrightsfirst.org

Kolid, Idham 2016. 'Bendahara Jadi Tersangka KPK, MUI: Kami Klarifikasi ke Fahmi Darmawansyah', *Detik News*, 23 December news.detik.com

Lindsey, Tim 2002. 'Indonesian Constitutional Reform: Muddling Towards Democracy', *Singapore Journal of International & Comparative Law* 6(1): 244–301

Lindsey, Tim 2012. *Islam, Law and the State in Southeast Asia. Volume I: Indonesia*. London and New York: I.B. Tauris

Lindsey, Tim 2016. 'Blasphemy Charge Reveals Real Fault Lines in Indonesia Democracy', *The Australian*, 24 November

Lindsey, Tim and Butt, Simon 2016. 'State Power to Restrict Religious Freedom: An Overview of the Legal Framework', in Tim Lindsey and Helen Pausacker (eds.), *Religion, Law and Intolerance in Indonesia*. New York: Routledge, pp. 19–41

Mardiastuti, Aditya 2017. 'Jadi Ahli di Sidang Ahok, Hamka Haq Bicara Sikap Keagamaan MUI', *Detik News*, 29 March https://news.detik.com

Mounk, Yascha 2018. 'The Undemocratic Dilemma', *Journal of Democracy* 29(2): 98–111

Nailufar, Nibras Nada 2016. 'Ahok Dilaporkan Dua Organisasi ke Polda Metro Jaya', *Kompas* 7 October https://megapolitan.kompas.com

Net.Z 2016. 'Ini Kata Polisi Soal Perkara Ahok dan Buni Yani', 6 November netz.id/news

Peterson, Daniel 2018. 'Sukmawati's Saving Grace', *New Mandala*, 12 April www.newmandala.org

Porter, Donald J. 2002. *Managing Politics and Islam in Indonesia*. Abingdon: RoutledgeCurzon

Prastiwi, Devira 2017. 'Ketua MUI: Ishomuddin Tidak Dipecat, Tapi...', *Liputan 6*, 27 March http://news.liputan6.com

Purnama, Basuki Tjahaja 2008. *Merubah Indonesia: The Story of Basuki Tjahaja Purnama*. Jakarta: Center for Democracy and Transparency

Putra, Putu Merta Surya 2016. 'Ini Isi Kontrak Politik Ahok-Djarot dengan PPP Djan Faridz', *Liputan 6*, 21 October pilkada.liputan6.com

Rimadi, Luqman 2016. 'MUI: Warga Jangan Mudah Terprovokasi Isu SARA Pilkada DKI', *Liputan 6*, 9 October pilkada.liputan6.com

Romadoni, Ahmad 2016. 'Kapolri: Bukan Membela, Ahok Tidak Bermaksud Menistakan Agama', *Liputan 6*, 5 November news.liputan6.com

Salim, Arskal 2008. *Challenging the Secular State: The Islamization of Law in Modern Indonesia*. Honolulu: University of Hawai'i Press

Tempo 2016. 'Al-Maidah 51, Kemenag: Awliya Diterjemahkan Sesuai Konteks', 23 October nasional.tempo.co

Wilson, Ian Douglas 2008. 'As Long as It's *Halal*': Islamic Preman in Jakarta', in Greg Fealy and Sally White (eds.), *Expressing Islam: Religious Life and Politics in Indonesia*. Singapore: Institute of Southeast Asian Studies

Legislation

1945 Constitution

Criminal Code (*Kitab Undang-Undang Hukum Pidana*, KUHP: Law No. 1 of 1946 as amended by Law No. 27 of 1999 on the Indonesian Criminal Code)

Criminal Procedure Code Law (*Kitab Undang-undang Hukum Acara Pidana*, KUHAP), Law No. 8 of 1981

Law No. 1 of 1965 on Prevention of the Abuse/Sullying of Religion

Law No. 8 of 1981 on Criminal Procedure

Law No. 39 of 1999 on Human Rights

Law No. 4 of 2004 on Judicial Authority

Law No. 11 of 2008 on Electronic Information and Transactions

Law No. 44 of 2008 on Pornography

Law No. 12 of 2011 on Lawmaking

Presidential Regulation No. 151 of 2014

Cases

Constitutional Court Decision No. 140/PUU-VII/2009

North Jakarta State Court Decision No. 1537/Pid.B/2016/PN.Jkt Utr.

Court documents

North Jakarta Attorney-General 2016a, *Indictment No. Reg. Perkara: PDM – 147/ JKT. UT/12/2016*, 1 December

North Jakarta Attorney-General 2016b. *Opinion of the General Prosecutor on the Objection of the Accused and Legal Counsel to the Indictment in Criminal Case No. 1537/Pid.B/2016/PN.JKT.UTR Accused Ir. Basuki Tjahaja Purnama alias Ahok*, 20 December

Tim Advokasi Bhinneka Tunggal Ika BTP 2016. *Notice of Objection to General Prosecutor's Statement of Alleged Facts in Criminal Case No. 1537/Pid.B/2016/PN.JKT.UTR at North Jakarta State Court*, 13 December

Tim Advokasi Bhinneka Tunggal Ika BTP 2017. *Notice of Defence – Legal Counsel Team for Ir. Basuki Tjahaja Purnama, M. M. In Criminal Case No. 1537/Pid.B/2016/PN.JKT.UTR – "Terkoyaknya Kebhinnekaan"*, 25 April

Interviews

Interview, Charles Honoris, 20 July 2018, Jakarta
Interview, Humphrey Djemat, 20 July 2018, Jakarta
Interview, K. H. Ahmad Ishomuddin, 24 July 2018, Jakarta
Interview, Dian Rositawati, 26 July 2018, Jakarta

16 Homosexuality and the law in Indonesia

Helen Pausacker

The situation for Indonesian lesbian, gay, bisexual and transgender (LGBT)[1] people has become increasingly perilous over the last few years. Homosexuality has never been illegal at the national level in Indonesia. However, with the granting of special autonomy in Aceh, homosexual acts have now been criminalised in Aceh and discriminatory laws have been passed in a number of other regions. Indonesian LGBT people now also face the possibility of imprisonment under different national laws, such as the 2008 Pornography Law, and discussions are underway about whether homosexuality should be included as a crime in the Criminal Code (*Kitab Undang-undang Hukum Pidana* or KUHP).

The current wave of hostility to LGBT people can be traced to 2016, when officials began to make strong homophobic remarks, which were used as a justification for Islamist gangs to attack LGBT groups and individuals, sometimes causing serious injury, without fear of prosecution from the authorities. Increasingly, too, police, together with groups of locals, have raided private residences and evicted the occupants, following tip-offs by neighbours. This chapter offers an historical account of legal attitudes to the LGBT community, focusing on the rise of homophobia and the increase in legal action against the LGBT community in the *Reformasi* ('Reformation') period, which began after Soeharto's New Order collapsed in 1998.

Historical attitudes to homosexuality in the Indonesian archipelago

A large number of societies in the Indonesian archipelago have traditionally had forms of indigenous 'ritualised cross-dressing', which provided the opportunity for different, not biologically-defined, gender roles and often also included sexual relationships between people who are genetically the same sex. For example, the Buginese in South Sulawesi have a classification of five genders: *oroane* ('male-acting' biological men), *makunrai* ('female-acting' biological women), *calalai* ('male-acting' biological women), *calabai* ('female-acting' biological men), and *bissu* (half-man/half-woman – although not necessarily biologically intersex – priests) (Graham 2001; 2002).[2] The *warok* (man of prowess) and his *gemblak* or *janthil* (kept boy, who dressed as a woman) are also a phenomenon in Ponorogo in East Java (Boomgaard

2012: 146–7). Such traditions continue to the present day, albeit less prevalent than in the past.

Javanese performing arts have often featured cross-dressing. To avoid the prohibition on male-female contact between dance partners, who were not married, the women in a number of Javanese dances (at least before 1914), including the *bedaya* and *wayang wong* (the dance adaptation of *wayang* kulit, the shadow puppet performance), were played by men in Yogyakarta. Although the roles in Yogyakarta were played by men, in the Mangkunegaran Court of the late nineteenth century in nearby Surakarta, women played both male and female roles. Carey and Houben (1987: 19) comment that

> [t]his interchangeability of sex roles and costumes was likewise reflected in the homosexual culture of the Yogyakarta court, a culture summed up in the pithy epigram […] in the 1930s, that, whereas the Pangérans [rulers] of Surakarta liked 'wine and women', those of Yogya preferred 'opium and boys'.
>
> (Carey and Houben 1987: 19)

Carey and Houben also mention a reference in the early-nineteenth-century text, the *Serat Tjentini* where two *talèdhèk* (male singer-dancers, dressed in female clothing) end up in bed with their male host; and a scandal in Surakarta during the reign of Pakubuwana V (reigned 1820–3), when one of the ruler's unofficial wives 'acted the male role in a series of lesbian relationships amongst the frustrated royal concubines' (Carey and Houben 1987: 20).

In *ludruk* drama, based in Surabaya (East Java), women characters are portrayed by men. Of this, Peacock (1987: 207) commented:

> Ludruk transvestites have traditionally shown more than professional interest in playing feminine roles. Almost all are markedly effeminate offstage. They wear women's clothes at home, sometimes in public. […] Some become the 'wives' of men […].

Peacock (1987: 206) commented that by the 1960s (in Soekarno's Old Order), there was an attempt to 'modernise' the art-form. Ludruk transvestites were encouraged to wear women's clothes only on stage and homosexual relationships were discouraged. Peacock (1987: 204) also comments:

> […] the Javanese case is complicated: 'Pure' Javanese tradition does not condemn homosexuality and regards a very wide range of behavior, from he-man to rather (in our terms) 'effeminate', as properly masculine. Therefore, Javanese who condemn the transvestite are probably doing so from the standpoint of Javanese morality influenced by Islam, but the transvestite legitimizes himself in terms of 'pure' (non-Islamized) Javanese ideals of alusness (refinement).

This discouragement of homosexuality in ludruk has continued to the present day. In Java, in *pesantren* (Islamic boarding schools), homoerotic relationships between pupils have been 'tolerated and condoned' (Boomgaard 2012: 148). Such relationships usually involve an older with a younger, prettier boy (*mairil*) and tend to be seen as a situational, temporary relationships before a heterosexual marriage and child-rearing (Izharuddin 2013: 543).

In late-nineteenth-century Hindu Bali, there tended to be a tolerant attitute to male–male relationships between adult men and youths (*menyelit*) and same-sex activities between women. Boys of 10–12 years old are reported to have cross-dressed as female dancers, and then had sex after the performance with the highest (male) bidder (Boomgaard 2012: 149).

Boomgaard (2012: 146–8) comments that attitudes to homosexual activity, however, vary throughout the archipelago and it was forbidden in some places. He mentions an Old Javanese text, *Caturyuga*, based on a pre-1500 Indian text, which mentions male-male sex as a 'sin' and an early-sixteenth-century text, *Agama* (religion), which instructs rulers to execute (married) homosexuals, along with thieves and tyrants.

The Muslim Javanese leader, Pakubuwana II (reigned 1726–49), appears to have gone through a particularly pious phase in the late 1730s. In addition to executing the son of a *pengulu* (religious official) and a royal concubine for having a (heterosexual) affair, in 1739 he banished his younger brother, Pangeran Blitar, for his homosexual behaviour. Pangeran Blitar was imprisoned in a stockade in the Pajimatan mosque at the foot of the Imagiri graveyard, with only women in attendance. On release after eight months, Blitar 'reoffended' and was again banished to Imagiri. His lover was executed, with his head impaled on a stake in the market place as a warning to others (Ricklefs 1997: 242–3).[3] In the general indigenous population, however, the most common sexual transgression which attracted the death penalty (usually drowning) was incest and, sometimes, adultery (Boomgaard 2012: 142, 154).

In Aceh, in the early eighteenth century, an Indian Muslim was tried in the local harbour master's court for 'attempting Soddomy on a Mallayan boy [sic]'.[4] Boomgaard comments that these attitudes to homosexual activity were the 'official orthodoxy' and adds:

> [...] how the indigenous population perceived same-sex activities of shamans, actors and dancers does not necessarily reflect how society dealt with 'homosexual' behaviour in general. Actors, dancers and shamans were, each in their own way, outsiders, even if, or perhaps rather because, they were regarded as spiritually powerful. Nevertheless, it is unthinkable that homoerotic behaviour of comparable people in Europe would have been condoned or even tolerated.
>
> (Boomgaard 2012: 147)

The Dutch response

As Boomgaard's remark suggests, in the nineteenth and first part of the twentieth centuries, homophobia was stronger in the West than in Indonesia.

Indeed, homophobia may well have been introduced to Indonesia by the negative attitudes of the Dutch colonisers and missionaries in the colonial period and through media in subsequent years.

The generally more tolerant indigenous attitudes to homosexuality sometimes led to misunderstandings between the Dutch colonisers and local rulers. In 1667, Sultan Alauddin, ruler of Bacan (North Moluccas) sent a male prostitute as a gift to the Governor General of the VOC in Batavia, presumably considering this a suitable gift (Boomgaard 2012: 147). Nagtegaal (1983/84) details a number of other misunderstandings between Dutch and Javanese, including Dutch confusion upon finding themselves confronted with transvestites, and a Javanese ruler, who was reported to be a 'hermaphrodite' and interested in men. The Javanese, on the other hand, found behaviour like men kissing other men's wives, or holding a member of the opposite sex in a ballroom dancing pose, to be repulsive.

Nevertheless, unlike many Western countries or, indeed, other Asian countries that inherited their legal systems from the English, homosexuality was not illegal in the Netherlands in 1915, when the Criminal Code was passed in the Dutch East Indies (entered into force on 1 January 1918). Nor was this altered, as the law changed in the Netherlands, to make it illegal. Indonesia left the Dutch Criminal Code in place upon independence. Given that the status of homosexuality varied over time in the Netherlands, it is a quirk of history that the Criminal Code was adopted at a point when homosexuality was not illegal, although it had been at other points in Dutch history, with pogroms and executions occurring at particular times.[5]

Such persecution of homosexuals also took place in the Dutch East Indies, where there had also been executions of sodomites by the VOC (Vereenigde Oost-Indische Compagnie, Dutch East Indies Company), under which homosexuality was a criminal offence.[6] One of these was Joost Schouten, a leading figure in the VOC, who had emigrated to the Dutch East Indies in 1622. In 1644 Schouten was accused, tried and convicted of sodomy. He was strangled and his body then burned at the stake. Three of his (younger) partners were tied in sacks and drowned. Boomgaard (2012: 152) comments that prior to 1652, it was common for the older partner to be burned (either alive or strangled prior to the burning) and the younger partners to be drowned. The authorities also sentenced non-European sodomites to death. Boomgaard found fewer sodomy trials, and fewer death sentences for the eighteenth century than the seventeenth century – possibly because of the death penalty had, in general, become rarer (Boomgaard 2012: 152).

In Holland in 1795, after the founding of the Batavian Republic, there was another spike in prosecutions for sodomy, including women who had sex with women, but the sanctions were less severe. In 1810, Napoleon Bonaparte incorporated the region into the French Empire and in 1811 Holland adopted the French legal code. Laws against sodomy had been removed from the French legal code in 1791, so homosexuality became legal. In 1911, Christian-based political parties in Holland added a new clause to the Dutch criminal code (article 248 bis) which raised the age of consent for homosexuals to twenty-one, while retaining the age of consent for heterosexuals at sixteen.[7] The Criminal Code of the Dutch East Indies (*Wetboek van Strafrecht voor Nederlandsch-Indie*) was based on the 1915 Dutch penal code (Tilemann 2016), so the age of consent initially adopted would appear to have been twenty-one for homosexuals and sixteen for heterosexuals. The current age of consent in Indonesia is sixteen for women, nineteen for men in heterosexual relations and eighteen for same sex relationships.[8]

Despite homosexuality in general not being illegal in the Dutch East Indies, there was a major crackdown between 1938 and 1939 on homosexuals suspected of having sex with minors (Boellstorff 2005: 52–4; Mader and Hekma 2016: 170). Bloemenbergen (2011: 121–2) comments that although the stated target was men having sex with minors, it was clear from police investigation methods that homosexuals in general were targetted. There were large numbers of men arrested in Bali and Surabaya. In Batavia (Jakarta), street youths were arrested by police and presented a police lineup of European men; if they indicated they had had sex with any of them, the men were arrested. The 'native' youths were usually assumed not to be homosexual – those above the minority age were imprisoned for prostitution, while those below the minority age were sent to juvenile re-education facilities (Boellstorff 2005: 52–4; Bloemenbergen 2011: 138). At least 223 men were detained (often for months) and most were tried and 171 received prison sentences for periods of two months to two years, under art. 292 of the Dutch East Indies Penal Code. Most of the men arrested were Dutch, but there were also nine Indonesians, one Armenian, four Chinese and one Arab detained. Those convicted included Fievez de Malines van Ginkel, the Resident of Batavia and head of the Batavia police (sentenced to one and a half years in prison), and the German painter, Walter Spies, in Bali, who was imprisoned for about eight months. Assistant Resident Coolhaas, a member of the Volksraad (the colonial legislature) was interrogated by police but was not imprisoned. He was allowed to go on leave but the government refused to take him back after his leave (Boellstorff 2005: 52–4; Bloemenbergen 2011: 5, 121, 138).

As would happen with the police detentions in 2017, the names of those arrested were published in the newspapers. Bloemenbergen (2011: 121) describes this as follows:

> The Netherlands Indies newspapers followed this remarkable mass arrest of homosexuals – which had never happened before on such a scale in the Netherlands Indies – with great interest and referred to it as '*de grote schoonmaak*' (the great spring-cleaning), '*zedenschoonmaak*' (moral cleaning) or '*het reiningsproces*' (the cleansing process). At the same time they introduced the suspects of homosexual sex – at first by full name, later on by initials, town, and occupation – as representatives of a '*poel der verwording*' (cesspool of vice) and '*vies gedoe*' (dirty stuff).

Bloemenbergen (2011: 141) speculates that the massive hunt for homosexuals was the result of the state feeling weak:

> At the end of the 1930s, this fake and enforced atmosphere of normalcy was extremely tense in reality, reflecting the essential weakness of the colonial state. This state was threatened by the continuous challenge of Indonesian nationalism and by a new danger, the possibility of war in Europe and Asia. Against this background, the police raids against homosexuals can be understood as an endeavour of the colonial authorities to stay firm by showing firmness. By catching the elusive, the unfathomable and the deviant as the weak spot, they emphasized the opposite: the male heterosexual strength of the colonial state. At the same time this moral cleansing was also meant to show the civilized face of the colonial state, and thus to legitimize colonial authority to appease possible indigenous critics.

The mass arrests of homosexuals in 1938 and 1939 does not seem to have been overtly on religious grounds but on a more secular version of 'moral cleanliness' – although it could be said that moral cleanliness has religious roots. These raids introduced a form of homophobia that had previously not existed in the Dutch East Indies, certainly not in indigenous societies.

LGBT in independent Indonesia before Reformasi

Although Indonesian governments have been more tolerant than the Dutch colonisers, there has been spasmodic violence against LGBT people in independent Indonesia before the Reformasi period. Violence has come in waves and at these times has been condoned, if not supported, by state apparatus. For example, in South Sulawesi, the 1960s saw an increase in the influence of the Islamist movement led by Kahar Muzakkar. This, combined with the violence that ushered in the New Order in 1966, led to Operasi Toba (Operation Repent) to stop practices considered un-Islamic. Bissu ceremonies were stopped and – in actions that would be repeated in Aceh in 2017 – gangs shaved the heads of bissu. Bissu were even tortured and murdered – Sanro Makgangke, the bissu leader of Boné, was decapitated, with his/her head being publicly displayed (Davies 2010: 197–8). This occurred at a time when the state was in turmoil, similar to the wave of persecutions in the 1930s, when, as mentioned above, the Dutch colonial state had felt threatened.

In general, however, the Indonesian state had, in the past, showed a fairly benign attitude to transvestites/sexuals (initially known as '*wadam*', later '*waria*'), who organised themselves before lesbians and gays.[9] Jakarta's Governor, Ali Sadikin, facilitated the setting-up of the first wadam organisation, the Djakarta Wadam Association (HIWAD) in 1969. In 1977, two wadam jumped to their death into the Malang River in the Taman Lawang district of Jakarta, while pursued by security officers. The following day a wadam delegation spoke to Ahmad Toha, the head of Social Affairs Board at Jakarta City Hall. Speaking to the press in 1984, Toha commented:

> Through that first meeting, I realised that waria should be treated as human beings. This new understanding has changed the policy of our department to deal with waria as our neighbours.
>
> (Suwito 1984)

The Jakarta Social Affairs Board planned to build a waria centre but had already established training programmes in hairdressing, cooking, dressmaking and beautician skills – by 1984, 280 waria had completed these courses. While the state was concerned with the morals of wadam, who were often forced by circumstance to work as prostitutes, the response was to provide them with the occupational training to find other employment. Ibrahim, from the West Jakarta Mayor's office, emphasised that the courses were to be freely chosen by the waria and no coercion would be used, because most waria would prefer not to become prostitutes but had too few choices, because 75 per cent of them had fled 'intolerable circumstances' (Suwito 1984).

As will be described below, radical Islamist groups like FPI (Front Pembela Islam, the Islamic Defenders Front), describe homosexuality as a 'disease from the West' – along with drugs and pornography. While this is, of course, patently incorrect, it has been suggested that the current wave of homophobia is caused both by the rise of radical Islamic groups and the increased visibility of LGBT groups. When Dédé Oetomo founded one of the first Indonesian lesbian and gay groups, Lambda Indonesia, in 1982 in Solo, he was inspired by the movement in America, and the terms 'lesbi' and 'gay' have been borrowed from English, to describe same-sex relationships, where neither of the partners have adopted the dress and roles of the opposite sex. However, both the word 'gay' and Gay Liberation itself are also relatively new in the West. It is an irony that the Islamist groups now seek to criminalise homosexuality, when the West has only just decriminalised homosexuality in the last (the twentieth) century.

Legislation affecting LGBT people

One of the first ways anti-LGBT legislation was introduced in the period after the New Order ended in 1998 was through Regional Regulations (*peraturan daerah*).

Regional Regulations

Regional Regulations affecting LGBT people were introduced from the early 2000s. Muthmainnah (2016: 22–4) discusses the introduction of six regional regulations between 2002 and 2010, which specifically mention lesbian and gay sexual activity, describing it as immoral, sinful, adulterous or equivalent to 'prostitution'. Katjasungkana and Wieringa (2016: 44–66) discuss a further twenty-two regional regulations affecting lesbians and gays (see Table 16.1). Some legislation describes homosexuality as 'disturbing public order' or 'violating religious norms and customs'. Many of the regulations specify a maximum prison sentence of three or six months and maximum fines ranging between Rp. 5.000.000 and Rp. 25.000.000 (approximately A$ 500 to A$ 2,500). There has been a pattern of different regions copy-and-pasting the regulations of other regions (Katjasungkana and Wieringa 2016: 10).

Aceh

Until the introduction of special autonomy and the passing of anti-homosexual laws, Aceh, like the rest of Indonesia had been reasonably tolerant of LGBT people.[10] There was a marked shift in the post-Reformasi era. In 2001, Acehnese *Qanun* (Regional Regulation) No. 23 of 2001 was passed. Article 32(1) of this law,[11] requires the Social Department to 'reintegrate' *waria* or return them to 'normal society'. Other people deemed to require 'reintegration' into 'normal' society include former prisoners, beggars and prostitutes. In January 2007, two men suspected of being gay were beaten up by police and the local community. This led, in the same year, to the formation on the LGBT rights group, Violet Grey (Jauhola 2013: 75–7). In 2008, the Acehnese ulama council (Majelis Permusyawaratan Ulama, MPU)[12] stated that (male to female) transgendered people and transvestites must have a complete set of female genitalia through surgical operation and that, in addition, *waria* should comply with Muslim dress regulations for women (Jauhola 2013: 71). The rules are, however, applied randomly. One transgender woman told Human Rights Watch (HRW) that the WH (Wilayatul Hisbah, or Shariah Police) detained her and another transgender woman, ostensibly for failing to wear Islamic attire, despite the fact that one was wearing women's clothing and the other was wearing men's clothing that conformed to the law (HRW 2010: 56).

Persecution of waria continues to the present day in Aceh. In January 2018, a group of twelve transgender women were arrested while at work in beauty salons, their heads were publicly shaved and they were forced to dress as men before they were released, after the inevitable humiliating press conference (Harvey and Guillanno 2018).

Since the passing of anti-homosexual laws in September 2014, in Qanun No. 6 of 2014 on Islamic Criminal Law (the Qanun Jinayat), people discovered engaging in same-sex sexual relations in Aceh can receive a sentence of up to a hundred lashes of the cane, these sentences being carried out in public. In 2017, two men were caned for same-sex relations, followed by another two in 2018, receiving eighty-three and eighty-seven lashes respectively (HRW 2018: 22; Reuters 2018: and see Mann and Afrianty, Chapter 19, and Butt, Chapter 20, this volume). One of the most disturbing aspects of these canings

Table 16.1 Regional regulations affecting lesbians and gays[1]

East Kalimantan	RR No. 2 of 2007 of Kabupaten Berau on the Prohibition of Prostitution
	RR No. 21 of 2000 of Tarakan on Indecent Acts
South Kalimantan	RR No. 10 of 2007 of Banjar Local on Public Order
Jakarta	RR No. 8 of 2007 of Jakarta on Public Order
Lampung	RR No. 15 of 2002 of Bandar Lampung on the Prohibition of Prostitution and Immoral Acts
	RR No. 7 of 2001 of Way Kanan on the Prohibition of Prostitution and Immoral Acts
	RR No. 11 of 2012 of Tulang Bawang Barat on the Prohibition of Immoral Acts, Prostitution and Immorality
	RR No. 4 of 2004 of Lampung Selatan on the Prohibition of Prostitution, Immoral Acts and Gambling and the Prevention of Sinful Acts RR of No. 7 of 2006 of Lampung Utara
	RR No. 7 of 2003 of Mandailing Natal on the Prevention and Eradication of Societal Diseases Juncto (in Relation to) RR No. 32 of 2007
	RR No. 6 of 2003 of Mandailing Natal on Clothing for Muslim Men and Women
	RR No. 32 of 2008 seri C No. 2 of Labuhanbatu on the Prohibition of Immoral Acts, Vagrancy and Beggars
	RR No. 25 of 2007 of Serdang Bedagai on the Prohibition of Immoral Acts, Vagrants and Beggars
West Sumatra	RR No. 9 of 2010 of Padang Panjang on the Prevention, Elimination and Repression of Social Diseases
	RR No. 2 of 2004 of Padang Pariaman on Prevention, Repression and Eradication of Immorality
South Sulawesi	RR No. 5 of 2003 of Bulukumba on Muslim Clothing
	RR No. 16 of 2005 of Maros on Muslim Clothing
	RR No. 9 of 2004 of Luwu Timur on Public Order
South Sumatra	RR No. 3 of 2003 of Lahat on the Prohibition of Prostitution and Indecent Acts
	RR No. 23 of 2006 of Ogan Komering on the Eradication of Immorality
	RR of Muara Enim No. 3 of 2005 juncto (in relation to) RR No. 13A of 1989 and RR No. 14 of 1993 on the Prevention of Immoral Acts
	Regulation No. 13 of 2002 on Combating Immorality in the Province of South Sumatra
	Local Regulation of Palembang No. 2 of 2004 on the Eradication of Prostitution
Jogjakarta	RR No. 5 of 2007 of Bantul on the Prohibition of Prostitution
West Java	RR No. 12 of 2009 of Tasikmalaya on the Development of Community Life Values Based on the Teachings of Islam and Societal Social Norms

[1] Table compiled primarily from Katjasungkana and Wieringa (2016) and Muthmainnah (2016).

has been the crowds of jeering spectators allowed to watch the caning, often photographing events on their mobile phones.

The 2008 Pornography Law

It is not just at the regional level that legislation affecting LGBT people has changed. The national 2008 Pornography Law makes specific mention of lesbian and gay sexual activity in the elucidation to art. 4(1)(a). Article 4 of the Pornography Law prohibits people from producing or making available pornography, which explicitly contains: '(a) sexual intercourse, including "deviant sexual intercourse"'. The elucidation then explains that '(a) [w]hat is intended by "deviant sexual intercourse" includes intercourse *or other sexual activity* with corpses, animals, oral sex, anal sex, lesbian and homosexuals'. Not only is this a poorly formed sentence – combining activities (oral sex, anal sex) with non-consenting partners (corpses, animals) and consenting partners (lesbians and homosexuals) – but the ambiguity of 'other sexual activity' makes it a clause that could be applied to representations of LBGT activity (for example, holding hands or kissing), which would not be considered pornographic if applied to heterosexuals.

Three petitions claiming the Pornography Law was unconstitutional have been brought to the Constitutional Court. The second (17-PUU-VII/2009) was brought by six organisations that included: groups involved in human rights and women's issues; Christian groups; and twenty individuals.[13] One section of this petition criticised the Pornography Law's inclusion of lesbianism and homosexuality in a list of deviant sexual activities (such as sexual activity with a corpse or animal, oral sex and anal sex). The petitioners argued that lesbianism and homosexuality were natural orientations, not sexual activities, and that including homosexuality and lesbianism as sexual deviancies was a form of discrimination (Mahkamah Konstitusi 2009b). Petition 17-PUU-VII/2009 was rejected, with Justice Maria Farida Indrati providing the only dissenting opinion (Lindsey 2012: 480).[14] This weakened the position of supporters of LGBT rights, a position which was yet further weakened when MUI issued a specific *fatwa* (opinion of a qualified scholar on a question of Islamic law) against LGBT activity.

Fatwa by MUI

In 2014, MUI issued Fatwa No. 57 Tahun 2014 on Lesbians, Gays, Sodomy and Indecency (*Pencabulan*). Its 'Legal Provisions' (*Ketentuan Hukum*) include:

> 4. Homosexual activity, including lesbian, gay and bisexual can incur *hadd* or *ta'zir* sentences from the authorities;[15] [...]
>
> 6. Sodomy can incur the maximum *ta'zir* sentence, the death penalty; [...]
>
> 10. Crimes against children can incur the death penalty.

While fatawa do not have legal status nationally, this fatwa also includes recommendations to the DPR that: it should not legalise the homosexual community, or other communities that are 'sexual deviants'; it should enact heavy penalties against sodomy and other lesbian and gay sexual activities and include these in the Criminal Code; there should be socialisation and rehabilitation against sexual deviance; the legislature must not legalise same sex marriage; and the legislature and the community must not allow the existence of homosexual activities, sodomy or other indecent acts to arise within the community.

People did not respond strongly to the fatwa at the time. Irwan Martua Hidayana, Associate Professor of Anthropology, Universitas Indonesia and board member of Suara Kita (Our Voice), an Indonesian LGBT rights organisation, for example, commented:

> The Lesbian, Gay, Bisexual and Transgender (LGBT) community in Indonesia has responded to the fatwa in a calm manner. Suara Kita (Our Voice), an LGBT rights organisation, wrote on its website that the MUI has a right to its opinion as much as Suara Kita has the right to dismiss the fatwa.
>
> (Hidayana 2015)

He does however, suggest that the existence of the fatwa could encourage vigilante groups to attack LGBT events. He also mentions that there is a precedent for fatwa to be used in drafting national laws – he mentions the laws on *halal* products and *hajj* management (Hidayana 2015). The 2008 Pornography Law was similarly preceded by a fatwa that supported its aims.[16] One possible reason for the passing of the 2008 Pornography Law is that it was too difficult to get the amended draft Criminal Code, a long, complex and much contested document, through the national legislature.

Moral crimes in the revised Criminal Code

As this suggests, the Criminal Code is undergoing revision (and has been for decades). There have been a number of drafts but each has stalled over controversial articles (Butt and Lindsey 2018: 200; and see Butt and Lindsey, Chapter 2, this volume). One of the current controversial issues is whether homosexual acts between adults should be criminalised.

Academic draft, March 2015

Each Bill in Indonesia must be accompanied by an 'academic draft' (Butt and Lindsey 2018: 44), which, in this case, recommended the criminalisation of homosexuality. The academic draft (*naskah akademik*) of the Draft Criminal Code in March 2015 was prepared by BPHN (the National Law

Development Agency, Badan Pembinaan Hukum Nasional) of the Ministry for Law and Human Rights, under the leadership of Dr Enny Nurbaningsih. The introduction to section 2.16 on moral crimes (*tindak pidana kesusilaan*) stated that the compilers of the draft had conducted research and sought input from focus groups. The academic draft stated that the Criminal Code must be reformulated to adapt to the moral values of Indonesia's legal community (*nilai kesusilaan masyarakat hukum Indonesia*), for example, legal concepts of adultery and morality (*zina dan kesusilaan*). It also suggested that the Criminal Code needed to take into account the legal norms contained in more recent laws such as the Pornography Law, the Electronic Transactions Law, the Domestic Violence Law and the Protection of Children Law. Finally, *adat* (customary) law and living law (*hukum yang hidup dalam masyarakat*)[17] should be sources for criminal legal norms (Naskah Akademik RUU KUHP 2015: 237–8). This commentary draws on the views of Oemar Seno Adji, fifth Chief Justice of the Supreme Court of Indonesia, who stated that religious values should have a role when formulating laws to deal with moral crimes (*kejahatan-kejahatan terhadap kesusilaan*) (Naskah Akademik RUU KUHP 2015: 239).[18] The commentary recommended that [laws about] moral crimes must include:

a. a definition (*rumusan*) which outlines the boundaries and the definition of violating morality (*melanggar kesusilaan*);
b. clarifies (*menegaskan*) actions that are moral crimes (*tindak pidana terhadap kesusilaan*), both through examining the laws in other countries and through creating new laws from religious norms, which relate to morality; and
c. improving the interpretation of existing criminal acts and aligning them with the thinking that the law must be closely founded on religious morals. (Naskah Akademik RUU KUHP 2015: 239).

Included among possible new moral crimes were 'conducting an indecent act with an adult of the same sex' (*melakukan perbuatan cabul dengan jenis kelamin yang sama antara sesama orang dewasa*) and 'sodomy'(*sodomi*) (Naskah Akademik RUU KUHP 2015: 240).

Apart from these, another moral crime was the vaguely-worded 'deviant behaviour in public' (*tindakan penyimpangan yang dilakukan didepan umum*) (Naskah Akademik RUU KUHP 2015: 240).

The academic draft therefore bore more similarity to the fatwa than to either the earlier draft of the Criminal Code or the later March 2018 draft (see below), in that it raised the possibility of criminalising adult homosexual acts in private. In addition, despite stating that there must be a clear definition of what a moral crime is, the academic draft did not make this any clearer than other Indonesian legislation.

Draft of February 2017

In the 24 February 2017 version of the draft amended Criminal Code produced by the Criminal Code Working Committee (Panitia Kerja R-KUHP) of the DPR, the only reference to homosexuality is a statement about the age of consent:

Article 495

(1) Everyone who conducts indecent acts with someone of their own sex, who is known to be, or could reasonably be considered to be, under the age of 18 (eighteen), may be sentenced to imprisonment for a maximum of 9 (nine) years.
(2) The sentence can be increased by a third if the indecent act mentioned in clause (1) is oral sex or anal sex or any form of touching a non-genital organ with a genital organ, which is conducted in a homosexual manner (*atau semua bentuk pertemuan organ non-kelamin dengan alat kelamin yang dilakukan secara homoseksual*).

Notes [by the drafting group]

A definition is needed for indecent acts (articles 491(2)a and article 495(2)) and rape.[19]

March 2018 Draft Criminal Code

The version produced on the 8 March 2018, did not differ greatly from the February 2017 version, although it did fill in items missing from the 2017 version. It raised the sanction for sex with a minor to twelve years' imprisonment.

Article 454

(1) Everyone who conducts an indecent act (*perbuatan cabul*) with someone of the same sex:

  a. in public may be may be sentenced to imprisonment for a maximum of 1 (one) year 6 (six) months or a Category II fine.
  b. violently or with the threat of violence, may be sentenced to imprisonment for a maximum of 9 (nine) years or a Category III fine.
  c. which is published with a 'pornographic flavour' (*muatan pornografi*) may be sentenced to imprisonment for a maximum of 9 (nine) years or a Category III fine.

(2) Everyone who conducts an indecent act with someone of the same sex, who is known to be, or could reasonably be considered to be, under the age of 18 (eighteen) may be sentenced to imprisonment for a maximum of 12 (twelve) years or a Category IV fine.

(3) Where the action in clause (2) involved violence or threats of violence, maximum sanctions of 15 (fifteen) years imprisonment or a Category V fine may be imposed.

The 8 March 2018 draft Criminal Code did not have an Elucidation attached but the 2015 version defines 'indecent acts' as follows:

Article 492

What is meant by 'indecent acts' (*perbuatan cabul*) are all acts which violate moral feelings (*rasa kesusilaan*) and other despicable (*keji*) acts, which are related to sexual desire (*nafsu birahi*).

Criminal acts according to this provision are not just forcing someone to commit an indecent act, but also compelling a person by use of force or threat of force to allow an indecent act to be committed upon him or her.

Such a loose definition makes it very difficult to know exactly what constitutes an indecent act – does it constitute sexual intercourse or simply kissing in public? If the draft Code were passed in this form, the interpretation of the term would be left to individual panels of judges at trial, and this would add greatly to the insecurity of the LGBT community.

July 2018 Draft Criminal Code

At time of writing (April 2019), the most recent draft was prepared on 9 July 2018. All reference to same sex relations – the entire art. 454 – has been deleted from this draft. The references to 'indecent acts' remain, but the deletion of the same sex articles is nevertheless a very positive sign for the LGBT community.

As will now be explained, the outcome of a petition to the Constitutional Court to criminalise homosexual acts by changing the Criminal Code likewise ultimately had a positive outcome. The petition was rejected in December 2017, about eighteen months after it was submitted (A'yun 2017).

AILA and the Constitutional Court

The Family Love Alliance (AILA), a conservative group composed of academics and community representatives, submitted a petition to the Constitutional Court in 2016.[20] In it, AILA sought changes to a number of articles in the existing Criminal Code, including art. 284 on adultery, to criminalise all extramarital sex (including, but not exclusively, homosexual sex).[21] They also asked that art. 285 (on rape) and art. 292 (on the age of consent for lesbian/gay relations) be altered to criminalise all gay relationships (Saputra 2017). Due to financial and administrative difficulties, a large portion of Indonesians are not legally married, particularly those living in remote areas or involved in polygamous marriages (Huis and Wirastri 2012; Platt 2009). This would have made the change impossible to enforce.

In December 2017, the Constitutional Court ruled that it was unable to grant the petition. It stated that its role is not to make laws but rather to strike out laws that conflict with the Constitution. This decision was supported by a bare majority of five out of nine judges (Da Costa and Kapoor 2017).[22]

Both the Chief Justice of the Constitutional Court, Arief Hidayat, and the Deputy, Dr Anwar Usman, decided in favour of AILA's petition. This was hardly surprising in the case of the former. In March 2013, when Hidayat was being interviewed by the DPR to determine his fitness for the job, he was asked whether human rights were 'compatible with the local context' and whether Indonesia should recognise same-sex marriage. He answered that while that might be acceptable in the United States, Indonesia 'cannot accept the concept of same-sex-marriage since it contradicts with our faith and local wisdom'. The Chair of Commission III, I Gede Pasek Suardika, commented to the media that Hidayat had demonstrated skills and knowledge needed to lead the legal institution: 'He [Hidayat] has provided us with convincing argument on same-sex marriage and human rights' (429 Magazine 2013; Festiani and Sasmita 2013: 2–13).

With such a small margin, the Decision could easily have gone another way. Justice Saldi Isra (who voted against the ALIA petition) replaced Justice Patrialis Akbar in 11 April 2017, after the latter was arrested on suspicion of corruption. Akbar had previously spoken out in favour of the Constitutional Court agreeing with the petition, which would have made extramarital sex illegal. Ironically, it was revealed during the trial that part of the reason Akbar had engaged in corruption was to raise money to pay for an apartment for his young mistress (Coconuts Jakarta 2017; Suparman, Andriyanto and Prasetyo 2017).

In passing down the Constitutional Court's decision about the AILA petition, Chief Justice Hidayat (dissenting) said that the petitioners should 'submit their petition to lawmakers, and there it should be an important input in the ongoing revision of the national criminal code' (Da Costa and Kapoor 2017).

However, although an amended Criminal Code is yet to be passed, the Pornography Law has been used to imprison gay men for their behaviour in gay bars and saunas, as will be discussed below.

Response to LGBT events by Islamist groups in early Reformasi era

In the post-Soeharto era, there has been a rise of vigilante Islamist groups, and a growing trend within the Muslim community to adopt more conservative religious views. Although there had been attacks by Islamist groups on LGBT gatherings in the past, these were spasmodic and isolated – and society was generally reasonably tolerant. In addition, both state officials and mainstream Islamic groups initially provided some protection for LGBT people.

The lack of anti-discrimination legislation that can protect sexual orientation has, however, left lesbians, gays and waria vulnerable.

Before and during the time that changes to legislation that would target LGBT Indonesians were being discussed, Islamist vigilante groups attacked LGBT events on a number of occasions. One of the first major attacks on LGBT gatherings took place in the early days of the Reformasi era, in September 1999, when FPI Surakarta[23] demonstrated against a meeting of Jaringan Lesbian dan Gay Indonesia (Indonesian Network of Lesbians and Gays) in Solo, threatening to burn down the Dana Hotel where the meeting was to be held and to kill the gay activists (Liang 2010; Oetomo 2001). The meeting was cancelled.

The following year, in November 2000, an event was held in Kaliurang in Central Java, with performances and comedy skits by waria attended by both waria and members of the general community, to observe National Health Day. This event was interrupted by about 150 members of GPK (Gerakan Pemuda Ka'bah, Ka'bah Youth Movement), who attacked participants with knives, machetes and clubs. At least twenty-five people were injured and at least three of these were hospitalised with severe injuries. Fifty-seven men were arrested following the incident but all were released without charges being laid (Boellstorff 2004a: 465–6).

Waria fashion parades and beauty contests have usually been well-attended by the general public (often in their thousands) and have often been opened by a local official, such as a mayor.[24] Even at the beginning of the Reformasi period, officials continued to attend these and less extreme Muslims provided support for the events. In July 2005, the Miss Waria Indonesia beauty contest, which was attended by dignitaries including Sutiyoso (then Governor of Jakarta), was gate-crashed by about one hundred FPI members, who demanded the event be disbanded. After some discussion, FPI members were escorted from the event by police. A number of days later, it was reported that about fifty members of FPI visited the office of Governor Sutiyoso. Ahmad Sabri Lubis from FPI commented to the press that they had come to ask about Sutiyoso's views on (gambling and) transsexuals, as they suspected that Sutiyoso had ignored regulations outlawing transsexual beauty pageants (The Jakarta Post 2005b). There is no specific legislation dealing with transsexual beauty contests, and I can only presume this is a reference to a 1980 local regulation banning beauty contests in general.[25]

FPI's demands did not lead to the event being stopped and in 2006 even more public figures attended Miss Waria Indonesia pageant. These included Abdurrahman Wahid (Gus Dur), former President of Indonesia and head for fifteen years (from 1984 until 1999) of NU (Nahdlatul Ulama). This is Indonesia's largest, mainstream Muslim organisation and it claims a membership of about 80 million. Gus Dur was photographed with the founder of Yayasan Putri Waria Indonesia, Megie Megawatie. It was reported that many of the dignitaries had specifically come to support the event, because of the 'visit' by FPI the year before (Jakarta Post 2005b; Kortschak 2007;

Taipei Times 2005). There was no reported action by FPI in 2006, despite the Pornography Bill being hotly debated in the wider community at the time.

During the debate over the pornography bill, tens of thousands of people marched in the streets, expressing strong feelings both for and against the Pornography Bill (Pausacker 2013: 85–6). For Islamist groups, pornography, like LGBT activity, is symptomatic of an amoral/immoral 'Western' influence (Pausacker 2013: 62–3). For their opponents, Islamist opposition reflects foreign 'Arab' values.

In March 2010, FPI and other Islamist groups disrupted a conference of ILGA (the International Lesbian, Gay, Bisexual, Transgender and Intersex Association) in Surabaya, forcing the conference to be disbanded. The three-day conference was hosted by Gaya Nusantara, the oldest gay organisation in Indonesia, and was to be held at the Mercure Hotel. After being approached by FPI and its supporters, who threatened demonstrations, Mercure withdrew from its contract with ILGA, forcing the ILGA board to find a new site, the Oval Hotel, at a few days' notice. Likewise, the South Surabaya police initially agreed to grant a permit for the event but then withdrew it after the Surabaya City Police (the level above the South Surabaya Police) received phone calls from conservative Muslim groups, United Madura Front (Formabes, Forum Madura Bersatu), MUI, and Hizbut Tahrir Indonesia. Police stated that the permit could not be issued for security and order reasons. Members of SBY's Democratic Party, KomnasHAM (Komisi Nasional Hak Asasi Manusia, National Commission on Human Rights) and Kontras (Komisi untuk Orang Hilang dan Korban Tindak Kekerasan, The Commission for Missing Persons and Victims of Violence) objected to the refusal of the permit.

A number of both conservative and extremist Muslim groups combined forces in the demonstrations against the conference. As well as FPI, Formabes, HTI and MUI, they included: the Indonesian Muslim Students' Action Front (KAMMI, Kesatuan Aksi Mahasiswa Indonesia); the Islamic Student Union of Airlangga University; Al-Irsyad; and the Islamic Community Forum (FUI, Forum Umat Islam). Simultaneously, Gaya Nusantara's office was spray-painted with the words, 'Gays and lesbians are moral terrorists'. On this occasion, Surabaya police did arrive and stood guard at the front entrance of the hotel. Likewise, Banser, the paramilitary wing of NU, also agreed (on payment of 'transportation money') to provide security and attempt to persuade the demonstrators to leave. Given the persistence of the demonstrators, however, the conference was disbanded (Bhinneka 2010; HRW 2016; Liang 2010; Tejo 2010).

A month later, in April 2010, the West Java branch of FPI raided a workshop on transgender rights in Depok, which was sponsored by the FKWI (Forum Komunikasi Waria Indonesia, Indonesian Transgender Communication Forum) and Komnas HAM. Once again, there were issues of whether the appropriate permission had been granted by the Depok Municipal Government. FPI broke into the session, verbally assaulted attendees, and broke glasses. As a result, the training session moved to Komnas HAM headquarters in Jakarta, where it was completed without incident (The Jakarta Post 2010; Liang 2010; Sufa and Setiawati 2010).

FPI also demonstrated against the first lesbian and gay Q! Film Festival in 2002, and then again in 2010 (Harkins et al. 2010; Maimunah 2008; Wijaya 2010). The Q! Film Festival was held at a number of venues throughout Jakarta, including the Goethe Institute and the Dutch cultural body, Erasmus House. Each of these venues were visited in turn by FPI. A video of the event at the Goethe Institute, for example, shows event organisers being presented with a petition. The protestors stated that the Goethe Institute promotes campaigns for free sex and that foreigners are purposely destroying Indonesia's next generation by 'supporting devilish activities that are against our constitution, our religious norms and our Eastern values'.[26] It was not stated which part of the constitution was being violated. The East/West comparison is, however, a very common one for FPI.[27] The video of the event shows that there was a police presence at the venue that kept the demonstrators from entering the compound, which was, after all, part of a diplomatic mission. On the other hand, there was pressure by the police for someone from the venue to speak to the protestors, implying that the responsibility for security was to rest, at least in part, on the shoulders of the venue owners. Showings continued at the Goethe Institute but the French cultural centre and the Japan Foundation advised they would not be showing further Q! films (Child 2010).

There are common factors in these early Reformasi attacks. The first is the threat of violence – or violence itself – by the Islamist groups. Although not all the attacks involved violence, there is enough of a history of the groups being prepared to carry out the violence (as, for example, at the Kaliurang event) to ensure that people take threats of violence seriously. In many cases, the organisers cancelled the event, rather than take the risk. State officials in all these cases are not supportive – for example, licences for events are withdrawn, violent demonstrators are held in custody and not charged – but, on the other hand, they are not antagonistic. Similarly, mainstream Muslim groups, such as NU, have been prepared to offer assistance. In Gus Dur's case, this was by himself attending a waria event and in the case of the ILGA conference, there was protection provided by Banser. By 2016, however, state officials and bodies were vocal against LGBT people.

Anti-lesbian, gay and waria hysteria in 2016

The current wave of anti-lesbian and gay hysteria began in January 2016, when state officials began to issue anti-LGBT statements publicly, thereby giving licence for anti-LGBT activities. On 23 January 2016, Indonesia's Higher Education Minister, Mohamad Nasir Djamil, was one of the first to make a public statement. He tweeted that he wanted all LGBT student groups expelled from campuses, a statement he later withdrew to some degree, saying, three days later, that LGBT groups would be allowed to host campus activities if they have permission from their university, and that the groups will be allowed on campus so long they do not promote indecent acts, such as intimacy and sexual intercourse (Sundaryani 2016).

Following Nasir's statement a long string of officials began issuing anti-gay statements. These ranged from a mayor advising young mothers not to cook instant noodles because more nutritious cooking would prevent their children becoming gay, to Defence Minister Ryamizard Ryacudu labelling LGBT rights activism as a proxy war on the nation, led by outsiders and more dangerous than a nuclear war (Knight 2018). Culture and Education Minister (now Governor of Jakarta), Anies Baswedan, advised that parents of small children needed to watch out for LGBT deviants preying on the children (Suryakusuma 2016).

On 12 February 2017, Administrative and Bureaucratic Reform Minister Yuddy Chrisnandi said that it was not appropriate for civil servants to be homosexual. He commented, however, that having more than one wife for a man was still normal, even though it was prohibited by regulations and ethical codes. Five days later, Religious Affairs Minister, Lukman Hakim Saifuddin, said that the LGBT community was a social problem that 'threatened religious life and the strength of family and national identity' (Sundaryani 2016).

The then Vice-President, Jusuf Kalla, commented on 15 February, that he had summoned the United Nations Development Programme (UNDP) to seek clarification on US$ 8 million in funding allocated for LGBT programmes in several countries in Asia, including Indonesia. This was in response to the UNDP and United States Agency for International Development (USAID) funding the 'Being LGBT in Asia' initiative. The Indonesia country report for this programme stated that there are about 119 LGBT groups in Indonesia, a figure that troubled conservatives (Frontline Defenders 2017: 10; The Jakarta Post 2016; Mann 2016; Sundaryani 2016).[28]

PKS (Partai Keadilan Sejahtera, Prosperous Justice Party) politician, Tifatul Sembiring, on 26 February then tweeted a verse said to be from the hadith (sayings and deeds of the Prophet Muhammad): '[...] kill the person and their partner who commit the acts of the people of Luth [homosexuals] and kill the person and the animal who have sexual intercourse' (Sundaryani 2016).

One minister stood apart from the general comments. Coordinating Political, Legal and Security Affairs Minister Luhut Pandjaitan commented on 12 February that whoever members of the LGBT community are, and wherever they work, they are still Indonesian citizens, and also have a right to be protected. He urged the public to 'restrain themselves and not be prejudiced toward the LGBT community' (The Jakarta Post 2016; Sundaryani 2016).

The negative comments by ministers were backed up by statements from social institutions. Despite the fact that the World Health Organization (WHO) removed homosexuality from its list of psychiatric disorders in 1990, the Indonesian Psychiatric Association (PDSKJI, Perhimpunan Dokter Spesialis Kedokteran Jiwa Indonesia) issued a statement that the association's Mental

Health and Mental Disorder Diagnostic Guidelines categorise homosexuals and bisexuals as 'people with psychiatric problems', while transgender people have 'mental disorders'. Echoing the concern for public acknowledgement of homosexuality, their spokesperson, Suzy Yusna Dewi, commented, 'What we are worried about is, if left untreated, such sexual tendencies could become a commonly accepted condition in society'. She added, 'We must respect Indonesian traditions, which culturally do not accept same-sex marriage, and we should not bow to the influence of foreign values that may not fit in with our values'. By contrast, the Indonesia Planned Parenthood Association (PKBI, Perkumpulan Keluarga Berencana Indonesia) issued a statement that people have different orientations and PKBI did not view these as disorders. Their spokesperson, Chatarina Wahyurini, commented that 'the LGBT community should have equal access to public services and space needed to freely express their identity, participate in dialogue and to contribute to the nation in a positive manner' (Yosephine 2016b).

NU called for DPR and the government to enact a law in order to criminalise homosexuality, LGBT activism and for the 'rehabilitation' of LGBT people, so they can return to 'normal' (Sundaryani 2016). As mentioned, NU was formerly headed by the late Gus Dur, known for his liberal views, and NU was the organisation that had provided protection for the ILGA conference in 2010, only six years earlier.

There has been little or no public response from President Jokowi to these statements. This is despite the fact that point 9 of Jokowi's and Jusuf Kalla's *Nawa Cita* ('nine-point plan', their platform for the 2014 presidential elections) calls for tolerance, diversity, education and creation of space for dialogue among citizens (Yosephine 2016a).[29] It has, however, been suggested that Jokowi reprimanded Muhammad Nasir and Anies Baswedan behind the scenes, stating that their statements went against the *Nawa Cita* (Mann 2016).

In an interview, Dédé Oetomo, founder of Indonesia's first gay rights organisation, Lambda Indonesia, discussing the wave of anti-LGBT feeling that erupted in 2016, commented:

> It has just exploded. It could have been triggered by anyone, there is no particular reason why Muhammad Nasir, the minister of higher education, research and technology, was the one who started it. Some people believe the whole thing has been planned, but I am not so sure.
>
> (Mann 2016)

Oetomo believes that when fewer LGBT people were public, there was less of a panic. Overseas news about the marriages of gay celebrities, such as Elton John and Ricky Martin may have made conservative people anxious. He believes it is not being driven solely by conservative Islam but that many in the society may have become afraid because the heteronormative template, established by the New Order, was being disrupted by a more public display of homosexuality (Mann 2016). He added:

> It also relates to the appearance of order that is so crucial in high Javanese society. Challenges to this order are perceived as threatening. People already know that things are in a mess, but when the mess starts to want legitimacy, when it starts to organise, that's when they get really frightened.
>
> (Mann 2016)

Gay sauna – men imprisoned

By 2017, the state was not just making anti-LGBT remarks but had imprisoned a number of people for their activities in gay saunas and clubs. In December 2017, shortly after the Constitutional Court rejected the AILA petition, ten men were sentenced by the North Jakarta District Court to two to three years' imprisonment each,[30] together with fines of one billion rupiah (A$ 73,700) for violations of the Pornography Law ('displaying nudity and sexual exploitation collectively in public'), at a gay sauna. These men had been arrested following a raid in May 2017, at the Atlantis Club in Kelapa Gading. One hundred and forty-one people were detained in a raid, with ten later charged (Pojoksatu 2017).[31]

Another venue was raided in October 2017 in Harmoni, Central Jakarta, with fifty-one people detained and possibly six being charged (Da Costa 2017; Irwanto 2017). The men were charged under the Pornography Law (arts. 4(2) and 30) and, in some cases, the Criminal Code (Art 296 on prostitution) (Nurita 2017; Okezone 2017).[32]

Police and residents cooperation in targeting LGBT residents

Police behaviour, unchecked – and perhaps encouraged – by the state has become increasingly aggressive towards LGBT people, even where arrest does not lead to conviction. Knight (2018) estimated that more than 300 LGBT Indonesians were arrested in 2017, many for alleged violations of the Pornography Law. In the raids on one of the gay saunas, for example, 80 men were arrested, their photos given to the press and, in some cases, their names and occupations were published.

The houses of LGBT people have also been targeted by police, army and residents. For example, in September 2017 in Tugu Jaya, in the Bogor district of West Java, a raid by police and village leaders forced twelve women suspected of being lesbians out of their homes and the community, following complaints by local Islamic youth groups and religious leaders that the women's cohabitation was 'against the teachings of Islam'. The women were suspected of being lesbians simply because of their appearance. One leader remarked, 'Some [of the women] have short hair, acting as the males. Some have long hair, acting as the females. It's against Islamic law. It's obscene.' The same women had already been chased out of Sukabumi before moving to Tugu Jaya (BBC 2017). Residents, accompanied by Babinsa (Bintara

Pembina Desa, army non-commissioned officers charged with keeping the peace locally), entered the house where five women were living in Medan (North Sumatra) in June 2017, after a passer-by saw two women kissing. These women were also asked to leave the area (Leandha 2017). These were not isolated incidents. In 2017, Arus Pelangi was receiving about ten reports of violence, intimidation and evictions a month (Lamb 2017).

Activists representing LGBT activists have been increasingly targeted. Yulita Rustinawati, from LGBT activist group, Arus Pelangi, commented, 'In Yogyakarta one LGBT activist I know slept in a different house every night because [he/she] was afraid' (Lamb 2017). Activists have received a rising number of anonymous, threatening phone calls at night. One activist received 500 violent comments on a poem she wrote condemning a minister's anti-LGBT tweet. Twenty-three of the twenty-five activists interviewed by Frontline Defenders had received death threats since the beginning of 2016. Activists have been forced to move offices following raids by extremist groups on both their offices and meetings. Police have ignored requests for help, which is a change in response. Online, the situation is no better – with extremist Islamist groups posting photos of activists, calling on the public to attack them (Frontline Defenders 2017). Even well-established, public groups like GAYa Nustantara have had to work underground – their postal address is not published, events are not announced and no banners are put up. They also often choose to work with interfaith organisations, who can provide the 'face' of the programme (Copland 2017).

In addition to violence against LGBT people, there has also been increasing casual, non-violent discrimination from the community, such as the case of a member of the public, Sri Mulyani, who uploaded a video to the Internet, which contained disapproving comments about two men on a motorbike showing affection. After it went viral, it was discovered they were brothers (The Jakarta Post 2017). Recently, there was the case of the 'colour run' (a world-wide event, where participants are sprayed with colour) in Bukittinggi being cancelled by the mayor out of fear that the multi-colours could be seen as the LGBT rainbow symbol (Coconuts Jakarta 2018). Similarly, after Brata Santoso, an executive at the transport app, Gojek, stated a non-discrimination policy toward LGBT people, some sectors of the community pressured others to delete the transport app, using the hashtags #TolakLGBT (reject LGBT) and #DeleteGojek being set up.[33] On the positive side, though, LGBT allies are also increasingly speaking up on social media ridiculing such negative responses. In the Gojek case, for example, responders commented that it was fine to uninstall the Gojek app but if people were going to do that, they needed to be consistent and uninstall multiple other apps and refuse to buy countless products[34] made by companies, which had supported LGBT rights. One netizen helpfully suggested, 'You could ride an *odong-odong* (colourful children's toy car, often a pedicab), sir. That would be *halal*'.[35] Unfortunately, Gojek itself was not so enthusiastic about the publicity, commenting that while it respected diversity, it also respected 'Indonesian values and culture', implying that this did not include Indonesian LGBT people (Techusijarana 2018). The airing of such constant, casual prejudice contributes to a general feeling of disquiet and provides the background for further legal discrimination.

Conclusion

As shown in this chapter, while the many and various societies of the Indonesian archipelago have historically tended to be tolerant of LGBT people, and there have been places in these societies for different genders, there have also been outbreaks of violence against LGBT people, particularly at times of crisis, such as during the violence of 1966. The growing visibility of LGBT groups, both internationally and nationally has perhaps fostered insecurity among many in the community. Together with a greater national piety, this has possibly been part of the cause of rising anti-LGBT behaviour and legislation in recent years.

While homosexuality and transvestitism have not (yet) been criminalised nationally, there has also been no anti-discrimination legislation introduced to protect LGBT people. This means that there are no obstacles to the passing of anti-gay laws apart from contested interpretations of some statements in the Constitution.[36] The introduction of discriminatory regional regulations and the application of the 2008 Pornography Law to prosecute LGBT people provides fertile ground for the possibility of either criminalising homosexual acts nationally through the Criminal Code – or, possibly, as happened with the 2008 Pornography Law, through a 'special' law.

The situation for LGBT people will obviously become worse if homosexuality is included as a crime in the Criminal Code. Even if this does not occur – or takes many more decades to occur – the discussion about the possibility of introducing homosexuality into the Criminal Code has had a damaging effect. Together with negative statements by politicians and community leaders, these potential legal changes indicate to the general public that there will be little or no protection from the state for any violence or persecution of LGBT people. This, in turn, provides legitimacy for extra-legal activity against LGBT people, both casual homophobic remarks and violence.

Notes

1 In many Western countries, it is now common to use the acronym LGBTIQ or LGBTQI, or even LGBTIQ++, which adds 'intersex' and 'queer' to the list of terms. It is currently rare for Indonesians to add these terms, so I have used just the four-letter acronym they usually prefer.
2 See also Katjasungkana and Wieringa (2016: 20–1) for descriptions of the Ngaju Dayak, Toraja and Bare'e Toraja of Central Sulawesi and Iban in Kalimantan.
3 Boomgaard (2012: 148) considers that marriage and producing an heir were more important factors than whether someone engaged in homosexual activities

before – or even after – the marriage. He suggests that Pakubuwana II himself had male lovers, although, unlike Pangeran Blitar, Pakubuwana II did get married and have a son.

4 Very close to what is now the Indonesian archipelago, in an area now covered by Malaysia, the fifteenth century *Undang-undang Melaka* (Laws of Malacca) proscribed death by stoning for sodomy (also the punishment for adultery with a woman) if a man was married, and 100 lashes and expulsion for a year, if he was not (Boomgaard 2012: 146).

5 The crime of sodomy was a public offence in the Dutch Republic from 1730 until 1811. In 1730 (during, ironically, the 'Age of Enlightenment', which promoted the ideas of 'liberty, progress, tolerance, fraternity, constitutional government and separation of church and state'), there was a pogrom directed at homosexual men in the Dutch Republic (Norton 2011: np). In the second half of the seventeenth century, sodomy trials were conducted behind closed doors but in 1730, death sentences for sodomites were again carried out in public and bodies were left to rot on the gallows or the corpses thrown in the sea or a river – or, more rarely, burned after execution (Boomgaard 2012: 144). It is estimated that between 250 and 300 such trials took place around 1730, many leading to death sentences. Outbreaks of disease in cattle, of shipworm in dikes, and disasters, such as flooding (1657) and an earthquake in 1692, were all seen to be signs of divine wrath, brought onto the nation by the existence of homosexuals. In the fifteenth and sixteenth centuries, the death penalty was usually by fire or beheading. In the seventeenth and eighteenth century, men found guilty of sodomy were usually strangled or hanged from gallows (Boomgaard 2012: 143–4).

6 The VOC, founded in 1602, ruled individual colonies in the region. From 1816, the Dutch state assumed sovereignty of the VOC's Indies territories. See Adams 1996: 13.

7 Subsequent changes to the Dutch penal code after 1915 were not adopted in the Dutch East Indies. During the World War II, for example, when the Netherlands was occupied by the Nazis, art. 175 was introduced into Dutch law from German law, making homosexuality illegal. This law was repealed at the end of the war and art. 248bis was repealed in 1971 (Meer 2008: 202, fns. 26 and 27).

8 Article 292 of the Criminal Code provides that same-sex relations with a minor can receive a sanction of up to five years' imprisonment. A minor is defined as under 18 years of age in Law No. 23 of 2002 on Child Protection, art. 1(1). Article 287(1) of the Criminal Code defines the age of consent for a woman as 15 years. Article 7(1) of Law No. 1 of 1974 on Marriage defines the minimum age of marriage as 19 for men and 16 for women.

9 Originally known as *banci*, a more polite term, 'wadam', a combination of 'Hawa Adam' (Eve and Adam), was adopted in the 1960s and later 'waria', a combination of *wanita pria* (woman-man) became the standard word. The term 'waria' was first introduced by Alamsyah, Minister of Religious Affairs in the 1978, after complaints by Islamic groups that the Prophet Adam's name was being associated with transgender and transsexual people (Boellstorff 2004b: 184, fn. 8). Safitri (2013: 105, fn. 4) states the change to 'waria' occurred in the 1970s, while Muthmainah (2016: 16) suggests 1980.

10 In the past, there were similar incidences in Aceh of the role in courts of androgynous courtiers and cross-dressing in the arts, as in other parts of the Indonesian archipelago (Jauhola 2013: 60).

11 Aceh Qanun No 23 of 2001 on the Social Organisation and Social Services Administration for the Special Region of Aceh (Susunan Organisasi dan Tata Kerja Dinas Sosial Propinsi Daerah Istimewa Aceh).

12 The MPU in Aceh is composed of *ulama* (Islamic scholars) and representatives of local government. The organisation can propose laws and issue *fatawa* on the religious acceptability of new laws and regulations (Bowen 2013: 149).

13 For a full description of the Articles impugned in petition 17/PUU-VII/2009, see Lindsey (2012: 477, fn. 57), and for a list of the groups involved see Lindsey (2012: 477–8), as well as Mahkamah Konstitusi (2009c).

14 Maria Farida Indrati was the only Constitutional Court judge who was on both the panel deciding the Pornography Law and the AILA petition against the Criminal Code, discussed below.

15 Oxford Islamic Studies Online (www.oxfordislamicstudies.com) defines *tazir* as

> 'Punishment for crime not measuring up to the strict requirements of *hadd* punishments, although they are of the same nature of those for which specific punishments have not been fixed by the *Quran*. Punishments range from the death penalty for espionage and heresy to flagellation, imprisonment, local banishment, and a variety of fines. Determination of punishment is left to the judge or chief executive, who can vary the punishment according to a number of criteria including who has inflicted the crime and upon whom'.

Oxford Islamic Studies Online defines *hadd* as 'Limit or prohibition; pl. *hudud*, punishment fixed in the Quran and hadith for crimes considered to be against the rights of God. The six crimes for which punishments are fixed are theft (amputation of the hand), illicit sexual relations (death by stoning or one hundred lashes), making unproven accusations of illicit sex (eighty lashes), drinking intoxicants (eighty lashes), apostasy (death or banishment), and highway robbery (death). Strict requirements for evidence (including eyewitnesses) have severely limited the application of *hudud* penalties. Punishment for all other crimes is left to the discretion of the court; these punishments are called *tazir*. [...]'

16 On the Pornography Law, see Pausacker, Chapter 17, this volume.

17 Literally, 'law that lives in society'. The Academic Draft gives the example of the 'crime of living together outside marriage' (Naskah Akademik RUU KUHP 2015: 237).

18 Oemar Seno Adji argued that religion was a fundamental basis of the state and was also adamant that an article on religious vilification should be included in the Indonesian Criminal Code (Ropi 2017: 120).

19 All drafts of the KUHP and the Academic Draft (*Naskah Akademik*) are from the National Alliance for the Reform of the Criminal Code (Aliansi Nasional Reformasi KUHP) website: http://reformasikuhp.org/r-kuhp/. The alliance is composed of a number of legal NGOs and advocacy groups, such as Walhi (Wahana Lingkungan Hidup Indonesia, Indonesian Forum for the Environment) and Arus Pelangi ('Rainbow Flow', an LGBT advocacy group).

20 Constitutional Court Decision No. 46/PUU-XIV/2016. AILA means 'big family' in Arabic (Hermawan 2016).

21 Article 284 of the Criminal Code states that extra-marital sex is an offence in Indonesia but a person can only be prosecuted at the request of the spouse and the request must be accompanied by a request for divorce.

22 The four judges in the minority who decided in favour of the AILA petition were: Dr Anwar Usman, Prof. Dr Arief Hidayat, Dr Wahiduddin Adams, and Prof. Dr Aswanto. The judges in the majority against the petition were Prof. Dr Maria Farida Indrati, I Dewa Gede Palguna, Dr Suhartoyo, Dr Manahan Sitompul, and Saldi Isra.

23 Most FPI branches are coordinated centrally, but FPI Surakarta (Central Java) claims to operate independently of the Jakarta branch (Jahroni 2008: 50; Wilson 2006: 283).

24 For further information see Blatt (1982); Boellstorff (2007: 104); Oetomo (1981).

25 On 9 August 1980, Governor Tjokropranolo signed Governor of Jakarta Letter (Surat Gubernur DKI Jakarta) No. 3554/VII/1980, which forbade the holding of Puteri Indonesia (Indonesian Princess) contests and the sending of beauty queens overseas. Achmad Tirtosudiro, the Director General of Tourism, issued a similar ban in Letter (Surat) No. 142/D.1/VI/1981 (FPI 2005).

26 See video at: www.youtube.com/watch?v=dYF10YZMXxc.

27 See Pausacker, Chapter 17 of this volume, for a discussion of the labelling of 'immoral' activities as 'Western'.

28 See USAID webpage, www.usaid.gov/asia-regional/being-lgbt-asia, for further details of the initiative.

29 The *Nawa Cita* is available at: https://polmas.wordpress.com/2014/09/20/visi-misi-dan-program-aksi-pemerintahan-joko-widodo-jusuf-kalla-2014–2019/

30 Only eight of the accused attended the trial but it was understood that all ten on trial were convicted (Associated Press 2017; Agence France Press 2017).

31 North Jakarta Court Decisions Nos. 852, 853 and 854/Pid.Sus/2017/PN.JKT. UTR, 14 December 2017. The Chief Prosecutor was Robertino Fedrik Adhar Syaripuddin (usually known by his two middle names), who was also one of the prosecutors in the Ahok case (Sumandoyo, 2016; and see Peterson, Chapter 15, this volume). The judge chairing the panel of judges was Judge Pinta Uli Boru Tarigan, who had sentenced a fifteen- and sixteen-year old to four months' prison for naked table-top dancing, and who had been criticised by Human Rights Watch for her poor treatment of Ahmadis, an Islamic sect (Hutton, 2017; Pausacker, 2014: 98), both decisions likely influenced by her conservative religious values.

32 I have been unable to find any evidence that this case has gone to trial.

33 https://twitter.com/espraszz/status/1051136168169943040.

34 These included many famous brands, such as iphone, apple, Google, Microsoft, Yahoo, Visa, Mastercard and Nike.

35 https://twitter.com/rio_damar/status/1050547808531406848.

36 Indonesia inserted a new chapter, XA, based on the Universal Declaration of Human Rights, into the Indonesian Constitution in 2000. See Robet and Primaldhi 2019. Article 28I(2) of the Constitution states that every person shall have the right to be free from discriminatory treatment on any grounds whatsoever and shall have the right to protection from such discriminatory treatment.

References

429 Magazine 2013. 'Letter from Indonesia: I'm Gay, I'm Not a Product of the West, and I'm Not Alone', 9 March http://fourtwonine.com/2013/03/09/1635-letter-from-indonesia-i-m-gay-i-m-not-a-product-of-the-west-and-i-m-not-alone/

Adams, Julia 1996. 'Principals and Agents, Colonialists and Company Men: The Decay of Colonial Control in the Dutch East Indies', *American Sociological Review* 61(1): 12–28

Agence France Presse 2017. 'North Jakarta Court Jails Men for Two Years over "Gay Sex Party"', 18 December www.thejakartapost.com/news/2017/12/18/north-jakarta-court-jails-men-for-two-years-over-gay-sex-party.html

Associated Press 2017. 'Indonesia Sentences Gay Club Workers to 2–3 Years in Prison', *New York Daily News*, 15 December www.nydailynews.com/newswires/news/world/indonesia-sentences-gay-club-workers-2-3-years-prison-article-1.3699368

A'yun, Rafiqa Qurrata 2017. 'AILA's Unsuccessful Petition: A Narrow Escape from Overcriminalisation', *Indonesia at Melbourne*, 19 December https://indonesiaatmelbourne.unimelb.edu.au/ailas-unsuccessful-petition-a-narrow-escape-from-overcriminalisation/

BBC 2017. 'Pengusiran "Terduga Lesbian": Antara Ekspresi Gender, Asumsi, dan Pemberitaan Media', 7 September www.bbc.com/indonesia/trensosial-41170875

Bhinneka 2010. 'Kronologi Pembubaran Paksa Konferensi ILGA', vol. 6, May: 2–8

Blatt, Emily 1982. 'Wadam and Bisu: Male Transexualism and Homsexuality in Indonesia', *Gay Community News* 4(6): 26–27, July

Bloemenberg, Marieke 2011. 'Being Clean is Being Strong: Policing Cleanliness and Gay Vices in the Netherlands Indies in the 1930s', in C. (Kees) Dijk and Jean Gelman Taylor (eds.), *Cleanliness and Culture*. Leiden: KITLV, pp. 117–45

Boellstorff, Tom 2004a. 'The Emergence of Political Homophobia in Indonesia: Masculinity and National Belonging', *Ethnos* 69(4): 465–86

Boellstorff, Tom 2004b. 'Playing Back the Nation: Waria, Indonesian Transvestites', *Cultural Anthropology* 19(2): 159–95

Boellstorff, Tom 2005. *The Gay Archipelago: Sexuality and Nation in Indonesia*. Princeton NJ: Princeton University Press

Boellstorff, Tom 2007. *A Coincidence of Desires: Anthropology, Queer Studies, Indonesia*. Durham NC: Duke University Press

Boomgaard, Peter 2012. 'Male–Male Sex, Bestiality and Incest in the Early-Modern Indonesian Archipelago: Perceptions and Penalties', in Raquel A. G. Reyes and William G. Clarence Smith (eds.), *Sexual Diversity in Asia, c. 600–1950*. London and New York: Routledge, pp. 141–60

Bowen, John R. 2013. 'Contours of Sharia in Indonesia', in Mirjam Künkler and Alfred Stepan (eds.), *Democracy and Islam in Indonesia*. New York: Columbia University Press

Butt, Simon and Lindsey, Tim 2018. *Indonesian Law*. Oxford: Oxford University Press

Carey, Peter and Houben, Vincent 1987. 'Spirited Srikandhis and Sly Sumbadras: The Social, Political and Economic Role of Women at the Central Javanese Courts in the 18th and Early 19th Centuries', in Elsbeth Locher-Scholten and Anke Neihof (eds.), *Indonesian Women in Focus: Past and Present Notions*. Dordrecht: Foris, pp. 12–42

Child, Ben 2010. 'Gay Film Festival Attacked by Masked Islamic Protestors', *The Guardian*, 29 September www.theguardian.com/film/2010/sep/29/gay-film-festival-jakarta-attacked

Coconuts Jakarta 2017. 'Former Constitutional Court Judge Patrialis Akbar Sentenced to 8 Years in Prison for Accepting Bribe', 4 September https://coconuts.co/jakarta/news/former-constitutional-court-judge-patrialis-akbar-sentenced-8-years-prison-accepting-bribe/

Coconuts Jakarta 2018. 'Indonesian Mayor Cancels Color Run Event over Suspicions Rainbow Theme Might "Represent LGBT"', 30 October https://coconuts.co/jakarta/news/indonesian-mayor-cancels-color-run-event-suspicions-rainbow-theme-might-represent-lgbt/

Copland, Simon 2017. 'Threats, Violence, Hope: What It's Like to be a Gay Activist in Indonesia', *SBS*, 30 May www.sbs.com.au/topics/sexuality/agenda/article/2017/05/30/threats-violence-hope-what-its-be-gay-activist-indonesia

Da Costa, Agustinus Beo and Kapoor, Kanupriya 2017. 'Indonesia Court Rejects Petition to Bar Consensual Sex outside Marriage', *Reuters*, 14 December www.reuters.com/article/us-indonesia-court-adultery/indonesia-court-rejects-petition-to-bar-consensual-sex-outside-marriage-idUSKBN1E80BI

Davies, Sharyn Graham 2010. *Gender Diversity in Indonesia: Sexuality, Islam and Queer Selves*. London and New York: Routledge

Festiani, Satya and Sasmita, Ira 2013. 'House Picks Arief Hidayat as Next Chief of Constitutional Court', 4 March http://en.republika.co.id/berita/en/national-politics/17/10/12/en/national-politics/13/03/04/mj595y-house-picks-arief-hidayat-as-next-chief-of-constitutional-court

FPI (Front Pembela Islam) 2005. 'Surat untuk Presiden tentang Miss Universe', 27 June www.fpi.or.id/artikel.asp?oy=sik-16

Frontline Defenders 2017. 'Attacks on LGBT Rights Defenders Escalating in Indonesia'. Dublin/Brussels: Frontline Defenders, December www.frontlinedefenders.org/en/statement-report/report-attacks-lgbt-rights-defenders-escalating-indonesia

Graham, Sharyn 2001. 'Sulawesi's Fifth Gender', *Inside Indonesia*, no. 66, April-June www.insideindonesia.org/sulawesis-fifth-gender-2

Graham, Sharyn 2002. 'Sex, Gender, and Priests in South Sulawesi, Indonesia', *IIAS Newsletter*, no. 29, November https://iias.asia/sites/default/files/IIAS_NL29_27.pdf

Harkins, Jessica; Pawas, Zaky; and Lutfia, Ismira 2010. 'FPI Browbeats "Liberal Infidels" over Hosting Gay Film Festival', *The Jakarta Globe*, 29 September www.thejakartaglobe.com/home/fpi-browbeats-liberal-infidels-over-hosting-gay-film-festival/398628

Harvey, Adam and Guillanno, Archicco 2018. 'Indonesian Police "Re-educate" Transgender Beauty Workers to "Yell like Men" after Public Humiliation in Raids', 4 February www.abc.net.au/news/2018-02-03/indonesian-police-re-educate-transgender-beauty-workers/9391972

Hegarty, Ben and Thajib, Ferdiansyah 2016. 'A Dispensable Threat', *Inside Indonesia*, no. 124, April-June www.insideindonesia.org/a-dispensable-threat

Hermawan, Ary 2016. 'Commentary: Why AILA is a Bigger Threat to Freedom than the FPI', *The Jakarta Post*, 30 August www.thejakartapost.com/news/2016/08/30/commentary-why-aila-is-a-bigger-threat-to-freedom-than-the-fpi.html

Hidayana, Irwan Martua 2015. 'Does the Fatwa on Homosexuals in Indonesia Matter?', *The Conversation*, 2 April https://theconversation.com/does-the-fatwa-on-homosexuals-in-indonesia-matter-39531

HRW (Human Rights Watch) 2010. 'Policing Morality: Abuses in the Application of Sharia in Aceh, Indonesia', December www.hrw.org/sites/default/files/reports/indonesia1210WebVersionToPost.pdf

HRW 2016. 'These Political Games Ruin Our Lives: Indonesia's LGBT Community under Threat' www.hrw.org/sites/default/files/report_pdf/indonesia0816_web_2.pdf

HRW 2018. '"Scared in Public and Now No Privacy": Human Rights and Public Health Impacts of Indonesia's Anti-LGBT Moral Panic', January www.hrw.org/report/2018/07/01/scared-public-and-now-no-privacy/human-rights-and-public-health-impacts-indonesias

Huis, Stijn Van and Wirastri, Theresia Dyah 2012. 'Muslim Marriage Registration in Indonesia: Revised Marriage Registration Laws Cannot Overcome Compliance Flaws', *Australian Journal of Asian Law* 13(1): 1–17

Hutton, Jeffrey 2017. 'Indonesia's Crackdown on Gay Men Moves from Bars into the Home', *The New York Times*, 20 December

Izharuddin, Alicia 2013. 'Same-sex Intimacies in Syariffudin's *Mairil* and the Queering of Authenticity', *Inter-Asia Cultural Studies*, 14(4): 538–50

Jahroni, Jajang 2008. *Defending the Majesty of Islam: Indonesia's Front Pembela Islam, 1998–2003*. Chiang Mai: Asian Muslim Action Network/Silkworm Books.

The Jakarta Post 2005b. 'FPI Quizzes Sutiyoso's Stand', 5 July http://asia-pacific-action.org/southeastasia/indonesia/netnews/2005/ind_26v9.htm

The Jakarta Post 2010. 'FPI Radicals Remain Free after Assault', 4 May www.asia-pacific-solidarity.net/southeastasia/indonesia/netnews/2010/ind17v14.htm

The Jakarta Post 2016. 'Kalla Requests UNDP to Not Fund LGBT Groups', *The Jakarta Post*, 15 February www.thejakartapost.com/news/2016/02/15/kalla-requests-undp-not-fund-lgbt-groups.html

The Jakarta Post 2017. 'Viral Video Uploader Who Accused Brothers of Being Lovers Apologizes' 28 December www.thejakartapost.com/news/2017/12/27/viral-video-uploader-who-accused-brothers-of-being-lovers-apologizes.html

Jauhola, Marjaana 2013. *Post-Tsunami Reconstruction in Indonesia: Negotiating Normativity through Gender Mainstreaming in Aceh*. London and New York: Routledge

Katjasungkana, Nursyahbani and Wieringa, Saskia 2016. *Creeping Criminalisation: Mapping of Indonesia's National Laws and Regional Regulations that Violate Human Rights of Women and LGBTIQ People*. New York: OutRight Action International www.outrightinternational.org/sites/default/files/Creeping Criminalisation-eng.pdf

Knight, Kyle 2018. 'Indonesia's Anti-LGBT Drive Should Concern All Asia: Panic over Sexuality Puts Reputation for Tolerance on the Line', HRW, 20 February www.hrw.org/news/2018/02/20/indonesias-anti-lgbt-drive-should-concern-all-asia (first published in Nikkei Asian Review)

Kortschak, Irfan 2007. 'Defining Waria: Indonesia's Transgendered Community is Raising its Profile', *Inside Indonesia*, no. 90, October-December www.insideindonesia.org/weekly-articles/defining-waria

Lamb, Kate 2017. 'Why LGBT Hatred Suddenly Spiked in Indonesia', *The Guardian*, 22 February www.theguardian.com/global-development-professionals-network/2017/feb/22/why-lgbt-hatred-suddenly-spiked-in-indonesia

Leandha, Mei 2017. 'Gara-gara Ciuman, 5 Perempuan di Medan Diusir Warga', *Kompas,* 8 June https://regional.kompas.com/read/2017/06/08/21020001/gara-gara.ciuman.5.perempuan.di.medan.diusir.warga

Liang, Jamison 2010. 'Homophobia on the Rise', *Inside Indonesia*, no. 100, April-June www.insideindonesia.org/weekly-articles-100-apr-june-2010/homophobia-on-the-rise-14061863

Lindsey, Tim 2012. *Islam, Law and the State in Southeast Asia. Vol I: Indonesia.* London: IB Tauris.

Mader, D. H. and Hekma, Gert 2016. 'Same Sex, Different Ages: On Pederasty in Gay History', in Thomas K Hubbard and Beert Verstraete (eds.), *Censoring Sex Research: The Debate over Male Intergenerational Relations*. London/New York, pp. 161–92

Mahkamah Konstitusi 2009b. 'Ringkasan Permohonan Perkara Nomor 17/PUU-VI/2009 tentang Undang-undang Pornografi (Kemajemukan Budaya yang Terlanggar)' www.mahkamahkonstitusi.go.id/Resume/resume_sidang_perkara%2017%20%20pornografi.pdf

Mahkamah Konstitusi 2009c. 'Ringkasan Permohonan Perkara Nomor 23/PUU-VII/2009 tentang Undang-undang Pornografi (Kemajemukan Budaya yang Terlanggar)'. Jakarta, Mahkamah Konstitusi, www.mahkamahkonstitusi.go.id/Resume/resume_sidang_perkara%2023%20%20pornografi.pdf

Maimunah 2008. 'Indonesia's Q! Film Festival', *Inside Indonesia*, no. 93, July-September www.insideindonesia.org/indonesia-s-q-film-festival

Mann, Tim 2016. 'Q&A: Dede Oetomo on the LGBT Panic', *Indonesia at Melbourne*, 17 March

Meer, Theo van der 2008. 'Eugenic and Sexual Folklores and the Castration of Sex Offenders in the Netherlands', *Studies in History and Philosophy of Biological and Biomedical Sciences* 39(2): 195–204

Muthmainnah, Yulianti 2016. 'LGBT Human Rights in Indonesian Policies', *Indonesian Feminist Journal* 4(1): 13–29

Nagtegaal, Luc 1983/84. 'Halzenkussers en Hermafrodieten: Nederlands-Javaans Cultuurcontact voor 1900', *Jambatan* 2: 3–20

Norton, Rictor 2011. 'Newspaper Reports, The Dutch Purge of Homosexuals, 1730', *Homosexuality in Eighteenth-Century England: A Sourcebook*. updated 13 September 2000; reorganized and expanded 21 July 2002; updated 17 November 2011 www.rictornorton.co.uk/eighteen/1730news.htm

Nurita, Dewi 2017. 'Pakar: KUHP Tidak Tepat Dikenakan dalam Kasus Gay di Spa Harmoni', *Tempo*, 9 October https://metro.tempo.co/read/1023015/pakar-kuhp-tidak-tepat-dikenakan-dalam-kasus-gay-di-spa-harmoni

Oetomo, Dédé 1981. 'Impressions of a Night Parade of Perwakos Actors', *Liberty*, 18 July, no. 1454. Reprinted in *Gays in Indonesia: Selected Articles from the Print Media*. North Carlton: Translation Group, 1984: 23–24

Oetomo, Dédé 2001. 'Gay Men in the Reformasi Era', *Inside Indonesia*, no. 66, April-June www.insideindonesia.org/edition-66-apr-jun-2001/gay-men-in-the-reformasi-era-3007481

Okezone 2017. 'Kasus Gay di Kelapa Gading Akan Naik ke Meja Hijau', *Metro*, 8 August https://metro.sindonews.com/read/1228328/170/kasus-gay-di-kelapa-gading-akan-naik-ke-meja-hijau-1502186139

Oxford Islamic Studies Online. www.oxfordislamicstudies.com

Pausacker, Helen 2013. 'Morality and the Nation: Law, Pornography and Indonesia's Islamic Defenders Front', PhD thesis, Melbourne Law School, the University of Melbourne

Pausacker, Helen 2014. 'Sanctions against Popstars… and Politicians? Indonesia's 2008 Pornography Law and its Aftermath', in Bernhard Platzdasch and Johan Saravanamuttu (eds.), *Religious Minorities in Muslim-Majority Localities of Southeast Asia: Areas of Toleration and Conflict*. Singapore: Institute for Southeast Asian Studies, ISEAS, pp. 89–112

Peacock, James L. 1987. *Rites of Modernization: Symbolic and Social Aspects of Indonesian Proletarian Drama, with a New Afterword.* Chicago: University of Chicago Press

Platt, Maria 2009. 'Not Just a Piece of Paper', *Inside Indonesia*, no. 97, July-September www.insideindonesia.org/not-just-a-piece-of-paper

Pojoksatu 2017. 'Sekuriti Bagikan Honor Penari Telanjang, Ratusan Gay Ditangkap Saat Pesta, Polisi Temukan…', 22 May http://pojoksatu.id/news/berita-nasional/2017/05/22/sekuriti-bagikan-honor-penari-telanjang-ratusan-gay-ditangkap-saat-pesta-polisi-temukan/

Reuters 2018. 'Indonesia's Aceh Resumes Public Caning Despite Pledge to Curb Access', 13 July www.reuters.com/article/us-indonesia-aceh-caning/indonesias-aceh-resumes-public-caning-despite-pledge-to-curb-access-idUSKBN1K31N1

Ricklefs, M. C. 1997. 'Islam and the Reign of Pakubuwana II, 1726–49', in Peter G. Riddell and Tony Street (eds.), *Islam: Essays on Scripture, Thought and Society: A Festschrift in Honour of Anthony H. Johns*. Leiden, New York, Köln: Brill

Robet, Robertus and Primaldhi, Alfindra 2019. 'Do Indonesians Still Care about Human Rights?', *Indonesia at Melbourne*, 8 February https://indonesiaatmelbourne.unimelb.edu.au/do-indonesians-still-care-about-human-rights/

Ropi, Ismatu 2017. *Religion and Regulation in Indonesia.* Singapore: Springer Nature

Safitri, Dian Maya 2013. 'The Politics of Piety in the Pondok Pesantren Khusus Waria Al-Fatah Senin-Kamis Yogyakarta', in Jajat Burhanudin and Kees van Dijk (eds.), *Islam in Indonesia: Contrasting Images and Interpretations*. Amsterdam: Amsterdam University Press, pp. 91–107

Saputra, Andi 2017. 'Nasib LGBT di KUHP Ditentukan MK Esok', *Detik News*, 13 December https://news.detik.com/berita/3767382/nasib-lgbt-di-kuhp-ditentukan-mk-esok

Sufa, Theresia and Setiawati, Indah 2010. 'FPI Sabotages Transgender Workshop', *The Jakarta Post*, 1 May www.thejakartapost.com/news/2010/05/01/fpi-sabotages-transgender-workshop.html

Sumandoyo, Arbi 2016. 'Rekam Jejak Empat Jaksa Penuntut Ahok', 13 December https://tirto.id/rekam-jejak-empat-jaksa-penuntut-ahok-b9Qy

Sundaryani, Fedina S. 2016. 'NU Joins Anti-LGBT Bandwagon with Edict', *The Jakarta Post*, 27 February www.thejakartapost.com/news/2016/02/27/nu-joins-anti-lgbt-bandwagon-with-edict.html

Suparman, Fana; Andriyanto, Heru; and Prasetyo, Eko 2017. 'Constitutional Court Judge Patrialis Akbar Named Suspect in Graft Case', *The Jakarta Globe*, 27 January http://jakartaglobe.id/news/constitutional-court-judge-patrialis-akbar-named-suspect-graft-case/

Suryakusuma, Julia 2016. 'View Point: State Hysteria: Leading the Nation with Homophobia', *The Jakarta Post*, 24 February www.thejakartapost.com/news/2016/02/24/view-point-state-hysteria-leading-nation-with-homophobia.html

Suwito, Hendro 1984. 'What Manner of People Are These?', *The Jakarta Post*, 9 January. Reprinted in *Gays in Indonesia: Selected Articles from the Print Media.* North Carlton: Translation Group, pp. 27–8

Taipei Times 2005. 'Indignant Islamists Crash Transvestite Beauty Contest', 28 June www.taipeitimes.com/News/world/archives/2005/06/28/2003261210

Tehusijarana, Karina M. 2018. '#UninstallGojek Trends after Executive Shows Support for LGBT Community', *The Jakarta Post*, 14 October www.thejakartapost.com/news/2018/10/14/uninstallgojek-trends-after-executive-shows-support-for-lgbt-community.html

Tejo, Amir 2010. 'Indonesian Radicals "Raid" Gay Conference', *The Jakarta Globe*, 27 March www.thejakartaglobe.com/home/indonesian-radicals-raid-gay-conference/366141

Tilemann, Hal 2016. 'Indonesia's Long Wait for its Own Criminal Code', *Indonesia at Melbourne*, 10 November

Wijaya, Megawati 2010. 'Glad to be Gay in Indonesia', *Asia Times*, 23 September www.atimes.com/atimes/Southeast_Asia/LI23Ae01.html

Wilson, Ian Douglas (2006) 'Continuity and Change: The Changing Contours of Organised Violence in post-New Order Indonesia', *Critical Asian Studies* 38(2): 265–97

Yosephine, Liza 2016a. 'Komnas HAM Slams Vilification of LGBT by Officials', *The Jakarta Post*, 5 February www.thejakartapost.com/news/2016/02/05/komnas-ham-slams-vilification-lgbt-officials.html

Yosephine, Liza 2016b. 'Indonesian Psychiatrists Label LGBT as Mental Disorders', *The Jakarta Post*, 24 February www.thejakartapost.com/news/2016/02/24/indonesian-psychiatrists-label-lgbt-mental-disorders.html

Legislation

National laws

Wetboek van Strafrecht Nederlandsch Indie, 1918, Criminal Code of the Dutch East Indies

Criminal Code (*Kitab Undang-Undang Hukum Pidana*, KUHP: Law No. 1 of 1946 as amended by Law No. 27 of 1999 on the Indonesian Criminal Code)

Law No. 1 of 1974 on Marriage

Law No. 23 of 2002 on Child Protection

Law No. 23 of 2004 on the Elimination of Domestic Violence

Law No. 11 of 2008 on Electronic Information and Transactions (amended by Law No 19 of 2016)

Law No. 44 of 2008 on Pornography

Regional regulations

Aceh: Regional Regulation No 23 of 2001 on the Social Organisation and Social Services Administration for the Special Region of Aceh (Susunan Organisasi dan Tata Kerja Dinas Sosial Propinsi Dearah Istimewa Aceh), http://jdih.setjen.kemendagri.go.id/files/P_ACEH_23_2001.pdf

Jakarta: Regional Regulation No. 8 of 2007 of Jakarta on Public Order

Kalimantan, East: Regional Regulation No. 2 of 2007 of Kabupaten Berau on the Prohibition of Prostitution

Kalimantan, East: Regional Regulation No. 21 of 2000 of Tarakan on Indecent Acts

Kalimantan, South: Regional Regulation No. 10 of 2007 of Banjar Local on Public Order

Lampung: Regional Regulation No. 15 of 2002 of Bandar Lampung on the Prohibition of Prostitution and Immoral Acts

Lampung: Regional Regulation No. 7 of 2001 of Way Kanan on the Prohibition of Prostitution and Immoral Acts

Lampung: Regional Regulation No. 11 of 2012 of Tulang Bawang Barat on the Prohibition of Immoral Acts, Prostitution and Immorality

Lampung: Regional Regulation No. 4 of 2004 of Lampung Selatan on the Prohibition of Prostitution, Immoral Acts and Gambling and the Prevention of Sinful Acts Lampung: Regional Regulation of No. 7 of 2006 of Lampung Utara

Lampung: Regional Regulation No. 7 of 2003 of Mandailing Natal on the Prevention and Eradication of Societal Diseases Juncto (in Relation to) Regional Regulation No. 32 of 2007

Lampung: Regional Regulation No. 6 of 2003 of Mandailing Natal on Clothing for Muslim Men and Women

Lampung: Regional Regulation No. 32 of2008 seri C No. 2 of Labuhanbatu on the Prohibition of Immoral Acts, Vagrancy and Beggars

Lampung: Regional Regulation No. 25 of 2007 of Serdang Bedagai on the Prohibition of Immoral Acts, Vagrants and Beggars

West Sumatra: Regional Regulation No. 9 of 2010 of Padang Panjang on the Prevention, Elimination and Repression of Social Diseases

West Sumatra: Regional Regulation No. 2 of 2004 of Padang Pariaman on Prevention, Repression and Eradication of Immorality

South Sulawesi: Regional Regulation No. 5 of 2003 of Bulukumba on Muslim Clothing

South Sulawesi: Regional Regulation No. 16 of 2005 of Maros on Muslim Clothing

South Sulawesi: Regional Regulation No. 9 of 2004 of Luwu Timur on Public Order

South Sumatra: Regional Regulation No. 3 of 2003 of Lahat on the Prohibition of Prostitution and Indecent Acts

South Sumatra: Regional Regulation No. 23 of 2006 of Ogan Komering on the Eradication of Immorality

South Sumatra: Regional Regulation of Muara Enim No. 3 of 2005 juncto (in relation to) Regional Regulation No. 13A of 1989 and Regional Regulation No. 14 of 1993 on the Prevention of Immoral Acts

South Sumatra: Regulation No. 13 of 2002 on Combating Immorality in the Province of South Sumatra

South Sumatra: Local Regulation of Palembang No. 2 of 2004 on the Eradication of Prostitution

Jogjakarta: Regional Regulation No. 5 of 2007 of Bantul on the Prohibition of Prostitution

West Java: Regional Regulation No. 12 of 2009 of Tasikmalaya on the Development of Community Life Values Based on the Teachings of Islam and Societal Social Norms

Court decisions

Constitutional Court Decision No. 17-PUU-VII/2009 on the 2008 Pornography Law

Constitutional Court Decision No. 46-PUU-XIV/2016 on the Criminal Code (LGBT-related sections)

North Jakarta District Court Decision No. 852/Pid.Sus/2017/PN.JKT.UTR

North Jakarta District Court Decision No. 853/Pid.Sus/2017/PN.JKT.UTR

North Jakarta District Court Decision No. 854/Pid.Sus/2017/PN.JKT.UTR

17 Habib Rizieq Shihab and Ariel Peterpan

Law, morality and the digital era

Helen Pausacker

In 2006, FPI (Front Pembela Islam, the Islamic Defenders Front) and other conservative Muslims campaigned ardently for the introduction of a national Pornography Law in Indonesia and were active in the lead-up to the passing of the Law. When the first issue of Indonesian *Playboy* – a toned-down version with no nudes – was published in April 2006, FPI ripped up copies of the magazine and burned it. FPI members also threw stones at the *Playboy* office in South Jakarta, breaking the windows (CBC 2006). In May 2006, FPI was also prominent when tens of thousands rallied across the country in favour of the pornography bill (AFP 2006). Around this time, Habib Rizieq Shihab, the head of FPI, commented:

> Right now, the most pressing danger is that pornography is destroying people's morals, drugs are also destroying the younger generation, gambling and alcohol also destroy our way of life.
>
> (Compass 2006)

FPI is one of the most notorious hardline Islamist groups in Indonesia. It was established in August 1998 by Rizieq Shihab, with backing from some politicians, senior military and police figures. It began as vigilante organisation running a criminal stand-over racket. However, it soon sought legitimacy by acting as a form of moral police, targeting small businesses and entertainment venues, before expanding to become a hardline political pressure group, with much online activity. It is noted for its ability to mobilise large mobs and deploy violence. FPI is estimated to have about 100,000 members, with branches in twenty-two provinces. It is perhaps best known for its paramilitary wing, Laskar Pembela Islam (Islamic Defenders Militia).

As a result of protests by FPI and others, in 2006, Erwin Arnada, the editor of *Playboy*, faced criminal charges under art. 282 of the Criminal Code (which prohibits public display, broadcasting or publishing of pornographic material). About fifty members of FPI attended Erwin Arnada's initial hearings and shouted slogans such as '*Allahu Akbar*' (God is Great), '*Playboy* damages morals', 'Torture in the grave' (*Ada siksa kubur*),[1] and even 'Porno Judge' (*Hakim porno*) (Gatra 2006). Later, protestors from FPI continued their demonstrations outside the court, joined by two other groups. When Andhara Early (a model from the first issue of *Playboy*) appeared as a witness, protesters, including FPI (now all banished to outside the court), yelled abuse at her, calling her a 'cheap prostitute' who would go to hell, saying they hoped her daughter would be raped. Scuffles broke out between police and the demonstrators (Patung 2006).

When pop star Nazril Irham, a.k.a. Ariel, lead singer of the popular boy band, Peterpan, was placed on trial in 2011, facing similar charges of pornography (under the 2008 Pornography Law[2] and the 2008 Electronic Information and Transactions Law[3]), he received similarly rough treatment from members of hardline Islamic groups, including FPI and the Gerakan Reformis Islam (Islamic Reformist Movement). They pelted the armoured police car that brought Ariel to court with rotten eggs (Hardi 2011).

At the point that members of FPI protested at Erwin Arnada's and Ariel Peterpan's trials, neither had yet been convicted. Given the attitudes towards pornography and immorality by FPI in general, and Rizieq Shihab, in particular, it was an ironic surprise that Rizieq Shihab himself was eventually charged with pornography – although it was less surprising that FPI stood by him, protesting his innocence.

In this chapter, I examine why hardline Muslims were interested in introducing a national Pornography Law, given there were already prohibitions against pornography in the Criminal Code. I will then briefly outline the Pornography Law and the degree to which it overlaps with the two existing national laws – the Criminal Code and the 2008 Law on Electronic Information and Transactions – as well as numerous regional laws. I then examine the cases of Rizieq Shihab and other Islamist politicians and activists accused of violating pornography prohibitions, contrasting these with the case of Ariel Peterpan. In the Conclusion, I discuss whether Rizieq Shihab did, in fact, violate the Pornography Law and whether the Pornography Law has achieved its aims.

Why were hardline Islamists interested in introducing a national Pornography Law?

The introduction of the 2008 Law on Pornography can be seen an example of the increasing influence of Indonesian conservative Muslim groups.[4] The influence of conservative Muslim groups could be argued to be greater than their numbers, as is true of the Christian Right in the United States. Conservative Muslims in Indonesia have often united to call on the state to introduce laws – and their sanctions – to bring about the standards of morality that they desire, in other words, they use the Pornography Law as a means to institute conservative Islamic norms by legal means. In doing so, they increase their own political power. In the case of the Pornography Law, this coalition of Islamic groups, included MUI (Majelis Ulama Indonesia or Indonesian Council of Ulama)[5] and FPI, but also more mainstream groups, all of which were engaged in lobbying for the introduction of the Law. PKS

(Partai Keadilan Sejahtera, the Justice and Prosperity Party), for example, talked in terms of the Pornography Law saving 'future generations from moral depravity' (PKS 2006).

Such efforts by conservative Muslims to introduce legal enforcement of morality have not gone uncontested. Progressive Muslims, together with ethnic and religious minorities, tend to view morality and religious belief as a personal issue, and are concerned that conservative Muslim views of morality should not dominate the whole society. Progressive Muslims formed a broad coalition, which fought against the Pornography Bill, focusing particularly on the idea of 'porno-action'. Ultimately, however, they were unsuccessful and the Law was passed.

Religion and pornography in former eras

During the *Reformasi* era (1998–), the fight against pornography became tied to religion, and pornography has been used by conservative Islamic groups as a means to assert their values. This has not always been the case. During Guided Democracy (1959–66, the later part of the Old Order, that is, Soekarno's rule) and the New Order (1966–98), Indonesia was under more autocratic leadership. Decisions tended to be top-down and administered by state officials loyal to the regime, rather than being driven by members of the community protesting about issues, and demanding action from the state, or agitating to change laws. Islamist groups were marginalised during both the Old Order and the first part of the New Order,[6] so it is not surprising that the state's definition of pornography tended toward the secular, rather than being based on religious norms.

Pornography cases during these periods were predominantly focused on the print media. One of the main differences in the treatment of pornography in films and print media at this time is that films were generally censored prior to distribution, whereas print media seen to violate the law was usually sanctioned after publication. [7]

Changing terms for pornography

The common usage of terms for pornography in Indonesia has also changed over time, although terms are not used exclusively in any one period. These terms have had both religious and secular flavours and have had their origins in Dutch, Arabic, English or Malay languages, depending on the emphasis of that particular period. The term *cabul*, meaning 'immoral, licentious, indecent, outrageous [acts], obscene, dirty, pornographic, lacivious' (Stevens and Schmidgall-Tellings 2010: 172) was most commonly used in the early days of the Old Order.[8] The concern about Western-influenced decadency 'allowed anti-pornography campaigns to cross periodically into other areas of life, such as dress [tight trousers or long-hair for men], popular culture [rock-and-roll] and prostitution' (Lindsay 2011: 179).

Under Guided Democracy, which began on 5 July 1959 with Soekarno's decree returning the country to the 1945 Constitution, the government for some time used *merugikan/merusak akhlak* (damaging morality), *akhlak* being an Arabic religious term, rather than the Malay *cabul* (Ginting 2003: 74–5). This shifted gradually until by the time of the New Order, the most common terms were *melanggar kesopanan* (violating decency) or *melanggar kesusilaan* (violating morality). All of these terms define something by what it is *not* (not decent or not moral), rather than what it is (pornographic). *Melanggar kesusilaan* is also the term used in art. 282 of the KUHP (Kitab Undang-undang Hukum Pidana, Criminal Code) and newspaper reports under the New Order. As Rachim (1977: 39, 42, 44) and Lindsay (2011: 173) comment, this term is a translation of the Dutch terms (*aanstotelijk voor de eerbarheid* and *openbare schennis der eerbarheid*), which is a result of the fact that the KUHP was originally a translation from the Dutch.

The use of the word *pornografi*, a loan-word from English, emerged in the New Order (Lindsay 2011: 177) and is the word incorporated in *Reformasi* era legislation.[9] In the early days of the New Order, pornography was also connected in a rather ambiguous manner to shady left-wing political forces, rather than the Western decadence described above in the Old Order. For example, the judges who tried a case involving short stories published in the newspaper, *Indonesia Djaya*, in October 1966, describe the stories as '*blue film* [term in English] on paper', which 'could produce excesses that could be used by [left-leaning] political guerillas (*gerpol-gerpol*)' (Ginting 2003: 79).

Lindsay (2011: 172) comments that 'in the post-Suharto period [...] the perception of pornography increasingly slips between media and behaviour'. However, given that '*cabul*' in the Old Order had already encompassed a number of meanings, it may be, in reverse, that the new word '*pornografi*' did not encompass all the meanings of '*cabul*', and so the notion of '*pornoaksi*' (porno-action) was created to cover this gap. 'Pornoaksi' is applied to actions deemed 'pornographic'.[10]

Old Order

In the Guided Democracy period, there was just one case of religion being mentioned in a pornography prosecution. This was in the 1963 court case of Chinese-Indonesians Go Tjing Hok and MF Liem Hok Liong, editors of *Liberty* (Surabaya), who, in addition to prison sentences of a month, were asked to apologise to religious leaders offended by an article they had published on prostitution (Lesmana 1995: 16).

In addition, on 12 October 1960, Peperti (Penguasa Perang Tinggi, the Supreme War Authority) issued a regulation that forbade the publication of writing, paintings, photos and pictures that were 'sensational and damaged morality [*akhlak*]'.[11] Shortly afterwards, in December 1960, the Department of Religion also held a seminar entitled 'Religious Elements in the Press', which stated that the press had to work towards forming an 'Indonesian identity' (*kepribadian*) with religious morals (*moral agama*) (Ginting 2003: 75).

Under the Old Order, pornography cases were brought to the courts. Although the government took action against pornography, judges made decisions about whether the accused was guilty and, if so, what their sentence should be. The evidence was openly displayed in court and the defendant had a chance to present a defence (Lesmana 1995: 12).[12]

New Order

During the New Order, there was some attempt to include religious leaders as part of the New Order's Attorney-General's Team on pornography, but religion as a reason for opposing pornography was given no more weight than the general societal problem of youth delinquency.[13] In discussing the issue in the later years of the New Order, academic Lesmana (1995: 17), for example, comments that pornography is a matter that covers 'legal, religious, moral, social and economic factors'.

Although the New Order administration used the law to enforce its views with regard to pornography, this was not always done by taking cases to court, particularly in the case of newspapers and magazines. Instead, the New Order enacted laws that made it essential to obtain a SIT (*Surat Izin Terbit*, Licence to Publish) or, as it was later known, SIUPP (*Surat Izin Usaha Penerbitan Pers* or Licence for a Publishing Firm) to publish a periodical. The Department of Information had the power to withdraw the SIT/SIUPP without trial. Periodicals faced with this arbitrary process either bowed to the demands of the Department of Information and ceased publication voluntarily, or had their SIT/SIUPP withdrawn (although sometimes not without a fight, or at least some comment).

In both the Old Order and the New Order, complaints about pornography were lodged privately, that is, the people complaining were supplicants, and the government then initiated the cases in its own name – the original complainant remained anonymous. During these eras, the state itself (principally, the president and his cronies) achieved a monopoly on power and imposed its own standards on pornography, but each regime still had to establish its power and enforce its regulations. Before Reformasi, Islamist agitation for law reform around the issue of pornography was weak. Islamist organisations rarely pressured the state to take action in particular cases of pornography because these groups were not yet in the position to assert political power, even in relation to matters of morality.

Reformasi

The SIT/SIUPP system was abolished soon after Soeharto fell in 1998.[14] This would have an additional, and perhaps unexpected, consequence for publications. Before the introduction of the Pornography Law, publications could be prosecuted under the 1999 Press Law. Without the possibility of cancelling a publication's SIT/SIUPP, the only way that critics could raise objections to a publication was through a criminal trial – or, at least, the threat of such a trial. This could occur even after the publication had ceased (as in the case of *Playboy*). Ironically, therefore, editors now face personally much heavier sanctions than they did, under Soeharto, when the worst that usually happened was the cancellation of their publishing licence.

In addition, in the Reformasi era, pressure groups such as FPI and PKS found new space to agitate publicly against pornography, and demand the government take action. As under the Old Order, both PKS and FPI clearly identify pornography with the amoral/immoral West, as opposed to the more generalised notion of 'Eastern culture', which is implicitly equated with 'moral' and 'Islamic'. Their use of 'Eastern culture' term makes many questionable assumptions of similarities between Asian countries, when the 'East' is, of course, very disparate, and many Indonesians might have little in common with Chinese, Japanese, Koreans or Thais on many issues, particularly those involving morality. Harding (2008) discusses the frequent use of the terms Eastern/Western in conservative Muslim publications. She comments that:

> The explicit ascription of the West as animal-like, morally depraved, associated with images of disease and illicit contamination (seeping) does not require any description of Indonesian society. Identity theory reveals how the epistemological dichotomy of Self/Other means that by default Indonesians are inherently moral and well-behaved. They only succumb to 'deviant' sexual practices when 'contaminated' by the immoral West.
>
> (Harding 2008: point 12)

By employing this sort of simplistic Western/Eastern dichotomy, FPI and PKS are able to broaden the application of their ideology to the whole of Indonesia, both Muslim and non-Muslim.

Often the offences of pornography reported by groups in the Reformasi era have been much tamer than many of the offences tried during the Old and New Orders, yet the sanctions have generally been higher in the Reformasi era. The 'Sexindo' 1984 calendar, for example, showed six naked women with their genitalia fully displayed. The sentences imposed by the High Court were two weeks' imprisonment, and some received a presidential pardon (Hamzah 1987: 146). Compare this to prison sentences received by people charged with offences of pornography during the Reformasi era (under the Pornography Law and, in the case of Erwin Arnada, under the KUHP), with sentences of up to seven years (see below).

FPI's involvement in opposing pornography has frequently been in coalition with other Islamic groups. In June 2000, for example, FPI members joined hundreds of others to demonstrate outside National Police headquarters, protesting the spread of pornography and urging the police to take action (Laksamana.net 2001).[15]

Support among conservative Muslims for the Pornography Bill had already become strong in 2001, when MUI issued its *Fatwa* [Islamic legal Opinion] on Pornography and Porno-action, discussed in the next section. This fatwa, in turn, influenced regional regulations (*peraturan daerah, perda*)[16] dealing with pornography and served as a benchmark for conservative Muslims in redrafting the Pornography Bill.

MUI Fatwa on Pornography and Porno-action, 2001

MUI issued Fatwa No. 287 of 2001 on 22 August 2001. Interestingly, the fatwa does not separately define *pornografi* (pornography) or *pornoaksi* (porno-action).[17] Instead, it uses the two concepts as a joint phrase. The fatwa begins with outlining the situation, stating that it takes into consideration (*menimbang*):

1. that **pornography and porno-action** and other similar matters recently have spread freely and been circulated widely in the community [...]
2. that in reality, **pornography and porno-action** have had a negative effect on the Islamic community in particular and the Indonesian nation in general [...]
3. that allowing **pornography and pornoaction** and other similar matters to continue to develop will result in the destruction of the nation [...] (emphasis added)

It could be suggested that this 'normalises' the terms, implying that everyone will understand them, whereas, in fact, the term 'porno-action' was a fairly new concept in Indonesia.

MUI's role during the New Order was typically conveying government policy to Muslim communities (Bruinessen 1990). In the post-Soeharto period, when multiple views were heard in the legislature, the media and on the streets, and multiple parties vied for power, MUI had to find a new role. Rather than being the state's mouthpiece, MUI is now able to influence the state, and is active in issuing its own fatwa and *tausiyah* (recommendations) on a wide variety of social issues, which range from yoga, women's clothing, Islamic sects and food to pornography. The group holds conservative views and its fatwa and tausiyah are often criticised by progressive or nationalist Muslims (Gillespie 2007; Ichwan 2005: 50). Progressive Muslims believe in a more personal approach to one's religion, and their views are therefore more diverse and less formulaic. As neither fatwa nor tausiyah are legally binding on either government or society, the influence of MUI's fatwa and tausiyah now depends on their indirect and long-term influence, and, in particular, whether they are accepted and adopted by the society (Hosen 2003: 169; Ichwan 2005: 71–2). MUI's views are influential, in a large part because of the legacy of the New Order government's support, and the fact that it expressed the 'official line' during that period, thus giving it the appearance of being a state agency, even though it is, in fact, an NGO. The fact that its leadership includes ulama from both NU (Nahdlatul Ulama, literally 'Awakening of Ulama') and Muhammadiyah, Indonesia's two largest Muslim organisations, also contributes to its influence, as a perceived representative and authoritative 'voice' of Indonesian Islam (Hosen 2003: 168).

The definition of pornography in Fatwa No. 287 of 2001, art. 1, describes pornography as depiction of erotic activities, through printed or electronic media:

1. Picturing, directly or indirectly, erotic activities, whether through painting, pictures, writing, voice, advertisements, or through utterances [*ucapan*], either through the printed media or the electronic media, which can arouse sexual desire [*membangkit nafsu birahi*] is forbidden [*haram*].

Showing one's *aurat* (parts of the body that one should not show, according to Islam, see further below) is also forbidden:

2. Allowing aurat to be shown either openly or by wearing tight or see-through clothes with the intention of having a picture taken, whether to be printed or to be viewed [*divisualisasikan*] is forbidden. (art. 2)

In addition, the duplicating, buying or selling of such photos, or even looking at a person who is showing their aurat, either directly or through the wearing of see-through clothing, is prohibited (art. 5). This proved particularly controversial, because the definition of aurat is debated, even among Muslims in Indonesia. The MUI fatwa echoes a reasonably conservative understanding of aurat, defining it as comprising everything except the face, hands and feet for a woman, and body parts from the navel to the knee for a man (Fatwa No. 287 of 2001, art. 7). A smaller and even more conservative minority in Indonesia interprets the proper covering of women's aurat to require wearing a *chador* (long, shapeless, drably-coloured garment), often with socks, gloves and a veil that covers all but the women's eyes (Smith-Hefner 2007: 390). For some, a woman's aurat even includes her voice – and a woman may be told she should lower and slow her voice when praying in mixed company. This is said to be one of the reasons that women usually do not conduct *azan*, the Muslim call to prayer (Hasyim 2006: 149–51). Progressive Muslims, however, quote the Qur'an to show that the requirements are simply for modesty of dress (Parker 2006). In Indonesia, despite the majority Muslim population, the wearing of the *jilbab* (headscarf that covers the head and neck but revealing the face) was not common outside some traditionally devout regions until the early 1990s, when it started to spread through the broader community (Smith-Hefner 2007: 389).

Prohibited 'porno-actions' under the fatwa also include sexual activity outside marriage; being alone with someone of the opposite sex who is not one's *mahram* (a close relative, who one is not allowed to marry, and who therefore can act as a chaperone) (art. 6); and showing one's aurat, directly or through see-through clothes, or showing the curves of one's body through tight-fitting clothes (Arts 7 and 8).

From fatwa to Pornography Law

This fatwa, together with the introduction of regional laws, may well have contributed to the impetus to re-introduce the Pornography Bill. The endorsement by a key Muslim body would have inspired many Muslims to have joined the campaign for the Law. In addition, in 2001, the year the fatwa was passed, Indonesia's oldest (and conservative) women's organisation, Kowani (Kongres Wanita Indonesia, Indonesian Women's Congress), expressed support for a Pornography Bill, which was ratified by Kowani members in 2004 (Maris 2006). In 2001, the national legislature, the DPR (Dewan Perwakilan Rakyat, People's Representative Assembly), issued an instruction to draft a Pornography Bill. Then in 2003, the Minister for Women's Empowerment stated that the Pornography Bill should be based on the MUI Fatwa of 2001.

The exact origins of the 2006 Pornography Bill are difficult to trace. It appears that a number of drafts were produced from 1998 onwards by bodies as various as the Ministry for Women's Empowerment under the Habibie administration; the Ministry of Religion under the Wahid administration; and the staff of the Faculty of Law at the University of Indonesia (Anjani and Ghosh 2006; Sherlock 2008: 162–4).

The 2006 Pornography Bill was hotly debated, with thousands marching in the street both in favour of the Bill and against it. The inclusion of 'porno-action' was one of the key points of contention, with those against the Bill arguing that it was too vague, creating a danger that it could lead to restrictions on activities ranging from wearing traditional, regional costume, kissing one's spouse goodbye at the airport, to censorship of the arts. After a number of revisions, during which the term 'porno-action' was deleted, the 2006 Pornography Bill became the 2008 Pornography Law.

Three national laws dealing with pornography

As a result, there are now three national laws that deal with pornography – the Criminal Code, the Pornography Law, and Law No. 11 of 2008 on Electronic Information and Transactions, each of which is slightly different. This further complicates the understanding of what is legal among both law enforcers and those who wish to obey the law.

Article 282 of the Criminal Code specifies that it is an offence to 'broadcast, display, or post publicly, writing, pictures or things which are known to have contents which violate morality [...]'.

Law No. 11 of 2008 on Electronic Information and Transactions was passed on 21 April 2008, before the passing of the Pornography Law later that year.

Article 27(1) of this law states that it is forbidden to 'knowingly and without authority distribute and/or transmit and/or cause to be accessible electronic information and/or electronic records with contents that violate morality (*melanggar kesusilaan*)', wording that is very similar to the Criminal Code. Later amendments to the Law have not clarified exactly what is considered to 'violate morality'.[18]

What is illegal under the Pornography Law?

Even though the controversial term *pornoaksi* was deleted in the passage from bill to law, the definition of 'pornography' in art. 1 in the 2008 Law is broad and includes, for example, movements of the body and performances in public that violate the moral norms (*kesusilaan*) of the society. It is, therefore, still possible to prosecute people for crimes of 'porno-action', even if the word is absent from the Law.

Article 4

(1) Everyone is prohibited from producing, making, reproducing, duplicating, circulating, broadcasting, importing, exporting, offering, selling, renting, or preparing pornography which contains:
  a. sexual intercourse, including deviant sexual intercourse;
  b. sexual violence;
  c. masturbation or onanism;
  d. nakedness or appearance which gives the impression of nakedness;
  e. sexual organs; or
  f. child pornography.

(2) Everyone is prohibited from making available pornographic services which:
  a. explicitly present nakedness or the impression of nakedness;
  b. explicitly present sexual organs;
  c. exploit or display sexual activity; or
  d. offer or advertise sexual services, whether directly or indirectly.

The sanctions in the Pornography Law are steeply increased from those in Criminal Code. For example, under the Criminal Code, distribution of pornography incurs a maximum prison sentence of one year six months or a maximum fine of Rp. 8,500,000 (approximately A$ 1,000).[19] However, as can be seen from some of the examples in Table 17.1, under the Pornography Law sanctions are much higher: prison sentences of up to fifteen years and/or considerably higher fines, well out of the reach of the average Indonesian.

On paper, therefore, the Pornography Law is much tougher in dealing with pornography, and conservative Muslims hailed its passing as a victory.

Table 17.1 Sanctions under the Pornography Law

Article	*Crime*	*Fines*	*Prison sentences*
29	producing, making, importing, exporting, buying and selling pornography	between Rp. 25,000,000 (A$ 3,423) and Rp. 6,000,000,000 (A$ 821,500)	6 months to 12 years
30	making available *jasa pornografi* (pornographic service, eg internet, television)	between Rp. 250,000,000 (A$ 34,200) and Rp. 3,000,000,000 (A$ 410,800)	6 months to 6 years
31	loaning or downloading pornography	maximum Rp. 2,000,000,000 (A$273,800)	maximum of 4 years
33	funding or facilitating pornographic acts	between Rp. 1,000,000,000 (A$ 136,900) and Rp. 7,500,000 (A$ 1,026,900)	2 to 15 years

Cases charged and tried: 'Immoral/pornographic' acts

Only a small number of cases prosecuted under Law No. 44 of 2008 on Pornography have been reported in the press. However, a portion of those that have been reported relate to what was known in the bill as 'porno acts'. In the first years, these seem to have focused on erotic dancers, where the women (and sometimes organisers) were charged but not the (male) audience, who could also possibly be said to have broken the law (Pausacker 2014: 98–100). The 2008 Pornography Law is ambiguous about whether it is illegal to attend sexual performances. Article 7 states that '[e]veryone is prohibited from funding or facilitating acts referred to in Article 4' but leaves unanswered the question of whether paying to attend a performance constitutes 'funding'.[20]

In 2017, 141 men were detained in a gay sauna, the Atlantis Club, in Jakarta. These men, including professional dancers and guests, were charged under the Pornography Law for dancing naked in public ('displaying nudity and sexual exploitation collectively in public'), even though events took place in a private club. In December 2017, ten of these men were imprisoned for between two and three years each.[21] This case highlights the difficulty of deciding what is considered 'public', and what is 'private' under the Pornography Law.

Under the Criminal Code, there was still a thriving black market in pornographic videos, sold openly in places like Glodok in Jakarta. Opponents of the Pornography Bill argued that the problem with the anti-pornography provisions in the Criminal Code was lack of enforcement (corruption), rather than poor legislation, and that a new law was unnecessary. There are still ongoing arrests for the sale of pornographic videos (online and as DVDs) that are often accompanied by police press conferences, with the arrests reported in the press. Surprisingly, these reports usually do not state under which law the accused will be charged, as is usually the case with Indonesian crime reporting.

One particularly prominent press conference, in January 2018, involved the West Java Police Chief Inspector, General Agung Budi Maryoto, together with his Deputy, the head of the West Java branch of P2TP2A (Pusat Pelayanan Terpadu Pemberdayaan Perempuan dan Anak, the Integrated Care Centre for the Empowerment of Women and Children), Netty Heryawan and, rather surprisingly, the head of MUI, Rachmat Syafe'i. Behind the four officials was a line of the six suspects, five (three men and two women) with their backs turned to the camera, the men wearing balaclavas. The man in the middle, the main suspect, did not wear a balaclava. Behind the suspects was a huge banner with a photo of the police chief and the words, 'Press Release: Disclosure of Pornography Case which Exploits Underage Children by the Police of West Java'. Although the case involved teenagers, there were photos of a baby and a very young child hiding behind a hand with 'Stop Child Porn' written on it. Despite the press conference being staged in so dramatic a fashion, the police only announced that they were delaying the case because one suspect was underage and one needed psychiatric assessment. Not surprisingly, there was also mention that the police were waiting to see if there were international child porn rings involved – suggesting that the source of the problem may be external to Indonesia (Dipa 2018). The press conference provided a sensational image, creating fear, but at the same time conveyed comfort to the general public, conveying the idea that the police and leaders of the Islamic community had the matter under control.

My examination of the cases of 'ordinary' people (that is, people who are not celebrities) available on-line on the court websites, as well as research theses over the last few years,[22] suggests that only a relatively small number of people have been charged under the Pornography Law – most district courts (and the Supreme Court) seem to handle only about two cases per annum. It is also clear that the Pornography Law is being used in respect of a wide range of crimes. In addition to the obvious cases of making and distributing pornography, the Law is used for prosecuting stalking, revenge porn, strip-tease dancing, and prostitution. Some rape cases are also classified as 'pornography', although, in a number of cases, it remains unclear what law was used. Table 17.2, however, shows that the majority of the charges are for the making and distributing pornographic material, whether by DVD or the internet, and the next most common category is for revenge porn. Charges for both of these clearly fall under the heading of pornography charges.

The category I focus on in this chapter involves electronic transmission, particularly cases where people made homemade pornographic videos for personal consumption (an activity that is legal under art. 4 of the Pornography Law), only to have them uploaded by an unknown third party onto the internet. The makers of these home movies rather than their uploaders were

Table 17.2 Prison sentences and fines resulting from charges under the Pornography Law

Category	*Number of cases*	*Prison sentence range*	*Fine range*
Pornographic DVDs, internet pornography	15	4 months to 7 years	Rp 100,000 to Rp 500,000,000
Revenge porn	7	10 months to 3 years	Rp 0 to Rp 250,000,000
Erotic dancers/prostitutes	5	1 month to 1 year.	Rp 2,000,000 to Rp 250,000,000
Rape (1 case also involving cyberporn violations, 2 cases involving rape of a child)	3	3 years to 15 years	Rp 1,000,000,000
Stalking, involuntary filming, exposing oneself	3	8 months to one year	Rp 0 to Rp 1,500,000
Sex outside marriage	1	6 months	--
Misclassified or unstated	5	n/a	n/a

charged, even though art. 4 clearly states that distributing pornography can incur sanctions under the Pornography Law. It would seem that law enforcers simply ignore the provisions of the law in order to punish high-profile examples they consider 'immoral'. What is evident from the Ariel Peterpan case, described below, is that the substance of the Pornography Law seems to have been blatantly disregarded. In this case, instead of charging the person who loaded the video onto the internet, it was the person in the video and his musical editor who were imprisoned.

Nazril Irham (Ariel) and Reza Rinaldi (Rejoy), Peterpan, 2011

The most publicised pornography case in Indonesia to date involved a celebrity who was eventually sent to prison: pop star Nazril Irham, aka Ariel, lead singer of the popular boy band, Peterpan.[23] The case involved the home-made videos showing Ariel involved (separately) in sexual activity with two high-profile celebrities, Luna Maya and Cut Tari. These were then uploaded to the internet. Cut Tari testified that the video did depict her and Ariel, and that the video was filmed in 2005–6, that is, before the Pornography Law was passed.

Peterpan's musical editor, Reza Rizaldi, aka Rejoy, also faced charges of distributing pornography, with respect to the videos. Rejoy testified that it was part of his job as music editor of Peterpan to back-up data from Ariel's computer and that, while doing this in 2006, he unintentionally copied the videos first onto the Peterpan office computer and then onto his own home computer. Rejoy stated that when he found the two files he rang Ariel, who asked him to delete them but Rejoy forgot to delete them from his home computer. Rejoy stated he did not distribute (*menyebarkan*) the videos.

It has been alleged that Rejoy's cousin, Anggit Gagah Pratama and three of his friends were involved in uploading the videos onto the internet in 2010, in the form of about ten clips from the originals. Anggit admitted to copying pictures and videos from Rejoy's personal computer in about 2009 but denied uploading the videos onto the internet. He said he only watched the videos and saved them. A computer expert (*ahli telematika*, one who deals with telecommunications and computer science) testified that after being installed on Anggit's computer, the files were distributed by about ten people by email, facebook and Bluetooth Blackberry and then put on the internet. In court, Anggit was only questioned for about five minutes as a witness in the trial of Rejoy but was not himself charged, nor were his friends.

Ariel and Rejoy were convicted in the Bandung District Court in January 2011,[24] and Ariel was sentenced to three and a half years in prison for violating art. 29[25] of the Pornography Law. Both Ariel and Rejoy were also charged under the 2008 Law on Electronic Information and Transaction. Although these acts had occurred between 2005 and 2006, the judge stated that the Pornography Law was not being applied retrospectively to when the acts (both the sexual acts and the storing of the video files) occurred, but to the fact that the video began to be circulated in June 2010, after the passing of the Pornography Law. He stated that Ariel was careless (*ceroboh*) in the way that he stored the video on his own computer, which led to Rejoy copying the video, and also careless in not checking that all copies of the files were indeed deleted. Presiding judge, Singgih Prakoso, deemed that through his carelessness, Ariel had effectively 'made the pornography available'.

As mentioned at the beginning of the chapter, the trial of Ariel triggered demonstrations from Islamic groups, including FPI and the Gerakan Reformis Islam that were violent and destructive. The police did not detain any of these demonstrators because, according to Bandung Police chief Sr Comr Jaya Subriyanto, the incident was 'merely a misunderstanding' (Suwarni and Dipa 2011; Krisna and Karana 2011). This may have sent a message to others that they could act outside the law with impunity.

Ariel appealed the decision but his appeal was rejected in the Bandung High Court,[26] which ruled that the original decision was correct (Krisna and Karana 2011). Presiding Judge Sjam Amansjah commented that the court had taken 'popular opinion' into consideration when it rejected the appeal (as is arguably permissible under Law No. 4 of 2004 on Judicial Power) (Hukumonline 2013). Given that there were both supporters and opponents of Ariel, it seems that the more violent group (that is, the conservative Islamic group) was the most persuasive.

Ariel was held in custody from the time of his arrest in June 2010 until July 2012, when he was released early for good behaviour. The prison sentence did not, however, diminish Ariel's popularity as a singer. His band was renamed 'Noah' in August 2012 and has continued to be successful, with one of Noah's videos being viewed by two million viewers in four weeks. The group has now toured nationally and internationally.[27]

Rizieq Shihab and Firza Husein, 2017

In late May 2017, as mentioned above, Rizieq Shihab, the head of FPI, was named a suspect in a high-profile pornography case. The Alliance of Anti-Pornography Students reported a website to police. This website had published photos and screenshots of a salacious WhatsApp conversation between two people, alleged to be Rizieq Shihab and a woman, Firza Husein, which had gone viral (Marhaenjati 2017). The conversation – more than one thousand words in total – detailed imagined sex acts together and naked photos of Firza. In amongst this is acknowledgment by the alleged Rizieq that he would like to marry Firza but didn't want to hurt his wife's feelings because his wife had served him well and made many sacrifices. He comments that if his wife permitted him to [marry] Firza, then Firza would have to respect his wife and love his children, as he would love those of Firza. He invites her to visit him out of town. They then resume their sex talk (Inotz 2017).

In the two years before this case, Rizieq had been heavily involved in protests against the ethnically Chinese, and Christian mayor of Jakarta, Basuki 'Ahok' Tjahaja Purnama, in late 2016 and early 2017, claiming that Ahok had committed blasphemy. This contributed to Ahok's loss in the Jakarta mayoral election in April 2017 and then to him being convicted for blasphemy in May 2017.[28] The city was divided over the question of Ahok's culpability, with an equally fervent group of people supporting Ahok, as evidenced by, for example, an estimated 2,700 flower boards being spontaneously sent by his supporters to the town hall, when he finally left office (Berita Satu 2017; CNN Indonesia 2017).[29]

There have been rumours, fanned by FPI lawyers and supporters but denied by the police, that the police brought charges against Rizieq (and Firza) because of Rizieq's role in bringing down Ahok, with insinuations against the police (who had confiscated Firza's mobile phone, and one of Rizieq's, at different stages). Novel Chaidir Hasan Bamukmin, then general secretary of FPI's Jakarta chapter, also referred, on an earlier occasion, to a 'global conspiracy to criminalise clerics' (Asmara 2017, Coconuts 2017). In January 2017, Rizieq was alleged to have slandered Jakarta Inspector General of Police, Mochamad Iriawan by saying that he had 'the rank of a general but the brain of a *hansip* (short for '*Pertahanan sipil*', civil defence force, a village security officer) (Asmara 2017), which would not have endeared him to the police.

It is not known who uploaded the material to the internet but the conversations first appeared after Firza's phone was confiscated by police as she was arrested for her alleged involvement in a plot to overthrow the government at the time of the 2 December 2016 anti-Ahok demonstration. Rizieq's lawyer, Eggi Sujana, has insinuated that there may have been a leak by a member of the police force (Kompas 2017).

Firza was a known supporter of Rizieq, who led his followers in the protests against Ahok. Police named Firza a suspect in the pornography case on 17 May 2017 and it was reported that she might be charged under one or all of arts. 4(1), 6 and 8 of Law No. 44 of 2008 on Pornography. In June 2018, however, the case was dropped (Jordan 2018).

Rizieq was initially only called for questioning as a witness but police said on 29 May 2017 that they had enough evidence to upgrade his status to 'suspect'. Rizieq twice ignored police summonses in April and May 2017, before fleeing to Saudi Arabia. Initially, one of his lawyers had said that he might stay there until President Joko (Jokowi) Widodo was no longer in power, presumably because he considered the charges to be politically motivated (Tribun Manado 2017), although he later said he would come home 'in the near future' (Anugerah 2017). Since 2017, there have been numerous suggestions that Rizieq was about to return to Indonesia but none of these have eventuated. In July 2019, there was a mention that he would now be facing fines of approximately US$ 7,099 per person for overstaying his visa in Saudia Arabia. As he has four other people (relatives and/or bodyguards) with him, this is a considerable sum (The Jakarta Post 2019).

The case was embarrassing for Rizieq, because FPI had actively campaigned for the introduction of the Pornography Law and demonstrated outside the court, first during the trials of *Playboy* editor Erwin Arnada (imprisoned under the Criminal Code), and then during the trials of Ariel Peterpan and Rejoy. Moral embarrassment is one thing – but did Rizieq break the law? Jakarta Police spokesperson, Argo Yuwono, commented that Rizieq would be charged under the provisions of the 2008 Pornography Law: arts. 4 (mentioned previously), 6 (making pornography available), and 8 (becoming a model for pornography) (Kompas 2017).

However, it is hard to know what legitimate case could be brought against Rizieq. As mentioned previously, it is clearly an offence to upload pornographic material onto the internet. Thus, whoever uploaded the chat onto the internet violated the law, the participants did not. It is not an offence under art. 4 of the Pornography Law for someone to make their own pornographic material for personal use, and face recognition analysis confirmed that the naked woman in the photos in the 'sex chat' was indeed Firza (The Jakarta Post 2017). In addition, art. 10 of the law prohibits public, but not private, nudity.

Other possible charges against Rizieq could be made under:

- Law No. 11 of 2008 on Electronic Information and Transactions, which is more ambiguous. Article 27 states that it is forbidden to 'knowingly and without authority distribute and/or transmit and/or cause electronic information to be accessible and/or electronic records that violate morality (*melanggar kesusilaan*)'. Unlike the Pornography Law, the Electronic Information and Transactions Law does not make a clear distinction between public and private. Technically, it might be possible to state that the discussion was 'transmitted' through WhatsApp, despite the fact that such chats are private (and encrypted) conversations.

The legal definition of 'violating morality' is also unclear. Whose morality should judges use as the standard in a multi-ethnic, multi-religious country like Indonesia?

- According to art. 284 of the Criminal Code it is an offence to have extramarital affairs in Indonesia but a person can only be prosecuted at the request of the spouse and the request must be accompanied by a request for divorce. In addition, the conversation through WhatsApp, even if true, was insufficient evidence of sexual contact. Further, Rizieq's wife had stood by him and Firza was a divorcee.

If the law was followed to the letter, it would seem that the only possibility for Rizieq to have been convicted was the Electronic Information Transfer Law but even that would be a longshot. As in Ariel Peterpan's case, it was the person who uploaded the images of the WhatsApp chat who had clearly broken the law. In Rizieq's and Firza's case, the police dropped the case in June 2018, stating that this was because 'they haven't found the uploaders [of the online chat]' (Lipson 2018). The noisy demonstrators from FPI, who had protested at Ariel's trial, remained loyal to Rizieq, and he stayed in Saudi Arabia. Without the force of the mob being deployed, the letter of the law was actually maintained in this case.

Rizieq is now free of the charges in the pornography case, and his suspect status in a case of alleged defamation of former President Soekarno and insulting the state ideology, Pancasila, has also been dropped.[30] He might still face charges for his claim that the new Indonesian rupiah note contained hidden communist symbols, and on the basis of a report that he may have blasphemed Christianity in one of his sermons (Coconuts 2018). Rizieq's stay in Saudi Arabia has not been without its legal difficulties either. He has been questioned by Saudi authorities both for overstaying his visa by a number of months and for displaying a black flag similar to that of Islamic State outside his home, although the latter seems to have been resolved (Anya 2018; Nathalia, 2018).

Politicians from Islamic parties

There have been a number of politicians and high bureaucrats reported in the media for issues involving pornography. Two well-known examples, which I will briefly mention, are politicians from Islamic parties, Arifinto and Iwan Fajarudin.

In April 2011, a journalist, Irfan, from *Media Indonesia,* photographed H Arifinto, a legislator from the Islamic party, the PKS, viewing a pornographic video on a tablet computer during a session of the the DPR. As mentioned above, PKS was a strong proponent of the Pornography Law. Although Arifinto claimed that he had accidentally opened the video, Irfan's photos proved that he had viewed the video for two minutes (Andriyanto, Rayda and Rachman 2011).

Watching the video clearly violated art. 6 of the Pornography Law, which states, 'It is illegal for anyone to allow pornographic products to be heard (*memperdengarkan*), to show (*mempertontonkan*), to use (*memanfaatkan*), to own (*memiliki*), or to save (*menyimpan*) pornographic products ....' (my underlining). It would seem that Arifinto used, owned and saved pornographic products, and that they were not homemade pornography of himself, which would have been legal.

Although Arifinto tendered his resignation and issued a public apology, the police did not summon witnesses, much less issue charges. With one of their own facing charges, a PKS official, Fahri Hamzah,[31] was quoted in the media, saying (in contrast to the provisions of the law), '[Punish] the one who distributes pornography and not the one who keeps it' (Andriyanto, Rayda, and Rachman 2011). Arifinto died of a heart attack, aged 55, in 2016 (Natalyn 2016).

Also in 2011, Iwan Fajarudin, a National Mandate Party (PAN, Partai Amanat Nasional) legislator in Purworejo's Legislative Council was embarrassed when a video of him and his second wife having sex circulated widely on the internet. Fajarudin admitted the video might have been taken from his laptop, which he had sold recently, and stated he may have been 'recklessness and foolish ...' in not deleting files, including those in the recycle bin of his computer (Jakarta Globe 2011). Although Ariel was, in effect, imprisoned for his 'carelessness' in not deleting videos of himself having sex, Iwan Fajarudin was not been charged, nor have hardline, radical Islamist groups demonstrated against him. Iwan Fajarudin was, of course, married to the woman he was having sex with, so while his moral position may have been different, legally he was in the same situation as Ariel.

The dangers of the Pornography Law providing opportunities to frame somebody are also highlighted by the fact that in the same week that Iwan Fajarudin's video circulated, another video went viral on the internet. Anis Matta, then Deputy Speaker of the DPR and PKS politician (now President of PKS), was implicated in a viral sex video on the internet. Like Iwan Fajarundin, Anis Matta also had a second wife and his marriage to his second wife, Szilvi Fabula, from Hungary, was controversial at the time he married her in 2006 (Tadjoeddin 2014). This may have contributed to a desire to target him. Investigation by police digital forensics unit indicated that the person in the video resembled him but was not Anis Matta himself (Arnaz 2011) and charges did not proceed.

Not all of the sex videos of politicians (or their look-alikes) are from Islamic parties, as Edward Aspinall (2014) demonstrates in the more than ten cases he documents. Of these, perhaps the only politician who has received a prison sentence is Karyawan Faturaham of Bogor district, West Java. He was imprisoned for *uploading*, not participating in, a sex video involving a rival in his own party, PDI-P. In other words, for many politicians the outcome of their cases does follow the intention of the law, that is, the distributors of home-made pornography are more commonly charged than those featured in the pornography. Politicians, in general, received better outcomes: Iwan Fajarudin was treated more leniently (and more correctly, according to the law) than Ariel, and Arifinto, who had clearly broken the law, escaped sanction, while Ariel was imprisoned.

Comments and conclusions

Aspinall (2014) comments that while 'black campaigns' (undermining candidates by spreading rumours through leaflets, sms messages and social network sites) and sex scandals are not a-typical, the use of uploading sex videos involving politicians (and, by extension other high-profile figures in authority) does seem particularly prevalent in Indonesia. Aspinall states that one of the reasons for this is the gap between publicly-stated conservative values on sexual matters and a very different lived reality, with pre-marital sex, extra-marital affairs and a strong commercial sex industry being commonplace. In recent times, the development of technology – both the ability to film and to distribute such images anonymously through social media – has made these 'black campaigns' more possible.

The Pornography Law may act as a deterrent. Both the threat of violence and of legal action (and likely imprisonment) is intended to bring about self-censorship. Given that there have been relatively few high-profile prosecutions, however, the main power of the Pornography Law is its symbolic value.

PKS and other conservative Muslim groups fought hard for the Pornography Law, and it could be said that the introduction of the Pornography Law was an attempt to institute Islamic norms and power by legal means. It would seem, however, that this law is not being applied any more systematically than the pre-existing articles in the Criminal Code. Rather than dealing with the difficult challenge of tackling the large hard-core pornography industry, individuals have been singled out as examples. In Ariel's case, this was perhaps because he was a high-profile teenage idol, who groups such as FPI wished to use as an example to demonstrate their power in influencing societal norms. In the case of Rizieq, it would appear that the leaking of his Whatsapp chat may have been done by people who opposed his actions (his campaign against Ahok, for example) and wished to expose his hypocrisy.

The (mis)application of the 2008 Pornography Law for political gain resulted in Ariel and Rejoy spending time in prison. The publicity surrounding this case may, in part, have inspired others to circulate sex videos of their opponents (or in some cases, lookalike actors), in the hope of sending them to prison – or, at minimum, embarrassing them. Politicians, bureaucrats and Islamic preachers, have however, mostly managed to survive these exposures. As Aspinall (2014) describes it:

> [...] most politicians simply tough it out and ignore the videos, or deny it was them. [...] Pornography is vigorously condemned right across the

> political spectrum in Indonesia, and some of the politicians who have been caught on film also cloak themselves in religion and morality when they campaign for office. Viewed in this light, surviving a sex video looks more like surviving a corruption scandal than standing up for the sanctity of the public sphere.

The 2008 Pornography Law has proved to be a toothless tiger in stamping out pornography (and the 'pornographic acts' it purports to eliminate) but a useful stimulus for those seeking to raise awareness of 'immorality' in the community, including for political reasons. While the passing of the law may have had symbolic value for conservative Islamic groups, their brand has now been tarnished by the exposure of the human flaws and the hypocrisy of some of its proponents. Given that there appears to be no diminishing of this trend, it is likely that in the future more sex videos and screenshots of salacious social media chats will continue to do little more than expose more hypocrisy on the part of both accusers and those accused.

Notes

1 This relates to a common Muslim belief (*ādhāb al-qabr*) that the physical body is beaten till bruised in the grave if the person has not been adequately punished for their sins during their lifetime. This belief may have its origin in pre-Islamic Arabic beliefs and is contested by a number of Islamic scholars. See Smith and Yazbeck 2002: 47–8.
2 Law No. 44 of 2008 on Pornography.
3 Law No. 11 of 2008 on Electronic Information and Transactions, subsequently amended by Law No. 19 of 2016.
4 Ichwan (2005) and Hosen (2003, 2008), among others, have examined the increasing influence MUI's fatwa have had on Indonesian society, politics and laws.
5 *Ulama* are Muslim religious scholars.
6 See Hefner 2000, particularly Chapters 3 and 4.
7 See Lindsay 2011: 175–6) for a discussion of censorship in the film industry.
8 For examples of Old Order press statements, see Ginting 2003: 57 [citing an example from 1953]; and 70 [from 1957]). While mainly used in the Old Order, I also came across '*cabul*' being used once in 1968 and once in 1991. See Ginting 2003: 81, 106.
9 The term *porno* (in abbreviated form) is often used in newspaper reports. In 1968, for example, KAPPI (Kesatuan Aksi Peladjar Indonesia, Union for Indonesian Youth and Student Action) declared 'total war against "porn morals"' (*perang total terhadap 'moral porno'*), see Ginting 2003: 83. Other examples can be seen in Ginting 2003: 83, 84, all from 1968.
10 See also Lindsay 2011: 177–8, 185–6, for further discussion of terminology and definition of pornography in Indonesia.
11 Article 17 of Peperti Regulation No. 10 of 1960 on the Licence for Publishing of Newspapers and Magazines (Haryanto 2006: 27–9).
12 See Pausacker 2013: 96, for the one example of a printing business, Tampomas, being shut down without court process. This was under the authority of art. 33 of

the Law No. 74 of 1957, which dealt with state security rather than the curtailing of pornography.

13 On 1 July 1971, the Indonesian Literature Department of the Arts Faculty of Gadjah Mada University held a discussion about erotic work in Indonesian literature (Lesmana, 1995: 11). This was followed in October 1971 by a further clampdown by the government on pornography, to 'curtail the wayward behaviour' (*kenakalan*) of young people in Indonesia. A Team to Curtail Youth Waywardness (Tim Penyusunan Pola Penanggulangan Kenakalan Remaja) was formed, to resolve the issue, particularly in relation to violations of sexual mores (Lesmana, 1995: 8–9).

14 Minister for Information Decision No. 133/SK/Menpen/1998 repealed previous Decisions No. 47/KEP/Menpen/1975 and No. 184/KEP/Menpen/1978, which had set up the SIUPP system.

15 Despite FPI's support of the Anti-Pornography Bill, FPI has rarely targeted local pornographic video industries. Wilson (2008: 202) suggests this might be because (unnamed) 'high-ranking military figures' are involved, and that the 'potential repercussions of disrupting military business interests would appear to outweigh any symbolic or material gains'.

16 See Bush 2008, for further information about regional regulations.

17 See section 'Changing Terms for Pornography' above, for further discussion of the term '*pornoaksi*'.

18 Law No. 19 of 2016, 27 October 2016 amended Law No. 11 of 2008. It: included revisions of the sanctions for defamation; added provisions on the right to be forgotten; strengthened the power of civil servants to investigate corporations; and increased the government's right to terminate access.

19 The sum in the actual Criminal Code is Rp. 8,500 (A$ 1) but fines were multiplied by 1,000 with the passing of Supreme Court Regulation No. 2 of 2012. Article 3 of this regulation increases all fines in the Criminal Code (except those in art. 303 of the Criminal Code) by 1,000 times. See Assegaf, Chapter 9 of this volume for further details of this Regulation.

20 Article 32(1) of the 2005–06 version of the Pornography Bill was much clearer, stating 'Everyone is prohibited from watching sexual performances'.

21 North Jakarta Court Decisions Nos. 852, 853 and 854/Pid.Sus/2017/PN.JKT. UTR, 14 December 2017. See Pausacker, Chapter 16, this volume, for further details of this case.

22 I examined thirty-nine cases: three from the Supreme Court; and the rest from the District Courts of Blora (Central Java), Denpasar (Bali), East Jakarta, West Jakarta, Jambi (Central Sumatra), Makassar (Sulawesi), Malang (East Java), Medan (North Sumatra), Pekanbaru (Riau), Semarang (Central Java), and Tamiang Layang (Central Kalimantan). The degree to which court decisions have been up-loaded to the internet varies widely from court to court, so the figures should not be taken to be reliable statistically but are offered to give some indication of use of the Pornography Law. See the list of cases at the end of this chapter.

23 The cases of Ariel and Rejoy are discussed in detail in Pausacker (2014: 100–2).

24 Bandung District Court Decision No. 1401/Pid/B/2010/PN.Bdg for Ariel; No. 1402/Pid/B/2010/PN.Bg for Rejoy, dated 31 January 2011 (see Bandung High Court website, www.pt-bandung.go.id/status-perkara-pengadilan-tinggi/perkara-pidana?field=&value=&v_f_date=01-07-2011&v_t_date=29-07-2011&show=100&fil=&start=1).

25 Article 29 forbids producing, making, duplicating, distributing, broadcasting, exporting, offering, selling, renting or preparing pornography according to the terms in art. 4(1). The Elucidation to art. 4(1) states that home-made pornography for one's own use is not illegal.

26 Bandung High Court Decision No. 67/Pid/PT-BDG for Ariel, No. 68/PID/2011/PT.Bdg for Rejoy, dated 19 April (Krisna and Karana 2011; Pos Kota 2011 and Bandung High Court website www.pt-bandung.go.id/status-perkara-pengadilan-tinggi/perkara-pidana?field=&value=&v_f_date=01-07-2011&v_t_date=29-07-2011&show=100&fil=&start=1).

27 See the official website, www.noah-site.com/.

28 See Butt (2017) for a description of this case.

29 See '2.700 Karangan Bunga Hiasi Balai Kota Jakarta' www.youtube.com/watch?v=ZnYiUQ_W3so

30 Rizieq was charged under arts. 154a and 320 of the Criminal Code for a sermon in which he compared the version of the Pancasila formulated by the founding fathers, including Soekarno, to the version that has the Jakarta Charter (which obliges Muslims to abide by sharia). Rizieq was reported to have said, 'In Sukarno's Pancasila, faith in God is placed in the butt, but in the Jakarta Charter's Pancasila, faith in God is placed in the head. Which one is better? Sukarno's or the Jakarta Charter's?' The case was dropped in May 2018, due to 'lack of evidence'. The police had asked for a video of the entire sermon, while the complainant, Sukmawati Soekarnoputri (Soekarno's third daughter), was only able to provide a short clip (Swaragita and Dwipa 2018).

31 For further details about PKS, see Fealy 2010.

References

AFP 2006. '"Say No to Porn", Say Jakarta Protesters', *ABC News*, 21 May www.abc.net.au/news/2006-05-21/say-no-to-porn-say-jakarta-protesters/1758452

Ambotang, Dalle 2016. 'Analisis Yuridis Tindak Pidana Pornografi dalam Media Elektronik (Studi Kasus Putusan No. 01/Pid.B/2015/PN.Mks)'. Thesis Sarjana. Faculty of Law, University Hasanuddin Makassar

Andriyanto, Heru; Rayda, Nivell; and Anita Rachman 2011. 'Can Arifinto Be Charged Under the Porn Law?', *The Jakarta Globe*, 12 April www.thejakartaglobe.com

Anjani; Karima and Ghosh, Arijit 2006. 'Miniskirts Clash with Islam as Indonesia Drafts Pornography Law', *Bloomberg*, 10 May www.bloomberg.com/apps/news?pid=10000080&sid=at7mE_oU2JiI&refer=asia

Anugerah, Pijar 2017. 'Saat Pulang, Rizieq Shihab "Berharap Disambut seperti Ayatullah Khomeini"', *BBC Indonesia*, 31 May www.bbc.com/indonesia/indonesia-40089552

Anya, Agnes 2018. 'Rizieq Has Overstayed His Visa: Envoy', *The Jakarta Post*, 28 September www.thejakartapost.com/news/2018/09/28/rizieq-has-overstayed-his-visa-envoy.html

Arnaz, Farouk 2011. 'Police "Digital Forensics" Clear Anis Matta in Sex Tape Scandal', *The Jakarta Globe*, 19 March www.thejakartaglobe.com/home/police-digital-forensics-clear-anis-matta-in-sex-tape-scandal/430190

Asmara, Tia 2017. 'Indonesia: Hate Speech Allegations Shadow FPI Leader', *Benar News*, 19 January

Aspinall, Edward 2014. 'Sex, Lies and Politicians', *Inside Indonesia*, no. 115, January-March www.insideindonesia.org/sex-lies-and-politicians

Aswad, Alfi Quthni 2016. 'Analisis Yuridis Tindak Pidana Menyiarkan dan Menyebarkan Pornografi "*Cyberporn*" (Studi Kasus Putusan Nomor 1302/Pid.B/2008/PN.Mks)', Thesis Sarjana, Faculty of Syariah and Law, UIN Alauddin Makassar

Bayani, Muhammad Tamyiz 2018. 'Tinjauan Hukum Pidana Islam terhadap Direktori Putusan Nomor 275/Pid.Sus/2015/PN. Jmb tentang Penyebaran Pornografi Anak di Bawah Umur', S1 Thesis, Faculty of Syariah and Law, Universitas Islam Negeri Sunan Ampel Surabaya

Berita Satu 2017. '2.700 Karangan Bunga Hiasi Balai Kota Jakarta', 27 April www.youtube.com/watch?v=ZnYiUQ_W3so

Bruinessen, Martin van 1990. 'Indonesia's Ulama and Politics: Caught between Legitimising the Status Quo and Searching for Alternatives', *Prisma: The Indonesian Indicator* 49: 52–69; also: www.let.uu.nl/~Martin.vanBruinessen/personal/publications/Ulama_and_politics.htm

Bush, Robin 2008. 'Regional Sharia Regulations in Indonesia: Anomaly or Symptom?', in Greg Fealy and Sally White (eds.), *Expressing Islam: Religious Life and Politics in Indonesia.* Singapore: ISEAS, pp. 174–91

Butt, Simon 2017. 'Why is Ahok in Prison? A Legal Analysis of the Decision', *Indonesia at Melbourne*, 6 June https://indonesiaatmelbourne.unimelb.edu.au/why-is-ahok-in-prison-a-legal-analysis-of-the-decision/

CBC (Canadian Broadcasting Commission) 2006. 'Playboy's Indonesian Office Hit with Violent Protest', 12 April www.cbc.ca/arts/story/2006/04/12/playboy-indonesia-protest.html

CNN Indonesia 2017. 'Karangan Bunga Untuk Ahok', 25 April www.youtube.com/watch?v=LAqbeQ8FIoI

Coconuts 2017. 'BREAKING: Police Officially Name FPI Leader Rizieq Shihab Suspect in Pornography Case Related to Sex Scandal Allegations', 29 May https://coconuts.co/jakarta/news/breaking-police-officially-name-fpi-leader-rizieq-shihab-suspect-pornography-case-related-sex-scandal-allegations/

Coconuts 2018. 'Porn Suspect Status Dropped, FPI Leader Rizieq Still Awaits Legal Certainty before Returning to Indonesia', 21 June https://coconuts.co/jakarta/news/porn-suspect-status-dropped-fpi-leader-rizieq-still-awaits-legal-certainty-returning-indonesia/

Compass 2006. 'Islam in Indonesia. Part 2: The Conservatives', 12 November www.abc.net.au/compass/s1766011.htm

Da Costa, Agustinus Beo 2017. 'Indonesia Police Detain 51 Men in Jakarta "Gay Spa" Raid', 8 October www.reuters.com/article/us-indonesia-lgbt-police/indonesia-police-detain-51-men-in-jakarta-gay-spa-raid-idUSKBN1CC0L7

Dipa, Arya 2018. 'Police Delay Detention of Bandung Child Porn Suspect', *The Jakarta Post*, 10 January www.thejakartapost.com/news/2018/01/10/police-delay-detention-of-bandung-child-porn-suspect.html

Fealy, Greg 2010. 'Front Stage with the PKS', *Inside Indonesia*, no. 101, July-September www.insideindonesia.org/weekly-articles/front-stage-with-the-pks

Gatra 2006. 'Hakim Ancam Tunda Sidang Pemred Playboy', 14 December www.gatra.com/2006-12-14/artikel.php?id=100267

Gillespie, Piers 2007. 'Current Issues in Indonesian Islam: Analysing the 2005 Council of Indonesian Ulama Fatwa No 7 Opposing Pluralism, Liberalism and Secularism', *Journal of Islamic Studies* 18(2): 202–40

Ginting, Alfred P. 2003. 'Sejarah Pornografi di Media Massa Cetak Indonesia: Analisis Sejarah dengan Metode Arkeologi Foucault tentang Pornografi di Media Massa Cetak Indonesia'. Jakarta: Sarjana Komunikasi Jurusan Jurnalistik. Fakultas Ilmu Komunikasi Universitas Padjadjaran

Hamzah, A. 1987. *Pornographi dalam Hukum Pidana: Suatu Studi Perbandingan*. Jakarta: Bina Mulia

Hardi, Erick P. 2011. 'Ariel Dilempari Telur Busuk', *Tempo*, 31 January https://seleb.tempo.co/read/310016/ariel-dilempari-telur-busuk

Hardi, Erick P. 2014. 'Dalang Video Mesum, Eks Wakil Bupati Bogor Ditahan', *Tempo*, 3 September https://nasional.tempo.co/read/604174/dalang-video-mesum-eks-wakil-bupati-bogor-ditahan

Harding, Claire 2008. 'The Influence of the "Decadent West": Discourses of the Mass Media on Youth Sexuality in Indonesia', *Intersections: Gender and Sexuality in Asia and the Pacific* 18, October http://intersections.anu.edu.au/issue18/harding.htm

Haryanto, Ignatius 2006. *Indonesia Raya Dibredel!* Yogyakarta: LKiS Pelangi Aksara

Hasyim, Irsan 2018. 'Rizieq Shihab Batal Pulang, Polisi: Ditunggu Kasus Firza Husein', *Tempo*, 24 February https://metro.tempo.co/read/1063903/rizieq-shihab-batal-pulang-polisi-ditunggu-kasus-firza-husein

Hasyim, Syafiq 2006. *Understanding Women in Islam: An Indonesian Perspective*. Jakarta: Solstice Publishing

Hefner, Robert W. 2000. *Civil Islam: Muslims and Democratization in Indonesia*. Princeton and Oxford: Princeton University Press

Hosen, Nadirsyah 2003. 'Fatwa and Politics in Indonesia', in Arskal Salim and Azyumardi Azra (eds.), *Shari'a and Politics in Modern Indonesia*. Singapore: ISEAS, pp. 168–80

Hosen, Nadirsyah (2008) 'Online Fatwa in Indonesia: From Fatwa Shopping to Googling a *Kiai*', in Greg Fealy and Sally White (eds.), *Expressing Islam: Religious Life and Politics in Indonesia*. Singapore: ISEAS, pp. 159–73.

Hukumonline 2013. 'Klinik Hukum. Pertanyaan: Masalah Independensi Hakim dan Rasa Keadilan Masyarakat', 26 May www.hukumonline.com/klinik/detail/cl3026/masalah-independensi-hakim-dan-rasa-keadilan-masyarakat

Ichwan, Moch. Nur 2005. 'Ulamā, State and Politics: Majelis Ulama Indonesia after Suharto', *Islamic Law and Society* 12(1): 45–72

Inotz, Tonz de 2017. 'Netizan Penasaran dengan Isi Chat Diduga Firza Husein dan Habib Rizieq', *Rancahpost*, 4 February www.rancahpost.co.id/20170268538/netizen-masih-penasaran-dengan-isi-chat-firza-husein-dan-habib-rizieq/

Irwanto, Deny 2017. 'Berkas 5 Tersangka Penyelenggara Pesta Gay Masih Digarap', 18 October http://news.metrotvnews.com/hukum/PNgJPL0K-berkas-5-tersangka-penyelenggara-pesta-gay-masih-digarap

The Jakarta Globe 2011. 'Another Lawmaker in Hot Water after Sex Video Leaks', 4 March www.thejakartaglobe.com

The Jakarta Globe 2014. 'Bandung Man Arrested for Alleged Child Porn Distribution', 24 February http://jakartaglobe.id/news/bandung-man-arrested-for-alleged-child-porn-distribution/

The Jakarta Post 2017. 'Naked Woman in Steamy WhatsApp Chat is Firza Husein, Police Confirm', 16 May www.thejakartapost.com/news/2017/05/16/naked-woman-in-steamy-whatsapp-chat-is-firza-husein-police-confirm.html

The Jakarta Post 2019. 'Rizieq May Leave Saudi Arabia. But Only if He Pays Fine for Overstaying, Indonesia's Envoy Says', 11 July www.thejakartapost.com/news/2019/07/11/rizieq-may-leave-saudi-arabia-but-only-if-he-pays-fine-for-overstaying-indonesias-envoy-says.html

Jordan, Ray 2018. 'Suara Firza Husein Setelah SP3 Kasus Chat Habib Rizieq', *Detik News*, 17 June https://news.detik.com/berita/d-4071871/suara-firza-husein-setelah-sp3-kasus-chat-habib-rizieq

Kompas 2017. 'Polisi Akan Keluarkan Surat Penangkapan', *Kompas*, 30 May https://kompas.id/baca/metro/2017/05/30/polisi-akan-keluarkan-surat-penangkapan/

Krisna, Yuli and Karana, Kinanti Pinta 2011. 'Ariel Verdict Leaves Sour Taste', *The Jakarta Globe*, 1 February www.thejakartaglobe.com

Laksamana.net 2001. 'A Chronology of Attacks by the Islamic Defenders' Front (FPI)', 16 October www.library.ohiou.edu/indopubs/2001/10/18/0068.html

Lesmana, Tjipta 1995. *Pornografi dalam Media Massa*. Jakarta: Puspa Swara

Lindsay, Jennifer 2011. 'Media and Morality: Pornography post Suharto', in Krishna Sen and David T. Hill (eds.), *Politics and the Media in Twenty-First Century Indonesia*. London/New York: Routledge, pp. 172–95

Lipson, David 2018. 'Pornography Charges Dropped against Indonesian Cleric Rizieq Shihab', *ABC News*, 18 June www.abc.net.au/news/2018-06-18/police-drop-pornography-charges-hardline-indonesian-cleric/9882386

Marhaenjati, Bayu 2017. 'Student Group Reports Viral Video Implicating Habib Rizieq in Sex Scandal', *The Jakarta Globe*, 31 January http://jakartaglobe.id/news/student-group-reports-viral-video-implicating-habib-rizieq-sex-scandal/

Maris, Inke 2006. 'Inul and Pornography Bill', *The Jakarta Post*, 7 June www.thejakartapost.com

Natalyn, Ezra 2016. 'Para Politikus PKS Melayat Arifinto', 10 September www.viva.co.id/berita/politik/820228-para-politikus-pks-melayat-arifinto

Nathalia, Telly 2018. 'Saudi Authorities Question Rizieq Shihab over Islamic State Flag', *Jakarta Globe*, 7 November https://jakartaglobe.id/news/saudi-authorities-question-rizieq-shihab-over-islamic-state-flag/

Nurita, Dewi 2017. 'Pakar: KUHP Tidak Tepat Dikenakan dalam Kasus Gay di Spa Harmoni', 9 October https://metro.tempo.co/read/1023015/pakar-kuhp-tidak-tepat-dikenakan-dalam-kasus-gay-di-spa-harmoni

Parker, Lyn 2006. 'Uniform Jilbab: The Islamic Headscarf is now Compulsory in Many High Schools', *Inside Indonesia* 83(July-September): 21–3

Patung 2006. 'The Trial of Playboy Editor Erwin Arnada', *Indonesia Matters*, 16 December www.indonesiamatters.com/995/erwin-arnada/

Pausacker, Helen 2013. 'Morality and the Nation: Law, Pornography and Indonesia's Islamic Defenders Front', PhD Melbourne Law School, the University of Melbourne

Pausacker, Helen 2014. 'Sanctions against Popstars… and Politicians? Indonesia's 2008 Pornography Law and its Aftermath', in Bernhard Platzdasch and Johan Saravanamuttu (eds.), *Religious Diversity in Muslim-majority States in Southeast Asia: Areas of Toleration and Conflict*. Singapore: ISEAS, pp. 89–112

PKS (Partai Keadilan Sejahtera) (2006) 'Dewan Syariah Pusat PKS Dukung Pemberlakuan UU Anti Pornografi dan Porno Aksi', 22 February http://pks-jepang.org/archives/340

Pojoksatu 2017. 'Sekuriti Bagikan Honor Penari Telanjang, Ratusan Gay Ditangkap Saat Pesta, Polisi Temukan…', 22 May http://pojoksatu.id/news/berita-nasional/2017/05/22/sekuriti-bagikan-honor-penari-telanjang-ratusan-gay-ditangkap-saat-pesta-polisi-temukan/

Rachim, Alex A. (ed.) 1977. *Pornografi dalam Pers Indonesia: Sebuah Orientasi* (Seri Monografi Dewan Pers). Jakarta: Dewan Pers

Rinaldo, Rachel 2013. 'Religion and the Politics of Morality: Muslim Women Activists and the Pornography Debate in Indonesia', in Yew-Foong Hui (ed.), *Encountering Islam: The Politics of Religious Identities in Southeast Asia.* Singapore: ISEAS, pp. 247–70

Safitri, Inge Klara 2017. 'Police Says Pornography Case of Firza Husein almost Complete', *Tempo*, 22 August https://en.tempo.co/read/news/2017/08/22/057902194/Police-Says-Pornography-Case-of-Firza-Husein-almost-Complete

Sherlock, Stephen 2008. 'Parties and Decision-Making in the Indonesian Parliament: A Case Study of RUU APP, the Anti-Pornography Bill', *Australian Journal of Asian Law* 10(2): 159–83

Sindonews 2017. 'Kasus Gay di Kelapa Gading Akan Naik ke Meja Hijau', 8 August https://metro.sindonews.com/read/1228328/170/kasus-gay-di-kelapa-gading-akan-naik-ke-meja-hijau-1502186139

Smith-Hefner, Nancy J. 2007. 'Javanese Women and the Veil in Post-Soeharto Indonesia', *The Journal of Asian Studies* 66(2): 389–420

Stevens, Alan M. and Schmidgall-Tellings, A. (ed.) 2010. *A Comprehensive 8Indonesian-English Dictionary*. Athens, Ohio: Ohio University Press

Suwarni, Yuli Tri and Dwipa, Arya 2011. 'Ariel Gets 3.5 Years; Unrest outside Court', *The Jakarta Post*, 1 February www.thejakartapost.com

Swaragita, Gisela and Dipa, Arya 2018. 'Police Drop Defamation Charges against FPI Leader', *The Jakarta Post*, 5 May www.thejakartapost.com/news/2018/05/05/police-drop-charges-against-fpi-leader.html

Tadjoeddin, Mohammad Zulfan 2014. 'Seeking Rational Choices on Polygamy', *The Jakarta Post*, 7 February www.thejakartapost.com/news/2014/02/07/seeking-rational-choices-polygamy.html

Tribun Manado 2017. 'Rizieq Tak akan Pulang Hingga Jokowi Tak Presiden Lagi', 17 May http://manado.tribunnews.com/2017/05/17/rizieq-tak-akan-pulang-hingga-jokowi-tak-presiden-lagi

Wilson, Ian Douglas 2008. '"As Long as It's *Halal*": Islamic *Preman* in Jakarta', in Greg Fealy and Sally White (eds.), *Expressing Islam: Religious Life and Politics in Indonesia.* Singapore ISEAS, pp. 192–210

Legislation

Criminal Code (Kitab Undang-Undang Hukum Pidana, KUHP: Law No. 1 of 1946 as amended by Law No. 27 of 1999 on the Indonesian Criminal Code)

Law No. 74 of 1957 on the 'Dangerous Situation' (Keadaan Bahaya)

Law No. 4 of 2004 on Judicial Power

Law No. 11 of 2008 on Electronic Information and Transactions

Law No. 44 of 2008 on Pornography

Law No. 19 of 2016, amending Law No. 11 of 2008 on Electronic Information and Transactions

Peperti Regulation No. 10 of 1960 on the Licence for Publishing of Newspapers and Magazines

Minister for Information Decision No. 133/SK/Menpen/1998 (repealed previous decisions No. 47/KEP/Menpen/1975 and No. 184/KEP/Menpen/1978, which had set up the SIUPP system)

Court decisions

Supreme Court Decision No. 123 PK/Pid.Sus/2015
Supreme Court Decision No. 132 K/PID.SUS/2015
Supreme Court Decision No. 276 K/Pid.Sus/2016
Bandung District Court Decision No. 1401/Pid/B/2010/PN.Bdg (Ariel Peterpan)
Bandung District Court Decision No. 1402/Pid/B/2010/PN.Bg (Rejoy)
Bandung High Court Decision No. 67/Pid/2011/PT.Bbg (Ariel Peterpan)
Bandung High Court Decision No. 68/PID/2011/PT.Bdg (Rejoy)
Blora District Court Decision No. 163/Pid.Sus/2016/PN Blora
Blora District Court Decision No. 237/Pid.Sus/2016/PN.Blora
Denpasar High Court Decision No. 29/Pid.Sus/2016/PT.Dps
Denpasar District Court Decision No. 462/Pid.Sus/2016/PN Dps
Denpasar District Court Decision No. 630/Pid.Sus/2016/PN Dps
Denpasar District Court Decision No. 631/Pid.Sus/2016/PN Dps
East Jakarta District Court Decision No. 217/Pid.Sus/2018/PN Jkt.Tim
North Jakarta District Court Decision No. 852/Pid.Sus/2017/PN.JKT.UTR
North Jakarta District Court Decision No. 853/Pid.Sus/2017/PN.JKT.UTR
North Jakarta District Court Decision No. 854/Pid.Sus/2017/PN.JKT.UTR
West Jakarta District Court Decision No. 751/Pid.B/2017/PN Jkt.Brt
Jambi District Court Decision No. 275/pid.sus/2015/pn.jmb
Makassar District Court Decision No. 1302/Pid.B/2008/PN.Mks
Makassar District Court Decision No. 01/Pid.B/2015/PN.Mks
Malang District Court Decision No. 450/Pid.B/2016/PN Mlg
Malang District Court Decision No. 556/Pid.B/2017/PN Mlg
Malang District Court Decision No. 557/Pid.B/2017.PN Mlg
Malang District Court Decision No. 210/Pid.B/2018/PN/Mlg
Medan District Court Decision No. 3634/Pid.Sus/2017/PN Mdn
Medan District Court Decision No. 515/Pid.B/2015/PN Mdn
Medan District Court Decision No. 567/Pid/2012/PT-MDN
Medan District Court Decision No. 701/Pid.B/2018/PN Mdn
Medan District Court Decision No. 807/Pid.B/2015/PN Mdn
Medan District Court Decision No. 1845/Pid.sus/2015/PN Mdn
Medan District Court Decision No. 194/Pid.Sus/2016/PN Mdn
Medan District Court Decision No. 2701/Pid.Sus/2015/PN Mdn
Medan District Court Decision No. 3745/Pid.Sus/2015/PN Mdn
Pekanbaru District Court Decision No. 475/Pid.B/2017/PN Pbr
Pekanbaru District Court Decision No. 489/Pid.B/2017/PN Pbr
Semarang District Court Decision No. 434/Pid.Sus/2017/Pn.Smg
Semarang District Court Decision No. 440/Pid.Sus/2017/PN.Smg
Semarang District Court Decision No. 520/Pid.Sus/2017/PN.Smg
Semarang District Court Decision No. 14/Pid.SUS/2015/PN Smg
Semarang District Court Decision No. 75/Pid.SUS/2015/PN Smg
Semarang District Court Decision No. 459/Pid.b\B/2017/PN Smg

18 *Hudud* and corruption

A critical analysis of proposals to cut off the hands of the corrupt in Indonesia

Nadirsyah Hosen

Corruption is a major problem in Indonesia, and many Islamist hardliners take the view that applying *hudud* (Islamic criminal law),[1] for example, by cutting off the hand of a thief, will end it. The idea behind this proposal is simple: the adoption of 'Western' anti-corruption reform has failed to free Indonesia from corruption, and therefore Indonesia needs to go back to the rules in the Qur'an and Hadith to combat corruption. The slogan of those who propose it is: 'Save Indonesia with Shari'a!' The government's inability to deal with corruption, collusion, nepotism (*Korupsi, Kolusi, Nepotisme*, or KKN), hardliners believe, forces them to offer another solution: the adoption of hudud law. They take the view that implementing a more Islamic legal system will bring Indonesia out of crisis (Kompas 2017).

More specifically, proponents of amputation believe that punishing the perpetrator of a crime (by producing pain) will generally push him or her to repent, so that he or she becomes wary (specific deterrence) and does not repeat the crime. Other people would likewise be afraid to follow the offender's path (general deterrence). In this sense, the implementation of this kind of Islamic law will protect the public good (Tempo 2011).

This chapter critically analyses these arguments. The main question addressed is would cutting the hands of thieves, as prescribed in the Qur'an, help Indonesia combat corruption? I test this by first looking at the current state of corruption in Indonesia and, second, by proposing a reinterpretation of the relevant Qur'anic verse in a modern context, and finally by comparing Indonesia with other countries. I would argue that, even from a Muslim perspective, Islamic hudud should not be the main solution, let alone the only one.

The complex nature of corruption

Corruption is closely linked to the way governments conduct their affairs in modern societies, and therefore also to the economic activity. It is unlikely that corruption can be substantially reduced without modifying the way governments operate. The fight against corruption is thus intimately linked to the reform of the state. This means that in order to combat corruption, attention must be paid to governance factors: corruption is principally a symptom of bad governance. In turn, it damages governance. It undermines democracy, reduces accountability and representation in policy-making, displaces the rule of law, and ultimately results in unequal provision of services.

Combating corruption became a formal national commitment in Indonesia with the issue of People's Consultative Assembly Decision No. XI/MPR/1998. This was then reflected in a range of laws and regulations, most notably, Law No. 31 of 1999 on the Eradication of the Criminal Act of Corruption. This Law widens the scope of the definition of corruption, increases penalties, and establishes an anti-corruption commission. It was followed by Law No. 30 of 2002 on the Anti Corruption Commission (KPK, Komisi Pemberantasan Korupsi) (Butt 2012).

Corruption manifests itself in various ways, from small bribes given to local officials to obtain a service, through to paying to avoid compliance with regulations. It has led to many much-publicised scandals in Indonesia, involving senior politicians and major businesses. Lack of transparency in rules, laws, and processes can create fertile ground for corruption. Rules are often confusing, documents specifying them are not publicly available, and, at times, rules are changed without properly publicised announcements. Laws, or regulations, including anti-corruption laws, are written in such a way that they can only be understood by trained lawyers, and they are often conceptually opaque on important issues, thus leaving grounds for different interpretations.

Nonetheless, issuance of these laws indicated that the Indonesian public expected that the government should be forced by law to be free from the practices of collusion, corruption and nepotism, and bring an end to the problems of corruption that emerged during the New Order Government under former President Soeharto, and which were beneficial only to certain elites.

Systemic and systematic corruption

Corruption in Indonesia can be seen as both systemic and systematic (Tempo 2001). 'Systemic corruption' within the public sector can be defined as 'the regular, habitual use of public office for private benefit, resulting in a reduction in the quality, or availability, of government-provided goods and services' (Buscaglia 1997). Corruption is systemic when a government agency supplies a good or service only if an unwilling and uncompensated transfer of wealth takes place between the market and the public sector (for example, bribery, extortion, fraud or embezzlement) (Buscaglia and Ratliff 2000: 87).

'Systematic corruption' is organised. It is not necessarily pervasive or institutionalised, but recurrent. It usually involves large gains and is often the subject of popular scandals. While it is entrenched, and is the norm among large numbers of officials, intermediaries and entrepreneurs, systematic corruption originates with high-level civil servants who recognise and exploit illegal opportunities in government departments and agencies. This practice contravenes the rule of law, but, unlike systemic corruption, if the offenders are removed, so too is corruption. Systemic corruption, by contrast, is pervasive, institutionalised (perhaps accepted but not necessarily approved), and built into economic and political institutions (Buscaglia and Ratliff 2000: 55).

The probability of detecting corruption decreases the more corruption becomes systemic, and, therefore, the traditional methods of detection and enforcement become less effective. Under these circumstances, Buscaglia and Ratliff (2000: 90) argue, such preventative measures as organisational change (the reform of the civil service by, for example, reducing procedural complexities in the provision of public services) and salary increases are more effective.

However, the mere imposition of preventative measures is not adequate. Corruption can only be effectively and systematically contained when anti-corruption strategies are consistent with the rule of law. Corruption of officials responsible for the rule of law impairs the institutions of government itself, and erodes the potential effectiveness of anti-corruption measures in other aspects of a society. Therefore, as well as taking preventative measures, imposition of repressive or punitive measures should also be considered.

In fact, C. V. Narasimhan identifies three types of anti-corruption measure: preventative, punitive and promotional. The term 'preventative measures' refers to those electoral and administrative reforms concerned with making all government transactions, 'more transparent and accountable to the people' (Narasimhan 1997: 251). Punitive measures include the 'laws, rules and the mechanism for effective investigation, court trial, departmental disciplinary action and other means, to deter the corrupt functionaries' (Narasimhan 1997: 251). Finally, promotional measures focus on the 'encouragement of value-based politics, inculcation of moral and ethical principles among the younger generation in schools and colleges, and the build-up of a kind of social ostracisation of corrupt people by society' (Narasimhan 1997: 252).

Robert Klitgaard (1988), by contrast, advocates eradicating systemic and systematic corruption by 'frying the big fish'. When there is a culture of engaging in corrupt acts with impunity, the only way to begin breaking it up, he argues, is for a number of major corrupt figures to be convicted and punished. However, any leader who undertakes this task will need support in the form of an enormous amount of political will from the ruling party and relevant government officials.

Do severe penalties for corruption work?

As mentioned, the question this chapter investigates is: would increasing the punishment for the corrupt such as by amputating hands or even executing offenders, as proposed by Islamist hardliners, have a big impact on combatting corruption? In other words, would increasing the penalty to this severe level automatically reduce the number of corruption acts?

Unlike the Criminal Code and the 1971 Anti-Corruption Law, Law No. 31 of 1999 has tried to follow this line of argument (to an extent at least) by setting minimum and maximum sentences, and increasing the penalties imposed by the two previous laws. However, although higher penalties could, theoretically, reduce the number of acts of corruption, they could just as easily lead to demands for higher bribes by those who commit corrupt acts. Susan Rose-Ackerman (1978: 109) has reminded us that 'a high fixed penalty will lower the incidence of corruption, but increase the size of bribes paid. If the penalty is high, officials must receive a high return in order to be willing to engage in bribery'. Therefore, she argues that 'the expected penalty should increase by more than a dollar for every dollar increase in the size of the bribe' (Rose-Ackerman 1978: 111).

A further problem is that there seems to be a wide gap between penalties specified for corruption and the penalties that are actually imposed. This means that increasing penalties will not help much in itself, if not accompanied by other measures such as effective and consistent enforcement. Also, there is the danger that an unscrupulous government could use the weapon of high penalties to go after political opponents. In other words, penalties could be used selectively or, worse, they could be used in connection with fabricated accusations.

It is worth noting that a basic conclusion of work done on the economics of crime is that the optimal amount of corruption is not zero, once one takes into account the costs of prevention. Deterrence expenditures should be set so that marginal benefits equal marginal costs (Rose-Ackerman 1978: 108–9). Deterrence of criminal behaviour depends on the probability of detection and punishment, and on the penalties imposed – those imposed by the legal system, and more subtle costs, such as loss of reputation, or shame. In addition, there should be a close connection between increasing the penalty and limiting judges' discretion. This is particularly important in the Indonesian context, when minimum and maximum sentences set by the law can be used as a 'bargaining chip' between all the parties involved before the court, including law enforcers.

In other words, corruption cannot be fought solely by imposing higher penalties or even more severe punishments. A serious anti-corruption effort requires the government to promote the rule of law, and conduct bureaucratic reform. This, in turn, requires a systematic approach involving criminal, administrative and civil laws. It would be too simplistic to just increase penalties or punishment.

Public participation is also important in combating corruption. Successful law enforcement and anti-corruption strategies are largely dependent upon both the willingness and availability of individuals to provide information, and/or to give evidence. Individuals will not be willing or available unless they have confidence that the government will protect their rights and safety. Potential accusers are often reluctant to come forward and spend the time and effort to go through the full process required to punish someone. Also, when corruption is widespread, the costs to accusers in terms of social capital can be high, such as loss of friends and family relations (Stapenhurst and Kpundeh 1998).

Witness protection usually starts with a risk-based assessment of the direct threat to the witness, and his or her vulnerability (Feneley 1997). Where the risk is assessed as very high, the person can be placed in a formal witness protection scheme, and this can involve the person and his or her family being relocated to another province, or even overseas, and given new identities. A substantial amount of witness protection involves counselling the witness and his or her family, to allay their fears. Witness protection legislation can encourage testimony by protecting material witnesses and improving the prosecution and conviction of corrupt people (Feneley 1997). In this context, Indonesia has issued Law No. 31 of 2014 on the Protection of Witnesses and Victims and established a witness protection agency (LPSK – Lembaga Perlindungan Saksi dan Korban), both of which are intended to ensure witnesses are adequately protected.

Another big factor in the success of any anti-corruption strategy is political will. The principal challenge in assessing political will is the need to distinguish between reform approaches that are intentionally superficial, and designed only to bolster the image of political leaders; and substantial efforts which are based on strategies to create change. It is, of course, difficult to objectively evaluate the intent of political reformers. Many well-intended regimes have engineered their own destruction through inept or ineffective efforts, while exploitative rulers have successfully hidden their motives behind a facade of cosmetic measures. (Abdulai 2009). Take, for example, what President Soeharto did during his thirty-two years of presidency in Indonesia. Despite his rhetoric of combatting corruption, the majority of the officials in judicial, executive and legislative branches of government became deeply corrupt (Assegaf 2002).

One indicator of genuine political will is the willingness of the government to bring those suspected of corruption to justice. An individual found guilty of corruption offences, regardless of his position or status in society, should be punished accordingly. Syed Hussein Alatas has reminded us that:

> Cases of high-level corruption are rarely truly punished. The regime has always been permissive towards its ruling elite. Corruption has developed to the extent that offices can be bought, as newspaper accounts reveal. Involvement of the highest leadership, in turn causes permissiveness towards corruption. This is the greatest cause of its perpetuation.
>
> (Alatas 1991: 121)

The enforcement of law depends primarily on the political will of the government. In other words, the key factor is strong political will demonstrated by a commitment from the leadership at all levels of government. 'Political will' refers to the demonstrated credible intent of political actors to attack perceived causes, or effects (of, here, corruption), at a systemic level (Kpundeh 1998). It is a critical starting point for sustainable and effective anti-corruption strategies and programmes. Without it, government statements of their determination to eradicate corruption remain mere rhetoric.

So far I have argued that corruption in Indonesia is a complicated matter that requires a whole package of strategies. Simply increasing penalties or imposing severe physical punishments ignores the complexity of the problem. In the next section I consider how the traditional punishment of hand amputation prescribed in the Qur'an can be reinterpreted to reject the proposal of Islamist hardliners to restore hudud as the solution to corruption in Indonesia.

Qur'an and its reinterpretation on *Hudud*

There is a view that Islamic teaching is immutable, because the authoritarian, divine and absolute concept of revelation in Islam does not allow change in Islamic teachings and institutions. On this view, the Qur'an and the Hadith[2] are immutable, regardless of history, time, culture and location. Muslims may change, but Islam will not. This means that the rulings pronounced by Shari'a are held to be static, final, eternal, absolute and unalterable. In other words, Islam's idealistic nature, religious nature, rigidity and casuistic nature lead inevitably to the immutability of Islamic teaching.[3] For Textualists, it is the Qur'an that should guide Muslims, rather than any so-called modern 'needs'. They consider the meaning of the Qur'an to be fixed and universal in its application (Saeed 2006: 3).

However, this view is only one side of the coin. Islamic teaching is, in fact, the product of a very slow and gradual process of interpretation of the Qur'an, and the collection, verification and interpretation of the Hadith during the first three centuries of Islam (the seventh to the ninth centuries CE). This process took place amongst scholars and jurists who developed their own methodology for the classification of sources, derivation of specific rules from general principles, and so forth (Gleave 2012). The Qur'an and the Hadith must involve human interpretation. They cannot be understood nor have any influence on human behaviour except through the efforts of (fallible) human beings. Therefore, even though Islam is based on the revelations of God, it cannot possibly be comprehended except through human understanding, which means there is both an inevitability of differences of opinion and the possibility of error, whether amongst scholars or in the community in general.

In modern times, most Muslim countries have abandoned or rejected the full application of classic Islamic criminal law, and many regard Islamic criminal law as a phenomenon of the past. However, from the 1970s, the number of countries applying Islamic criminal law has slowly increased. One recent example of the application of Islamic criminal law that garnered world-wide media attention occurred in October 2008, when a thirteen-year-old girl, Aisha Ibrahim Dhuhulow, was buried up to her neck at a Somalian football stadium, before being stoned to death in front of more than 1,000 people.

The stoning occurred after she had allegedly pleaded guilty to adultery in a Sharia court in Kismayo, a city controlled by Islamist insurgents. Similarly, since the Sharia legal system was introduced in the predominantly Muslim north of Nigeria in 2000, more than a dozen Nigerian Muslims have been sentenced to death by stoning for sexual offences ranging from adultery to homosexuality. In 2008, it was reported that six people convicted by Islamic Sharia courts in a northern Nigerian state were awaiting death by stoning, while forty-six others were waiting for amputation. In 2010, the world was shocked by the news that Sakineh Mohammadi Ashtiani had been sentenced in Iran to stoning to death. She had two sentences, one for adultery, for which she was sentenced to stoning, and the other for being an accomplice to the murder of her husband, for which she received a ten-year prison term. Ashtiani's two children began a campaign to overturn their mother's conviction. In June 2010, they wrote a 'letter to the world' asking for help to save their mother, which was first published on 26 June 2010, by Mission Free Iran's International Committee against Stoning. The letter brought widespread attention in 2010, as a result of grassroots campaigning through social networking sites that led to the letter being passed to mainstream mass media. Her stoning sentence was suspended but she remained in prison in Tabriz, Iran (News.com 2011) until 2014, when her sentence was commuted for good behaviour after nine years on death row.

Hudud and theft

It is beyond the scope of this chapter to examine all aspects of hudud in classical Islamic criminal law. Instead, I will focus on the punishment for a thief prescribed in the Qur'an and practised by the Prophet Muhammad fifteen centuries ago. Is it possible to offer a reinterpretation of this classic punishment?

The punishment for the crime of theft is amputation is stated clearly in the Qur'an: 'As to the thief. Male or female, cut off his or her hands: a punishment by way of example, from God, for their crime: and God is Exalted in Power.'[4] However, classically, a number of conditions must be fulfilled before the hand of a thief is cut off. These include: first, the thing stolen should have been taken by stealth; if it was not taken by stealth, then the punishment cannot applied, for example, if the property was seized by force in front of other people, because in this case the owner of the property could have asked for help to stop the thief. Second, the stolen property should be something of worth, and that which has no sanctity is of no worth, such as wine and pigs, all forbidden in Islam. Third, the value of the stolen property should be above a certain limit, namely three Islamic dirhams or a quarter of an Islamic dinar. Fourth, the stolen property should have been taken from a place where it had been put away, that is to say, a place where people usually put their property, such as a cupboard. Fifth, the theft itself has to be proven, either by the testimony of two qualified witnesses or by the confession of the thief, made twice.

Finally, the person from whom the property was stolen has to ask for it back; if he or she do not do so, then the thief's hand does not have to be cut off.[5]

The discussion below will demonstrate how it is possible to reinterpret hudud, specifically focusing on the punishment (*had*) for theft. The point to be made is that it is possible to reform and reinterpret Islamic criminal law in a manner that is not only compatible with human rights principles but which can also be justified under the Islamic legal tradition. If such an interpretation could be accepted, then one might argue that Western-inspired penal codes, which are already practised in most Muslim countries, should be considered Islamic. If this is the case, then the attempts of Islamist hardliners to restore old interpretations of Islamic criminal law cannot be considered 'Islamic' and should be rejected.

The approach taken in this chapter is a contextual understanding of the Qur'anic texts founded on the functions and objectives of punishment, and a reinterpretation of the Qur'anic texts that contain an *ihtimal*, or possibility, for an understanding that differs from the popular understanding. A new approach should be followed that protects the public interest and makes offenders aware and fearful, so another crime will not be committed or repeated. Any kind of punishment that meets these criteria can be accepted by modern Islamic law (Hosen 1993). Thus, the enactment of this law as Shari'a becomes *ta'aqquli* (reasonable), not *ta'abbudi* (ritual only) or *gayr ma'qul al-ma'na* (unreasonable) (Hosen 1993).

On this view, the categories of punishment determined in the Qur'an and the hadith do not have to be applied literally. Any type and form of punishment may be approved, so long as it can function to protect public interest and be capable of realising the objectives of Islamic criminal law (Hosen 1993). On this basis, the formulation of punishment that is in line with the conditions of this day and age may also be approved. In contrast, the punishments determined in the Qur'an and hadith should be seen as only maximum penalties that must be applied only where other forms of punishment cannot realise the objectives of the punishment.

For instance, for the crime of theft, the punishment stated in the Qur'an (Súra Máida 5:38) is, as mentioned, amputation of the hand (*qat'ul yad*). Concerning this matter, the opinion among Muslim religious scholars (*ulama*) is divided. First, some argue that this punishment must be followed literally as it is part of *ta'abbudi* (rituals that cannot be challenged) and therefore cannot be replaced with another punishment – imprisonment or anything else. This is the general view of the classical *ulama*.

The second view is that this punishment is *ma'qul al-ma'na*, that is, it has a rational intent and understanding. Because of this it can be replaced with a different punishment, which does not have to be amputation. Some of the modern *ulama* are of this opinion (asy-Syahawi 1961: 9–13). According to the supporters of this second opinion, what is meant by 'amputation of the hand' as mentioned in the Qur'anic verse is 'prevention of theft'. This prevention may be brought about by detention in a prison or by other means, and does not have to be by amputation of the hand. Thus, the verse could mean: '[a]s to the thief[:] Male or female, [to prevent them stealing]: a punishment by way of example'.

This group of ulama reasons that the word 'amputation' *(al-qat'u)* originally meant only 'prevention' (*al-man'u*), on the basis of the following: First, according to a narration (a Hadith), the Prophet gave a gift to Aqra' ibn Habis at-Tamimi and 'Uyainah ibn Hisn al-Fazari of a hundred camels each, whereas to 'Abbas ibn Mardas, the Prophet gave gift of less than a hundred camels. Then 'Abbas started to recite a poem in front of the Prophet that stated that his position and struggle, if not more than, could not be viewed as less than, Aqra' and 'Uyainah. When he heard 'Abbas's poem, which he repeated over and over again, the Prophet said to his Companions: *'Iqta'u 'anni lisanah'* (literally, 'cut me off from his tongue'). The Companions then gave 'Abbas more camels, until he had a hundred, as the Prophet had given to Aqra' and 'Uyainah (asy-Syahawi 1961: 9–13; Hosen 1981: 15–16).

If the word *qat'a* meant 'amputation', then the Companions would surely have cut off 'Abbas's tongue. But they interpreted the Prophet's statement as meaning preventing 'Abbas's tongue from talking and expressing his protest, by increasing the amount of camels until it reached a hundred. Hence, the Prophet's statement was not interpreted as 'cut off his tongue', but as 'prevent (or stop) his tongue' (asy-Syahawi 1961: 9–13; Hosen 1981: 15–16).

Second, according to another Hadith, Laila al-Akhiliah once recited a poem to praise Commander Hajjaj. Hajjaj said to his aide, *'Iqta' 'anni lisanaha'*. Hearing this command, the aide took Laila to a blacksmith to cut off her tongue. When she saw the blacksmith taking out his knife, Laila said, 'That is not what Hajjaj meant, rather he ordered you to cut off my tongue with a gift, not with a knife'. When the aide returned to the Commander to ask him, he confirmed Laila's opinion, and the Commander then rebuked the aide for his stupidity. If the word *qat'a* was interpreted narrowly to mean 'to cut' with a knife, it would not have been reasonable for Hajjaj to rebuke his aide thus.

Commander Hajjaj and Laila are renowned as Arab poets and literary figures during the Umayyad period, whose words may be used as evidence or argument in understanding the Arabic language. Also, language experts are agreed that the Arabic language during the Umayyad period and the beginning of the Abbasid period, up to the time of Abu al-'Atahiyah (a renowned Arab literary figure of the Abbasid period, who died in 211 AH), can be used as *hujjah* (evidence, proof) (asy-Syahawi 1961: 9–13; Hosen 1981: 15–16).

Further, according to Abu Hanifah, as-Sauri, Ahmad and Ishak, the punishment for the crime of theft is in the form of a choice: amputation of the hand or returning (replacing) the item that was stolen to its owner (Al-Mawardi 1966: 228; ar-Razi n.d.: 228), or – according to other *ulama* – spending it 'in the path of God'.[6] This means that these scholars did not regard the hand amputation as mandatory. The judge has other options available.

Finally, there is a decision of Umar bin Khattab, the second Caliph, to suspend hudud punishment during a time of famine (Hasan 1970: 120). Here the law was suspended as an exceptional measure in an exceptional situation. Yahya ibn Abi Kathir reported: 'Umar bin Khattab, may God be pleased with him, said, "Do not cut the hand of the thief who steals dates in the year of famine"'.[7] As-Sa'di reported: 'I asked Ahmad ibn Hanbal about this narration and he said, "No, the hand is not cut for theft when there is a need for that and the people are in famine and hardship"'.[8] This illustrates that the application of hand amputation is the past was not absolute and could be modified in certain circumstances. This is a strong indication that reinterpretation based on the actual situation is possible.

In summary, it may be possible to state that as long as the criminal law texts contain a possibility for re-interpretation based on the wording of Qur'anic verses, or as a result of their reading being seen as ambiguous (*mushtarak*), reinterpretation and a change of understanding remains open, alongside, of course, an emphasis on the *zawajir* (deterrence) function of punishment, together with the objective (*maqasid*) and spirit of its enactment. On this view, the implementation of Islamic punishments becomes more elastic.

Comparing other countries

In this section, I will review and compare the corruption perception index ratings of Indonesia, Saudi Arabia, a Muslim country that applies hudud, with countries that do not.

As mentioned, Saudi Arabia applies hudud, and that includes hand amputation. One unidentified scholar claimed that:

> Due to the harshness of punishment in Islam, both the hand of the thief and the life of the victim have been protected, at one and the same time, and tranquillity is secured for all. The execution, which is done publicly, serves to set an example.
>
> (Souryal, Potts and Alobied 1994: 263)

What the scholar refers to here is the deterrent effect. Do not look only at the harshness of the punishment, the scholar argues, as such punishment can act as a deterrent to save the hands of those who might otherwise be tempted to steal. This is an often-used argument in favour of hudud. Rudolph Peters (2006: 146) explained that:

> The amputation of the hand of one thief, it is repeatedly asserted, will deter many others from violating the property of other people. The advocates always contend that the crime rate in countries such as Saudi Arabia, where fixed punishments are carried out, is much lower than elsewhere.

But is it true that the corruption rate in Saudi Arabia is much lower? The data from Transparency International is relevant here. Transparency International is widely known as the leading international non-governmental organisation devoted to combating corruption. It brings civil society, business, and governments together in a powerful global coalition. Transparency International, through its International Secretariat and more than ninety independent national chapters around the world, works at the national and international levels to curb the supply of, and demand for, corruption.[9]

Every year Transparency International releases a Corruption Perception Index. It scores countries on how corrupt their public sectors are seen to be. There are criticisms of this Index[10] but the numbers are the product of daily realities for people living in these countries.

So, what are the positions of Saudi Arabia and Indonesia? In 2017, Saudi Arabia ranked 57 and Indonesia ranked 96, that is, Indonesia is ranked as significantly more corrupt than Saudi Arabia. Does this mean that Indonesia must follow the application of hand amputation in Saudi Arabia? I argue that we should not jump to such a conclusion. The Index also contains other Muslim countries that have better rankings than Saudi Arabia, namely UAE (21), Qatar (29) and Brunei Darussalam (32). These are all rich countries, just like Saudi Arabia and unlike Indonesia, which is relatively much poorer. The corruption level might therefore also relate just as much to the economic conditions of those countries as to the application of hudud.

Singapore does not apply hudud but it ranks six on the Index, while the overall champion is New Zealand, at number one. So, the question might not be why Saudi Arabia ranks better in comparison with Indonesia, but rather why countries that do not apply hand amputation like Singapore and New Zealand rank higher than Saudi Arabia? My answer would be that a higher penalty or severe punishment is only a small element of an effective anti-corruption strategy. Checks and balances and the rule of law can constrain the arbitrary exercise of power by governments. Judicial and administrative institutions, devoted to providing clear and transparent mechanisms for private and public sector interaction, are also essential to prevent corruption. Indeed, it is worth noting that both New Zealand and Singapore have much better governance systems than the other countries mentioned above.

Conclusion

Domestic and foreign investors want to be assured of a politically stable and economically predictable environment in a country before they commit their resources. Good governance – the rule of law, along with transparency and accountability in the public sector – not only affects economic development, but also plays a critical role in the administration of a nation. The two concepts of transparency and accountability go hand-in-hand, since, without adequate information on performance, outputs, and justifications, it is difficult to hold governments accountable for their actions. Transparency and accountability serve as checks against mismanagement and corruption on the part of public officials. Thus they are pillars of sound governance, which is crucial to winning and maintaining the confidence of citizens, investors, and the international community.

Anti-corruption strategy should not rely solely on the type of penalty or punishment applied. Law enforcement institutions are crucial in the struggle against public and private corruption and the integrity of these institutions is essential for the credibility of that struggle. The proposal to apply hand-amputation as it is understood in traditional understandings of Islamic hudud will only create problems.

While this chapter has demonstrated that reinterpretation of traditional Islamic hudud is not only a possibility, but even a necessity, it is safe to argue that the success of anti-corruption law will depend on a complex and challenging combination of strong political will, clean and solid law enforcement agencies, preventative measures to eliminate opportunities for corrupt actions, repressive measures to provide legal standards, civil and criminal penalties for corruption, and the encouragement of public participation. There is no simple or magic solution.

Notes

1. *Hadd* or *had* (pl. *hudud*): Ar. A specific punishment fixed in the Quran for a particular crime.
2. *Hadith*: Ar. records of the words, deeds, descriptions and circumstances of the Prophet Muhammad.
3. See the discussion in Masud (1995: 17).
4. The Qur'an, al-Ma'idah 5:38; Ali 2005: 254.
5. See `Audah 1992; Bahansi 1963; Zahrah 1990.
6. Al-Alusi, *Ruh al-Ma`ani*, Beirut, Dar Ihya' at-Turas al-`Arabi, juz VI, p. 135.
7. Ibn Qayyim, *I'lam al-Muwaqqi'in*, Vol. 3, p. 17.
8. Ibid.
9. See Transparency International website: www.transparency.org/about
10. See, for instance, Campbell 2013: 247.

References

Abdulai, Abdul Gafaru (2009) 'Political Will in Combating Corruption in Developing and Transition Economies: A Comparative Study of Singapore, Hong Kong and Ghana', *Journal of Financial Crime* 16(4): 387–417

Al-Alusi n.d. *Ruh al-Ma`ani*. Beirut: Dar Ihya' at-Turas al-`Arabi, juz VI

Al-Mawardi 1966. *al-Ahkam as-Sultaniyah*. Beirut: Dar al-Fikr

Alatas, Syed Hussein 1991. *Corruption: Its Nature, Causes and Functions*. Kuala Lumpur: S. Abdul Majeed

Ali, Abdullah Yusuf 2005. *The Qur'an: Text, Translation and Commentary*. New York: Tahrike Tarsile Qur'an

Ar-Razi, Imam al-Fakhr n.d. *at-Tafsir al-Kabir*. Tehran: Dar al-Kutub al-'Ilmiah

Assegaf, Ibrahim 2002. 'Legends of the Fall: An Institutional Analysis of Indonesian Law Enforcement Agencies Combating Corruption', in Tim Lindsey and Howard Dick (eds.) *Corruption in Asia: Rethinking the Governance Paradigm*. Sydney: Federation Press, pp. 127–9

Asy-Syahawi, Ibrahim Dasuqi 1961. *As-Sariqah.* Cairo: Maktabah Dar al-'Urubah

`Audah, `Abd al-Qadir 1992. *at-Tasyri` al-Jina'i al-Islami*. Beirut: Mu'assasah al-Risalah

Bahansi, Ahmad Fathi 1963. *Nazariyat fi al-Fiqh al-Jina'i al-Islami.* Cairo: al-Sharikah al-'Arabiyah

Buscaglia, Edgardo 1997. 'Introduction', in Edgardo Buscaglia, William Ratliff, and Robert Cooter (eds.), *The Law and Economics of Development*. Greenwich: JAI Press, pp. 1–8

Buscaglia, Edgardo and Ratliff, William 2000. *Law and Economics in Developing Countries*. Stanford: Hoover Institution Press

Butt, Simon 2012. *Corruption and Law in Indonesia*. London: Routledge

Campbell, Stuart 2013. 'Perception is Not Reality: The FCPA, Brazil, and the Mismeasurement of Corruption', *Minnesota Journal of International Law* 22(1): 247–81

Feneley, John 1997. 'Witness Protection Schemes- Pitfalls & Best Practice & Covert Investigations', paper presented at 8th International Anti-Corruption Conference (IACC), held by Transparency International, 7–11 September

Gleave, Robert 2012. *Islam and Literalism: Literal Meaning and Interpretation in Islamic Legal Theory*. Edinburgh University Press

Hasan, Ahmad 1970. *The Early Development of Islamic Jurisprudence*. Islamabad: Islamic Research Institute

Hosen, Ibrahim 1981. 'Ukhuwwah Islamiyah Jangan Menjadi Retak Dikarenakan Masalah Khilafiyah [Let Not Islamic Brotherhood Become Fractured Because of Khilafiyah Problems]', *Studia Islamika* 15(6): 15–16

Hosen, Ibrahim 1993 'Jenis-Jenis Hukuman dalam Pidana Islam dan Perbedaan Ijtihad Ulama Dalam Penerapannya' [Different Types of Punishments in Islamic Criminal Law and its Application], paper presented at Seminar Kontribusi Hukum Islam Terhadap Pembinaan Hukum Nasional, Fakultas Syari`ah, IAIN Syarif Hidayatullah Jakarta, 17 July

Ibn Qayyim, n.d. I'lam al-Muwaqqi'in, vol. 3, p. 17. Beirut: Dar al-Kutub al-'Ilmiah

Klitgaard, Robert 1988. *Controlling Corruption*. Berkeley: University of California Press

Kompas 2017. 'Potong Tangan Koruptor', 17 May https://nasional.kompas.com/read/2011/05/17/22443881/Potong.Tangan.Koruptor

Kpundeh, Sahr J. 1998 'Political Will in Fighting Corruption', in Kpundeh Sahr J. and Irene Hors (eds.) *Corruption and Integrity Improvement Initiatives in Developing Countries*. New York: UNDP, pp. 91–110

Masud, Muhammad Khalid 1995. *Shatibi's Philosophy of Islamic Law*. Pakistan: Islamic Research Institute

Narasimhan, C. V. 1997. 'Prevention of Corruption: Towards Effective Enforcement', in S. Guhan and Samuel Paul (eds.), *Corruption in India: Agenda for Action*. New Delhi: Vision Books, pp. 251–85

News.com 2011. '"Stoning" Woman Sakineh Mohammadi Ashtiani Could Be Hanged Instead', 26 December www.news.com.au/world/stoning-woman-sakineh-mohammadi-ashtiani-could-be-hanged-instead/story-e6frfkyi-1226230371831

Peters, Rudolph 2006. *Crime and Punishment in Islamic Law: Theory and Practice from the Sixteenth to the Twenty-First Century*. Cambridge University Press
Rose-Ackerman, Susan 1978. *Corruption: A Study in Political Economy*. New York: Academic Press
Saeed, Abdullah 2006. *Interpreting the Qur'an: Towards a Contemporary Approach*. New York: Routledge
Souryal, Sam S.; Potts, Dennis W.; and Alobied, Abdullah I. 1994. 'The Penalty of Hand Amputation for Theft in Islamic Justice', *Journal of Criminal Justice* 22(3): 249–65
Stapenhurst, Frederick and Sahr J. Kpundeh 1998. 'Public Participation in the Fight Against Corruption', *Canadian Journal of Development Studies* 19(3): 491–508
Tempo 2001. 'The Aksara Journal', 19 February: 40
Tempo 2011. 'MUI: Potong Tangan Koruptor Harus Masuk UU', 27 May https://nasional.tempo.co/read/337185/mui-potong-tangan-koruptor-harus-masuk-uu
Zahrah, Abu 1990. al-`Uqubah fi al-Fiqh al-Islami. Cairo: Dar al-Fikr al-'Arabi

Legislation

Criminal Code (*Kitab Undang-Undang Hukum Pidana*, KUHP: Law No. 1 of 1946 as amended by Law No. 27 of 1999 on the Indonesian Criminal Code)
Law No. 3 of 1971 on Corruption
Law No. 31 of 1999 on the Eradication of the Criminal Acts of Corruption
Law No. 31 of 2014 on the Protection of Witnesses and Victims

Part VI

Criminal law in Aceh

19 Aceh's Islamic Criminal Code

Formalising discrimination

Tim Mann and Dina Afrianty

Indonesia was condemned around the world when, on 23 May 2017, two men from Aceh, aged twenty and twenty-three, received eighty-three strokes of the cane as punishment for engaging in gay sex, or *liwath*, under Aceh's 2014 Islamic Criminal Code, or *Qanun Jinayat*. A few months earlier, the men had been caught in bed together by vigilantes, who broke into their private accommodation. The pair were reportedly the first two men caned for gay sex under the Qanun Jinayat since its implementation began in 2015.

Many international media outlets were there to cover the event, capturing graphic images and video of officials wearing sinister brown hoods with white strips across the eyes, standing over the kneeled and wincing men receiving the punishment. Most reports described the crowd waving smart phones and cheering and yelling, calling for the hooded officials to 'Do it harder' (BBC 2017; Straits Times 2017a). International condemnation was swift and widespread. Amnesty International described the caning of the two men as an outrageous act of cruelty (Amnesty International 2017a). Australian Prime Minister Malcolm Turnbull, meanwhile, said it was 'barbaric' to be caning people because of their sexual orientation (SBS 2017), a criticism that was quickly picked up by Indonesian media outlets (Republika 2017).

Following the enormous backlash, President Joko 'Jokowi' Widodo reportedly instructed Aceh Governor Irwandi Yusuf and Deputy Governor Nova Iriansyah to ensure canings were conducted behind closed doors, because of the potential to damage foreign investment in Aceh (Afrianto 2017). This was, in fact, an argument that Irwandi, a known opponent of the practice, has made in the past, and there were claims that he was also behind the proposal this time (AJNN 2017).

Conducting caning behind closed doors would, in fact, be contrary to the express terms of art. 262(1) of Aceh's Islamic Criminal Procedure Code (*Qanun Acara Jinayat*), which says caning should be implemented in an open space and can be viewed by people attending (art. 262(1). In April 2018, Irwandi responded by introducing Governor's Regulation No. 5 of 2018 on the Implementation of Qanun Jinayat Provisions on Caning, which states that caning should be conducted in an open space but inside a prison complex (art. 30(1), (3)). This appeared to be a compromise between the government and the legislature, which has insisted that caning behind closed doors would lessen the intended deterrent effect of the policy (Saidi 2017). In any case, few local officials appear to have paid heed to Jokowi's suggestion or the new regulation – several public canings have been held since (see, for example, Anwar 2017; Setyadi 2018).

Aceh has been permitted to implement varying degrees of Islamic law for more than a decade now and the introduction of the Qanun Jinayat in October 2015 has resulted in dozens of Acehnese women and men being caned in public. Human rights and civil society organisations at the international and national levels continue to challenge the implementation of the Qanun Jinayat, arguing that it contradicts Indonesia's constitution and other national legislation. As the only Indonesian province permitted to implement Islamic law, Aceh observes a combination of 'secular' criminal law – regulated through the Criminal Code (KUHP, *Kitab Undang-Undang Hukum Pidana*), which operates across Indonesia's entire territory – and Islamic criminal law in the form of a select number of offences derived from Islamic traditions or shari'a, regulated through the Qanun Jinayat and other *Qanun* (as regional regulations or *peraturan daerah* [*perda*] are known in Aceh).

This chapter starts with a brief discussion of the context for the introduction of Islamic law in the province. Following this, the chapter examines the content of the Qanun Jinayat in detail, focusing on offences and punishments, and examining how it creates conflicts with the Criminal Code and other national level statutes. We provide a brief overview of the implementation of the Qanun Jinayat during its first three years, highlighting how it has a strong focus on regulating consensual sex. Finally, the chapter discusses responses to the implementation of the Qanun Jinayat from national and local civil society activists and speculates on prospects for reform.

Modern history of Islamic Law in Aceh

The autonomous province of Aceh is the only Indonesian province authorised to implement Islamic criminal law. Although small populations of religious minorities live in the province, Acehnese identity has long been strongly tied to Islam. This conceptualisation is so deeply embedded that Acehnese people will often remark that 'Aceh is identical with Islam' (Aspinall 2007a: 247). Despite ongoing debate on the subject, the Acehnese proudly claim that the region is the place where Islam was first established in the Indonesian archipelago, in the thirteenth century (Brown 2003: 32). As such, many Acehnese and Indonesians describe the region as 'the veranda of Mecca'. The history of Aceh as home to an influential Islamic sultanate in the sixteenth and seventeenth centuries has been passed on from older to younger generations of Acehnese, creating a collective memory of their glorious past and shaping notions of Acehnese identity (Shaw 2008: 2). In the public consciousness, this glorious past is 'rightly or, more often, wrongly' associated with a more complete implementation of shari'a (Lindsey and Hooker 2007: 217), and goes some way to explaining the persistent attraction of Islamic law in the region.

The province also has a reputation for being fiercely independent, and it resisted Dutch colonial control until the early twentieth century. In the 1950s, many Acehnese joined the Darul Islam movement to revolt against the newly formed Indonesian state, aiming to transform the new republic into an Islamic state (Aspinall 2007a: 245). A series of drawn-out negotiations between Acehnese rebels and central government authorities eventually put an end to this rebellion in 1962. Although attempts to establish an Islamic state were unsuccessful, the central government made some concessions, recognising the province as a 'special region' and providing it with nominal autonomy over religious, cultural and education affairs (Robinson 1998: 130).

The suspension of hostilities between Aceh and Jakarta was relatively short-lived. The New Order government, which came to power in 1966, soon sought to assert greater control over the region and in 1974 passed a new law on local government that essentially treated Aceh like any other regional province. Resentment over Jakarta's exploitation of Aceh's rich natural resource wealth and the New Order's centralised government led to the establishment of the secessionist Free Aceh Movement (GAM, Gerakan Aceh Merdeka) in 1976 (Aspinall 2005). Over the next three decades, GAM waged an armed separatist conflict in the province, attracting varying degrees of public support through this period. Human rights abuses by the military in the 1990s intensified Acehnese grievances. Following the fall of Soeharto's New Order in 1998, GAM grew in strength and guerrillas controlled most of the rural areas of the province at one point (Aspinall 2007a: 245).

With Indonesia's political reform in 1998 and the introduction of regional autonomy, the national leadership under President Habibie initiated policies to appease the Acehnese and offered some solutions to end the military conflict. To assuage the demands of separatists, Jakarta offered the province increasing degrees of autonomy, beginning in 1999 with the passage of Law No. 44 of 1999 on the Special Status of the Province of Aceh Special Region. Special status was granted in the fields of religion, education, customary law (*adat*), and the role of religious leaders (*ulama*, Muslim religious scholars) in policy formulation (art. 3(2)). In the field of religion, Aceh's provincial government was permitted to implement Islamic law for its adherents 'in social life', in a manner that 'safeguarded harmony among religious communities' (art. 4(1–2)). Soon after, the local legislature passed Regulation No. 5 of 2000 on the Implementation of Islamic Law. It stated that the implementation of shari'a would include criminal law (art. 5(2)) but the local government and the Acehnese ulama council of Ulama (MPU, Majelis Permusyawaratan Ulama) first needed to formulate provisions, 'socialise' and refine them, before passing local regulations on these matters (art. 18). This regulation also stated that the government must set up a body to monitor and control the implementation of shari'a, the so-called 'Shari'a Police' or WH (Wilayatul Hisbah) (art. 20(1)).

Although the Acehnese have a reputation for being among the most pious Muslims in Indonesia, there was no consensus among Acehnese over the introduction of Islamic law. GAM often drew on religious language and had, at times, promised the people that it would establish Islamic law after independence. However, it framed its struggle in largely secular-nationalistic terms (Aspinall 2007a: 245). Some of its leaders, including prominent women in the organisation, questioned moves to make Aceh an Islamic province. In the end, Islamic law was introduced in Aceh through a top-down process that was influenced by the political dynamics of the time (Aspinall 2007b). National government and military officials, as well as local Acehnese religious and bureaucratic elites, reportedly believed that the granting of Islamic law was a way of undermining one of the 'selling points' of GAM and pacifying the Islamic communities in the province (ICG 2006: 4).

The introduction of Islamic Law in Aceh

Law No. 18 of 2001 on Special Autonomy for the Province of Aceh Special Region granted the Acehnese the authority to control their own political, religious affairs, economic revenues (Aspinall 2005). It allowed the local legislature to pass qanun, Islamic local regulations, on the implementation of Islamic law. This Law also allowed the creation of the shari'a courts (Makamah Syariah).

Several qanun were passed over the following years, further regulating the Shari'a Courts, as well as matters such as Islamic dress, gambling, alcohol and 'seclusion', or *khalwat,* which is generally defined as being alone in an enclosed space with a member of the opposite sex.[1] Qanun No. 10 of 2002 on the Shari'a Courts first provided the courts with authority over Islamic criminal law *(jinayah)* (art. 49(c)), beyond the family and inheritance law matters typically handled by Indonesia's religious court (*peradilan agama*) system (Hooker 2008: 252). The explanatory memorandum to art. 49 introduced the types of Islamic criminal law offences under the jurisdiction of the courts, dividing them into three categories: *hudud* offences (offences for which a specific punishment is mandated under Islamic law); *qishash/diat* offences (offences for which compensation or retaliation may be part of the punishment); and *ta'zir* offences (offences for which no specific punishments are mentioned in the Qur'an and hadith, and so punishment is left to the discretion of judges). Notably, hudud, qishash/diat and ta'zir were not defined in the regulation, they were simply used as category headings. The three qanun on alcohol, gambling and seclusion, passed the following year, were significant for introducing caning as a punishment, and included definitions of hudud and ta'zir.

Following the 2004 Indian Ocean earthquake and tsunami and the cessation of conflict between GAM and the central government, there was a significant escalation in the implementation of shari'a in Aceh. The massive destruction of the tsunami and the new peace following the Helsinki agreement of 2005 triggered discussions about not just reconstruction of damaged physical property but also the complete reconstruction of Acehnese society (Feener 2013a: 252). This widespread discourse about the 'total reconstruction' of Aceh provided greater space for advocates of shari'a to promote Islamic law as a tool for reshaping Acehnese society (Feener 2013a: 261).

Efforts to compile an Islamic criminal code began soon after, and in May 2007, Aceh Governor Irwandi Yusuf instructed the Aceh Shari'a Agency (Dinas Syariat Islam Aceh) and the provincial Legal Office (Biro Hukum) to compile a unified code to replace the qanun on alcohol, gambling and seclusion (Großmann 2015: 100). Following a lengthy drafting process, the Aceh People's Representative Council (Dewan Perwakilan Rakyat Aceh, DPRA), the provincial legislature, passed a highly contentious version of the Qanun Jinayat (criminal code) and Qanun Acara Jinayat (procedural code) on 14 September 2009, at the end of their term in office. This *Qanun Jinayat* included provisions criminalising homosexuality and the death penalty by stoning for adulterers, a penalty that was not present in the draft law submitted to the legislature by the executive (Salim 2015: 94). The provisions on stoning, in particular, prompted considerable debate and backlash from civil society within Aceh, as well as at national and international levels (see, for example, Hukumonline 2009; Wibow 2009). Even before it was passed, Governor Irwandi made public statements against the penalty and then refused to sign the bill into law, despite large protests from some members of the Muslim community. Law No. 11 of 2006 on the Governing of Aceh states that if a bill is not signed by the governor then it automatically becomes law after thirty days (art. 234(1)). Although this suggested that the Islamic Criminal Code would still become law, even if not signed by the governor, art. 232(1) also states that qanun are formally passed by the governor following mutual agreement with the DPRA, which had not occurred in this case. It was generally accepted that the operation of art. 232(1) means the two quanun had not come into force, and so both sat idle and unenforced (Großmann 2015: 109).

Irwandi was voted out of office in 2012. When new Aceh Governor Zaini Abdullah, from the Aceh Party (formerly the GAM Party), came to power, he vowed to implement a 'purer' version of shari'a that could be accepted by all Acehnese (Hasan 2012). On 13 December 2013, ahead of the legislative elections, which were to be held in April 2014, Zaini signed Law No. 7 of 2013 on the Islamic Criminal Procedure Code (Qanun Acara Jinayat). Arskal Salim (2015: 97) has suggested this was a political move, designed to bolster the Aceh Party's Islamic credentials ahead of the election.

In late September 2014, again at the end of their term, the DPRA passed a revised version of the Qanun Jinayat, Qanun Aceh No. 6 of 2014 on Islamic Criminal Law (*Hukum Jinayat*) (Zamzami 2014). This version still criminalised adultery and homosexuality but the provisions on stoning were removed. The fact that both attempts to pass Islamic criminal law occurred during the period between the legislative election and when the new group of legislators took up their posts is significant. As Salim noted with respect to the first attempt to pass the Qanun Jinayat in 2009, 'the outgoing legislature was less interested in whether the qa*nun* would be implemented and more interested in being able to claim that they were the legislators who should be remembered by future generations for making tougher Islamic penal laws in Aceh' (Salim 2015: 97). This time, there was no resistance from the governor. Zaini signed the law and, in accordance with art. 75, it came into force one year later, on 22 October 2015. It replaced and consolidated the previous qanun on *khamar, maisir* and *khalwat,* and broadened the scope of Islamic criminal law.

The Qanun Jinayat, Aceh's Islamic Criminal Code

Supporters of Islamic law in Aceh welcomed the introduction of the Qanun Jinayat and saw it as evidence of the government's commitment to promoting '*Islam kaffah*', or 'Islam in its totality'. As noted, the Qanun Jinayat is a regional regulation, or perda, passed by the DPRA under regional autonomy. According to the hierarchy of laws laid out in art. 7(1) of Law No. 12 of 2011 on Lawmaking, perda (and therefore the Qanun Jinayat) are at the bottom of the hierarchy and should not conflict with the statutes above it or the Constitution. Until recently, the Minister of Home Affairs had the power to cancel problematic perda through the 2014 Law on Local Government. However, in mid-2017, the Constitutional Court struck down these provisions, leaving the only options available review by the Supreme Court, or issue by the DPR of a higher-level statute (Fachrudin 2018). As Simon Butt demonstrates in Chapter 20, the Supreme Court has rarely used its power to review or strike down regulations inferior to statutes in the hierarchy of laws, and has never done so in the case of Aceh's qanun.

This section discusses the principles and key provisions of the Qanun Jinayat, focusing on how it regulates offences and punishments. Despite its wide scope, the Qanun Jinayat is a relatively slim document. It is only twenty-three pages long, consisting of seventy-five articles, with eighteen pages of explanatory memorandum (*penjelasan* or elucidation). It contains ten chapters: General Provisions (which consists largely of definitions); Principles and Scope; Legal Justifications and Excuses, Offences and Punishments; Concurrent Offences; Offences and Punishments for Minors; Compensation and Rehabilitation; Other/Miscellaneous Provisions (which consists of three clauses relating to permits for businesses that violate the Qanun); Provisions on Transition; and Concluding Provisions.

Principles and scope

As with many Indonesian laws and regulations, the section on 'principles' begins with a lofty statement about guiding standards. The Qanun Jinayat states that it is based on the principles of Islam, legality, justice and equality, welfare, protection of human rights and community education (art. 2). The explanatory memorandum provides some guidance on these seemingly vague principles.

The explanation to art. 2(b) on legality in many ways mirrors art. 1(1) of the Indonesian Criminal Code (KUHP). It states criminal liability can only be established for conduct prohibited by laws and regulations that were in effect at the time the Qanun Jinayat was passed. The Qanun Jinayat can therefore not be applied retrospectively. Article 2(c) on justice and equality states that in determining the severity of punishments, judges must consider: the dignity and right of the victim to receive fair and appropriate restitution for the suffering and losses experienced; the dignity of the perpetrator and their right to receive a fair punishment that protects them from cruelty; and protection of the wider population, to create social security, order, comfort, and camaraderie. Popular discourse on shari'a in Aceh tends to lean heavily on this third aspect, justifying harsh punishments as a means to provide a 'deterrent effect' (*efek jera*) or encourage the population to practise shari'a more completely. Indeed, Feener has described the legal project of shari'a implementation as existing within a broader project to transform society in line with Islamic norms (Feener 2013b: 287). It appears that notions of appropriate justice are typically interpreted through this lens.

The explanation of art. 2(e) on human rights is particularly revealing. It states that 'protection of human rights' means that offences and punishments are formulated in line with efforts to protect and respect the nature and dignity of humanity, in accordance with the Indonesian Muslim community's understanding of human rights. This last component of the provision would therefore appear to be a form of defence against criticisms that universal human rights are violated by some offences in the Qanun, for example, adultery or same-sex relations, and punishments like caning. Rather than shying away from human rights debates, proponents of Islamic law in Aceh have, at times, directly referenced human rights principles in this way to argue that Islamic law in Aceh does not violate these standards (Feener 2013a: 247).

Most of the controversy over the Qanun Jinayat stems from the Islamic law offences (*jarimah*) and punishments (*'uqubat*) that it regulates. Punishments may take the form of hudud (as noted, a specific punishment mandated in the Qur'an or hadith, in this case, caning is the only one described) or ta'zir (offences for which no specific penalties are mentioned in the Qur'an or hadith, so the type of punishment is left to the discretion of judges) (art. 4(1),(2)). Under the Qanun Jinayat, these 'variable punishments' include caning, fines, imprisonment or restitution (art. 4(4)). The code also describes 'additional ta'zir punishments' of: guidance by the state; restitution by parents or guardians; return to parents or guardians; dissolution of marriage; revocation of permits or rights; confiscation of certain goods; and social work (art. 4(5)). These additional punishments are regulated further by Gubernatorial Regulation No. 5 of 2018, in accordance with art. 4(7) of the Qanun Jinayat.

The Qanun Jinayat is internally inconsistent with regards to its scope, although in general it seeks to apply its provisions to both Muslims and non-Muslims. Uncontroversially, the Qanun Jinayat applies to Muslims who commit an offence in Aceh (art. 5(a)). It is the regulation's treatment of non-Muslims, however, that gives rise to confusion. Article 5 enshrines two provisions established under art. 129 of Law No. 11 of 2006 on Governing Aceh.[2] Article 5(b) states that the Qanun Jinayat applies to non-Muslims who conduct an offence together with a Muslim and voluntarily choose to be subject to Islamic law. Article 5(c), meanwhile, states that the Qanun Jinayat also applies to non-Muslims in Aceh who commit offences that are regulated by the Qanun Jinayat but not the Criminal Code or other national criminal law (art. 5(c)). However, art. 72 of the Qanun Jinayat seems to seek to expand the operation of the Code, stating that if an offence is regulated by the Qanun Jinayat and the KUHP or national criminal statute, then the Qanun Jinayat is the regulation that applies. This provision would therefore appear to provide for the punishment of non-Muslims under the Qanun Jinayat, conflicting with the voluntary principle established in art. 5. The elucidation to art. 72 sheds no further light on whether art. 72 also applies to non-Muslims.

The overlapping nature of these provisions appears to have resulted in some confusion as to their application, even among state officials responsible for implementing the shari'a regime. Statements by Indonesian legal scholars and representatives of the Aceh Shari'a Agency (Dinas Syariat Islam) seem to suggest that there is a common understanding that the Qanun Jinayat should only apply to non-Muslims who commit an offence with Muslims and voluntarily submit themselves to the law (see, for example, Hidayat 2016; Hukumonline 2015). Yet there are examples of non-Muslims who have been punished under the law, despite conducting an offence alone. Consider the case of Remita Sinaga, 60, a Christian woman from Takengon, Aceh Tengah District, who in 2016 received thirty strokes of the cane for selling alcoholic drinks. On learning that she had not conducted the offence in conjunction with Muslim perpetrator, the head of the Aceh Shari'a Agency, Syahrizal Abbas, told journalists that this suggested the Qanun Jinayat had been erroneously applied (Hidayat 2016). This, of course, ignores the more likely explanation that she was simply unaware of the issue.

Another major problem is that neither the Qanun Jinayat nor the Qanun Acara Jinayat mention when and how a non-Muslim might make a statement declaring that they are willing to subject themselves to Islamic law. Neither do they cover what might happen if the accused wanted to revoke such a statement. Demonstrating the problematic nature of this omission, one of the judges hearing Remita's case said that the fact that she had not protested during investigation or trial and had not filed an appeal was sufficient evidence that she had voluntarily submitted herself to the Qanun Jinayat (Hidayat 2016).

Until further clarification is issued, however, we must read these provisions at face value and conclude that the Qanun Jinayat can be applied to non-Muslims. The extent to which it is applied to non-Muslims in practice will largely depend on how officials continue to interpret these provisions. This is one of the core problems with the Qanun Jinayat – it introduces overlapping and unclear provisions.

Offences and punishments

The most controversial aspect of the Qanun Jinayat is how it regulates offences and punishments. The Qanun Jinayat covers ten separate offences, most of which are related to issues of morality and sexuality (art. 3(2)). As mentioned, the Qanun Jinayat replaced three previously issued qanun on alcohol, gambling and seclusion, and introduced a number of new Islamic law offences, such as those covering adultery or sexual relations outside marriage (*zina*) and sodomy (*liwath*) and lesbian sex (*musahaqah*). Most offences are described using Arabic terms, although sexual abuse (*pelecehan seksual*) and rape (*pemerkosaan*) follow the Indonesian. Many of the morality and sexuality offences are described in quite graphic detail, while others, such as sexual abuse, remain somewhat vague and open to interpretation. There are several serious offences mentioned in the Qur'an that are not covered by the Qanun Jinayat, such as murder, theft, and robbery, which continue to be covered by the KUHP. A number of the offences override or conflict with principles of evidence long established under the national Criminal Procedure Code (*Kitab Undang-Undang Hukum Acara Pidana*, KUHAP), in many cases to the detriment of women. This section looks at the offences and their punishments in more detail.

Khamar

The Qanun Jinayat introduces heavy punishments for drinking, producing, storing, selling, importing, buying, carrying/transporting or gifting alcoholic drinks (*khamar*), which are defined as drinks with an alcohol content of 2 per cent or more (arts. 1(21) and 15–16). Punishment ranges from up to twenty strokes of the cane, or up to 200 grams of gold or up to twenty months in prison for buying, carrying/transporting or gifting alcoholic drinks (art. 16(2)), to up to eighty strokes of the cane, or up to 800 grams of gold or up to eighty months in prison for involving children in any khamar-related offence (art. 17). Intentionally drinking alcoholic drinks carries a compulsory hudud punishment of forty strokes of the cane (art. 15(1)). The Code contains exceptions for certain alcohol offences. It excuses people who consume alcoholic substances as part of medication prescribed by a doctor (art. 14(1)). Accordingly, chemists, doctors and hospitals cannot be accused of producing, buying, selling or storing alcoholic substances (art. 14(2)).

The khamar offences differ markedly from those contained in the KUHP. There are a few offences in the KUHP relating to alcohol, the most significant of which is art. 300. Under art. 300, intentionally selling or providing alcoholic drinks to a drunk person, or a minor under sixteen years old, or forcing a person to drink alcohol through violence or threat of violence, carries a punishment of up to one year in prison. If this behaviour results in serious injury, or death, the perpetrator may face up to seven or nine years in prison, respectively. The remainder of provisions in the KUHP relating to alcohol are misdemeanours (*pelanggaran*) and the maximum punishment described is three weeks of 'light imprisonment'. Two relate to public drunkenness (art. 536) and disturbing public order while drunk (art. 492); others relate to selling alcohol to members of the armed forces (art. 537), or children (art. 538) and providing free alcohol at a public event (art. 539). There are numerous other presidential and ministerial regulations regulating production, import and sale of alcoholic drinks.[3]

The most problematic of the khamar offences is arguably that relating to drinking alcohol. The earlier qanun on alcoholic substances (Qanun No. 12 of 2003) differentiated between punishment of Muslims and non-Muslims. Article 26(1) of Qanun No. 12 of 2003 is nearly identical to 15(1) of the Qanun Jinayat, and states that every person who intentionally drinks alcohol faces a hudud punishment of forty strokes of the cane.[4] However, the elucidation to the article states that 'every person' should be interpreted to mean 'every Muslim'. Non-Muslims found drinking alcohol, therefore, could not be caned under the 2003 qanun.[5] According to the provisions of the 2003 regulation, if a non-Muslim caught drinking alcohol was referred to a state court, he or she could receive a lighter punishment or escape punishment altogether. No such explanation or differentiation exists in the Qanun Jinayat. It is not clear whether this was an oversight or whether it was intentionally omitted to extend the hudud punishment to non-Muslims, however, the fact that the phrase was also omitted from similar articles on gambling and seclusion in the Qanun Jinayat suggests drafters did likely intended to extend the application of the Qanun Jinayat to non-Muslims. Notably, under the 2003 qanun, offences and ta'zir punishments (which do not include caning) related to producing, making available, selling, importing, circulating, carrying, storing, trading, gifting or promoting alcoholic drinks applied to all people in the territory of Aceh.[6]

Gambling (Maisir)

The Qanun Jinayat describes gambling (*maisir*) as any activity that involves betting between two or more people (arts. 1(22) and 18–22). Punishment ranges from up to twelve strokes of the cane, or a fine of up to 120 grams of gold, or up to twelve months in prison for gambling amounts equivalent to 2 grams of gold or less (art. 18), to up to thirty strokes of the cane, or a fine of up to 300 grams of gold or up to 30 months in prison for gambling amounts equivalent to more than 2 grams of gold (art. 19). Conducting, providing the facilities for or funding gambling, or involving children in gambling are subject to heavier penalties: up to forty-five strokes of the cane, or a fine of up to 450 grams of gold or up to forty-five months in prison (arts. 20 and 21).

Like the 2003 qanun on alcohol, the 2003 qanun on gambling (Qanun No. 13 of 2003) excused non-Muslims from the punishment of caning, although they could still face fines if they held (*menyelenggarakan*) a gambling event, or provided facilities for, or, 'protected' gambling.

Gambling is also covered in the KUHP and this is one of the few offences for which the penalty is harsher in the KUHP. Personal gambling offences are described under art. 303 bis (which was introduced through Law No. 7 of 1974) and carry a maximum sentence of four years. Repeating the offence within two years carries a maximum punishment of up to six years in prison. Offering, providing an opportunity for gambling, or making it a source of income, carries a maximum sentence of up to ten years in prison, or a fine of up to Rp. 25 million (art. 303).

In 2017, two Buddhist men were punished for gambling (cockfighting) under the Qanun Jinayat – reportedly the first time Buddhists had been caned for violating the Islamic Criminal Code (Simanjuntak and Ompusunggu 2017). On 10 March, Alem Suhadi, fifty-seven, and Amel Akim, sixty, both Chinese members of the Buddhist minority, received nine and seven lashes respectively. The sentences were carried out in the city of Jantho, Aceh Besar District. They had been caught by police in January, with two chickens and Rp. 400,000 of betting money (Straits Times 2017b). The pair reportedly chose to be subjected to the Qanun Jinayat in preference to the KUHP, which, as noted above, could have seen them face years in prison. The judgment referred to their decision to voluntarily be punished under the Qanun Jinayat (Wahono 2017).[7]

Khalwat

One of the most controversial Islamic law offences has been that of 'seclusion' (*khalwat*), which is defined as being alone (in an enclosed or private place) with a member of the opposite sex who is not a spouse or relative (arts. 1(23) and 23–24). Committing a khalwat offence carries a ta'zir punishment of up to ten strokes of the cane, or a fine of up to 100 grams of gold or ten months in prison (art. 23(1)) to fifteen strokes of the cane. A fine of 150 grams of gold or fifteen months in prison may be imposed for providing facilities for, or promoting, khalwat (art. 23(2)).

The Qanun Jinayat provides some exemptions for the offence of khalwat. For example, employees cannot be accused of khalwat with their colleagues at the workplace (art. 12(1)). Likewise, residents of a house cannot be accused of khalwat with other residents of the house if they are members of the same family or have village head approval, or equivalent, to live in the house (art. 12(2)). Similarly, any person who helps someone of the opposite sex during an emergency does not commit khalwat or *ikhtilath* (intermingling, see below) (art. 13).

Like the earlier local regulations on alcohol and gambling, the now invalid Qanun No. 14 of 2003 on Khalwat (*Mesum*) sought to exclude non-Muslims from the punishment of caning. Articles 22(1) and 22(2) describe ta'zir punishments for violating the offence of khalwat. The elucidations to both these provisions state that 'every person' should be read as 'all Muslims in Aceh'. As noted above, the Qanun Jinayat seems to remove this different treatment of Muslims and non-Muslims, allowing non-Muslims to face caning for khalwat offences.

Ikhtilath

The Qanun Jinayat introduces the offence of 'intermingling' (ikhtilath), which is defined as consensual intimate relations, such as flirting, touching, hugging and kissing, between a male and female who are not married in a private or public area (arts. 1(24) and 25–32). The Qanun Jinayat describes punishment of up to thirty strokes of the cane, or a fine of 300 grams of gold or thirty months in prison for a basic ikhtilath offence (art. 25(1)). Conducting, providing the facilities for or promoting ikhtilath, or involving children above the age of ten years in ikhtilath offences involves heavier penalties: up to forty-five strokes of the cane, or a fine of up to 450 grams of gold or up to forty-five months in prison (art. 26). Committing ikhtilath with a relative (*mahram*) involves an additional punishment of up to thirty grams of gold or up to three months in prison (art. 27).

Articles 28–32 describe the procedures for admitting to committing ikhtilath and accusing others of doing so. If a person admits he or she has committed ikhtilath, investigators do not need to uncover evidence of the offence – simply admitting (verbally or in writing) that one has committed ikhtilath is considered sufficient. Investigators only need to prove that the statement was made, and do not need to know with whom the offence was committed (art. 28). If the person who conducted ikhtilath mentions the name of his or her partner in the act, he or she must be able to provide evidence (art. 29). Accusing someone of conducting ikhtilath and not being able to provide evidence carries a ta'zir punishment of up to thirty strokes of the cane, or a fine of 300 grams of gold or thirty months in prison (art. 30(1)).

Adultery (Zina) and Qadzaf

Adultery (*zina*) is described as consensual sexual relations between one or more men with one or more women who are not married (arts. 1(26) and 33–45). The standard punishment for adultery is a hudud punishment of a hundred strokes of the cane (art. 33(1)). Additional punishments are applied for repeating the behaviour (another hudud punishment of a hundred strokes of the cane, plus a ta'zir punishment of up to 120 grams of gold or up to twelve months in prison) (art. 33(2)). Providing facilities for, or promoting, adultery carries a ta'zir punishment of up to a hundred strokes of the cane, and/or a fine of up to 1,000 grams of gold and/or up to a hundred months in prison) (art. 33(3)). Meanwhile, committing adultery with a child carries a hudud punishment of 100 strokes of the cane, plus a ta'zir punishment of up to a hundred strokes of the cane, or up to 1,000 grams of gold, or up to a hundred months in prison (art. 34).

Like the provisions on ikhtilath described above, according to the Qanun Jinayat, a person who has admitted committing adultery does not need to mention the name of the person with whom they committed adultery (art. 42(4)). However, if the person who has admitted to committing adultery names their partner, but the partner denies it, and the 'accuser' cannot provide four witnesses, the accuser is considered to have committed *qadzaf* (art. 43(4)).

Qadzaf is a new Islamic law offence introduced under the Qanun Jinayat and is defined as accusing someone of rape without being able to present four witnesses (arts. 1(31) and 57–62). The offence carries a hudud punishment of eighty strokes of the cane (art. 57(1)). Repeat offences carry the additional hudud punishment of eighty more strokes of the cane, plus an additional punishment of up to 400 grams of gold or up to forty months in prison (art. 57(2)).

A key change introduced through the Qanun Jinayat is that adultery is now considered a 'regular offence' (*delik biasa*) for which charges can be brought regardless of whether one of the involved parties makes a complaint to investigators. In the KUHP, by contrast, adultery is considered a 'complaint offence' (*delik aduan*), meaning that police investigators can only begin preliminary investigation if they receive a complaint. Article 284 of the KUHP states that it is an offence to have extra-marital affairs, but a person can only be prosecuted at the request of the spouse and this report should be accompanied by a request for divorce.

Human rights activists have also expressed particular concern over art. 36, which states that women who are pregnant outside marriage can be accused of committing adultery, without the support of sufficient evidence. This overrides evidentiary procedures long established under Indonesia's national Criminal Procedure Code (KUHAP). Under art. 184 of the KUHAP, valid evidence includes witness testimony (*keterangan saksi*), expert testimony (*keterangan ahli*), documents (*surat*), circumstantial evidence (*petunjuk*), and testimony from the accused, including a statement of guilt.[8] In 2014, the Constitutional Court ruled that the phrases 'preliminary evidence', 'sufficient preliminary evidence' and 'sufficient evidence' in arts. 1(14), 17 and 21(1) of the KUHAP were unconstitutional if they were not read to mean at least two forms of evidence as listed under art. 184.[9] Article 36 of the Qanun Jinayat, meanwhile, specifically states that support of 'sufficient evidence' is not required. This leaves open the possibility that a woman who is pregnant as a result of rape, for example, could be accused of committing adultery simply because she is pregnant.

*Sexual abuse (***pelecehan seksual***)*

The Qanun Jinayat defines sexual abuse as immoral or obscene acts committed in public on or towards a male or female without his or her consent (arts. 1(27) and 46–47). The offence involves a ta'zir punishment of up to forty-five strokes of the cane, or a fine of up to 450 grams of gold or up to forty-five months in prison (art. 46). The maximum punishments are doubled for sexual abuse of children (art. 47). The definition of sexual abuse in the Qanun Jinayat could be considered an improvement on the equivalent articles in the KUHP, at least because it places greater emphasis on consent. The KUHP does not mention 'sexual abuse', although there are several articles that cover indecency (*cabul*), many of which relate to underage children (see arts. 289–96). Perhaps the closest equivalent article in the KUHP is art. 289, which states that anyone who uses violence or threat of violence to force someone to commit or tolerate an obscene act will be accused of behaviour that threatens honour and decency and face up to nine years in prison. Although not explicitly described as such, verbal sexual abuse or harassment could be considered to be covered by art. 281(2) and art. 315 of the KUHP.[10]

Rape

Rape is the most problematic of the offences described in the Qanun Jinayat. Rape is defined as 'using violence, force or the threat of violence to conduct a sexual act towards the vagina or anus of a victim, using the penis, mouth, or other object used by the perpetrator, or towards the mouth of the victim with the penis of the perpetrator' (arts. 1(30) and 48–56). Rape involves a discretionary (ta'zir) punishment of between 125 and 175 strokes of the cane, or a fine of 1,250–1,750 grams of gold, or 125–75 months in prison (art. 48). The punishment for rape of a relative (mahram) or child is 150–200 strokes of the cane, or a fine of 1,500–2,000 grams of gold, or 150–200 months in prison (arts. 49 and 50). If the victim requests, the accused may also be liable for compensation of up to 750 grams of gold (art. 51).

The Qanun Jinayat is extremely discriminatory toward women victims of rape. Organisations like the Women's Association for Justice and Legal Aid (Lembaga Bantuan Hukum Asosiasi Perempuan Indonesia untuk Keadilan, LBH Apik) and other women's rights organisations have long complained that under the Indonesian national justice system, female victims of sexual violence already face significant discrimination and considerable difficulty in proving that an offence had occurred, particularly if they do not have a medical report (CNN Indonesia 2018). These problems are amplified in Aceh. Under the Qanun Jinayat, rape victims must provide preliminary evidence when they submit their case to police (art. 52(1)). If police investigators determine that the evidence provided is insufficient, the victim can make an oath, which is said to 'strengthen' the evidence (art. 52(3)). The oath is made five times (art. 53(1)). The first four times the victim must declare that she (or he) is honest and serious in her accusation, and the fifth time she must declare that she is willing to face God's wrath if she is lying (art. 53(2),(3)). If the victim is unwilling to state the oath in front of a court, he or she will then be considered to have committed qadzaf (art. 54(1)) (see above) and faces a hudud punishment of eighty strokes of the cane (art. 54(2)).

Meanwhile, those accused of rape can defend themselves simply by declaring their innocence in an oath five times. Like the oaths taken by the victim, he (or she) declares that he is not guilty for the first four oaths, and the fifth time declares his or her willingness to receive God's wrath if lying (art. 55). If both the victim and accused take these oaths, neither will receive punishment (art. 56). These provisions clearly make it very difficult for a victim of rape to obtain justice: all the alleged perpetrator need do is deny it.

The equivalent article on rape under the secular KUHP is art. 285, which states that any person who uses violence or the threat of violence to force a woman to sleep with him outside wedlock faces up to twelve years in prison. As noted above, to begin investigating a case, police investigators must obtain 'sufficient preliminary evidence', or two forms of legal evidence. This was already difficult to establish in many rape cases processed under the KUHP – the Qanun Jinayat provides an even greater window for rapists to escape justice.

*Sodomy (*liwath*) and lesbian sex (*musahaqah*)*

One of the most controversial aspects of the Qanun Jinayat, at least among international observers and human rights activists, has been its introduction of offences for same sex relations. The Qanun Jinayat describes sodomy (*liwath*) as consensual penetrative anal sex between men (arts. 1(28) and 63). Lesbian sex (*musahaqah*), meanwhile, is defined as a consensual act of two or more women involving mutual 'rubbing' of body parts or vaginas to obtain sexual pleasure (arts. 1(29) and 64). Both offences carry ta'zir punishments of up to 100 strokes of the cane, or a fine of up to 1,000 grams of gold or up to 100 months in prison. Repeating the offence carries a penalty of up to 100 strikes of the cane, and can include an additional penalty of 120 grams of gold and/or twelve months in prison. A person who commits the offence of liwath or musahaqah with a child can face an additional penalty the same as the original penalty.

It is worth noting that the Qanun Jinayat does not appear to outlaw homosexual or lesbian identity, only particular sexual acts. There are, of course, many sexual acts that same sex couples could perform, if the definitions provided under the Qanun Jinayat are interpreted narrowly. Oral sex between two people of the same sex, for example, does not appear to be an offence according to the Qanun Jinayat. This is likely to be little comfort for lesbian or gay people in Aceh, however, as history suggests the provisions will be interpreted loosely. In 2015, for example, one month before the Qanun Jinayat came into force, Shari'a Police detained two suspected lesbians, aged eighteen and nineteen years, for cuddling in public. Head of the Shari'a Police Evendi Latief commented that the pair would undergo 'rehabilitation' with the local

Department of Social Affairs, as they could not be charged under the Qanun Jinayat, which would only take effect in October 2015 (VOA Indonesia 2015).

Homosexuality has never been criminalised at the national level in Indonesia. The criminalisation of homosexual and lesbian sex under the Qanun Jinayat is therefore a significant departure from the KUHP, which only criminalises same-sex relations with minors, under art. 292.[11] Over the past few years, however, there has been a push from conservative Muslim groups to criminalise homosexuality across the entire country. In early 2016, numerous public figures made a series of hateful and offensive statements about lesbian, gay, bisexual and transgender (LGBT) individuals.[12] Around this time, a conservative group known as the Family Love Alliance (AILA, Aliansi Cinta Keluarga Indonesia) submitted a challenge to art. 292 of the KUHP to the Constitutional Court.[13] The petitioners hoped to extend the scope of art. 292 so that it applied to all same-sex relations, not only sexual relations with minors. The Constitutional Court rejected their challenge in December 2017, noting that it was the job of the legislature to criminalise behaviour, not the Constitutional Court.[14] Subsequent deliberations on a revised Criminal Code (RUU KUHP) have included harsher provisions on same-sex relations. Discussions on revisions to the KUHP have extended for decades, and although legislators pledged to pass the revised code by Independence Day on 17 August 2018, this deadline was missed. Another deadline was missed in 2019. At the time of writing it remained unclear whether or when the revised code would be passed.

Is caning legal under Indonesian law?

In addition to the multiple inconsistencies with the KUHP outlined above, there is a question over whether caning is, in fact, a legal form of punishment under Indonesian law. Human rights groups such as Amnesty International have stated that caning as a form of punishment in Aceh may be considered a form of torture (Amnesty International 2017b). The UN Convention Against Torture and Other Cruel, Inhuman or Degrading Treatment or Punishment (which Indonesia ratified through Law No. 5 of 1998) defines torture as:

> …any act by which severe pain or suffering, whether physical or mental, is intentionally inflicted on a person for such purposes as obtaining from him or a third person information or a confession, punishing him for an act he or a third person has committed or is suspected of having committed, or intimidating or coercing him or a third person, or for any reason based on discrimination of any kind, when such pain or suffering is inflicted by or at the instigation of or with the consent or acquiescence of a public official or other person acting in an official capacity. It does not include pain or suffering arising only from, inherent in or incidental to lawful sanctions.
>
> (art. 1)

One problematic aspect of this definition is the 'lawful sanctions' exception. Including this clause would appear to undermine the universality of the definition, allowing the concept of what constitutes torture to vary between countries (Coracini 2006: 310). Some countries, especially Muslim majority countries, have argued that this allows for corporal punishment, such as caning, provided in Islamic law (Karapetyan 2016: 145). While there is some debate over this clause, in general 'lawful sanctions' is defined in the context of international law or practices that the international community widely consider to be permissible (Miller 2005).

Aceh authorities do, however, argue that the form of caning practised in Aceh cannot be considered torture – they claim that it inflicts less pain and suffering than the type of caning used in Singapore and Malaysia (Feener 2013a: 247). Indeed, officials in Aceh usually frame caning as part of the broader project to shape Acehnese society in line with Islamic norms. The primary goal of caning is said to be not to apply a painful punishment but to 'increase awareness' in the community and create a sense of shame (Feener 2013a: 236–7). Claims about caning in Aceh being less painful than forms in Malaysia or Singapore may be true, but officials would have a much harder time defending caning in Aceh against accusations that it constitutes cruel, inhuman or degrading treatment or punishment.[15] The fact that caning continues to be carried out in public, in front of large crowds who openly take photos and record videos – despite the governor's recent attempts to limit this practice – causes considerable emotional pain and suffering. On 2 February 2017, for example, a female sentenced to 26 lashes of the cane had to be taken down from the stage after 15 strikes, because she was suffering from psychological distress (Asri 2017). UN Special Rapporteur on Torture Manfred Nowak, following a visit to Indonesia in 2008, noted that victims of caning are often subject to prolonged stigmatisation and social sanctioning well beyond the implementation of the punishment. Women who have been punished under Islamic law may be labelled immoral by their husbands, families and communities. This treatment, he said, can amount to degrading and inhuman treatment (UN Human Rights Council 2008: 11).

If caning is considered not to be torture but to be at least degrading and inhuman treatment it still violates the following provisions of the Constitution and national statutes:

- art. 28G (2) of the Constitution;[16]
- art. 33 of Law No. 39 of 1999 on Human Rights;[17]
- Law No. 5 of 1998 on the Ratification of the Convention Against Torture and Other Cruel, Inhuman or Degrading Treatment or Punishment; and
- Law No. 12 of 2005 on the Ratification of the International Covenant on Civil and Political Rights (art. 7).

As mentioned, the Supreme Court has the power to review regional regulations (Peraturan daerah, perda) like the Qanun Jinayat to ensure their consistency with higher level statutes. However, it has historically been quite reluctant to use this power, and on the only occasion that it was asked to review the Qanun Jinayat, it avoided doing so on technical grounds, a matter that is discussed further below, and in more detail in Simon Butt's chapter in this volume.

Implementation of the Qanun Jinayat

Public canings have been carried out in Aceh since the early days of the implementation of its shari'a regime. The first public caning was reportedly implemented in Bireuen on 24 June 2005, when eighteen people received between four and eight strokes of the cane for the offence of gambling (Großmann 2015: 90; Afrianty 2015: 76). As noted, until the Qanun Jinayat was introduced in late 2015, caning only existed as a punishment for the offences relating to alcohol, gambling, and khalwat (Afrianty 2015: 73–6). Before the Qanun Jinayat was implemented, Feener (2013b: 300) wrote that Aceh's Shari'a Courts only heard a relatively small number of cases for these offences, and focused more on divorce and inheritance cases, much like religious courts in other provinces. In fact, he noted that between 2007 and 2009, there had been a marked decrease in the number of cases involving violations of provisions on sexual morality, gambling and alcohol (Feener 2013b: 300). While jinayat cases still comprise only a small fraction of the cases heard by Aceh's Shari'a Courts, there does not appear to be any evidence that the decline in shari'a criminal law cases has continued.

It is difficult to find accurate figures on the types of sentences handed down since the Qanun Jinayat came into effect in October 2015, although overall numbers can be obtained relatively easily through the Shari'a Court website. In 2016, Aceh's twenty first instance shari'a courts decided 330 jinayat cases. During the same period, shari'a courts decided 11,090 civil cases (Mahkamah Syar'iyah Aceh 2017: 34–6). In 2017, meanwhile, Aceh's first instance courts decided 288 Islamic criminal law cases and 10,633 civil cases (Mahkamah Syar'iyah Aceh 2018: 165–7). In 2018, first instance courts decided 315 jinayat cases and 11,571 civil cases (Mahkamah Syar'iyah Aceh 2019a: 182–3). According to monitoring conducted by the Institute for Criminal Justice Reform (ICJR), from January to December 2016, 339 offenders were punished with caning (this figure would presumably include cases decided during 2015) (ICJR 2017b). In 2017, meanwhile, ICJR reported that 188 people were caned between January and September (ICJR 2017a).

As mentioned, the Qanun Jinayat focuses heavily on regulating morality and sexuality. Of the ten offences regulated under the Islamic Criminal Code, eight relate to consensual or non-consensual sexual activity. A significant proportion of sentences continue to be handed down for gambling offences (Mahkamah Syar'iyah Aceh 2019a), although recent cases decided by the Banda Aceh District Shari'a Court tell a slightly different story. From January to June 2018, the court heard twenty-four Islamic criminal cases. Of these, fourteen involved consensual and non-consensual sexual activity, ranging from khalwat, to ikhtilath, liwath, and sexual harassment. The court handed down punishments of between twenty-five and ninety strokes of the cane, depending on the type of offence. The heaviest punishments were delivered for liwath, or gay sex.

Publicly available judgments for these fourteen cases indicate several critical issues about the investigation and trial process. They suggest that the process is failing to meet even the standards and principles outlined in the Qanun Jinayat and Qanun Acara Jinayat. A particular concern relates to the cases on ikhtilath, khalwat and sexual harassment. The published decisions reveal that most of the couples were 'caught' by neighbours or members of the community, who followed couples home, and sometimes conducted their own vigilante raids. During court hearings, the people who caught and reported the accused couples were considered 'witnesses', despite sometimes only seeing a couple enter a private dwelling and having no knowledge of what occurred inside.

Despite often lacking direct witness accounts, court decisions were often incredibly graphic in their description of the sexual activities of the defendants, to the extent that they read more like adult literature than a legal document (Afrianty 2018). In almost all ikhtilath cases, court decisions included details of how the defendants removed their clothes, which parts of their bodies were touched and by whom, and how long they engaged in particular acts – information that would have been near impossible for the members of the public who caught them in the act to obtain. Many of the decisions state that defendants confessed to their crimes, raising questions about how this 'evidence gathering' was conducted.

A second concern is that of these fourteen cases, there was only one where the defendant was accompanied by a lawyer, despite this being a basic requirement under the Qanun Acara Jinayat (see art. 2(i) and its elucidation). Further, this was the sole prosecution for non-consensual sex. Interestingly, there seemed to be a relationship between the duration of the court proceedings and representation. Most cases lasted between thirty and fifty days, whereas the one case in which the defendant did get legal representation took more than 100 days. Further, the court found this defendant not guilty, suggesting that more prosecutions might fail if defendants were properly represented (Afrianty 2018).

Beyond questions about the legality of caning, there is clearly grounds to question whether the Qanun Jinayat is really protecting and respecting 'the nature and dignity of humanity' as stated in its guiding principles. The fact that in many cases defendants are not accompanied by lawyers makes it very difficult to protect defendants' rights. Further, the emphasis on the criminalisation of consensual sex seems to be having the effect of encouraging vigilante behaviour and intimidation.

Civil society response and prospects for reform

The Qanun Jinayat has provoked widespread criticism internationally for violation of human rights norms (see, for example, Human Rights Watch 2017). This international criticism, especially when framed in terms of human rights and coming from organisations like Human Rights Watch and Amnesty International, is unlikely to have any impact in Aceh. Within the province, international criticism of shari'a based on human rights arguments is typically dismissed as a western attack on Islam (Serambinews.com 2013; StatusAceh.net 2018). Indeed, the introduction and expansion of shari'a was viewed by Islamic leaders precisely as a means to protect Aceh from 'Westernising globalisation' that might result from the post-tsunami reconstruction process (Feener 2013a: 259).

More than ten years since Islamic law was first introduced, and about four years after the passage of the Qanun Jinayat, Acehnese civil society remains divided on the issue of Islamic criminal law. However, the intensity of antipathy towards Islamic criminal law, and, indeed, civil society activism focused on reforming or revoking the Qanun Jinayat, has been relatively muted compared to when shari'a law was first introduced. Conversations with several Acehnese academics and activists revealed that practices such as caning and headscarf checks have become somewhat normalised. The spirited public debate about the role of Islam in a newly reconstructed post-tsunami Aceh has now faded. As other scholars have also noted, the conversation appears to have shifted from the place of Islamic criminal law in Acehnese society to a focus on tinkering with practical details so that shari'a can be implemented more effectively (Feener 2013a: 235; Missbach 2016: 216).

One possible reason for this lack of opposition is a broader decline in the strength of civil society in Aceh. During the post-tsunami reconstruction process, Aceh was flooded with large numbers of national and international organisations, many of which partnered with and supported local organisations. Civil society in Aceh was actively engaged in discussions about the future of shari'a law in the province. Seminars, workshops, and international conferences involving local, national and international speakers debated ideas and arguments about human rights, shari'a law, gender equality, and civic participation (Afrianty 2015).

Over the past five to ten years, however, donor support for Acehnese organisations has fallen dramatically. The Acehnese have been left largely to define their future for themselves. In a region where identity is so closely linked to Islam, and criticism of Islamic law is often perceived as an attack on Islam itself, there has been little vigorous public debate over the implementation of Islamic law. While many Acehnese civil society organisations still express reservations about Islamic criminal law in the province, local organisations have largely avoided public condemnation of the Qanun Jinayat. For example, the caning of two gay men in May 2017 might have provoked outrage in

Jakarta and around the world but there were few, if any, dissenting voices within Aceh (Interview, Banda Aceh, 1 December 2017).

In addition to declining donor support, civil society organisations have found that it is politically unwise, and even dangerous, to express views against shari'a. This is partly because many Acehnese members of the public see the Qanun Jinayat as enforcing existing standards of morality. One of the few civil society movements advocating for reform of the Qanun Jinayat within Aceh is the Civil Society Network for Shari'a (Jaringan Masyarakat Sipil Peduli Syariah, JMSPS). This network of local civil society organisations was highly active in protests against the original 2009 Qanun Jinayat but its opposition has not been without risks. One of the JMSPS' previous spokespeople faced threats to her life, and had to be evacuated to Jakarta for expressing public views considered critical of shari'a law (Interview, Melbourne, 23 November 2017). This has also dampened local civil society activism.

Further, academics from the two leading tertiary education institutions in Aceh, Ar-Raniry State Islamic University (UIN Ar-Raniry) and Syiah Kuala University, which were heavily involved in discussions about the place of shari'a in the reconstructed Acehnese state, have also become less active in advocating reform of the Qanun Jinayat. A senior academic from UIN Ar-Raniry, for example, publicly suggested that the implementation of Islamic criminal law in Aceh was effectively beyond the point of no return. It was the right of the people to implement Islamic criminal law, and on the whole, the people of Aceh were happy with it, he commented (Interview, Banda Aceh, 1 December 2017). Other academics from the same institution expressed similar views, saying that they believed the public now considered Islamic criminal law to be part of Acehnese identity and that it would bring about positive changes for society. Female students at UIN Ar-Raniry said that the rest of Indonesia should follow in Aceh's footsteps and introduce Islamic law, as they believed it would lead to members of the public performing good deeds (Interview, Banda Aceh, 30 November 2017).

At the national level, however, the Qanun Jinayat has faced heavy criticism from Jakarta-based women's and human rights activists, especially organisations like Komnas Perempuan (the National Commission on Violence against Women) and Solidaritas Perempuan (Women's Solidarity). In October 2015, for example, prominent gender activist Tunggal Pawestri described the Qanun Jinayat as a misogynistic document that was hostile towards women (BBC 2015). This is typical of the concerns expressed by women's activists, who have focused, quite rightly, on the provisions on rape.

Notably, the Institute for Criminal Justice Reform (ICJR) and Solidaritas Perempuan submitted a request for Judicial review of the Qanun Jinayat to the Supreme Court in 2015. The Supreme Court rejected this challenge,[18] because Law No. 12 of 2011 on Lawmaking, which they used the basis for their challenge, was under review at the Constitutional Court. It based its reasoning on art. 55 of Law No. 24 of 2003 on the Constitutional Court, which states that 'examination of regulations against statutes by the Supreme

Court must be stopped if the statute that is the basis for the regulation is being examined by the Constitutional Court, until the Constitutional Court reaches a decision'. Simon Butt discusses the grounds for the challenge, and questions the Court's somewhat unusual reasoning, in the following chapter.

In 2017, national civil society organisations began ramping up advocacy efforts, using the third anniversary of the passage of the Qanun Jinayat as a rallying point. In October, the so-called Civil Society Network for Qanun Jinayat Advocacy (a coalition of about twenty mainly Jakarta-based civil society organisations, including Solidaritas Perempuan and ICJR) made a renewed push for review of the regulation. Unfortunately, this momentum was not sustained. Efforts to revise or repeal the Qanun Jinayat will not be successful unless there is also a strong push from within Aceh, and this does not look likely to be forthcoming.

Some Aceh-based organisations and individuals have, in fact, said that they felt a press release issued by the Civil Society Network for Qanun Jinayat Advocacy at that time was highly counterproductive. They felt that placing such a strong emphasis on human rights language and gender equality would only end up promoting further resistance in Aceh. One women's activist in Aceh said she considered the efforts made by national-level activists to be irrelevant. Drawing on a long history of hostility toward Jakarta and popular ideas of Acehnese exceptionalism, she said that Jakarta-based activists did not understand the situation in Aceh and had no real-life experience of living under Islamic law. According to her, Acehnese people had no serious problems with living under Islamic law. At the same time, however, she admitted that there was a problem with the way Islamic law was being implemented, in that women were often victims of discrimination.[19] For this activist, however, the Qanun Jinayat was an issue for the Acehnese to debate among themselves. The Acehnese, she said, have the right to determine what is in their best interests. Another women's activist echoed these sentiments, arguing that although there were instances of discrimination, these were only a small number of cases, involving small numbers of Acehnese people. Most people in the province, she said, had no problems with living under shari'a or the Qanun Jinayat.

Conclusions

The Qanun Jinayat introduces some of the harshest punishments for offences relating to sexuality and morality in all of Indonesia. In addition to the existing offence of khalwat, particularly problematic are the new offences of ikhtilath, liwath and musahaqah, which criminalise consensual sexual activity between adults. While further data is needed, media reports and examination of case data suggest that these offences have promoted vigilante behaviour by some members of the public. Even if the form of caning practised in Aceh is less painful than forms implemented in nearby Malaysia or Singapore, there can be little question that it constitutes cruel, inhuman or degrading treatment. Indeed, even its supporters acknowledge its express purpose is to generate shame.

It is worth noting that, at present, the number of people being charged and punished under the Qanun Jinayat remains relatively low, at around 300 people annually. Three years into the implementation of the Qanun Jinayat it is still too early to assess whether this represents a high point of its implementation, or whether there will be calls for stricter and more expansive implementation of Islamic criminal law.

Despite these concerns, about a decade into the introduction of Islamic law in Aceh, and more than three years of implementing the Qanun Jinayat, the debate about the introduction of shari'a appears to have petered out. While there is criticism of the application of the Qanun Jinayat, there is little questioning of the place of Islamic criminal law in Acehnese society. Aceh is not exempt from the wider, so-called 'conservative turn' (van Bruinessen 2013) in Indonesian Islam. Many Acehnese people seem to have accepted arguments about the need for strict Islamic law. In a region where local identity is so closely intertwined with Islam, openly criticising Islamic law can be viewed as an attack on Islam itself. Despite criticism of the way the Qanun Jinayat has been implemented, the majority of the community and officials in Aceh continue to publicly support the 'implementation of shari'a in its totality' (*penerapan Syariat Islam secara kaffah*). They remain adamant that it is the right of Acehnese to live under Islamic criminal law and it is the right way to make people better Muslims. The dominant narrative about Islamic criminal law as helping to shape Acehnese society for the better (Feener's notion of social engineering) appears deeply embedded.

Only a small number of Acehnese share concerns that the Qanun Jinayat in its current form is discriminatory and was not formulated in the spirit of equality, as its supporters claim. This appears to be true even among Acehnese civil society. It therefore seems unlikely that despite the legal conflicts that it introduces, its violations of human rights, and its discrimination against women and LGBTIQ individuals, that the Qanun Jinayat will be revoked or revised in the near future. At the time of writing, Governor Irwandi Jusuf, a reluctant supporter of shari'a and one of the few government officials willing to express public views about limiting its scope, had been arrested for corruption. There are few other public officials willing to make public statements critical of Islamic criminal law. In the absence of a major effort from civil society or the public within Aceh, it seems likely that for the time being, at least, the Qanun Jinayat is here to stay. That will be to the detriment of the men and women who are punished under it, as well as Indonesia's reputation in the eyes of the international community.

Notes

1 Qanun No. 10 of 2002 on the Shari'a Courts; Qanun No. 11 of 2002 on the Implementation of Islamic Law in the Areas of Belief (*Aqidah*), Worship and

Dissemination of Islamic Teachings; Qanun No. 12 of 2003 on *Khamar* (alcohol); Qanun No. 13 of 2003 on *Maisir* (gambling); Qanun No. 14 of 2003 on *Khalwat* (seclusion).

2 Article 129 states: 1) If an offence is committed by two or more people together (and among them are non-Muslims), the non-Muslims can choose whether to voluntarily submit themselves to hukum jinayat; 2) Every non-Muslim who commits an Islamic law offence that is not regulated in the KUHP or other criminal provisions outside the KUHP is subject to the Qanun Jinayat.

3 See, for example: Presidential Regulation No. 74 of 2013 on the Control and Monitoring of Alcoholic Drinks; Presidential Regulation No. 44 of 2016 on Fields of Business Closed and Open to Investment; Trade Ministerial Regulation No. 20 of 2014 on the Control and Monitoring of Procurement, Circulation and Sale of Alcoholic Drinks (as amended by Trade Ministerial Regulation No. 74 of 2014, Trade Ministerial Regulation No. 6 of 2015, Trade Ministerial Regulation No. 32 of 2016 and Trade Ministerial Regulation No. 47 of 2018); Finance Ministerial Regulation No. 158 of 2018 on Tax Rates for Ethyl Alcohol, Drinks Containing Ethyl Alcohol and Concentrates Containing Ethyl Alcohol; and Industry Ministerial Regulation No. 63 of 2014 (as amended by Industry Ministerial Regulation No. 62 of 2015). Many local administrations have also passed regional regulations (*perda*) on control of alcoholic drinks (see, for example, Depok Municipal Regulation No. 6 of 2008 on Monitoring and Control of Alcoholic Drinks).

4 See art. 5 and art. 26(1) of Qanun No. 12 of 2003.

5 See also Salim (2015: 85) for a discussion of this matter.

6 See art. 6 and art. 26(2) of Qanun No. 12 of 2003.

7 The decision reportedly stated: 'The accused, as Buddhists, have declared that they have voluntarily submitted to be subjected to Islamic law that operates in Aceh Province. The accused therefore have no objection to and are willing to be tried in the Sigli Shari'a Court.

8 Article 1(14) of the KUHAP defines a 'suspect' as a person who, because of his or her actions, and based on preliminary evidence, is suspected of being the perpetrator of a criminal act. Similarly, art. 17 states that detention may only be ordered based on 'sufficient preliminary evidence'. Article 183 of the KUHAP, meanwhile, states that a judge can only hand down a criminal penalty if, based on two forms of valid evidence, he or she is convinced that a crime was committed by the accused.

9 Constitutional Court Decision No. 21/PUU-XII/2014, 109.

10 Article 281(2): Any person who in public, intentionally and against the wishes of others at the location, violates decency, faces up to two years and eight months in prison.

Article 315: Every intentional insult towards a person that is not defamatory in nature, whether conveyed verbally or in written form in public or verbally, through behaviour or in written form directly to the person, results in up to four months and two weeks in prison.

11 Although no national laws criminalise homosexual or lesbian sex, several regional administrations have enacted regulations (perda) that discriminate against sexual minorities through provisions on immorality or indecency. For further details, see Katjasungkana and Wieringa 2016.

12 Human Rights Watch compiled a thorough account of the anti-LGBT backlash that occurred in early 2016. See Human Rights Watch 2016.

13 AILA also challenged art. 284 on adultery in an attempt to outlaw all sex outside marriage, and art. 285 on rape, hoping to extend the offence of rape to cover same-sex rape. The current definition of rape under art. 285 does not yet cover rape of men.
14 Constitutional Court Decision No. 46/PUU-XIV/2016.
15 Article 16 of the Convention Against Torture states: 'Each State Party shall undertake to prevent in any territory under its jurisdiction other acts of cruel, inhuman or degrading treatment or punishment which do not amount to torture as defined in Article I, when such acts are committed by or at the instigation of or with the consent or acquiescence of a public official or other person acting in an official capacity…'
16 Article 28G(2): 'Each person has the right to be free from torture or inhuman and degrading treatment and shall be entitled to obtain political asylum from another country'.
17 Article 33(1) states: 'Every person has the right to freedom from torture, or cruel, inhumane and degrading punishment or treatment'.
18 Supreme Court Decision No. 60 P/HUM/2015.
19 Interview, Banda Aceh, 2 December 2017.

References

Aceh Kita 2016. 'Qanun Jinayat tidak Berlaku bagi Non-Muslim', 14 April www.acehkita.com

Afrianto, Dedy 2017. 'Aturan Hukum Cambuk di Aceh Akan Dimodifikasi', *Okezone*, 11 July https://news.okezone.com

Afrianty, Dina 2018. 'Aceh's Obsession with Sex: Why the Province has its Priorities Wrong', *Indonesia at Melbourne*, 7 August http://indonesiaatmelbourne.unimelb.edu.au

Afrianty, Dina 2015. *Women and Sharia Law in Northern Indonesia: Local Women's NGOs and the Reform of Islamic Law in Aceh.* London and New York: Routledge

AJNN 2017. 'Irwan Djohan Sebut Irwandi Yusuf Penggagas Modifi kasi Hukum Cambuk', *Aceh Journal National Network*, 13 July www.ajnn.net

Amnesty International 2017b. 'Indonesia: Revoke the Caning Sentence of Gay Men in Aceh', 17 May www.amnesty.org

Amnesty International 2017a. 'Indonesia: Caning of Gay Men an Outrageous Act of Cruelty', 23 May www.amnesty.org

Anwar 2017. '18 Warga Aceh Barat Dicambuk di Depan Umum', *Antara*, 30 November www.antaranews.com

Aspinall, Edward 2005. *The Helsinki Agreement: A More Promising Basis for Peace in Aceh?* Washington DC: East-West Center Washington

Aspinall, Edward 2007a. 'From Islamism to Nationalism in Aceh, Indonesia', *Nations and Nationalism* 13(2): 245–63

Aspinall, Edward 2007b. 'The Politics of Islamic Law in Aceh', Association for Asian Studies Annual Meeting, 22–5 March, Boston.

Asri, Misran 2017. 'Terpidana Kesakitan Hukuman Cambuk Dihentikan', *Serambinews.com*, 5 February https://aceh.tribunnews.com/2017/02/05/terpidana-kesakitan-hukuman-cambuk-dihentikan

BBC 2015. 'Perda Jinayat Aceh Terus Dikecam', 23 October www.bbc.com

BBC 2017. 'Indonesian Men Caned for Gay Sex in Aceh', 23 May www.bbc.com

Brown, Colin 2003. *A Short History of Indonesia: The Unlikely Nation?* Crows Nest, NSW: Allen & Unwin

Coracini, Celso Eduardo Faria 2006. 'The Lawful Sanctions Clause in the State Reporting Procedure before the Committee against Torture', *Netherlands Quarterly on Human Rights* 24(2): 305–18

CNN Indonesia 2018. 'Kekerasan terhadap Perempuan Terganjal Proses Pembuktian', 1 December www.cnnindonesia.com/

Fachrudin, Fachri 2018. 'Putusan MK Cabut Kewenangan Mendagri Batalkan Perda Provinsi', *Kompas.com*, 14 June https://nasional.kompas.com

Feener, R. Michael 2013a. *Shari'a and Social Engineering: The Implementation of Islamic Law in Contemporary Aceh.* Oxford Islamic Legal Studies. Oxford University Press

Feener, R. Michael 2013b. 'Social Engineering through Shari'a: Islamic Law and State-Directed Da'wa in Contemporary Aceh', *Indonesia Law Review* 3(3): 285–310

Großmann, Kristina 2015. 'Women's Rights Activists and the Drafting Process of the Islamic Criminal Law Code (Qanun Jinayat)', in R. Michael Feener, David Kloos, and Annemarie Samuels (eds.), *Islam and the Limits of the State: Reconfigurations of Practice, Community and Authority in Contemporary Aceh.* Leiden: Brill, pp. 87–117

Hasan, Nurdin 2012. 'Indonesia's Aceh Province Elects Ex-rebel as Governor', *Yahoo News Singapore*, 18 April https://sg.news.yahoo.com

Heriansyah, M. 2017. 'Irwan Djohan Sebut Irwandi Yusuf Penggagas Modifikasi Hukum Cambuk', *Aceh Journal National Network*, 13 July www.ajnn.net

Hidayat, Rafki 2016. 'Cambuk Perempuan Non-Muslim, Pusat Diminta Tegur Aceh', *BBC Indonesia*, 15 April www.bbc.com

Hooker, M. B. 2008. *Indonesian Syariah: Defining a National School of Islamic Law.* Singapore: Institute of Southeast Asian Studies

Hukumonline 2009. 'Kontroversi Qanun Jinayat di Serambi Mekah', 15 September www.hukumonline.com

Hukumonline 2015. 'Dua Kategori Non-Muslim yang Bisa Terjerat Qanun Jinayah', 11 February www.hukumonline.com

Human Rights Watch 2016. '"These Political Games Ruin Our Lives": Indonesia's LGBT Community Under Threat', August www.hrw.org

Human Rights Watch 2017. 'Indonesia: Stop Public Flogging of Gay Men', 19 May www.hrw.org

Institute for Criminal Justice Reform (ICJR) 2017a. 'Caning as Legal Corporal Punishment Ruins the Image of Indonesia Human Rights', 11 October http://icjr.or.id

Institute for Criminal Justice Reform (ICJR) 2017b. 'Praktek Hukuman Cambuk di Aceh Meningkat, Evaluasi atas Qanun Jinayat Harus Dilakukan Pemerintah', 6 February http://icjr.or.id

International Crisis Group (ICG) 2006. *Islamic Law and Criminal Justice in Aceh*, http://old.crisisgroup.org

Karapetyan, Anna 2016. 'A Recurring Phenomenon: The Lawful Sanctions Clause in the Definition of Torture and the Question of Judicial Corporal Punishment Under International Human Rights Law', *Polish Yearbook of International Law* 36: 137–61

Katjasungkana, Nursyahbani and Wieringa Saskia E. 2016. *Creeping Criminalisation: Mapping of Indonesia's National Laws and Regional Regulations That Violate*

Human Rights of Women and LGBTIQ People. New York: OutRight Action International

Lindsey, T. and Hooker, M. B., with Clarke, R. and Kingsley, J. 2007. 'Shari'a Revival in Aceh', in R. Michael Feener and Mark E. Cammack (eds.), *Islamic Law in Contemporary Indonesia: Ideas and Institutions*. Cambridge, Massachusetts: Harvard University Press, pp. 216–54

Mahkamah Syar'iyah Aceh 2017. 'Laporan Tahunan Mahkamah Syar'iyah Aceh Tahun 2016'

Mahkamah Syar'iyah Aceh 2018. 'Laporan Tahunan Mahkamah Syar'iyah Aceh Tahun 2017'

Mahkamah Syar'iyah Aceh 2019a. 'Laporan Perkara Jinayat Yang Putus Pada Mahkamah Syar'iyah Se-Provinsi Aceh, Bulan Januari-Desember Tahun 2018'

Mahkamah Syar'iyah Aceh 2019b. 'Laporan Tahunan Mahkamah Syar'iyah Aceh Tahun 2018'

Miller, Gail H. 2005. *Defining Torture*. New York: Benjamin N. Cardozo School of Law

Missbach, Antje 2016. '"That is Jakarta's Project": Views from the Acehnese Diaspora on Shari'a, Self-Determination and Political Conspiracy', in R. Michael Feener, David Kloos and Annemarie Samuels (eds.), *Islam and the Limits of the State: Reconfigurations of Practice, Community and Authority in Contemporary Aceh*. Leiden: Brill, pp. 212–41

Republika 2017. 'Kritik Hukum Syariah Aceh, PM Australia: Menghukum Cambuk Gay Aksi Barbar', 26 May www.republika.co.id

Robinson, Geoffrey 1998. '*Rawan* Is as *Rawan* Does: The Origins of Disorder in New Order Aceh', *Indonesia* 66: 127–57

Saidi, Juli 2017. 'Ketua Komisi VII DPR Aceh: Upaya Mundur dan Jangan Cepat Pancing Suasana', *Modus Aceh,* 12 July www.modusaceh.co

Salim, Arskal 2015. *Contemporary Islamic Law in Indonesia*: Sharia and Legal Pluralism. Edinburgh University Press

SBS 2017. 'Gay Men Caning in Indonesia "Barbaric": PM', 26 May www.sbs.com.au

Serambinews.com 2013. 'HAM Barat Sudutkan Islam', 17 March http://aceh.tribunnews.com

Setyadi, Agus 2018. 'Mengapa Pasangan Gay di Aceh Dihukum Cambuk di Halaman Masjid?', *Detik*, 13 July https://news.detik.com

Shaw, Robert 2008. 'Aceh's Struggle for Independence: Considering the Role of Islam in a Separatist Conflict', *Al Nakhlah: The Fletcher School Online Journal on Southwest Asia and Islamic Civilization*, Fall: 1–14

Simanjuntak, Hotli and Ompusunggu, Moses 2017. 'Buddhists Caned for Violating Sharia in Aceh', *The Jakarta Post*, 13 March www.thejakartapost.com

StatusAceh.net 2018. 'YARA Gelar Diskusi Publik "Mempidanakan Perilaku Menyimpang LGBT"', February www.statusaceh.net

Straits Times 2017a. 'Gay Indonesians Caned in Front of Jeering Crowd in Aceh for Having Sex', 23 May www.straitstimes.com

Straits Times 2017b. 'Non-Muslims Caned for First Time under Aceh's Syariah Law', 13 March www.straitstimes.com

United Nations General Assembly, Human Rights Council 2008. 'Report of the Special Rapporteur on Torture and Other Cruel, Inhuman or Degrading Treatment or Punishment, Manfred Nowak, Addendum: Mission to Indonesia', A/HRC/7/3/Add.7, 10 March

Van Bruinessen, Martin 2013. *Contemporary Developments in Indonesian Islam: Explaining the 'Conservative Turn'*. Singapore: Institute of Southeast Asian Studies.

VOA Indonesia 2015. 'Aceh "Rehabilitasi" 2 Tersangka Lesbian', 5 October www.voaindonesia.com

Wahono, B. M. 2017. 'Warga Buddhis yang Dicambuk, dan Qanun Jinayat Aceh', *Berita Tagar,* 13 March https://beritagar.id/artikel/berita/warga-buddha-yang-dicambuk-dan-qanun-jinayat-aceh

Wibow 2009. 'Pakar Hukum: Qanun Jinayat Agar Dibahas Ulang', *Antara*, 26 October www.antaranews.com

Zamzami, Daspriani Y. 2014. 'Hukum Pidana Islam, DPR Aceh Sahkan Qanun Hukum Jinayat', *Kompas.com*, 27 September http://regional.kompas.com

Legislation

The Indonesian Constitution, Undang-Undang Dasar 1945

Criminal Code (*Kitab Undang-Undang Hukum Pidana*, KUHP: Law No. 1 of 1946 as amended by Law No. 27 of 1999 on the Indonesian Criminal Code)

Criminal Procedure Code Law (*Kitab Undang-undang Hukum Acara Pidana*, KUHAP), Law No. 8 of 1981

Law No. 7 of 1974 on Marriage

Law No. 5 of 1998 on the Ratification of the Convention against Torture and Other Cruel, Inhuman or Degrading Treatment or Punishment

Law No. 39 of 1999 on Human Rights

Law No. 44 of 1999 on the Special Status of the Province of Aceh Special Region

Law No. 18 of 2001 on Special Autonomy for the Province of Aceh Special Region ('the Special Autonomy Law')

Law No. 24 of 2003 on the Constitutional Court

Law No. 12 of 2005 on the Ratification of the International Covenant on Civil and Political Rights

Law No. 11 of 2006 on Governing Aceh

Law No. 12 of 2011 on Lawmaking

Qanun No. 10 of 2002 on the Shari'a Courts

Qanun No. 11 of 2002 on the Implementation of Islamic Law in the Areas of Belief (Aqidah), Worship and Dissemination of Islamic Teachings

Qanun No. 12 of 2003 on Khamar (alcohol)

Qanun No. 13 of 2003 on Maisir (gambling)

Qanun No. 14 of 2003 on Khalwat (seclusion)

Qanun No. 7 of 2013 on the Islamic Criminal Procedure Code (Qanun Acara Jinayat)

Qanun No. 6 of 2014 on Islamic Criminal Law (Qanun Jinayat)

Governor of Aceh's Regulation No. 5 of 2018 on the Implementation of the Qanun Jinayat

Decisions

Constitutional Court Decision No. 21/PUU-XII/2014

Constitutional Court Decision No. 46/PUU-XIV/2016

Supreme Court Decision No. 60 P/HUM/2015

20 Aceh and Islamic criminal law in the courts

Simon Butt

In 2014, the Aceh provincial government enacted a *Qanun Jinayat* or Islamic Criminal Code.[1] The Qanun came into force on 22 October 2015, one year later. Hundreds of citizens have since been flogged after being found guilty of engaging in various acts considered impermissible or *haram* under Islamic law as defined by the Code, including homosexual intercourse, prohibited physical 'proximity' between unmarried males and females, gambling, adultery, and alcohol consumption and distribution. A smaller number of citizens have been prosecuted under the Qanun Jinayat for acts that are also illegal under Indonesia's national criminal law, such as sexual abuse and rape (Elnizar 2017).

The Qanun has been controversial for many reasons. One is that it significantly expands the scope and application of substantive Islamic criminal law in Aceh, including some of its punishments, which many groups argue violate human rights standards, including prohibitions on torture and discrimination against women. It is also controversial that the Qanun asserts that its provisions, and the Islamic precepts it imposes, prevail over national laws and even international human rights law.[2] Many advocates and lawyers argue that the Qanun Jinayat is, therefore, illegal under Indonesian law because it violates the Constitution, which contains these human rights guarantees. Others argue that it violates Indonesia's legal order as represented in the 'hierarchy of laws', which appears to hold that a regional regulation (*peraturan daerah* or *perda*), of which the Qanun is a type, must not contradict national statutes (*undang-undang*).

The Supreme Court is the only institution in Indonesia with power to formally determine whether a Qanun is legal. It can do this by exercising its judicial review power to invalidate lower-level laws – such as national and subnational government or executive regulations, or regulations issued by subnational legislatures, including Qanun – if they do not accord with national statutes. The Supreme Court also has the final say on the interpretation and application of the Qanun Jinayat by the Islamic courts in Aceh, the Mahkamah Syariah. It does this by hearing cassation (*kasasi*) appeals from Aceh's Syariah courts and overturning decisions when it identifies judicial errors.

The available evidence, presented in this chapter, suggests that in cases involving Islamic criminal law the Supreme Court has exercised neither its judicial review nor its cassation functions with the rights of citizens and the order of the legal system in mind. Instead, it has preferred to avoid making decisions about the application of the Qanun Jinayat wherever possible. This means that, despite genuine concerns about the oppressiveness of the Qanun Jinayat and its application by Aceh's courts, and the strength of legal arguments pointing towards the Qanun Jinayat's invalidity, the legality of the Code and its enforcement by officials in Aceh has not been judicially tested in any meaningful way.

This chapter examines the Qanun Jinayat in light of the previous piecemeal attempts by the Aceh government to regulate the Islamic offences of gambling, proximity and alcohol-related activities. It provides an overall picture of how these laws have been applied, and the types of penalties Aceh's Syariah courts hand down. These observations are based on academic studies, press reports and the relatively few publicly available decisions of these courts. I then turn to consider the role of the Supreme Court in the two categories of cases relating to the Qanun Jinayat just mentioned. The first type is cassation cases, of which the Supreme Court has heard five on appeal from the Aceh provincial High Court in Islamic criminal cases.[3] These cases were decided in 2007 and 2008, before the 2014 Qanun Jinayat was enacted, but relate to crimes also prohibited under the Qanun Jinayat. No Supreme Court cassation cases concerning the Qanun Jinayat itself were publicly available. The second type of case is judicial review. The Supreme Court has heard one such challenge, brought by a human rights NGO against the Qanun Jinayat.[4] As we shall see, in both types of cases, the Court has maintained the status quo, refusing to disturb either the decisions of the provincial court (in the cassation cases) or the Qanun Jinayat itself (in the judicial review case). By so doing, the Supreme Court has taken a path that does not draw the ire of religious conservatives.

Before turning to discuss these various issues, I first provide some background about Islamic law in Indonesia and the process by which Aceh came to have authority to impose it, including Islamic criminal law, in the province.

Background

The positions of Islam in the state and of Islamic law in the legal system have long been highly vexed issues in Indonesia.[5] Given that Muslims are said to comprise around 85–90 per cent of Indonesia's population, Muslim groups have long pushed for an Islamic state or for some type of formal recognition of Islam. As Indonesia's first independent constitution was being discussed in 1945, it was decided that Indonesia should be a state based on 'Almighty God', and Muslim politicians successfully negotiated the inclusion, in the penultimate draft, of a constitutional obligation for Muslims to follow Islamic law (the so-called 'Jakarta Charter' or *Piagam Jakarta*) (Anshari 1997). However, Indonesia's first president, Soekarno, removed this obligation before the Constitution was promulgated, in response to protests from Christians, particularly in Eastern Indonesia, who threatened not to join the new nation, and even from moderate Muslims, who saw religion as a private matter and did not want the state to enforce Islamic law against them (Butt 2016; Lindsey 2012; Ricklefs 1993). Nevertheless, the declaration that the state is based on 'Almighty God' – which is the first of the five-principle national ideology, the *Pancasila* – was retained in the Preamble to the Constitution.[6]

Because the state is not secular, it has assumed a role in the administration of religion, but because Islam is the religion with which most Indonesians associate, the state has dedicated more resources to supporting Islam than to other religions (Shah 2017). For example, Indonesia has a Religious Affairs Ministry that purports to help administer all officially recognised religions in Indonesia (other than Confucianism) but most of its operations relate to Islam (Lindsey 2012).[7] Likewise, Indonesia has a system of 'religious courts' (*peradilan agama*), but it only has jurisdiction over Muslims and particular issues of Islamic law (Cammack and Feener 2007; Hooker 2008; Lev 1972).

Because Pancasila mandates such a role for religion in matters of state, the ideological door has remained ajar for some Muslim groups to continue seeking a more prominent place for Islamic principles in the operation of government. Many of them continue to see the Pancasila compromise as a betrayal of Islam, and have made sustained and spirited calls for Islamic law to be given more prominence in Indonesia's constitutional and legal systems. However, most of their efforts have been unsuccessful, with the state being able to resist calls for Islamic law to be accorded legal authority independent of the nation state.[8] For example, the religious courts apply a state-sanctioned version of Islamic law, the Compilation of Islamic Laws (*Kompilasi Hukum Islam*, Presidential Instruction No. 1 of 1991), rather than classical Islamic sources, and their jurisdiction is limited primarily to family law.[9] Their decisions can be appealed to the Supreme Court in Jakarta. This apex court has a religious chamber, but its decisions generally uphold Islamic law only to the extent that it has been adopted in the laws of the government (Butt 2008; Hooker 2008; Nurlaelawati 2010). In this context, the national government has continually rejected calls to apply Islamic criminal law across the archipelago, even if only to Muslims.

Also important to note by way of background are the decentralisation reforms initiated after the fall of Soeharto in 1998. Under these reforms, many subnational governments received powers to make laws on a wide range of matters, with only several areas remaining within the exclusive purview of the central government (Butt 2010b). Some of these subnational governments have used this authority to pass bylaws that reflect Islamic norms, including those imposing dress codes, or banning gambling, and alcohol consumption and distribution (Buehler 2011; Bush 2008). Human rights groups and others have called for the central government to revoke these bylaws, primarily on grounds that they often discriminate against minorities and women, and impose draconian punishments, but it refused, and in 2017, the Constitutional Court invalidated the central government's revocation powers in any case (Butt 2017a). As mentioned, this leaves the Supreme Court as the only institution with power to review and, if necessary, invalidate subnational laws.

Aceh is the only province of Indonesia where the legislature has formal authority to issue laws expressly based on Islamic norms, including those relating to criminal law. This power was confirmed and consolidated as part of a peace accord – the Helsinki Agreement – signed by Aceh representatives and the Indonesian national government (Aspinall 2006). The Agreement, inked within a year of the 2004 Boxing Day Tsunami, aimed to end decades-long civil war in the province. This was led on the Aceh side by GAM (Gerakan Aceh Merdeka, Free Aceh Movement), which sought Aceh's independence from Indonesia. Under the Agreement, aspects of which were later embodied in Law No. 11 of 2006 on Aceh Special Autonomy, the Aceh government received similar powers to those of other Indonesian subnational governments, plus the power to issue Islam-based laws. Using this lawmaking power, the Aceh provincial legislature issued the 2014 Qanun Jinayat, and various other Qanun, which I now turn to discuss.

The Qanun Jinyat and its predecessors

The 2006 Aceh Special Autonomy Law authorises the Aceh government to 'implement' Islamic law in Aceh, expressly mentioning criminal law (*jinayat*) as being encompassed (art. 125(2)). The 2006 Law also grants broad powers to the Aceh government itself to regulate how Islamic law is implemented, by issuing Qanun. The Law also appears to have the effect of adopting a local equivalent to the Jakarta Charter in Aceh: art. 126(1) states that 'Every adherent to Islam in Aceh must adhere to and observe Islamic law'. Article 126(2) adds that 'Every person living in or present in Aceh must respect the application of Islamic law'. However, art. 127(2) requires the Aceh government to respect the religious values of the adherents to other religions. As we shall see, the Aceh government does not appear to have met this obligation – at least to the extent to which the Qanun Jinayat applies to non-Muslims.

The Qanun are applied and enforced by Aceh's Syariah courts. Their decisions can be appealed to the Supreme Court (art. 131(1)) and are subject to the Supreme Court's PK (*peninjauan kembali*, reconsideration) processes (art. 131(3)) under which the Supreme Court can reopen any case – even one of its own (Butt and Lindsey 2018; and see Lindsey, Chapter 6, this volume). The Supreme Court recommends Syariah Court judges for appointment, and administers the organisation, administration and financial affairs of the Syariah courts (art. 135(1)).

Early Qanuns and the 2009 draft Qanun Jinayat

In the earlier years of regional autonomy, and even before the enactment of the 2006 Law, Aceh's provincial legislature issued several laws prohibiting activities such as gambling and alcohol consumption, and enforcing strict dress codes.[10] These laws were widely enforced by the Aceh religious police (Wilayatul Hisbah), sometimes heavy-handedly (International Crisis Group 2006), and resulted in significant numbers of prosecutions, as indicated in the case statistics set out below.

These piecemeal efforts were later consolidated into a draft Qanun Jinayat, which also incorporated prohibitions on *zina* or adultery with severe penalties. On 14 September 2009, just two weeks before the end of its 2004–9 term, the Aceh provincial legislature passed this Code.[11] However, it never came into law and was never enforced. The Aceh provincial executive refused to approve the Bill and the Aceh governor refused to sign it (Karni 2009). The main objection of the governor and his administration, echoed by human rights groups,[12] related to the draft Qanun's imposition of punishments associated with Islamic law: caning and stoning, even to death. Most controversial was art. 24 of the Draft, which stated:

> Any person who deliberately engaged in adultery faces … 100 strokes of the cane for those who are not yet married, and stoning/death penalty for those who are married.

The 2014 Qanun Jinayat

As mentioned, in 2014 the Aceh provincial legislature enacted a new Qanun Jinayat which, this time, the provincial executive endorsed and the governor signed. The 2014 Qanun Jinayat retained caning as a punishment, but stoning was dropped.[13]

The Qanun Jinayat prohibits various offences (*jarimah*) that are not otherwise expressly covered by national law.[14] These include prohibited 'seclusion' (*khalwat*) – that is, being alone in an enclosed or private place with a member of the opposite sex who is not a spouse or relative;[15] and 'intermingling' (*ikhtilath*) – that is, consensual intimate relations between an unmarried male and female, such as flirting, touching, hugging and kissing.[16] Punishment for *khalwat* is up to ten strokes of the cane, a fine of 100 grams of gold or ten months in prison (art. 23(1)); and for *ikhtilath*, is 30 strokes, 300 grams or 30 months (art. 25).[17]

The Qanun prohibits drinking, producing, selling or carrying alcohol, and giving it as a gift, although use of alcohol for medical purposes as prescribed by a doctor is permitted (art. 14(1)).[18] It also criminalises gambling, with applicable penalties, depending on whether the potential winnings are worth more than two grams of gold, or equivalent. If under two grams, then the punishment is up to 12 strokes, 120 grams, or 12 months (art. 18), but if more than two grams, the punishment increases to up to 30 strokes, 300 grams or 30 months (art. 19). Funding or providing facilities for gambling, or involving children in gambling, attract higher penalties.[19]

The Qanun's prohibition on 'adultery' (*perzinaan*, or *zina*) is much broader that art. 284 of the national Criminal Code, which prohibits a married person having sex with someone who is not their husband or wife. Under the Qanun, adultery includes any sex between people who are not married. This covers sex between people who are married, but not to each other, between one person who is married and one person who is not, and between two unmarried people. Unlike other offences, where offenders appear to be able to choose between alternative punishments of caning, a fine or imprisonment, the only penalty for first-time perpetrators of *zina* is up to 100 strokes of the cane (art. 33).[20]

The Qanun also prohibits consensual sex between people of the same gender, distinguishing between sodomy (*liwath*) and lesbian sex (*musahaqah*) but imposing the same penalties: 100 strokes, 1000 grams of gold, or 100 months' imprisonment (arts. 63–4). This is broader than the national Criminal Code, which only prohibits same-sex intercourse with a minor (art. 292).

The Qanun also prohibits sexual abuse (*pelecehan seksual*) and rape (*pemerkosaan*). For sexual abuse – an 'immoral or indecent act deliberately performed by a person in public or against another person as a victim, whether male or female, without the consent of the victim' (art. 1(27)) – a penalty of up to 45 strokes, 450 grams or 45 months applies (art. 46).[21] The Code also punishes rape (*pemerkosaan*) with 125–75 strokes, 1250–1750 grams of gold or 125–75 months' imprisonment (art. 48).[22]

Controversially, if an alleged victim reports an alleged rape to police, he or she must provide initial evidence (art. 52(1)).[23] This can be in the form of an oath, made five times, with the fifth time constituting willingness to receive the wrath of God if the oath is untrue (art. 53(3)). The Qanun also provides a punishment of eighty strokes of the cane for making an unproven allegation of adultery (*qadzaf*),[24] with the person making the allegation also liable to pay restitution of up to 400 grams of gold to the person accused of rape (art. 58). An alleged rape victim who promises to make an oath before a judge but then resiles from that promise also commits *qadzaf*. Problematically, a person accused of rape based on an oath can avoid responsibility, simply by uttering a counter-oath five times (art. 55(4)). If both victim and alleged perpetrator make such oaths, then the alleged victim and the alleged perpetrator cannot be found guilty of *qadzaf* or rape, respectively (art. 56). Of course, this means that where the only evidence of rape is the victim's word against the perpetrator's, the perpetrator will escape responsibility.

Legal predominance

Also contentious is the Qanun's claim to trump national law – particularly, the national Criminal Code. Article 72 states that if an offence is regulated in *both* the Qanun *and* the KUHP, then the Qanun prevails. Presumably, art. 72

indicates that the Aceh legislature wants the Qanun's broader prohibitions on *zina* and same-sex intercourse to prevail over the narrower prohibitions in the Criminal Code, mentioned above.

While art. 72 appears to constitute an overt attempt by the Aceh provincial legislature to assert its own authority over that of the national government, art. 72 can also be interpreted as an attempt to assert the authority of Islam over the nation state, particularly considering the 'contest' between Islam and the state discussed above. There is support for this interpretation in the Qanun itself. The Preamble to the Qanun commences with a statement that the *Qur'an* and *Hadith*[25] are the main bases for Islam, and that Islam has become the conviction and basis for life of the Aceh community. And, in the list of instruments that provide a legal basis for the enactment of the Qanun, the national Criminal Code is absent. On one view, the ordering of these references is symbolically important, and indicates that the Aceh provincial legislature views Islamic law as the predominant source of law in general and of the Qanun in particular. However, regardless of the intent of art. 72, it appears to be clearly illegal, as discussed below.

The Qanun also appears to assert predominance over widely-recognised international human rights norms. Article 2 lists various principles that are said to underlie the Qanun's implementation, including 'protection of human rights' (*perlindungan hak asasi manusia*) (art. 2(e)). The Elucidation to art. 2(e) defines 'protection of human rights' as the:

> guarantee that the formulation of Islamic offences and punishments will accord with efforts to protect and respect human characteristics, honor and dignity, in accordance with the understanding of Indonesian Muslim communities about human rights.

As discussed below, this definition of human rights is limited and appears to contradict both Indonesia's national Human Rights Law,[26] and Indonesia's obligations under international human rights treaties it has signed and ratified.

It bears noting, too, that the Qanun applies not only to Muslims in Aceh, but also to non-Muslims who, in collaboration with a Muslim, violate the Qanun and voluntarily submit to the Qanun (art. 5(b)). It also applies to a non-Muslim who commits an offence under the Qanun that is not otherwise prohibited by national law (art. 5(c)). In this respect, the Qanun does not significantly diverge from the 2006 Aceh Government Law, which provides that the Mahkamah Syariah is the court for 'every person whose religion is Islam and is in Aceh' (art. 128(2) of the 2016 Law). It also provides that, if an Islamic crime is committed by two or more people and that there are non-Muslims amongst them, the non-Muslims can choose to submit to Islamic criminal law (art. 129(1)). Islamic criminal law is also applicable to non-Muslims who commit an Islamic crime that is not regulated in national criminal law (art. 129(2)).

Applying Islamic law to non-Muslims is very controversial. On the one hand, the Qanun is a valid exercise of legislative power of the Aceh provincial legislature – and is therefore prima facie applicable to all people in the physical jurisdiction of Aceh. But on the other hand, the Qanun's adoption of Islamic norms makes its application to people of other religions legally problematical, perhaps even violating the religious freedoms of defendants and convicts (Butt 2018).

Judicial application

The available information about the number and type of Islamic criminal cases the city, county and provincial Mahkamah Syariah hear in Aceh is patchy. Nevertheless, data obtained, primarily from Feener (2014: 172–5) and Supreme Court annual reports, allow identification of broad trends. In addition to these criminal cases, the Syariah courts in Aceh hear the same cases as the religious courts in other parts of Indonesia. Like those other courts, their caseload is dominated by divorce applications, as well as inheritance, matrimonial property and *wakaf* administration matters. By contrast, criminal matters comprise a relatively small part of their caseloads (Feener 2014: 172).[27] Feener's statistics cover 2005–8, as indicated in Figure 20.1, and decisions brought under the various abovementioned Qanun regulating individual jinayat offences, issued before the 2014 Code was enacted. They appear to indicate that these courts have tended to hear fewer cases over time.

The data from the Supreme Court's annual reports presented below in Figure 20.2 should only be taken as being indicative, for several reasons. First, the reports generally disclose the number of cases each branch of the judiciary handles in any given year, though in some years only the number of cases *received* are given and in others only the cases *decided* are reported. Second, while it was possible to obtain statistics on the number of jinayat

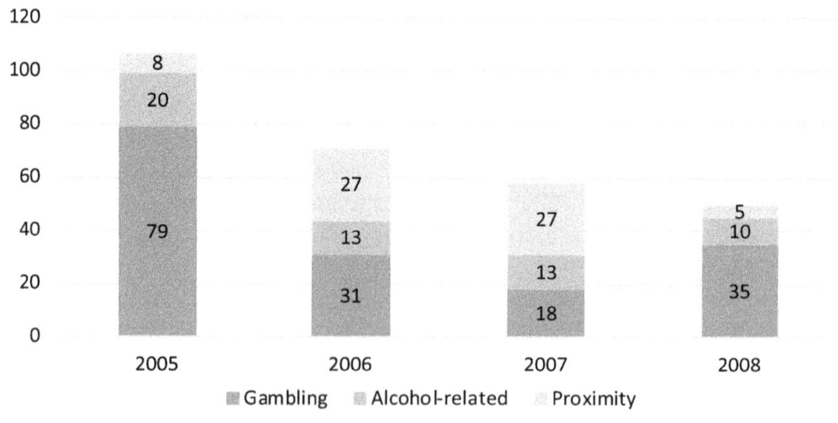

Figure 20.1 Jinayat cases, 2005–8.

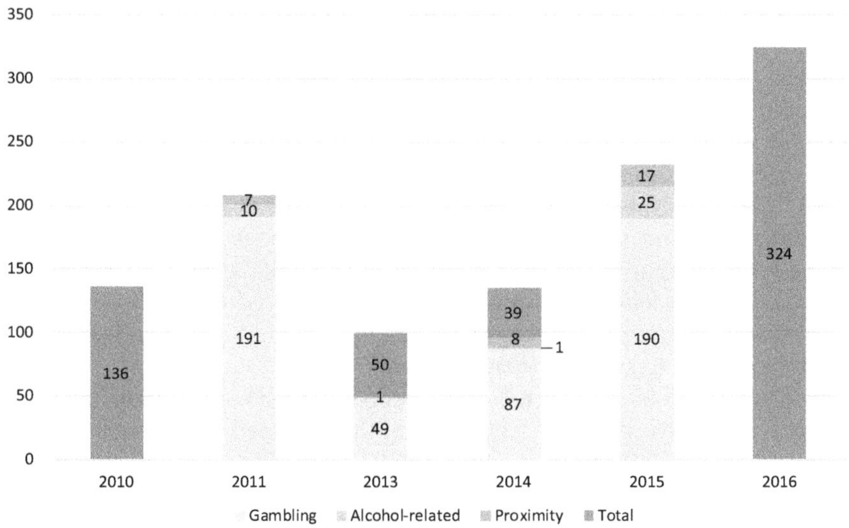

Figure 20.2 Jinayat cases, 2010–16.
Source: Supreme Court of Indonesia (*Mahkamah Agung*) (2017: 94; 2016: 51, 73; 2015: 93; 2014: 65–6; 2012: 80–1)

cases handled (that is, received *or* decided) by the Aceh courts from 2011–16, the annual report for 2012 could not be obtained. Third, in some years, the annual reports did not differentiate between first instance and appeal cases, instead giving a combined case disposition figure.

Despite these data inadequacies, it seems relatively clear that the number of cases the Syariah courts are hearing is now increasing, and that significant resources are being allocated to pursue gambling offences.

Decision-making

Only seventeen judgments in jinayat cases were publicly available at time of writing, from the Aceh provincial Mahkamah Syariah webpage.[28] In all of them, the names of the defendants had been redacted. Ten of them are provincial Syariah High Court appeals, two are first instance decisions, and five are Supreme Court cassation decisions. Given the small sample size relative to the number of cases the Syariah courts hear, it is only possible to draw several general conclusions about broad trends, rather than provide representative and specific observations about judicial decision-making in jinayat cases.

First, the Aceh Syariah High Court appears to generally uphold the decisions of first instance courts. It did so in all available cases, except two. In one of these, the High Court found that the lower court had convicted based on inadequate evidence. In the other, the Court acquitted the defendant after finding that the evidence pointed to the defendant attempting a crime rather than completing one.[29]

Second, most of the cases related to gambling offences, for which the Court almost always imposed caning as punishment, rather than imprisonment or a fine. This probably reflects the socio-economic background of most defendants, who were found guilty of gambling with very small amounts of money. For example, in one case, the defendants were convicted of gambling and sentenced to six strokes of the cane.[30] The main physical evidence against them was the cards they used for gambling and thirteen Rp. 1,000 notes, sixteen Rp. 5,000 notes, two Rp. 10,000 notes, and two Rp. 20,000 notes, which were confiscated and transferred into local government coffers. In another case, the total amount confiscated was only Rp. 60,000, around AUD$6.[31] In this context, the defendants would likely have preferred to avoid a fine and imprisonment, particularly because confinement would prevent them from earning an income to support their families.

Third, the decisions are short, at least compared with many judgments from the general courts in criminal cases that the author has read. However, although they ran to only a few pages, many of these judgments provided significant detail about the criminal act that the defendant had allegedly committed. In some of the gambling cases, for example, the Court gave a detailed explanation of the rules of the game the defendants were caught playing. Particularly noteworthy were the cases of prohibited 'proximity' that led to sexual intercourse between couples not married to each other. In many of these cases, the Court included an account of the lead-up to the encounter – including how the defendants met and came to be in proximity with one another in a secluded place – and an explicit description of the sexual act itself, including the timing of the alleged ejaculation.[32] The graphic nature of the descriptions of these acts seems at odds with the climate of conservatism in which these acts were allegedly perpetrated and then adjudicated and punished.

Fourth, these decisions did not appear overly concerned to explain the relevance of evidence inventorised in the judgment that, the prosecution argued and the court decided, pointed towards guilt. Many of them also did not refer to any witness statements or testimony, despite the references in the various Qanun to need for the evidence of witnesses to prove particular crimes. The only notable exceptions were first instance cases,[33] but even in these, key evidence and/or a discussion of the probity of that evidence was missing. For example, in a case involving the sale of alcohol,[34] the defendant's residence was raided by the Islamic police (Wilayatul Hisbah), the civilian police force, the police, and the military. Around 350 bottles of alcohol were discovered and seized. While the decision explained that the beverages had been tested for their alcohol content, the decision did not specify the legal authority for this search and seizure, as one sees as a matter of course in other Indonesian criminal decisions. One is left wondering whether due process was ignored in the police investigation, or whether the search warrant was simply left out of the evidence. Another example comes from the proximity cases. In almost all of them, the undergarments of the defendants were seized and held as evidence, but no mention was made about the relevance of this, and what it 'proved' beyond the fact that the defendants were wearing them, which is hardly surprising.

Of course, one explanation for the apparent lack of concern to fully interrogate the evidence, at least in appeal cases, is that appeals are formally intended only to deal with legal issues, not matters of fact (Subekti 1982). However, Indonesia's other courts routinely ignore this formality and rarely confine themselves to legal issues. They will usually consider the evidence used, and its weight, in appeals. Indeed, the Supreme Court itself is quite notorious for doing this (Pompe 2005).

Finally, in none of the decisions analysed did the court indicate how it arrived at the punishment it handed down. There was, for example, no explanation about how the court determined how many strokes of the cane should be administered to the defendant, and no attempt to standardise or compare punishments across similar cases. For example, while gambling seemed to attract a penalty of six or seven strokes of the cane in many cases,[35] in other cases it was less and in other cases many more, but the court did not explain why.[36]

Supreme Court cases

As mentioned, only five Supreme Court cassation appeals are publicly available. In all of them, the Supreme Court refused to overturn the decisions of the Aceh courts. In all but one case,[37] the Court refused to intervene because it characterised the main issues in dispute as being related to the facts of the case rather than the relevant law. It declared that it could only hear cassation appeals on issues of law.

So, for example, in Decision No. 01K/AG/JN/2008, the Supreme Court considered an appeal against a proximity conviction by the Aceh provincial Mahkamah Syariah. A couple had claimed that they were married, even though there were not, in an effort to secure access to a room, presumably at a hotel. According to the case file, they had sexual intercourse on two occasions, thereby violating Qanun No. 14 of 2003.[38] At first instance, they were sentenced to eight and seven strokes of the cane respectively, but on appeal, the first defendant's punishment was reduced to five strokes and the second defendant escaped with a fine. The Supreme Court case file explains neither why the defendants had received different punishments, nor the reasons for the appeal court reducing their sentences.

In the Supreme Court appeal, the defendants' arguments centred on the evidence used to convict them. They argued: first, that one of the witnesses was lying and had engineered the case against the first defendant because of a dispute about a debt; second, that another witness was the husband of one of the defendants, and was, therefore, not sufficiently impartial to provide reliable testimony; third, that the arrest and detention was not performed by a member of the police force but someone who merely claimed to have authority to perform the arrest; and, finally, that some of the evidence used against them had been obtained through violence. The Supreme Court refused to entertain these arguments, stating:

> These reasons cannot be justified, because the *judex facti* did not wrongly apply the law, and, indeed, the evaluation of evidence, which takes the form of evaluating fact, cannot be considered during cassation examinations, because cassation examinations only touch upon the implementation or wrong application or violation of applicable law, as referred to in art. 30 of Law No. 14 of 1985 as amended by Law No. 5 of 2004.[39]

This decision has little to commend it. As mentioned, in other types of cases, the Supreme Court rarely limits itself to considering only clearly legal issues, such as an erroneous application or misinterpretation of the law by a lower court judge. Also, it is arguable that some of the issues here that related to admissibility of evidence were actually issues of law, not fact. For example, whether husbands or wives of defendants can legally give evidence against their spouses, and the consequences of an illegal arrest or detention on subsequent legal proceedings, appear to be matters about which a lower court could have misapplied the relevant law.

Similar observations can be made about Supreme Court Decision No. 04K/AG/JN/2008, which was an appeal against a gambling conviction. At first instance, the defendant was sentenced to two strokes of the cane but, on appeal, the provincial Mahkamah Syariah acquitted him after finding that the defendant had not committed the alleged crime, but rather had merely made preparations to run an illegal lottery. The prosecution appealed to the Supreme Court, arguing that even though the relevant Qanun did not capture attempted crimes, art. 50 of the Criminal Code, which covers attempted crimes, should be applied in this case.

Again, the Supreme Court refused to intervene, employing a passage virtually identical to that extracted above from 01K/AG/JN/2008 and then adding two further possible grounds for cassation that, for the Court, did not apply in this case: 'whether the way of adjudication was not performed according to statute, and whether the Court has exceeded its jurisdiction, as referred to in art. 253 of the KUHAP'.[40] Again, the Supreme Court may have ignored a significant legal issue raised by this case: whether art. 50 of the national Criminal Code can apply to a case alleging breach of the relevant Qanun. This appears to be a legal issue because it involves the application of the hierarchy of laws, contained in art. 7(1) of Law No. 12 of 2011 on Lawmaking, and determination of whether there was a 'conflict' between the Qanun and art. 50.

The Court's contestable categorisation of these issues as factual rather than legal could indicate that the Supreme Court is wary of disturbing the decisions of Aceh courts in Mahkamah Syariah cases and, therefore, will avoid doing so if possible. While the small sample size renders this a necessarily speculative conclusion, it seems to be supported by the Supreme

Court's use of 'cut and paste' responses in these cases. The passage extracted above from Decision No. 01K/AG/JN/2008 was reproduced verbatim by the Supreme Court to dismiss an appeal in Decision No. 05K/AG/JN/2008;[41] and the equivalent passage in Supreme Court Decision No. 04K/AG/JN/2008 appears verbatim in Decision No. 03 K/AG/JN/2008.[42] This gives the impression that the Court did not give much consideration to the circumstances of each case.

Caning as a punishment

The 2013 Qanun Jinayat Procedual Code[43] establishes caning procedures. Canings are to take place in public and are to be visible to the people in attendance (art. 262(1)). People under the age of eighteen years are not permitted to attend canings (art. 262(2)). The caning is to be performed on a three-by-three-metre platform, with a gap of at least 12 metres between the person to be caned and the public (art. 262(3) and (4)), with a doctor, prosecutor and supervising judge positioned near the platform (art. 262(5)). The caner's face must be covered, and must stand between 700 millimetres and 1 metre from the left or right of the person to be punished (arts. 264(1) and (2)). The caner is not permitted to swing the cane higher than his or her shoulder (art. 264(4)). The person being caned is to wear a shirt provided by the prosecution, and can choose to kneel or stand (art. 265(1) and (2)). The caning can be stopped on the instructions of the doctor, for medical reasons (art. 266(a)).

According to one estimate, 527 people were flogged from 2015 to 2017 (Hodge and Rayda 2017). ICJR (the Institute for Criminal Justice Reform) estimates that at least 339 people were caned in Aceh in 2016, and 118 in January–September 2017, but the number is likely much higher given that ICJR does not monitor canings in all parts of Aceh, and the Mahkamah Syariah, which oversees the punishments, does not publish statistics (ICJR 2017).

Criticisms

Unsurprisingly, the 2014 Qanun Jinayat drew heavy criticism from gender and human rights activists in Indonesia and abroad.[44] Human Rights Watch, for example, pointed out that the UN Committee Against Torture had recognised flogging as torture. Torture is a violation of the Convention against Torture and the International Convention on Civil and Political Rights, (both of which Indonesia has ratified), as well as domestic Indonesian law (HRW 2014; HRW 2016). Indeed, in 2008, the Committee had already singled out other laws in Aceh imposing corporal punishment and called for their immediate abolition for violating the Convention.[45] Amnesty International, Indonesia's National Human Rights Commission, and various Indonesian non-government organisations, voiced similar concerns, particularly about the physical and psychological aspects of canings (Acehkita.com 2009; Afif 2014; Amnesty International 2017; Florene 2017).

Although some have claimed that the primary purpose of caning is to shame perpetrators rather than cause physical injury, some of those caned have suffered such injury. As they point out, some canings have needed to be stopped on medical advice, and then continued once the convict has recovered sufficiently (Aziz 2017). In 2017, a thirty-year-old woman was hospitalised after receiving 100 lashes for adultery before a crowd in the capital, Banda Aceh (Hodge and Rayda 2017). At least partially because of the negative psychological consequences of public canings, a gubernatorial regulation[46] was issued to provide for canings to take place in detention rather than in public, although of course, this makes independent monitoring more difficult, if not impossible (ICJR 2017). It also appears that this regulation has been ignored, with press reports indicating that canings continue to take place in public (Voanews 2018).

Several cases resulting in canings have drawn significant public attention, in Indonesia and internationally, such as where the punishment has been imposed upon non-Muslims. This occurred in a case involving the playing of electric games at a Funland entertainment centre at a mall in Peunayong, Banda Aceh. About a dozen people were arrested after a month-long police investigation, including players, workers, and providers of the premises, primarily for playing, or being involved in the provision of, the 'Seafood Paradise' electronic game, which officials deemed to involve gambling (Setyadi 2017). The media reports about this case contained no convincing explanation of the elements of the game that involved gambling. It was not possible to obtain a copy of the decision in this case at time of writing. According to one description of the game, players purchased coins to play a game in which they attempted to shoot fish. If they were able to reach 600 points playing the game, they received tickets, which they could then exchange for cash (Setyadi 2017). Two of those arrested and tried were Christians, who were found guilty of breaching art. 18(1) of the Qanun Jinayah on gambling. Each was found guilty and was initially sentenced to eight strokes, but this was reduced to six and seven strokes respectively on appeal because they had already been imprisoned for over one month before the Syariah court decision finding them guilty was handed down (Setyadi 2018). Their punishment was carried out before a crowd of 300 people (Jakarta Post 2018).

Other cases have involved non-Muslims. In one, a sixty-year-old Christian woman was whipped for selling alcohol. And, in another, two Chinese Buddhists were caned for running a cockfighting betting scheme (Jakarta Post 2018). Although Aceh officials are often quick to explain that non-Muslims have freely chosen to be caned instead of fined or imprisoned (Setyadi 2017), human rights activists claim that non-Muslim offenders are usually deprived of legal assistance (Jakarta Post 2018). Also controversial has been the caning of homosexuals for having consensual sex. In 2017, two gay men were the first to be punished, with each receiving eighty-five lashes (Hodge and Rayda 2017).

Supreme Court review

One of the most vocal domestic critics of the Qanun Jinayat has been the Institute for Criminal Justice Reform (ICJR), which advocates for criminal justice reform and human rights protections. It has long been concerned about many aspects of the Qanun, including caning as a punishment. ICJR engages in what it describes as 'strategic litigation' – providing *amicus curiae* submissions in some matters and even bringing its own cases.[47] In one such case, ICJR sought judicial review of various provisions of the Qanun before the Supreme Court.[48] This had been preceded by the unsuccessful efforts of several NGOs to convince the government to review and revoke the law using its executive review powers.[49] The Ministry of Home Affairs quite correctly responded that it lacked power to do this (Jakarta Post 2018).[50]

Applicants' arguments

The ICJR lodged its application with the Court on 22 October 2015 – the very day the Qanun came into force. ICJR compellingly argued that the Qanun clearly contradicted various higher-level laws, or at least was not supported by them. ICJR argued, for example, that the use of caning as a punishment was not supported by the national Criminal Code, which sets out an exhaustive list of punishments that do not include caning.[51] Similarly, an oath is not recognised as a determinative form of evidence under national criminal law, yet the Qanun permitted alleged rapists to use oaths to avoid prosecution. ICJR also alleged that caning breached: constitutional provisions and various domestic human rights laws that seek to protect against torture, inhumane or undignified treatment;[52] national child protection laws;[53] international treaties that Indonesia has signed; and United Nations Human Rights Committee recommendations.[54]

ICJR argued that the Qanun also violated various provisions of the Law No. 12 of 2011 on Lawmaking that required maintenance of the legal order (*ketertiban hukum*). For ICJR, the Qanun compromised the legal order because: many of its provisions were not supported by or contradicted higher level laws; it duplicated offences already prohibited by national law; and for some offences, perpetrators could choose whether to be prosecuted under the national criminal law or the Qanun (which imposed different penalties). The Qanun also contained inconsistencies: on the one hand, art. 52(1) states that people who report allegations that they have been raped to police must provide initial evidence of the rape; on the other, art. 52(2) requires police to investigate to find initial evidence of 'every rape it knows about'. It is unclear why art. 52(1) is necessary, given once the allegation is reported to police, they will 'know about' it and must then investigate to find evidence under art. 52(2) in any event. The applicant also claimed that the Qanun contained unclear drafting, thereby violating the Lawmaking Law, which requires clear drafting. As an example, ICJR pointed to the Qanun's definition of *khalwat* as the voluntary act of an unrelated and unmarried man and woman being in a closed space, which 'tended towards the act of *zina*'. ICJR argued that the meaning of 'tended towards' was unclear and thus susceptible to subjective interpretation.

In response, the respondent, the Aceh governor, complained that the Ministry of Home Affairs should have been joined as a respondent and emphasised that all formal enactment procedures had been followed in respect of the Qanun. He also argued that the 2011 Aceh Autonomy Law gave power to the Aceh provincial legislature to enact the Qanun and claimed that the Law overrode the various national and international laws cited by the applicant, on grounds of *lex specialis derogat lege generalis*. This maxim of statutory interpretation is well known in Indonesia and provides that a law of specific application prevails over a law of general application if they conflict (Hamzah 1986). In this context, he argued that the Aceh Autonomy Law was specific and therefore the powers it granted overrode any limitation otherwise placed on it by these other laws.

The Decision

The Supreme Court did not consider any of the arguments from the applicant or respondent, deserving of attention though they may have been. The Court simply threw out the case, giving its reasons in only two paragraphs.[55] This was that art. 55 of the Constitutional Court Law[56] requires it to stop hearing a review of a lower level law against a statute if the constitutionality of that statute is being reviewed by the Constitutional Court. The Supreme Court observed that the Constitutional Court was examining the constitutionality of the 2011 Lawmaking Law,[57] and, citing art. 55, refused to proceed with the case. It mattered not that the Supreme Court and Constitutional Court cases were otherwise unrelated, brought by different parties for different purposes, and the Supreme Court did not seem to consider the obvious alternative of simply adjourning the hearing until the Constitutional Court handed down a decision.

Analysis and implications

On a narrow reading of art. 55, the Supreme Court's decision appears to be correct. After all, the Constitutional Court was reviewing art. 7(1) – one of the very provisions the ICJR asked the Supreme Court to review the Qanun against. If the Constitutional Court invalidated art. 7(1) and the Supreme Court invalidated Qanun provisions for violation of art. 7(1), then much uncertainty and disputation would have undoubtedly resulted. The Constitutional Court has identified avoiding this uncertainty as the main rationale for art. 55, the constitutionality of which was unsuccessfully challenged in a 2012 case.[58]

However, this narrow view was only one of many open to be adopted by the Supreme Court. In particular, it is arguable that meeting this purpose of avoiding uncertainty requires only that art. 55 be read to prevent the Supreme Court from proceeding with applications that rest entirely on statutory provisions under review in the Constitutional Court. It makes no sense for the Supreme Court to refuse to proceed when only one statute or statutory provision is subject to constitutional review. In other words, there seems nothing to stop the Supreme Court from refusing to proceed only with the applicant's arguments based on the Lawmaking Law (the only statute in the application subject to simultaneous constitutional review) and continuing to consider the applicant's and respondent's arguments based on the human rights law, KUHAP and the Aceh Regional Government Law. After all, these alleged violations stood independently of the Lawmaking Law arguments. This way there could have been no overlap between the Supreme Court and Constitutional Court cases, and the Supreme Court could have addressed the serious legal problems with the *perda*, including the apparent violation of fundamental rights, and its attempt to override the Criminal Code. There is nothing in the words of art. 55 to preclude this reading. Only if the Constitutional Court is testing the constitutionality of all statutes used as a basis for a simultaneous Supreme Court review should the Supreme Court refuse to proceed and, even then, the better course would be to simply adjourn the hearing until the Constitutional Court hands down its decision.[59]

Conclusions

Aceh's Qanun Jinyat, like its predecessors, has proved to be more than just symbolically important. It has been enforced with some enthusiasm, with regular canings being performed in public, at least until recently, when they began being performed in detention centres. This application of Islamic criminal law, though specific to Aceh, has occurred as other many parts of Indonesia have experienced a 'conservative turn' (van Bruinessen 2013). It corresponds, too, with the growing influence of conservatism on politics at both national and regional levels, combined with a growing intolerance for liberalism and for religious and other minorities (Butt 2016; Crouch 2014; Menchik 2016). Conservative sentiment appears to have found its way into other Indonesian courts, including the Constitutional Court, which in 2017 only barely rejected a constitutional review application urging it to expand the definition of adultery and prohibit homosexual intercourse in the national Criminal Code to fit generally-recognised Islamic norms (Butt 2018). Another prominent example of the courts upholding Islamist interests was the North Jakarta District Court blasphemy trial of former governor of Jakarta, Basuki Tjahaja Purnama (for more details, see Peterson, Chapter 15 of this volume). The prosecution was able to produce almost no evidence to support the charges against him, yet the Court found him guilty and sentenced him to two years' imprisonment, after the Council of Islamic Scholars (Majelis Ulama

Indonesia) issued a ruling declaring a statement he made to be blasphemous and urging authorities to take legal action against him (Butt 2017b).

Ahok's conviction without convincing evidence suggests that his trial was far more political than legal. The same might be said for many of the Jinayat cases heard in Aceh discussed above, in which convictions were secured without clear evidence. The same might be said, too, for the Supreme Court's decision in the Qanun Jinayat review case. There, the Supreme Court was able to deflect convincing arguments that might have led to the invalidation of the Qanun Jinayat in Aceh, citing technicalities that need not have been applied. It seems clear that the Supreme Court deliberately sought to avoid hearing this case on its merits.

Why have the Aceh courts and the Supreme Court adopted this position? Answering this question necessarily involves speculation, but it is possible that at least some judges share conservative sentiment, or are afraid of a backlash from Islamists if they decide cases in ways that are inconsistent with that sentiment. The Supreme Court's cassation appeals from the Aceh Mahkamah Syariah in Mahkamah Syariah matters appear to betray a court reluctant to 'engage' in genuine legal debate about the application of Islamic criminal law. Instead, it appears to prefer to defer to the decisions of the provincial Aceh court, using legal justifications that sit uncomfortably alongside long-standing Supreme Court practices. If this speculation is correct, then Indonesian judges are failing to perform their main constitutional function: impartially interpreting and applying the law. And, by so doing, they are also failing to protect citizens, particularly minority groups.

Notes

1 'Qanun' is an Arabic term for 'law' (Esposito 2017). In Aceh, it is synonymous with the term '*perda*', used to refer to regional regulations in other provinces (Aspinall 2006).
2 As per art. 75 of the Qanun.
3 Supreme Court Decisions Nos. 01K/AG/JN/2008; 02K/AG/JN/2008; 03K/AG/JN/2008; 04K/AG/JN/2008; and 05K/AG/JN/2008.
4 Supreme Court Decision No. 60 P/HUM/2015.
5 See Benda (1958) for debates surrounding Islam that occurred in colonial Indonesia, and the Dutch response to it. This background discussion draws on Butt (2018) and (2010a).
6 That Indonesia is a state based on belief in Almighty God is restated in art. 29(1). Also included in the Constitution is freedom of religion and to worship in accordance with that religion (art. 29(2)).
7 The officially recognised religions are: Islam, Catholicism, Protestanism, Hinduism, Buddhism and Confucianism.
8 For example, proposals for increased constitutional recognition for Islam and Islamic law were rejected during constitutional debates in 1955–9 and 1999–2002 (Nasution 1992; Indrayana 2008; Butt and Lindsey 2012). Yet, Islamic conservatives have won some legal ground. For example, the national legislature

has enacted some statutes that appear to adopt Islamic norms or prefer Islam over other religions, although not expressly. An example at the national level is the Law No. 44 of 2008 on Pornography (Pausacker 2009).

9 The subject-matter jurisdiction of the religious courts is marriage (*perkawinan*); succession (*waris*); gifts (*hibah*); bequests (*wakaf*); payment of alms (*zakat*); charitable gifts (*infaq*); gifts to the needy (*shadaqah*); and the 'shari'a economy' (*ekonomi syari'ah*): art. 49(1) of Law No. 7 of 1989 on the Religious Courts, as amended by Law No. 3 of 2006 and Law No. 50 of 2009.

10 See, for example, Qanun No. 11 of 2002 on the Implementation of Islamic Law in the Fields of Aqidah, Ibadah and Syi'ar Islam; Qanun No. 12 of 2003 on Alcoholic Beverages and the Like; Qanun No. 13 of 2003 on Gambling; and Qanun No. 14 of 2003 on Prohibited Proximity. For discussion of these Qanun, see Feener (2014: 143–5). It bears noting that, before the Helskini Agreement and the enactment of the 2006 Law, Aceh had already been granted a measure of special autonomy, through Law No. 18 of 2001, under which these Qanun were enacted.

11 Only one political faction disagreed, arguing instead for a term of imprisonment and forcing fornicators to marry.

12 The National Women's Human Rights Commission and other human rights groups had strongly objected to the inclusion of both stoning and caning in the 2009 draft, claiming the punishments were unconstitutional and violated human rights. They had also objected to the Aceh legislature's failure to seek community input about the draft. See Hukumonline 2009.

13 There are some notable differences between the 2009 draft and the 2014 Qanun Jinayat, besides the removal of stoning. For example, under the 2009 draft, sexual intercourse between married couples was excluded from the definition of rape.

14 The following description of offences under the Qanun Jinayat draws on Butt (2018).

15 The offence is not committed if the two are co-employees (art. 12(1)) or live in the same house (art. 12(2)).

16 Although punishment for *khalwat* and *ikhtilath* do not apply if helping a person of opposite sex in emergency (art. 13).

17 Accusing someone of *ikhtilath* without being able to prove the allegation attracts the same punishment applicable to *ikhtilath* itself (art. 30(1)).

18 Drinking alcohol can attract up to 40 strokes of the cane, with repeat offenders facing 80 strokes, a fine of 400 grams of gold or 40 months in prison (art. 15); producing or selling alcohol can lead to up to 60 strokes, or 600 grams or 60 months (art. 16(1)); and carrying alcohol or giving it as a present can result in up to 20 strokes, 200 grams or 20 months (art. 16(2)). If the perpetrator involves children in drinking or producing alcohol, then he or she faces 80 strokes, 800 grams or 80 months (art. 17).

19 For the former, up to 45 strokes, 450 grams, 45 months; for the latter, 45 strokes, 450 grams or 45 months (arts. 20–1).

20 Repeat offences, or *zina* with a family member or a child, attract up to 100 strokes, 1000 grams of gold or 100 months imprisonment in addition to this base penalty (arts. 33–5). Unmarried women who fall pregnant can be accused of *zina* without further evidence (art. 36).

21 The penalty doubles if the victim is a child (art. 47).

22 An additional 150–200 strokes, 1500–2000 grams and 150–200 months applies if the victim is related to the perpetrator (art. 49) or is a child (art. 50). The Qanun allows the victim to seek 750 grams of gold as restitution from the perpetrator if the perpetrator can afford it (arts. 51(1) and (2)).

23 Police are also able to commence investigations if they come to hear of an alleged rape (art. 52(2)).

24 Repeated offences attract up to 80 additional strokes of the cane, though this can be substituted by 400 grams of gold or 40 months' imprisonment (art. 57(1) and (2)).

25 *Hadith: Ar.* records of the words, deeds, descriptions and circumstances of the Prophet Muhammad.

26 Law No. 39 of 1999 on Human Rights.

27 Although, as Feener (2014: 175) points out, these statistics certainly do not reflect actual incidents of gambling, alcohol-related crime and prohibited proximity, many of which might not get to court, with offenders instead undergoing 'moral instruction' at the offices of Wilayatul Hisbah, or being dealt with under local custom.

28 https://ms-aceh.go.id/layanan-publik/pelayan-informasi-perkara/putusan-jinayat.html.

29 01/JN/2008/MSy-Prov; 02/JN/2008/MSy-Prov.

30 02/JN/2010/MS-Aceh.

31 04/JN/2011/MS-Aceh.

32 01 K/AG/JN/2008: 2; 05 K/AG/JN/2007: 2; 03/JN/2010/MS-ACEH: 3–4; 05/JN/2011/MS-ACEH: 3; 04/JN/2008/MSy-BNA: 2.

33 See, for example, 04/JN/2006/MSy. Lsm, in which the testimony of several witnesses was set out.

34 22/JN/2009/MS.Mbo.

35 04/JN/2011/MS-Aceh; 02/JN/2010/MS-Aceh.

36 03/JN/2011/MS-Aceh.

37 In this case, Decision 02K/AG/JN/2008, the Supreme Court refused to hear the cassation appeal because the defendant did not lodge it within fourteen days of the appeal court decision.

38 Specifically, arts. 5 and 22(1).

39 01K/AG/JN/2008: 6.

40 04K/AG/JN/2008: 5.

41 05K/AG/JN/2008 was an appeal against a conviction for proximity, based on facts that clearly alleged adultery. The defendant was sentenced to nine strokes of the cane, which was upheld on appeal. At the cassation level, the defendant argued that because he was a member of the local legislature, he should have been called for questioning and interrogated in accordance with the legislature's standing orders, but was not. Therefore, he argued, the investigation and prosecution was flawed and should be declared invalid by the Court.

42 See page 5 of the Decision. This was an appeal against a first instance decision, confirmed by the Aceh provincial Mahkamah Syariah, imposing a fine on a defendant for providing facilities to others for gambling. On cassation, the defendant argued that he did not know about the gambling, even though it occurred at his residence. He also promised, perhaps contradicting this claimed lack of knowledge, not to repeat the offence and or be involved in criminal activity.

43 Qanun No. 7 of 2013 on the Jinayat Procedural Code.

44 See, for example, Kine 2017.

45 UN Committee against Torture (2 July 2008) 'Concluding Observations: Indonesia', CAT/C/IDN/CO/2, para. 15, www.hri.global/files/2011/11/08/IHRA_Corporal PunishmentReport_Web.pdf.
46 Government Regulation No. 5 of 2018 on the Implementation of Jinayat Procedure.
47 http://icjr.or.id/category/special-project/strategic-litigation/.
48 Supreme Court Decision No. 60 P/HUM/2015.
49 For an explanation of these review powers see Butt and Parsons (2014).
50 The Ministry pointed to art. 235(4) of the 2006 Aceh Autonomy Law, which states that Qanun that implement Islamic law can only be invalidated by the Supreme Court through judicial review.
51 See art. 10 of the KUHP, which specifies only death, incarceration, fines, revocation of particular rights, confiscation of particular property and announcement of the judicial decision.
52 Namely, arts. 28G(1), 28G(2) and 28I(1) of the Constitution; arts. 5(1) and 33(1) of Law No. 39 of 1999 on Human Rights; arts. 7 and 10 of Law No. 12 of 2005, which ratified the ICCPR; and arts. 1 and 5 of Law No. 5 of 1998, which ratified the Anti-Torture Convention.
53 See art. 71(1) and 71(2) of Law No. 11 of 2012 on the Children's Criminal Justice System, which limit the punishments that can be applied to children under the age of 18, whereas art. 65 of the Qanun allows for a person aged 12–18 years to receive one-third of the penalty of an adult.
54 Including arts. 7 and 10 of the ICCPR and the Convention against Torture.
55 Supreme Court Decision No. 60 P/HUM/2015, p. 72.
56 Law No. 24 of 2003 on the Constitutional Court.
57 Constitutional Court Decision No. 59/PUU-XIII/2015.
58 Constitutional Court Decision No. 74/PUU-X/2012.
59 Incidentally, the Constitutional Court ultimately threw out the challenge for lack of standing, because the applicants established no clear constitutional ground to object to art. 7(1): 59/PUU-XIII/2015: 47–8.

References

Acehkita.com 2009. 'Qanun Jinayat Melanggar HAM', 15 September

Afif 2014. 'KontraS Sebut Pelaksanaan Qanun Jinayat di Aceh Melanggar HAM', *Merdeka.com*, 3 October

Amnesty International 2017. 'Indonesia: Revoke the Caning Sentence of Gay Men in Aceh', Amnesty International, 18 May

Anshari, H. E. Saifuddin. 1997. *Piagam Jakarta 22 Juni 1945: Sebuah Konsensus Nasional tentang Dasar Negara Republik Indonesia (1945–1949)*. Jakarta: Gema Insansi Press

Aspinall, Edward. 2006. *The Helsinki Agreement: A More Promising Basis for Peace in Aceh?* Washington, DC: East-West Center

Aziz, Abdul. 2017. 'Suara-Suara yang Menentang Hukum Cambuk', *Tirto.id*, 3 February

Benda, Harry. J. 1958. *The Crescent and the Rising Sun: Indonesian Islam under the Japanese Occupation, 1942–1945*. The Hague; New York: W. van Hoeve

van Bruinessen, Martin (ed.) 2013. *Contemporary Developments in Indonesian Islam: Explaining the 'Conservative Turn'*. Singapore: Institute of Southeast Asian Studies

Buehler, Michael 2011. 'Whodunit? Politicians Affiliated with Secular Parties Implement Most Syariah Regulations', *Tempo*, 6 September

Bush, Robin 2008. 'Regional "Sharia" Regulations in Indonesia: Anomaly or Symptom?', in Greg Fealy and Sally White (eds.), *Indonesia: Islamic Life and Politics*. Canberra: Indonesia Update Series

Butt, Simon. 2008. 'Polygamy and Mixed Marriage in Indonesia: Islam and the Marriage Law in the Courts', in T. Lindsey (ed.), *Indonesia: Law and Society*, 2nd edn. Annandale, NSW: Federation Press

Butt, Simon. 2010a. 'Islam, the State and the Constitutional Court in Indonesia', *Pacific Rim Law & Policy Journal* 19(2): 279–301

Butt, Simon. 2010b. 'Regional Autonomy and the Proliferation of Perda in Indonesia: An Assessment of Bureaucratic and Judicial Review Mechanisms', *Sydney Law Review* 32(2): 177

Butt, Simon. 2016. 'Freedom of Religion under the Constitution', in T. Lindsey and H. Pausacker (eds.), *Religion, Law and Intolerance in Indonesia*. London: Routledge, pp. 42–67

Butt, Simon. 2017a. 'Constitutional Court Lets Local Governments off the Leash', *Indonesia at Melbourne*, 4 July

Butt, Simon. 2017b. 'Why is Ahok in Prison? A Legal Analysis of the Decision', *Indonesia at Melbourne*, 6 June

Butt, Simon. 2018. 'Religious Conservatism, Islamic Criminal Law and the Judiciary in Indonesia: A Tale of Three Courts', *Journal of Legal Pluralism and Unofficial Law* (under review)

Butt, Simon. and Lindsey, Tim. 2012. *The Indonesian Constitution: A Contextual Analysis*. Oxford: Hart

Butt, Simon. and Lindsey, Tim. 2018. *Indonesian Law*. Oxford University Press

Butt, Simon. and Parsons, Nicholas. 2014. 'Judicial Review and the Supreme Court in Indonesia: A New Space for Law?', *Indonesia* 97: 55–85

Cammack, Mark E. and Feener, R. Michael. 2007. 'The Indonesian Islamic Judiciary', in R. M. Feener and Mark E. Cammack (eds.), *Islamic Law in Contemporary Indonesia: Ideas and Institutions*. Cambridge, Mass.: Islamic Legal Studies Program, Harvard Law School

Crouch, Melissa. 2014. 'Proselytization, Religious Diversity and the State in Indonesia: The Offense of Deceiving a Child to Change Religion', in J. Finucane and R. M. Feener (eds.), *Proselytizing and the Limits of Religious Pluralism*. Singapore: Springer

Elnizar, Norman. E. 2017. 'Qanun Jinayat untuk Pemerkosa Anak Kandung', *Hukumonline*, 11 March

Esposito, John L. 2017. 'Qanun', *The Oxford Dictionary of Islam*. Oxford Islamic Studies Online

Feener, R. Michael. 2014. *Shari'a and Social Engineering the Implementation of Islamic Law in Contemporary Aceh, Indonesia*. Oxford University Press

Florene, Ursula. 2017. 'Komnas HAM Kritik Penerapan Qanun Jinayat', *Rappler*, 24 May

Hamzah, Andi. 1986. *Kamus Hukum*. Jakarta: Ghalia Indonesia

Hodge, Amanda, and Rayda, Nivell 2017. 'Sharia Law in Aceh to Face Legal Challenge', *The Australian*, 27 October

Hooker, M. B. 2008. *Indonesian Syariah: Defining a National School of Islamic Law*. Singapore: ISEAS

HRW (Human Rights Watch) 2014. 'Indonesia: Aceh's New Islamic Laws Violate Rights: Same-Sex Relations Banned; Whipping Imposed as Punishment', 2 October www.hrw.org/news/2014/10/02/indonesia-acehs-new-islamic-laws-violate-rights

HRW 2016. 'Human Rights Watch Complaint on the Rights of LGBT People in Indonesia's Aceh Province', 29 March www.hrw.org/news/2016/03/29/human-rights-watch-complaint-rights-lgbt-people-indonesias-aceh-province

Hukumonline 2009. 'Kontroversi Qanun Jinayat di Serambi Mekah', 15 September

ICJR 2017. 'Hukuman Cambuk Mencoreng Wajah Hak Asasi Manusia di Indonesia', Institute for Criminal Justice Reform, 23 September

Indrayana, Denny. 2008. *Indonesian Constitutional Reform 1999–2002: An Evaluation of Constitution-making in Transition*. Jakarta: Penerbit Buku Kompas

International Crisis Group 2006. *Islamic Law and Criminal Justice in Aceh*. Southeast Asia/Brussels: International Crisis Group (ICG)

Jakarta Post 2018. 'Q&A: What You Need to Know about Sharia in Aceh', 4 March

Karni, Asrori S. 2009. 'Rajam Setitik Ganjal Qanun Sepasang', *Gatra*, 6 November

Kine, Phelim. 2017. 'Indonesia's Aceh Authorities Lash Hundreds Under Sharia Statutes', Human Rights Watch <www.hrw.org/news/2017/02/08/indonesias-aceh-authorities-lash-hundreds-under-sharia-statutes>

Lev, Daniel S. 1972. *Islamic Courts in Indonesia: A Study in the Political Bases of Legal Institutions*. Berkeley: University of California Press

Lindsey, Tim. 2012. *Islam, Law and the State in Southeast Asia: Volume 1 Indonesia*. London: I. B. Tauris

Mahkamah Agung 2012. *Laporan Tahunan 2011*. Jakarta: Mahkamah Agung

Mahkamah Agung 2014. *Laporan Tahunan 2013*. Jakarta: Mahkamah Agung

Mahkamah Agung 2015. *Laporan Tahunan 2014*. Jakarta: Mahkamah Agung

Mahkamah Agung 2016. *Laporan Tahunan 2015*. Jakarta: Mahkamah Agung

Mahkamah Agung 2017. *Laporan Tahunan 2016*. Jakarta: Mahkamah Agung

Menchik, Jeremy. 2016. *Islam and Democracy in Indonesia: Tolerance without Liberalism*. New York: Cambridge University Press

Nasution, Adnan Buyung. 1992. *The Aspiration for Constitutional Government in Indonesia: A Socio-Legal Study of the Indonesian Konstituante, 1956–1959*. Jakarta: Pustaka Sinar Harapan

Nurlaelawati, Euis. 2010. *Modernization, Tradition and Identity: The Kompilasi Hukum Islam and Legal Practice in the Indonesian Religious Courts*. Amsterdam University Press

Pausacker, Helen. 2009. 'Indonesia's New Pornography Law: Reform Does Not Necessarily Lead to More Liberal Attitudes to Morality and Censorship', *Alternative Law Journal* 34(2): 121–3

Pompe, Sebastiaan. 2005. *The Indonesian Supreme Court: A Study of Institutional Collapse*. Ithaca, NY: Southeast Asia Program, Cornell University

Ricklefs, Merle C. 1993. *A History of Modern Indonesia since c. 1300*, 2nd edn. Stanford University Press

Setyadi, Agus. 2018. 'Pasutri di Aceh Dicambuk Karena Berjudi, Warga Rekam dengan HP', *Modusaceh*, 27 February

Setyadi, Agus. 2017. 'Polisi Bongkar Perjudian di Permainan Anak di Aceh, 13 Orang Dibekuk', *Detik News*, 10 November

Shah, Dian. A. H. 2017. *Constitutions, Religion and Politics in Asia Indonesia, Malaysia and Sri Lanka*. Cambridge University Press

Subekti, R. 1982. *Law in Indonesia*, 3rd edn. Jakarta: Center for Strategic and International Studies

Voanews 2018. 'Indonesia's Aceh Resumes Public Caning Despite Pledge to Curb Access', 13 July www.voanews.com/a/indonesia-aceh-resumes-public-caning-despite-pledge-to-curb-access/4481427.html

Legislation

Constitution of 1945
Wetboek van Srafwet Nederlandsch Indie (WvS) 1918
Criminal Code (*Kitab Undang-Undang Hukum Pidana*, KUHP: Law No. 1 of 1946 as amended by Law No. 27 of 1999 on the Indonesian Criminal Code)
Law No. 7 of 1989 on the Religious Courts, as amended by Law No. 3 of 2006 and Law No. 50 of 2009
Law No. 5 of 1998 on the Ratification of the Convention Against Torture and other Cruel, Inhuman or Degrading Treatments or Punishments
Law No. 39 of 1999 on Human Rights
Law No. 18 of 2001 on the Special Autonomy of Aceh
Law No. 24 of 2003 on the Constitutional Court
Law No. 12 of 2005 on the Ratification of the ICCPR
Law No. 11 of 2006 on the Governing of Aceh
Law No. 44 of 2008 on Pornography
Law No. 12 of 2011 on Lawmaking
Law No. 11 of 2012 on the Children's Criminal Justice System
Presidential Instruction No. 1 of 1991on the Compilation of Islamic Laws (*Kompilasi Hukum Islam*)
Qanun No. 11 of 2002 on the Implementation of Islamic Law in the Fields of Aqidah, Ibadah and Syi'ar Islam
Qanun No. 12 of 2003 on Alcoholic Beverages and the Like
Qanun No. 13 of 2003 on Gambling
Qanun No. 14 of 2003 on Prohibited Proximity
Qanun No. 7 of 2013 on the Jinayat Procedural Code
Qanun No. 6 of 2014 on Islamic Criminal Law (*Hukum Jinayat*)

Court cases and decisions

Aceh High Syariah Court Decision No. 01/JN/2008/MSy-Prov
Aceh High Syariah Court Decision No. 02/JN/2008/MSy-Prov
Aceh Syariah Court Decision No. 02/JN/2010/MS-Aceh
Aceh Syariah Court Decision No. 03/JN/2010/MS-Aceh
Aceh Syariah Court Decision No. 04/JN/2011/MS-Aceh
Aceh Syariah Court Decision No. 05/JN/2011/MS-Aceh
Aceh Syariah Court Decision No. 03/JN/2011/MS-Aceh
Banda Aceh Syariah Court Decision No. 04/JN/2008/MSy-BNA
Constitutional Court Decision No. 74/PUU-X/2012
Constitutional Court Decision No. 59/PUU-XIII/2015
Lhokseumawe Syariah Court Decision No. 04/JN/2006/MSy. Lsm,
Meulaboh Aceh Syariah Court Decision No. 22/JN/2009/MS.Mbo
Supreme Court Decision No. 01K/AG/JN/2008
Supreme Court Decision No. 02K/AG/JN/2008
Supreme Court Decision No. 03K/AG/JN/2008
Supreme Court Decision No. 04K/AG/JN/2008
Supreme Court Decision No. 05K/AG/JN/2008
Supreme Court Decision No. 60 P/HUM/2015

Index

For Product Safety Concerns and Information please contact our EU
representative GPSR@taylorandfrancis.com
Taylor & Francis Verlag GmbH, Kaufingerstraße 24, 80331 München, Germany

www.ingramcontent.com/pod-product-compliance
Ingram Content Group UK Ltd.
Pitfield, Milton Keynes, MK11 3LW, UK
UKHW020156200926
475702UK00016B/2742
* 9 7 8 0 3 6 7 6 4 3 9 4 2 *